WASN'T THAT A MIGHTY DAY

WASN'T THAT A MIGHTY DAY

African American Blues and Gospel Songs on Disaster

Luigi Monge

University Press of Mississippi / Jackson

The University Press of Mississippi is the scholarly publishing agency of the Mississippi Institutions of Higher Learning: Alcorn State University, Delta State University, Jackson State University, Mississippi State University, Mississippi University for Women, Mississippi Valley State University, University of Mississippi, and University of Southern Mississippi.

www.upress.state.ms.us

The University Press of Mississippi is a member of the Association of University Presses.

First printing 2022
∞

Library of Congress Control Number: 2022940584
Hardback ISBN 978-1-4968-4169-8
Trade paperback ISBN 978-1-4968-4176-6
PDF single ISBN 978-1-4968-4177-3
PDF institutional ISBN 978-1-4968-4178-0
Epub single ISBN 978-1-4968-4179-7
Epub institutional ISBN 978-1-4968-4180-3

British Library Cataloging-in-Publication Data available

This book is dedicated to my wife Enrica and my son Lorenzo
because they are, and
to my sister Roberta and my mother Elda
because they were and always will be

CONTENTS

ACKNOWLEDGMENTS

Among the experts who contributed to drawing up the final version of this book, I would like to warmly thank: British researcher Tony Russell and Australian "information finder" and internet magician Bob Eagle, who were repeatedly bothered by my desperate questions, which they invariably and swiftly answered with the common sense, expertise, and humility they are appreciated for in music circles all over the world; Dutch blues and gospel historian Guido van Rijn, whose vision and dedication inspired me to follow his lead of dealing with topical songs' lyrics; American author and editor Edward Komara, for publishing my first tentative research on disaster songs, the longest of the twenty-nine items I contributed to the two-volume *Encyclopedia of the Blues* he edited; English researcher and compiler Rob Ford for providing rare information and material; Craig Gill, Jackson Watson, Will Rigby, and the staff at the University Press of Mississippi for believing in an unknown researcher's project and for patiently accepting its irritatingly slow progress; and Norm Cohen, for reading and making enlightening remarks on the whole manuscript. Finally, I want to acknowledge two people without whom this book would not even be in your hands: my brightest beacon, music scholar and ethnomusicologist David Evans, and British researcher Chris Smith. Evans is the editor of my book as well as a friend. He was a supporter and motivator in times of difficulty, a wise and sympathetic advisor, and a regular supplier of research material. He also put me in contact with informants and experts in different fields, and was instrumental in helping me transcribe parts of the song lyrics analyzed in the book. I know I must consider myself very lucky to have met him and to have worked with him on several other projects and publications. Besides being another victim pestered by my continuous questions while I was in the process of writing the book, Smith was brave enough to accept the grueling task of reading the whole manuscript, making constructive criticism and meticulous remarks on my approach, and providing not only insightful suggestions but what it is altogether accurate to define as "second editing."

Hoping not to have forgotten anyone and to be forgiven if I have, the following critics, discographers, musicians, record label owners, and so on have also assisted me in various ways in writing the book, and I extend my sincerest thanks to them all: Lynn Abbott, Ashley Adair, Gőrgen Antonsson, Gary Atkinson, Alan Balfour, Scott Barretta, Matthew Barton (curator of Recorded Sound at the Library of Congress), Davide Bianchi, Eric Bibb, Gigi Bresciani, Patrice Champarou, William Clements, Larry Cohn, John Cowley, James G. Cusick, Stefano Danielli, Ralph Elder, William Lee Ellis, William Ferris, Daniel Fleck, Tyler Fritts, Dario Gaggero, Stefano Espinoza, Cary Ginell, Alan Govenar, Marino and Davide Grandi, Judith Gray (referent specialist, American Folklife Center, Library of Congress, Washington, DC), Jerry Hatfield (public services assistant, Motion Picture, Broadcasting, and Recorded Sound Division, Library of Congress, Washington, DC), Joe Hickerson, David Horn, Bruce Jackson, Brian Jannsen, the late Big Jack Johnson, David Johnson, Eliot Kleinberg, Dean Klinkenberg, Roberto Lijoi, Melissa Lindberg (reference librarian, Prints & Photographs Division, Library of Congress, Washington, DC), the late Giorgio Lombardi and musicologist Guido Festinese, Kip Lornell, Marina Mazzoli, Thomas A. McKean, Mary-Jo Miller, Allan Moore, the late Arnold Dwight "Gatemouth" Moore, Bettye J. Mullen, Bruce Nemerov, Jim O'Neal, the late Paul Oliver, Harriet Ottenheimer, Ted Ownby and Charles Reagan Wilson, Ann J. Abadie, Odie Lindsey, and James G. Thomas, Sam Perryman (music specialist, Music Division, Library of Congress), the prewar blues list, Philip R. Ratcliffe, Joel Collin Roberts, Pio Rossi, Robert Sacré, Gianfranco Scala, Stefano Scalich, Maria "Meripi" Simonetti, John Slate (Dallas city archivist), Aaron Smithers and Jason Tomberlin, Robert Springer, Elizabeth Surles (Starr-Gennett Foundation Inc.), Paul Swinton, Alex van der Tuuk, Libero "Bibo" Verda, Elijah Wald, Sandy Waring, Susan Watson and Marilyn Clune (American Red Cross), Steven M. Weiss, Stefan Wirz, and Jerry Zolten.

Although this book has benefited from the professional competence and disinterested help of several scholars who have given me a lot of their time and knowledge, the mistakes herein remain my own.

The "gestation time" of this book has been so long that many "facts of life" have happened to me since I started to write it. Among them, my newborn baby boy Lorenzo has grown up to become a smart teenager and university student, my sister Roberta has left this world too early, and my Mum Elda reached her in 2020. This book is dedicated to them and to my wife Enrica, who has shared my feelings throughout this journey, all along the way bearing the burden.

FOREWORD

I am writing here both as a friend and research colleague of Luigi Monge and as editor for the University Press of Mississippi's American Made Music Series. Luigi was a recent graduate from the University of Genova and a budding blues researcher when he and I met briefly at the Chicago Blues Festival in 1987 and exchanged our first correspondence. Two years later we became better acquainted when I was touring in France and Italy as guitar accompanist to the great bluesman Johnny Shines. The organization of which Luigi was secretary, Associazione Culturale "Liguria Blues—Genova," sponsored one of our concerts, and it was among the more memorable ones of the tour, especially because the Association put us up in a small hotel redolent of nineteenth-century splendor on the outskirts of the city overlooking the Mediterranean and a topless beach.

It was not until 1997, however, the year after I became series editor, that we began to correspond more regularly, with Luigi sending me English translations of his writings on blues lyrics for my commentary. Up to that time I had encountered hardly any writing in English by Italian scholars on African American blues, much less on blues lyrics. It was a topic that required a high degree of cultural knowledge as well as an ear for idiomatic speech and dialect, qualities that were rare even among American scholars at the time. I recognized immediately that here was someone possessing unusual insight into the creative literary processes of blues singers and composers, and I began to hope that our correspondence and my encouragement of his efforts might someday result in a book for the series. Little did I realize that it would take another quarter-century for the result to appear, but it has been well worth the wait and the interim has hardly been unproductive on Luigi's part.

We had several more visits in Italy when I was touring as a musician on my own, as well as in America when Luigi came to do research and lecturing. One of the most notable of the latter visits was in 1999, when he and I and our wives did research in Texas on the life of the great blues singer and poet Blind Lemon Jefferson (ca. 1893–1929). These visits and our prolific correspondence resulted in a number of important articles and chapters by Luigi that I was able to critique or edit—on the covert theme of blindness in Jefferson's blues lyrics; on the same theme more generally in early blues and gospel songs by blind performers; on some newly discovered songs by Jefferson found in submissions to the US Copyright Office (co-authored by Luigi and me); and on blues songs about the 1940 Natchez Rhythm Club fire, the 1928 Florida hurricanes and floods, the 1912 sinking of the *Titanic*, and the 1930 dry spell. As his stature as a blues scholar grew and came to be internationally recognized, Luigi was chosen to write over thirty entries in standard blues and gospel encyclopedias, and he published books in Italian on the blues lyrics of Robert Johnson and Howlin' Wolf. With all the above as background and preparation, we can now enjoy and appreciate Luigi Monge's *magnum opus*, this comprehensive work on African American blues and gospel songs about disasters, eighteen years in the making.

Although the particular insights expressed here are unique to the author, the book stands in a more general sense within a great tradition of overseas, and especially British and European, writing about American blues, jazz, and gospel music, and it joins a list of some twenty books in the American Made Music Series by authors or editors from England, Scotland, France, Belgium, The Netherlands, Austria, and New Zealand. These overseas scholars of American music, perhaps because they are physically and culturally distanced from their subjects (though no less attracted to them), have tended to produce comprehensive genre studies, such as discographies and other broad surveys, or biographies of great artists, usually ones who are long deceased. For example, almost all of the major discographies and bibliographies of American blues, jazz, gospel, and country music have been compiled by overseas, especially British, scholars. These writers tend to treat their material as factual data to be gathered in their entirety, organized systematically, compared, and correlated with other facts, then perhaps to be interpreted. This is in contrast to some American researchers and writers who may feel more culturally familiar with their subjects and therefore confident enough to begin with an interpretation or a hypothesis and then marshal selected data to support it.

Wasn't That a Mighty Day is truly comprehensive and systematic, at least for songs on disasters up to the mid-1950s, after which, with the exception of Hurricane Katrina (2005), there were very few such events that inspired songs by Black singers or composers. The book covers folk and popular, sacred and secular, field-collected and commercially printed or recorded, previously published and unpublished, narrative, descriptive, and impressionistic songs on a host of natural and accidental disasters as well as epidemics and infestations. It even compares them to songs by white singers and composers on the same specific events. It is doubtful that more than a tiny handful of songs on disasters from the period covered will be found or identified in the future, and those are likely to be the few that are known to have been recorded but have not been located up to now or ones that are buried deep in uncatalogued archives. With these few potential exceptions, it can be stated with confidence that this book cites every relevant song example for the disasters under discussion. It will thus become a major resource and reference work on this subject as well as in the growing field of disaster studies in general and broader fields such as American folk and popular music and African American studies.

So how did Luigi Monge accomplish the task of creating this book? He first had to identify and gather recordings or transcriptions of all the disaster songs by Black singers and composers for the period covered in the study. This is not an easy process, especially for someone living and working a continent away from the sources of the material. Some of the songs are found in published collections organized by state or region rather than specifically by ethnicity. Finding aids and indexes for these collections help the researcher only to a limited extent, and many publications need to be read or scanned from beginning to end in the hope of finding one or more relevant items. Other songs exist on paper but only in the form of field-collected versions placed in archives. The majority of the songs exist as recordings, both commercial and archival. Once again, there may be title indexes, but some important disaster songs have such unassuming titles as "Jesus Is Coming Soon," "No More Ball and Chain," and "Coal Mountain Blues." The task of merely identifying the relevant material therefore involves leafing through hundreds of publications, searching finding aids of archival collections, scanning title indexes of discographies and track lists of albums, listening to thousands of recordings, and asking research colleagues to dredge up obscure items from their memories. Acquiring usable printed or recorded copies of relevant songs can also be extremely time consuming as well as expensive.

Once the songs have been identified and gathered, they must be transcribed accurately. The lyrics of some of the better-known ones have been printed previously in books, articles, or on internet sites, but it would be hazardous merely to accept these well-meaning but sometimes naïve attempts at achieving meaning. Some may be fairly accurate, but others are downright ludicrous or, while appearing plausible, are in fact incorrect and have led to faulty interpretations by scholars who accepted them without actually listening to the recordings. For someone who speaks fluent and correct English but with a noticeable Italian accent, Luigi Monge has an extraordinary ability to understand dialect and idiomatic and nonstandard expressions, one that would put most Americans making the attempt to shame.

Once the songs have been transcribed, one must identify the disasters to which they refer. This is usually easy, but not always. Some of the song lyrics give no clue to where the event described occurred. Fortunately, it is generally the case that songs identify the location of the event or in any case were recorded or collected shortly after the event took place, and by using such resources as the *New York Times* annual index and searching under such topics as "floods," "fires," and so on, one can usually pinpoint the event. There are, however, a few disaster songs whose referents remain a mystery. After the event has been identified, the song lyrics need to be compared to the facts about the disaster as reported in newspapers and government publications. Sometimes these published reports are premature, incomplete, inaccurate, or inconsistent, and in a few cases the song lyrics may actually be more accurate. Singers were sometimes closer to the events, or knew people who were, than newspaper reporters and government relief agents.

Next comes the interpretation of the song in respect to broader themes in African American and American social life, culture, and history. Sometimes one needs to consider factors in the life of the song's performer or composer. It helps, for example, to know that blues singer Son House was a former preacher when we try to understand the sermon-like structure of his "Dry Spell Blues." Sometimes there are different interpretations to be made for different songs about the same disaster, particularly if it is given both a blues and a gospel treatment. Finally, one can try to make general interpretations and draw general conclusions about all the songs on a particular disaster, or about disasters of a certain type (fires, floods, tornados, train wrecks, and so on), or even disasters as a whole.

The more general matters of interpretation of large bodies of song or of African American disaster songs as a whole are likely to be of greatest interest to scholars in the field of African American studies. After all, the focus in this book on songs by African American singers and composers (a not unusual delimitation when one also considers the many studies of African American literature, art, and music) begs the question of what relationship the songs have to widely recognized Black social, cultural, and historical patterns. Although he approaches interpretation from a personal background far outside the culture itself, Luigi Monge does not avoid these issues. He is cautious, however, in drawing broad conclusions about the material as a whole, often even in drawing conclusions about the treatment of specific disasters in song. He follows the material where it leads him, and sometimes it leads to contradictory interpretations, due to differences in personality and personal experience of the singers and composers, or differences in secular and sacred outlooks on the events, and other factors, some of which may never be fully understood. Luigi avoids the temptation to privilege one singer's treatment of an event over another's or songs that support a particular ideology or social stance over another.

Luigi's main conclusion concerns the abstract concept of memory in its various forms as remembrance, retention, and commemoration. He finds little preoccupation in the songs with brave and virtuous heroes in the midst of disasters, or with a spirit of rebuilding. Instead, there is greater concern in them for victims on the receiving end of the disasters. Often the singer or composer portrays himself or herself as a victim, and in some cases they actually were victims. Rather than reclaiming the site of a disaster and rebuilding, Black singers tend to express personal grief for the loss, sympathy with the community, and sometimes a desire or a vow to move on to something better or at least to something new and different. While white singers tend to look to the future by reconstructing the past, Black singers mostly look for a new, though uncertain, future, often in a new location, with the old slate having been wiped clean by the disaster, while the memory of its demise is kept alive in song. There are exceptions to all of these generalizations, however, and Luigi never downplays them or covers them up.

One can, of course, interpret African American history, beginning with enslavement and continuing through the long years of Jim Crow and further incidents of racism and discrimination up to the present day, as in many ways a prolonged disaster. The isolated incidents studied here that have struck the Black community and individual singers and composers, most of them occurring without racial causation although sometimes with racial implications, and the responses to them in song might serve as a baseline to tell us something about a more general Black response to disaster, including social disaster. It can be instructive, therefore, to compare African American songs about natural and accidental disasters to this broader social history and the responses of individuals and communities to it. In the songs surveyed here, one finds protest, heroism, faith, and a sense of community identity and solidarity, but also acceptance of fate, individualism, universalism, and cynicism. Disasters are described variously as acts of God, as punishments for sin in general or of individuals or communities, and as random occurrences of bad luck not directed at any particular individual or group. All together, the songs display the rich complexity of Black American thought and culture, both its unities and divisions. Individually and in their totality, as compiled, organized, and interpreted by Luigi Monge, they will provide material for further study and interpretation for many years to come.

David Evans

WASN'T THAT A MIGHTY DAY

INTRODUCTION

As I write this introduction in mid-2020, I am conscious that in these troubled times due to the COVID-19 pandemic and the appalling series of killings of Black people, a book dealing with African American blues and gospel songs on disasters may be perceived as an insignificant or superfluous addition to Black cultural studies. However, in the last few years disaster has become a matter of global interest and preoccupation. Questionable though it may be, a widespread belief that disaster is imminent is shared by prophets of doom and many reputable scientists. Still-frequent natural disasters, and studies of the possibly devastating effects of global warming, are reminders of the need to change our behavior and our attitude to nature. The popularity of disaster movies and other flesh-creeping artistic expressions, and predictions of the "big one" in California or an eruption of the Yellowstone supervolcano, are examples of a generalized fear, uncertainty, and pessimism: the coronavirus pandemic is only the latest contributor to this zeitgeist.

My seventeen-year-long research draws on the publications of scholarly and amateur writers from around the world who have specialized in African American music and on a number of reference books and miscellaneous sources to verify the truthfulness of data. I acknowledge such literature here to avoid repeated reference to it in the endnotes.[1] My book also owes a particular debt to those who have dealt with disasters from any cultural perspective, but especially that of music.[2] Nevertheless, this book is important as the first comprehensive study of its subject. In themselves, the number and quality of the songs analyzed justify a book-length study, but it is the comparison of written accounts of disasters with the songs that has proven particularly revealing. The patterns of cross-reference and borrowing between songs, and their adaptation to different disasters, would not have been revealed without a wide-ranging approach.

In the late nineteenth and early twentieth centuries, before radio broadcasting and with a scarcity of widely circulated newspapers aimed at African Americans, topical songs were an important medium for recounting and commenting on historical, social, and political events that involved or concerned them. Sacred and secular music are accordingly a window into Black communities' feelings and world views.

After I had conducted research on songs related to specific events, including the 1930 Dry Spell and the 1940 Natchez Fire, the idea of this book came to me in 2003, as I was working on the *Encyclopedia of the Blues* entry "Topical Blues: Disasters."[3] The encyclopedia entry was almost wholly confined to blues and related secular music, but I repeatedly became aware of sacred songs covering the same events, and disasters not mentioned in blues songs. A much wider and more intricate picture than I had expected began to emerge. This book's broader perspective enables a more general approach to the analysis of African American songs dealing with disasters, demonstrating that they describe events that should not be seen exclusively as individual tragedies but as also closely interrelated and often mutually influenced.

The large body of material has forced me to impose a time limit—the first half of the 1950s—on the consideration of both disasters and songs about them. Deserving though they are of a similar study, comparatively fewer songs have been composed and recorded about disasters since the mid-1950s; the only exceptions are the many songs created in response to Hurricane Katrina (2005).[4] The case for the chosen cutoff date was strengthened as the important role played by broadsheets (or "ballets") in the circulation of disaster songs became apparent—and equally by the fact that Black composers had stopped creating and selling them by the mid-1950s. Reverend Ruben Lacy's response to David Evans makes the case for me:

> EVANS: Have you seen ballets being distributed since that time, since '52?
> LACY: I sure haven't.
> EVANS: That was the last time you ever saw people selling them in the street? Were these colored people or white people that were selling them?
> LACY: Colored. All these ballets I speak of about these tornadoes just like that, they mostly made by colored people.[5]

In the introduction to my encyclopedia entry, I divided disaster songs into "Natural Disasters" and "Accidental Disasters." Scholarly literature on disasters has often pointed out that the adjective "natural" is not always the most scientifically appropriate: calamities can be caused by natural phenomena, but these in turn can be brought about by environmental policies or political decisions.[6] I agree with this theory, but the purpose and scope of this book is to analyze responses rather than causes, and for want of better alternatives, the terms "natural" and "accidental" have been adopted to define and categorize disasters under clearly distinct categories. Broadly speaking, Black singers seem to understand disasters as either "acts of God" (natural) or of people (accidental). Environmental disasters begin with a "natural" event (heavy rains, tornadoes, hurricanes, and so on), which is not exclusively caused by human actions.

Since my research began, the World Wide Web has made it easier to trace historical material relating to natural and accidental disasters in scattered and out-of-print books and other printed resources, as well as in blogs and other online sources. It is a welcome development that some cultural and social historians have begun to cite blues (and less frequently gospel) music in their books and to use the lyrics of disaster songs to contextualize tragic events.

The downside is that some historians use lyrics as "flavoring" and/or chapter headings. Seeing them as secondary tools rather than key interpretive elements, they often cherry-pick lyrics to support their theories. Sometimes they also reveal inadequate knowledge of blues history, of the available literature on blues and gospel music, and even of the historical background to the facts analyzed. In the worst cases sources are cited wrongly, proving that the authors have not read them. As a result, their works, though sometimes excellent contributions to their specific fields, are diminished and sometimes invalidated in relation to the study of Black music.

The greater space offered by a book-length study enables me to be more comprehensive and to analyze as many African American songs dealing with communal (as opposed to personal) catastrophic events as possible. However, some limitations must be pointed out:

1) This is mainly a study of disaster *songs*, so recordings of spoken narratives such as poems and toasts are considered only when their content is relevant to both the disaster and to songs about it. The few sermons dealing with disasters are transcribed in full or commented upon when they include pertinent sung verses or refrains.[7]

2) Full discussion of songs covering personal tragedies and accidents is excluded because they constitute a scattered corpus of recordings which is numerically negligible (however important the event may have been to the singer personally) when juxtaposed to songs about collective tragic events. A cursory analysis of the songs dealing with "private" tragedies has shown that songs about personal accidents come to conclusions about meaning and causation similar to those reached in songs dealing with disasters striking a community.[8]

I have added a chapter on "Infestations, Pandemics, Epidemics, and Diseases," a category excluded from my earlier encyclopedia entry. Consistent with the treatment of natural and accidental disasters, it considers pandemics, epidemics, and poisonings which came on rather suddenly, with a terrific spike in deaths and serious illnesses, such as the 1918–20 Influenza Pandemic, the 1930 Jamaica Ginger Paralysis, and the 1951 Poisoned Moonshine Tragedy. I have also investigated recordings about tuberculosis, meningitis, syphilis, and other diseases, which were not always localized "tragedies and disasters" ascribable to a specific event or epidemic but were more or less chronic problems. Blindness is not discussed in this study because when blues and gospel singers address it directly, they seem to treat it as a personal problem, like bad luck or mistreatment, rather than a social or epidemiological issue.

David Evans's view, arising from consideration of Bessie Smith's "Back-Water Blues," that "[t]opical blues are almost always composed immediately after the event, both because the inspiration to compose is at its highest and because public interest is greatest," has been adopted as a general working hypothesis in this book.[9] The lyrics of 181 disaster songs (155 Black, 26 white) have been transcribed, omitting repetitions of verses in order to save space. Thirty unpublished Black disaster songs, and one by a white singer, held at the American Folklife Center of the Library of Congress in Washington, DC, are analyzed and/or transcribed here for the first time, and new information about their pertinence to the relevant disasters has been unearthed.

Using printed and recorded sources, this book aims to show the historical importance of sacred and secular songs about natural disasters (storms, floods, tornadoes, droughts, earthquakes, and the like), accidental disasters (sinkings, fires, train wrecks, explosions, air disasters, and so on), and infestations, pandemics, epidemics, and diseases (the boll weevil, the jake leg, the influenza pandemic, and more). Most of the analyzed material is derived from African American singers and informants. Some printed sources and recordings by white singers dealing with disasters that Black performers also sang about are scrutinized for comparative purposes.[10] All the lyrics are accompanied by textual analysis, including a comparison of song lyrics to historical facts, enabling answers to such questions as:

a) how deeply and directly the catastrophes discussed affected the Black communities where they occurred;
b) how African Americans in general, and blues and gospel singers in particular, faced and reacted to such events, whatever the cause, scope, and resonance of the disaster;
c) whether, in the light of answers to the above, and other factors, these collective tragedies prompted different reactions among white people and, if so, why; and
d) how the role of memory in recounting and commenting on historical and cultural facts shaped African American society in the period under consideration.

As is inferable from printed broadsides, early song collections, and discographies, several Black disaster songs—not all of them recorded—were composed and sung in the late nineteenth century and the first quarter of the twentieth. The coincidental release of Bessie Smith's "Back-Water Blues" just as the 1927 Mississippi River flood was about to occur started the vogue for commercially recorded African American songs on natural disasters, and the flood inspired the largest number of compositions. Yet musicians Black and white, professional and amateur, recorded songs both secular and sacred about other disasters, regardless of the severity of the loss of life and damage caused by the specific event that inspired them. Some tragedies that were minor in terms of casualties and damage spawned a comparatively high number of songs, whereas some massively destructive events or fatal calamities were overlooked, or perhaps deliberately ignored.

An example of a natural disaster not addressed by Black singers and composers is the great New England hurricane of September 1938, also known as the "Long Island Express," which swept along the Atlantic Coast from Delaware to Québec. This calamity brought about no recordings, possibly because of its minimal effect on the Black community. As for disasters pre-dating the beginning of systematic commercial recording of African American blues and gospel music in 1920, it should not be forgotten that in the United States "there were 938 disasters in the forty-eight years from 1881 to 1928."[11] Most disaster songs by Black people in those years appeared in printed broadsides, or in folksong collections by scholars, where scattered songs were printed.

Original African American compositions and recordings on natural disasters are more numerous than those on accidental disasters, and usually they describe events that were more severe for the Black community than for the white one. Only disasters that elicited more than one song are examined in separate chapters; tragedies memorialized in a single song are grouped together in the "Unidentified and Miscellaneous" chapters. This is because isolated disaster songs do not constitute a large enough sample to supply useful input toward the four conclusions drawn in the final chapter. Notably, they are not good starting points for comparison of Black and white approaches to writing disaster songs, nor do they help us understand the different ways in which African American blues and gospel singers coped with tragic events.

This is my third full-length book, and the first not in my native Italian. It has been much harder for me to write than the previous ones, not just because English is not my mother tongue, but because the book covers a lot of space and time as well as several fields of research other than blues and gospel. I hope that it will be obvious that it has been a labor of love triggered by my passion for blues and gospel. I also hope and believe that it provides new information about, and new insights into African American music.

Chapter One

NATURAL DISASTERS

Their Eyes Were Watching God: Storms and Hurricanes

THE WONDERFUL POWER OF GOD:
THE 1893 SEA ISLANDS HURRICANE

The 1893 Sea Islands Hurricane is the first natural disaster known to have been dealt with in Black songs. Many of the people affected were African American: "As many as 2,000 people, maybe more, were killed in the hurricane that hit coastal Georgia and walloped South Carolina with winds up to 120 miles per hour and a ten- to twelve-foot storm surge. Another 1,000 may have died afterward from injury, dehydration, starvation, and illness."[1]

This was one of the five deadliest storms in US history, as well as the largest and most powerful of the several nineteenth- and twentieth-century hurricanes to hit South Carolina. About 70,000 people were left destitute, and the cost of damage has been estimated at $10 million (equivalent to over a quarter of a billion in 2018 dollars). Landfall took place on Tybee Island, just east of Savannah, Georgia, on Sunday evening, August 27, but most of the destruction and loss of life were caused the day after by the storm surge. The mainly Black and rural Sea Islands residents in South Carolina were directly exposed to the surge, and flooding was especially severe in Beaufort County, Port Royal, St. Helena, Hilton Head, and Daufuskie, Edisto, and Parris Islands.

No relief funds were appropriated by either South Carolina's governor "Pitchfork" Benjamin Tillman or the US Congress to help the stricken people. The notoriously racist governor's refusal to provide relief is consistent with his ideological stance. A ten-month relief effort was run by the American Red Cross under the pioneering and effective supervision of Clara Barton. On October 13 of the same year, another hurricane hit slightly to the north, near Charleston, South Carolina. Usually known as "the Flagg Storm," after Dr. Ward Flagg, who survived but lost all his family, it considerably hampered recovery

8

Figure 1.01. "Lillie Knox (front) and Hagar Brown in the kitchen of Genevieve W. Chandler's home." Bayard Morgan Wootten Photographic Collection #P0011, North Carolina Collection, University of North Carolina Library at Chapel Hill

from the previous calamity. There is a historical marker commemorating the August 1893 hurricane at Frogmore, St. Helena Island, in Beaufort County.[2]

On Monday, August 31, 1936, two field recordings were collected by folklorist John Avery Lomax in Murrells Inlet, South Carolina, which lies on the border between Horry and Georgetown counties. The first recording is a spoken account of the tragedy, "Story of the '93 Storm" (AFS [Archive of Folk Song] 830-A-3). The second is titled "Ballad of the '93 Storm" (AFS 830-B-1), and is sung by Mrs. Lillie Knox, with vocal accompaniment by Mamma Hagar Brown (see fig. 1.01), Uncle Cato Singleton, Professor Collins, and Mrs. Mattie Brown Collins.

Chorus:
The wind that blowed/blowing so hard,
They knowed not what to do
And yet they recognized in it
By the wonderful power of God.

The tin from the roof was shaken
And they was watching the wind
How many more are waiting?
How many more God only knows.

Chorus

[They] found four hundred bodies
And they was watching the wind,
How many more are missing?
How many more God only knows.

Chorus

Hagar Brown, a native of Columbia, South Carolina, was born into slavery during the Civil War but grew up free. Aged about seventy-six at the time of the Library of Congress recordings, she was a matriarchal figure and a midwife for many of the families in her community.[3] Lillie Knox was the housekeeper for local folklorist Genevieve Chandler's family. Born on September 2, 1902, she died of cancer in Knoxville in 1959.[4] Uncle (Reverend) Cato Singleton, whose nickname was "Black Cat," was born into slavery circa 1859 on the Singleton plantation, on the banks of the Pee Dee River.[5] A published interview with Reverend Singleton contains an account of the later hurricane known as "the Dr. Flagg Storm," and at the end of this chapter there is a transcription of part of a ballad that Singleton sang to Genevieve Chandler.

De wind so high
He blow so hard
We just doan know what fer do.
Den we recognize in it de wonderful power o' Gawd.
Two hundred body come floatin by.
We ain't know jes what fer do.
Den we recognize in it de wonderful power o' Gawd.
Two hundred body . . . [6]

The recording is akin to the lyrics of an untitled song contributed to the Works Progress Administration's (WPA) South Carolina files by Chlotilde Martin of Beaufort County, South Carolina, in 1937. Chlotilde Rowell Martin (1895–1991) was a writer who interviewed former slaves for the Federal Writers' Project and published a number of books and articles about African Americans in the Low Country area.[7]

> It was on the 27th of August
> Eighteen-ninety and three,
> A cyclone begin ragin'
> En' de people begin to pray
> Islant [Islands] around us did suffer
> And we tremble' here een our home
> And when we recognize een it
> 'Twas de wonderful power of Gawd.
>
> De tin from the roof were taken
> Great tree was deah lie low
> De houses was broken een pieces
> By de wonderful power of Gawd.
>
> Preachers were preaching Gawd gospel,
> En de ooman [women] was singing His praise
> All were pleadin' for sentence
> An' beggin' Him to be saved.[8]

The two songs' lyrics differ considerably, but the correspondence of the date when the disaster occurred, the word-for-word reprise at the beginning of the second stanza ("De tin from the roof were taken"), and some other textual similarities leave no doubt that they are different versions of the same composition.

All these recorded and unrecorded performances may derive from a song, later preserved in print, which was composed in the aftermath of the hurricane by "a St. Helena Island minister [who] wrote a ballad about what his congregation experienced on the night of the hurricane. It so captured the spirit of the people of the time that it became a part of Beaufort County's folklore, sung by old-timers well into the twentieth century. Rivers Varn,[9] well known as a bass soloist in St. Helena's Episcopal Church in Beaufort and as the county's treasurer for almost forty years, recorded the song in the hopes of preserving it for future generations."[10]

The Storm of 1893

'Twas the twenty-seventh of August
In Eighteen and Ninety-Three
The wind from the north did blowing
The people begin to fear.

Chorus:
Oh the wind did blow so high
And de storm was all abroad
But yet we recognize in it
The wonderful power of God.

Was the midday of Sunday
The wind from the north did blow
The cyclone did come to rage us.
The people beginning to pray.

Chorus

Have been four hundred bodies
Have been washed ashore
The islands surrounded with sufferers
So God knows how many more.

Chorus

Now we come to persuade you
Persuade you to come to Christ.
Cast all your sins upon him.
You'll have everlasting life.

Chorus

This song was presumably written down by Varn from a Black person's singing. Its lyrics share so many lines with the field recordings that their common
origin cannot be questioned.

The last recording about the hurricane is Lavinia Simmons's "Twenty-
seventh of August, 1893" (AFS 3150 B-1), where she accompanies herself with
clapping. This song was recorded on Edisto Island, South Carolina, on Friday,
June 23, 1939, by Herbert Halpert (1911–2000). Before the recording, Halpert
asks Simmons whether the song she is going to sing is a true one and how she

learned it. She replies that it is a true spiritual song and that she learned it when she was a little girl around the time of the *Titanic* disaster (1912):

On the Twenty-Seventh of August of Eighteen Ninety-Three
When the wind began to blow and the trees began to fall

Chorus:
I'm gwine home [to] see my [Jesus]
I'm gwine home to see my Jesus (x2)
When the first trumpet sound.

Ask God to hear me that when I come to die
I'll meet one hundred or a thousand home in yonder sky.
Chorus

People all so wicked and they wonders to perform,
God moved the wicked children and yet controlled the storm.
Chorus

Biographical information on Lavinia Simmons is scarce and unconfirmed. From what is stated above, one can infer that she was born in the first decade of the twentieth century, but this seems unlikely, given that her song was collected in 1939 and that her voice sounds much older than that of a woman in her mid- to late thirties. She cannot be confidently identified in official records.

Consideration of known songs about the Sea Islands hurricane suggests that it was above all an African American tragedy. When a catastrophe mainly affected the Black population, almost invariably only Black singers were moved to preserve the memory of the event in song. There are some exceptions, but when a disaster was particularly obscure, remote, or controversial, it was usually amateur rather than professional African American singers who felt the urgent need to express themselves. A disaster was "obscure" or "remote" when record companies saw no market for songs about it or were unaware of such a possibility. Conversely, a disaster was "controversial" when the companies would not want to risk getting involved. The 1893 Sea Islands hurricane is "remote" in time, as it happened over three decades before the first field recordings and over two decades before systematic commercial recordings of blues and gospel songs. Therefore, all the songs dealing with this disaster were collected by folklorists and not recorded commercially.

THE PEOPLES IN MIAMI RUN: THE 1926 MIAMI HURRICANE

The Great Miami Hurricane, also known as "Big Blow," a Category 4 storm, made landfall on the east coast of Florida near Coral Gables, south of Miami, in the early morning of September 18, 1926, blowing at about 130 miles per hour. After devastating the coastal area for four and a half hours, the wind speed fell abruptly to a few miles an hour as the thirteen-mile-wide eye of the hurricane loomed over Miami Beach. Many residents were recent arrivals during the Florida land boom and were unaware of the behavior of hurricanes. They poured into the streets, only to be caught by surprise thirty-five minutes later when the wind started to blow again in the reverse direction at a recorded speed of 138 miles per hour. Alongside Miami and Miami Beach, the hardest-hit towns and communities were Hialeah, Ojus, Pompano, Hollywood, Hallandale, Dania, Fort Lauderdale, and Moore Haven, but others were also affected. The barometric pressure went down to 27.61 inches, one of the lowest ever recorded. According to some contemporary official sources, "a total of 327 persons lost their lives, and 6,327 were injured, 1,000 of which were seriously hurt. Property damage has been variously estimated as between $75,000,000 and $150,000,000. Most estimators agree that it was not under $100,000,000."[11] More recent estimates have established the number of fatalities (excluding 811 missing persons) as 373, with over 8,000 injured.[12] Between 130 and 300 inhabitants perished in Moore Haven alone, where the dikes on Lake Okeechobee broke and a ten- to fifteen-foot-high wall of water swept over the small town.

Two hillbilly songs were recorded about this disaster. "The Miami Storm" (OKeh 40692) was cut by country music star Vernon Dalhart (1883–1948) in New York City on September 22, 1926, only four days later. Composed by Carson J. Robison (1890–1957), it was published by Triangle Music Publishing Company.[13] In the next few days Dalhart recorded this number no fewer than nine times for different labels. The version transcribed here, from Gennett 3378, was recorded ca. September 28, 1926.[14]

> Way down by the sea was a city
> A spot that was bright and fair,
> A city of palm trees and flowers,
> A garden of beauty rare,
> A haven of rest for the weary,
> Where cool breezes flow from the sea,
> Where youth and old age smile together,
> With a heart ever light and free.

And then on a night in September,
The bright lights shone everywhere.
Miami was proud in her splendor,
And sweet music filled the air.
The breeze seemed to whisper a story.
The stars seemed to smile from the sky.
And no one would dream for a moment
That death would come riding by.

And then in the darkness of midnight
Their laughter was turned to tears.
The wrath of a storm was upon them
That filled every heart with fears.
The wind was the voice of a demon
That howled as it crashed through the town,
And great ships were torn from their anchor
And broken upon the ground.

And then when the gray dawn came stealing,
The toll of the storm was known,
And sad were the cries of the injured,
The streets with the dead were strewn.
We cannot explain this disaster,
We know not what fate may befall,
And we should be ready each hour
To answer the Master's call.

Fiddlin' John Carson's "The Storm That Struck Miami" (Bluebird B-5483) was recorded in Camden, New Jersey, more than seven years after the catastrophe, on February 27, 1934.[15]

> *Spoken:* This is old Fiddlin' John himself with Moonshine Kate. Look
> out! Here she comes!

Oh, come and hear my story, the saddest was ever told,
Of the storm that struck Miami, a town of wealth and gold.

The water fell in torrents for nine long hours or more,
The wind it blew at a hundred miles an hour swept ashore.

Eight hundred dead and many who never will be found
And buildings that cost millions wrecked there upon the ground.

Ships were wrecked and bodies were carried out to sea,
And all is desolated where beauty used to be.

Little children lost their parents, and husbands lost their wives,
There were thousands torn and bleeding, escaped with just their lives.

'Twas at the midnight hour when those souls were called away,
To face their earthly record at the great judgment day.

Some say that in Miami folks had forgotten God.
They did not keep the Sabbath; in sinful ways they trod.

People all take warning, and don't forget to pray
For you too may meet your Maker before the break of day.

Apart from a brief mention in a sermon by Rev. J. M. Gates,[16] the first African American recording about the 1926 Miami hurricane was collected for the Library of Congress by Carita Doggett Corse and Robert Cornwall of the Federal Writers' Project, part of the New Deal's WPA. Recorded at Caruja Ranch, Kenansville, Florida, in July 1940, "Hurricane" (AFS 3898-A) was sung by James Brown Jr., accompanied by Walter Van Bass and Ned Hugh Bass, two white teenagers who played banjo and guitar, respectively.[17] The song is transcribed as "[Miami] Hairikin" in Alton C. Morris's book *Folksongs of Florida*, where it is introduced as follows:

Mrs. Carita Doggett Corse, of the Federal Writers' Project of Florida, reports a song similar in pattern and content to that of the "West Palm Beach Storm" from the singing of Mr. James Brown, a young ranch hand, Kenansville, who said he learned the song at Dawson, Georgia.[18]

After the transcription, Morris states:

Several people have said that they know this song, thus indicating that it has achieved some currency among the folk of South Florida. This song is patterned closely on "God Moves on the Water," a folk song that recounts the tragic sinking of the *Titanic*.[19]

Spoken: Miami Hurricane.

Chorus:
God Almighty just moving on the water [ocean]

Peoples in Miami run.
God Almighty just moving on the water [ocean]
And the peoples in Miami run.

When the Ninety left Miami
Well, she left it in lightning speed.
When every time that lightning would flash
She would think about her dirty deeds.

Chorus

Well, the ships went down in that ocean,
It was most too sad to tell;
Ten thousand peoples got drownded,
And they all went to hell but twelve.

Chorus

Well, yon' stand a lady,
She was standing in the back door.
Says, "If I get back to Georgia,
Lord, I won't go to Florida no more."

Chorus

Well, the rich white folks and the well-to-do
They was playing five-up and pool;
God Almighty got angry in glory,
And they forgot He's on the move.

Chorus

Some was floating on the ocean,
Some was floating on the sea;
Sinners fell on knees and said,
"Lord, have mercy on me."

Chorus

Spoken by Robert Cornwall: You have just heard a ballad sung by the
    Negroes of South Florida.

Brown's stanza about "the Ninety" (later referred to as "she") seems to refer to a train, perhaps one that failed to take on people trying to flee the hurricane. His statement that ten thousand people drowned is an exaggeration, of course, probably designed to intensify the comment that "they all went to hell but twelve." The specific reference to "the rich white folks and the well-to-do" as God's victims reflects the racial tension in Miami after the storm. The nature and cause of the tension was the race riot that resulted in "the shooting of a naval militiaman and three negroes when several men in uniform sought to impress negro men for relief work."[20] The shooting was allegedly the direct consequence of some Black people being caught looting. In the aftermath of the disaster, Black people were conscripted to do up to sixty or ninety days of hard labor to clear the rubble out of greater Miami. Tension surged because many men carried weapons with or without a license. This gloomy picture was reversed in a follow-up newspaper article where the charges of racism were refuted, and a brighter light was cast on the presumed strained relationships between Miami's Black and white citizens.[21]

Eight years later, on December 2, 1948, "Florida Storm" (Decca 48189)[22] was recorded in New York City by singer and pianist Marie Roach Knight.[23]

> It was in Miami, Florida, that city by the sea,
> When God almighty sent a disaster, and He killed both man and beast.
> Oh, it was an awful sight what my God sure worked that night
> When God poured down His judgment on man.
>
> Oh, down the streets of Miami how those salty billows rolled
> And the water came out of the ocean in twelve feet tide wave tall
> Then it laid the buildings low, Lord, how that wind did blow
> But God poured down His judgment on man.
>
> Short skirts and filthy dances they've caused my heart to bleed
> And now our country is filled up with every wicked deed
> But all that's all right, my God's gonna visit you one night
> He's gonna pour down His judgment on man.

The tune of this song closely resembles that of both "The 1927 Flood" (OKeh 8647), Elders McIntorsh and Edwards's gospel song about the Mississippi River flood of that year, and "Tupelo Destruction" (AFS 2958-B), Lulu Morris's gospel song about the 1936 Tupelo tornado.[24] McIntorsh and Edwards and Lulu Morris were members of the Church of God in Christ. The striking melodic similarities between McIntorsh's sacred recording and "Florida Storm" suggest that the latter was likely composed well before 1948, probably in the aftermath of the Miami disaster, and that it circulated within the Church of God in Christ, possibly with the aid of a broadside version.[25]

In New York City in January 1960, Katie Bell Nubin, Sister Rosetta Tharpe's mother, recorded "Miami Storm," a jazz-gospel ballad on which she was accompanied by the rhythm section of trumpeter Dizzy Gillespie's orchestra.[26] Nubin and her daughter were both members of the Church of God in Christ. This recording is a variant of the song recorded by Marie Knight, featuring a refrain and other interesting differences:

> Well, down in Miami, Florida, a big city by the sea,
> God almighty sent a disaster, and He killed both man and beast.
> A man couldn't understand how those ships were brought to land
> And the water became as salty as could be.
>
> *Chorus:*
> God made a path by the sea way down in sunny land
> He made the clouds and thick darkness just to move at His command.
> Oh, wasn't that an awful sight? God sure did work that night
> When He sent down His judgment on man.
>
> This storm began in the morning on an island on the sea
> And then it swept across the ocean, oh, what a sight to see,
> The citizens they didn't know, and felt the wind begin to blow
> God sent down His judgment on man.
>
> *Repeat chorus twice*
>
> Short skirts and filthy dance have caused our heart to bleed
> Now our country's filled up with every wicked deed
> But all that's all right, God's gonna visit you one night
> He's gonna pour out His judgment on man.
>
> *Repeat chorus*

Except for the first two lines and the last stanza, the two songs' lyrics differ considerably. In Nubin's version, some of the words that are in Knight's stanzas are found in the refrain, and Nubin's main text includes some striking original images, which bear both a narrative and commentative meaning. Knight's approach is more straightforward and unemotional, yet no less effective. Nubin's statement that "This storm began in the morning on an island on the sea" does not solve the dilemma of whether this song refers to the 1926 Miami hurricane or to the 1928 Lake Okeechobee hurricanes and floods: the former storm was first observed near St. Kitts on the morning of September 14, while the latter originated in Puerto Rico. Nevertheless, her specific references to Miami, rather than inland Florida, and to a specific feature of the earlier disaster ("The citizens they didn't know"), strengthen the hypothesis that this song refers to the 1926 Miami hurricane. So, too, does the reference to "those ships [being] brought to land," as can be seen in a striking image, wryly captioned "Miami's new drydock."[27] Despite their differences, both songs are closed by slight variations of the same highly accusatory stanza containing the customary indictment of and warning to sinners.

On April 5, 1975, at the Minot Sound Studios in White Plains, New York, Marie Knight cut "The Florida Storm," a revival of her 1948 recording, accompanied by her sisters Bernice Henry and Virgie, and blues guitarist Louisiana Red, among others.[28] Gospel authority Tony Heilbut's liner notes state that this is a "topical song the Roach sisters learned as children," which is consistent with Knight's age of six at the time of the disaster and with the religious milieu where the song very likely originated. All this seems to confirm that the song was composed soon after the event by an unknown member of the African American community. Knight's later version is not transcribed here because it is a mixture of her 1948 recording and Nubin's lyrics, including the chorus that Nubin sang in 1960, which was possibly part of the original composition.

Another composition certainly dealing with the Great Miami Hurricane of 1926 is "Florida Storm," a "shape note" song printed in Judge Jackson's *The Colored Sacred Harp*.[29] Judge Jackson (1883–1958) was a "self educated Alabama farmer . . . born March 12, 1883, in Montgomery County," who became "the most creative and talented African American musician to express the depths of his soul by composing songs in four-shape notation."[30] The heading to "Florida Storm" in *The Colored Sacred Harp* claims that the song was composed by Jackson himself on July 13, 1928.

> September Eighteenth, Nineteen Hundred and Twenty-six,
> The people cried mercy in the storm
> Their cries were too late, their crying was in vain
> Crying, Lord, have mercy in the storm.
>
> A pity and a shame all the people in the rain
> But God show'd His mercy in the storm
> It was very sad that they lost all they had
> Crying, Lord, have mercy in the storm.

The wind with a mighty sound laid many buildings down
But God show'd His mercy in the storm
Night comes on, you know, they had nowhere to go
Crying, Lord, have mercy in the storm.

The streets were all a mess, it was so no one could pass
Mothers look'd for children in the storm
Fathers tried in vain, it was a shame, I know
Crying, Lord, have mercy in the storm.

The doctors got the news, so many that were bruised
Together with the Red Cross on the train
They all came in haste to see about their case
Crying, Lord, have mercy in the storm.

Chorus:
The people cried mercy in the storm (x2)
The colored and the white stay'd awake all the night
Crying, Lord, have mercy in the storm.

The origin of Judge Jackson's "Florida Storm" is recounted by Sacred Harp expert Joe Dan Boyd:

> [In 1969,] when the Jacksons and I were rummaging through Judge Jackson's papers, we came across an old (but undated) broadside sheet that was headlined, "subject: The Florida Storm" which was "Composed by Frank Spencer, Ph.D." and carried a ten cent price tag. Spencer's long broadside contained no music though it denoted one section as the "chorus." Apparently [Judge] Jackson selected five stanzas which appealed to him and rewrote them slightly to conform to his metrical requirements. Spencer's ten-cent asking price may have also been Judge Jackson's model for determining the value of his own later broadside.[31]

Four recordings of Jackson's original composition are available. The first was made during a "coin-operated RecorDisc session" in Dothan, Alabama, around 1950, where Judge Jackson himself sings tenor and leads the ensemble. The second recording comes from a September 29, 1968, WOZK-AM radio program in Ozark, Alabama.[32] Neither version includes all the verses printed in Jackson's book.

On August 23 or 24, 1980, in Campbellton, Florida, the Southeast Alabama and Florida Union Sacred Harp Singing Convention recorded a third version of Judge Jackson's "Florida Storm," led by Henry Japheth Jackson.[33]

In April 1993, the Wiregrass Sacred Harp Singers of Ozark, Alabama, recorded selections from Jackson's book, including a fourth version of "Florida Storm," sixty-five years after it was reworked by Jackson from Dr. Spencer's broadsheet.[34] The performance again derives from Jackson's book, but includes only the first, second, and last of the five printed verses.

Some general conclusions on the singers' attitudes to this disaster may be drawn. Not surprisingly, the white hillbilly and the Black gospel-oriented songs differ considerably in style and content. In general, the former compositions adopt a descriptive and fatalistic approach, leading to a moralistic finale. The latter develop a more interpretive and eschatological view of the tragic event.

THEIR EYES WERE WATCHING GOD:
THE 1928 FLORIDA HURRICANES AND FLOODS[35]

A search of the *New York Times* front-page headlines of 1928 shows that two catastrophes hit Florida in the latter part of the summer, both causing flooding in the Lake Okeechobee area. The first storm struck Florida from Palm Beach to Titusville on August 7, 1928. The *Times* only reported the consequences in passing, on August 8 and 10, not giving them appropriate prominence until August 14.[36] On September 16, 1928, a more severe Category 4 hurricane moved over Palm Beach. The storm was first detected on September 10, two days before it swept toward the Leeward Islands. It reached about 150 mph before striking Puerto Rico on September 13, the feast day of San Felipe, where it caused about 300 deaths, then made an unexpected northerly turn toward Florida.[37] It made the front-page headlines in a more timely manner than the earlier storm, on September 18, but at first the vast extent of the disaster around Lake Okeechobee was greatly underestimated.[38] Barometric pressure there fell to 27.43 inches, making this one of the most intense storms recorded in the continental United States during the twentieth century. It was particularly severe in the Lake Region's northern and southwestern shores, where the lake's shallow waters reached a height of several feet, flooding the area. Pahokee, Canal Point, Chosen, Belle Glade, and South Bay were hardest hit (see fig. 1.02).[39] The American Red Cross estimated that over 12,000 people were injured and 32,414 buildings destroyed or damaged. Three quarters or more of the many people lost in the floodwaters were nonwhite migrant field workers, most of them from the Bahamas. Estimates of the death toll in Florida alone range from 1,836 to 2,500, making this one of the deadliest hurricanes ever to strike the United States. It has also been estimated that property damage in Florida alone amounted to $25 million.

Figure 1.02. "Wreckage in Pahokee, in the Everglades area." Fred William Papers, Box 1, Folder 5, Images of the 1928 Okeechobee Hurricane. Florida. P. K. Yonge Library of Florida History, Special & Area Studies Collections, George A. Smathers Library, University of Florida

The 1928 Florida storms and ensuing floods elicited at least five African American recordings, the first of them being the only commercial one. Ruby Gowdy's "Florida Flood Blues" (Gennett 6708) was cut in New York City ca. September 28, 1928, about seven weeks after the first, and less than two weeks after the second disaster.[40]

> Water all around me, I ain't got no place to stand (x2)
> Hurricanes has been here, killed all the crops on my land.
>
> Blew down my log cabin, there's no shelter left for me (x2)
> Food is all exhausted; I'm as weary as can be.
>
> That old tornado came upon us yesterday (x2)
> Pulling down in anger everything that's in its way.
>
> Hear the wind a-howling, hear the roaring thunder crash (x2)
> Lord, looks like the wreckage. Just see that lightning flash.
>
> Watch the buildings crumble, crumble like a piece of clay (x2)
> Shows the gods are angry. Got the blues so bad today.

Nothing definite is known about the singer, not even whether Ruby Gowdy was her real name.[41]

"Florida Flood Blues" has all the features of a generic disaster blues. Its lyrics are not very accurate, and no place names, details, or dates are given. We can safely assume that Gowdy's song combines the two 1928 Florida storms, since she mentions a tornado as well as a hurricane. The reference to a "log cabin" being blown down may indicate that she or the composer was a migrant laborer who witnessed and survived the hurricane, but this image, with its romantic overtones, suggests that the songwriter was not familiar with southern architecture. Some people still lived in log cabins, but most of the houses destroyed by the hurricane would have been cheap frame houses, such as shotgun shacks. One would not expect the conclusion "the gods are angry" from the average blues singer or from a churchgoer, which suggests that the composer was a professional songwriter with a certain level of cultural sophistication.

Four Library of Congress recordings deal with the 1928 Florida hurricanes and floods. The first, "God Rode on a Mighty Storm" (AFS 327-A-1), was collected by Mary Elizabeth Barnicle, Alan Lomax, and Zora Neale Hurston ca. June 15–22, 1935, and was sung by Lily Mae Atkinson and a group of women at Fort Frederica, St. Simons Island, Georgia. This recording presents several serious technical problems, but it is similar to the 1937 version by Viola Jenkins discussed below. Atkinson's is the only field recording about the event that was not collected in Florida.

There is evidence that the lyrics were composed in the immediate aftermath of the event. The *Atlanta Constitution* dated October 25, 1928, carried an AP wire story from West Palm Beach, Florida, stating that the files of the American Red Cross contained the text of a Negro spiritual created in the aftermath of the hurricane. The first three verses of Atkinson's song display only minor differences from the two stanzas and chorus quoted in the report.[42]

The second and third field recordings are two takes of "In That Storm" (AFS 715-A and 715-B), both sung by George Washington and a quartet of African American convicts for John A. Lomax at Camp No. 28 in Gainesville, Florida, on May 13, 1936. Both takes have the same refrain and structure as the Atkinson recording, although the lyrics differ from her version. The recordings contain technical problems that make it impossible to transcribe them in their entirety, but the existence of two takes enables us to conflate their lyrics and reconstruct an almost complete text. The following transcription only includes stanzas related to this disaster. The word in square brackets is sung only in the second take.

Chorus:
In that storm, oh in that storm,
Well, it's somebody got drownded in that storm.

Wasn't it in that storm, [Lord] wasn't it in that storm,
Lord, it's somebody got drownded in that storm.

Well, my God works in a mysterious way
His wonders to perform.
He planted His footsteps out on the sea
And He rode out in that storm.[43]

Chorus

On the sixteenth day of September
In Nineteen Twenty-Eight
(inaudible) God moved on the water
And He moved till very late.

Chorus

The fourth field recording, "West Palm Beach Storm" (AFS 977-A), is a longer and flawless variant of "God Rode on a Mighty Storm," performed by Viola Jenkins in 1937.[44] A transcription of both music and lyrics is included in A. C. Morris's *Folksongs of Florida*,[45] which states that it was "Communicated by Mrs. J. R. York, Pahokee, who received it from Mr. C. A. Knowles, of the same city. Tune obtained from the singing of Mrs. Viola Jenkins, Gainesville, who learned the song from oral tradition." It is very likely that Morris got the lyrics from a printed broadside supplied by Mrs. York, and the tune from Jenkins. A common printed source would also explain the close similarity between the Jenkins and Atkinson versions.

What follows is the transcription of the song as Jenkins sang it to Morris. The recording makes it clear that she is reading its text.

On the sixteenth day of September,
Nineteen Twenty-Eight,
God start to riding early,
He rode till very late.

Chorus:
In the storm, oh in the storm;
Lord, somebody got drownded in the storm.

He rode out on the ocean,
Chained the lightning to his wheel,

Stepped on the land of West Palm Beach,
And the wicked hearts did yield.

Chorus

Out in Okeechobee,
Families rushed out at the door,
And somebody's poor mother
Haven't been seen anymore.

Chorus

Some mothers looked at their children,
As they began to cry,
Cried, "Lord, have mercy,
For we all must die."

Chorus

I tell you wicked people,
What you had better do:
Go down and get the Holy Ghost
And you'll live the life too.

Chorus

Out around Okeechobee,
All scattered on the ground,
The last account of the dead they had
Were twenty-two hundred found.

Chorus

South Bay, Belle Glade, and Pahokee,
Tell me they all laid down,
And out at Chosen,
Everybody got drowned.

Chorus

Some people are yet missing,
And haven't been found, they say.
But this we know, they will all come forth
In the Resurrection Day.

Chorus

When Gabriel sound the trumpet,
And the dead begin to rise,
I'll meet the saints from Chosen,
Up in the heavenly sky.

Chorus

The principal difference between Viola Jenkins's "West Palm Beach Storm" and Ruby Gowdy's "Florida Flood Blues" is that Jenkins provides a highly informative and accurate description giving an exact date and the number of fatalities and naming the hardest-hit communities. In a further contrast to Gowdy's blues, Jenkins's song is imbued with the moralistic style typical of a ballad.

Jenkins's and Atkinson's texts and tunes clearly have a common origin, sharing as they do their first five stanzas, with some minor differences; but Jenkins's song contains three additional stanzas, and the two versions' last stanzas are different. After some minor textual differences in the first halves of the two recordings, from the last line of its fifth stanza Jenkins's version continues with a more detailed description of the effects of the catastrophe and a more focused moral.

It is generally thought that the 1928 hurricane and flood inspired the ending of anthropologist and novelist Zora Neale Hurston's masterpiece *Their Eyes Were Watching God* (1937), where a similar catastrophe is described.[46] In fact, real places, such as Palm Beach and Lake Okeechobee, which were considerably devastated as a result of this natural calamity, are mentioned in chapter 18 of Hurston's novel.[47]

WORLD BLACK AS MIDNIGHT: TORNADOES

World Black as Midnight: The 1927 St. Louis Cyclone

In just five minutes, the significant tornado that struck St. Louis on the afternoon of September 29, 1927, killed between seventy-two and eighty-four people, many of them Black, destroyed five thousand buildings, and caused damage costing many millions of dollars.[48] Winds reached a maximum velocity of 96 miles per hour, and when the event began at 1:02 p.m. the barometric pressure fell to as low as 28.80 inches.[49]

This disaster inspired two blues and a sermon by Reverend J. M. Gates.[50] St. Louis resident Lonnie Johnson (1894–1970) recorded "St. Louis Cyclone Blues" (OKeh 8512) only four days after the tornado had occurred.[51] The song is credited to pianist and songwriter Porter Grainger, but the idea came from Johnson's wife, blues singer Mary Johnson, née Smith (1898–1983), who was in St. Louis when the cyclone swept through the city.[52]

> I was sitting in my kitchen, looking way out 'cross the sky,
> I was sitting in my kitchen, looking out 'cross the sky,
> I thought the world was ending, I started in to cry.
>
> The wind was howling, the buildings beginning to fall (x2)
> I seen that mean old twister coming just like a cannonball.
>
> The world was black as midnight, I never heard such a noise
>   before (x2)
> Sound like a million lions, when they turn loose their roar.
>
> Poor people was screaming and running every which-a-way,
> Poor people was screaming, running every which-a-way,
> *Spoken:* Lord, have mercy on our poor people.
> I fell down on my knees, I started in to pray.
>
> The shack where we was living, she reeled and rocked but never fell,
> *Spoken:* Lord, have mercy.
> The shack where we were living, it reeled and rocked but never fell,
> *Spoken:* Have mercy.
> How the cyclone spared us nobody but the Lord can tell.

The vagueness typical of blues descriptions of events is here embellished with an impending (and eventually pervasive) religious sentiment, which is only waiting for a spark to be ignited. From the first spoken aside onward, the focus of the song shifts from what happened (in the first three stanzas plus the A lines of the fourth) to what might have happened but did not because of God's intervention (from the B line of stanza 4 until the end). At this turning point the singer reacts to the storm by kneeling to pray. As a result, divine providence and grace save the lives of the whole family of believers from the fury of the tornado, and there turns out to be no need to explain the (in any

Figure 1.03. "Rev. J. M. Gates's 'God's Wrath in the St. Louis Cyclone'" (Luigi Monge).
Courtesy Museo del Jazz Gianni Dagnino, Genova, Italy; Luigi Monge collection

case inexplicable) ways of God. The spirituality inherent in the lyrics sets this recording apart from most blues songs about natural or accidental disasters, making it into a sort of undercover gospel song within a blues structure: it is neither fully secular and iconoclastic, nor does it resort to the blues praying of Son House's two-part composition "Dry Spell Blues."[53]

Three days later, the extremely popular and prolific Reverend J. M. Gates (1884–1945)[54] recorded his first topical sermon on a disaster. Assisted by Deacon Leon Davis and Sisters Norman and Jordan, Gates preached on "God's Wrath in the St. Louis Cyclone" (OKeh 8515)[55] (see fig. 1.03). exactly one week after the catastrophe, and only two days after his previous recording session. Chris Smith has plausibly suggested that "Gates may have been asked to preach on the topic by the record company."[56]

> *Spoken:* I want to speak to you from this subject, "God's Anger for Sin in the St. Louis Cyclone." You'll find in the Book of Nahum where He said in the first chapter and the third verse, "He has His way in the whirlwind and in the storm, and the clouds are the dust of His feet. He plants His footsteps on the sea, and He rides in every storm." God rode through St. Louis in the cyclone, and, ah, and ah, not only did he ride through St. Louis in the cyclone, ah, but He rode—ah,

glory to God—ah, He rode, mmm, through Memphis; and He rode through Sodom and Gomorrah. All of their mothers, brothers and sisters, they lost their lives. But He rode, Lord knows He rode. God not only rode through St. Louis, in the cyclone, but He passed through Louisiana, and Arkansas, Mississippi and Tennessee in the flood of water. He rode, ah, through Miami, Florida, in a storm, and in a flame of fire He rode through Atlanta, Georgia. A long time ago He rode through Chicago, Illinois, in a flame of fire. Are you ready for Him to ride through your city and through your land? Ohoh, are you ready now?

Sung: Oh, be ready when He comes again.
    Ah, be ready when He comes again. (x2)
    He's coming again so soon.

Spoken: Oh, Lordy. Oh, He's coming again. After a while and by and
    by, he's planted His feetsteps in the mighty cloud and ride down
    through blue ether space. He's coming again.

Sung: Oh, be ready when He comes again.
    Ah, be ready when He come again. (x2)
    He's coming again so soon.

As well as the St. Louis cyclone, the text mentions the hurricane that hit Miami in September 1926 and the Mississippi River flood that began near Greenville on April 21, 1927. Gates also alludes to the fires that occurred in Chicago in 1871 and in his home city of Atlanta on May 21, 1917. The latter burned out several blocks and caused $5 million worth of damage.[57]

On October 11, 1927, still less than two weeks after the calamity, blues singer Luella Miller (possibly 1889–unknown), then a resident of St. Louis,[58] entered Brunswick-Balke-Collender's studio in Chicago, where she recorded "Tornado Groan" (Vocalion 1147), released on December 22.[59] On January 24, 1928, Miller came back to Chicago to cut another version of "Tornado Groan," which was released with the same issue number.[60]

Tornado swept out this little town today (x2)
And taken away everything I had.

The lightning flash, wind rattle around my door,
Lightning flash, wind rattle around my door,
Every since that time, I haven't seen my house no more.

It ruined my clothes and blowed my bed away,
It ruined my clothes, blowed my bed away,
I ain't got no place to lay my worried head.

The storm come back and blowed my man away,
Storm come back and blowed my man away,
That's the reason why I ain't got a good man today.

I'm lonesome now, I have to walk the street,
Lonesome now, I have to walk the street,
Seems like a stranger to everyone I meet.

Mmm, tornado's ruined my home (x2)
And left me standing with the tornado groan.

The second part of "New St. Louis Blues," a sequence of three poems by Sterling A. Brown (1901–1989), is "Tornado Blues," one of Brown's sporadic yet outstanding poems employing the three-line structure typical of blues compositions.[61] The main title's reference to St. Louis, and the date of publication (1931), make it very likely that "Tornado Blues" is about the 1927 cyclone, and is a rare treatment of a disaster in African American literature. In the last two stanzas of his poem Brown shows no sympathy for the "ofays" (white people)[62] and the Jews who hold the mortgages that Black people were unable to pay in the aftermath of the disaster:

Foun' de moggidge unpaid, foun' de insurance long past due,
Moggidge unpaid, de insurance very long past due,
All the homes we wukked so hard for goes back to de Fay and Jew.

De Black wind evil, done done its dirty work an' gone,
Black wind evil, done done its dirty work an' gone,
Lawd help de folks what de wind ain't had no mercy on.

In the final verse, the poet's concern focuses on the aftermath of the catastrophe. He seems to adopt Lonnie Johnson's spiritual approach, and place his trust in God, but in fact he sounds closer to Son House's more articulated blues praying in "Dry Spell Blues." Because there is nothing left for Black people to lose, Brown resorts to a mixture of pleading and subtle psychological blackmail in asking God to have mercy on them.

There Is a God Somewhere: The 1936 Tupelo, Mississippi, and Gainesville, Georgia, Tornadoes

The F5 twister that raged in Tupelo from 8:30 p.m., with windspeeds ranging from 261 to 318 miles an hour, "was probably a member of a tornado family beginning near Coffeeville, Yalobusha County [Mississippi]. . . . [The tornado's] massive funnel moved east-northeast across central Lee County, passing through residential areas in the northern half of Tupelo [see fig. 1.04]. Entire families were killed, up to 13 individuals in a single home. The Mississippi State Geologist estimated the final death toll at 233."[63] However, this figure does not include African American fatalities, which were not taken into account until the 1950s. One of the most thorough accounts of the Tupelo tornado, by historian Martis D. Ramage Jr., lists all the known casualties, and his total of 287 significantly exceeds the official figure,[64] probably because it includes African Americans living in the Black settlement of Elephant Hill, which was wiped out by the storm. Around thirty-five drowned bodies were found in Gum Pond, a fifteen-acre city lake on the edge of town.[65] The estimated population of Tupelo in 1936 was 7,350, which means that almost 4 percent of the inhabitants lost their lives in the tornado.

The first two recordings about the Tupelo tornado were made by white hillbilly artists. "The Terrible Tupelo Storm" (Decca 5223) was recorded in New York City by Willie Phelps, accompanied by Norman Phelps's Virginia Rounders, five weeks after the event on May 8, 1936.[66]

> The storm clouds have vanished and silence there is,
> But all of the town is forlorn,
> For death and destruction are left in the path
> Of the terrible Tupelo storm.
>
> The homes that they strived for were all blown away,
> That's where their children were born,
> And sickness and sorrow are left in the way
> Of the terrible Tupelo storm.
>
> May God show His mercy and help them to save
> The lives that are tattered and torn,
> They'll carry the memory right on to their grave
> Of the terrible Tupelo storm.
>
> Mothers are homeless and fathers are sad,
> Their bodies are tired and worn,

Figure 1.04. "Tupelo Tornado of 1936." Courtesy of the Special Collections Department, University of Memphis Libraries

> They've lost all the courage and hope that they had
> In the terrible Tupelo storm.
>
> When honors are given for bravery and such,
> Let's think of the burden they've borne,
> They gave all they had, though it wasn't so much,
> In the terrible Tupelo storm.
>
> *Repeat stanza 3*

These meticulously rhymed lyrics do not focus on the event itself, but on its aftermath and on the ensuing concept of memory. Whereas the healing power of memory is inherent in most Black sacred and secular disaster songs, here it is viewed negatively, as a heavy burden the survivors of the catastrophe must bear for the rest of their lives.

The second song on the Tupelo disaster was "1936 Tornado" (ARC 6-08-57), recorded by white country music artist Elton Britt in New York City on May 23, 1936, seven weeks after the catastrophe.[67] This song, composed by white recording artist Bob Miller, is in marked stylistic contrast to Black religious and secular recordings about this disaster:

When God sent out His angels to sow
His precious blessings on earth below,
They traveled through the land till they came to Dixieland.
There they sowed those precious blessings to grow.

But the Elements got jealous at the wonders that they saw,
So they called a million Furies on to war.
Through Tupelo and Gainesville these Furies went to kill
Scattering desolation everywhere.

Chorus:
The storms raged while hearts bled,
Leaving sorrow and leaving dead;
Surely angels looked and wept from way up there
At the misery they saw down here.

Though hearts were crushed by sorrow and pain,
Lost souls shall sing in glory again;
For the Master oh so grand will induct His guiding hand
To rebuild a stronger refuge for all.

And the Elements and Furies they can store [*sic*] and screech and roar,
But they'll never, never harm us anymore.
And Dixieland shall arise, again a paradise,
As a resting place till we reach the eternal shore.

Chorus

Following the typical "white" viewpoint, destruction is attributed to Nature ("the Elements") and to non-Christian mythological creatures ("Furies"). Even God and the angels are unable to stop these forces, and are limited to the reconstruction of Dixieland.

The first four known African American recordings related to the Tupelo tornado are sacred. The first three were field recordings collected by Herbert Halpert for the Archive of American Folk Song. Two of them are songs, by Lulu Morris and Will C. Thomas, and both are titled "Tupelo Destruction." They were collected in churches in Tupelo, Mississippi, and in Iuka, Mississippi, respectively on May 8 and 17, 1939.

Morris's "Tupelo Destruction" (AFS 2958-B), on which she is accompanied by a congregation of the Church of God in Christ, is preceded by another track credited to her and titled "Introduction to Tupelo Destruction" (AFS

2958-A-2). It consists of an interview by Halpert, which reveals that the song was composed immediately after the catastrophe by Elder Felton Williams of the Church of the Living God, the Pillar and Ground of the Truth, located in Tupelo. Morris states that Williams said it took him about two or three weeks to get the words together, after which he had copies of the song printed to sell for ten cents apiece. Lulu Morris clearly sounds annoyed by Halpert's persistent questioning, but it is thanks to his curiosity that we know the origin of one of the few compositions about the tornado.

Chorus:
God just sent out a warning through the land (x2)
Oh, the white or Black, rich and the poor, all alike they had to go,
So He sent out a warning through the land.

In Tupelo, Mississippi, a very sinful town
The people were as wicked as anywhere was found.
They would drink, cheat, and rob, and they would not obey God,
So He sent out a warning through the land.

Chorus

It was late one Sunday evening just about nine o'clock
When the cyclone struck in Tupelo and the town began to rock.
There was wind, hail, and fire, for God surely was passing by
And He sent out a warning through the land.

Chorus (with the congregation)

I heard women screaming, I heard children groan
I heard men a-crying, "Oh, Lord, I'm out there alone."
Oh, it all sounds so hard, but the folks just wouldn't hear God,
So He sent out a warning through the land.

Chorus (with the congregation)

Somebody was torn in pieces and somebody had to drown,
Some was burning to ashes and some could not be found.
Oh, it was an awful sight, for God sure did work that night,
He just sent out a warning through the land.

Chorus (with the congregation)

Well, some was floating on water; some was sailing through the air,
People, you may not believe it, but there is a God somewhere.
He can wound, He can heal, and He can do just as He feel
And He sent out a warning through the land.

Chorus (with the congregation)

Now people, heed that warning and quit your sinful ways,
So God'll spare you over. He's coming again someday.
You may be rich and you may be poor [interrupted][68]

Like other sacred songs analyzed in this book, Lulu Morris's "Tupelo Destruction" describes God's reaction to man's misdeeds. The lyrics and melody are
closely similar to those of Elders McIntorsh and Edwards's "The 1927 Flood."
The melody had evidently been circulating in Black Pentecostal circles for
some years, and first McIntorsh and Edwards, then Elder Williams, set their
own words to it.

In 1942 blind singer Turner Junior Johnson told Alan Lomax that the only
song he had ever composed was about the Tupelo disaster:

Just one time . . . when the great storm come to Tupelo, Mississippi.
You must remember that. I heard about it over the radio. Said the folks
was dancin and raisin sand in some great big tavern. Had three or four
Seabirds playin.[69] Didn't hear that God was workin, raisin up a storm.
Then that tornado hit the juke and I was layin in my room that night and
listenin to the rain and wind on the glass and this song come to my mind:

Sung: It was late one Friday evenin
In wicked Tupelo,
The storm begin to risin
And the wind begin to blow.
Wasn't that a storm at Tupelo?
Wasn't that a storm, wasn't that a storm?[70]

Johnson interrupts his song to explain to Lomax that God sent the twister
because "four or five" years earlier "three or four hundred" African Americans
had been lynched, and one of them had cursed the town:

You must know the real reason for all that. Tupelo was a town where they
had done some mighty mobbin. They took and hung three or four hundred colored folks, hung um unmerciful. And one of them colored boys

they hung spoke to um—up there where they gonna hang him—and said
Tupelo wouldn never do no good no more. And that's what happened.
Four or five years later come this big tornado, like a ball of fire turning
over and over till you couldn't hear nothing but it lumberin and roarin,
and it tore Tupelo all to pieces. Only eight folks were saved in the whole
town. Because those people had forgot there was a God. Is that right or
not, Rev'run? . . . Now I don't know what them colored boys had been
doin. Maybe had touched something they should have left alone. Maybe
they should have been punished. Maybe it was somebody else and the
wrong ones were caught. Maybe so and maybe not. But we don't know.
They didn't wait for no trial. They took God's justice in they own hands,
what they say. . . . These Tupelo folks didn't wait on the mercy of the Lord.
And look what happen to um.

> A mother and a father
> Standin lookin and cryin.
> The storm had dashed their house down
> And all their children lay dyin.
> Wasn't that a storm at Tupelo?
> . . . .
> . . . . . Wasn't that a storm?

Turner Johnson's recollection is unreliable and exaggerated. Neither the fragment of his song nor his statement is available on any recording, but the search
for a historical basis behind his statement shows that there may be a kernel of
truth in it. His figures, for the numbers both of Black people hanged and of tornado survivors, are not supported by written evidence, but the story that Tupelo
was cursed by a Black person about to be killed without trial is widely believed
in the African American community.[71] Black belief in a mass lynching in Tupelo
may reflect folk memory of a real event, which may not have become wider
public knowledge because of fear of retaliation against anyone disclosing it.

Although there are inconsistencies with regard to the date and the nature of
the underlying event, local belief that a curse was placed on Tupelo is reflected
in an account by white musician John Murry, raised in the town, in "Tupelo,
Mississippi, 1936," composed with Bob Frank as a tribute to "a black man who
was abducted and lynched on the town square. . . . The murder took place in
1926. The '1936' of the title refers to a tornado . . . that ravaged the city a decade
later and, according to local lore, was predicted by the lynching victim before
his death."[72]

Reverend Charles Haffer Jr., a preacher who had been making a living by
singing his compositions and selling typescripts of them in the streets and in

front of churches for over thirty years, was from Clarksdale, Mississippi, and was sightless like Turner Junior Johnson.[73] The chorus of "The Tupelo Disaster" was transcribed by Alan Lomax in *The Land Where the Blues Began*[74] to the tune of Haffer's song about the Rhythm Club fire, "The Natchez Theatre Fire Disaster" (AFS 6623-B-2), which is obtainable from the Library of Congress's Archive of Folk Song. The undated typescript of Haffer's "The Tupelo Disaster," which is available at the Library of Congress, is printed here in full and includes some amendments (in brackets) I made to spelling and punctuation, as well as statistical data and the Biblical references that Haffer used to introduce the song.[75]

Two hundred and six dead, more than a thousand injured, three thousand homeless, property damage more than three million dollars. A warning song: from Job 27:13–21 and Nahum 1:3.

On one Sunday night in April,
Between nine and ten o'clock,
The Beautiful city of Tupelo
Began to reel and rock.

Chorus:
Oh, what a storm in Tupelo
Heard of [for] miles around,
What a storm in Tupelo
So many people went down.

Many people had returned from service
And put their children to bed,
And [in] less than seven minutes
Hundred[s] of souls were dead.

The thunder began to roar,
Clouds hung very low,
Signs appeared in the Elements
They never had seen before.
The wind commenced blowing,
Began to uproot trees.
All over town people cried
Lord save me if you please.

Some of them started running,
And tried to make their escape:

But the dashing wind overtook them
And blew them in the lake.
Many was killed by the storm
And quite a number drowned,
If the lake is ever drained,
Many more bodies may be found.

As buildings crumbled
The lights went out
Darkness all over town;
Men, Women, and Children lie dying
On the ground.
The moans, groans and helpless cries
Were heard from everywhere
Dead men like small timber
Were sailing through the air.

It was a night of terror
Very bad and sad
Thousands of men and women
Lost everything they had.
Many of them had no money,
Food, shelter nor clothes;
The storm having blown away their homes,
They had nowhere to go.

Now Tupelo is a city
Located in the Miss. hills.
When it was visited by the storm
Many hundred people were killed.
God works in a mysterious way
His wonders to proform [sic],
He maketh the cloud his chariot
And haves his way in the storm.

Doctors, Medicines, and Nurses
Were rushed there, it is said;
Undertakers, Embalmers, and Hearses
Were sent to bury the dead.
Hospitals were quickly established
To care for the injured souls,

Homeless victims were given
Shelter, food and clothes.

And you my dear young friends
Who may this warning read
To silly, sly and flattering words
I pray you will never take heed.
But be a consistent Christian
And live a righteous life.
And when the master calls
You can answer here I am.

As with other compositions of his dealing with disasters, Haffer obtained details of the news item he wanted to write a song about from his wife, who read newspaper articles to him.[76] As often occurs in sacred songs on disasters, Haffer refers to William Cowper's poem "Light Shining out of Darkness" (1774, commonly known as "God Moves in a Mysterious Way"). However, in the statistics preceding the text, Haffer rather unusually underestimates the number of dead people, probably because he couldn't gain more accurate and timely information from the newspapers. Haffer's composition is as descriptive as his other disaster songs, especially the stanza accurately describing Black people's death in the Gum Pond lake, but he does not focus on God's judgment on man, and his recurrent "warning" to get right with God in order to be ready for Doomsday is given only in the last stanza.

Two more unrecorded testimonies by white authors about the Tupelo tornado are printed in Ramage's book.[77] "The Tupelo Disaster," a broadsheet that sold for twenty-five cents, was composed by J. W. Allen from Greenwood, Mississippi, for his daughter Marjorie Glazier Allen Gassman:

Way down in Southern Dixie, where cotton blossoms grow
There's a beautiful little city, and its name is Tupelo.

Then on one fatal evening, after the day had gone,
Her lights were beaming brightly, the clouds began to mourn.

Then homes and buildings trembled, and went whirling to the ground,
The town was thrown in darkness, and rest could not be found.

The old and young were screaming, and dying everywhere,
The cries and moans from broken hearts, were sent to God in prayer.

No human tongue can ever tell, no pen will ever write,
And none will know, but those who saw, the horrors of that night.

When daylight came next morning, a thousand broken hearts
Were searching for their loved-ones, that the cyclone tore apart.

But many of them lay sleeping, beneath their fallen homes,
And their lips were closed forever, they heard no cries or moans.

It's just another message, from God up in the sky,
To warn all you good people, that He still reigns on high.

The time is surely coming, no one can tell just when,
So we should all stay ready, to meet the final end.

The second document reproduced by Ramage is Irene Cox's fifteen-stanza text without music, "The Tupelo Storm." It is not known whether it was written to be sung, nor if it ever was. The first eleven verses describe the storm and its impact; the last four are printed here because they are an excellent example of the acquiescent and sermonizing white attitude toward disasters.

We will never know the tragedy
Of how these people went
But let us all take warning
While time is here "REPENT."

Oh, build your home in Heaven
For nothing else will stand
And then we'll meet our loved ones
Across the mystic land.

For time is swiftly passing
And wrecks of different kinds
Oh, let us all get ready
To meet our Lord Divine.

We will never know the morning
Our lives will have to go
To meet an awful ending
Of sorrows, pains and woes.

As well as stating accurately that there was another storm through Tupelo after the people had begun rebuilding from the first, bigger one,[78] blues and gospel singer Jessie Mae Hemphill (1923–2006) told music scholar David Evans an anecdote that seems to be based on the biblical story of Paul and Silas and is very similar to what Turner Johnson had said to Alan Lomax. Blues singer Aleck "Rice" Miller, better known as Sonny Boy Williamson II, was arrested in Crenshaw, Mississippi, for singing in the streets about "the big tornado."[79] He played his harmonica in the jail cell; the door opened, the guard seemed paralyzed, and Sonny Boy walked out and came up the road. He went to the home of Sid Hemphill (Jessie Mae's grandfather), near Strayhorn, and told them what had happened.[80] Perhaps Miller sang a version of Elder Felton Williams's broadside or perhaps the one by Haffer.

The other song about the Tupelo tornado that Herbert Halpert collected in 1939 is Will C. Thomas's "Tupelo Destruction" (AFS 3020-B-3), a shorter and far less impressive version of Lulu Morris's song. There is no information available on Will C. Thomas except that he lived in Iuka, Mississippi, a few miles from Tupelo.

On June 5, 1951, over sixteen years after the Tupelo tragedy, Henry Green[81] recorded "Storm Thru Mississippi" (Chance 1109). Accompanied by his own guitar, it is a version of the gospel song that Lulu Morris had sung for Herbert Halpert twelve years earlier.[82] This recording both attests to the persistence of some Black sacred songs and illustrates their stylistic evolution.

Of all the tragic events dealt with in this book, the Tupelo disaster songs show the greatest discrepancy between facts and lyrics. This has caused a series of inaccuracies by critics and historians. In some of his recordings about this disaster, John Lee Hooker (1912 or 1917–2001) states that the catastrophe took place on a Friday in 1932, and always wrongly describes it as a flood. In fact, Tupelo, Mississippi, was struck by the tornado on Sunday evening, April 5, 1936,[83] and was not flooded as a result.[84] Hooker's biographer, Charles Shaar Murray (followed by other writers and musicians), adds to the confusion by stating that "'Tupelo' evokes the terrible flood which devastated the Delta in 1927."[85] Tupelo was not affected by the 1927 flood because the town is in the hills, not the Delta.[86]

A series of cross-references and coincidences suggests that Hooker's errors are the result of his muddling the date of this natural calamity with that of the burning of the Rhythm Club in Natchez, Mississippi, on April 23, 1940, as I contended in my earlier study of the Rhythm Club disaster: "[T]he fact that they occurred in the same month four years apart and in the same state when Hooker was working outside music in the Cincinnati, Ohio, area, and that he recorded ["Natchez Fire" and "Tupelo"] for the same label in the same year [1959] certainly had something to do with his possible confusion."[87]

The first of John Lee Hooker's several recordings about the Tupelo tornado (the only one transcribed here), recorded in Detroit, Michigan, in April 1959 as "Tupelo Blues" (Riverside LP 838), focuses on the concept of memory as remembrance and commemoration:[88]

Spoken: D'you read about the flood? Happened a long time ago in Tupelo, Mississippi. There were thousands of lives destroyed. It rained, it rained both night and day. The poor people was worried, didn't have no place to go. Could hear many people crying, "Lord, have mercy! 'cause You're the only one that we can turn to." It been a long time ago. A little town way back in Mississippi, in Tupelo. Mmmmm, mmm, mmm. There was women and there was children. They was screaming and crying, crying, "Lord have mercy! 'cause You're the only one now that we can turn to." Way back down in Mississippi, a little country town. I know you read about it 'cause I'll never forget it. The mighty flood in Tupelo, Mississippi. It been years ago. Mmmmm. Ohhhhh. Ohhhh. Mmmmmm. Oh, oh. Lord, have mercy! Wasn't that a mighty time. Tupelo is gone.[89]

Ten years later in Memphis, Roebuck "Pops" Staples recorded "Tupelo" (Stax LP 2020), Hooker's composition, with Albert King on guitar.[90] As well as a number of studio versions, John Lee Hooker made another live recording of "Tupelo" (Tomato 2LP 7009) at Palo Alto, California, in September 1977. For the first time, he gave the right year for the event. This recording also includes a tribute to the then recently deceased Elvis Presley, born in East Tupelo in the year before the twister.[91]

The day after the tragedy in Tupelo, an F4 category tornado resulting from the same weather system ripped through downtown Gainesville, Georgia, at 8:27 a.m., after devastating the surrounding area of Hall County. Just above Grove Street, two different funnel paths merged, and the twister suddenly changed direction, seeming to dodge the Catholic Church at Spring Street before resuming its earlier route. The official death toll was 203 fatalities and forty missing. Between sixty and seventy of the dead were young workers at the Cooper Pants Factory, which collapsed and burst into flames. This tragedy within the tragedy still accounts for the highest number of tornado victims to perish in a single American building. Around 1,600–1,800 people were injured, 750 houses had to be pulled down, and the total damage was estimated at about $13 million.[92]

No African American recordings about this event are known to exist, but thanks to researcher Bruce Nemerov, it is known that Atlanta-born guitar evangelist Sister O. M. Terrell (1911–2006), real name Ola May Long, was renowned among church people in Gainesville for "The Georgia Storm," a song she composed after miraculously surviving the disaster:

April, the sixth in Nineteen and Thirty-Six,
A storm visit Gainesville and left the people in a bad shape.

Nemerov explains:

Sister Terrell was living in Gainesville "right in Jewell Alley and the house fell down on the ground, but here I am living." After she chanted the first stanza to "The Georgia Storm," Sister Terrell told of "running to the printer when I had a new composition in time and get some ballets printed with my picture at the top." These she'd sell to the crowds attracted by her street corner singing.[93]

A study of the Tupelo disaster highlights the importance of accurate historical information; shows that some commercial recordings, initially assumed to be original compositions, are traceable to earlier sources; and shows that recordings made well after the event may play an important role in bringing long-forgotten disasters back to public awareness.

HELL AND HIGH WATER: FLOODS

Back-Water Blues: The 1926 Cumberland River Flood

By the mid-1920s, topical songs on natural and accidental disasters were fairly popular in the Anglo-American folk tradition, and were being recorded by hillbilly artists; but only after the release of Bessie Smith's composition "Back-Water Blues" (Columbia 14195-D), recorded in New York City on February 17, 1927, did Black performers begin to offer similar thematic compositions to record companies in significant numbers.[94] Three related factors contributed to this trend: a) the well-established popularity of Bessie Smith (1892–1937) among African American and white audiences;[95] b) the coincidence that "Back-Water Blues" was released on March 20, one month before the breaching of the Mississippi River levee system at Mounds Landing, near Greenville, Mississippi, which marked the beginning of one of the greatest catastrophes in US history; and c) the fact that the song is nonspecific and can fit almost any flood. This fortuitous association between the record and the disaster explains both the high sales of Smith's composition, with initial and follow-up orders of 13,275 and 6,000 copies respectively, and the multitude of both cover versions and original songs clearly inspired by it.

> When it rained five days, and the skies turned dark as night (x2)
> Then trouble taking place in the lowlands at night.

> I woke up this morning, can't even get out of my door (x2)
> That's enough trouble to make a poor girl wonder where she want to go.

> Then they rowed a little boat about five miles 'cross the pond (x2)
> I packed all my clothes, throwed 'em in, and they rowed me along.

> When it thunders and lightning, and the wind begins to blow (x2)
> There's thousands of people ain't got no place to go.

> Then I went and stood upon some high old lonesome hill (x2)
> Then looked down on the house where I used to live.

> Backwater blues done caused me to pack my things and go (x2)
> 'Cause my house fell down, and I can't live there no more.

> Mmmm, I can't move no more (x2)
> There ain't no place for a poor old girl to go.

A *backwater* is defined as either "water turned back in its course (as in a sewer or river channel) by an obstruction, an opposing current, or the flow of the tide" or "a body or accumulation of water resulting from this, esp. when overflowing lowlands or forming a body fed by a side channel from the main current or sea."[96]

Many listeners, blues singers, and music and cultural historians have mistakenly considered "Back-Water Blues" to be about the 1927 flood of the lower Mississippi.[97] Noting that the song's recording and release dates precede the event by two and one months respectively, blues scholar David Evans conducted research in the newspapers of the period and delved into Smith's touring itinerary, evidence rendered by Smith's colleagues, and literature on floods. Evans proved that the song is in fact Smith's response to the flooding that took place in Nashville, Tennessee, on December 25, 1926, as a result of the Cumberland River bursting its banks.[98] Taking into account casualties caused by the simultaneous flooding of the Tennessee River in Chattanooga, Smith's birthplace, at least sixteen people died in Tennessee.

Bessie Smith's seemingly generic description of a flood in fact conceals an accurate account of events in Nashville. The song's solemn incipit may have been inspired by the Bible's description of the rainfall that caused Noah's flood: "And the flood was forty days upon the earth; and the waters increased" (Genesis 7:11–17).[99] It is more likely, however, that Smith read newspaper accounts that reported five consecutive days of heavy rain before the flood.[100] Her line would appear in dozens of blues about different floods, both reworkings of "Back-Water Blues" and original songs. The reference to the time and place where the flood hit ("in the lowlands at night") is far from generic and accidental. The flood did occur overnight, and many residents woke up to flooded homes on Christmas morning.

In the second stanza, Bessie Smith casts herself as a flood victim, unable to leave her house for a safer place. This was indeed the predicament in which the predominantly African American population living in northeastern Nashville found themselves. Her rescue by a rowboat that came "five miles 'cross the pond" perfectly corresponds to what was reported in many local newspapers. Smith's mention of thousands of homeless refugees in the next verse is also anything but fictional: the final official estimate was that 10,400 people had been displaced. The fifth stanza's reference to viewing the aftermath of a catastrophe from hills around town would become quite common in blues songs about disasters. In stanza six, Smith is still playing the role of someone made homeless by the collapse of her house, again a result of the flood covered in newspaper accounts. The final verse finds the singer stranded and with no prospect of finding a place to live.

Smith's "Back-Water Blues" has been interpreted as alluding to racial issues. This is certainly true for some of the recordings dealing with the 1927 Mississippi flood, and it is more generally undeniable that there is a context of segregation implied when a song mentions that Southern Blacks lived in the lowland areas which were inevitably the first to be submerged by flooding. However, as far as this specific event and song are concerned, the assumption that there was "racism underlying the differential relief provided black and white victims" does not hold.[101] From reports published in the *Chicago Defender* and other African American newspapers, it is clear that interracial cooperation in the Nashville relief efforts exceeded all expectations.[102]

The popularity of Bessie Smith's "Back-Water Blues" is attested, among other things, by the three covers made by different artists in the same year[103] and by the myriad other recordings of the song (commercial and noncommercial, studio and live) that have followed.[104] In the years immediately following its release, "Back-Water Blues" "took on a life of its own, becoming *the* flood blues, an all-purpose generic blues on the theme, suitable for commemorating any particular flood, or floods in general."[105]

Another topical song on the Nashville flood deserves closer scrutiny for comparative purposes: "Backwater Blues" (Vocalion 5164), recorded in New York City on May 11, 1927, by the white Tennessean stars of country music, Uncle Dave Macon (1870–1952) and Sam McGee (1894–1975).[106] Despite its similar title, the song is completely different from Smith's composition.

> *Spoken:* Well, good people, you all know water will put out fire, but when water backs up, it makes you put out. Right up the mountain, just like old Wreck of '97, going down grades ninety miles an hour. Now I'm gonna give you a little imitation how that old train was a-going. [Plays "Wreck of the Old 97" as a banjo solo.]
>
> *Spoken:* Hot dog! I'm old but I'm 'round here!
>
> Backwater's up and the people's a-running
> I'm a-going to the mountain, I'm a-going hunting
> Fare you well, oh my little darling
> Lord, Lord, ain't I gone.
>
> *Chorus:*
> Oh my love, lonesome road
> Oh my love, lonesome world
>
> I love you and you can't help it
> You love me, but you won't confess it
> No, you don't, oh my little darling
> Lord, Lord, ain't I gone.
>
> *Chorus*
>
> Two little children lying in the bed
> The water was a-rising over their head
> Their mother's up town, was never found
> Lord, Lord, wasn't that sad
> Oh how bad! Oh how sad!
>
> I heard a man talking to a feller
> The water was a-rising in his cellar
> Rise any more and a-coming through the floor
> Lord, Lord, open the door.

Chorus

Nashville is a favorite town
The backwater's got us a-running around
Lord have mercy, ain't I gone.
Lord, Lord, fare you well.

Chorus

After the spoken introduction, the first two stanzas and chorus only hint at the Nashville flood; the third and fourth introduce the subject, and the fifth makes explicit reference to the adoptive city where Uncle Dave Macon and Sam McGee matured artistically and became stars of the Grand Ole Opry radio show.[107] There was a vigorous interchange of mutual influences between Black and white music, but Macon's approach is so "Black" in style and compositional technique that he was sometimes thought to be African American by Black listeners to his records.[108] All in all, this topical disaster song can be defined as "pre-blues" not only musically, but also textually in its descriptive indefiniteness and lack of historical details.

A comparison between Smith's and Macon's lyrics shows obvious stylistic and metrical differences, typical of their respective musical genres. Smith's heartfelt delivery is no surprise, given that she was an eyewitness to the tragedy and the writer of the song. Considerable emotional involvement on Macon's part is also evident, and as will be seen below, his approach differs from that of other whites who were shortly to sing about the 1927 Mississippi River flood. Macon's tone is highly personal, and he presents himself as a participant in the catastrophe, as happens in most African American blues songs on natural disasters.[109]

Greenville Levee Blues: The 1927 Mississippi River Flood

The widespread disaster known as the Mississippi River Flood resulted from a combination of torrential rains along the Yazoo River in the Mississippi Delta in the winter of 1926, and along the Ohio River and its tributaries in January 1927. The lower Mississippi Valley experienced flooding in February and was hit by tornadoes in March. Pittsburgh was flooded in late January and March, and Cincinnati in mid-April. Among other places, the levees broke at Laconia, Arkansas; Hickman, Kentucky; Dorena and near New Madrid (thirty miles south of Cairo, Illinois), Missouri. At 7:30 a.m. on Thursday, April 21, there was a massive breach of the levee at Mounds Landing, near Greenville, Mississippi.[110]

Although other natural disasters claimed higher death tolls, the 1927 Mississippi River flood affected and changed the lives of millions of Americans like

Figure 1.05. "Flood, 1927 Mississippi River. Birdsong Camp at Cleveland, Mississippi, April 29, 1927" (Illinois Central Railroad Company). Courtesy of the Archives and Records Services Division, Mississippi Department of Archives and History

no other disaster. According to the US Weather Bureau, 313 deaths were directly attributable to the flood, but the true total was probably over a thousand; several hundred plantation workers are thought to have been swept away when the Greenville levee broke. Almost a million people were left homeless in the lower Mississippi basin alone. Approximately one third of them fled to safety; another third or so (mostly white) were fed and clothed by the Red Cross; the rest (90 percent Black) were also taken care of, but were forcibly confined in segregated refugee camps (see fig. 1.05).

Total economic losses, direct and indirect, have been estimated at almost a billion 1927 dollars (equivalent to $14 billion in 2018). Most of the several million acres that were flooded in the seven hardest-hit states (Illinois, Missouri, Kentucky, Arkansas, Tennessee, Mississippi, and Louisiana) belonged to white landowners, but the mainly Black farmers, laborers, and sharecroppers who worked for them were utterly ruined.[111]

Thousands of Black people were urged or forced to work on combating the flood, especially in Greenville, where the levee required constant monitoring, and raising thousands of sandbags weighing between sixty and eighty pounds, which rain or other water increased to more than 100 pounds. The workforce shoveled the earth, filled the sandbags, carried them up the slope, and stacked them by hand atop the levee. They were paid seventy-five cents a day, less than the wage for picking cotton. In the early morning of April 21, when the first small break in the levee appeared, hundreds of Blacks refused to work in such life-threatening conditions, but were compelled to do so by the guns of a white foreman and his guards, mostly World War I veterans ready to shoot anyone who attempted to escape.[112]

In the Louisiana parishes of Plaquemines and St. Bernard, on the east bank of the Mississippi near New Orleans, the tension was based less on race than on class and the division between urban and rural inhabitants. After prolonged debate, the local authorities, fearing that New Orleans would be flooded, resolved to dynamite the levee at Caernarvon, thirteen miles southeast of Canal Street, on April 29. This futile measure inundated the surrounding countryside and destroyed some 10,000 people's crops and homes.

David Evans's definitive study of the response to this natural disaster in African American blues and gospel music transcribes and analyzes all the relevant African American lyrics dealing with this catastrophe and explicates some other songs that have been dubiously or erroneously associated with it.[113] In order to consider aspects not dealt with in Evans's survey, only some lyrics pertaining to the 1927 flood are transcribed here. My emphasis is on songs recorded as the catastrophe was still raging, and on the most significant songs that consider the event from an unexpected perspective. I also expand coverage to hillbilly songs in order to comment on Black and white approaches to this and other disasters, and to discuss more recent original songs and thematic developments related to the event.

Possibly the earliest popular song to mention the flood was "High Water Blues" by Daryl Sinclair Conner and Clarke Tate, published in 1927 by the Conner Publishing Company of Augusta, Arkansas.[114] Born in Missouri in June 1895, by 1920 Daryl Sinclair had married William Bolivar Conner, and was living in Augusta. A farmer at the time of the flood, her husband had become a bank vice-president by 1940.[115] Clarke Tate was a Memphis singer and music teacher, probably hired to write the music. Both lyricist and composer were white.

Augusta was unaffected by the flood, but the lyrics depict its effects in the neighboring area, where three hundred people were marooned at Peach Orchard Bluff with limited food supplies.[116] The description of the song as "a real southern blues," the cover image of a Black man sitting on the porch of a shack, surrounded by rising flood waters, and the use of a version of Black speech are all attempts to represent the lyrics as mimetic of African American culture. In fact, they emerge from and reinforce stereotypes of Blacks as being fatalistic.

I got the blues, blue as can be,
My front yard looks like the deep blue sea.
Just sittin' round, can't see de ground,
Keeps me wonderin' when de flood's goin' down.

Chorus:
I got de high water blues (x2)
Nobody home but de fishes and me.
Water's all aroun' me
Just like the sea!
I got de high water blues (x2)
Holes in my roof an' there's holes in my shoes,
I can't see nobody,
Can't hear no news.

Trains can't run 'cause the tracks washed away,
Can't do a thing but sit here all day.
I got the high water blues,
I said the high water blues,
You ol' high water blues.
I got de blues.

Can't plant cotton an' I can't plant no hay,
Can't plant no corn, it's raining all day,
I got the high water blues,
I said the high water blues,
Those muddy water blues,
I got de blues.

Extra choruses

I got de high water blues (x2)
Sittin' here smokin'
Just my thots [*sic*] and me,
Wonderin' when somebody,
I'll ever see,
I feel like old Noah
In the Ark,
I'm lonesomer than one bear
Out in the park.
I got de high water blues

Those triflin' high water blues
You ol' high water blues.

I got de high water blues (x2)
The bacon's all gone
And 'lasses, too
Corn meal almost gone
What shall I do?
Boat's full of holes
An' I can't swim
Lawd heah mah prayers
I'm trustin' in Him.
I got de high water blues
Those muddy high water blues
You ol' high water blues.

The first recording directly associated with the disaster is "South Bound Water" (OKeh 8466) by Lonnie Johnson, recorded in St. Louis, Missouri, on April 25, 1927, only four days after the levee breach at Mounds Landing. The song has little topical interest because it merely depicts a generic flood.[117]

I live down in the valley; people comes from miles around (x2)
Their little homes was washed away; they had to sleep on the ground.

Through the dreadful nights I stood, no place to lay my head (x2)
Water was above my knees, and the water had taken my bed.

I climbed up on the mountain to find some place to stay (x2)
'Cause the south bound water had washed my little valley home away.

The water was roaring down the valley just like a thunderstorm.
Water was roaring down the valley just like a thunderstorm.
Washed my little valley house away; there's no place I can call my home.

In New York City, six days after the levee was breached at Greenville, white country singer Vernon Dalhart recorded the first of his ten versions of Carson Robison's composition "The Mississippi Flood" (Victor 20611):[118]

Another great disaster has come upon our land,
Down where the Mississippi flows on its way so grand.
The springtime flowers were blooming, the world was bright and gay,
And folks along the levee were happy all the day.

And then the skies grew cloudy and rain came falling down.
For days a mighty torrent came pouring to the ground.
The streams throughout the country kept swelling day by day
Until the angry river was roaring on its way.

And then there came a warning: "The levee cannot stand,"
And brave men fought and struggled to save their native land.
But still the raging water kept pounding at the shore
Until it broke the levee and through the country tore.

So many lives were taken, and brave men knelt to pray.
There's all that they had cherished was madly swept away.
The world will gladly help them to pay the awful cost,
But gold can never bring them a loved one who is lost.

We can't explain the reason these great disasters come,
But we must all remember to say, "Thy will be done."
And though the good may suffer for other people's sins,
There is a crown awaiting where eternal life begins.

This song's stylistic and lyrical approaches are completely different from those in all Black compositions about the flood. Its formulaic text shows the composer's detachment from the event, which is hardly surprising, given that Robison had no involvement in it, and was motivated by commercial considerations.[119]

Paramount Records played their ace late in April, when their Texan star Blind Lemon Jefferson (1893 or 1894–1929) recorded "Rising High Water Blues" (Paramount 12487), credited on the record label to his accompanist, pianist George Perkins, but probably composed by Jefferson himself.[120]

Backwater rising, southern peoples can't make no time,
I said, backwater rising, southern peoples can't make no time,
And I can't get no hearing from that Memphis girl of mine.

Water all in Arkansas, people screaming in Tennessee,
Oh, people screaming in Tennessee,
If I don't leave Memphis, backwater been all over poor me.

Paper states it's raining; it have been for nights and days,
Paper states it's raining, has been for nights and days.
Thousand people stands on the hill looking down where they used to stay.

Children sadly pleading, "Mama, we ain't got no home."
"Oh, mama, we ain't got no home."
Papa says to childrens, "Backwater left us all alone."

Backwater rising, come in my windows and door.
Ah, backwater rising, come in my windows and door.
I'll leave with a prayer in my heart, backwater won't rise no more.

In typical blues fashion, the song shifts between deep concern for the victims of the flood and expressions of personal preoccupation and self-pity. Thus, Jefferson begins with the "southern peoples" who are unemployed ("can't make no time") because of the flood, and then states that he cannot get through on the phone to his girl in Memphis. In the second stanza, his description of flooding in Arkansas, and the indirect mention of a refugee camp in Memphis (probably the Tri-States Fairgrounds) are accurate reporting of events, although its location on a bluff meant that Memphis was little affected by backwater. Verse three alludes to newspaper accounts of the disaster[121] and to a hill (possibly Crowley's Ridge in Arkansas) where refugees found shelter, and from where they could see the devastation caused by the flood. After the pleading from children which features in at least one more blues recording about disasters ("Hi" Henry Brown's "Titanic Blues"), the song closes with a prayer (or more accurately, a hope, since it is not explicitly addressed to God) that the waters will stop rising.

On May 2, Blue Belle (real name Bessie Martin),[122] later also known on disc as Bessie Mae Smith, St. Louis Bessie, and May/Mae Belle Miller, recorded "High Water Blues" (OKeh 8483):[123]

The rivers all are rising, ships sinking on the sea,
The rivers all rising, ships sinking on the sea,
I wonder do my baby think of me.

The waves is dashing and roaring like a lion (x2)
My baby's in the river drifting up and down.

I want to go to Cairo, but the river's all over town (x2)
I want to ride the train, but the track's all out of line.

I'm gonna build me a ship and buy me a rocking chair (x2)
If this water keep on rising, gonna rock on 'way from here.

My daddy's got something make you talk in your sleep,
My daddy have got something make you talk in your sleep,
But these high-water blues will make you hang your head and weep.

Blue Belle's song presents two simultaneous scenes: a shipwreck and a snapshot of the Mississippi River flood between her hometown, St. Louis, and Cairo, Illinois, further south, at the confluence of the Mississippi and Ohio Rivers. The lost ship may be the American freighter *Elkton*, which had recently disappeared in the Pacific; her references to the danger of flooding and the disruption of the railroad network in Cairo accurately depict the situation just a few weeks before the song was recorded.

Born in Plum Bayou, Arkansas, and raised in Houston, Texas, Sippie Wallace, née Beulah Thomas (1898–1986), was living in Chicago by the time she recorded "The Flood Blues" (OKeh 8470) there on May 6.[124] Despite her claim that she wrote the song with her brother, George Thomas, the composer credits are to "Wallace and Granger" [*sic*]. The latter may be pianist Cleo Grainger, with whom she had previously recorded, and who may be a member of the band on this recording, alongside Louis Armstrong on cornet and others.

> I'm standing in this water, wishing I had a boat (x2)
> The only way I see is take my clothes and float.
>
> The water is rising, people fleeing for the hills (x2)
> Lord, the water will obey if you just say, "Be still."
>
> They sent out alarms for everybody to leave town (x2)
> But when I got the news, I was high water bound.
>
> They dynamite the levee, thought it might give us ease (x2)
> But the water still rising, doing as it please.
>
> I called on the Good Lord and my man too (x2)
> What else is there for a poor girl to do?

These original lyrics provide a vivid portrait of a woman trying to escape the rising waters. Her references to "alarms" sent before the breaking of levees, and to the dynamiting at various sites to divert the course of flood waters, are historically accurate. In the last stanza, the singer pleads to both God (as she had previously done in verse two, quoting Mark 4:39) and her man for help, in a daring juxtaposition of sacred and secular solutions to the disaster.[125]

Besides Dalhart's, two more recordings by white musicians were made at the time of the disaster.[126] Philadelphia-born vaudeville vocalist and songwriter Arthur Fields (Abe Finkelstein, 1888–1953) recorded "The Terrible Mississippi Flood" (Grey Gull/Radiex 2334) in New York City ca. May 1927.[127]

Down in the sunny Southland, where the Mississippi flows,
The skies were fair, and the people there were living in sweet repose,
Till the Father of the Waters arose in angry might,
And overflowed its muddy banks, 'twas an awe-inspiring sight.

The people were horror-stricken when they realized their plight,
And many were drowned without a chance of putting up a fight.
Thousands were forced to flee for their lives and their happy homes
    forsake,
While the rushing water left its toll of destruction in its wake.

Here was a land where all was peace a few short hours before,
Turned into a land of horror with the Angel of Death at each door.
While the cruel waters were rising, thousands of men were on hand,
Struggling in vain to build up the levees with millions of bags of sand.

A lot of men lost all they had, their homes and loved ones gone,
Till the hearts of a nation were beating for them, as they tried to carry on.
Just picture the mother who lost her babe, perhaps her husband too,
Try and put yourself right in her place and imagine what you would do.

Think of the poor little boys and girls who are now left all alone,
Little orphans of Dixieland, without the shelter of home.
Let's hope this great stream can be harnessed, so its name won't be
    written in blood,
In the hearts of the grieving survivors of the Mississippi flood.

Initially the perfectly rhymed lyrics are descriptive, then they become sentimental, especially in the verses describing the loss of loved ones and the sympathy of the nation. Divine Justice goes unmentioned, no religious comfort is
provided, and there is a sense that hope may be groundless and action futile.
This is quite an innovative thematic approach, especially in white disaster songs,
which seldom eschew the chance to plead for God's intervention, help, or mercy.
On the whole, the text of this Tin Pan Alley number reveals a more secular
consciousness than the typical hillbilly disaster song. This probably reflects the
presumably northern and urban background of its composer, identified only
as "Ryder" on the record label.

    "The Story of the Mighty Mississippi" (Victor 20671) was recorded in New
York City on May 21 by country music star Ernest "Pop" Stoneman (1893–1968),
from Galax, Virginia. It was composed by his fellow Virginian Kelly Harrell
(1889–1942).[128]

Way out in the Mississippi Valley, just among those plains so grand,
Rolled the flooded Mississippi River, destroying the works of man.

With her waters at the highest that all men have ever known,
She came sweeping through the valleys, and destroying lands and
   homes.

There were children clinging in the treetops who had spent a sleepless
   night,
And without a bit of shelter, or even a spark of light.

With their prayers going up to the Father for the break of day to come,
That they might see some rescue party who would provide for them a
   home.

There were some of them on the housetops with no way to give an
   alarm,
There were mothers wading in the water with their babies in their arms.

Let us all get right with our Maker, as He doeth all things well,
And be ready to meet in judgment when we bid this earth farewell.

Five mainly descriptive stanzas, narrating the sad plight of people clinging to housetops and treetops,[129] or wading through troubled waters, are rounded off with a typical exhortation to behave as good Christians in order to be ready for Judgment Day.

On the same day, Stoneman also recorded "Joe Hoover's Mississippi Flood Song" (Victor, unissued). Stoneman reportedly adapted a song learned from a Black janitor who was working in the Victor building,[130] and indeed Joe Hoover is credited as songwriter in the Victor files.[131] However, in 1934 the white pianist-composer J. Russel Robinson wrote topical songs as "Joe Hoover." These compositions, about Bonnie and Clyde, John Dillinger, and kidnapping (probably of the Lindbergh baby) were recorded (as Joe Smith) by hillbilly yodeler Dwight Butcher. Robinson seems a more likely source for Stoneman's unissued song.[132] The matter-of-fact descriptions and aloof tone of the hillbilly songs, and Arthur Fields's Tin Pan Alley number, mirror sympathy rather than grief. However, Fields's song introduces a touch of originality to the stereotyped formula in its subtly threatening and fatalistic final stanza.

On June 7, 1927, Black vaudeville singer Laura Smith (1882–poss. 1932) recorded two flood songs in Chicago, accompanied by Clarence M. Jones on piano. "Lonesome Refugee" and "The Mississippi Blues" were released on Victor

20775.[133] Written by vaudeville singer-comedians Sidney Easton and Joe Simms respectively, they have little blues flavor and display a pop style typical of the previous decade when their composers were very popular on the theatrical circuits. Despite the generic character of the two lyrics, a reference to current events is present in the second song, where the apparently negligible line "The water is still rising from Memphis down to New Orleans" conceals Black people's fear that the Mississippi River might rise again. Indeed, work on the levee near Greenville was carried out throughout the first week of June and finished on the day Laura Smith's two songs were recorded.[134]

With "Mississippi Heavy Water Blues" (Columbia 14222-D), recorded in New York City on June 15, 1927, Atlanta twelve-string guitarist Robert "Barbecue Bob" Hicks (1902–1931) recorded a song that focuses on the aftermath of the 1927 flood and on themes as diverse as death, sex, and the post-flood clearance of mud:[135]

I was walking down the levee with my head hanging low,
Looking for my sweet mama, ah, but she ain't here no more.
That's why I'm crying Mississippi heavy water blues.

Lord, Lord, Lord, I'm so blue; my house got washed away,
And I'm crying "How long 'fore another payday?"
That's why I'm crying Mississippi heavy water blues.

I'm sitting here looking at all of this mud,
And my gal got washed away in that Mississippi flood.
That's why I'm crying Mississippi heavy water blues.

I hope she comes back some day kind and true.
Can't no one satisfy her like her sweet papa do.
That's why I'm crying Mississippi heavy water blues.

I think I heard her moan on that Arkansas side,
Crying "How long before sweet mama ride?"
That's why I'm crying Mississippi heavy water blues.

I'm in Mississippi with mud all in my shoes.
My gal in Louisiana with those high water blues.
That's why I'm crying Mississippi heavy water blues.

Spoken: Lord, send me a sweet mama.

Got plenty mud and water, don't need no wood or coal.
All I need's some sweet mama to slip me jelly roll.
That's why I'm crying 'sippi heavy water blues.

Nothing but mud and water far as I could see.
I need some sweet mama come and shake that thing with me.
That's why I'm crying Mississippi heavy water blues.

Listen here, you mens. One more thing I'd like to say.
Ain't no womens out here, for they all got washed away.
That's why I'm crying Mississippi heavy water blues.

Lord, Lord, Lord, Mississippi's shaking, Louisiana's sinking.
The whole town's a rinking [sic]; Robert Hicks is singing.
That's why I'm crying Mississippi heavy water blues.

Reportedly composed by Barbecue Bob with the help of a passenger on the train taking him to New York to record,[136] the song played an important role in his short recording career, as it was a big seller and was mentioned by the preacher at Hicks's funeral.[137] Barbecue Bob may also have drawn on newspaper reports when writing his song; his instinct for what would appeal to listeners probably accounts for his references to the three most devastated states: Arkansas, Mississippi, and Louisiana. There may be an implied reference to Greenville, which is in Mississippi, across the river from Arkansas and about forty miles above the Mississippi-Louisiana border.

In the first six verses, Bob casts himself as a man searching the levee for his woman who has been "washed away." The spoken interlude marks a thematic shift, from an implicitly unsuccessful search for a specific missing woman, to a search for sexual satisfaction with any available woman. Given contemporary attitudes, the difficulties of achieving and maintaining sexual relationships were not a subject mentioned in official accounts of the flood, but they must have been a very real problem for the refugees packed into the camps.

In the week of May 23 to 28, 1927, Alice Pearson, probably then living in Memphis, made her only recordings for Paramount in Chicago, accompanied by pianist Freddie Coates. The six titles included songs (with no composer credits) about the Memphis earthquake of May 7, 1927 (see "Hell Broke Loose in This Land: Unidentified and Miscellaneous Natural Disasters"), and the 1927 Mississippi Flood.[138] On "Greenville Levee Blues" (Paramount 12547), Pearson borrows the melody and portions of her lyrics from Bessie Smith's "Back-Water Blues," and achieves similarly distinctive artistic results, recounting a shocking situation with great urgency, but clearly and effectively.

I woke up this morning, couldn't even get out of my door (x2)
The levee broke, and this town is overflowed.

And you could hear people screaming all over town (x2)
And some was hollering, "Please don't let me drown."

When the water was rising, creeping up in my door (x2)
I had a mind to leave, and I didn't know where to go.

They was rowing little boats five and ten miles away,
They was rowing little boats, Lord, five and ten miles away,
They were picking up people didn't have no place to stay.

Living on the levee, sleeping on the ground (x2)
I will tell everybody that Greenville's a good old town.

Delta water caused me to lose my clothes and shoes (x2)
You can tell by that it's left me with the Delta water blues.

The two singers' perspectives are very different: Smith sang about the Nashville flood from the privileged position of a visiting star who arrived after the flooding and was accommodated, reluctantly but in reasonable comfort, above an undertaker's parlor. Pearson, on the other hand, presents herself as a homeless refugee in the Greenville levee camp.

Pearson sounds as heartfelt as Smith, but like Smith she may not have experienced the flood she sings about. In 1960 Johnny Watson (Daddy Stovepipe), recalling his time in Greenville, told Paul Oliver that "there was another lady used to sing—Alice—Alice Pears think her name was and she had a pianner player call him Freddy. They used to be there."[139] However, it is not clear whether Watson was in Greenville at the time of the flood, and consequently his recollection does not prove that Pearson was. Moreover, Daddy Stovepipe was probably replying to a leading question by Oliver. Pearson may have had some connection to Greenville, but it is more likely that she simply saw the flood and the Memphis earthquake as good song topics.[140] Whether she experienced them personally or not, her allusion to conditions in the levee camp at Greenville seems deliberately ambiguous: she may be describing Greenville as "a good old town" ironically, because people had to sleep "on the ground," or sincerely, because there was assistance, however inadequate, for people displaced by the flood.

At the beginning of "Water Bound Blues" (Paramount 12507), the flip side of "Memphis Earthquake," Pearson sings that she is in poor health—quite a common occurrence after a flood—before recalling the high waters covering her house and forcing her to flee:

> High fever and suffering really got me barred (x2)
> I can't even get away. High water's all in my yard.
>
> I went to bed last night, water was easing over my white floor (x2)
> I got up this morning, water creeping all in my door.
>
> Hey, hey, hey, hey, hey, hey.
> Hey, hey, hey, hey, hey, hey, hey.
> Hey, hey, hey, hey, hey, hey, hey, hey.
>
> I went and climbed a tall old lonesome tree.
> I went and climbed up a tall old lonesome tree.
> I couldn't stand to see my house float away from me.
>
> All down the road the water's all 'cross the tracks (x2)
> And I've left my home; you see I can't go back.

If the song is autobiographical after all, its final line seems to tally with a move from Mississippi to Memphis, where in 1928 Pearson "is listed in the Memphis City Directory as rooming at 249 S. 3rd St., in the Beale Street entertainment district. She had said in 'Memphis Earthquake' that it would take her until the next summer to 'overcome.'"[141]

After the success of Bessie Smith's "Back-Water Blues" and other songs on the Mississippi flood, Columbia Records commissioned a follow-up from her, to be released before Christmas. The seldom dependable Big Bill Broonzy told Paul Oliver that African American recording director Mayo Williams "chartered a boat for a number of the blues singers to witness [the victims of the flood]. Including Lonnie Johnson, Kansas Joe McCoy, Springback James, Sippie Wallace and Broonzy himself the party was joined by Bessie Smith."[142] There is some doubt as to whether the boat trip actually took place or that Smith's recording was inspired by it. Whether it was or not, "Homeless Blues" (Columbia 14260-D), composed by Porter Grainger, was recorded in New York City on September 28, 1927, accompanied by Grainger on piano and alto saxophonist Ernest Elliott.[143]

> Mississippi River, what a fix you left me in,
> Lord, Mississippi River, what a fix you left me in,
> Potholes of water clear up to my chin.

House without a steeple,[144] didn't even have a door (x2)
Plain old two-room shanty, but it was my home sweet home.

Ma and Pa got drownded; Mississippi, you're to blame.
My Ma and Pa got drownded; Mississippi, you're to blame.
Mississippi River, I can't stand to hear your name.

Homeless, yes, I'm homeless, might as well be dead.
Ah, you know I'm homeless, homeless, yes, might as well be dead.
Hungry and disgusted, no place to lay my head.

Wished I was an eagle, but I'm a plain old black crow. (x2)
I'm gonna flop my wings and leave here and never come back no more.

Porter Grainger's lyric sets the Empress of the Blues on a new metaphorical
stage, but as a touring artist she would have been as familiar with Mississippi
and its suddenly deadly river as with her native Tennessee, and the Cumberland River that had inspired "Back-Water Blues." The lament of a homeless
person is made poignant by verbal and musical quotations from "Home Sweet
Home," but Grainger adds a strong sense of racial pride, seasoned with irony,
self-awareness, and realism. These are embedded in the lines "Plain old two-
room shanty, but it was my home sweet home" and "Wished I was an eagle,
but I'm a plain old black crow." The singer's solution to her plight is found in
many secular disaster songs, and one that many African Americans in the
devastated region were considering: departure in search of a better and less
hostile place to live.[145]

In contrast to the flow of blues songs about the 1927 Mississippi flood, only
one topical sermon was recorded: "Red Cross the Disciple of Christ Today"
(Paramount 12601) by Moses Mason (1871–1934),[146] recorded ca. January 1928 in
Chicago.[147] Described by Paramount in the Black newspaper *Chicago Defender*
as "Uncle Mose Mason, the singing elder from the Delta land,"[148] Mason and
his family were living in Lake Providence, Louisiana, when he recorded the
sermon, but in the previous decade they had lived in Greenville.[149]

Mason focuses on the Red Cross's relief effort, and likens it to the Feeding
of the Five Thousand, the story in the Bible in which Jesus Christ took five
little loaves and two fishes and fed five thousand people (Matthew 14:13–21;
Mark 6:30–44; Luke 9:10–17; John 6:1–15). He thus rejects the critical stance of
some *Chicago Defender* journalists, who accused the Red Cross of discriminat-
ing against Black refugees,[150] but he does indirectly criticize the compulsion
imposed on them by the National Guard. Mason sees the Red Cross as an
unbiased organization devoted to helping flood victims regardless of race, but

his reference to Christ riding in "heaven's chariot [with] no gun on His side" implicitly reproaches the threatening behavior of armed National Guardsmen, forcing Black people to work on the levee.

At the October 11, 1927, session where she recorded "Tornado Groan," Luella Miller also made "Muddy Stream Blues" (Vocalion 1147). This transcription is of her second version, recorded on January 24, 1928. Neither recording has any songwriter credit.[151]

> Mississippi muddy water rose from bank to bank (x2)
> Prayed to the good Lord that the man I love won't sink.
>
> Sun rise in the east, and it sets in the west (x2)
> The way rain have did the people, left all their homes in a mess.
>
> I'm going back south, going back there to stay,
> Going back south, going back there to stay,
> And I'll see you, daddy, 'most any old rainy day.
>
> I got the muddy stream blues; I ain't got no time to lose,
> I got the muddy stream blues; got no time to lose,
> All this rain down south give all the farmers the blues.

Miller's preoccupation with the fate of her man and her longing to go home ("back south") and be reunited with him are juxtaposed to sympathy for people living there, and especially for farmers, whose crops have been ruined and who are unable to raise another.

Almost a year after the levee broke, African American people's increasing frustration and anger at their mistreatment during and after the flood are openly expressed in Lonnie Johnson's "Broken Levee Blues" (OKeh 8618), recorded in San Antonio, Texas on March 13, 1928.[152]

> I wants to go back to Helena; the high water's got me barred. (x2)
> I woke up early this morning, high water all in my back yard.
>
> They want me to work on the levee; I had to leave my home,
> They want to work on the levee, then I had to leave my home,
> I was so scared the levee might break, Lord, and I may drown.
>
> The water was 'round my windows and backing all up in my door,
> The water was all up 'round my windows and backing all up in my door,
> I'd rather to leave my home 'cause I can't live there no more.

The police run me from Cairo all through Arkansas,
The police run me all from Cairo all through Arkansas,
And put me in jail behind those cold iron bars.

The police say, "Work, fight, or go to jail." I say, "I ain't toting no sack."
Police say, "Work, fight, or go to jail." I say, "I ain't toting no sack.
And I ain't building no levee; the planks is on the ground, and I ain't
driving no nails."

It is not known—but is irrelevant to the song's impact—whether Johnson actually went through the unpleasant experiences he describes. Helena was protected by five miles of levees, but its southern outskirts had been flooded since April 15, 1927, and a refugee camp was established there, with its inhabitants used on work to reinforce the levees. Local Black laborers and even visitors were often conscripted, under the threat of being arrested for vagrancy, to carry out the hazardous work day and night. In this blues, and notably in his refusal to obey in the last verse, Johnson gives vent to Black people's (and especially his own) indignation; expressed in real life, it would probably have resulted in a severe beating.

Further evidence of some historians' unfamiliarity with blues lyrics is found in Richard M. Mizelle's interpretation of Johnson's song, which is basically correct but marred by his faulty transcription of the last verse as:

The police say work right or go to jail, I say I ain't totting no sacks,
I won't drown on that levee and you ain't gonna break my back.[153]

Leaving aside the mistaken "totting" for "toting," the impudence of Johnson's reply to the police does not lie in his refusing to "work right" but in his rejection of the coercive alternatives to work offered by the police. If accepted, their challenge to him to fight would simply have been an excuse to beat him; his refusal to rise to the bait, seemingly passive or even cowardly, is in fact as defiant as his bold (and in prewar blues lyrics, most unusual) rejection of white authority by refusing to work at all. This is much stronger than Mizelle's seemingly resolute, but in fact weak, "I won't drown on that levee."

Some later recordings on the 1927 flood fail artistically because of lack of originality. Some are so generic that they may be about other, later floods in other states. Barbecue Bob's "Mississippi Low-Levee Blues" (Columbia 14316-D) was recorded in Atlanta on April 21, 1928,[154] the anniversary of the breaking of the levee at Greenville. It is a sequel to "Mississippi Heavy Water Blues," probably requested by the recording company, looking to cash in on the earlier song's commercial success. It revisits some of the themes in his earlier song—mud, the death of his woman and the indifference of other women, the ensuing lack of sex, apathy due to unemployment, the loss of his house. This time, however, the themes are strung together, less coherently but with a surprisingly more incisive comic effect.

Other songs were nondescript, like James Crawford's "Flood and Thunder Blues" (Gennett 6536) and Mary Dixon's partial cover of it, "Fire and Thunder Blues" (Columbia 14459-D).[155] Recorded at Crawford's only session, "Flood and Thunder Blues" has the peculiarity of creating a hillbilly atmosphere with the yodeling in the fourth verse, but it also hints at racial discrimination and prejudice in the otherwise unmotivated mention of color in "Black cats whining, white dogs want to bite." "Flood and Thunder Blues" also resonates with the eschatology found in numerous sacred songs and sermons about floods and other disasters ("Heaven's angry, someone's done some wrong"). Credited to "Cole," vaudeville singer Mary Dixon's "Fire and Thunder Blues" is a cover of this song, omitting Crawford's opening verse and adding two new ones.

Elders McIntorsh and Edwards's "The 1927 Flood" (OKeh 8647), recorded in Chicago on December 4, 1928, is the only gospel song on the event.[156] The leaders' duetting vocals and (probably) guitars are finely enhanced by the powerful singing of Sisters Bessie Johnson and Melinda Taylor.

> It was in Nineteen Twenty-Seven. It was an awful time to know.
> Through many Delta countries God let the water flow.
> The people worked in vain, but God wouldn't stop the rain.
> Lord, He poured out His flood upon the land.
>
> He sent a flood to the land, (Oh, glory) and He killed both beast and man,
> 'Cause the people got so wicked, they wouldn't hear God's command.
> All praying [They prayed] the water would yield, but for God they had
>   no zeal.
> Well [And/So], He poured out His flood upon the land.
>
> Many sacks of dirt was gathered; (Oh, yeah) men worked with all their
>   power,
> But the levees still was breaking, water rising more each hour.
> They did all they could do, but God's judgment must go through,
> So He poured out His flood upon the land.
>
> *Repeat stanza 2*
>
> The evil hearts of men have brought this land to shame,
> But God looked down from heaven to invade the Delta plain.

"This land will be brought down, with the flood it will have to drown,"
And He poured out His flood upon the land. (Glory)

Repeat stanza 2 twice

Repeat stanza 3

The song's message—that the flood is God's punishment for sin—is unoriginal, and the wickedness it blames is implicitly universal, not attributed to any group or race. This perhaps reflects the danger of making explicit accusations of racism. They may nevertheless underlie the stanza describing the reinforcement of the levees, a task that Black workers in Greenville and elsewhere performed unwillingly or at gunpoint.

"When the Levee Breaks" (Columbia 14439-D) was among the first recordings of Wilber McCoy, better known as Kansas Joe (1905–1950), and his wife Memphis Minnie (1897–1973), whose real name was Lizzie Douglas. It was recorded in New York City on June 18, 1929, more than two years after the Greenville levee broke.[157]

If it keeps on raining, levee's going to break (x2)
And the water gon' come, and have no place to stay.

Well, all last night I sot on the levee and moaned (x2)
Thinking 'bout my baby and my happy home.

If it keeps on raining, levee's going to break (x2)
And all these people have no place to stay.

Now look here, mama, what am I to do?
Now look here, mama, now what I should do,
I ain't got nobody to tell my troubles to.

I worked on the levee, mama, both night and day (x2)
I ain't got nobody to keep the water away.

Oh, crying won't help you, praying won't do no good,
Now crying won't help you, praying won't do no good,
When the levee breaks, mama, you got to move.

I works on the levee, mama, both night and day,
I worked on the levee, mama, both night and day,
Done worked so hard to keep the water away.

I had a woman; she wouldn't do for me (x2)
I'm going back to my used to be.

Oh, mean old levee, caused me to weep and moan,
It's a mean old levee, caused me to weep and moan,
Gonna leave my baby and my happy home.

Notwithstanding its late recording date and lack of geographical or temporal references, the song pertains to the 1927 Mississippi River flood, as Memphis Minnie's sister-in-law Ethel Douglas pointed out:

> When we lived on the levee, right near Walls, [Minnie] and her oldest brother lived with us then. The levee *did* break, and we left from there. I'm sure that's what she was singing about "when the levee broke" 'cause we were scared to death when it broke, 1927.[158]

It was Kansas Joe who sang the song, however, and it is very likely that he at least contributed to writing the lyrics; he may have also witnessed the deluge when he was living in the flooded area below Vicksburg, Mississippi. Regardless of who wrote them, and regardless of Joe's garbling of stanzas one and five, the lyrics paint a vivid picture of a frustrated and exhausted Black worker, toiling on the levee night and day. Nevertheless, I entirely agree with Memphis Minnie's biographers that "'When the Levee Breaks' was not so much a cry of pain as an announcement of a new beginning."[159]

The last, but by no means the least, song certainly dealing with the 1927 Mississippi River flood was "High Water Everywhere Part I" (Paramount 12909) by Delta bluesman Charley Patton (ca. 1885–1934), who recorded it in Grafton, Wisconsin, ca. February 1930.[160]

The backwater done rose all around Sumner, drove me down the line,
Backwater done rose at Sumner, drove poor Charley down the line,
And I'll tell the world the water done struck Drew'ses town.

Lord, the whole round country, Lord, creek water is overflowed,
Lord, the whole round country, man, it's overflowed,
Spoken: You know, I can't stay here. I'm . . . I'll go where it's high, boy.
I would go to the hill country, but they got me barred.

Now looky here now at Leland, river was rising high,
Looky here, boys around Leland tell me river is raging high,
Spoken: Boy, it's rising over there. Yeah.
I'm gonna move over to Greenville. Bought our tickets. Good-bye.

Looky here, the water dug out, Lordy (*Spoken:* Levee broke), rose most everywhere,
The water at Greenville and Leland, Lord, it done rose everywhere,
Spoken: Boy, you can't never stay here.
I would go down to Rosedale, but they tell me it's water there.

Lord, the water now, mama, done struck Shaw'ses town,
Well, they tell me the water done struck Shaw'ses town,
Spoken: Boy, I'm going to Vicksburg.
Well, I'm going to Vicksburg on a high[er] mound.

I am going on dry water where land don't never flow [*sic*]
Well, I'm going on a hill where water, oh, it don't never flow,
Spoken: Boy, Sharkey County and Issaquena's drowned and inched over.
Bolivar County was inching over in Tallahatchie's shore.
Spoken: Boy, I went in Tallahatchie. They got it over there.

Lord, the water done rushed all over that old Jackson Road,
Lord, the water done raised over the Jackson Road,
Spoken: Boy, it got my clothes.
I'm going back to the hill country. Won't be worried no more.

Patton's artistry manifests itself to the full in his ability to sing about an event that had occurred almost three years earlier with as much urgency as if it were taking place at that instant. Despite some geographical incongruities, such as his nonsensical escape from the safe town of Sumner in Tallahatchie County to flooded areas like Greenville and Leland, his and the other flood victims' hopelessness and bewilderment is vividly conveyed.

Patton was leading a peripatetic life in Mississippi in 1927, but it is unlikely that he was present at all the places mentioned, and "[t]he specific details and locations in the lyrics . . . are probably based on a combination of personal experience, experiences of friends, news reports, and perhaps even Patton's imagination."[161] The events in the song most likely to be real may be his attempt to reach safety in either his native "hill country," south of the Delta, or Vicksburg, where he had relatives. His failure to reach the hill country is ascribed to white people, often cautiously referred to in both speech and song by the deliberately indefinite and ambiguous "they," as here in the phrase "they got me barred."[162]

The most extensive discussion of Bessie Smith's "Back-Water Blues" is included in a recent cultural study of the 1927 Mississippi River flood.[163] In her book, Susan Scott Parrish disregards the earlier flood that occurred in Nashville at Christmas. Her choice of Smith as a towering figure in music (as well as, admittedly, the first and commercially most successful Black composer of a flood blues song) and her idea of connecting only Smith's song to the concept of a "super-flood" are indicative of some cultural historians' tendency to "exploit" selected or even isolated blues (albeit unforgivably few gospel) lyrics as a secondary and isolated tool rather than as a primary source to support conceptually valid and accurately researched theories without appreciating their significant global impact on popular culture.

In my opinion, this reflects a shortsighted view of Black culture as a whole, in that African American popular music (especially vaudeville, blues, and gospel) is not a monolith but rather a many-sided geometric figure with different interrelated facets. In this particular case, Parrish manipulates the transcription of the text to avoid the fact that it mirrors newspaper accounts alongside Smith's own probable personal experience. Parrish's brilliant general reading of the lyrics as displacement is marred by her parallel between Smith's song and the classical "eclogue," which in my opinion draws on totally different cultural backgrounds in the tradition of nature writing.

David Evans's thorough study of African American songs on the 1927 Mississippi River flood may justify (yet not fully explain) why Parrish barely mentions (and provides no analysis of) all the other songs on the 1927 Mississippi River flood. Thus, Parrish's otherwise remarkable and enlightening insight into the disaster loses momentum. Even though nowadays historical evidence has proven that a more accusatory treatment of the subject by African American singers would have been more than justified, Parrish's focus on racial and gender identity issues clashes with the few overt references or indictments of racial conflict in the bulk of 1927 disaster recordings. Some uncomfortable stereotypes (such as Moses Mason's sermon and Barbecue Bob's secular song) and the attribution of the flood to divine agency (as in McIntorsh and Edwards's sacred song) that are detectable in the recordings confute Parrish's one-sided reading of this complex subject.

As for her idea of a "super-flood," it remains doubtful whether the 1927 flood that started in April can be seen as a direct consequence of the December 1926 Nashville flood rather than as a separate event. Of course, a flood can linger on for several weeks (receding water, mud, clean-up, and so on), and the case can be made that the high water of Nashville flowed into the Mississippi River and contributed to the more disastrous flood in April, but the 1926 Nashville flood was a minor and localized disaster and was likely to have been essentially over by April 1927. In fact, no newspaper coverage of flooding on the Mississippi or Ohio Rivers is reported in the period from January to March 1927 except in early January, shortly after the rain system affected Nashville.

The relatively large number of songs on the 1927 Mississippi flood enables us to draw some conclusions. The first is the high incidence of Black topical compositions on the disaster, which arises from the African American population's having been harder hit than the white, and from the flood having struck in the heart of blues country.

Most white performers interpret the calamity as an inscrutable and inevitable expression of God's will, and "God's will be done" is their only moral to be drawn. The white response to the tragedy was to rebuild in the same place. The African American workforce had received relief supplies, and were consequently seen as indebted to both local landowners and society at large, a debt which they should discharge through unpaid work. Most African Americans, whether or not they were committed Christians, conceived the flood as the act of an angry God punishing mankind for its sins. We might say that they reversed the meaning of Woody Guthrie's as yet unwritten song, "This Land Is Your Land": this land had never been their land, and a new life was awaiting them elsewhere.

Pop music largely trivialized the event. Hillbilly music treated it from a distance, expressing solidarity with the sufferers through themes of sympathy, rebuilding, and "harnessing" the river. Black blues singers put themselves right in the midst of the flood as victims; Black gospel artists sang or preached with extreme fervor, seeing the flood as a sign of God's wrath (McIntorsh and Edwards) or mercy (Moses Mason). It is noteworthy, however, that the 1927 Mississippi flood was handled fairly profusely by blues singers and rarely in gospel. This is probably largely due to the fortuitous and incorrect association of "Back-Water Blues" with this disaster, and its consequent commercial success.

The memory of the disaster is still vivid today, having been handed down in people's stories from generation to generation,[164] but by the end of World War II the 1927 flood theme had largely been forgotten by the blues and gospel communities. Postwar secular and sacred musicians very occasionally revived songs about it,[165] and Kansas Joe McCoy's song was an improbable hit for the white rock group Led Zeppelin.

However, there were several covers of Bessie Smith's recording, by singers who mistakenly associated it with the Mississippi River flood. Possibly the most significant of them is Big Bill Broonzy's "Back-Water Blues," recorded live in Amsterdam, The Netherlands, on February 28, 1953. In his spoken introduction, the composition is correctly credited to Smith, but Broonzy's account of how he and his family lived through the disaster is quite unreliable, as often was the case with him. However, this is more usefully seen as an example of Broonzy's self-presentation as an African American Everyman, making history and communal experience vivid to white audiences by personalizing them. It is significant that Broonzy presents the song as a token of memory, and that

Figure 1.06. Eric Bibb, Chattanooga, Tennessee, 2008 (Brian Jannsen). Courtesy Eric Bibb

he devoted all the proceeds of his two Dutch concerts to the National Disaster Fund, set up in the wake of the January 31, 1953, Zeeland floods that had killed 1,836 people.[166]

Among the few recent compositions inspired by the 1927 flood is "Flood Water," recorded by Eric Bibb (1951–) in Burton, Ohio, on November 11 or 12, 2008 (see fig. 1.06).[167]

> Flood water spreading all around (x2)
> People everywhere trying to make higher ground.
>
> Many met their Maker in a watery grave (x2)
> If your neighbor had a boat, well, you mighta been saved,
> Mighta been saved.
>
> Bibles floating in the water, had to leave it all behind (x2)
> Sister had a vision, church paid her no mind,
> Paid her no mind.

People straddling their rooftops, water reaching to their knees (x2)
Heard the preacher holler, "Lord, Lord, Lord have mercy, if You please!"

Don't you know, it rained, Noah, where were you? (x2)
Cows couldn't swim, drowning two by two.

Flood water far as my eyes could see (x2)
Nineteen hundred, twenty-seven never leave my memory,
Never leave my memory.

Bibb's song is quite atypical of blues on this topic in its challenge to the value
and effectiveness of religious faith (stanzas 2–5), which seems to be the main
theme of the song. Bibb was born almost a quarter of century after the disaster,
and this may explain why his song differs in outlook from older treatments,
probably reflecting his background growing up in a politically conscious leftist
folk scene. The concept of memory is at work here in all its different meanings
of remembrance, retention, and commemoration. His song is not a distortion or
interpretation of history, but a resolute and modern point of view. The manifold
meanings of the word *memory* come to the fore throughout the analysis of
songs on the 1927 Mississippi River flood, thus permeating over ninety years
of American history.

Southern High Waters Blues: The 1929 Alabama, Georgia, Kentucky, and Tennessee Floods

In March 1929, severe floods submerged large areas of Alabama, Georgia, Kentucky, and Tennessee, and several dozen people lost their lives, thirteen in
Alabama.[168] Elba, the county seat of Coffee County, Alabama, was the most
seriously affected town, although there was only one fatality, a blind African
American man. A series of articles in the Laurel, Mississippi, *Morning Call*
provides a vivid account of events.[169] On the afternoon of Thursday, March 14,
a dam on the Pea River broke and many people, including two hundred children, were marooned in the Elba schoolhouse; thousands more were stranded
on rooftops for up to three days, and were supplied with food and clothing
dropped from airplanes.[170] An enormous volume of rain fell: "At Elba alone a
rainfall total of 21.4 inches was measured in a period of 32 hours ending at
16:00 CST [Central Standard Time], March 14, 1929."[171] In the early afternoon
of the following day, the river crested at 43.5 feet.

In the study of disaster songs, the 1929 flood is particularly interesting for
comparative purposes because it elicited songs, both sacred and secular, from
Blacks and whites. Twelve-string guitarist George Carter's "Rising River Blues"

(Paramount 12750), recorded in Chicago, was possibly the first related blues recording.[172] The recording date for this session is generally given as ca. February 1929, but if it relates to the flooding that began on the last day of that month, March is more likely. However, the song probably describes a generic flood, or at most foreshadows what was going to happen in its reference to rising rivers:

> Rising river blues running by my door (x2)
> They running, sweet mama, like they haven't run before.

> I got to move in the alley, I ain't 'lowed on the street (x2)
> These rising river blues sure have got me beat.

> (Hummed stanza)

> Come here, sweet mama, let me speak my mind (x2)
> To cure these blues, mama, take a long, long time.

Despite its indefiniteness, there may be some personal experience elements in the text. The line "I got to move in the alley, I ain't allowed on the street" may refer to a curfew or some ordinance against looting. The singer's last stanza is also ominous, and if read in context, it might turn these apparently harmless and vaguely descriptive lyrics into a song of "resistance" or of forthright commentary similar to some of Charley Patton's creations.

After his 1927 "God's Wrath in the St. Louis Cyclone" (and again perhaps at the record company's urging), Rev. J. M. Gates committed "The Flood of Alabama" (OKeh 8678) to wax in Atlanta on March 21, 1929.[173]

> Ah. The flood of Alabama. God rode through Alabama in a flood of water. My God is able to whip the world with a drop of water. God rode through Elba, Alabama, in a flood of water. Men and women, men and women, children as well, rushed into Judgment. Tell me water was in West Point, Georgia, floating six feet in the street. He's riding, God rode in a flood of water. It rained from above until it woke up the sleeping animals of the water. Yes, it did there below. It rained, rained on until it woke up a turtle. And they tell me he weighed one thousand three hundred and fifty pounds. It taken four horses to pull him out of the Gulf of Mexico. It rained right on. Rained, it rained, and they tell me that this turtle about three hundred years old, but it rained right on. Rained until it baptized the hills and the valleys. It rained on. Rained on the peoples in Alabama, in Georgia, and in Florida as well. It rained on till the water got so high. Aeroplanes moving through the air. It

rained right on. Rained until men and women clinged to the trees floating down the water. And it rained, God knows it rained. It rained, you
remember ah, that storm that moved through the country over in Tennessee. Oh, it rained, God knows it rained. After a while, and by and
by, my God's gonna rain, gonna rain down fire on high. Instead of the
aeroplanes moving in the air, angels from glory, ooooh oohhh, gonna
build a platform in the air, and it's gonna rain down fire. Oh, it rained,
God knows it rained.

The landing of a huge sea turtle near Port Arthur, Texas, is accurately described
from contemporary reports.[174] Gates's linking of this incident to the flood is
consistent if the turtle is interpreted as a sign of God's wonders. Gates does see
the flooding as God's judgment: he refers to God "whip[ping] the world with
a drop of water," and characterizes the flood as a forerunner of the Last Judgment, with an intertextual evocation of "God gave Noah the rainbow sign / No
more water but the fire next time," a couplet that later supplied James Baldwin
with a book title.

On the same day, for the same company and in the same city, white singer,
preacher, and composer Andrew Jenkins (1888–1956) recorded "The Alabama
Flood" and "The Fate of Elba, Alabama," both released on OKeh 45319 under
the moniker Blind Andy.[175] In the former song, assisted by second vocalist Mary
Lee Spain, Jenkins sings:

> On a dark and stormy night
> I saw an awful sight
> The water in the rivers rising high.
> In an Alabama town
> Not a resting place was found
> The thunder and the lightning pierced the sky.
>
> A message of despair
> Came flashing through the air,
> It told the story of that little town.
> All rescue seemed in vain
> By car, and boat, and plane,
> It seemed that all the people there must drown.
>
> Amidst the falling rain,
> The lightning flash and flames,
> The people in that town were filled with fright.
> And while they cried and screamed

On came that mighty stream,
No tongue can tell the terrors of that night.

From shelter in that hour
The flood in all its power
Drove thousands from their homes into the street [town].[176]
From tranquil resting place,
The people rose to face
A mighty wall of water rushing down.

The flood was at its worst
With hunger and with thirst,
The little town of Elba met its fate.
With cries and screams and groans
The people fled their homes.
They tried to leave that town; it was too late.

The countryside was sad
When they received the word
They started out to save that little town.
With car and boat and plane
Amidst the falling rain
While the mighty flood came rushing rolling down.

Its recording date, June 11, 1929, suggests that Lonnie Johnson's "The New Fallin' Rain Blues" (OKeh 8709), recorded in New York City, may relate to the flooding of three months earlier.[177] The song is a mishmash of scarcely original verses drawn from his and other singers' flood recordings. Featuring Johnson's violin playing, it draws inspiration from Noah's flood and Bessie Smith's "Back-Water Blues," and reprises a stanza from his first commercially successful recording— otherwise unrelated except in its title—"Falling Rain Blues" (OKeh 8253). David Evans suggests, however, that the song was inspired by the 1927 Mississippi River flood, and that Johnson is "capitalizing on his earlier hit, [borrowing] phrases and imagery from the Biblical flood and Bessie Smith's 'Back-Water Blues.' . . ."[178] This is certainly true, but Johnson was a prolific and fast composer of flood songs, therefore "The New Fallin' Rain Blues" is more likely to pertain to the 1929 flood. Johnson also mines his own back catalog when he describes the flood as roaring like a lion; vivid in 1927's "St. Louis Cyclone Blues," here the simile is no more than a cliché:

Storm is rising, rain begin to fall (x2)
Think some poor people ain't got no home at all.

The dark clouds rising, trouble in the low land, I know,
Dark clouds rising, trouble in the low land, I know,
Lord, I wants to leave this old shack, but I'm afraid to go.

It's been raining in this town forty days and nights,
Been raining in this town forty days and nights,
When the world turned dark, know it was trouble in the low land that
    night.

Storm started at midnight and never stopped until day (x2)
Seen nothing but empty houses floating down the river all day.

Started to raining on Monday, rained forty days and nights (x2)
When the world turned dark, I know it's trouble in the low land that
    night.

When the wind start to howling, poor people begin to scream and
    cry (x2)
The water roared like a lion and taken poor people as it passed by.

The only apparently factual statements in the lyrics (the storm and flood beginning on a Monday at midnight) are inaccurate, and probably as conventional
as the references to "forty days and forty nights."

   "Southern High Waters Blues" (Gennett 7101) was recorded by Cow Cow
Davenport's wife Ivy Smith (1892–1937, real name Iva France)[179] in Richmond,
Indiana, on August 27, 1929. It carries no composer credit, but undoubtedly
describes the March 1929 flooding. The reference to Monday is again incorrect.[180]

Mmm, thundered and rained (x2)
You, southern high water, driving me insane.

In Georgia and Alabama, even Tennessee,
The southern high water's rising, and it's sure hurting me.
The southern high waters rising night and day,
They rising so fast, they driving me away.

On Monday morning 'bout half past four,
Skies got cloudy, and the wind began to blow.

The southern high waters rising fierce and fast,
If they keep on rising, I sure can't last.

Way up North it ain't rained a drop,
I can't go there 'cause the trains done stopped.
Says, the southern high waters rising all the time,
If they keep on rising, I will lose my mind.

Lord, lightning flashed, thunder rolled,
Skies got cloudy, and the rain began to pour.
Says, the southern high waters rising night and day,
Lord, Southern high waters driving poor me away.

Sonny Scott's composition "Rolling Water" (Vocalion 02533), which he recorded in New York City on July 19, 1933, with piano accompaniment by Walter Roland, may relate to the March 1929 Alabama flood.[181]

Rolling water rolling in my rider's door,
Well, it's rolling water rolled up in my rider's door,
It got so cloudy that evening, didn't have no place to go.

Lord, I went fishing in the rolling water, caught a fish, a eel, and a snake,
I went fishing in the rolling water, caught a fish, eel, and a snake,
I saw a frog and a terrapin do the shimmy down on that lake.

Lord, I saw the cloud rising; I tried to get back home,
Lord, I saw the cloud rising, eeeh; I tried to get back home,
But I got the news my baby got lost in that storm.

Lord, I didn't want to go home, baby; I tried to die myself. (x2)
Lord, my baby got killed, and I can't love nobody's else.

When it dried off, baby, sky was purple red,
When it dried off, baby, eeeh, sky was purple red,
But that wasn't my trouble; the woman I love was dead.

The generic descriptions fit any flood disaster, but despite the late recording date, Scott—resident in Birmingham, Alabama, in the 1930s and possibly before, and an associate of Walter Roland, also based in Birmingham—may have been singing about an event that had affected the state where he was living.

Besides those by Andrew Jenkins (Blind Andy), there was one more composition by a white singer about the Alabama flood, notably by Jack Waite.[182] Dalhart made as many as nine recordings on this disaster, but only two are different songs. They bear different titles and were composed by Jack Waite or Andrew Jenkins. Dalhart's following version of "Alabama Flood" (Edison 52566) was recorded on April 11 and released in July. It is credited to Jack Waite.[183]

Everyone was happy where the cotton blossoms grow,
Working and a-singing where the southern breezes blow,
When suddenly there came a cry that froze up each one's blood,
For down the levee came a man who cried, "Here comes the flood."

The waters came a-rushing while the people were asleep,
And then before they knew it round their homes did quickly creep.
Though many did escape it, oh so many met their fate,
They tried to get away, but they awakened just too late.

Chorus:
Down in Alabama, in the water and the mud,
Many souls are homeless from the Alabama flood.

Little babies perished and husbands lost their wives,
The cruel waters took their toll of many, many lives.
And down in Alabama you can hear an awful moan
For those who lost their dear ones and for those who lost their home.

Thousands who have suffered now are heartbroken and sad,
Some have lost their dear ones, some lost everything they had.
We know they must have help and so throughout this wondrous land
Each one of us will do our share and lend a helping hand.

Chorus

The strong impact that the 1929 Alabama flood had on both the African American and white communities is mirrored by the topical songs' diversity of styles and lyrical approaches.[184] Of all the natural disasters, the 1929 Alabama flood was the one that elicited a more balanced proportion of Black and white recordings, a possible reflection of the even racial distribution of victims and casualties in comparison with other catastrophes.[185] The speed with which songs, and a sermon, were composed, recorded, and released in the wake of the disaster suggests that the record companies had taken note of the success of topical recordings (most notably "Back-Water Blues") after the 1927 Mississippi flood, and were hoping for a repetition.

Some Peoples on Tallahatchie Done Lost Everything They Had: The 1930 Arkansas and Mississippi Floods

The Tallahatchie River flows eighty-five miles in Mississippi, from Tippah County to Leflore County, where it merges with the Yalobusha to form the Yazoo. "Tallahatchie River Blues" (Vocalion 1480) was recorded by blues singer-guitarist Mattie Delaney (1904–unknown) in Memphis, Tennessee, ca. February 21, 1930.[186] The song relates to a series of floods that submerged large areas of Tallahatchie and Quitman Counties in the Mississippi Delta, the town of Blytheville in northeast Arkansas, and parts of other states from the second half of January 1930 onward. The flooding was particularly severe on January 22.

> Tallahatchie River rising; Lord, it's mighty bad. (x2)
> Some peoples on Tallahatchie done lost everything they had.
>
> The people in the Delta all wondering what to do. (x2)
> 'f they don't build some levees, I don't know what become of you.
>
> High water rising, got me troubled in mind. (x2)
> I got to go and leave my daddy behind.
>
> Lord, this water rising, and I sure can't swim,
> High water rising, and I sure can't swim,
> But if it keep on rising, sure gon' follow him.
>
> Gon' pack my suitcase, go back to Tennessee (x2)
> For this Tallahatchie River done got the best of me.

David Evans has found newspaper coverage reporting that the floods were "accompanied by bitter cold and ice. No one died in the flood in Mississippi, but many families lost their possessions and livestock in flood waters that were three feet deep and turning to ice over 20,000 acres north of the town of Swan Lake."[187] Evans has also shed new light on Mattie Delaney: a person by that name, aged 25, was listed in the 1930 US Census of Glendora in Tallahatchie County, Mississippi. Delaney's lyrics describe the effect of the flood on the Delta's population as a whole, before zeroing in on personal experience in a narrative that is possibly fictionalized but historically quite accurate. This calls to mind Alice Pearson's account of the 1927 Mississippi River flood in the way they portray themselves as "typical" flood victims.[188] Glendora and Swan Lake are only two miles apart and are on the banks of the Little Tallahatchie River, so it is very likely that Delaney actually experienced the flood or knew people who did.

Another song on this series of floods was Charley Patton's "High Water Everywhere Part II" (Paramount 12909).[189] Because it is "Part II" of a record whose "Part I" is definitely about the 1927 Mississippi River flood, it has usually been associated with that earlier disaster, but more likely describes these later floods, and their impact on northeastern Arkansas. It was recorded in Grafton, Wisconsin, ca. February 1930. Paramount caused long-running confusion among blues and other historians by giving two songs about different disasters the same title, suffixing them "Part I" and "Part II," and releasing them on the same disc.[190]

> Backwater at Blytheville, backed up all around,
> Backwater at Blytheville, done struck Joiner town,
> It was fifty families and children, some of them sink and drown.
>
> The water was rising up in my friend's door. (x2)
> The man said to his womenfolk, "Lord, we'd better go."
>
> The water was rising, got up in my bed,
> Lord, the water was rolling, got up to my bed,
> I thought I would take a trip, Lord, out on the big ice sled.
>
> Oh, I heard the horn blow, blowing up on my shore,
> *Spoken:* Blowing; couldn't hear it.
> I heard the iceboat, Lord, was sinking down,
> I couldn't get no boat, so I let 'em sink on down.
>
> Oh-ah, the water rising, islands sinking down.
> Saying, the water was rising, airplanes was all around.
> *Spoken:* Boy, they was all around.
> It was fifty men and children, some o' them sink and drown.
>
> Oh, Lordy, women is groaning down,
> Oh, women and children sinking down,
> *Spoken:* Lord, have mercy.
> I couldn't see nobody at home, and wasn't no one to be found.

Blytheville and Joiner are close to the Mississippi River, and mentions of Blytheville and northeast Arkansas abound in newspaper accounts of the flooding.[191] The lyrics of "High Water Everywhere Part II" strengthen the hypothesis that the song describes not the 1927 Mississippi River flood but that of 1930, far less disastrous and less widespread. The repeated (and, on the second occasion, garbled) reference to "fifty families and children, some o' them sink and drown" probably reworks (and exaggerates for dramatic effect) an incident reported in Mississippi's *Greenwood Commonwealth*: "One report from Blytheville, Ark., center of relief operations, said that between 40 and 50 families, marooned on the little river district, southwest of that city, were in a serious plight with provisions running low and ice blocking efforts of rescue parties to reach them. Rising water was forcing them into a smalled [*sic*] area and it was reported that several persons had been forced to the roof of their cabin."[192] Patton's references, unique in blues lyrics, to "the big ice sled," "airplanes . . . all around," and "the ice boat" may be accurate descriptions of what he either experienced or read about in the Memphis *Commercial Appeal* of January 24 and 25 referenced above.

As David Evans has pointed out, Patton seems to have developed a literary "technique of multiple perspectives" on the facts narrated.[193] He simultaneously plays the roles of local reporter, volunteer helper (which he may actually have been) in a failed rescue, passive observer, and victim of the flooding. It is quite common for a blues singer to be at once an eyewitness, a reporter, and a more or less directly affected sufferer in a disaster, but Patton does not remain passive or adopt an aloof and ironic attitude. Instead, and in contrast to the rather obsessive and almost chaotic approach of "High Water Everywhere Part I," he takes manifold perspectives and a more focused view.

To conclude, the lack of any song by whites about this mainly Black disaster may result from the fact that flooding was not always reported in the white newspapers as tragedy, but merely as a commonly occurring event that inevitably causes inconvenience and some suffering. Yet such neglect may also be due to what the whites considered as part of normal life in the region for Blacks. Indeed, it is significant that two Black singers were concerned enough to offer a counternarrative conflicting with the white songwriters' general approach to emphasize heroism and to find it when they are the victims of disasters. Floods mainly affected the poorest Black people because they had to leave in low-lying areas that were more likely subjected to catastrophic events.

Flood Water Blues: The 1936 Pennsylvania Flood

On May 31, 1889, more than 2,000 people died in Johnstown, Pennsylvania, when a dam burst upstream. Forty-seven years later, Johnstown was again struck by flooding, together with Pittsburgh, Washington, DC, and eleven states in the northeast and mid-Atlantic regions.[194] Because it happened on March 17, 1936, this disaster is known as "the Great St. Patrick's Day Flood." The day before, unusually warm temperatures and heavy rain had caused snow and ice on the upper Allegheny and Monongahela Rivers to melt. On St. Patrick's Day, the waters reached the officially defined flood level, twenty-five feet, and peaked at forty-six feet on March 18, thanks to torrential rainfall. The death toll varies according to sources, but it is generally given as twenty-five people in Pittsburgh and 200 in the surrounding area.[195] Some 100,000 buildings collapsed or were seriously damaged, including steel mills and other industrial plants, which employed scores of workers, and many offices in Johnstown's business section, "the Golden Triangle." Fires added considerably to the injury toll. Estimated total damage amounted to $250 million.[196] Johnstown was again devastated, but deaths, at around two dozen, were far fewer than in 1889.[197] The smaller towns of Altoona and Hollidaysburg were also seriously flooded.

There were no recordings by white artists about this disaster, but two African American musicians recorded songs. On March 25, 1936, in Chicago, Kansas City–based Casey Bill Weldon (born Nathan Hammond, probably 1901–1972) made "Flood Water Blues No. 1" and "Flood Water Blues No. 2" (Vocalion 03220).[198]

It's high water in the east, has flooded all the river towns. (x2)
Everybody's getting warning, better go to the hills before they drown.

So I caught a train, I got back home at the break of day,
Oh, I caught a train, got back home about the break of day,
I looked for my house, the river had taken my house away.

I rowed a boat across the river, the water was rough as it could be,
I rowed a boat across the river, water was rough as it could be,
I heared the women and children screaming, hoo-oo, "Please save poor me."

And then I tried so hard to turn my boat around,
Then I tried so hard to turn my boat around,
But the water was so rough, it turned my boat upside down.

Oh, I was satisfied, I didn't have to moan and cry,
I was satisfied, I didn't have to moan and cry,
Because when I looked upstream, I seen a mule come swimming by.

I caught that mule that was swimming down the stream. (x2)
Then I rode that mule, hoo-oo, to the nearest hill I seen.

Despite the lack of reference to locations more specific than "the east," this and the following song were probably inspired by the 1936 Pennsylvania flood, since they were recorded only eight days later. Casey Bill Weldon shows great talent as a lyricist and seems to epitomize the bluesman who tells "the truth, although it was not an autobiographical truth. . . . [I]t was a truth based in universal human experience or at least a kind of experience that was known to the singer and audience."[199]

It was dark as midnight and everything was still. (x2)
It was a thousand of people, hoo-oo, trying to make it to the hills.

I'm gonna tell you, people, the strangest thing I ever seen (x2)
Was cats and dogs on housetops a-floating down the stream.

There was thousand of people in the hills didn't have no place to stay,
There was a thousand of people in the hills didn't have no place to stay,
Was watching the high water, hoo-oo, taking the houses away.

Spoken: Lord, have mercy. Wonder what the people's gonna do.

It was cold and it's raining, some people didn't have no shoes on their
feet,
It was cold and it was raining, some people didn't have no shoes on
their feet,
Women and children was crying, hoo-oo, because they didn't have a
thing to eat.

Well, I'm gonna build me a house in the mountains, in the highest
mountains I know,
Gonna build me a house in the mountains, in the highest mountains I
know,
So I don't have to worry 'bout the high water and floods no more.

In the opening stanza, the dark stillness of midnight is clichéd but enables a highly effective, quasi-cinematic cut to the panic-stricken flight of people suddenly menaced by a roaring flood. A fixation with animals runs through Weldon's lyrical output, and manifests itself here in the imaginative image of abandoned cats and dogs floating downstream, stranded on housetops.

Less than a month later, on April 18, and again in Chicago, Virginian Carl Martin (1906–1979) recorded "High Water Flood Blues" (Champion 50074).[200]

> Well, it rained, it rained, and the rivers began to rise,
> Banks began to overflow, thousands lost their lives.
> The water kept on flowing, flowing on and on,
> There's thousands of people have done lost their happy home.
>
> Well, the whistles began blowing and the bells began to ring,
> People running and screaming, but they couldn't do a thing,
> 'Cause the water kept on flowing, flowing on and on,
> There's thousands of people have done lost their happy home.
>
> Well, that Johnstown flood left the people in an awful fix,
> Nothing like that flood started in Pittsburgh in 1936.
> The water kept on flowing, flowing on and on,
> There's thousands of people have done lost their happy home.
>
> Well, high water's here, high water's everywhere,
> High water's here, high water's everywhere,
> I believe if you go to China, you'd find high water's there.

Unlike Weldon, Martin names towns devastated by the flood, and appears to compare the severity of the 1889 flood in Johnstown with the more recent one in Pittsburgh. Martin's possible allusion to the 1931 flooding in central China, which killed perhaps two million people through drowning, famine, and disease,[201] is too wide-ranging for a blues singer, especially considering that he seems indifferent to accuracy, and formulaically exaggerates the number of fatalities in the Pennsylvania flood ("thousands lost their lives").

The final comments on the lack of topical songs by whites recalling the 1930 Arkansas and Mississippi River floods also apply here even if the 1936 Pennsylvania flood was a less localized and more extensively covered event in the newspapers of the time than the earlier flood. Again, it was two blues (and no gospel) singers who felt the need to remind the African American record-buying public that Black people were the main victims of these catastrophic events.

Wild Water Blues: The 1937 Ohio and Mississippi River Floods

In January and February 1937, severe flooding of the Ohio River and Mississippi River valleys affected Pennsylvania, Ohio, West Virginia, Indiana, Illinois, Kentucky, Tennessee, Arkansas, and Louisiana. The Ohio River rose to record levels

Figure 1.07. "Three refugees from the 1937 flood in their tent of the camp in Marianna, Arkansas, February 1937" (Edwin Locke). Courtesy Prints and Photographs Division, Library of Congress, Washington, DC

in Cincinnati, Ohio (80 feet), and Paducah, Kentucky (60.8 feet). On January 24 (known as "Black Sunday"), martial law was declared in Evansville, Indiana, where the water level had reached 54 feet. The following day, with 70 percent of Louisville, Kentucky, under water, Mayor Neville Miller asked Governor Albert Benjamin "Happy" Chandler to declare martial law there also. The flood in Louisville crested at 57 feet on January 27. Portsmouth, Ohio, was also hard-hit. Nearly 400 people (90 in Louisville alone) died by drowning and other causes, a million were left homeless, and estimated property losses amounted to $500 million dollars.[202] The thriving town of Cairo, Illinois, situated a few miles from where the Ohio River flows into the Mississippi River, was miraculously spared, but further south the Mississippi River and some of its tributaries flooded west and middle Tennessee, eastern Arkansas, and Louisiana. Over a thousand people, mainly from west and middle Tennessee and eastern Arkansas (see fig. 1.07), quartered at the flood refugee camp at Memphis fairgrounds,[203] and by February 3 the city had registered about 28,000 refugees.[204]

The 1937 floods struck African Americans' imagination more than any other natural disaster after the 1927 Mississippi River flood, and prompted a number of bluesmen and a gospel composer to write songs about it. It is also reported that in 1937 "rivergees" (a whimsical spelling of "refugees") at the Memphis fairgrounds sang:

Down at the Fairgrounds on my knees,
Prayin' to the Lord to give me ease—
Lord, Lord, I got them high-water blues![205]

Three commercial blues recordings (two with alternate takes) were made within days of the first overflow. Two more songs were recorded within the next twelve months, a song was composed but not recorded, another recording three months later contains a possible reference to the flood, and an otherwise unrelated song recorded four years after the event includes a passing mention of it. Only one sacred song on this natural disaster, Charles Haffer's "The 1937 Flood," is known to have been composed. Its broadside, which is dated January 1937 and is subtitled "A National Disaster (Part One)," was sold by Haffer for ten cents a copy in the streets and in front of churches. Haffer's usual introductory statistics about the event and the biblical extracts that inspired the song precede the text.[206]

More than 400 dead, and more than 1,000,000 People Homeless. Property Damage Estimated $550,000,000. A Prophetical Song from the following Scriptures: 2 Peter 1:21; Jeremiah 47:2–3; Joshua 10, 11; Judges 5:20–21.

The Bible is said to be written by Holy Men of old,
As they were moved by the Spirit of God[, they] wrote down what they
    were told;
They wrote about these troubled times which we are passing through;
These days got everybody troubled—So they don't know what to do.

Chorus (after every verse):
These days got everybody troubled, not only me and you—
It's got the rich and the poor, and every nationality—
So they don't know what to do. (Repeat chorus twice.)

In nineteen thirty-seven there was awful times you know;
Through many towns and countries God let his water flow;
People were so distressed [they] could hardly make it through;
These days got everybody troubled so they don't know what to do.

This flood is Bible prophesy in harmony with God's will;
Recorded thousands of years ago and now it's being fulfilled;
Chunks of ice falling from the heavens, men dying all around;
Multitudes swept away, rivers breaking through dry ground.

The water commenced rising—rose higher and higher
Until it filled up every creek, river, lake and bayou;
The rain continued falling about 23 nights and days,
Until the water had covered a portion of eleven states.

There are people living in this world who have seen many floods years
    ago,
But the flood of nineteen thirty-seven is the worst ever seen before.
There's thousands of acres of land that's never been flooded before;
There was thousands of people driven from their homes and no place
    to go.

Many sacks of dirt was gathered, men worked with all their power,
But the levees still were threatening, water rising more each hour;
They did all they could do, but the water went through;
These days got everybody so troubled so they don't know what to do.

Many camps were established to care for the refugees,
Thousands of doctors and nurses to battle with disease.
Soup kitchens were soon erected to feed the hungry souls,
While thousands and thousands of others were shivering in the cold.

With more than four-hundred people dead, half-billion-dollar prop-
    erty loss;
More than a million cared for by the Red Cross;
Whole cities were in darkness, communication lines were down,
Short wave stations were set up to broadcast news around.

Now goodbye refugee people, and in my last appeal
If you will put your trust in the Lord, He will surely heal;
God almighty is the prince of peace, He's true, good and kind;
If you call on Him in time of need He will ease your troubled mind.

As pointed out in the study of the 1926 Miami hurricane and the 1936 Tupelo tornado, the reprise of portions of lyrics and melodic similarities with Elders McIntorsh and Edwards's "The 1927 Flood" are further evidence of the popularity of the song within the Church of God in Christ well before 1926. From the earlier recording, Haffer borrows the stanza after the chorus and stanza six, merging both text and melody with one of his own compositions unrelated to disasters, namely "These Days Got Everybody Troubled" (AFS 6623-A).

The widely popular Bumble Bee Slim (Amos Easton, 1905–1968) recorded the first song about the flood, "Rising River Blues" (Vocalion 03473), on January 27 in Chicago.[207]

> If the river keeps on rising, soon it will overflow. (x2)
> Thunder keeps on rolling, I believe I've got to go.
>
> Storm keeps on raging, rain keeps on falling down. (x2)
> I'm gon' get myself a rowboat, and ride from town to town.
>
> Should it rain forty days, we will have another flood. (x2)
> Well, I can see lying women deep down in the mud.
>
> *Green Pastures* showed everybody just the way the world began. (x2)
> After so much water had washed away the sand.
>
> Well, my baby bought her ticket and she watched it endless times,
> My baby bought her ticket and she watched it endless times,
> But she was so hardhearted, she didn't even change her mind.

The main point of interest in this song is that it does not depict the aftermath of the disaster, but the hours immediately preceding it. The high waters had already reached record levels in Evansville and Cincinnati, and they did so in Louisville on the very day that Bumble Bee Slim recorded the song. The 1936 feature film *The Green Pastures*, directed by William Keighley and Marc Connelly, was an adaptation of the latter's 1930 play of the same name. Not without some racial stereotyping, it attempted to portray rural African American religion by using an all-Black cast to perform Old Testament stories, including Noah's Flood. There seems to be a link between Slim's reference to "lying women" (rather than all mankind) being punished by "another flood" and his girlfriend's failure to be improved by repeated viewings of the film.

Two days later, and again two days after that, Big Bill Broonzy (born Lee Conley Bradley, 1903–1958)[208] entered a Chicago recording studio to perform "Southern Flood Blues" and "Terrible Flood Blues" (see fig. 1.08), which were released back-to-back on the American Record Corporation's five "dime-store labels," with catalog number 7-04-68.[209]

In the former song, Broonzy sings:

> Eh, early one morning water was coming in my door,
> Early one morning water was coming in my door,
> It was the Ohio River telling us to get ready and go.

Figure 1.08. ARC promotional handbill: Big Bill Broonzy's "Terrible Flood Blues"/"Southern Flood Blues." *Record Research* magazine, 1937

It was dark and was raining, you could hear that howling wind,
Yeah, it was dark and was raining, babe, you could hear that howling
     wind,
If I get away this time, I will never come here again.

Yeah, my baby was crying, I didn't have a thing to eat,
Yeah, I didn't have a thing to eat,
Yeah, the water had come in, washed everything I had down the street.

I was hollering for mercy and it were no boats around,
Yeah, I was hollering for mercy and it were no boats around,
Yeah, that looks like, people, I've gotta stay right here and drown.

Babe, my house started shaking, started floating on down the stream,
Hey, my house started shaking, went floating on down the stream,
It was dark as midnight, people begin to holler and scream.

Apart from the mention of the Ohio River in the first stanza, "Southern Flood Blues" is a generic flood blues. "Terrible Flood Blues," with its references to Cincinnati and Louisville, and to refugees in Memphis, is more specifically related to current events:

The flood caught me in Cincinnati, my own people in Louisville,
Yeah, flood caught me in Cincinnati, and my people in Louisville,
I asked Uncle Sam to help me, please do that if you will.

I'm looking for my mother and my brother; I was wondering where
   can they be,
Yeah, looking for my mother and brother; I was wondering where can
   they be,
Yeah, maybe they in Memphis, I believe I'll go and see.

I started walking down the levee, I was looking high and low,
Yeah, start walking down the levee, I was looking high and low,
Yeah, if they ain't in Memphis, I wonder where did they go.

Crying, Lord, have mercy, do something for me,
Yeah, Lord have mercy, do something for me,
Yeah, I seed my baby drownding underneath a willow tree.

Yes, I'm going to Wyoming where the water don't get so high,
Yeah, I'm going to Wyoming where the water don't get so high,
I'm gon' go up on the highest mountain and stay there till I die.

"The Ohio River Flood" (Bluebird B6852) is apparently the only song on
this disaster by a white combo. Recorded by the Dellinger Family in Charlotte,
North Carolina, on February 20, 1937, it was released in May.[210]
   "Wild Water Blues" (Decca 7285), recorded on March 12 in Chicago by James
"Kokomo" Arnold (1896–1968), is also about this flood, in view of its repeated
references to Cairo, Illinois, which lies at the confluence of the Ohio and Mississippi Rivers, and underwent serious flooding.[211]

I woke up this morning; I couldn't even get out of my door. (x2)
Said this wild water got me covered and I ain't got no place to go.

Now, I hear my mother crying, but I just can't help myself. (x2)
Now, if this wild water keep on rising, I've got to get help from someone else.

Now, good morning, Mister Wild Water, why did you stop at my front
   door? (x2)
Said you reaches from Cairo clean down into the Gulf of Mexico.

Now, don't you hear your mother crying, weeping and moaning all
   night long? (x2)
'Cause old man Wild Water done been here, took her best friend and
   gone.

Now, look-a-here, Mister Wild Water, why do you treat me so doggone
    mean? (x2)
Says you took my house outta Cairo, carried it down in New Orleans.

The influence of Bessie Smith's "Back-Water Blues" is evident in the opening
stanza, which reprises lines from Smith's second and last verses, but then the
song introduces Mister Wild Water, a personification of the flood. Thereafter,
the mention of the singer's house being washed away reflects reality but is
unlikely to be autobiographical; the only description of the flood otherwise is
a reference to its length, from Cairo to the mouth of the Mississippi. This is an
exaggeration; the flood did not reach New Orleans.

    Definitely autobiographical, "Floating Bridge" (Decca 7442), recorded in
New York City on August 2, 1937, is an account of his near drowning by Sleepy
John Estes (1900–1977).[212]

Now, I never will forget that floating bridge. (x3)
Tell me five minutes' time under water I was hid.

When I was going down, I throwed up my hands,
Now, when I was going down, I throwed up my hands. (x2)
Please, take me on dry land.

Now, they carried me in the house and they laid me across the
    bank. (x3)
'Bout a gallon and a half muddy water I had drank.

They dried me off and they laid me in the bed,
Now, they dried me off and they laid me in the bed. (x2)
Couldn't hear nothing but muddy water run through my head.

Now, my mother often taught me, quit playing a bum,
Now, my mama often taught me, quit playing a bum,
Now, my mama often taught me, "Son, quit playing a bum,
Go somewhere, settle down and make a crop."[213]

Now, people was standing on the bridge screaming and crying,
Peoples on the bridge was screaming and crying,
Now, the people on the bridge stand screaming and crying,
Lord, have mercy while we gwine.

The personal rather than communal approach in this song sets it apart from most topical blues on natural disasters. This enables the bluesman to make rueful fun of himself, while still preserving the drama of the event. Also unusual in disaster songs is that Estes resorts to four- rather than three-line stanzas.

Estes said that "Floating Bridge" recounts an automobile accident that befell him and his friend and fellow bluesman Hammie Nixon on a temporary bridge across the Ohio at Paducah, Kentucky, when "there was that high water and rain."[214] After his rediscovery, Estes recorded the song two more times.[215] At the end of the first of these covers, recorded for Pete Welding on April 22, 1962, Estes added one whole stanza to the otherwise almost identical version of the original song:[216]

> Now, I was sitting [in] the back seat lacing up my shoes,
> Now, I was sitting [in] back seat lacing up my shoes,
> Now, I was sitting [in] back seat, I was lacing up my shoes,
> It was so uncertain I didn't know what to do.

On November 8, 1937, almost a year after the floods began, Lonnie Johnson—the most prolific writer of blues disaster songs up to 1943—recorded "Flood Water Blues" (Decca 7397) in Chicago.[217]

> It's been snowing forty days and nights, lakes and rivers begin to freeze,
> It's been snowing forty days and nights, rivers and lakes begin to freeze,
> Some places through my old hometown, water's up above my knees.

> Storm begin rising and the sun begin sinking down. (x2)
> I says, "Mother and dad, pack your trunk, we ain't safe here in this town."

> When it lightning, my mind gets frightened, my nerves begin weaken-
>   ing down,
> When it lightning, my mind get frightened, my nerves begin weaken-
>   ing down,
> And the shack where we was living begin moving 'round.

> Women and children were screaming, saying, "Mama, where must we go?"
> Women and children were screaming, saying, "Lord, where must we go?"
> The flood water have broke the levees and we ain't safe here no more.

> And began cloud [sic] as dark as midnight, keep raining all the time,
> I say, "Oh, I wonder why the sun don't ever shine,"
> And the way it keeps raining, it's driving me out my mind.

Despite its generic character, this song is generally thought to be about the Ohio-Mississippi River flood. This cannot be said of one, and probably both, of the two flood-related songs Johnson recorded on March 31, 1938, again in Chicago. The first stanza of "The New Fallin' Rain Blues" (Decca 7461) reprises the opening verses of the original "Falling Rain Blues" (OKeh 8253, recorded on November 4, 1925), but then develops into a generic flood song. Its flip side, "South Bound Backwater," is "an ingenious reworking of Bessie Smith's 'Backwater Blues' describing the disastrous effects of the Spring thaw,"[218] and may be "about severe flooding in eastern Arkansas in late February 1938, or indeed about any flood."[219]

According to his stepsister, Robert Johnson (1911–1938) put lyrics to a song about the 1937 floods: "I didn't see Brother Robert again until he came home for Christmas. He did a song about the flood that he called '1937 Waters.' He sang it to the tune of an old gospel everyone knew, 'Didn't It Rain.' It had different words. He could rock on that one."[220]

Singer and pianist Walter Davis (1909–1963) recorded the mistitled "West Coast Blues" (Bluebird B7064) at the Leland Hotel in Aurora, Illinois, on May 5, 1937. The song is not about a flood, but contains the following stanza, which may refer to the 1937 flood:[221]

> Now the backwater has been dreadful; I wonder how is my baby get-
> ting along,
> Lord, the backwater has been dreadful; wonder how is my baby getting
> along,
> I hope she didn't get washed away; I hope nothing didn't go on wrong.

Davis's song should have been titled "Water Coast Blues." Among the place names he mentions in his other verses are Dallas, the "Water Coast" (the Gulf Coast), and Smoky Mountain.

Although it is not part of a topical song on this flood, a stanza in "Machine Gun Blues" (Bluebird B8876) by Willie "61" Blackwell (1905–ca. 1972), recorded on July 3, 1941, in Chicago, highlights the strong impact that the Ohio and Mississippi River floods had on Black people's imagination. In a context of violence against his woman, Blackwell sings:

> Some of these mornings, it's gonna be another 1937 flood,
> Some of these mornings, it is going to be another 1937 flood,
> I'm going to shoot my woman, man, I'm going to wade out in the blood.[222]

On May 10, 1959, long after one might have thought that the 1937 flood had been completely forgotten, Roosevelt Charles, a prisoner in the Louisiana

State Penitentiary at Angola, sang an unaccompanied (and unissued) song for folklorist Dr. Harry Oster. Its title, probably assigned by Oster, is "Where Were You When the Archeta River Went Down?"[223] The correct spelling of the river's name is Ouachita, and Oster's transcription, reproduced below, has been amended accordingly. Six hundred and five miles long, it rises in the Ouachita Mountains in Polk County, Arkansas, and runs south through Arkansas and the northern half of Louisiana, before flowing into the Tensas River near Jonesville, Louisiana, to form the Black River.

> *Spoken:* That happened back in the year of 1937, during the high water. There was an ole boy, was standin' on the levee when the water was beginnin' to rise, an' the back water begin to run away. He had [a] woman, she was down in the bottom, an' he was wonderin' whichaway did she go; did she go to a high hill, or was she down in the bottom below. Which he knowed, if she was in the bottom, the poor girl had to be drowned. But if she was up on the high hill, the little girl had to be saved, so the little boy begin to sing the blues, he got blue as a man can be, he begin to holler, an' he hollered out loud—

> *Sung:* Well, tell me, baby, woh, little girl, where were you when that old
>   Ouachita River went down?
> Please tell me, baby, please tell me, little girl, where were you when that
>   ol' Ouachita River went down?
> Was you up on that high hill, baby? Or was you in the valley below?

> Now backwater has been dreadful,[224] wonder where that little girl o' mine,
> Backwater has been dreadful, wonder where that little girl o' mine,
> Did the poor girl get drowned, or did the poor girl get saved?

> I been aroun' the town, been all out through the hill,
> I can't find my little woman, no matter where I go,
> I ain't heard nobody tell me they seen any little girl call' Irene,
> An' I wonder did she get drowned, or did the poor girl get saved?

> I been all aroun' in Texas, all down in Tennessee,
> I been aroun' in Texas, baby, been roun' in Tennessee,
> I can't find my baby, no matter where I go.

> I'm gonna ring up St. Peter, man, gonna ring up old St. Paul,
> If my baby ain't in heaven, she must be on the earth somewhere.

Like Estes's, Charles's recollection is not devoid of humor ("I'm gonna ring up St. Peter, man, gonna ring up St. Paul"), but Charles's characteristic use of an unrhymed and irregular strophic scheme makes it very different. Charles's introductory narrative, which may or may not be factually based, makes his song about a third party, rather than autobiographical.

The varied stylistic (including lyric) approaches used, mostly within the blues genre, to describe this flood collectively make it a precious source for drawing general conclusions about songs on natural disasters. Composers take different perspectives: descriptive, humorous, narrative, interpretive, and so on. Estes's and Charles's approaches to this catastrophic event are realistic, in the former case certainly, and in the latter possibly relating events that actually occurred, but they differ from more traditional approaches by adopting a mainly subjective mode of expression. Typical blues humor is added to increase liveliness and avoid purely narrative, ballad-like depictions. Instead, Bumble Bee Slim, Big Bill Broonzy, Kokomo Arnold, and Lonnie Johnson, none of whom was directly involved in the tragedy, follow in Bessie Smith's footsteps, alternating and juxtaposing stanzas containing subjective (but not real-life) and objective (but descriptive rather than narrative) experiences, in order to convey a sense of participation and sympathy for the victims.

DRY SPELL BLUES: DROUGHTS

Dry Spell Blues: The 1930–31 Drought

The drought of 1930–31 was one of twentieth-century America's most serious natural disasters, lasting almost a year and affecting twenty-three states. It was the first of four droughts in the 1930s, which were factors in the Dust Bowl disaster, but it constitutes a separate disaster. The monetary and social costs were on a par with those of the 1927 Mississippi River flood, even though the drought did not cause much loss of life or high levels of displacement. Rainfall started to decrease in the North and Midwest from March to May, then in the South during July and August, especially in the plantation counties of the Arkansas and Mississippi deltas.[225] At first the Federal government paid no attention to the 1930 drought, despite extensive coverage in magazines and newspapers.[226] It is difficult to ascertain the number of people affected and the financial effects, but an indication of the disaster's severity is that in 1930–31 the American Red Cross spent almost $11 million on drought relief for 600,000 families in Mississippi and adjacent states, $500,000 of it in Mississippi alone (see fig. 1.09).[227]

At least on disc, the Dry Spell of 1930 elicited only three topical blues by African Americans, all of them recorded by the end of September that year.[228]

Figure 1.09. *"Some colored beneficiaries of the Red Cross drought relief work near Cleveland, Mississippi, 1930 or 1931" (Lewis Wickes Hine).* Courtesy Prints and Photographs Division, Library of Congress, Washington, DC

In February 1931, a solitary song by a white singer was recorded. The first two blues were recorded in Grafton, Wisconsin, circa August 1930, when the drought's consequences in the Mississippi Delta were at their most severe.[229]

"Dry Spell Blues" (Paramount 12990) by Eddie "Son" House (1902–1988), recorded in two parts because of the time limitations of 78 rpm records, is essentially a blues prayer.[230]

Part One

The dry spell blues have fallen, drug me from door to door,
Dry spell blues have fallen, drug me from door to door,
The dry spell blues have put everybody on the killing floor.

Now the people down south soon won't have no home,
Lord, the people down south soon won't have no home,
'Cause this dry spell have parched all this cotton and corn.

Hard luck's on everybody, ain't missing but a few. (x2)
Now besides the shower, ain't got a help but You.

Done got [*sic*] fold my arms, and I walked away,
Oh, I fold my arms, Lord, I walked away,
Just like I tell you, somebody's got to pay.

Pork chops forty-five cents a pound, cotton is only ten. (x2)
I can't keep no women, Lord, Lord, nowhere I been.

So dry, old boll weevil turned up his toes and died. (x2)
Now ain't nothing to do, [but] bootleg moonshine and ride.

Part Two

It have been so dry, you can make a powder house out of the world,
Well, it has been so dry, you can make a powder house out of the world,
Then all the money men like a rattlesnake in his quirl.[231]

I done throwed up my hand, Lord, and solemnly swore (x2)
"It ain't no need of me changing towns, it's a drought everywhere I go."

It's a dry old spell everywhere I been,
Oh, it's a dry old spell everywhere I been,
I believe to my soul, this old world is bound to end.

Well, I stood in my back yard, wrung my hands and scream,
I stood in my back yard, I wrung my hands and scream,
And I couldn't see nothing, couldn't see nothing green.

Oh, Lord, have mercy if You please. (x2)
Let Your rain come down, and give our poor hearts ease.

These blues, these blues is worthwhile to be heard,
Oh, these blues, worthwhile to be heard,
God fed Elijah by the raven bird(s).[232]

Although split by the constraints of recording, "Dry Spell Blues" is a single composition, comprising an eleven-stanza blues prayer, pleading with God for rain, and an envoi, explaining the purpose of the song to listeners and relating the 1930 drought to a biblical one. Its seemingly conventional structure conceals an intricate and original treatment of the main theme of drought, whose complexity is enhanced by the intertwined development of at least three subthemes (wandering, death, and bootlegging); but in a book on disasters, it is appropriate to focus chiefly on the theme of drought.

The term drought may be interpreted in both a literal and metaphorical sense throughout the song. After introducing the drought with a verb that arrestingly denotes its opposite, rain ("The dry spell blues have fallen"), Son House provides generic yet incisive descriptions of its effects on the natural world and its inhabitants. The drought turns people into helpless victims, like animals about to be slaughtered ("The dry spell blues have put everybody on the killing floor"), and can even kill the proverbially unkillable boll weevil.

House makes a connection between natural and economic disasters, vividly contrasting low cotton prices, which have depressed sharecroppers' income, and high food prices. His comparison of "the money men" (white bankers and planters) with rattlesnakes, taking advantage of the drought to strike with chicanery, eviction, and foreclosures, is remarkable in its time and place. The only hope House can envisage is that God, propitiated by his blues prayer, will be "a help" to Mississippians. The song's penultimate stanza constitutes its musical and lyrical climax, as House pleads with God for the rain that will relieve people's misery and save the world from the end that he hyperbolically prophesies. The transcription of the last line conforms with 1 Kings 17:1–7, which could be considered as a likely biblical reference text for Son House, as it includes mentions of Elijah, a drought, and Elijah's feeding by the ravens. The transcription is not only meaningful and phonetically acceptable, but it is almost identical to a line in the Reverend C. H. Savage's "Elijah and Ahab" sermon.[233]

In contrast, House refers only indirectly to the metaphorical drought, Prohibition, which was in force in Mississippi since 1908, and nationally from 1920. It makes its appearance in stanza six, where House alludes to bootlegging, implicitly suggested as a way of surviving the drought's economic stresses by selling illegally produced alcohol, and its psychological stresses by drinking it. It is no accident that the parallel, indeed antithetical motifs of drought as a lack of rain and a lack of liquor are presented in the same stanza. Their simultaneous contrast and connection underlie the whole song. The heavy-drinking Son House implicitly compares lack of access to alcohol (a figurative drought, and a personal disaster) to the impact of literal drought on a society as dependent on water as he is on alcohol. He thereby renders his personal "blues prayer" universally relevant, and "worthwhile to be heard."[234]

Charley Patton's "Dry Well Blues"[235] (Paramount 13070) depicts the effects of the drought in Lula, Mississippi, the small town north of Clarksdale where Patton and House were then living.

When I was living at Lula, I was living at ease. (x2)
Lord, the drought come and caught us and parched up all the trees.

Oh, today over in Lula, we'll bid the town goodbye,
'Day in Lula bidding you and the town goodbye,
Well, we have come to know the day, Lord, the Lula well was gone dry.

Lord, the citizens around Lula all was doing very well,
Citizens around Lula all was doing very well,
Lord, they all met together, and they done bored a well.

I ain't got no money, and I sure ain't got no home,
Lord, I ain't got no money and sure ain't got no home,
The hot weather done come in; parched all the cotton and corn.

Oh, look down the country, Lord, it'll make you cry,
Look, country, Lord, it'll make you cry,
'Most everybody, Lord, had a water bayou.

Lord, the Lula women, Lord, putting the Lula mens down,
Lula mens [sic] all putting the Lula men down,
Lord, you oughta been there, Lord; see the womens all leaving town.

As with House, there was a dichotomy in Patton's life between the sacred and the profane,[236] but his song is strictly a blues, without prayer or preaching. Occasional formulae ("I sure ain't got no home," "parched all the cotton and corn") resemble lines in Son House's song, but they are set in a different context: the response of Lula's inhabitants to the drought, and the relations between the town's men and women. The last verse's humorous reference to the Lula women "putting the Lula mens down [and] leaving town" depicts an impending sexual drought.[237]

These songs by Patton and House can be read from both a personal and a communal perspective, and both have a more complex structure than one might expect. House and Patton both address the pressing concerns of their Delta audience, and strive for maximum vividness.

Patton's shifts from first-person singular to first-person plural, and from past to present tense, enable a realistic, empathetic, and tangible description of the catastrophic effects of the drought on both himself and his audience. He seems to share the concerns of both Black tenant farmers and white "citizens," but he also points out that the latter group's efforts to increase the water supply have literally and metaphorically run dry. In late July, shortly after municipal bonds had been issued to raise $5,000 toward the cost of a second well, the town's water supply ran dry, inspiring Patton's composition.

Reading between its lines, one can detect irritation at the privileged position of Lula's white "citizens," "all doing very well" and having a "water bayou" (irrigation ditch) despite the drought. Even as a second well was being bored to mitigate the drought's effects, the town installed a sprinkler system to keep the streets dust-free. Simultaneously, however, Patton seems to suggest that the drought has subjected Black farmers and white "citizens" to the same hardships and reduced them to the same level. This is inferable from the ambiguity introduced when Patton fails to specify the race(s) of the women and men who are "leaving town" in his final stanza.[238]

The third recorded blues on the 1930 drought, which bears the same title as Son House's, was written by St. Louis resident "Spider" Carter. He recorded the song in Chicago on September 13, a few weeks after House and Patton's session, and it was released on Brunswick 7181 on December 18, 1930.[239] This beautiful piano blues is sung in the first person, but its references to displacement, hard times, and crop failure seem to be based on reports rather than firsthand experience, and it presents no original perspective on the drought.

> The dry spell's on, many a man ain't got no home. (x2)
> They have caused poor me to wander and roam.
>
> I woke up this morning just about half past four. (x2)
> All I could feel was hard luck knocking on my door.
>
> Hard times are driving me mad. (x2)
> They are the worst old feelings that I've ever had.
>
> It's so dry down home, folks can't plant cotton and corn,
> It's so dry down home, folks can't plant taters and corn,
> And it's all or nothing since the dry spell's been on.
>
> Everywhere that I went was nothing [but] bad news,
> Everywhere that I went was nothing but bad news,
> That's why I'm singing these worrisome dry spell blues.

White recording artist and composer Bob Miller (1895–1955) recorded "1930 Drought" (Columbia 15664-D) in New York City on February 25, 1931.[240]

> Oh, listen now, good people, and I'll tell you of a spot,
> A certain spot in the South and West it seems the Lord forgot.
> There's hunger and there's poverty among the young and old.
> The days are long when hope is gone, the weather's mighty cold.

Chorus:
These good folks are hard workers, earning bread by the sweat of their
    brow.
It's more than prayers that they need, it's food and clothes right now.
Remember that they're human, be they from the West or South.
And we that have should not forget the 1930 drought.

Just picture how they tilled and toiled and worked with all their might,
With calloused hands and aching backs from dawn until the night,
And when their crops were planted and the hardest work was done,
That awful drought is slowly on with its old scorching sun.

Chorus

When soles are worn from trudging and feet worn to the quick,
With hunger-weakened bodies, heart and spirits sick,
There's things we do not understand about the land and sea,
But there's one thing we understand, and that is misery.

Chorus

Bob Miller was raised in Memphis but based in New York from the mid-1920s. A prolific lyricist and proficient ragtime pianist, he wrote and recorded a myriad of Tin Pan Alley songs about contemporary political and social issues affecting his native South. As with "1936 Tornado," his song on the Tupelo disaster, Miller's composition about the Dry Spell epitomizes his knack for catchy tunes and schmaltzy lyrics. It also stands in marked contrast to blues songs about the drought, which use straightforward language, free of Miller's patronizing condescension ("Remember that they're human") toward both the listeners he is addressing and the people he is singing about.

"Dry Spell Blues" had no enduring significance for Son House, who did not re-record it after his "rediscovery" in 1964. In the twenty-first century, the drought has faded from memory among African Americans, and not surprisingly, no modern Black blues artist has created a new song about it, although Corey Harris has sung House's "Dry Spell Blues" in concert. Rather, it is mainly white blues artists who have appropriated "Dry Spell Blues" in recent years, but it is clear that their motivation is to express their admiration for House as an artist (and in some cases mentor) rather than interest in the song's historical content.[241]

HELL BROKE LOOSE IN THIS LAND:
UNIDENTIFIED AND MISCELLANEOUS NATURAL DISASTERS

In chronological order, this chapter considers miscellaneous African American songs about natural disasters. Deriving from commercial and field recordings, or from printed folk song collections, each of them is the only known song inspired by a particular disaster. Collectively they make up an impressive body of work, and offer important insights into African American responses to disasters.[242]

Wasn't That a Mighty Storm: The 1900 Galveston Hurricane

The deadliest natural disaster in United States history took place on Saturday, September 8, 1900, at Galveston, a port and island resort known as the "Jewel of Texas." A category 4 hurricane raised twenty-foot waves and winds gusting to an estimated 120–30 miles per hour. Their impact devastated twelve blocks (about three fourths of the city) at the east end of Galveston Island, which is about thirty miles long and two miles off the Texas coast. Estimates of the death toll range from 6,000 to 8,000 of about 37,000 inhabitants. Most sources state that the lower figure is for fatalities in the city of Galveston, with the additional 2,000 being in the surrounding area (see fig. 1.10). The cost of damage was $20,000,000, with 3,600 buildings destroyed.[243]

The only African American song about the Galveston disaster was recorded by John A. and Alan Lomax at Darrington State Farm, Sandy Point, near Houston, Texas, probably on March 25 or April 1, 1934.[244] "Wasn't That a Mighty Storm" (AFS 185-B-2) has been credited in discographies and other sources to Reverend "Sin-Killer" Griffin, who was "employed by the State as Chaplain to the Negro convicts of the Texas Penitentiary system,"[245] but Griffin only preached a remarkable sermon, "The Man of Calvary." "Wasn't That a Mighty Storm" was sung by a "penitentiary song leader" (perhaps Washington, nicknamed "Lightnin'"), and a chorus of inmates.[246]

The song's refrain can be traced in "'Mighty Day' by Charles H. Sheffer, [which is] included in the circa-1880 *Olympia Quartette Songster* collecting songs performed by that group on its U.S. tour."[247] Sheffer was a white comedian and composer of "coon songs"; the Olympia Quartette were also white. It seems likely that Sheffer borrowed his refrain from an African American source. "Under the title 'Wasn't That a Mighty Day,' [the refrain] turned up in Anna Kranz Odum's article 'Some Negro Folk Songs from Tennessee' in the July-September 1914 *Journal of American Folklore* as a gospel number: 'Wasn't That a Mighty Day When Jesus Christ was Born?'"[248]

Figure 1.10. "Galveston disaster: I'm glad Ise living, Galveston, Texas, ca. 1900" (M. H. Zahner). Courtesy Prints and Photographs Division, Library of Congress, Washington, DC

. . . Galveston with a sea wall
To keep the water down,
But the high tide from the ocean
Pushed water over the town.[249]

Chorus (after each stanza):
Wasn't that a mighty storm?
Oh, wasn't that a mighty storm with water?
Wasn't that a mighty storm
[That] blew the people [all] away!

Their prophets gave them warning,
"You had better leave this place."

They never thought of leaving
Till Death looked them in the face.

The trains they were loaded
With peoples leaving town.
The tracks give away on the ocean,
The trains they went on down.

Death like a cruel Master,
As the wind began to blow,
Rode out on his pale horses,
Said, "Death, let me go."

Now, Death, in 1900,
That was fifteen years ago,
You throwed a storm at my mother,
With you she had to go.

Now, Death, your hands is icy,
You've got them on my knees.
You done carried away my mother,
Now come back after me.

The trees fell on the island,
The houses give away.
Some peoples crushed and drownded,
Some died 'most every way.

The lightning played its kindling,
The thunder began to roll.
The winds, it began blowing,
The rain began to fall.

The sea, it began roaring,
The ships could not stand.
I heard the captain crying,
"Please, save a drownding man."

If compared to most religious songs and sermons about natural disasters, the lyrics are narrative and descriptive rather than accusatory.[250] The lines "Now, Death, in 1900 / That was fifteen years ago" suggest a date of composition around 1915, when another storm hit Galveston in August. This suggestion is supported by the truncated opening stanza, with its anachronistic reference to the seawall that was built after the 1900 storm.[251]

Study of the 1900 Galveston hurricane leads to the conclusion that there is no correlation between the severity of a disaster and the number of songs it elicits. The meager response to this disaster from singers both Black and white is unsurprising, however, for the creation of ballads was not yet a consistent response to disasters in either community. The dearth of disaster songs on this event may also depend partly on the fact that we have few data on folksongs from the nineteenth century and earlier.

Gilliam Town Was Such a Wicked Town: The 1908 Gilliam Storm

The F4 tornado that struck Louisiana at 5:30 p.m. on Wednesday, May 13, 1908, wiped out the small town of Gilliam, in Caddo Parish, near the borders with Texas and Arkansas. It killed forty-nine people (thirty-four in Gilliam, nine in Caddo Parish, and six in Bolinger in neighboring Bossier Parish); 135 people were injured, and at Gilliam only one out-of-town house was left standing.[252]

Remarkably, it was nearly eighty years later that two contemporary artistic responses to the hurricane were recorded. Singer and poet Osceola Mays (1909–2004) was recorded in 1987 at her home in Dallas by Texas writer, filmmaker, and photographer Alan Govenar. After reciting the poem "Gilliam's Town," written by her mother Azalene Douglas, Mays sang unaccompanied her father's setting of it, "Gilliam's Storm."[253]

> *Chorus:*
> Oh, wasn't that a mighty time,
> Wasn't that a mighty time that evening,
> Wasn't that a mighty time,
> When the storm struck Gilliam town.
>
> Gilliam town was such a wicked town,
> There weren't but one church house in Gilliam town,
> Seemed like all of the people there had laid God's army down.[254]
>
> Late one Wednesday evening, the cloud rose dark and blue,
> People were running and crying, crying, "Lord, Lord, what must I do?"
>
> Said, the cloud started toward Shreveport, God turned that cloud around,
> 'Cause you know there was some unsaved people lived in Shreveport
>   town.

Well, a woman said to her husband, "I believe that cloud's about gone."
God works in a mysterious ways His wonders to perform.
He plants His footsteps on the sea and rides on every storm.

The chorus shares its melody with "Wasn't That a Mighty Storm." In stanza
two, "wicked" is used to pinpoint discriminatory or violent behavior by white
inhabitants of Gilliam, described as a sinful (meaning racist) town. The song
concludes with the well-known opening lines of "Light Shining out of Darkness" by English poet and hymnodist William Cowper.

The poem is also collected in a children's book, where Osceola Mays recalls: "I
was almost six when I learned 'Gilliam's Storm.' . . . I don't remember the storm,
but I know the poem. Mama and Daddy used to live there in Gilliam, Louisiana.
They said that Gilliam was wicked because there was only one church house in
the town and the people there weren't very nice to the Black folks."[255]

Trinity River Blues: The 1908 Trinity River Flood

The Trinity River, which runs southeast through Texas for 700 miles, underwent
minor flooding in 1844, 1866, 1871, and 1890. On May 26, 1908, there was a major
overflow in Dallas, with the river rising to a height of 52.6 feet, and running 1.5
miles wide. Five people were killed and 5,000 left homeless. Dallas's Oak Cliff
neighborhood was completely cut off by the flood, and the city suffered $2.5
million in property damage.[256]

Nineteen-year-old "Oak Cliff T-Bone," later much better known as Aaron "T-Bone" Walker (1910–1975), recorded "Trinity River Blues" (Columbia
14506-D) in Dallas on December 5, 1929.[257] Its connection with remote or recent
floods in the area has been altogether overlooked in blues literature. The storm
of May 22–26, 1908, is unlikely because in 1929 the recording was not topical.
Indeed, Walker was not yet born when that flooding took place, but as his
recording pseudonym indicates, he grew up in one of the areas that had been
worst affected. If the 1908 flood is Walker's source of inspiration, his projection
of himself two decades back to an event that he had doubtless heard about from
family members is unusual in a blues context. Another possibility is that Walker
was referring to the May 24–31, 1929, storm, which affected "the entire area of
the Trinity River Basin between the mouth of East Fork and Liberty gage."[258]

That dirty Trinity River sure have done me wrong. (x2)
It came in my windows and doors, now all my things are gone.

Trinity River blues keeps me bothered all the time. (x2)
I losed all my clothes, baby, believe I'm going to lose my mind.

They are building a levee now, I have no more to worry about. (x2)
If that river should happen to rise, won't have to move my things out.

Trinity River rising, it came in my windows and doors (x2)
It is with a swear in my heart, baby, Trinity River won't rise no more.[259]

There are derivative elements in Walker's lyrics: the B-line of stanza 1 and the closing half-line are from Blind Lemon Jefferson's "Rising High Water Blues" (1927), and stanza 4 is related to one in Lonnie Johnson's "Broken Levee Blues" (1928). However, Walker's recasting of them in a new context, featuring original lines of his own, is a remarkable creative feat by a teenager who had been unexpectedly offered a recording session after a Columbia talent scout spotted him at a show in Houston.[260]

When he became a star in later years, Walker's elegant suits were much admired, and "I lost all my clothes, baby, believe I'm going to lose my mind" suggests that even as a youth he was a dandy. Also original is the stanza about "building a levee." This seems to refer, with poetic license, to the construction of the viaduct that linked Oak Cliff to downtown Dallas, replacing a wooden bridge washed away in 1908. Financed by a $650,000 bond issue, the Oak Cliff Viaduct (now the Houston Street Viaduct) was opened in 1912.[261] Alternatively, it may refer to the 1928 city bond package that was passed to build the levee two years after the Levee Improvement Association was formed for this purpose.

God Was in the Windstorm: The 1909 Grand Isle Hurricane

A song commemorating the category 3 hurricane that struck Louisiana and Mississippi in September 1909 appears as an untitled text in two books on folk culture.[262] The hurricane, which is generally known as the "Grand Isle Hurricane" because of the devastation it caused there, killed at least 371 people, but the actual death toll is not known. Of the ascertained fatalities, 353 took place in Louisiana and eighteen in Mississippi. Damage throughout the two states was estimated at $10 million (in 1909 dollars).[263]

In the last day of September
In the year 1909
God Almighty rose in the weather
And that troubled everybody's mind.

The storm began on a Sunday
And it got in awful rage.

Not a mortal soul
In the globe that day
Didn't have any mind to pray.
And God was in the wind storm,
And troubled everybody's mind.

God Almighty and his ministers
They rode up and down the land;
All God Almighty did that day
Was to raise the wind and dust.

God he is the wind storm and rain
And everybody ought to mind.

The date and day above ("In the last day of September . . . The storm began on a Sunday") are wrong, but the text certainly refers to this disaster.

In an unpublished interview by David Evans, Rev. Ruben Lacy (1901–1969) was discussing Mrs. Lacy's collection of hymnbooks and broadside "ballets" when he recalled the words of the chorus above:

> LACY: That was the time they had a tornado. I don't know where that was. I can't think what tornado that was. It was a tornado come through the state of Mississippi. It done a whole lot of destruction, and somebody made that song. And, you know, I done forgot that song. . . . All I remember is, "God moves in the windstorm, and troubled everybody's mind."[264] This song I'm talking about, this ballet, it went on to tell in what date and what year, practically what night, what time of night this storm hit in this certain place. I never would think of that. No use of me messing with talking.[265]

The chorus Lacy recalled can also be found in the text describing the Tri-State tornadoes of 1925. Unless Lacy made a mistake, he specifies that this tornado came "through the state of Mississippi," and not through the three states hit by the Tri-State tornadoes. The song's origins remain unknown, but at least the chorus of this song was probably sung by the congregation reading a broadside "ballet" similar to (if not the same as) the one mentioned by Lacy to Evans.

God Was Worried with Their Wicked Ways: The 1913 Omaha Tornado

On March 23, 1913, Easter Sunday, a series of at least seven tornadoes hit Nebraska, Iowa, Illinois, and Indiana. Omaha, Nebraska, was hardest hit, being the point where two tornadoes converged shortly before 6:00 p.m.[266] The number of casualties in Omaha is estimated at 101 to 140.[267] A further thirty-seven people are believed to have died elsewhere in Nebraska, and fourteen in Iowa. Property loss in Omaha alone is estimated at about $8,700,000.

Only one song is known to have been composed about this natural disaster. "Flood in Omaha" was sung for John A. Lomax by Sister Crockett in San Antonio, Texas, where she and her husband were co-pastors of the Church of the Holy Ghost in the town's West End district.[268] Recent research has produced information about Sister Crockett. On June 8, 1900, Tennie Crockett (née Brown) was enumerated in the census, living in Indianapolis, Marion County, Indiana. Born in Tennessee in October 1866, to Tennessean parents, she was 33 years old and had been married to Wyatt Crockett, a day laborer, for ten years. She had borne seven children, of whom a son and two daughters had survived. By 1920 the Crocketts and a twelve-year-old son were living in San Antonio, where Wyatt was a minister and Tennie a peddler.[269]

An article by John Lomax, published in the *Dallas Morning News* of May 3, 1936, states that Sister Crockett sold lye hominy from a buggy drawn by a pony. This tallies with her occupation in the 1920 census report. Probably in January 1936,[270] Lomax collected from Sister Crockett the six songs that are listed in *Adventures of a Ballad Hunter*, but unfortunately none of them could be traced at the Library of Congress or anywhere else.[271]

In *Adventures of a Ballad Hunter*, Lomax printed only two stanzas and a chorus from "Flood in Omaha," but the *Dallas Morning News* article includes the complete song:

Oh, just look at Omaha;
Children there without Ma or Pa (x2)
For a tornado swept through Omaha.

Chorus:
God was worried with their wicked ways (3)
And God's getting worried with your wicked ways.

They went out Easter morning dressed in white,
They went out again on Easter night (x2)
And the tornado put all them to flight.

It was a sorrowful time, that you know,
Right behind the tornado came the snow (x2)
And they couldn't pull out dead bodies no mo'.[272]

There was a place in Omaha,
They called a pool room, and I guess it was a bar;
The tornado came and blew it down,
And thirty-six bodies in there was found.

The Governor was trying to do his best,
He called for help for his suffering guest,
The horrors was worse than words could tell,
The Governor cried out it was hell.
But God knew His business and He knew it well.

In the ninth chapter of Psalms and seventeenth verse,
God says that it's a-going to be worse,
When you read it, read it well,
For God says that the wicked shall be burned into hell.

Your cities and towns are stuffed with pride,
And you hardly want Jesus to come inside,
You hardly want Jesus to come inside,
And God sends tornadoes and sweeps them aside.

All the people in Omaha went to the show,
But never got back to their homes any mo',
They never got back to their homes any mo',
And that ought to stop you from running to the show.

While they was at the show, looking at the play,
A tornado came and swept them away,
They had their show on Sunday night,
And everybody knows that wasn't right.

Sister Crockett said that the song came to her on a street in Lake Charles, Louisiana, after she had read newspaper reports about the Omaha storm. A key textual element is her mention of a pool room. People's corruption and vice ("their wicked ways") as the cause of God's anger is a common theme in sacred songs,[273] but Sister Crockett's statement to John Lomax that she was inspired by "reading the newspaper about the Omaha storm" is significant in the light of a report in the *New York Times* of March 25: "From the ruins of a negro pool hall the body of a negro was taken out along with many others. In one hand of the dead man was a roll of bank notes."[274] On the same page, the *Times*'s list of victims includes "C. W. Dillon, proprietor pool hall." The *Times* was drawing on

Figure 1.11. "Easter Sunday at Idlewild Pool Hall, 24 & Grant Streets, Omaha. March 23, 1913" (unknown).
Courtesy History Nebraska

a wire service story: the quoted sentence appears in at least thirty-four other newspapers between March 25 and April 3, and Dillon's name and occupation appear in many casualty lists.[275] On March 25, the *Coffeyville Daily Journal* in Kansas carried an Associated Press report: "Sixteen more bodies were taken from the Idlewild Pool Hall at Lake and Twenty-fourth today, making a total thus far from that place of thirty-one. The building after being wrecked caught on fire from an overturned stove. Many of the bodies taken out were placed in baskets, not being in a position to be handled intact."[276]

The death toll at the "negro pool hall" seems likely to have been about forty, certainly almost all African Americans (see fig. 1.11).[277] Sister Crockett's condemnation of the people who went to "the show" on a Sunday is also significant. This refers to the destruction of the Diamond Moving Picture Theatre, a block away from the Idlewild Pool Hall, in which at least sixteen and possibly thirty people were killed.[278]

The African American population of Omaha was 4,426 in 1910, so we might estimate a total of around 5,000 in 1913.[279] On this assumption, about 1 percent of the city's African American inhabitants were killed, and they accounted for at least one third of the total fatalities. The true proportion may well have been higher. It is no surprise that Sister Crockett was moved to sing about a tragedy that had so grievously afflicted Black people.

Wasn't It a Storming Time? The 1915 New Orleans Hurricane

On September 29, 1915, a Category 4 hurricane came ashore very close to Grand Isle, Louisiana, where the 1909 hurricane discussed above had made landfall. Known locally as "The Great Storm of 1915," it is more generally called "The New Orleans Hurricane of 1915," because of the damage and loss of life there. The storm passed over the city in the afternoon, with sustained wind speeds reaching 86 mph and gusting to 130 mph. The death toll was at least 275 people, making it one of the deadliest hurricanes in Louisiana. Twenty-one people died in New Orleans, twenty-three in Venice, and about as many fatalities were reported in the coastal towns of Fremier and LaBranche. The town of Saint Malo was destroyed, and Plaquemines Parish was also hard hit. Thousands of people were left homeless, and damage amounted to $13 million.[280]

Reverend A. C. W. Shelton's "Wasn't It a Storming Time?" appears to be the only African American composition about this storm.[281] It appears in a book on Louisiana folk culture, and was probably transcribed from a printed ballet.[282]

'Twas on the 29th day of September
In the year 1915
Many lost souls that went and slept
Just because of that raging storm.

Chorus:
Wasn't that a raging and a storming time? (x3)
People had to run and pray and cry.

The storm held people day and night
And God was playing just the same.
Wasn't it a pity and a shame,
Seems that God was calling everybody's name.

Business was very quiet all night and day,
Glasses were broken down to the ground.
God playing in New Orleans, just the same,
People knows that he was God anyhow.

The hurricane making eighty miles an hour,
So we learn to know.
People of New Orleans they did run,
God broke the power and cars couldn't run.

The weight of the gale everybody felt,
Gambling men and dancing women,
You want [*sic*] serve God, men and women,
You are wicked and you seldom pray.

I have warned you by lightning,
People mourning, weeping did pray,
Just keep on with your sinful ways,
I am able to stop you people's way.

Many souls lost that floated
Down the stream to New Orleans,
Yet the people were caught,
Not a single soul would tell their name.

Many telegraph and telephone wires
Leading out the city of New Orleans,
Milneburg had washed away,
And they rush to the city for aid.

People had left their happy homes,
With all what they possessed,
Cry, Jesus, will you hear us,
And help us in our distress?

One is immediately struck by the similarity of the chorus and final stanza with Texas gospel singer Blind Willie Johnson's fourth stanza in "God Moves on the Water" (Columbia 14520-D), a disaster song on the sinking of the *Titanic* composed by Blind Butler presumably in 1912 and recorded by Johnson in New Orleans on December 11, 1929. The reference to people leaving "their happy homes" and possessions is out of place in a song about a shipwreck, which suggests that Johnson may have acquired this stanza from Butler's ballet, from Shelton's song, or from another singer. Conversely, the final stanza could also be a general disaster stanza used in many songs.

God He Rode in the Wind and Storm: The 1925 Tri-State Tornado

The "Great Tri-State Tornado" of March 18, 1925, was the deadliest American tornado, and one of America's ten deadliest catastrophes. It ripped through Missouri, Illinois, and Indiana, killing around 700 people, injuring more than 2,000, destroying about 15,000 homes, and causing about $500 million worth of damage across more than 164 square miles.[283] It elicited only one known song, "God, He Rolled in the Wind and the Storm" (AFS 264-B-1), which was sung nine years later by four male convicts at Reid State Farm, Boykin, South Carolina, surprisingly distant from the location of the disaster. It was collected by John Avery Lomax, assisted by his son Alan and Lead Belly, ca. December 19, 1934.[284]

Chorus:
God He rode in the wind and storm (x3)
And He troubled everybody's mind.

So sad, some day in 1925,
God rode in a mighty storm and destroyed a-many people's lives.

Chorus

Listen now, people, I'm going to sit and tell
How I prayed to my God and I shunned both death and hell.

Chorus

Wind began to stir and the rain began to fall,
Hundreds and thousands of people they didn't have no way to call.

Chorus

Lord God spoke from Mount Sinai's top to the people of the stubborn will,
He spoke so loud until the mountain shook, and trembled like a common hill.

Chorus (x2)

Yes, God moves in a mysterious way His wonders to perform,
He plants His footsteps in the sea and He rides upon the storm.

Chorus

Yes, when I die won't you bury me low? Bury me where no liars don't go.
When I rise won't you carry me high? Yes, carry me back to Jericho mile.

Chorus (x2)

It is noteworthy that "God Moves/Rode in the Windstorm" was already traditional, and was published in broadside "ballets" for congregational use. It could be sung as a general song about God's power or adapted to refer to specific windstorms.

Earth Quaked Last Night: The 1927 Memphis Earthquake

Between 2:30 and 2:35 a.m. on Saturday, May 7, 1927, an earthquake of considerable intensity shook Memphis, Tennessee, and the surrounding area. It hit several states but lasted for only six to seven seconds, causing little damage and no fatalities.[285]

Later in May, Alice Pearson would record "Greenville Levee Blues" about the ongoing Mississippi flood, but she began her only recording session with "Memphis Earthquake" (Paramount 12507).[286]

> Earth quaked last night just about two o'clock (x2)
> You might have seen my bed began to reel and rock.
>
> I wheeled and turned in my bed from side to side (x2)
> I'll overcome next summer someday by and by.
>
> (Hummed verse)
>
> When the sun looked funny and the doves began to moan (x2)
> Lord, I knowed right then that something was going on wrong.[287]
>
> 'Fore the sun went down, I felt so sad and blue,
> When the sun went down, I felt so sad and blue,
> I knowed something was going to happen, and I didn't know what to do.

"Memphis Earthquake" stands out as a fully developed song. Rather than focusing on the disaster itself, Pearson reports its effect on her state of mind, and her premonitions the day before. It is indicative of her distress that at her sole recording session she recorded as many as three natural disaster songs (including two songs on the 1927 Mississippi River flood) out of a total of six sides. It is likely that she connected the two events as somber presages of an imminent end of the world.

It Seemed Like Hell Was Broken: The 1930 Frost Tornado

"Frost Texas Tornado Blues" (OKeh 8890), recorded by Alger "Texas" Alexander (1900–1954) in San Antonio on June 9, 1930, is the only known song about the tornado that hit the eponymous small town just a month earlier, on May 6, 1930.[288]

> I was sitting looking, way out across the world (x2)
> Says the wind had things twisting almost in a twirl.
>
> Says, I've been a good feller, just as good as I can be,
> Says, I've been a good feller, good as I can be,
> Says, it's Lord, have mercy, Lord, have mercy on me.
>
> Mmmm mmmm mmmmm,
> Mmmm mmmm mmmmm,
> Says, I been a good feller, just as good as a man could be.
> *Spoken:* Have your way.
>
> Some lost their babies, was blown for two, three miles around,
> Some lost their babies, blown for two, three miles around,
> When they come to they right mind, they come on back to town.
>
> Says the rooster was crowing, cows was lowing, never heard such a
>   noise before,
> Ah, oh Lordy, Lord.
> Says it seemed like hell was broken in this place below.

The tornado caused about forty deaths and considerable damage. According to another source, "Sixty-six persons were killed, many were injured and property damage estimated at more than $500,000. . . . Of Frost's population of 600, half were left homeless."[289] Some stylistic and lyric similarities with Lonnie Johnson's "St. Louis Cyclone Blues" are evident in the A-lines of the opening and closing stanzas. The generic nature of stanzas two and three, which are unrelated to tornadoes, suggests that OKeh asked Alexander to come up with a topical song at short notice.

Mean Twister: The 1932 Alabama Tornado

Several states, including Alabama, Georgia, Tennessee, Kentucky, and South Carolina, were struck by a series of tornadoes on March 21–22, 1932. "The Deep

South Outbreak" left at least 330 people dead.[290] There was extensive coverage in the *New York Times*, which stated that the majority of casualties in Alabama were black, whereas all the people killed in other states were white.[291] Central and western Alabama, and especially the towns of Marion, Northport, Demopolis, Faunsdale, Linden, and Columbiana were hardest hit. Unofficial estimates put the number of injured at over 3,000, with 8,500 left homeless. Property damage amounted to between three and five million dollars.

The Deep South Outbreak probably inspired Bessie Jackson's "Mean Twister" (Banner 33059), recorded on July 20, 1933, in New York City, with piano accompaniment by Walter Roland.[292] Bessie Jackson was a pseudonym. Her real name was Lucile Anderson (1897–1948), who was born in Birmingham, Alabama. Until 1933 her records were credited to Lucille Bogan, her married name.

> I'm gon' tell everybody what that mean old twister done. (x2)
> It tore down my house and hardly left a one.
>
> It went in my house, tore down my bed and frame. (x2)
> It broke my man's back and tried to do me the same.
>
> It set the town on fire and it weren't no water around,
> Set the town on fire and it weren't no water around,
> Let's whoop and holler, women, try to save that burning town.
>
> Fell down on my knees and I raised my hands to God above,
> Fell down on my knees, raised my hand to God above,
> Say, "You tore down my house and you killed the man I love."
>
> Lord, searched the ashes for twenty-five miles around,
> Say, I searched the ashes for twenty-five miles around,
> And my man's body, Lord, could not be found.
>
> I went and I stood upon some high old lonesome hill,
> Say, I went and I stood, high old lonesome hill,
> And looked down on my house, Lord, where me and my daddy lived.[293]

Some descriptive elements in this blues are very generic ("hardly left a one" and "for twenty-five miles around") and cannot be taken as evidence that Bogan was referring to the Deep South Outbreak, but her reference to the twister "[setting] the town on fire" is more specific and revelatory, for there are newspaper reports of fires following the tornadoes.[294] Tornadoes in Alabama had killed two people on December 31, 1931, and twelve on January 13, 1932, but these were minor incidents in a relatively mild year for storms in the South. In March and May 1933, tornadoes killed several dozen people in other states, but Alabama was unaffected. By elimination, it seems more likely that Bogan was singing about the major Alabama tornado of March 1932, especially if we consider that she had not recorded since 1930. In fact, she might have composed the song in 1932 and saved it, or perhaps she had been personally affected by it.

I'm Coming to You If through Twenty Feet of Water I Wade: The 1935 Crenshaw, Mississippi, Rescue

On Sunday, January 27, 1935, the *New York Times* reported that the Coldwater River basin between Marks and Crenshaw, Mississippi, was flooded. There were at least twenty-seven dead, most of them Black, in Tennessee, Arkansas, and Mississippi, with 25,000 people homeless and property damage of over $5 million.[295]

The story of John Little, a Black man who became known as "the hero of the flood" or the "Crenshaw Life Saver," inspired the only topical song on this disaster. "[I]n the dead of night and at freezing temperature" he "rowed through the icy waters, dug the oars out of the ice with his fingers and rowed the boat back to Crenshaw, where white men used it to bring out 100 people." His "hands were frozen and his clothes had to be cut from his body."[296] Similar reports, including John Little's brave feat, were published in the Baltimore *Afro-American* and the *Chicago Defender*, but not until Saturday, February 2, six days after the flood on January 27, because they were published weekly. The *Afro-American* mainly recycled a wire story but added: "Only a few deaths of white persons have been reported. The heaviest toll has been among colored women and children who were caught by the rapidly rising flood water, and lost before rescuers could rush to their aid and carry them to higher grounds."[297] The *Defender*'s reporting was much more exhaustive, and identified "Marks, Darling, Crenshaw, Hinchcliffe [*sic*, actually Hinchcliff], Falcon, and Sledge" as the towns hardest hit.[298]

On the evidence of the newspaper coverage, Joe Pullum's "Mississippi Flood Blues" (Bluebird B5844) was inspired by this minor flood. Born in Alabama and living in Houston, Pullum (1905–1964) recorded his composition in San Antonio on January 29, 1935.[299]

> The wind howled, and the rain began to fall,
> The wind howled, and the wind began to fall. [*sic*]
> My woman was out in Mississippi; that was my one and all.

I received a telegram saying, "Baby, won't you please come here?"
I received a telegram saying, "Baby, won't you come here?
Hell broke loose on the Delta, and your baby is way down here."

Love is like this Depression; it lingers on and on (x2)
But better times will greet me when I fall in my baby's arms.

I'm coming to you, baby, if through twenty feet of water I wade (x2)
For I can't stand to see my baby fill a watery grave.

Knee deep in the water; treetops men and women did choose (x2)
But I'm back in my baby's arms with those Mississippi flood blues.

As David Evans was first to note, Pullum was not looking back eight years to the 1927 Mississippi River flood. Placing himself in the role of the rescuer, he probably drew on an Associated Press wire service story published two days before his recording session.[300]

What a Storm That Evening: The 1942 Mississippi Tornado

Perhaps because of the huge area it struck, the storm system that ravaged Mississippi, Tennessee, and the Midwest in 1942 did not acquire a soubriquet.[301] The outbreak occurred on Monday, March 16, between 4:15 and 5:30 p.m. Parts of Mississippi, Tennessee, Illinois, Indiana, Kentucky, Missouri, and probably also Alabama were struck. Mississippi and Tennessee suffered the most fatalities and damage. Reported deaths in the daily newspapers consulted average out at over 100 in Mississippi alone. As was customary at that time, most of the dead listed were white. Updated statistics give 153 dead and 1,284 injured.[302] The loss of life was heaviest in and near the Mississippi towns located (approximately in this order) along the path of the storm: Itta Bena, Greenwood, Avalon, Holcomb, Grenada, Water Valley, and the nearby school at O'Tuckalofa, Belden, the little town of Tula fifteen miles east of Oxford, Baldwyn, Spring Hill, Michigan City, and near Selmer and Lexington, Tennessee. The effects of the twister were particularly severe on African Americans because it swept through rural areas, especially the Wade and Phillips plantations. The Black section of Itta Bena, Mississippi was also hard hit.[303] The path of the storm extended from Fort Pemberton, three miles west of Greenwood, Mississippi, which was spared, to Henry County, Tennessee, on the Tennessee–Kentucky state line.

Reverend Charles Haffer Jr. was drawn to catastrophic events as subjects for songs. Having afflicted Mississippi more severely than any other state, the 1942 tornado inevitably attracted his attention. "The Song of the Great Disaster

(Storm of '42)" (AFS 6624-A-1) was among the recordings Haffer made for Alan Lomax on July 23, 1942, at Nelson's Funeral Home in Clarksdale during the joint study of Coahoma County by the Library of Congress and Fisk University.[304]

In Haffer's own estimation, "the people seemed to appreciate that song *mighty* well."[305] Fisk University's John Wesley Work III titled his transcription of the recording "What a Storm," and noted that "passages in [it] are very similar to passages found in the 'Elijah and Ahab' sermon by Reverend C. H. Savage, indicating common racial exhortative devices of musical expression."[306]

> *Spoken:* Song of the great disaster, March 16, 1942. Passed . . . Storm passed through six states, eleven hundred and five injured, a hundred and forty-seven dead, property damage run far in the millions. What a storm.

> *Chorus:*
> Oh, what a storm that evening
> In different parts of the land.
> What a storm that evening
> Men [folks] died on every hand.

> *Repeat chorus*[307]

> On a Monday evening in March, between four and five o'clock,
> Great buildings like play toys began to leave the blocks.
> A fierce storm was raging, which passed through six states,
> Leaving a trail of death and destructions in the wake.

> *Chorus*

> Two clouds commenced rising in the East and in the West,
> They rose higher and higher until they finally met.
> They clashed against each other as it were a ball of fire,
> Then went a terrible roaring like a hundred Fourth of Julys.

> *Chorus*

> People started running and screaming, falling everywhere,
> Water Valley, Grenada and Greenwood, Itta Bena and Berclair.
> The rain it commence falling, thundering and lightning, too,
> The wind started blowing, brethren, as it never blew before.

Chorus

You talk about your Twenty-Seven waters, how many of our friends
  were drowned,
About your storm in Tupelo where so many people went down,
Your Natchez fire disaster, which happened some years ago,
But the storm that happened that Monday is the worst ever happened
  before.

Repeat chorus twice

There was a man and his wife became frightened, and give themselves
  up to die,
Put their arms around each other, together they wanted to die.
Their house was blown to pieces, goods scattered everywhere,
But when it was all over, brethrens, they were left standing there.

Chorus

There was a woman with a baby she was carrying in her arms,
The storm destroyed the woman, but the babe was left unharmed.
God works in a mysterious way, brethren, His wonders to perform,
He hears His children when they pray and makes the storm be calm.

Chorus

Satan is the god of this world, he's the prince and power of the air,
By him all nations is disturbed, and there's trouble everywhere.
He tried to tempt the Savior while He was hungry and weak,
And then sent a storm on the ocean, brethren, to destroy Him while He
  sleep.

Chorus

Now Christians, let's be careful, and don't forget to pray,
Lest anytime He send a storm and take us all away.
The sun that rose this morning was shining in our face,
Maybe this time tomorrow's sun may shine upon our grave.

Chorus

The second half of the fifth stanza is another occurrence in a disaster song of the opening couplet—here slightly varied—of William Cowper's "Light Shining out of Darkness." In addition to the instances in this chapter, George Washington and his fellow convicts sang it in "In That Storm" about the 1928 Florida hurricanes and floods.[308] The couplet's recurrence in disaster songs doubtless results from its being the most familiar reference, for African American Christians, to God's presence in storms. More strikingly original are Haffer's biblical references to Satan's temptation of Christ (Matthew 4:1–11), and to the storm on the Sea of Galilee, mentioned in the three synoptic Gospels (Haffer does not add that Christ calmed the storm, having alluded to it in the previous stanza).

A comparison of Haffer's lyrics with contemporary newspaper accounts reveals his concern for factual accuracy. In the spoken introduction, Haffer states that 147 people were killed and 1,105 injured. The *Memphis Press-Scimitar* reported similar figures, which Haffer's wife must have read to him. "Between four and five o'clock" is not inconsistent with the hour and a half's duration reported in the press, and probably refers to the time the storm took to cross Mississippi before entering southwest Tennessee. Of the places hit by the tornado which Haffer mentions, Water Valley, Grenada, and Greenwood were the north-central Mississippi towns most severely struck by the twister and reporting the most fatalities.

Haffer clearly also drew some anecdotes and details from the Memphis *Commercial Appeal*. A map in that paper, which Haffer's wife perhaps described to him, shows that the more destructive tornado passed through all the towns he mentions, although he lists them in the reverse order of impact, probably constrained by the demands of scansion and rhyme. "Two clouds commenced rising in the East and in the West" may relate to the storm's path through Mississippi from southwest to northeast.[309] The related line, "They clashed against each other as it were a ball of fire" is undoubtedly inspired by eyewitness accounts in the press of a ball of fire, which accompanied the tornado as it ravaged Itta Bena.[310] Haffer's comparison of the wind's noise to a hundred Fourth of July firework displays is vividly imaginative. "Great buildings like play toys began to leave the blocks" may refer to the *Commercial Appeal*'s report of a galvanized iron building smashed in Grenada.[311]

Haffer compares the tornado's impact to those of the 1927 Mississippi flood, the 1936 tornado in Tupelo, and the 1940 Natchez Rhythm Club fire. He had composed songs about the latter two events, and the tragic results of all three would still have been vivid in the collective memory of Black Mississippians. Contrary to Haffer's assertion, made for dramatic effect, the Tupelo tornado caused more fatalities than were suffered in 1942.

The broadside of the song available at the Library of Congress website doesn't fully correspond to the transcription of the recording above.[312] Besides several minor variations in spelling, punctuation, and choice of words and structures that don't affect the meaning conveyed in the recording, the broadside doesn't include Haffer's spoken introduction but prints the customary reference to the Scriptures from which the Reverend drew inspiration (Job 1:11–22; Ephesians 2:2; 2 Corinthians 4:3–4; Nahum 1:3; Luke 8:23).[313] More importantly, the broadside prints an additional stanza, the fifth, that Haffer probably just forgot to sing to Alan Lomax:

> The train was at Itta Bena, but by the time it got to Moor(e)head,
> The storm was practically over and many a soul was dead.
> The wind, somehow, got angry, and it did just as it pleased,
> Blew churches and schools in the river, set automobiles in trees.

Again, newspaper articles are the source of Haffer's unrecorded stanza.[314]

God's Chariot: 1952 Mid-South Tornado

The Mid-South tornado outbreak of March 21–22, 1952, was one of the deadliest in the history of the United States. A series of eleven F4 tornadoes caused 209 deaths, most of them in Arkansas, Tennessee, Missouri, and Mississippi; there were also fatalities in Alabama and Kentucky. The first tornado developed in southwestern Arkansas, and struck the town of Dierks during the early afternoon of March 21. The next tornado hit White County, Arkansas, and leveled the town of Judsonia, killing fifty of its 1,100 inhabitants. In the next twenty-two hours nine more F4 tornadoes killed 123 more people.[315]

This disaster is the subject of the two-part "God's Chariot" (Duke G-1), recorded in Memphis ca. 1952 by a local quartet, one of the many groups who called themselves the Gospel Travelers.[316] The personnel were the song's composer Eugene Walton (lead), Ray Hurley (tenor and guitar), John Spencer (baritone), and Troy Yarborough (bass). There are also overdubbed sound effects of wind and thunder.[317]

Part 1

Chorus:
Well, you know God rode (God rode in a mighty storm)
Yes, He rode (God rode in a mighty storm)
Oh, I know God rode (in a mighty dark cloud)
(Oh, He rode through the Southland in a storm.)

Well, in the year of 1952, on the 21st day of March,
It was late one Friday evening, along about seven o'clock

God took the cloud for His chariot, He used the wind for His horse
He rode on across the Southland, where many a soul was lost.

And the first stop He made was over in Arkansas,
He loosed His zig-zag lightning, mighty wind began to blow
So the peoples beginned to run, trying to find somewhere to hide
But you just can't hide from Jesus, no matter where you go.

Those houses began to rock, green trees began to pop
Little childrens crying for mother, 'cause mother couldn't be found
You sure better stop and pray, He's coming back one day.

Chorus

Yes, that mighty Son of Man, He rode on across the land
He stopped, trying to stop over in the state of Missouri
Well, He spoke with a voice of thunder, so heavy it shook the earth
Those people, they saw Him coming in a big black ball of smoke.
With a long red streak of fire, zigzagging from east to west
They didn't know what to do, 'twas Jesus passing through.

It was a blind man in the door, couldn't see nowhere to go
He just fell down on the floor, cried, "Lord, I'm ready to go."
Those buildings began to shake, windowpanes began to break
Well, it blowed the building down, but he was safe and sound
Well, that shows you what God will do if you've been living true.

Chorus

Part 2

Chorus (x2)

Well, he stepped back in His chariot, and He rode on across the land
And the next time He stopped, He was over in Tennessee
Those people heard a roaring they never had heard before
Well, it hit like a 'tomic bomb, peoples began to run.

It was death and destruction, all up and down the road,
So the hospitals sent out a call for doctors one and all.
"We ain't got no more room, but they still coming in,
They just laying all over the floor, just groaning more and more."
Well, they worked both day and night, trying to save those people's lives.

Chorus

Well, He moved on across the way, He didn't have long to stay
Well, He stopped in Mississippi, He dropped a ball of fire
Those houses began to burn, prayer wheels began to turn
It sure was a sad time, seeing so many peoples dying.

Well, He stepped right on time, 'cross the Alabama line
Every time the chariot stopped, Southland would reel and rock
You people that's living wrong, you know by the mighty storm
You sure better stop to pray, He's coming back one day.

Good God, He's coming (He's coming back)
Yes, He's coming, He's coming back
Oh Lord, He's coming, He's coming back.
You better get ready,
You better get ready, better get ready for you don't know when.

The last stanza of Part 1 refers to an incident reported in the *New York Times* of Sunday, March 23, 1952: "At the town of Marked Tree, [Arkansas,] Henry Wilkins, a 77 year old blind man, sat unhurt while his house was blown over his head, but his wife was injured seriously."

In the interview by David Evans already referred to, Rev. Ruben Lacy probably also recalled this tornado:

EVANS: Now you said there was another song that was written, a ballet, about a storm that came through this town . . .
LACY: I never did know that one there, but I heard it. But I never did know that one.
EVANS: What town was that?
LACY: Brinkley, Arkansas.
EVANS: And the year was . . .
LACY: 1952.
EVANS: And you said you saw people selling this on the streets?
LACY: Yes, I saw people selling that ballet on the streets. That didn't last long though. Seems that that storm wasn't publicly known. I don't see why. The storm should have been known all over the world, 'cause it did a lot of destruction. A little small place, Brinkley is. It's not a large place. And the most damage was did was out in the rural routes. That's another thing.[318]

It's Praying Time: The 1955 Mid-South Tornado

Circa 1955, and again in Memphis, the Gospel Travelers recorded "Praying Time" (Chariot 30), also credited to Eugene Walton. An unidentified drummer was added to the lineup.[319] This song is an account of tornadoes that struck Arkansas and Mississippi on Tuesday, February 1, 1955, before dissipating near Huntsville, Alabama. No one was seriously injured in Arkansas, but in Mississippi 125 people were injured and thirty-one killed: twenty-eight on the Leatherman Plantation in Commerce Landing, and three in Olive Branch. All of the dead and most of the injured were Black. Elementary schools were hit in both settlements, and in each of them a teacher and two children (possibly more at Commerce Landing) were killed.[320]

Chorus:
Well, it's praying time, it's praying time.
Death went a-riding through the land.
My God waved His mighty hand.
He brought destruction in/to the land.

February, Nineteen Fifty-Five,
You know, I seen a storm arise.
God himself stepped upon a cloud.
He rocked the world, He was rocking loud.
He rolled crossed the Mississippi line
You could see the peoples dying.

Two little children, I want you to see,
They ran and hid, down in a tree.
God looked down from Heaven and smiled.
Told Old Death, "Don't you ride.
Go down, Mercy, spare their lives."
Strong houses was torn down.
The church houses was moved around.
He brought destruction in/to the land.

You know my Jesus kept on His way.
Many a soul was blown away.
There was a mother, fifty-one years old,
She cried, "Lord, save our souls."
She took the children into her arms.
She said, "Dear Lord, save our home."

God looked down, He heard her cry.
He told Old Death, "Pass on by.
[Ex]'cuse their lives, 'cause I'm watching you."
He brought destruction in the land.

Chorus

The reference to the "two little children [who] hid down in a tree" draws on contemporary press reports. The tree, actually a hollow stump near the Commerce Landing school, is said to have sheltered several children. It appears in a photograph of the destroyed school's site in the *Philadelphia Inquirer*.[321]

As well as expressing African American Christians' belief in God's omnipotence, and the need to prepare for the Second Coming by living in accordance with Christian precepts, these songs attest to Black gospel singers' accurate factual reporting of dates and incidents of apparently miraculous survival.

Unidentified and Miscellaneous Natural Disasters

Other recordings are not easily associated with a specific disaster. Among them is Kokomo Arnold's "Mean Old Twister" (Decca 7347), recorded in Chicago on March 30, 1937.[322] The first of its two generic stanzas mentioning the twister refers to the need of "lower[ing] your airplane down," and then the lyrics shift the focus on personal recollections and universal worries. In the line "Everybody's on a wonder what's the matter with this cruel world today," Arnold "reveals that the sudden appearance of the twister ... forced people to ponder on the atrocious state of the world," and in the final stanza he "ponders on his inevitable death"[323] and claims he deserves to go to heaven ("Now, I'm going home, I done did all in this world that I could / Says I got everybody happy 'round here in my neighborhood"). Paul Oliver's general assumption that "blues songs that tell of disasters are about something that the singer has probably witnessed" is questionable, although they are certainly more likely to be "familiar to his audience."[324] No concrete evidence could be found that Kokomo Arnold's song describes one of the "tornadoes that sweep up from the Texas coast as far as St. Louis and beyond."[325]

Likewise, only the first stanza of Tom Bell's "Storm in Arkansas" (AFS 4066-B-1), collected by John Lomax and his wife, Ruby Terrill, in Livingston, Alabama, on November 3, 1940, relates to an unidentified disaster; the rest of the song is a series of formulaic verses:[326]

> ... the storm they had in Arkansas (x2)
> ... that storm they had in Arkansas,
> It killed one hundred, uhm, and ninety-nine.

Although not unique, it is unusual for a noncommercial recording, made in a rural community, to refer to an event that took place elsewhere. This song may be an account of the tornado that hit Arkansas, Louisiana, Texas, Oklahoma, and Alabama in April 1939, killing at least forty-three people, nineteen of them in the little community of Center Point, near Collins, Arkansas.[327]

The first in the long and diverse list of disaster songs by Texas bluesman Sam "Lightnin'" Hopkins (1911–1982) was "That Mean Old Twister" (Aladdin 167), recorded in Los Angeles on November 9, 1946.[328]

> Yes, I was sitting in my kitchen, I was looking way out 'cross the west,
> I was sitting in my kitchen, I was looking way out 'cross the west,
> I see that mean old twister coming, I started in to pray.
>
> I fell down on my knees, this is the words I begin to say (x2)
> I said, "Oh Lord, have mercy, and help us in our wicked ways."
>
> Yeah, you know, the wind was blowing, coming in my windows and
>   door (x2)
> Yeah, you know my house done fell down, and I can't live there no more.
>
> I said, "Lord, Lord, what shall we do?"
> "Oh Lord," I said, "Lord, what shall we do?
> Yes, it ain't no other help I know, oh Lord, but You."

This patchwork of stanzas, partly inspired by Lonnie Johnson's "St. Louis Cyclone Blues" and Bessie Smith's "Back-Water Blues,"[329] describes an unidentified East Texas tornado possibly experienced by Hopkins. The natural disaster that probably inspired him was the March 1943 St. Augustine tornado.[330] Mack McCormick wrote:

> His "Backwater Blues" (an alternative title to "That Mean Old Twister") has only the barest hint and glimpse of the song as Lightnin' first heard it from Lonnie Johnson (and as it became famous through Bessie Smith's recording). This memory mingles with his recollection of Blind Lemon Jefferson's singing "Rising High Water Blues" and of Texas Alexander's singing "Frost, Texas Tornado Blues." It crosses his own experience with *a tornado slashing across the "Piney Woods."* [my italics][331]

Hopkins himself explained the creative process underpinning his song:

Once it was a twister come through a farm not far from where I was living and kill quite a few people and tore up homes and things like that—
and that just give me the idea. . . . That's the reason I tell you—that's the
way I get practically all my songs. Something happen. I just go ahead
and make a song. Practically all my songs are *true* songs.[332]

Also unidentified and generic is the disaster in St. Louis Jimmy Oden's
"Florida Hurricane" (Aristocrat 7001), recorded in Chicago in 1948.[333] After
getting hurricanes and tornadoes mixed up in the first stanza, the lyrics veer
to wry humor in the third stanza when the singer winks at the listeners and
says that if a hurricane strikes, the victims don't need to spend their money
on unnecessary clothes and can afford to rebuild their homes instead. In the
last stanza, his love for Florida depends on whether the wind will never blow
him away if he decides to live there all his life.

Another original treatment of a natural disaster not easily associated with
a specific historical event is "Georgia Flood" (Red House RHR 113), recorded
by bluesman Guy Davis (born 1952) in 1998 in New York.[334] Not only does this
song once more prove Black musicians' creativity and the allure of tragedies
rooted in tradition, but it also reasserts and strengthens the power of memories
(albeit reported, vague, or mythical) handed down in blues lore from generation
to generation. As explained by Davis before performing a videotaped version
of the song:

I wrote that song on my way to the supermarket one day. I had no idea
where it came from, but the basic verses to that song were in me by the
time I got back to the supermarket and I jiggled around with a tune for
it. And I know that there were tunes about floods, the "Backwater Blues"
and things that Charley Patton sang. And, you know, various blues musicians have sung songs about the floods and the disasters. After writing
this song I found out years later that in my own, I'll say, family, I don't
know exactly how they related, but back during my grandmother and
grandfather's time, somebody somehow related to us, there was a man
and a woman [who] had ten children, and there was a flood in their
community, I think this may have been in the thirties, and the whole
community had to go up hillside and watch while the floodwaters wiped
out their town. And like any good mother, this woman took attendance,
she called out to her kids one by one. Ten kids, nine of them answered,
one did not. . . . She became convinced that her child was down in the
waters of the flood. She ran down the hill, grown men could not hold
her. She jumped into that water to look for her child and she drowned.
And as if that's not tragedy enough, it turns out that her little baby child

was up on that hillside and he chose the wrong time to be willful and when he heard his mother call his name, he didn't answer, not realizing the effect that it would have. And then I found out that this was part of our extended family history after I wrote the song.[335]

Despite Davis's accurate description, I haven't been able to find any factual evidence that this disaster occurred, but the song's lyrics stand out as one of the best modern and innovative recreations of a blurred yet inspiring incident:

> Well, let me tell you a story
> For there's no one else alive
> Who can tell you about the Savannah flood
> Of Nineteen and Twenty-five, of Nineteen and Twenty-five.

Finally, there are a few unpublished compositions or unreleased recordings related to natural disasters. Among the former, one of the oldest is "Marshfield Tornado," a programmatic piece by Black ragtime pianist John William "Blind" Boone (1864–1927) commemorating the storm that struck Marshfield, Missouri, on April 18, 1880.[336] Allegedly inspired by Blind Tom's "Battle of Manassas," Boone always concluded his concerts with "Marshfield Tornado," but never published it.[337] A concert program describes the piece's content as "The Chimes ringing, as the storm happened at the beginning of evening church services; Opening Hymn; Approaching Storm; Fire Bells heard giving alarm; the Raging Storm; it dies away in the distance while the water drips from the eaves of the house."[338]

Perhaps the most intriguing unissued topical recording on a natural disaster is Mose Andrews's "Mississippi Storm" (ARC unissued), recorded in Chicago on June 21, 1935. Born around 1913 in Lobdell, Bolivar County, Mississippi, Andrews was in his early twenties when he recorded.[339] His recording was probably related either to the April 7 tornadoes that ravaged Gloster and Gillsburg in southern Mississippi, and the area around Lake Providence, Louisiana, or (more likely) to a series of storms on May 3, which killed five Black people in Mississippi, and another five, as well as a white woman, in Mississippi County, Arkansas.[340]

CONCLUSION

This chapter reveals an unsystematic attitude among African American musicians to the creation of disaster songs, an activity that seems to be contingent on the responses of individual composers and performers to a particular event.

It is also evident that the amount of interest aroused, nationally or even internationally, by a catastrophe is not correlated to the number of songs about it. The 1900 Galveston hurricane and the 1925 Tri-state tornado, two of America's greatest natural disasters, yielded just one known song each, while calamities that were mainly local (the 1926 Miami hurricane) or less deadly (the 1926 Cumberland River flood) inspired more songs and cover versions. Factors involved include the time and place where a calamity occurred, and how seriously and directly it affected the Black community. Likewise, some songs may have been composed and sung but never published or collected.

Even when songs are about different disasters, the melody and lyrics of a later song can be influenced by or derived from earlier ones. "Wasn't That a Mighty Storm," in particular, made a strong impact on later singers and composers.

Chapter Two

ACCIDENTAL DISASTERS

God Moves on the Water: Transportation Disasters

SOME PEOPLE SAY THAT MISTER KASSIE COULDN'T RUN: THE 1900 CASEY JONES TRAIN WRECK

Railroad engineer Jonathan Luther "Casey" Jones has become a mythic figure in American folklore and the subject of hundreds of recordings by singers both Black and white. He was the only fatality in the wreck of the Illinois Central Railroad's prestigious Cannonball Express, which occurred at 3:52 a.m. on April 30, 1900.[1] Behind time on its run from Chicago to New Orleans, the Cannonball crashed into the rear of a caboose and some freight cars, which were standing on the main track at Vaughan, Mississippi, a few miles north of Canton. Jones only had time to tell fireman Sim Webb to jump from Engine 382. After the collision, Jones was found dead "because either a metal bolt, or a piece of wood, pierced his throat."[2] Express Messenger Miller suffered two broken ribs, and some passengers were slightly injured, but because of Jones's efforts to slow the train before the collision, most of them survived unhurt, as did Sim Webb.

It was determined that among the causes of the crash were the Cannonball's excessive speed, and not surprisingly, the presence of the caboose and freight cars standing on the main track around a sharp bend. Webb initially confirmed that Jones had disregarded flagman John Newberry's warning signals, but in retirement he claimed that there had been no warning at all.[3]

The origin of the "Casey Jones" ballad has been the subject of much speculation and controversy because different texts have been traced as recurrent standard forms, making it impossible to separate the various song clusters assumed to have contributed to the two main threads that fed into later versions: the non-copyright lyrics of a text reportedly sung by African American Wallace (a.k.a. Wallis or "Wash") Saunders, a Black engine-wiper from Canton, Mississippi,[4] and the pop song "Casey Jones," published and copyrighted by

Figure 2.01. Casey Jones music sheet, p. 1 (E. Newton). Luigi Monge collection

white vaudevillians T. Lawrence Seibert (words) and Eddie Newton (music) in 1909 (see fig. 2.01).[5]

Saunders's original text is not available. The first published reference to a song about Casey Jones was printed in *Railroad Man's Magazine* in 1908.[6] It is thought to derive from the combination of original material contributed by Saunders with Black and white songs and fragments:

Come all you rounders, for I want you to hear
The story told of an engineer.
Casey Jones was the rounder's name,
A heavy right-wheeler of a mighty fame.

Caller called Jones about half past four;
He kissed his wife at the station door,
Climbed into his cab with his orders in his hand,
Says, "This is my trip to the holy land."

Through South Memphis yards, on the fly,
He heard the fire-boy say, "You've got a white eye."
All the switchmen knew, by the engine moan,
That the man at the throttle was Casey Jones.

It had been raining some five or six weeks,
The railroad track was like the bed of a creek;
They rated him down to a thirty-mile gait,
Threw the south-bound mail about eight hours late.

Fireman says, "Casey, you're running too fast,
You run the block-board the last station you passed."
Jones says, "Yes, I believe we'll make it through,
For the steam's better than I ever knew."

Jones says, "Fireman, don't you fret;
Keep knocking at the fire-door, don't give up yet.
I'm going to run her till she leaves the rail,
Or make it in on time with the Southern mail."

Around the curve and down the dump
Two locomotives were bound to bump.
Fireman hollered, "Jones, it's just ahead;
We might jump and make it, but we'll all be dead."

'Twas around this curve he spied a passenger-train.
Reversing his engine, he caused the bell to ring.
Fireman jumped off, but Jones stayed on—
He's a good engineer, but he's dead and gone.

Poor Casey Jones was all right,
For he stuck to his duty both day and night.

They loved to hear his whistle and ring of number three,
As he came into Memphis on the old I.C.

Headaches and heartaches, and all kinds of pain,
Are not apart from a railroad train.
Tales that are in earnest, noble and grand,
Belong to the life of a railroad man.[7]

The most important combination of original material contributed by
Saunders with Black and white songs and fragments is the Black ballad that
Howard W. Odum published in 1911, having collected it in Lafayette County,
Mississippi, sometime between 1905 and 1908.[8] It is significant as an unmis-
takably African American text and because it is clearly orally transmitted: the
penultimate stanza's sexual reference (comically misunderstood by Odum as
referring to unemployment) has migrated from "Take Me Back Blues."

Casey Jones wus engineer
Told his fireman not to fear.
All he wanted was a boiler hot,
Run in Canton 'bout four o'clock.

One Sunday mornin' it wus drizzlin' rain,
Looked down de road an' saw a train;
Fireman says, "Let's make a jump;
Two locomotives an' dey bound to bump."

Casey Jones, I know him well,
Tole de fireman to ring de bell;
Fireman jump an' say "Good-bye,
Casey Jones, you're bound to die."

Went on down to de depot track,
Beggin' my honey to take me back;
She turned 'roun' some two or three times;
"Take you back when you learn to grind."

Womens in Kansas, all dressed in red,
Got de news dat Casey was dead;
De womens in Jackson, all dressed in black,
Said, in fact, he was a cracker-jack.[9]

Seibert and Newton's sheet music was available by April 1909, when it was demonstrated at the Broadway Department Store in Los Angeles.[10] Its cover carries the subtitle "The Brave Engineer," and the phrases "Greatest Comedy Hit in Years" and "The Only Comedy Railroad Song." The text, which is erratically punctuated, transfers the crash to the Western states, reflects negative opinion about Jones's supposedly unprofessional behavior, and makes allegations about his wife Janie Brady's infidelity, which as a widow she spent many years rebutting.

> Come all you rounders if you want to hear
> A story about a brave Engineer.
> Casey Jones was the rounder[']s name
> On a six eight wheeler boys he won his fame.
>
> Put in your water and shovel in your coal
> Put your head out the window watch them drivers roll
> I'll run her till she leaves the rail
> Cause I'm eight hour[s] late with that western mail.
>
> Casey pulled up that Reno hill
> He tooted for the crossing with an awful shrill
> The switchmen knew by the engine's moan
> That the man at the throttle was Casey Jones.
>
> Casey said just before he died
> There's two more roads that I'd like to ride.
> Fireman said what could that be
> The Southern Pacific and the Santa Fe.
>
> The caller called Casey at a half past four
> He kissed his wife at the station door
> Mounted to the Cabin with his orders in his hand
> And he took his farewell trip to that promised land.
>
> *Chorus*
> Casey Jones! mounted to the cabin,
> Casey Jones, with his orders in his hand,
> Casey Jones, mounted to the cabin,
> And he took his farewell trip to that Promised land.
>
> He looked at his watch and his watch was slow
> He looked at the water and the water was low

He turned to the Fireman and he said,
We're going to reach Frisco but we'll all be dead.

Chorus
Casey Jones! going to reach Frisco,
Casey Jones, but we'll all be dead,
Casey Jones, going to reach Frisco,
We're going to reach Frisco but we'll all be dead.

He pulled up within two miles of the place
Number Four stared him right in the face
He turned to the Fireman said, Boy, you'd better jump
Cause there's two Locomotives that's a going to bump.

Chorus
Casey Jones! two Locomotives,
Casey Jones, that's a going to bump,
Casey Jones, two Locomotives,
There's two Locomotives that's a going to bump.

Mrs. Jones sat on her bed a sighing
Just received a message that Casey was dying
Said, Go to bed, children, and hush your crying
Cause you got another papa on the Salt Lake line.

Chorus
Mrs. Casey Jones! got another Papa,
Mrs. Casey Jones, on that Salt Lake Line,
Mrs. Casey Jones, got another Papa,
And you've got another Papa on that Salt Lake Line.[11]

There are many recordings of Seibert and Newton's song, most of them displaying little or no variation from the published text. They are performed in many genres, including among others pop, vocal group harmony, country, folk, and blues.

It appears that songs, and fragments of songs, from various thematic families coalesced around the Casey Jones theme soon after the 1900 wreck of the Cannonball Express. The songs that are African American or that draw on African American constituents can be divided into three thematic groups, which include only two songs about a train wreck.

The first group contains songs about hobos and ramblers, such as "Wreck of the Six-Wheeler," "Hobo John," "Milwaukee Blues," and (because it also deals with hoboes and is from a hobo point of view) possibly also verses titled "Old Jay Gould" or "Jay Gould's Daughter," some fifty of which were stated to exist by a hobo nicknamed "Kelley the Rake" in a letter published in the *Kansas City Star* of August 5, 1911.[12]

> Old Jay Gould said, before he died:
> I'll fix the blind so the 'boes [hoboes] can't ride.
> If they ride, they will ride the rod,
> And place their life in the hands of God.
>
> Old Jay Gould said, as he was about to die,
> There's two more railroads I'd like to buy.
> We were wondering what they could be.
> He said, "The New York Central and the Santa Fe."

Gilded Age robber baron Jay Gould owned the Missouri Pacific Railroad from 1879 to his death in 1892, which seems to imply a date of composition in the last decade of the nineteenth century. In 1925, but probably drawing on Odum's fieldwork two decades earlier, Odum and Johnson reported in *The Negro and His Songs* that verses similar to those above were "favorites with Negro railroad workers."[13]

On September 9, 1930, in Johnson City, Tennessee, country music star Charlie Poole, leading the North Carolina Ramblers, recorded "Milwaukee Blues" (Columbia 15688-D):

> One Tuesday morning and it looked like-a rain,
> Around the curve come a passenger train;
> On the blinds sat old Bill Jones,
> Good old hobo and he's trying to get home.
> Trying to get home, he's trying to get home,
> He's a good old hobo and he's tryin' to get home.
>
> Way down in Georgie on a tramp,
> Roads are getting muddy and the leaves are getting damp;
> I got to catch a freight train and leave this town,
> 'Cause they don't allow no hoboes a-hanging around.
> Hanging around, yes, a-hanging around,
> 'Cause they don't 'low no hoboes a-hanging around.

I left Atlanta one morning 'fore day,
The brakeman said, "You'll have to pay."
"Got no money, but I'll pawn my shoes,
I wanta go west, got the Milwaukee blues.
Got the Milwaukee blues, got the Milwaukee blues,
I wanta go west, got the Milwaukee blues."

Ol' Bill Jones said before he died,
"Fix the road so the 'boes can ride;
When they ride, they will ride the rods,
Put all trust in the hands of God.
In the hands of God, in the hands of God,
They'll put all trust in the hands of God."

Ol' Bill Jones said before he died,
There's two more roads he'd like to ride;
Fireman said, "What can it be?"
"Southern Pacific and the Santa Fe.
Santa Fe, yes, Santa Fe,
Southern Pacific and the Santa Fe."[14]

"Milwaukee Blues" and "Casey Jones" appear to have a shared ancestor in a fragment titled "Jimmie Jones." Wash Saunders had died by the time John and Alan Lomax went to Canton in search of him in August 1933, but they did find his seventy-year-old friend and former co-worker Cornelius Steen. While paying a visit in Kansas City, Steen had heard a street guitarist sing "Jimmie Jones."[15] Steen could only remember one of its stanzas:

On a Sunday mornin' it begin to rain,
Around the curve he spied a passenger train;
On the pilot lay poor Jimmie Jones,
He's a good old porter, but he's dead and gone.
Dead and gone, oh he's dead and gone;
He's a good old porter but he's dead and gone.[16]

Back in Canton, Steen sang the song to Saunders, who liked it so much that he started to add verses describing Jimmie Jones's death in a wreck. When Casey Jones died in 1900, Saunders changed the song's protagonist and title to "Casey Jones" and adapted the lyrics to the recent train wreck. Steen recalled three verses from among those that Saunders sang:

On a Sunday mornin' it begin to rain,
Around the curve he spied a passenger train;
Under the cab lay po' Casey Jones,
He's a good engineer but he's dead and gone.

Casey being a good engineer,
Told his fireman not to have fear;
"All I wan's a little water and coal,
I'll peep out the cab and see the drivers roll."

On a Sunday mornin' it begin to rain,
Around the curve he spied a passenger train;
Told his fireman he's [sic] better jump,
Cause there's two locomotives that are bound to bump.[17]

Norm Cohen notes that "analogs of [the 'Jimmie Jones' fragment] appear in more than twenty texts, only five of which mention Casey Jones."[18] This seems to support the suggestion that "Jimmie Jones" contributed both to "Casey Jones" and to other songs about hoboes and train wrecks.

The second group, which appears to draw on material predating "Casey Jones," does deal with train wrecks. "Joseph Michael" (or "Joseph Mica"), apparently in circulation in the late nineteenth century, was preserved by "Kelley the Rake" in his 1911 letter to the *Kansas City Star*. He said it was about an engineer on the Rock Island Line named James A. Michaels, and claimed to have chosen the following verses at random from three hundred he knew:

Songs are sung about the heroes of old,
I'll tell you of one that skins them cold.
James A. Michaels was the eagle eye's name,
And when he died he died dead game.

James A. Michaels was a brave engineer;
He told the tallow pot[19] not to fear.
Says he, all you got to do is keep her hot,
And we'll make it in about four o'clock.

Just grab the shovel and heave the coal;
Put your head out the window and watch the drivers roll.
Then he looked at his watch and mumbled and said,
We may make it, but we'll all be dead.

They pulled out of —————— about forty minutes late,
Dragging behind thirty-six cars of freight.
The conductor didn't keep any tab,
'Cause James A. Michaels was in the cab.

But when they got to the whistling post,
James turned as pale as any old ghost.
He had the tallow pot out on the top,
Helping the brakies to make the stop.

The Cannon Ball come splitting the air
He threw her over and unloaded right there.
He yelled to the fireman, You'd better jump,
'Cause two locomotives is about to bump.[20]

"Ben Dewberry's Final Run" was written by the prolific white evangelist and musician Andrew "Blind Andy" Jenkins in 1927, and recorded by Jimmie Rodgers on November 30 that year (Victor 21245). In *Long Steel Rail*, Norm Cohen theorizes that "Ben Dewberry's Final Run," although apparently a recomposition of "Casey Jones," "represents an older family of texts and tunes than does the popular vaudeville version."[21] At that time, Cohen had been unable to discover a historical basis for Jenkins's composition.

Ben Dewberry was a brave engineer,
He told his fireman, "Don't you ever fear;
All I want is the water and coal,
Put your head out the window, watch the drivers roll.
  Watch the drivers roll, watch the drivers roll,
  Put your head out the window, watch the drivers roll."

Ben Dewberry said before he died,
Two more roads that he wanted to ride;
His fireman asked him what could they be,
Said, "The old Northeastern and the A and V."
  "The A and V," he said, "the A and V,
  It's the old Northeastern and the A and V."

On the fatal morning it begin to rain,
Around the curve come a passenger train;
Ben Dewberry was the engineer,
With the throttle wide open and without any fear.

> He didn't have no fear, he didn't have no fear;
> He had her runnin' wide open without any fear.
>
> Ben looked at his watch, shook his head,
> "We may make Atlanta but we'll all be dead."
> The train went flyin' by the trestle and switch,
> Without any warning then she took the ditch.
>   Yeah, she went in the ditch, well, she took the ditch,
>   Without any warning then she took the ditch.
>
> The big locomotive leaped from the rail,
> Ben never lived to tell that awful tale;
> His life was ended and his work was done,
> When Ben Dewberry made his final run.
>   He made his final run, he made his final run,
>   When Ben Dewberry made his final run.

When he came to write about it again in 2008, Cohen was aware that "Ben Dewberry's Final Run" commemorates a wreck at Buford, Georgia, on August 23, 1908, in which Dewberry and his African American fireman, Mason Wadkins, were killed. The cause of the crash was a bolt placed on the track by twelve-year-old Lewis Cooksey, who wanted to see what a train wreck would look like. Tried for murder and train-wrecking, Cooksey was acquitted, after which he stated that he had indeed placed the bolt.

On the basis of this information, Cohen concluded that "Jenkins, contemplating for a railroad song to capitalize on the commercial success of 'The Wreck of the Old 97,' 'Casey Jones' and similar songs, cobbled together some familiar verses and structured them around an engineer he had remembered from years before."[22] It may be added that the song is short on detail, and inaccurately blames the crash on excessive speed to make up time. There is an obvious parallel here with the historical facts of the "Casey Jones" crash and songs about it.

The third cluster of songs including material that predates "Casey Jones" is represented on records titled "J. C. Holmes Blues," "Hobo Blues," and also, confusingly, "Casey Jones."[23] These songs are about rounders leading a fast and dissolute life. The first commercial African American recording in this song cluster was Bessie Smith's "J. C. Holmes Blues" (Columbia 14095-D), recorded in New York City on May 27, 1925.[24] Composed by Gus Horsley, it is a parody of "Casey Jones" that seems to incorporate older material. It features strong sexual innuendos, including the use of the train as a phallic symbol.

Listen, people, if you want to hear
A story told about a brave engineer;
J. C. Holmes was the rounder's name,
A heavyweight wheelman with a mighty fame.

J. C. said with a smile so fine,
"Woman gets tired of one man all the time;
Get two or three, if you have to hide,
If the train go and leave, you've got a mule to ride."

In the second cabin sat Miss Alice Fry,
Going to ride with Mister J. C. or die;
"I ain't good looking and I don't dress fine,
But I'm a rambling woman with a rambling mind."

Just then the conductor hollered, "All aboard,"
Then the porter said, "We've got a load."
"Look-a here, son, we ought to (have) been gone,
I feel like riding if it's all night long."

J. C. said just before he died,
Two more roads he wanted to ride;
Everybody wondered what road it could be,
He said, "The Southern Pacific and the Santa Fe."

J. C. said, "I don't feel right,
I saw my girl with a man last night;
Soon as I get enough steam just right,
I been mistreated and I don't mind dying."

The three groups of songs discussed thus far contributed elements to the popular "Casey Jones" ballad. Two ballad texts, both probably containing elements that predate the Casey Jones wreck, have been attributed to Wash Saunders, the alleged composer of "Casey Jones." What has hitherto been thought to be the earliest published text of the first of these was published in 1908, but a recent discovery pushes its composition back to before June 20, 1903, on which date a Paducah, Kentucky, newspaper carried this story:[25]

Many of the "old times" [sic] will pleasantly remember Engineer Jones, familiarly dubbed as "Casey Jones," who ran between this city and

Memphis back in the 80's.[26] Down in Mississippi on the I.C. one day last year [sic] "Casey" was "splitting the wind" on a delayed mail train eight hours late. When rounding a curve he met another train. There was loud blasts of whistles, air brake set and then a mighty crash and after all was over the mangled, dead body of "Casey" was extricated from the wreck. A former companion of the old engineer has indicated his sorrow for his old friend's taking-off in the following lines which he sings as mournful as a funeral dirge as he accompanys [sic] himself on the guitar.

CASEY JONES

Come all you "railroaders," I want you to hear,
The story, I'll tell of a brave engineer,
"Casey Jones" was the old "eagle eye's" name.
And he was a heavy "right-wheeler" of fame.

The rain had poured for more than a week,
The track was like the bed of a creek.
The "slow orders" rated him to a thirty-mile gait,
And caused the fast mail to be eight hours late.

The caller yelled—"Jones" at half-past four,
He kissed his wife "good-bye" at the door.
He mounted his cab—with his orders in his hand,
And then started on his trip to the holy land.

Went on down through the Memphis yards,
On number 3's daily schedule cards,
And the switchmen knew, by the enger's [sic] groans,
That the man at the throttle was Casey Jones.

"Casey" threw his leg over the window sill,
Blew for the crossing with a peculiar thrill,
Said to the fireman, "We're sure to go through,
For she's steaming better than I ever knew."

"Casey Jones" was a great engineer,
And said to his fireman—"Bud, don't you fear,
But that I'll run her to Canton by six o'clock.
If only you will keep her boiler hot."

The fireman answered—"Ain't you running too fast?
You run by the last station board that you passed."
Casey said, "I'll run her till she leaves the rail,
Or make up the eight hours with the Southern mail."

Rounding a curve, he met another train,
Reversed his engine, rung the bell—but all in vain,
The fireman jumped—but Casey stayed on,
He was a h–ll of a "wheeler," but now he's gone.

Mrs. Jones was sitting on the side of the bed,
When a telegram told her old Jones was dead,
She said to the children, "go to bed and hold your breath,
You are sure to draw a pension four [sic] your dady's [sic] death."

There are close similarities between this lyric and that published in 1908, the main difference being Mrs. Jones's callous reaction in the final stanza.

Discussing the 1908 text, Norm Cohen notes that it displays all the characteristics of an Anglo-American ballad, and that it was composed within a railroad subculture.[27] The same is true of the precursor 1903 text. Even though its language is not particularly "Black," the lyrics have a syncopated rhythmic quality suggesting an origin in the environment of Black–white musical interchange. Blacks composed narrative ballads in a variety of styles. Not all were humorous or on "badman" themes or in the three-line rhymed couplet-plus-refrain form (for example, "Frankie"). In fact, some were also heroic, tragic, or moralistic. In the complex of songs examined in this chapter, the disaster/tragedy theme is only one among several.[28]

In a 1927 interview, Casey Jones's widow adds the significant information that "In 1901 Ed Newton, a song writer from California, came to Jackson[, Tennessee, her and Casey's hometown]. He heard the song [composed by Wallace Saunders] around the hotel where he was staying and began asking questions about it."[29] In the same interview, Mrs. Jones accuses Newton of adding the verse about having "another papa on the Santa Fe" to Saunders's lyric. It appears, then, that Newton was performing the song well before it was published, although there seems no doubt that it was the 1909 sheet music, and subsequent recordings, that made the song widely known.[30]

The second ballad supposedly deriving from Saunders stems from the mainly (albeit not exclusively) Black blues-ballad tradition,[31] and includes full or fragmentary elements also found in songs transcribed or sung by Cornelius Steen, the Lomaxes, Howard Odum, musician and hobo Harry "Haywire Mac"

McClintock, and folklorist E. C. Perrow, who published fragments of ballads he had collected in Mississippi in 1909.[32]

The similarity of the texts of the various versions of the ballad that probably derived from Saunders argues for a single source; and in 1951, "Haywire Mac" McClintock told Sam Eskin that he had learned the song from Wallace Saunders himself when switching box cars in Memphis in 1909.[33]

> Casey Jones was an engineer,
> Told his fireman to have no fear;
> "All I want is water and coal,
> And my head out the window when the drivers roll.
> > When the drivers roll, when the drivers roll
> > And my head out the window when the drivers roll."
>
> Through south Memphis yard on the fly,
> The fireman hollered, "Ya got a white eye";
> The switchman knew by the engine's moans
> That the man at the throttle was Casey Jones.
> > Oh, Casey Jones, oh Casey Jones,
> > That the man at the throttle was Casey Jones.
>
> Well, the engine rocked and the drivers roll,
> The fireman hollered "Lordy, save my soul!"
> Casey said, "I'll roll her till she leaves the rails,
> 'Cause I'm way behind time with the Southern mail."
> > With the Southern mail, oh, that South bound mail,
> > I'm way behind time with the southbound mail."
>
> Got within about a mile of the place,
> A big old headlight stared him right in the face;
> He told his fireman, "Boy, you'd better jump,
> 'Cause there's two locomotives that's a-goin' to bump.
> > That's a-goin' to bump, that's a-goin' to bump,
> > There's two locomotives that's a-goin' to bump."
>
> You ought to have been there to see that sight,
> The women stood cryin', both colored and white;
> I was there for to tell the fact,
> They flagged him down but he never looked back.
> > No, he never looked back, no, he never looked back,
> > They flagged him down but he never looked back.

Oh, Casey said, just before he died,
"There's lots more railroads that I'd like to ride";
But the good Lord whispered, "It's not to be,"
And he died at the throttle on the Y and MV.
 On the Y and MV, on the Y and MV,
 He died at the throttle on the Y and MV.

However, Norm Cohen is surely right to note the difficulties posed by the attribution to Saunders of two such culturally and linguistically different texts, and to be skeptical about the convenience of the testimonies of Cornelius Steen and Haywire Mac.[34]

There seem to be two "perspectives" in this entire body of material. The figure of the hobo (generally comic, sometimes sexual, and mainly Black) is antagonistic to the one of the railroad man (generally heroic and white), but they intersect because there were white hoboes and Blacks who worked for the railroad. Also, many railroad men (like Jimmie Rodgers) were sometimes hoboes. Many of the song texts are "mixed" by the time they are collected or published.

Although it is likely that Saunders incorporated elements of "Joseph Michael," "Hobo John," and others that were being sung before the Casey Jones wreck, the uncertainties surrounding the sources of the two lyrics attributed to Saunders are an obstacle to attempts to determine a reliable origin for the Casey Jones ballad. One way to draw conclusions on the song's thematic evolution and significance for Black and white singers is to transcribe and analyze the most representative and meaningful Black and white recordings, and compare them with the earliest transcriptions in folksong collections.

Although the first printed songs about Casey Jones were from African American informants, the first recordings were by white singers and were derived from the Newton and Seibert sheet music.[35] However, African American husband-and-wife team Butler "String Beans" May and "Sweetie" Matthews May (prob. 1891–1917) are known to have performed "Casey Jones" as early as November 10, 1910,[36] and the song was regularly in the repertoires of the Black vaudevillians Tom Young (1910), Wayne "Buzzin'" Burton (1910), Laura Smith (1911), and Virginia Liston (1913).[37] Unfortunately, there are no recordings of "Casey Jones" by any of these artists, but they probably sang Newton and Seibert's recently published hit.

Fiddlin' John Carson (1868–1949) made the first hillbilly recording of "Casey Jones" (OKeh 40038) in New York City on November 7 or 8, 1923.[38]

Come all you rounders if you want to hear
The story I'm a-telling on a brave engineer.

Casey Jones was the rounder's name,
On a six-eight wheeler, boys, he won his fame.

Caller called Casey at a half past four,
Kissed his wife at the kitchen door.
Mounted to the cabin with his orders in his hand,
Took a farewell trip unto the Promised Land.

Casey Jones a-mounted to the cabin,
Casey Jones, with his orders in his hand.
Casey Jones a-mounted to the cabin,
Took a farewell trip unto the Promised Land.

'Twas on a Friday morning, she's a looking like rain,
Around the curve come a passenger train.
On the pilot lay little Bill Jones,
A good old rounder, but he's dead and gone.

He looked at his watch and his watch was slow,
Looked at his water and his water was low.
Turned to his fireman, "Pick your place to jump
For the two locomotives are a-bound to bump!"

Casey Jones, two locomotives,
Casey Jones, are a-bound to bump.
Casey Jones, two locomotives,
There was two locomotives, that are bound to bump.

You oughta been there and a-seen the sight,
People were screaming, both Black and white.
Flier was there, it is an actual fact,
Seen four boxcars when they left the track.

They're at the Four Mile Curve
But Johnny Devine he lost his nerve,
Poor old Casey didn't weaken a bit,
Had his hands on the throttles and his engine hit.

Casey went to Heaven, went straight from here,
He told Saint Peter he's a brave engineer.
Saint Peter says, "Well, you're looking mighty bold,
I guess I'll have to put you back to shoveling coal."

"Mama, mama, I can't see
How Papa got killed on the Santa Fe";
"Go to bed, children 'fore you cry yourselves hoarse,
I've got you 'nother daddy on the police force."

Casey Jones, I got another papa,
Casey Jones, on the police force.
Casey Jones, I got you 'nother daddy,
And I got another daddy on the police force.

During the next four years, several other white musicians recorded versions of "Casey Jones."[39] Among citybilly Vernon Dalhart's versions, Victor 20502 was recorded in New York City on June 25, 1925, with Carson Robison on guitar. It is similar to Fiddlin' John Carson's recording, including stanzas referring to the Promised Land and Mrs. Jones's infidelity. However, Dalhart mentions a different railroad line (the Salt Lake) and different place names (Frisco and Reno Hill), the latter evidently originating in the Newton and Seibert version.

Also similar to Carson's version is "Casey Jones" (Columbia 15237-D) by Gid Tanner and His Skillet-Lickers, recorded in Atlanta on March 28, 1927.[40] The only variation worth noting is the inclusion of the stanza about Alice Fry, already recorded by Bessie Smith on "J. C. Holmes Blues" and regularly featured in subsequent Black and white recordings of the song.

The first issued African American version[41] was the two-part "Kassie Jones" (Victor 21664), a blues ballad recorded in Memphis on August 28, 1928, by Walter Furry Lewis (prob. 1899–1981), born in Greenwood, Mississippi, and residing in Memphis.[42]

Part 1

I woke up this morning, four o'clock,
Mister Casey told his fireman [to] get his boiler hot;
Put on your water, put on your coal,
Put your head out the window, see my drivers roll;
See my drivers roll,
Put your head out the window, see my drivers roll.

Lord, some people said Mister Casey couldn't run,
Let me tell you what Mister Casey done;
He left Memphis, was quarter to nine,
Got in Newport News, it was dinner time;
Was dinner time,
Got in Newport News, it was dinner time.

I sold my gin, I sold it straight,
Police run me to my woman's gate;
She come to the door, she nod her head.
She made me welcome to the folding bed;
To the folding bed,
Made me welcome to the folding bed.

Lord, the peoples said to Casey, "You're running over time,
You're having a collusion [sic] with the one-o-nine."
Casey said, "This engine's mine,
I'll run her in glory 'less I make my time."
Said to all the passengers, "Better keep yourself hid,
Naturally gon' shake it like Chainy did;[43]
Like Chainy did,
I'm naturally gon' shake it like Chainy did."

Mister Casey run his engines in a mile of the place,
Number Four stabbed him [sic] in the face;
Then Dep[uty] told Casey, "Well, you must leave town,"
"Believe to my soul I'm Alabama bound;
Alabama bound,
Believe to my soul I'm Alabama bound."

Missus Casey said she dreamt a dream,
The night she bought the sewing machine;
The needle got broke, she could not sew,
She loved Mister Casey 'cause she told me so;
Told me so,
Loved Mister Casey 'cause she told me so.

There was a woman named Miss Alice Fry,
Say, "I'm gonna ride Mister Casey or I'll die;
I ain't good looking but I takes my time,
A rambling woman with a rambling mind;
Got a rambling mind."

Part 2

Casey looked at his water, water was low;
Looked at his watch, his watch was slow.
On the road again,
Natural born eastman on the road again.[44]

Lord, the peoples telled by the throttle['s] moan,
The man at the [throttle] Mister Casey Jones,
Mister Casey Jones.

Mister Casey said before he died,
One more road that he wants to ride;
People telled Casey, "Which road is he?"
"The Southern Pacific and the Sancta Fe [*sic*],
Sancta Fe."[45]

This morning I heard someone was dying,
Missus Casey's children on the doorstep crying;
"Mama, mama, I can't keep from crying,
Papa got killed on the Southern line,
On the Southern line,
Papa got killed on the Southern line."

"Mama, oh mama, how can it be?
Killed my father in the first degree."
"Children, children won't you hold your breath?
Draw another pension from your father's death.
From your father's death."

On the road again.
I'm a natural born eastman, on the road again.

Tuesday morning, it looked like rain.
Around the curve came a passenger train.
Under the bar laid Casey Jones.
Good old engineer, but he's dead and gone.
Dead and gone.

On the road again.
I'm a natural born eastman, on the road again.

I left Memphis to spread the news.
Memphis women don't wear no shoes.
Had it written in the back of my shirt.
Natural born eastman don't have to work.
Don't have to work.
I'm a natural born eastman, don't have to work.

"Kassie Jones" is the first and longest of Lewis's many versions; he recorded others from the 1950s to 1971.[46] The stanza beginning "Lord, the peoples telled by the throttle['s] moan" and portions of stanzas beginning "Mister Casey run his engines in a mile of the place," "The caller called Casey at a half past four," and "Mister Casey said before he died" resemble the Newton-Seibert lyrics. Stanzas beginning "I sold my gin, I sold it straight," "Missus Casey said she dreamt a dream," "There was a woman named Miss Alice Fry," and "I left Memphis to spread the news" are not about a train wreck, while stanzas beginning "Lord, some people said Mister Casey couldn't run" and "Mama, oh mama, how can it be?" mention Jones but do not deal with the 1900 accident. In an interesting study of blues formulas in some of Lewis's lyrics, the author argues that Lewis's "near-complete departure from the well-known story is exemplary of obfuscating a narrative for poetic and/or cultural effect. Eventually, Lewis's 'Casey Jones' loses all connection to the conductor both historically and emotionally. This shift in subject matter is reinforced by the change in title from 'Casey Jones' to either 'Natural Born Eastman' or 'On the Road Again.'"[47] In this connection it is worth remembering that in 1916 Furry lost a leg in a hoboing accident and thus might have felt a personal connection to the Casey Jones story. Lewis's sources predate 1900 and belong "to that body of folksong . . . that Wash Saunders must have drawn on in fashioning the Casey Jones elegy."[48] Lewis's postwar recordings of "Casey Jones" are lyrically and structurally quite similar to his prewar treatment of the topic, showing that he conceived the song as a blues ballad, containing stanzas about the train wreck, but not dealing with it exclusively, or in either logical or chronological order.

As well as two unreleased commercial recordings by African American musicians[49] and some by white performers,[50] there are a number of field recordings, most of them unissued, made by singers of both races for the Library of Congress.[51]

One of the early African American versions is Henry Truvillion's "Casey Jones" (Cylinder 12-6), recorded in Wiergate, Texas, ca. July 11, 1933 (see fig. 2.02). The song's music and lyrics are transcribed as "Nachul-Born Easman," and ascribed to "Henry Trevelyan," in John A. and Alan Lomax's *American Ballads and Folk Songs* (1934). The elder Lomax reports that Truvillion was the "section gang foreman of the Wier Lumber Company of Wiergate," and first heard the song "when he went to work on the Illinois Central line that runs through Canton, Mississippi."[52]

> Casey Jones, befo' he died,
> Fixed de blinds so the bums couldn't ride;
> "Ef dey ride, gotta ride de rods,
> Trust dey life in de han's of God."

Figure 2.02. "Henry Truvillion and Wife in his Garden, Rt. #1; Newton, Texas, October 3, 1940" (Ruby T. Lomax). Courtesy Prints and Photographs Division, Library of Congress, Washington, DC

Chorus
Oh, my honey, who tol' you so?
Nachul-born easman, ev'rywhere I go.

Casey Jones was a li'l' behin',
He thought prob'ly he could make de time,
Got up in his engine, an' he walked about,
Gave three loud whistles an'-a he pulled out.

Right-hand side dey was a-wavin' of flags,
Wavin' of flags to save Casey's life,
Casey blowed de whistle an' he never look back,
Never stopped a-runnin' till he jumped de track,

Oh, my baby, till he jumped de track,
Never stopped a-runnin' till he jumped de track.

On de right-hand side was a tuzzle switch,
On de left-hand side was a ten-foot ditch,
Fireman looked out, got ready to jump,
Two locomotives here, bound to bump.

Number 3 got within a mile of the place,
Number 4 stared him straight in de face,
Casey tol' his fireman to keep his seat and ride,
"It's a double-track road, we're runnin' side by side."

When Casey's wife heard dat Casey was dead,
She was in the kitchen, makin' up bread,
She says, "Go to bed, chilluns, an' hol' yo' breath,
You'll all get a pension at yo' daddy's death."

Casey called up his wife and son,
Willed them an engine, had never been run.
When Casey's son did come of age,
Says, "Daddy's done willed me a narrow gauge."

Cincinnati pianist Jesse James's "Southern Casey Jones" (Decca 7213), recorded in Chicago on June 3, 1936, is an interesting African American account.[53]

I heard that people said Casey Jones can't run.
I'm 'on' tell you what the poor boy done.
He left Cincinnati 'bout half past nine.
Got to Newport News 'fore dinner time.
'Fore dinner time, that's 'fore dinner time.
Got to Newport News 'fore dinner time.

Now, Casey Jones said before he died.
He'd fix the roads so a bum could ride.
And if he ride, he had to ride the rod.
Risk his heart in the hand of God.
Hand of God, in the hand of God.
Had to risk his heart in the hand of God.

Now, the little girl says, "Mama, is that a fact,
Papa got killed on the I.C. track?"
"Yes, yes, honey, but hold your breath,
Get that money from your daddy's death.

From your daddy's death, from your daddy's death.
You'll get money from your daddy's death.
Lord, your daddy's death, from your daddy's death.
You'll get money from your daddy's death."

When the news reached town Casey Jones was dead,
Women went home and outed out in red.[54]
Slipping and sliding all across the streets,
With their loose Mother Hubbard and their stocking feet.
Stocking feet, stocking feet,
Loose Mother Hubbards and their stocking feet.[55]

Now, Casey Jones went from place to place.
Another train hit his train right in the face.
People got off but Casey Jones stayed on.
Natural born eastman, but he dead and gone.
Dead and gone, he's dead and gone.
He's a natural born eastman, but he dead and gone.

Here come the biggest boy, coming right from school,
Hollering and crying like a doggone fool.
"Look here, mama, is our papa dead?
Womens going home and outed out in red.
No good shoes and their evening gown,
Following papa to the burying ground.
To the burying ground, to the burying ground.
Following papa down to the burying ground."

"Now, tell the truth, mama," he says, "is that a fact,
Papa got killed on the I.C. track?"
"Quit crying, boy, and don't do that.
You got another daddy on the same damn track.
On that same track, on the same track,"
Said, "You got another daddy on the same track."

In *Folk Song U.S.A.*, Alan Lomax prints stanzas adapted from James's third, fourth, and sixth, omitting those that focus on the supposed infidelity and greed of Casey Jones's widow.[56] Jones was indeed "killed on the I.C. track," but it was the C & O, not the Illinois Central, that ran from Cincinnati to Newport News.

In Los Angeles in July 1949, African American vocal group the Dixie-Aires recorded a very different version of "Casey Jones" (Exclusive 116). The text is close to Seibert and Newton's (they are credited as composers on the record label) and to other sources, including the version in *Railroad Man's Magazine*, but it is performed in the vocal group harmony "jive" style popular at that time.[57]

African American bluesman K. C. Douglas (1913–1975) recorded an a cappella "Casey Jones" (Cook 5002) in Oakland, California, around 1952.[58] The recording begins with part of the hillbilly gospel standard "Life Is Like a Mountain Railroad." "Casey Jones" has the Jesse James version as its main source, but the final stanza appears to be unique to Douglas:

> Old big angel with the starlit face,
> Come on around about the lonesome place.
> The whistle blowed and the bell it rung.
> He's a good engineerman, but he's dead and gone.
> He's dead and gone,
> He's a good engineerman, but he's dead and gone.

Although Douglas's rendition clearly resembles Jesse James's recording, it is likely that he first heard a version of "Casey Jones" in Canton, where he moved in 1934 from Sharon, Mississippi, his birthplace.

Black songster Mance Lipscomb (1895–1976) made four recordings of "Casey Jones," of which the earliest (and only) released version dates from July 9, 1961.[59] Lipscomb's main sources appear to be the Seibert-Newton version and Fiddlin' John Carson's recording, including the stanza about Saint Peter sending Casey "down yonder" to "shovel coal."

Thirty-five years after cutting an unreleased version, Mississippi John Hurt (1892 or 1893–1966) made his first issued recording of "Casey Jones" (Piedmont PLP 13157) at Sandy Fisher's house in Annapolis, near Washington, DC, during four days of recording on March 24, 26, 29, and April 2, 1963.[60]

> Casey Jones was an old engineer,
> He told his fireman to not to fear.
> "All I want is my water and my coal,
> Look out the window, see my drive wheel roll."
>
> Early one morning came a shower of rain,
> 'Round the curve I seen a passenger train.
> In the cabinet [*sic*] was Casey Jones,
> He's a noble engineerman but he's dead and gone.
>
> Casey's wife she got the news
> Sitting on the bedside, she was lacing up her shoes.

Said, "Go away, children, and hold your breath,
Gonna draw a pension at your Daddy's death."

"Children, children, get your hat."
"Mama, oh mama, what you mean by that?"
"Get your hat, put it on your head,
Go down in town, see your daddy's dead."

Casey said before he died,
Fix the blinds so that the bums can't ride.
If they ride, let 'em ride the rod,
Trust their lives in the hands of God.

Casey said before he died,
One more road that he want to ride.
People wonder what road could that be:
Gulf Colorado [sic] and the Santa Fe.

It is likely that Hurt's unreleased 1928 recording resembled his Piedmont LP version in that "John learned 'Casey Jones' from his cousin who also worked on the railroad. He added, 'Of course some of them verses I didn't get them from him. I got 'em all together by hearin' people talk about what happened.'"[61] In his many subsequent songs bearing the same title, and in different songs titled "K. C. Jones Blues," Hurt only sang a few stanzas, interspersing them with spoken asides. They are instrumental train imitations, with a tragic angle based on the domestic theme.

There are still mysteries around the origins of "Casey Jones," but there is no doubt of its remarkable role in American folklore and music. Despite many painstaking studies, untangling the threads of tradition is still a daunting task, but in light of the survey above, it is possible to offer suggestions toward future research.

When the ballad of Casey Jones was developing, before its mass media popularization from 1909, the variously named protagonists (Casey Jones, Jimmy Jones, and others) were treated as heroes, at least in Black compositions. The earliest sources available (the 1903 newspaper text antedating the better known 1908 publication, the text collected by Odum between 1905 and 1908, and the Saunders and Steen fragments) are all African American in origin, and they say nothing negative about Jones. The text collected by Odum portrays Casey as mourned by both white and African American women: the "womens in Kansas all dressed in red" are wearing a color associated with "sinful" women, the verse coming from the culture of pimps and prostitutes, while the "womens in Jackson, all dressed in black [who] said, in fact, he was a cracker-jack" are implicitly identified as white by their contrasting mourning garb.

However, when Seibert and Newton's version, with its added humorous and sexual elements, became a hit, its denigration of the heroic engineer spread among white and Black singers alike. Rather than depicting Casey Jones as a comic figure, most subsequent songs by both African American and white singers focus on the unfounded allegations of his wife's adultery.

In Furry Lewis's 1928 recording, however, infidelity by "Mrs. Casey" is denied. Her Freudian dream about buying a sewing machine with a broken needle implies temptation resisted, and ultimately "She loved Mister Casey 'cause she told me so." Lewis does allude to Mrs. Casey's uncaring avarice, however ("Children, children won't you hold your breath / Draw another pension from your father's death"), and he also implies possible adultery on Casey's part with his references to "Miss Alice Fry" and the sexual feats of Stavin' Chain. Most singers, whether Black or white, describe events from their own point of view, prominently inserting themselves into the song as witnesses, participants, or alter egos. This is especially evident in Furry Lewis's versions.

"Casey Jones" was "the last train-wreck song originating from Tin Pan Alley that achieved great popularity on a national scale."[62] It was also a rare example of a "confluent song" which merged the matter-of-fact treatment of disasters in late nineteenth- and early twentieth-century ballads with more creative, personal and imaginative ways of addressing large-scale tragedy.

Regardless of the song's origins and early development, the Seibert-Newton version unquestionably redirected the evolution of "Casey Jones," which soon lost most of its tragic connotations. Despite Norm Cohen's exhaustive list of parodies of the Seibert-Newton text,[63] and John Garst's efforts to explain "the psychology that makes it 'fun' to sing about 'tragic events,'"[64] establishing why and how the comic transformation of a song about a tragedy was so readily accepted remains problematic. A key may come from the toast that Joe Cal recited to Samuel C. Adams Jr. on the King and Anderson Plantation in Coahoma County, Mississippi:

> On one Sunday morning, it look like rain
> Round the curve come a passenger train
> On the bump[er] was Casey Jones
> Two locomotives and they bound to bump
>
> Casey Jones was a son-of-a-bitch
> And run his engine on an open switch
> The boiler busted
> The whistle split

The fireman fotted [i.e. farted]
And Casey shitted

When I make a hundred
I make a hundred and a half
Going back to Memphis
To sit on my Black ass.

A key point about this text lies in Cal's introductory remark: "I knows lots of them old tales and songs, and when I'm by myself I sings them, but I just don't like to do that kind of stuff among folks that ain't like me."[65] "That kind of stuff" is obscenity, and the "folks that ain't like me" may be white people, higher-status Black people like Samuel Adams and his fellow researcher Lewis Jones, or both.[66] Casey Jones, who is speeding, and who loses control of his bowels in the face of danger, is not granted heroic status. Seibert and Newton's reference to adultery was daring in a song aimed at mass audiences in 1909, but Joe Cal's scatology takes the rejection of respectable norms to another level. His declared intention "to sit on my Black ass," defying stereotypes of Black laziness by embracing them, is also significant. Assuming that Joe Cal's protagonist is white, like the historical Casey Jones, there seems to be a parallel with toasts about the *Titanic*, in which white people are portrayed as "rather opaque and clumsy," and outsmarted by the African American trickster Shine.[67]

On June 24, 1964, Bruce Jackson collected a toast in Jefferson City, Missouri, from a convict, to whom he assigned the pseudonym "Slim Wilson." The speech patterns of the sexual prodigy given the identity "Casey Jones" suggest that he is African American.[68]

They tell me that Casey Jones was a railroad man
And he jumped outta his train with his dick in his hand.
Said, "All a you whores that want to be screwed—"
At the word he had a hundred and ninety-two.
So he lines 'em all up against the wall,
Bet his fireman five dollars he could fuck 'em all.
He got a hundred and ninety and his balls turned blue,
He took a shot of corn and fucked the other two.

Then Casey died and he went to hell,
He fucked the Devil's wife and he fucked her well.
Two little devils started runnin' through the halls,
Said, "Papa, catch him 'fore he fuck us all."
Now there set old Satan high on the shelf:
"You better run, motherfucker, I'm tryin' to save myself."

But Casey said, just before he died,
"There's a couple more things I'd like to ride:
Tricycle, bicycle, automobile,
A crapped-up cart, and a Ferris wheel.
Say, you know, man, it's a goddamned shame,
I'm forty years old and haven't rode nothin' but a motherfuckin' train."

This toast and other examples suggest that Furry Lewis's passing reference to Stavin' Chain may be the tip of an iceberg: sexual toasts featuring Casey Jones may have existed quite soon after the train wreck. It is possible that Casey's name was inserted into toasts that predated his fame, in the same way that earlier ballads were adapted to tell the story of the accident.

Leaving aside the accretion of comic and sexual material to the song and its chief actor, we are still confronted by the question of why African Americans should have celebrated a white hero. Part of the explanation may be that the historical Jones saved his African American fireman, by ordering him to jump as he was trying to slow the train. On a more general level, a comparison of John Henry's unequal contest against the steam drill with Casey Jones's unsuccessful attempt to slow his train is enlightening. Just as Lawrence W. Levine said of John Henry's contest, Casey Jones's heroism is "never purely individual," and Casey, too, can be seen as "a representative figure whose life and struggle are symbolic of the struggle of the worker against machine, individual against society, the lowly against the powerful."[69]

Levine naturally adds "Black against white" to his description of "John Henry," a dichotomy also present in songs and toasts about the *Titanic*, but not—except in Joe Cal's toast—in "Casey Jones." This is partly explained by the racial egalitarianism found to some degree in hobo circles, a world on the outskirts of society that seems to have played an important part in generating and perpetuating the "Casey Jones" ballad and its predecessors. Black firemen and white engineers (like Sim Webb and Casey Jones, or Ben Dewberry and Mason Wadkins) also rode trains together, creating further opportunities for the movement of songs between the races.

The ballad of "Casey Jones" is a special case in Black disaster songs because its hero is white.[70] Like some African American folk heroes, but unlike Shine in the *Titanic* toasts, Casey Jones becomes a hero not through extraordinary powers or by self-aggrandizement, but by bravely confronting his enemy. (Jones's opponent is a train, John Henry's a steam drill.)

Initially, Casey Jones captured the imagination of African Americans, who celebrated his heroism without regard to race. However, he swiftly became an object of ridicule by white and Black artists alike, particularly after Seibert and Newton made their comic additions to the historical reality.

As noted above, it seems likely that in the 1910s it was Seibert and Newton's hit version of "Casey Jones" that African American vaudevillians added to their acts, simply because it was a hit, and one which transcended racial boundaries. Nevertheless, the possible early existence of toasts about Casey Jones suggests that their lyrics may have differed according to whether their audiences were Black, white, or mixed (although they would have been spatially segregated in the latter case). We may never know, but the search is worth pursuing.

GOD MOVES ON THE WATER: THE 1912 SINKING OF THE *TITANIC*[71]

Introduction

Between them, the boll weevil infestation and the sinking of the RMS (Royal Mail Ship) *Titanic* on the night of April 14–15, 1912, have generated the largest number of disaster songs in African American and white American folklore. Most of the *Titanic* songs were composed in or soon after 1912, in the immediate aftermath of the disaster, but new songs were written into the twenty-first century. The loss of some 1,500 people on the *Titanic*'s maiden voyage has been sung about in genres including country music, blues, rhythm and blues, gospel, reggae, and pop, as well as inspiring instrumentals, sermons, and toasts. There has been extensive research into published and recorded songs,[72] but this chapter aims at a comprehensive and systematic study of blues, gospel songs, toasts, and hillbilly songs engendered by the disaster. Variants of the same composition are cited but not transcribed or analyzed.

Historical Background

Hundreds of books have been written about the sinking of the *Titanic* and its social, historical, and cultural significance.[73] There are still controversies about what happened on the fatal night, but only one is closely pertinent to this study.

The White Star Line's RMS *Titanic* departed Southampton, England, on her maiden voyage on April 10, 1912, calling at Cherbourg, France, on the same day, and Queenstown (now Cobh), Ireland, the next morning. Bound for New York, the liner was 400 miles south of Newfoundland when she struck an iceberg at 11:40 p.m. on April 14. Despite wireless warnings of ice ahead, sent by six craft on the day of the foundering alone, the *Titanic* maintained an average speed of around 22 knots. Contrary to what is often asserted, this was not because of an attempt to break the Atlantic crossing record. Captain Smith had been instructed "to dismiss all idea of competitive passage with other vessels," but received professional wisdom was that for large ships, the way to deal with danger from ice was to get through it as quickly as possible.[74] At first, the collision with the iceberg was not thought to be serious, the more so because the vessel's advanced construction was widely believed to render it unsinkable, but the gravity of the situation soon became apparent. Captain Edward James Smith gave orders to send out distress calls and fire rockets, and instructed his crew to lower the lifeboats, which were initially not filled, and which in any case only had space for just over half those on board. (The provision of lifeboats sufficient for all passengers and crew only became a legal requirement after the loss of the *Titanic*.) The Cunard liner *Carpathia* hastened to the rescue (other ships that were nearer the scene of the accident did not), but it only picked up the first lifeboat at 4:10 a.m. The *Titanic* had sunk at 2:20 a.m.

The death toll, mostly by hypothermia rather than drowning, was unprecedented in maritime history. Definitive data are not available because the exact number of people on board is unknown, and there are inconsistencies between lists of survivors. The liner was carrying at least 1,309 passengers (324 first-class, 277 second-class, and 708 third-class) and 897 crew members, and 1,495 of these 2,206 people are reckoned to have died. Only 38 percent of the passengers (most of them first-class) and 24 percent of the crew survived. Most of the dead were adult males, and foreigners of all ages and both sexes in steerage. One study calculates that there were 2,224 people on board, of whom 1,514 died, divided by class as follows: 329 first-class passengers (60 percent survived), 285 second-class passengers (44 percent survived), 706 third-class passengers (25 percent survived).[75] First-class passengers mentioned in songs include hotel magnate John Jacob Astor IV and his pregnant wife Madeleine, American millionaire Benjamin Guggenheim, and Isidor Straus, co-owner of Macy's department store in New York, whose wife, Ida, refused to board a lifeboat without her husband, and died alongside him.

The question of the presence of Black people on the ship (which is relevant to some African American songs) has been resolved. It seems that the only Black passenger was 26-year-old Haitian engineer Joseph Philippe Lemercier Laroche, who was traveling back to Haiti with his pregnant French wife and their two mixed-race children. Lemercier Laroche died; his family survived.[76] One early, sensationalist account reports that an armed "Negro stoker" was killed by wireless operator Harold Bride, who caught the man stealing his colleague Jack Phillips's life belt.[77] Stokers were referred to as "the black gang" because they were smeared with coal dust, and this tale seems to be either a misunderstanding or a racist fabrication, intended to add a dramatic frisson. Bride's testimony about the incident to the British inquiry mentions neither a gun nor the race of the stoker.[78]

It was Bride who provided reliable information about the two songs being played by the band as the last lifeboat—Collapsible D—departed, fifteen minutes before the *Titanic* sank by the head. They were a ragtime tune and "Autumn," the latter probably a then-popular waltz, rather than the obscure hymn tune of the same title. It is unlikely that the band played "Nearer My God to Thee," as was reported by one survivor, some contemporary newspapers, and several songs about the tragedy, because "the hymn at that time was sung to two different settings in Britain and a third in the U.S., so British and American passengers would not have recognized it from the music alone."[79]

Titanic Song Types

Global interest in the sinking of the *Titanic* is attested by commercial and field recordings of songs in many different languages and cultures.[80] Joseph C. Hickerson, former head of the Archive of Folk Song at the Library of Congress (1974–1988), reported that over one hundred songs were copyrighted in the United States alone between 1912 and 1915:

> The sinking of the Titanic on April 14, 1912, . . . produced a host of songs, 106 of which I have thus far discovered through the files of the Copyright Office for the years 1912–1915. Of the 106, 44 were published by H. Kirkus Dugdale Co., Inc., 14th and U Streets, Washington D.C. Of these 44, the music for 22 was composed by M. C. Hanford, and the music for 9 was composed by Charles J. W. Jerreld. The Dugdale Co. apparently had a particularly active and effective method for soliciting songs, usually lyrics only, through such "come-ons" as "Have your song published" or "Earn thousands," perhaps with a contest for the best *Titanic* song. Of course, the author of the song had to submit a "fee" which "covered" (actually exceeded) the cost of copyright registration (always in the author's name) and a minimal printing. A summary description of the well-known *Titanic* event need not have accompanied Dugdale's solicitations, although it does seem surprising that the reported facts through a multiplicity of sources should have given rise to the universal use of "Nearer My God to Thee" in all of the 106 Titanic pieces which contain words.[81]

Forty-four of the 106 songs found by Hickerson were published by a firm operating a "song-poem" scam, but the industriousness of amateur lyricists provides evidence of popular fascination in the years immediately following the disaster.

The shipwreck took place before the commercial recording of blues, and most of the earliest African American compositions about it are ballads, many ultimately derived from white traditions, or varyingly moralistic gospel commentary.[82] Songs about the Titanic that are members of a song family are analyzed in discrete sections. Those that are not are considered together as "Other *Titanic* Songs."

(Wasn't It Sad) When That Great Ship Went Down

One of the most popular song types about the sinking among both Black and white singers is "The (Great) Titanic," also known as "The Sinking of the Titanic" and "When That Great Ship Went Down." In 1915–16, it was collected from a Black man in the streets of Hacklesburg, Marion County, in northwest Alabama, a blind white man in Fayetteville, Tennessee, and another Black man, also blind, in Tuscumbia, Colbert County, Alabama, thirty-six miles from Hackleburg.[83]

> It was on one Monday morning just about one o'clock
> When that great *Titanic* began to reel and rock;
> People began to scream and cry,
> Saying, "Lord, am I going to die?"
>
> *Chorus:*
> It was sad when that great ship went down. (x2)
> Husbands and wives and little children lost their lives,
> It was sad when that great ship went down.
>
> When that ship left England it was making for the shore,
> The rich had declared that they would not ride with the poor;
> So they put the poor below,
> They were the first to go.
>
> While they were building, they said what they would do,
> We will build a ship that water can't go through;
> But God with power in hand
> Showed the world that it could not stand.
>
> Those people on that ship were a long ways from home,
> With friends all around they didn't know that the time had come;
> Death came riding by,
> Sixteen hundred had to die.
>
> While Paul was sailing his men around,
> God told him that not a man should drown;

If you trust me and obey,
I will save you all to-day.

You know it must have been awful with those people on the sea,
They say that they were singing, "Nearer My God to Thee."
While some were homeward bound,
Sixteen hundred had to drown.[84]

Different versions of this composition are held, as broadsides and in type-script, in the Frank C. Brown collection at Duke University, Durham, North Carolina. There are two songs titled "(The) Destruction of the *Titanic*." The first, an undated broadside, was purchased on May 26, 1920, for five cents from William O. ("Bill") Smith, who had driven a horse cab in Durham ca. 1912–15, and who claimed to have composed it with his daughter, Irma.[85]

Come all you dear people, listen and hear me tell
How that great *Titanic*, that was in its great swell,
It went down on Sunday night in nineteen and twelve.

Chorus:
Wasn't it sad about the *Titanic*, how it got lost. (x2)
Women and children saved their lives,
Husbands parted with their wives,
Wasn't it sad about the *Titanic*, how it got lost.

It left the port of London, it was bound for New York shore.
An iceberg struck the vessel, which caused a leaking hole.
The engineer said, "Captain, no, we cannot reach the goal."

It was more than a thousand people who did lose their lives;
There were fathers and mothers, husbands and their wives;
Yet some of them were saved from their watery graves.

The officers were commanding, "The women must be saved."
It wasn't pleasing to male passengers, but yet it did prevail;
Some men had to be shot down, that women might not drown.

One husband said unto his wife, "Go take the little boat,
To try and save your own self, for they will be on float."
"No" (her eyes were filled with tears), "we've been together forty years."

Upon her he insisted to do just as he said,
But still she lingered to him, waiting for her watery grave.
"I will not leave you for another, we will both go down together."

And yet some were hiding in the little boat;
They laid down in the bottom, thinking their presence would not be
    known;
And as little as one would think, from their weight the boat would sink.

Now as the boat was sinking, it was sadness to behold.
There was darkness all around them, and it was so very cold;
The boat was sinking in the sea, the band played "Nearer My God to Thee."

The second text appeared without a composer credit in a ballet printed by the
Black-owned Reformer Publishing Company of Durham for Reverend J. H.
Brown, who had probably collected fragments and put them together.

It was in the month of April,
In 1912:
Will you listen to the story
As I begin to tell?
How it happened on Sunday night,
When the ship went out of sight.
It was sad about the *Titanic* when it got lost.

Chorus:
It was sad about the *Titanic* when it got lost. (x2)
Women and children saved their lives
Husbands parted with their wives,
It was sad about the *Titanic* when it got lost.

It was about two thousand people
Who have lost their lives.
There were fathers and daughters, and some sons' wives;
They are in their watery graves,
And I hope their souls are saved,
It was sad about the *Titanic* when it got lost.

They left the shore of London;
To New York they tried to come.
An iceberg struck the vessel,

And she couldn't make the run.
Many have fallen asleep
In waters two thousand fathoms deep.
It was sad about the *Titanic* when it got lost.

It was commanded by the officers
To have the women and children saved.
It was not satisfactory to some,
Though it did prevail.
The men saw they could not be saved;
So they knelt and prayed.
It was sad about the *Titanic* when it got lost.

You have never read it
In the history of your lives,
How they separated
The husbands from their wives.
But some took their rathers
And agreed to die together.
It was sad about the *Titanic* when it got lost.

There were the millionaires and captains
And mighty men of wealth
From all over the country
Who were on the ship that night.
On there they had to stay;
Money could not pay their way.
It was sad about the *Titanic* when it got lost.

Have you heard of such destruction,
How it happened on that night,
About three o'clock in the morning,
When the ship went out of sight?
How sad the band did play
"Nearer My God to Thee"!
It was sad about the *Titanic* when it got lost.

The Frank C. Brown collection also holds "The Great Titanic," a slightly different transcription of the William O. and Irma Smith composition, contributed by Miss Fanny Grogan on November 30, 1920, and several other compositions presenting slight variations.

The earliest issued hillbilly recording, Ernest "Pop" Stoneman's "The Titanic" (OKeh 40288-B, recorded in New York City, ca. January 8, 1925) belongs to this song family. Stoneman accompanies himself on harmonica and autoharp.[86]

> It was on Monday morning just about one o'clock
> That the great *Titanic* began to reel and rock.
> Then the people began to cry saying, "Lord, I'm-a going to die."
> It was sad when that great ship went down.
>
> *Chorus:*
> It was sad when that great ship went down.
> Husbands and wives, little children lost their lives
> It was sad when that great ship went down.
>
> When they were building the *Titanic*, they said what they could do
> They were going to build a ship that the water could not go through.
> But God with His mighty hand showed to the world it could not stand.
> It was sad when that great ship went down.
>
> *Chorus*
>
> When they left England, they were making for the shore,
> The rich they declared they would not ride with the poor.
> So they sent the poor below, they were the first that had to go.
> It was sad when that great ship went down.
>
> *Chorus*
>
> Then the people on the ship were a long way from home,
> With friends all around them did know that time had come.
> For death came riding by, sixteen hundred had to die.
> It was sad when that great ship went down.
>
> *Chorus*

New York–based light opera singer turned hillbilly star Vernon Dalhart's eight recordings of *Titanic* songs are all versions of Stoneman's song.[87]

Several African American songs were recorded for the Archive of Folk Song before World War II. The earliest were two renditions of "The Titanic" (AFS A-294 and A-295), collected by Robert Winslow Gordon (1888–1961) in

Brunswick, Georgia, on April 2, 1926. Sung by Jack Silence, they are unaccompanied standard versions of the "When That Great Ship Went Down" song type.[88]

The first Black commercial recording deriving from this cluster of songs was "When That Great Ship Went Down" (Paramount 12505), recorded in Chicago, probably on June 22, 1927, by William and Versey Smith, an elusive gospel duo who accompanied themselves on guitar and tambourine.[89] Their lyrics are very similar to those in Stoneman's recording. It has often been suggested that William O. Smith and Irma Smith of Durham may be William and Versey Smith, but Erma Smith (spelled thus on the certificate) died in 1919, aged 28. More likely candidates are another father and daughter: William Smith, a farmer from Henry County, Alabama, aged about fifty in June 1927, and his daughter, Versey, then seventeen.[90]

A little-known Black version belonging to this song model and titled "Sinking of the Titanic" (AFS 15679-A-3) was collected by Walter C. Garwick on Edisto Island, South Carolina, ca. mid-May 1936.[91] The singer is not named by the Library of Congress, but she is certainly Lavinia Simmons, by aural comparison with two variants of the song titled "Old Titanic" (AFS 3150-B-2 and AFS 3151-A-1), recorded by Herbert Halpert on June 23, 1939, also on Edisto Island.[92] Simmons's more complete later version presents interesting variations from the usual "When That Great Ship Went Down" text:

It was on a Wednesday morning, just about four o'clock,
When that old *Titanic* began to reel and rock,
While some were taking their rest,
God was summoning them to death
In that awful time of fear, God knows (x3)
When that great ship went down
Sixteen thousand souls got drowned.
In that awful time of fear, God knows.

When that ship was leaving England, it was making for the shore
And they cried to the captain that they will not ride with the poor
They put the poor below
They was the first ones caught the blow
In that awful time of fear, God knows.

Black South Carolinian songster Pinkney "Pink" Anderson (1900–1974) recorded two versions of the "When That Great Ship Went Down" model: "The Ship Titanic" (Riverside RLP 12–611, recorded in Charlottesville, Virginia, May 29, 1950), and "The Titanic" (Bluesville BVLP 1071, recorded in Spartanburg,

South Carolina, August 14, 1961).[93] Anderson uses the less common stanza referring to St. Paul's shipwreck on Malta (Acts 27).[94] Apparently unique are Anderson's mangling of "John Jacob Astor" as "Jakewood Ascott," and his reference, in the second recording, to the ship's builder as "Captain Workfield."

African American singers adapted this and other song models to conform with changing music fashions. In December 1947, New York gospel group the Dixiaires [sic] recorded a close-harmony jubilee version of "When That Great Ship Went Down" (Sittin' In With 2013) in Newark, New Jersey.[95]

> *Chorus:* (twice)
> Well, it was sad when that great ship went down,
> It was sad when that great ship went down,
> Well, it was an awful sight, everybody stayed awake all night,
> It was sad when that great ship went down.
>
> Well, in the year of 1912, in the year of our good Lord,
> From the way they told the story, there were mighty men aboard,
> Now they're all lying asleep way down in the briny deep.
> It was sad when that great ship went down.
>
> *Chorus*
>
> Well, that ship began to rock (Oh, Lord) when the iceberg struck the ship.
> Captain and his crew didn't have nowhere to dock (in the morning)
> In their watery grave, and I hope their souls'll be saved.
> It was sad when that great ship went down.
>
> *Chorus* (twice)
>
> Well, they started out from London, to New York tried to come,
> When the iceberg struck the vessel, and they could not make the run,
> Now, they're in their watery grave, Lord, I hope their souls'll be saved.
> My Lord, it was sad when that great ship went down.
>
> *Chorus*

This song is an interesting revision of the standard version. The main point seems to be the fall of the "great ship" and the "mighty men aboard," with some uncertainty whether their souls were saved.

During recording sessions on the first three days of 1962 in Philadelphia, Pennsylvania, African American songster Bill Jackson (1906–1975), born in

Granite, Maryland, recast "When That Great Ship Went Down" as a twelve-bar "Titanic Blues" (Testament T-201).[96]

> The *Titanic* pulled out from England bound for New York shore (x2)
> But when she struck that iceberg, poor old ship was lost.
>
> She was sailing 'cross the water, sailing 'cross the deep blue sea (x2)
>
> (instrumental line)
>
> Now when the *Titanic* was sinking, sinking in the deep blue sea (x2)
> Oh, then the band began to play "Nearer My God to Thee."
>
> Now Captain Smith walked out with a shotgun under his arm (x2)
> Crying, "Let the women get off, let the men go down."
>
> Now wasn't it sad, sad when that great ship went down? (x2)
> There was husbands and wives, little children lost their lives.

Jackson's third stanza is shared with "Hi" Henry Brown's "Titanic Blues," discussed below, but whether it derives from it is uncertain. The fourth stanza is unusual, and perhaps unique. Fifth Officer Harold Lowe testified that he fired warning shots to prevent men capsizing his lifeboat by leaping into it, and other officers may also have fired shots. First Officer William Murdoch is even said to have killed one or more men,[97] but Captain Smith is not known to have used a weapon, although an early and unverified account said that he had sent armed men to the boiler rooms to ensure that stokers and engineers stayed at their places.

The last African American version of this song pattern is "The Titanic" (L+R 42.030) by Flora Molton (1908–1990), recorded in Washington, DC, on November 28, 1980.[98] Molton recalled learning the song from her father.[99]

Among the *Titanic* song types, "When That Great Ship Went Down" is the model most commonly used by both Black and white singers. This is because of the song's flexibility and complexity of meaning, and the hit status of the Stoneman and Dalhart recordings. The rhetorical question in the refrain is ambiguous; it can carry a religious, social-critical, or racial message, depending on what the singer wishes to convey, and how the listener reads it. The lyrics are often selected and recombined from other versions, which in turn derive from an unknown and probably untraceable original. As a result, it is sometimes difficult to discern an overall message, because singers seem to move inconsistently from one aspect of the disaster to another.

The Lost Ship

"The Lost Ship," composed ca. 1913 by the blind white Kentuckian Richard D. Burnett (1883–1977), would prove particularly influential among hillbilly musicians:

> Titanic was the ship just on her maiden trip
> To sail across the Atlantic Ocean wide;
> It was a pleasure trip—millionaires aboard the ship,
> But they never lived to reach the other side.

> *Chorus:*
> *Titanic* was her name; sailing Atlantic was her fame;
> She sank about five hundred miles from home;
> Sixteen hundred were unsaved—went down in the angry waves,
> Went down in the angry waves to rise no more.

> It was a dreadful scene, like a sad and awful dream,
> To see so many perish beneath the waves;
> There were children, husbands and wives were pleading for their lives,
> But they all went down beneath the angry waves.

> It was a dark and moonless night, and there was not a gleam of light
> To light them from the darkness o'er the sea;
> It was a solemn sound, just as the ship went down,
> To hear the band playing "Nearer, My God, to Thee."

> Miss Esidora Strauss [*sic*], the wife and husband lost;
> They were to each other noble, true and brave—
> As they sung that Evening Hymn, she preferred to die with him,
> And they both went down beneath the angry waves.

> There was an eager, watching crowd, who had gathered like a cloud,
> To watch the ocean steamer as she came,
> But the captain and the crew went down in the ocean blue,
> And they never, never heard them call their names.[100]

The popularity of Richard D. Burnett's composition is attested by three recordings. The first was "The Great Ship Went Down" (OKeh 45137), recorded by Hancock County, Georgia, duo the Cofer Brothers (guitarist and vocalist Leon, 1899–1968; fiddler and vocalist Paul, 1901–1967) in Atlanta on March 19, 1927.[101] Only the first three of Burnett's five stanzas are used, probably because of the time limitations of 78 r.p.m. recording, but the Cofer Brothers' version retains the original's drama and appeal.

"Sinking of the Titanic" (AFS 3283-B), collected by Sidney Robertson Cowell in July 1937 from Kentucky-born Clyde Spencer (1900–1967) and Harry Fannin (1900–1966) in Crandon, Wisconsin, is also a shortened version of Burnett's song with minor variations.[102]

The third white recording inspired by Burnett's composition is "Down with the Old Canoe" (Bluebird B-7449), recorded in Charlotte, North Carolina, on January 25, 1938, by the Dixon Brothers (slide guitarist and vocalist Dorsey, 1897–1968; guitarist and vocalist Howard, 1903–1961), who were cotton-mill workers from Darlington, South Carolina.[103]

It was twenty-five years ago
When the wings of death came low
And spread out on the ocean far and wide.
A great ship sailed away
With her passengers so gay
To never, never reach the other side.

Chorus:
Sailing out to win her fame
The *Titanic* was her name
When she had sailed five hundred miles from shore
Many passengers and her crew
Went down with that old canoe
They all went down to never rise no more.

This great ship was built by man
That is why she could not stand
"She could not sink" was the cry from one and all.
But an iceberg ripped her side
And it cut down all her pride
And they found the hand of God was in it all.

Chorus

Your *Titanic* sails today
On life's sea you're far away
But Jesus Christ can take you safely through
Just obey His great command
Over there you'll safely land
You'll never go down with that old canoe.

Chorus

When you think that you are wise
Then you need not be surprised
That the hand of God should stop you on life's sea
If you go on in your sin
You will find out in the end
That you are just as foolish as can be.

Chorus

What is strikingly different about Dorsey Dixon's recasting of Burnett's original is his privileging of theodicy (the vindication of divine providence in view of the existence of evil) over historical narrative, and his apparent lack of compassion for the drowned. The *Titanic* and its passengers function symbolically, and their fate is an inevitable judgment, the result of sin, pride, and the displacement of divine omnipotence by a delusion of human omnipotence.[104]

Fare Thee, Titanic, Fare Thee Well

In 1916, the white popular singer Marie Cahill recorded "Fare Thee, Honey, Fare Thee Well" (Victor 45125), copyrighted by John Queen and Walter Wilson (New York: Howley, Haviland & Dresser).[105] In fact, the song sung by Cahill derives from an influential "coon song" of the same title, with a marked blues quality and much use of Black dialect, first published and sung in 1901.[106] It is almost certainly the inspiration for the refrain "Fare thee, *Titanic*, fare thee well," used by later singers both Black and white.

The first recording by an African American singer to mention the *Titanic* co-opted the catastrophe to describe a personal disaster. In "Titanic Man Blues" (Paramount 12374), a cheating man, dumped by the singer, is personified as the ship in the refrain "It's the last time, *Titanic*, fare thee well." Recorded by Gertrude "Ma" Rainey (maiden name Gertrude Pridgett, 1882–1939) in New York City ca. December 1925,[107] its composer credits are to Rainey and its producer and publisher, J. Mayo Williams.[108]

Vaudeville blues singer Virginia Liston (possibly ca. 1890–1932; birth name Crawford)[109] made the first Black commercial recording specifically about the sinking. "Titanic Blues" (Vocalion 1031) was cut in Chicago on May 29, 1926.[110]

Pay attention while I sing this song
About that *Titanic* that went down.
It was the last time, *Titanic*, fare you well.

When the *Titanic* had got a load,
The Captain he hollered, "All aboard!"
It was the last time, *Titanic*, fare you well.

Just then there came a shout,
Everybody wondered what that noise was about.
They cried, "Fare thee, *Titanic*, fare you well."

Didn't have to sink that fast
They found the *Titanic* had broke in half.
They cried, "Fare thee, *Titanic*, fare you well."

When Captain Smith received the sound,
He ordered the lifeboats down.
They cried, "Fare thee, *Titanic*, fare you well."

Then some of the men they raved and cursed
When the Captain said, "Women and children off first."
They cried, "Fare thee, *Titanic*, fare you well."

It was out in the midst of the sea,
Nothing but water and icebergs could be seen.
They cried, "Fare thee, *Titanic*, fare you well."

When Mr. Astor kissed his wife goodbye,
Didn't know that he kissed his wife to die.
He cried, "Fare thee, Miss [*sic*] Astor, baby, fare you well."

Liston's is the only song to mention the ship's breaking in half. This was only confirmed after the wreckage was discovered in 1985, but several survivors told the American and British enquiries that they had seen the *Titanic* break apart, which is not unusual when large ships sink.[111] This is not the only African American song to mention John Jacob Astor IV, but his imagined farewell to his teenaged wife, after being told that he could not join her in Lifeboat 4, is unusual.

The best-known recording of the "fare thee well, Titanic" song type is "The Titanic" (Folkways FA 24), recorded in New York City on September 27, 1948, by songster Huddie "Lead Belly" Ledbetter (1888–1949).[112] It differs slightly from his earlier version, transcribed here, which was recorded for the Library of Congress (AFS-136-A) by Alan Lomax at Wilton, Connecticut, in February 1935.[113]

Captain Smith when he got his load,
Might have heard him hollering, "All aboard."
Crying fare thee, *Titanic*, fare thee well. (*stanza repeated*)

Jack Johnson wanted to get on board,
Captain Smith hollered, "I ain't hauling no coal."
Now it's fare thee, *Titanic*, fare thee well. (*stanza repeated*)

Titanic was sinking down,
They had them lifeboats around.
Crying fare thee, *Titanic*, fare thee well. (*stanza repeated*)

Had them lifeboats around,
Saving the women, letting the men go down.
Crying fare thee, *Titanic*, fare thee well. (*stanza repeated twice*)

Jack Johnson heard about that mighty shock,
Might have seen the Black bastard doing the Eagle Rock.
Crying fare thee, *Titanic*, fare thee well. (*stanza repeated*)

It was at midnight on the sea,
Singing "Nearer My God to Thee."
Crying fare thee, *Titanic*, fare thee well. (*stanza repeated*)

When the women got on the land,
Crying, "Lord, have mercy on my man."
Crying fare thee, *Titanic*, fare thee well. (*stanza repeated*)

Black man oughta shout for joy,
Never lost a girl and either a boy.
Crying fare thee, *Titanic*, fare thee well. (*stanza repeated*)[114]

Lead Belly dated the start of his association with Blind Lemon Jefferson to around 1912 because he recalled that they played "Fare Thee Well, Titanic" in the streets. His assertion, here and elsewhere, that African American world heavyweight champion Jack Johnson was refused passage because of his color ("I ain't hauling no coal") is apocryphal; Johnson had returned to New York from England aboard the White Star Line's *Celtic* the previous December.[115]

Lead Belly's beliefs about Johnson and the *Titanic* were historically incorrect, but to him and many African Americans, Johnson was a hero because of his victories over white opponents, notably James Jeffries, "the great white hope,"

BLIND BUTLER,

Figure 2.03. Blind Madkin Butler. *Kansas City Sun* (Kansas City, MO), June 2, 1917

and his flouting of the social and economic taboos of racism by flaunting his wealth, marrying white women, taunting white opponents, and operating an integrated restaurant. The song's artistic conceit is that Johnson's "visibility" to the Captain as "coal" causes him to be "invisible" (absent) aboard the vessel. Johnson's being saved from drowning makes the sinking an exclusively white tragedy, hence the recommendation that Black people should "shout for joy."[116] Lead Belly's defiance of racism is as striking as Johnson's: he triumphantly co-opts the racist epithet "Black bastard," no doubt often applied to Johnson in real life, and depicts him derisively dancing the Eagle Rock to celebrate his escape from the "mighty shock" that had killed so many white people.

God Moves on the Water

By far the most widespread song family among African Americans is that deriving from "God Moves on the Water." This song was composed shortly after the sinking by the blind evangelist Madkin Butler (1873–1936) (see fig. 2.03) of Hearne, Texas, with his second wife, Ophelia, who read a newspaper account to him from the editorial of the *Houston Chronicle* published on April 16, 1912. Printed first by the *Hearne Democrat* and then sold by Blind Butler as a "ballet" for ten cents a copy, this song spread widely.[117]

In her 1919 book *From a Southern Porch*, a sort of celebration of the "southern porch" with descriptions of Black people, their songs, and sayings, "southern writer" Dorothy Scarborough from Waco, Texas, published two texts collected from fictionalized (or possibly loosely based on real people) singers named Ahasuerus and Jake, two ghosts who appear to Scarborough on the porch. The Ahasuerus text reads:[118]

It was in the year nineteen hundred an' twelve
On April the fourteenth day,
When de great *Titanic* struck a iceberg,
An' de people hab to run an' pray.

Chorus:
God moved on de waters, God moved on de waters,
God moved on de waters
An' de people had to run an' pray.

While the guards who had been watchin',
Were asleep fo' dey was tired,
Dey heard de great excitement,
An' many guns was fired.

Chorus

Some people had to leabe dey happy homes,
An' all dat dey possessed.
Lawd Jesus, will you hear us,
Hear us in our distress.

Chorus

When de captain gib his orders,
It was women an' children first;
Many lifeboats was let down,
An' many libes was crushed.

Chorus

Some women had to leave dey loved ones,
An' flee fo' de safest place.
But when dey seen dey loved ones drown,
Dey hearts did almost break.

Chorus

The survivors in general did escape to de lan',
Dey lives dey tried to save.
But de torture an' de price dey paid fo' life
Is a warnin' to ebery man brave.

Chorus

Watchers' hearts on de boats was touched,
An' dey eyes was moved to tears,
When widows inquired ob dey loved ones,
Wid nothin' in dey hearts but fears.

Chorus

It's bes' to stay away fum de ocean,
De dry ol' land am de best.
Fo' den you don't get drownded,
When you lay down to rest.

The text collected from Jake, who is said by Scarborough to be originally from Waco, where he was a shoeshine boy at Baylor University, is derived from performances by Butler "String Beans" May's self-composed "Titanic Blues":[119]

Come all you people, ef you want to know
Something dat happened not so long ago.
I guess yo' heard bout dat misteree,
Bout de *Titanic* sinkin' in de deep, blue sea.
Dey was people on dat ship
Had Elgin movement in dey hip.
Captain Smith had de worry-blues.
I got de *Titanic* movement in my hip,
Wid a twenty-year guarantee.
I ain't good-lookin' an' I don't dress fine,
But I angles in my hips, an' I'm goin' to take my time!

Circa 1920 in Durham, North Carolina, Will "Shorty" Love (1876–1963), a janitor at Duke University's Trinity College, sang the following seven-stanza "God Moved on the Waters" for Dr. Frank C. Brown, whose transcription is held in the Frank C. Brown collection at Duke:[120]

Chorus: (after each stanza)
God moved on de waters
On April the fifteenth day;
He just moved on the waters,
And de people had to run and pray.

De rich dey had decided
Dat dey would not riduh wid the pore.
Dey placed de pore on the deck of de ship
And de pore was de first to go; but . . .

Twas on one Monday morning
Just about one o'clock
When de iceberg struck de *Titanic*
And it began to reel and rock; but . . .

Those people were enjoying themselves,
Of de trouble dey had no dream,
When de iceberg struck the boat,
Prayed [*sic*] "Nearer My God to Thee"; [but] . . .

When the large boat was in building,
They said what dey could do;
They said that dey could build one boat
That the water wouldn't ever break through; but . . .

Women tried to save dey children,
Husbands tried to save dey wives,
But after all dey hard struggles
More than fifteen hundred died; for . . .

My people, let me say to you,
It's nothing but a thing of naught
To say what you yourself will do
And never give God a thought; [for] . . .

You read about that mighty ship,
In Nineteen Hundred and Twelve,
That moved upon the mighty seas
And landed those people in hell; [for] . . .

Most versions of "God Moves on the Water" condemn the unequal treatment of
rich and poor passengers, the consequent higher proportion of deaths among
those in steerage, and the claim that the ship was unsinkable, seen as defiance
of God's power. These messages are found in other songs about the *Titanic*, by
both Black and white musicians, but "those people" in Love's text seems to be
a coded reference to white people specifically.[121]

Almost twenty years later, on December 9, 1939, Frank C. Brown recorded
Will "Shorty" Love singing a truncated "God Moved on the Waters" (AFS
8792-A-2) for the Library of Congress.[122] The recording quality is poor, but
some differences from the earlier transcribed text are detectable. The harsh,
accusatory verse in which "those people" are landed in hell (instead of New
York) concludes the printed text but opens the recording; the narrative stanza
beginning "'Twas on one Monday morning" is omitted, as is the one about the
boast that the ship was unsinkable. The recording breaks off before the song is
completed, but the text is coherent. Condemnation to hell is the (teleo)logical
fate of those who see human destiny as determined by technology rather than
God. They are not explicitly identified as white, but it seems clear that in Love's
view, which was probably widespread among African Americans, this disaster
was visited specifically on whites because of their arrogance.

A decade earlier, on December 11, 1929, guitar evangelist Blind Willie Johnson (1897–1945) recorded "God Moves on the Water" (Columbia 14520-D) in
New Orleans.[123] His slide guitar completes the song's title, which is never sung
in full. These completions, and one other, are shown in square brackets below.

Year of nineteen hundred and twelve, April the fourteenth day,
Great *Titanic* struck an iceberg. People had to run and pray.

Chorus:
God moved [on the water]
Moved [on the water]
God moved [on the water]
And the people had to run and pray.[124]

The guards who had been a-watching sleeped 'cause they were tired.
When they heard the great excitement, many gunshots were fired.
Chorus

Captain Smith gave orders, "Women and children first."
Many the lifeboats couldn't let down, many the lives were crushed.
Chorus

Oh, many had to leave their happy home, all that they prossess [*sic*].
"Lord Jesus, will you hear us now? Help us in our distress."
Chorus

Women had to leave their loving ones, before the safety's [sake].
When they heard their loved ones doomed, hearts did almost break.
Chorus

A.G. Smith, mighty man,
Built a boat that he couldn't understand.
Named it a name of God in a tin.[125]
Middle of the sea, Lord, it folded in.
Chorus

It is uncertain how closely Madkin Butler and Blind Willie Johnson were associated, and how much influence Butler, twenty-nine years older, had on Johnson. Johnson would visit Hearne, where his father was a member of Adam Booker's church, and where Blind Butler also had a church; but Paul Oliver and Mack McCormick concluded that there was "little direct link between them" beyond the younger man's admiration for the older.[126] It's also impossible to know whether Johnson learned "God Moves on the Water" directly from Butler, from having Butler's widely distributed "ballet" read to him, or in some other way, and in the absence of a copy of the "ballet" it is difficult to assess the degree of originality in the lyrics that Johnson recorded. Yet it is worth noting that the Ahasuerus version printed in Scarborough's *From a Southern Porch* (1919) is very close to Blind Willie Johnson's lyrics, with some additional verses that Johnson was probably unable to sing because of time limitation. Ahasuerus's and Johnson's versions are probably derived from the Blind Butler ballet. As Johnson wouldn't have known of Scarborough's book, it's very likely that the two lyrics ultimately stem from an earlier common source.

   Johnson's recording combines a montage-like narrative, sympathetic to the plight of the trapped passengers and crew, with a refrain that conveys the usual gospel message: "God plants his footsteps in the sea," and prayer is the only hope in time of danger. The last verse, where the most pungent remarks in Black sacred songs about disasters often seem to be placed, comments specifically on God's reasons for moving on the water on "April the fourteenth day." Captain E. J. Smith, misidentified as "A. G. Smith," is also misidentified as the builder

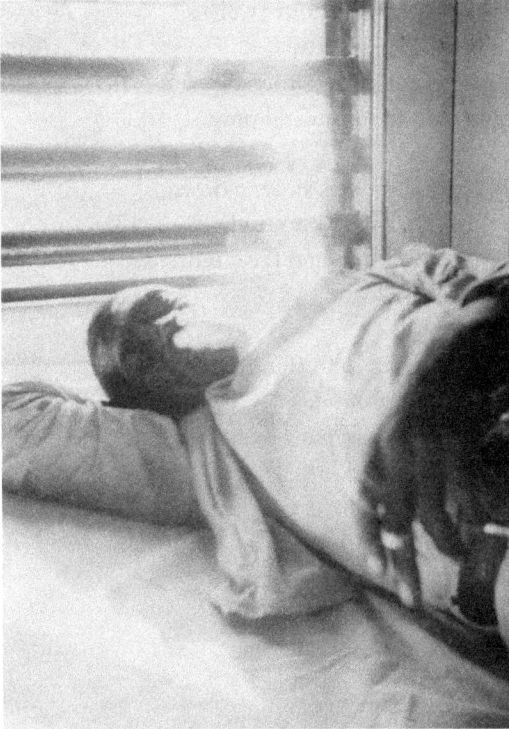

Figure 2.04. Washington ("Lightnin'"), an African American prisoner, in the prison hospital at Darrington State Farm, Texas, April 1934 (Alan Lomax). Courtesy Prints and Photographs Division, Library of Congress, Washington, DC

of "a boat that he couldn't understand." This is a unique way of referencing the widespread belief that the ship was wrongly claimed to be unsinkable. There seems to be a generalized, encoded criticism here, with Captain Smith used as an exemplar of white people and their pursuit of dominance, through technology and otherwise.

Many versions of the "God Moves on the Water" music and lyric pattern followed. The Archive of Folk Song holds three, of which the last recorded is the Will "Shorty" Love version discussed above. The earliest is "God Moves on the Water" (AFS 188-B-2), sung by Washington ("Lightnin'") (see fig. 2.04) and a group of convicts for John and Alan Lomax at Darrington State Farm, Sandy Point, Texas in December 1933.[127]

> *Chorus* (before each stanza)
> God moves on the waters (x3)
> And the people had to run and pray.

It was the year of Nineteen and Twelve,
On-a April the thirteenth day,
When the great *Titanic* was sinking down,
Well, the peoples had to run and pray.

When the great *Titanic* was sinking down,
Well, they throwed lifeboats around,
Crying, "Save the womens and the childrens
And let the men go down."

When the lifeboats got to the landing
The womens turned around,
Crying, "Look 'way 'cross that ocean, Lawdy,
At my husband drowned."

That Captain Smith was a-lying down,
Was asleep for he was tired;
Well, he woke up in a great fright
As a many gunshots was fired.

That Jacob Nash he was a millionaire,
Lord, had plenty of money to spare;
When the great *Titanic* was sinking down,
Well, he could not pay his fare.

Well, the sun stood still and refused to shine,
Lord, silence in Heaven for a space of time;
The rocks did burst, a tempest rushed of wind,
And "My Father, forgive Thy sinful men."

Well, they taken my Jesus, well, they led Him away,
Lordy, up on the mountain called Calvary,
They roughed up His feet, well, they roughed up His hands,
Well, they troubled God's peoples in Jerusalem.

Galveston with a sea wall
To keep the waters down,
But the high tide from that ocean, Lord,
Brought the water all over the town.

Well, they taken my Jesus down from the cross
They wrapped Him up in a fine linen cloth,
All Nature suspended at three o'clock
At the foot of that cross was a gambling flock.

Well, there's Peter, Saint James, Saint John start to weep,
Uh, Mary Magdalena [sic], her sisters alone,
Well, they wondered who could roll away the stumbling stone.[128]

[Bell tolling]

If anybody should ask you, well, who composed this song,
Well, the bullying Dave Tippen and Lightnin' Smith the verse
And bully Charley Rogers, and Baker Whittaker didn't compose it
wrong.[129]

Despite the credit assigned on the Library of Congress file cards, the last stanza may indicate that Dave Tippen, rather than Washington, is the lead singer. Whoever is leading, the song is melodically similar to Blind Willie Johnson's recording. The text lacks Johnson's judgmental final verse, but presents some interesting variations and misdates the sinking by a day. "Jacob Nash" (John Jacob Astor IV), unable to escape death despite his wealth, symbolizes the impartiality of God's judgment on rich and poor. The song's concluding six stanzas take the song away from the *Titanic* but correspond with its somber mood. (So does the eerily tolling bell, perfectly timed but clearly coincidental; it surprises the singers, who pause before their sign-off verse.) Four stanzas describe events connected with the crucifixion and resurrection of Christ. In the middle of them is the first stanza of the song about the 1900 Galveston flood, which the Lomaxes recorded at the same location in 1934 (see "Hell Broke Loose in This Land"). This strengthens the assumption that Washington or Dave Tippen may have been that song's lead singer.

In May 1936, at the State Farm in Raiford, Florida, John Lomax collected "Sinking of the Titanic" (AFS 686-A-2), sung by Walter Roberts and a group of singers, one of whom may have been named Emanuel Duke.[130]

Chorus:
God almighty, just moved on the water,
April, the fifteenth day,
God almighty, just moved on the water,
And the people had to run and pray.

It was on the fifteenth day of April
Nineteen Hundred and Twelve,
The vessel struck an iceberg,
And she had to sink in hell.

Chorus

There was women and little children,
Husbands and their wives,
Lord, the day that vessel sunk
They all lost their lives.

Chorus

Oh, the mate said to the captain,
"Oh, what kind of burst is this?"
Oh, the captain told him to drive on,
"A burst won't sink our ship." (x2)

Chorus

Oh, the rich they decided
That they would not ride with the poor.
Oh, they placed the poor on the deck of the ship,
And they was the first to go.

Chorus

The third verse, describing a dialogue between the captain and the mate after the collision with the iceberg, is not commonly found in other recordings. It offers another perspective on the arrogance arising from the ship's supposed unsinkability.

    A later variant is "The Titanic" (Prestige International LP 25008), recorded on St. Simons Island, Georgia, in April 1960, by Bessie Jones (1902–1984) with the Georgia Sea Island Singers.[131]

Chorus:
God moved on the water[s],
April the fourteenth day,
Children, God moved on the water,
Everybody had to run and pray.

Titanic left South Hamilton [sic]
With all their spoil and gain,
But when they struck that iceberg,
I know their minds was changed—children

Chorus

Their mothers told their daughters (Oh, Lord)
On a pleasure trip they may go (Oh, yeah)
But when they struck that iceberg,
They haven't been seen anymore.

Chorus

One man, John Jacob Astor (Oh, yeah)
Was a man with pluck and brains (Oh, Lord)
While this great ship was sinking,
All the womens he tried to save.

Chorus

He was warn-ded by a freight boat (Oh, Lord)
Captain Smith would not take heed (Oh, yeah)
But instead of giving a warning,
He ran with a greater speed.

Chorus

He kissed his wife the last time (oh, yeah)
When the boiler did explode (oh, Lord)
He holped her in the lifeboat,
Saying, "I won't see you anymore."

Chorus

The story of this shipwreck (Oh, yeah)
Is almost too sad to tell (Oh, Lord)
One thousand and six hundred
Went down forever to dwell.

Chorus

Yeah, the fourteenth day of April (Oh, yeah)
It was in Nineteen Hundred and Twelve,
The ship had a wreck by the iceberg (oh, Lord)
It went down forever to dwell.

Chorus

Like Blind Willie Johnson's song, Jones's version seems extremely critical of the rich and proud white people on the ship and of Captain Smith, who is blamed for recklessly increasing the ship's speed despite warnings. However, she also points out individual instances of bravery and heroism. Indeed, the verse about Captain Smith appears between two about John Jacob Astor, who is presented as a hero trying to save the women, and with more historical accuracy, as a tragic figure bidding his wife farewell. Jones's lyrics seem to be influenced by an unidentified song about a pleasure boat excursion where a boiler exploded.

Texas songster Mance Lipscomb made nine recordings about the *Titanic*, variously titled but all versions of "God Moves on the Water."[132] The most easily accessible version is "God Moves on the Water (The Titanic)" (Arhoolie LP 1023).[133]

That was a very distressful time out on the ocean when the *Titanic* struck the iceberg and went down, all those people had to drown. And the main part of it was so sorry, the womens had to, you know, look at they mens go down on the ocean. And they put out the lifeboats just to save the womens and let the mens went down. So we're gon' play you "The Titanic":

On the fourteenth day of April, year of nineteen twelve,
When the *Titanic* struck a iceberg, almost too sad to tell.

Chorus:
God moved [on the water] (x3)
Oh, the people had to run and pray.

When the *Titanic* was sinking, they put the lifeboats all around,
Said, "Let's save the women and children, either let the men go down."
Chorus

When the lifeboats got to the landing, the women looked around,
Saying, "Look out on that ocean. Look at all the men go down."
Chorus

Captain he was laying down, 'sleep 'cause he was tired,
But he woke up in a great fright 'cause a-many gunshot was fired.
Chorus

Jacob Astor was a millionaire, had plenty of money to spare,
But when the *Titanic* was sinking, Lord, he could not pay his fare.
Chorus

Lipscomb met Blind Willie Johnson around 1918, and it is clear that he learned the slide guitar arrangement of "God Moves on the Water" directly from Johnson. According to Mack McCormick, Lipscomb learned the song itself in 1914,[134] but his lyrics are less developed—or perhaps less well remembered—than Johnson's: as his spoken introduction foreshadows, he concentrates on the saving of the women rather than the men, adding two stanzas about Captain Smith and John Jacob Astor, the most famous male protagonists in the sinking.

In his oral autobiography, Lipscomb stated that "anothuh blind fella from Houston put that song out. . . . He couldn play a lick. An he couldn read, but his wife read it off a newspaper, he would rememorize it, an he made him a song out of it. Cause he got the schedule of it an made the verses comepair. An he made a record of it."[135] Lipscomb may be describing Madkin Butler, whom he never met, although his assertion that the "blind fella" recorded the song is mistaken. Mack McCormick interviewed Butler's widow, Ophelia, in 1962, and introduced her and her daughter at a concert in Houston, where he asked Lipscomb to play "The Titanic." As Lipscomb recalled, "she sot there an cried like a baby."[136] It is rare that a ballad can be traced to its author. Madkin Butler's "God Moves on the Water" was most often sung in the state where it was composed, but it spread widely and rapidly among African Americans. No doubt it owed much of its appeal to one of the lessons of the *Titanic*'s fate: there was a power greater than white supremacy, which was not invincible.

Out on the Ocean

In 1927 the Chicago poet Carl Sandburg's anthology *American Songbag* included "De Titanic," with an arrangement "based on the singing of Miss Bessie Zaban, formerly of Georgia and now of Chicago; a number of verses were sent to her by C. H. Currie of Atlanta, Georgia. . . . Negro troops sang the song crossing the submarine zone and in the trenches overseas."[137] Born in Atlanta to Jewish parents who had emigrated from Austria, Bessie Zaban (1898–1997, later Zaban Jones) moved to Chicago in 1920 to attend university.[138]

De rich folks 'cided to take a trip
On de fines' ship dat was ever built.

De cap'n presuaded [sic] dese peoples to think
Dis Titanic too safe to sink.

Chorus:
Out on dat ocean,
De great wide ocean,
De *Titanic*, out on de ocean,
Sinkin' down!

De ship left de harbor at a rapid speed,
'Twuz carryin' everythin' dat de peoples need.
She sailed six hundred miles away,
Met an icebug [sic] in her way.

De ship left de harbor, 'twuz runnin' fas'.
'Twuz her fus' trip an' her las'.
Way out on dat ocean wide
An icebug ripped her in de side.

Up come Bill from de bottom flo'
Said de water was runnin' in de boiler do'.
"Go back, Bill, an' shut yo' mouth,
Got forty-eight pumps to keep de water out!"

Jus' about den de cap'n looked aroun',
He seed de *Titanic* wuz a-sinkin' down.
He give orders to de mens aroun':
"Get yo' life-boats an' let 'em down!"

De mens standin' roun' like heroes brave,
Nothin' but de wimin an' de chillun to save;
De wimin an' de chillun a-wipin' dere eyes,
Kissin' dere husbands an' friends good-bye.

On de fifteen day of May nineteen-twelve,
De ship wrecked by an icebug out in de ocean dwell.
De people wuz thinkin' o' Jesus o' Nazaree,
While de band played "Nearer My God to Thee!"

Zaban was not culturally African American, but the lyrics that she sang
appear to be. (This is determined from the attempt to represent dialect, which

Sandburg himself described as "imperfectly rendered.") It has not been possible to trace C. H. Currie, who contributed "a number of verses," to determine whether he was African American. Particularly striking is the stanza about "Bill," a prototype of "Shine," the African American trickster who features in toasts (orally transmitted narrative poems, usually obscene) about the *Titanic*, which are discussed in more detail below.[139] Like this lyric, toasts typically place the disaster in May, which is easier to rhyme and scan than April.

The "Out on the Ocean" song model seems to have been fairly widely known but seldom recorded. The first African American recording is "The Titanic" (AFS A-552), collected by Robert Winslow Gordon from an unidentified female singer in the area around Darien, in McIntosh County, Georgia, circa May 21, 1926.[140] The quality of this recording is too poor to allow a transcription, but the song belongs to a different model from other versions of "Titanic." The first verse mentions "Southampton," but the chorus is different from that of "De Titanic" as printed in Sandburg's anthology. At the end of the recording it is possible to discern a reference to "Nearer My God to Thee."

Collected by John Lomax at the Bellingrath Gardens, Mobile, Alabama, on March 15, 1937, "Great Titanic" (AFS 991-A-1), by Frank Woodward with Sallie Howard, Floreta Jenkins, and Hattie Jenkins, is much better recorded.[141] This is a concise but effective version of the song, with little narrative or commentary, and no reference to a Shine figure trying to warn the captain. As Woodward's lyrics present no additional material, it is reasonable to assume that the Zaban and Woodward texts are derived from a ballet.

On May 14, 1954, near Sprott, Alabama, songster Horace Sprott (1899–unknown)[142] recorded "The Great Titanic" (unissued), a fragmentary and sometimes incoherent variant, for Frederick Ramsey Jr.

In 1955, probably in either Florida or the Bahamas, the Bimini Harmonizing Four recorded "The Great Titanic" (Maytag EAR 234), another version of the song. Once again, there is no stanza about the Shine character, "Bill."

> Now the white folks decide[d] to take a trip to sea
> Upon the finest ship that was ever built.
> Oh, the captain made those people think
> That the great *Titanic*, she could never sink.
>
> *Chorus*:
> She's out on the ocean, oh baby, oh, the deep wide ocean.
> Oh, the great *Titanic*, she's out on the ocean sinking down.
>
> Now she left Southampton with a rapid speed.
> She was carrying out all of the people['s] needs.

Oh, the ship was a-keeping up a jubilee.
Yes, she ranned [*sic*] on plunging through the sea.
Chorus

Now six o'clock at the eventide
When the iceberg struck her in her side,
Oh, the captain's orders was sent around.
They said, "Take those lifeboats, lower them down."
Chorus

Now women and children came a-wiping their eyes,
Come a-bidding their husband[s] and friends goodbye.
Oh, they thought of Jesus of Nazaree
While the ship come plunging through the sea.
Chorus

Now John Jacob Astor was a millionaire.
Oh, he died like a soldier, he was there.
When the trumpet of God shall sound,
That great Titanic will be still sinking down.
Chorus

Now this (is) the last of *Titanic's* song.
Then seventeen thousand [*sic*] soul got lost.
Oh, they thought of Jesus of Nazaree
While the band played "Nearer, My God, to Thee."
Nearer, my God, to Thee, nearer to Thee.
Nearer, my God, to Thee, nearer to Thee.

This song is a strong indictment of the arrogance of "white folks," who are implicitly blamed for their own fate after they "decided to take a trip." The Sandburg/Zaban text refers to "de rich folks," but living in or migrating from majority Black societies, singers from the English-speaking West Indies seem readier than African Americans to be openly critical of whites.[143] It seems possible that the song originated in the Bahamas, and made its way to Alabama and Georgia; versions were recorded in Mobile, a seaport on the Gulf of Mexico, and in McIntosh County, on the coast of Georgia. African Americans in this area, and on the offshore Sea Islands, have strong linguistic and cultural connections with the Bahamas, where many Loyalist planters settled with their slaves after the American War of Independence.[144]

Other Titanic Songs

Some original songs or fragments from Black singers and composers predating the systematic recording of "race" and old-time music in the 1920s are known from printed sources and sheet music. In 1915–16 riverboat and farm hands in Auburn,[145] Andalusia, and Jackson County, Alabama, and also in southwestern Georgia were reported as singing these or similar lines:[146]

> Oh! where was you when de old *Titanic* went down?
> I wuz on de back of er mule singing "Alabama Bound."[147]

A very similar stanza about the sinking of an unspecified steamer had already been reported from Mississippi in 1909.[148] The alteration of such songs to refer to the *Titanic* would have been a straightforward process.

Among fully developed compositions is "The End of the Titanic in the Sea," by William Jackson and Charles E. Wright, published in 1912. It focuses on the fate of the steerage passengers, doomed to be forgotten, unlike the rich and famous in first class:

> 'Twas on a Monday morning in the Springtime,
> The folks were all in bed, fast asleep.
> *Titanic* struck an iceberg in the meantime,
> The folks are all now sleeping in the deep.
> The rich folks with their millions had to go down,
> Such as Astor, Mister Straub [*sic*] and Guggenheim,
> The poor folks on the vessel were not mentioned,
> We'll know them at the end of future time.

> *Chorus*:
> Now the days and nights are long and dreary,
> Tho' the world seems bright, our hearts still grieve,
> We'll watch and wait and pray for the souls that passed away,
> The Titanic ends its days in the sea.

> America and England are in mourning,
> For souls that passed away so suddenly,
> From recklessness of leaders who had warning
> Of icebergs that were floating in the sea.
> They had a great reception on a Sunday,
> Belshazzar's feast will make a simile,
> But when they saw the ending of their pleasure,
> The band played, "Nearer My God to Thee."[149]

Jackson and Wright were

> two African Americans from Western New York. . . . "The End of the
> Titanic in the Sea" features the only known Titanic song sheet cover
> that depicts a black performing duo. Wright and Jackson are seen pho-
> tographed posing in smart tuxedos with their instruments in hand—the
> former holding a mandolin and the latter a dual-neck guitar. . . . In late
> June 1912, barely two months after the *Titanic* sank, Wright and Jackson
> came to Medina [New York] to perform "their latest success" and other
> musical selections at the Cook Theatre. As promoted in the *Medina
> Daily Journal*, patrons who wished to hear "The End of the Titanic in
> the Sea" needed only to pay 10 cents admission.[150]

Sightless preacher Charles Haffer Jr. composed a song immediately after
the disaster. Part of it was transcribed by Alan Lomax in The Land Where the
Blues Began.[151]

> If you'll stop and listen,
> I'll sing to you a song
> About the time on the ocean
> When the *Titanic* went down.
>
> I'll tell you about John Jacob Astor
> With his handsome bride,
> Refused to get in the lifeboat
> And remained on the vessel and died.
>
> *Chorus*:
> Wasn't that a mighty time (x3)
> When the *Titanic* vessel went down.

Trying to learn "whether Haffer's was the original of the many *Titanic* songs,"
Lomax asked Haffer if he had heard any of them before he wrote his own
composition:

> Nossuh, but after I *wrote* that one, other people began to write, and
> I heard one or two more on the same things. But they wrote differ-
> ent. I reckon I sold two or three thousand of mine round over Missis-
> sippi, Arkansas, and Tennessee. Ten cents each, two for fifteen, three for
> twenty, and four for twenty-five.[152]

Haffer's claim is unverifiable, but as A. E. Perkins wrote in 1922:

> Negro folk-song making still goes on. The "Titanic" sank on Sunday, April 14, 1912. The following Sunday I saw on a train a blind preacher selling a ballad he had composed on the disaster. The title was "Didn't That Ship Go Down?" I remember one stanza: "God almighty talked like a natural man/Spoke so the people could understand."[153]

This blind composer's couplet is another way of expressing the accusation, found in songs performed by Blind Willie Johnson and others, that white people's belief that they had built an unsinkable ship proved that they "couldn't understand" God's power and human limitations.

The unrecorded vaudeville singer and pianist Butler "String Beans" May was performing his "Titanic Blues" by 1913.[154] An "irreverent" rendition in Chicago reportedly included:

> I want all you ladies in dis house
> To nestle up close to me.
> I was on dat great Titanic
> De night dat she went down;
> Ev'rybody wondered
> Why I didn't drown—
> I had dem Elgin movements in ma hips,
> Twenty-years' guarantee![155]

This is the song's only mention of the *Titanic*, and it is clearly "more referential than topical in nature."[156] It is striking, however, that in the metaphor of "Elgin movements in [his] hips"[157] the singer simultaneously celebrates his sexual prowess and his superhuman swimming ability. In doing so, he foreshadows Shine, the mythic trickster who survives the sinking of the *Titanic*.

Some *Titanic*-themed songs are related partially or not at all to the song types detected above. Their lyrical originality, and the relationships between their texts and themes, shed new light on the evolution of African American and white approaches.

On March 11, 1927, Black songster Richard "Rabbit" Brown (ca. 1880–1937, unconfirmed) recorded the ballad "Sinking of the Titanic" (Victor 35840) in his hometown, New Orleans. A vivid narrative of the disaster, it includes some interesting imagery:[158]

> 'Twas on the tenth of April
> On a sunny afternoon.

The *Titanic* left South Hamilton [*sic*]
Each one as happy as bride and groom.
No one thought of danger,
Or what their fate may be
Until a gruesome iceberg
Caused fifteen hundred to perish in the sea.

It was early Monday morning,
Just about the break of day.
Captain Smith called for help from the *Carpathia*,
And it was many miles away.
Everyone was calm and silent
They asked each other what the trouble may be,
Not thinking that death was lurking
Way out upon that northern sea.

The *Carpathia* received the wireless:
"SOS" (mean distress)
"Come at once, we are sinking,
Make no delays and do your best.
Get your lifeboats all in readiness,
'Cause we are going down very fast.
We have saved the women and the children,
And try and hold out to the last."

You know, at last they called all the passengers,
Told them to hurry to the deck.
Then they realized that the mighty *Titanic*
Had turned out to be a wreck.
They lowered the lifeboats one by one,
Taking women, children from the start.
The poor men, they were left to care for themselves,
But they sure played a hero's part.

You know, they stood out on that shrinking deck,
And they was all in great despair.
You know accidents may happen 'most any time,
And we know not when and where.
The music played as they went down
On that dark blue sea,
And you could hear the sound, that familiar hymn,
Singing, "Nearer, My God, to Thee."

They played, "Nearer, My God, to Thee.
Nearer my soul shall be.
Nearer, My God, to Thee.
Nearer to Thee.
Though, like a wanderer,
As the sun goes down,
Darkness be over me—"
Just then the *Titanic* went down.

The hallmark of this song is its concern for exact details and precise chronology, typical of ballads, rather than the freely associative stanzas of blues. At first the narrative proceeds as smoothly as the ship, perhaps making a subtle reference to Colonel Astor's recent, controversial marriage; but the collision with the iceberg soon turns idyll into tragedy. Successive mentions of Captain Smith, the *Carpathia*, the lifeboats and the "women and children first" rule follow the chronology of events and are succeeded by the observation, more common in white disaster ballads, that such events are both inevitable and unpredictable. The concluding verses are less accusatory than those in some other African American lyrics and quote the hymn "Nearer My God to Thee," then universally, if mistakenly, believed to have been played as the ship foundered.

On April 29, 1927, hillbilly guitarist Frank Hutchison (1897–1945) from Logan, West Virginia, recorded "The Last Scene of the Titanic" (OKeh 45121) in St. Louis. The song is a hallucinatory spoken narrative with masterly slide guitar accompaniment.[159]

The *Titanic*, the greatest ship ever was known,
Making its first sail to cross the sea.
Everybody's loaded up and waving their glad hands goodbye.
Captain Smith said, "How's your machinery?" "All right."
"How's your compass?" "Setting dead on New York."
"Keep a-trucking on down. Let's go! Right on down the pike."
Blowed his old whistle, went right on down.

Everybody's fiddling and dancing, having a big time on the lower deck
"Now you're right if you don't get wrong.
Get that girl and promenade on.
Good morning, baby, hello now,
Go on, mule."

Captain Smith says, "Gonna make a world's record out of this ship,

Gonna make it to New York about two days and a half or three days
　　ahead of time.
How's the machinery now? All right?
How's your compass?" "It's all right."
"Keep a-trucking on down, let 'er go! Right on down the pike."
Blowed his old whistle, went right on down.

Everybody's still having a big time.
"Now you're right, if you don't get wrong,
Get that girl with the red dress on
Good morning, baby, hello now."

Captain Smith got a message it was foggy on the sea
Couldn't see how to travel, all boats was tied up.
In a little while there was an iceberg from the North Pole
Biggest one ever was known, 'bout a mile square.
Impossible for any ships to run.

Captain Smith said, "Don't mind that fog on the sea.
We've got the strongest dynamite headlight ever was known.
Otherwise [*sic*] the ship is unsinkable,
Plow through all icebergs.
Now, how's your machinery? All right?
How's your compass?" "Still on New York."
"Keep her trucking on down, let 'er go! Right on down the pike."
Blowed his old whistle, went right on down the pike.

Everybody's still having a big time
"Now you're right, but don't get wrong,
Get that girl and go right on.
Good morning, baby, hello now."

The last seen and heared [*sic*] of the *Titanic* before it hit the iceberg,
Twenty miles it passed the lighthouse,
Just could hear the music on the lower deck.

The complete absence of either sentimentality or religious moralizing, perhaps unique in white songs about the *Titanic*, is a breath of fresh air. Equally
unusual is Hutchison's concentration on the ship's smooth sailing, Captain
Smith's attempt to break the Atlantic crossing record, and the passengers' enjoy-
ment of the trip. The fatal iceberg, hyperbolically described as "a mile square,"

is mentioned only in passing, and the song ends before the fatal collision. Listeners are left to decide for themselves whether there is a moral to be drawn from the behavior of the passengers, dancing to a caller's instructions as doom approaches.

Another proficient white slide guitarist, Jimmie Tarlton (1892–1979), born in South Carolina but living in Columbus, Georgia, recorded "After the Sinking of the Titanic" (Columbia unissued) in Atlanta on December 3, 1930.[160]

When the moon rose in its glory
And it drifted to the golden west,
It told a sad new story
Sixteen hundred had gone to rest.

Captain Smith surely must have been a-drinking
Not knowing that he was doing wrong.
He tried to raise a record
And let the *Titanic* go down.

Well, the porter had retired and was sleeping,
He was dreaming of some sad dream.
He dreamed the *Titanic* was sinking
Way out on the bottom of the sea.

Mr. Smith, he says to the rich man
"Oh, try and come to life,
Try and save your baby
Also your little loving wife."

Mrs. Smith heard her husband was a-drowning
Way out on the deep blue sea.
She cried out, "Oh Lord, have mercy,
Oh Lord, send him back to me!"

When the sad news reached the city
That the *Titanic* had gone down,
Many widows and poor little orphans
Was walking all 'round the town.

Tarlton's lyrics derive from "The Titanic," a ballad reportedly composed, presumably in the early 1920s, by fiddler and guitarist Seth Newton Mize from Searcy County, Arkansas.[161] It is not known how Tarlton came to learn it. The notes to the Bear Family boxed set suggest that this could be "the only version ... in which the captain's drinking is blamed for the disaster,"[162] but a fragment sung by a Black farmhand in Jackson County, Alabama, in 1915–16 ran:

> Oh, the captain must 'er been drunk
> When the big ship sunk,
> You could hear her whistle blowing
> Forty miles or more.[163]

"Hi" Henry Brown's "Titanic Blues" (Vocalion 1728) is the only known pre-war twelve-bar AAB commercial blues recording about the *Titanic*. It was recorded in New York City on Monday, March 14, 1932, with second guitar by Charley Jordan.[164]

Nothing certain is known about Brown's life. Reportedly born in Pace, Bolivar County, Mississippi, around 1884,[165] he was active in the St. Louis area and recorded six sides for Vocalion. His nickname (possibly a pun on "high brown," indicating either his color or his taste in women) was probably adopted to distinguish him from the St. Louis pianist of the same name.[166]

> Early one morning, just about four o'clock,
> It was early one morning, just about four o'clock,
> When the old *Titanic* 'gan to reel and rock.
>
> Smith took his glasses and walked out to the front,
> Captain Smith took his glasses and walked out to the front,
> And he spied the iceberg a-coming, oh Lord, had to bump.
>
> Some was drinking, some was playing cards,
> And it's some was drinking, some was playing cards,
> Some was in the corner praying to their God.
>
> Little children crying, "Mama, mama, what shall we do?" (x2)
> Captain Smith said, "Children, I'll take care of you."
>
> '*Tanic* sinking in the deep blue sea,
> *Titanic* sinking in the deep blue sea,
> And the band all playing "Nearer My God to Thee."

In this recording, Brown converts gospel and ballad rhetoric into a blues structure. In particular, he borrows from older gospel and ballad texts on the theme, such as the "God Moved on the Water" and above all the "When That Great Ship Went Down" models, to state that sinners and saved both had to die.

The song opens with a temporal distortion, since the collision with the iceberg happened at 11:40 p.m., and the sinking at 2:20 a.m., but Brown is unconcerned with historical accuracy, and intends only to convey that the drama began unexpectedly, in the small hours of the night. Within the framework of a realistic narrative, a subtle irony pervades the subsequent stanzas, possibly concealing a racial subtext.

In each of the last three stanzas, the last line makes an abrupt shift of focus. The third tercet, at the midpoint of the song, is especially significant. The initial (and historically accurate) indifference to the collision of some of the passengers, who continue their sinful pursuits ("Some was drinking, some was playing cards") is sharply contrasted with the fearful piety of others ("Some was in the corner praying to their God").[167] The phrase "praying to their God" is particularly interesting, since the possessive adjective can be held to imply "praying to the God of white people." Brown is certainly contrasting the reactions of the saved, who are praying, and the sinners, who are drinking and playing cards. The chiming of "playing" and "praying" is significant.

There is a less acerbic shift of focus in the fourth stanza, where the dismayed children's plea to their mothers for help is answered by Captain Smith's pitying and humane, but ultimately futile promise to take care of them. In the final verse, irony becomes extremely sharp. The horrifying sight of the sinking ship clashes with the would-be poetic cliché of the "deep blue sea," and is then associated with the false, but then universally believed account of the band playing "Nearer My God to Thee." The first word of the hymn's title, "Nearer," symbolizes Brown's and God's condemnation of the ship's passengers, who are now physically very near the death brought about by "their God," much "nearer" than before when, unaware of the risk, they were drinking and playing cards. Brown's delivery strongly emphasizes the word "playing," which is contrasted with the different sense of "playing" in the third stanza.

Brown's composition is a blues recasting of a sentimental, moralizing original, with the moralism made implicit rather than explicit. It is a significant and powerfully evocative addition to the corpus of *Titanic* songs.

Although it is marginal, we should finally note "Little Willie Got Drownded in the Deep Blue Sea (Titantic)" [*sic*], collected by Lawrence Gellert (1898– probably 1979) from an unknown male singer in the Carolinas or Georgia between 1933 and 1937. The only element related to the *Titanic* disaster is a reference to the band playing "Nearer My God to Thee." It is not possible to determine whether the misspelled subtitle was added speculatively by Gellert, or supplied by the singer.[168]

The Toast Tradition

As well as songs about the sinking of the *Titanic*, a narrative poem developed in the genre known as the toast. Toasts are oral narrative poems, almost invariably both obscene and recited in all-male groups. Their forthrightness and use of rhyme, alliteration, and other devices makes them a precursor of rap. "Shine and the Titanic" toasts, and songs related to them, are important because they are the only instances of African Americans appearing as protagonists in folklore related to the sinking. There are many versions of the toast, but they usually display considerable textual similarity. Being a spoken genre, toasts about the *Titanic* are peripheral to a study of disaster songs, and readers are referred to the extensive literature available.[169] However, some songs have drawn inspiration from the toast, and a brief summary of its content is therefore necessary before a consideration of the most representative musical examples.

After a prologue about the disaster, the Black stoker Shine informs the captain that the ship is taking on water. The Captain repeatedly orders him to pump the water out of the boiler room. (These events appear in the lyrics printed by Sandburg.) Shine's repeated warnings are ignored, and he decides to escape by jumping overboard. As he starts swimming, the Captain (or a millionaire or "a big fat banker") offers him money in exchange for rescue, and the Captain's daughter (and/or wife, or less frequently a pregnant woman) similarly offers him marriage and/or sexual favors. Turning down these offers, Shine is challenged by a shark and/or a whale, but outswims it, and makes landfall in places as varied as New York (especially Broadway and Harlem), Liverpool (England), Los Angeles, and Florida. He is last seen lying in bed half-drunk, wandering the streets, playing craps, or recovering from an orgy: the common factor is that Shine has survived, and is ashore well before news of the sinking reaches land.

African American poet Langston Hughes heard (or perhaps expurgated for print) a rather mild version of "Sinking of the Titanic" on Eighth Avenue in Harlem in 1956.[170]

> It was 1912 when the awful news got around
> That the great *Titanic* was sinking down.
> Shine came running up on deck, told the Captain, "Please,
> The water in the boiler room is up to my knees."
>
> Captain said, "Take your black self on back down there!
> I got a hundred-fifty pumps to keep the boiler room clear."
> Shine went back in the hole, started shoveling coal,
> Singing, "Lord, have mercy, Lord, on my soul!"

Just then half the ocean jumped across the boiler room deck.
Shine yelled to the Captain, "The water's round my neck!"
Captain said, "Go back! Neither fear nor doubt!
I got a hundred more pumps to keep the water out."

"Your words sound happy and your words sound true,
But this one time, Cap, your words won't do.
I don't like chicken and I don't like ham—
And I don't believe your pumps is worth a damn!"

The old *Titanic* was beginning to sink.
Shine pulled off his clothes and jumped in the brink.
He said, "Little fish, big fish, and shark fishes too,
Get out of my way because I'm coming through."

Captain on bridge hollered, "Shine, Shine, save poor me,
And I'm make you as rich as any man can be."
Shine said, "There's more gold on land than there is on sea."
And he swimmed on.

Jay Gould's millionairy daughter[171] came running up on deck
With her suitcase in her hand and her dress 'round her neck.
She cried, "Shine, Shine, save poor me!
I'll give you everything your eyes can see."
Shine said, "There's more on land than there is on sea."
And he swimmed on.

Big fat banker begging, "Shine, Shine, save poor me!
I'll give you a thousand shares of T and T."[172]
Shine said, "More stocks on land than there is on sea."
And he swimmed on.

When all them white folks went to heaven,
Shine was in Sugar Ray's Bar[173] drinking Seagrams Seven.

This text is heavily censored, and either omits or never included Shine's dialogue with the shark.

It has been suggested that some Black songs that included verses about the *Titanic* were precursors of the toast.[174] They feature an African American folk hero, the "traveling coon" or "traveling man." The origins of this song type are unclear, but it dates back to at least 1919, when it was collected by Percy F.

Dilling from "a traveling minstrel at King's Mountain, Cleveland County, North Carolina," and in 1928 Newman Ivey White noted that "several years ago the song circulated in Durham, N.C. as a printed ballet."[175] White suggests that the song is related to "Oh! Didn't He Ramble," copyrighted in 1902 by Bob Cole and J. Rosamond Johnson, which derives from the British folksong "The Derby Ram."

A 1920 article by Newman Ivey White refers to "the hero of a song about the *Titanic*, on deck when the ship strikes, [who] bestirs himself so briskly that he is shooting craps in Liverpool when she sinks."[176] This seems certain to be derived from the song reported by Percy Dilling in 1919, but the last two stanzas of "Travelin' Man," sung by Kid Ellis from Spartanburg, South Carolina, are the earliest known text collected directly from a Black singer, and referring to an African American who escapes drowning by abandoning the sinking *Titanic*:

> The coon[177] got on the *Titanic*
> An' started up the ocean blue,
> But when he saw the iceberg,
> Right overboa'd he flew.
>
> The white folks standin' on the deck,
> Said, "Coon, you are a fool."
> But 'bout three minutes after that
> He was shootin' craps in Liverpool.[178]

The first commercial recording belonging to this song cluster is "Traveling Coon" (Victor 20957), made by Virginian songster Luke Jordan in Charlotte, North Carolina, on August 16, 1927. Its two stanzas about the *Titanic* are very similar to Kid Ellis's, but Jordan refers to his protagonist as "a [or this] shine," an abusive term for Blacks.

The "travelin' coon/man" character seems likely to have developed before the use of "Shine" as a proper name became attached to the character in the toast, although a "character named Shine" is reported (with no evidence cited) to have "appeared in some early nineteenth-century minstrel routines."[179] Roger D. Abrahams's uncertainty is reasonable "whether these fragments [of "The Traveling Coon"] are echoes of the toast in an old version, or the toast is made up of fragments derived from these sources."[180] The use of "Shine" as a proper name seems to have been popularized by "That's Why They Call Me Shine," composed in 1910 by African Americans Cecil Mack and Ford Dabney. Originally featured by Aida Overton Walker, it was a hit for Louis Armstrong in 1931. The lyrics, including the verse understandably omitted by Armstrong, co-opt the abusive term and turn it into a badge of racial pride:

When I was born they christened me plain Samuel Johnson Brown,
But I hadn't grown so very big, 'fore some folks in this town
Had changed it 'round to "Sambo." I was "Rastus" to a few,
Then "Chocolate Drop" was added by some others that I knew.
And then to cap the climax, I was strolling down the line
When someone shouted, "Fellas, hey! Come on and pipe the shine!"
But I don't care a bit.
Here's how I figure it:

Well, just because my hair is curly,
And just because my teeth are pearly;
Just because I always wear a smile,
Likes to dress up in the latest style;
Just because I'm glad I'm living,
Takes trouble smiling, never whine;
Just because my color's shady,
Slightly different maybe,
That's why they call me Shine.

As already noted, "De Titanic," printed by Sandburg in 1927, contains a clear echo of the *Titanic* toasts in its reference to "Bill":

Up come Bill from de bottom flo'
Said de water was runnin' in de boiler do'.
"Go back, Bill, an' shut yo' mouth,
Got forty-eight pumps to keep de water out!"

The song as received by Bessie Zaban may have referred to "Shine," and she or Sandburg may have changed the character's name to "Bill" because the term "shine" was used by racists. If Sandburg's assertion that the song was sung by troops in World War I (that is in 1917–18) is correct, its reference to "Shine" would have been widely known among African Americans by then. This is further evidence of an early date for the creation of the toast. Yet it is not evidence that the name "Shine" was used in connection with the *Titanic*, nor that Shine was a racially oppositional figure in the toast at this time. It was simply an epithet in common use. There *is* a racially oppositional figure on the *Titanic*, or one is quickly developed by singers and composers in the aftermath of the sinking, but he has no agreed-upon name. He can be Jack Johnson, "Bill," or a "traveling coon." The toast that elaborates the theme of a Black "superhero" worker (or passenger) on the ship who escapes the disaster began to develop in the 1910s (cf. Butler "String Beans" May), but became an original creation ca. 1940, when references to escape by swimming fitted easily into songs about "the traveling man."

"The Titanic Ship," sung and, he claimed, written by a longshoreman nick-named Carolina Slim, is the earliest extended text definitely associated with the toast tradition. First printed in 1945, it was collected by the Louisiana Writers' Program of the Works Progress Administration (WPA) during a project that began in 1936:[181]

> I always did hear that the fif' of May was a wonderful day,
> You believe me, everybody had somethin' to say,
> Telephones and telegraphs to all parts of town,
> That the great *Titanic* ship was a-goin' down.
>
> The captain and the mate was standin' on deck havin' a few words,
> 'Fore they know it, the *Titanic* had done hit a big iceberg.
> Had a colored guy on there called Shine, who came down from below,
> And hollered, "Water is comin' in the fireroom do'!"
>
> Shine jumped off that ship and begun to swim,
> Thousands of white folks watchin' him.
> Shine say, "Fish in the ocean and fish in the sea,
> This is one time you white folks ain't gonna fool me!"
>
> There was thousands of people waitin' to shake his hand.
> Shine said, "Push back, stand there and hear my pedigree.
> I don't want nobody messin' with me."
>
> "My pillow was an alligator and a boa-constrictor was in my den.
> I lived on the water and I didn't have to pay no rent.
> And I don't owe nobody a damn red cent.
> When the great *Titanic* in the river sank."

The compilers of the book in which this text appears say that Carolina Slim could "sing a dozen or two verses," but they do not print the whole text, and appear to have censored what they do print ("Fish in the ocean and fish in the sea" will almost certainly have been "Pussy on land, and pussy on the sea"). It is also possible that this text was censored by Carolina Slim himself when he created his song from the toast.

The first recordings of "Shine and the Titanic" as a toast were made in July 25, 1942, when twenty-eight year old O. C. King recited two versions (AFS 6632-A-6 and 6632-B-2) for Alan Lomax at Ulisses "Buck Asa" Jefferson's house on the Hobson Plantation, Clarksdale, Mississippi.[182] However, most *Titanic* toasts were collected in the next two decades by folklorists, notably Roger D. Abrahams, in Philadelphia and Texas in the 1950s and 1960s, and Bruce Jackson, in Missouri and Texas prisons in the 1960s.

After the "traveling man/coon" songs, the first African American music recording with an unquestionable debt to the toast tradition is "Titanic" (Westside WESM 539), recorded in New York City for the Josie label on August 1, 1956, by Paul "Hucklebuck" Williams (1915–2002) with his Orchestra, featuring Bobby Parker (1937–2013) on vocals. It was not issued at the time.[183]

> May the fifth was a terrible day
> Great *Titanic* sailed away.
> Left my baby standing on the other side,
> I told my baby I'd be back alive.

> *Titanic* roared like a thundering herd
> Just been struck by a small iceberg.
> Big ship rocked and everybody screamed
> [The most] disgusting sight I've ever seen.

> Well, I came running, yeah, a-running from the deck below,
> Yelling, "Captain there's a water coming
> She's a-coming right through the floor."

> So I jumped in the water and began to swim,
> Told Mr. Whale I can swim faster than him.
> About the time the whale opened his mouth
> I swam five miles north and eighty miles south.

> *Chorus*:
> Well, I'm coming on back to baby,
> Well, faster than the *Queen Mary*,[184]
> Swimming home to you, baby,
> Your loving sends a message to me.

> I don't care who's the king of the ocean
> Shark can't swim fast as me,
> 'Cause I was raised drinking muddy water
> And I drank all the water in the sea.

> *Chorus*:

> That's why I'm coming on back to you baby,
> Well, faster than the *Queen Mary*,
> Coming home to you, baby,
> Your loving sends a message to me.

The chorus aside, the lyrics rework traditional material, but the song is less overtly hostile to the ship's white builders and passengers than the toasts proper, although it's striking that the iceberg is described as "small," and the panic after the collision as "disgusting." This restraint is probably because the song was intended to gain sales, radio airplay, and spins on jukeboxes. There is still a racial subtext, but the tragedy seems to have receded into history, becoming a peg on which to hang more trivial themes, couched in more generic language.

Altogether more vigorous and confrontational is "Hey Shine" (Kent KST-557), recorded in Los Angeles in 1969 as part of an LP of "adult" songs titled *Snatch and the Poontangs*, an identity that disguised singer Delmar "Mighty Mouth" Evans, musician-producer Johnny Otis, and Otis's son, Shuggie, then aged sixteen:[185]

> The eighth of May was a hell of a day,
> The day the *Titanic* sunk;
> They looked for Shine to save the ship,
> But he was in the shithouse drunk.
> He came up to the first deck,
> And said, "There's water on the boiler-room floor";
> The captain said, "Back, you dirty black,
> We're gonna let the water flow."
> He came up to the second deck,
> And then he started to think;
> Said, "I don't know what y'all gonna do,
> But this motherfucker gon' sink."
>
> *Chorus*:
> "Hey Shine, oh Shine, hey Shine,
> Save this ass of mine."
>
> The captain's daughter said, "Save poor me,
> I'll give you more pussy than your eyes can see."
> "Pussy is good while it last;
> You can't swim? Huh! That's your ass."
> The captain's wife said, "Save poor me,
> I'll give you more money than your eyes can see."

"Money is good, and that I know;
There's better bullshit on yonder shore."

Chorus

He told a shark out in the sea,
"You got to be a swimming ass to outswim me."
He couldn't swim and he couldn't float
He hit more licks than a motorboat.
He came upon a whale and he started to smile,
He say, "I think I'll thumb a ride 'bout a thousand mile."
Him and the whale, they begin to talk;
It wasn't too long before they reached New York.

Chorus

Walked into a greasy spoon just to get a little bite to eat,
The bottom of the glass was stale goat piss and a three-month old pig
    feet.
The Goddamnedest shit you ever seen, you can believe it or not,
Boiled boogers and barbecued snot, and a mule dick tied in a knot.

Chorus (x2)

A bitch say, "Shine, I got this ten, I'd like to suck your dick,"
He said, "Get away from me, you nasty whore, 'cause I don't turn no
    tricks."
Before I climb up on your ass and dabble with that funk,
I'd rob the mail and go to jail and fuck a clappy punk.
A fine young fox said, "Mr. Shine, you make my pussy twitch."
Said, "Get away from me, you nasty whore, I wouldn't fuck you with a
    egg-noodle dick.
Before I climb them scabby legs, and suck them flabby tits,
I'd drink a glass of panther piss and die of the grizzly shits."

Chorus

"Hey Shine" is a lively and creative recombination of material from the *Titanic*
toasts with equally obscene and colorful imagery drawn from other toasts.

The 1976 LP *Get Your Ass in the Water and Swim Like Me!* made the 1970s
the most prolific decade for the commercial availability of toasts; it was ironic

that the audience for the disc was almost entirely white. Doubtless the *Titanic* toast continued to be recited from time to time when African American males got together, but the 1970s and 1980s were virtually bereft of original musical treatments of the disaster. An exception, almost certainly inspired by Bob Ballard's location of the wreck on September 1, 1985, was "What a Tragedy" (Great Southern Records GS 11011), recorded in New Orleans by Louisiana pianist and singer Cousin Joe (real name Pleasant Joseph, 1907–1989).[186]

> What a tragedy when the *Titanic* ship went down,
> Oh, what a tragedy when the *Titanic* ship went down,
> I used strategy during the tragedy, that's why I wasn't nowhere around.
>
> Yeah, the women and the children, they was having fun,
> Yeah, the women and the children, they was really having fun,
> But when the ship started sinking, that's when the trouble begun.
>
> It was an awful thing when that ship hit that big iceberg,
> Yeah, it was an awful thing when that ship hit that big iceberg,
> Well, I wasn't worried: I was the best swimmer in the world.
>
> Now a rich man asked me to save his life,
> He would give me half his wealth;
> I said, "I'm very sorry, mister,
> But really I got to save myself."
>
> When I jumped in the water,
> Everybody said, "Look at that fool";
> But when that *Titanic* ship hit the bottom,
> I was in Harlem shooting pool.
>
> Oh, what a tragedy when the *Titanic* ship went down. (x2)
> I used strategy during the tragedy, that's why I was nowhere around.

In "What a Tragedy," with its mocking title and understated lyrics, "Shine" and the "Traveling Man" are conflated into a unique Black trickster "in a rewrite that . . . has all the wit, irony, and multiple meanings of its predecessors."[187]

Recent Treatments of the *Titanic* Disaster

Not related to the toast tradition nor derived from any of the "Titanic" song models analyzed above, two recordings testify to the resilience of the topic among African American singers.

Collected by Vaughan Webb and Fred Williams and held in Ferrum College, Ferrum, Virginia, at the Blue Ridge Institute Archives, "The Titanic"[188] was recorded by African American guitarist Bobby Buford (1934–2020) at his home in Pulaski, Virginia, on March 27, 1984. Unissued in any format, Buford's song is available online.[189]

> Tell me, have you ever read in the history of your life
> How they separated husbands from the wives?
> When the iceberg struck the vessel,
> She couldn't make the flight
> On the morning the *Titanic* sank out of sight.
>
> It was way back in the year of Nineteen and Twelve
> Listen to the story I'm about to tell
> When the iceberg struck the vessel,
> She couldn't make the flight
> On the morning the *Titanic* [sank out of sight].
>
> *Spoken:* Yeah!
>
> *Scat singing*
>
> 'Cause it was way back yonder in the year of Nineteen Twelve
> Won't you listen to the story I'm about to tell
> When the iceberg struck the vessel,
> She couldn't make the flight
> On the morning the *Titanic* sank out of sight.
>
> *Repeat verse with slight variations*

Buford's repertoire is strongly influenced by hillbilly music and this song's lyrics vaguely resemble the uncredited text printed by the Reformer Publishing Company of Durham in a ballet for Reverend J. H. Brown, who had collected fragments of different songs.

As almost always after 1997, James Cameron's movie looms like an iceberg before "Titanic Blues" (Electro-Fi 3364), recorded in September 1999 in Toronto, Canada, by Fruteland Jackson (born 1953).[190]

A moderately condemnatory attitude to the white passengers and crew emerges from the narrative, which is conveyed in a strange blend of gospel and blues rhetoric, reminiscent of "Hi" Henry Brown. Irregular AAB and ABC stanza patterns alternate before the final verse introduces a variation on the usual mention of "Nearer My God to Thee."

Conclusion

After World War II the *Titanic* became a less-visited theme for singers, but not as markedly as for other increasingly distant disasters. The discovery of the wreck in 1985, which inspired the making of *Titanic* (1997), one of the most popular feature films of all time, revived public awareness of the sinking, as did the centenary commemorations in 2012. All this has certainly prompted some musicians to record original songs and covers.

Most white treatments of the topic seem to be tragic and/or religious, though a few, notably Frank Hutchison's, escape these bounds. Few white singers deal with the tragedy in a highly original way, most of their songs being recompositions or slightly modified versions of earlier songs.

In contrast, there is no single pattern in the responses of African American singers, who display a dichotomy between treating the event seriously—as a tragedy and/or a religious warning—and approaching it humorously, ironically, and sometimes ambiguously. This is mainly due to the different meanings, and the differing psychological impact, of the tragedy on the two communities. Also relevant are cultural differences related to the creation of disaster songs, which are typically more factual and objective in white treatments, and more discursive and associative among vernacular, and especially blues-influenced, Black composers. As always, there are exceptions: Frank Hutchison, heavily blues-influenced, on the white side, and William Jackson and Charles E. Wright (as well as Richard "Rabbit" Brown) seemingly catering to majority culture, on the African American.

Black themes of protest in songs about the *Titanic* are overtly concerned with the hubris of challenging God, class discrimination, and racial discrimination. The first two issues are not restricted to Black performers, but the last of them is magnified in the toasts by humor, exaggeration, and obscenity. Black people were conscious that the sinking of the *Titanic* was a "whites only" disaster, and the racial factor is always present. The escapes from death of the "traveling coon," Shine, and Jack Johnson symbolize the hope of escaping or avoiding white supremacy, and in this respect these survivors are avatars of all Black people.

The sinking is frequently interpreted as God's judgment on white claims to racial (often covertly equated to technological) supremacy. The overt and covert condemnation of white people's hubris and racism seems to traverse the boundaries between Black secular and sacred treatments of the subject.

IT WAS UP IN THE WORLD JUST A LITTLE TOO HIGH: THE 1937 *HINDENBURG* DISASTER

The destruction by fire of the German airship LZ 129 (Luftschiff Zeppelin) *Hindenburg* was an accident second only to the sinking of the *Titanic* in its effect on the collective imagination. A symbol and pride of the Nazi regime, the *Hindenburg* was attempting to moor at the Lakehurst Naval Air Station, Manchester Township, New Jersey, when disaster struck at 7:25 p.m. on May 6, 1937.

Coming after the losses of the British *R101* on its maiden flight in 1930, and of the US Navy scout airship *Akron* in a storm in 1933, this tragedy ended the commercial use of dirigibles.[191] Thirteen of the *Hindenburg's* thirty-six passengers, twenty-two of the sixty-one crew members, and one member of the Lakehurst ground crew died.[192] Several hypotheses have been put forward to account for the outbreak of fire, including (unconvincingly) sabotage and incendiary paint, static electricity, lightning, a fuel leak, and engine failure. Whatever the cause, the hydrogen used to supply buoyancy ignited, and destroyed the *Hindenburg* in thirty-two seconds.

Despite worldwide horror at the disaster, only two topical songs are known to exist. "The Hindenburg Disaster" (Bluebird B-4621) was recorded in New York City by Wilf Carter, alias Montana Slim (1904–1996) on May 7, 1937, the day after the catastrophe, and shows some signs of high-speed writing.[193]

> Kind friends if you will listen to a story sad but true,
> The disaster of the *Hindenburg* once sailed through sky so blue.
> She left her native homeland, headed for our friendly shore,
> Today it lies a twisted wreck near the Lakehurst landing moor.
>
> Many voyages she conquered as she proudly rode the breeze,
> Defied the great Atlantic with its angry rolling seas.
> She rode the storms and seemed to scorn at nature's queer demand,
> But now it lays a twisted wreck far from its distant land.
>
> So proudly sailed this silver craft with all aboard so gay,
> Above the New York skyline, across the Great White Way.
> Then clouds so gray rolled o'er the sky and hid the heavenly blue,
> The thunder rolled, the lightning flashed, the great ship rode it through.

While hovering o'er the great airport a-waiting for to land,
Just waiting gliding to and fro for the captain's skilled command.
Friends were gay while waiting there to clasp their loved one's hand,
The great ship slowly settled, landing ropes were dropped to ground.

But fate, it seemed, must play its hand, right then, we don't know why,
There was a sudden burst of flame, explosion followed nigh.
The *Hindenburg* a mass of flame, great billows leaping high,
A deafening roar, the silver mass came crashing from the sky.

Heroic men rushed to the scene determined in their quest,
Helping victims to escape from their most certain death.
It seemed that death must take its toll and tear loved ones apart,
And start their heartstrings throbbing, carrying many a broken heart.

What caused this great disaster that has shocked the whole wide world?
Another mystery of mankind that keeps us in a whirl.

The first two stanzas contrast the technological triumph that the airship seemed to embody with its dismal fate. The song's largely objective description of the event is glossed by the final two lines, which draw the conclusion often found in white songs about accidents and disasters: we are in the hands of fate and nobody can explain why such things happen.

The second recording about the tragedy is "The Hindenburg Disaster" (AFS 998-B-1 and 998-B-2), a two-part song recorded by Louisiana songster Lead Belly in the Coolidge Auditorium at the Library of Congress, Washington, DC, on June 22, 1937.[194]

Part One
On one evening just about half past four,
The *Hindenburg* was coming along, it was running along a little slow.
Just a little while, just before night,
The *Hindenburg* had burnt clean out of sight.
Oh, Lord, burnt clean out of sight,
Hindenburg burnt clean out of sight.

The people all thought the *Hindenburg* was supposed to begin to roll,
The people in New York City, they all begin to stroll.
The *Hindenburg* when it caught afire,
It was up in the world just a little bit too high.

Oh, Lord, little bit too high,
Just up in the world a little bit too high.

Part Two
Oh, the *Hindenburg*, oh the *Hindenburg*,
Whole town's talking 'bout the *Hindenburg*.
On one evening 'bout half past four,
Hindenburg come along running slow.
Oh, the *Hindenburg*, oh, the *Hindenburg*,
Largest ship was in this world,
Whole town's talking 'bout the *Hindenburg*,
Largest ship was in this world.

The people saw the boat when it 'gin to roll,
The people on the ground they 'gin to stroll.
Whole town's talking 'bout the *Hindenburg*,
Largest ship that was in this world.

Oh, boys, when it caught afire,
It was up in the world a little bit too high.
Oh, the *Hindenburg* down on the ground,
Woman kept throwing her little chilluns down.
Oh, chilluns down, chilluns down,
Woman kept throwing her chilluns down.
Whole town's talking 'bout the *Hindenburg*.
Largest ship that was in this world.

It's a sin and a shame, sin and a shame,
Look at that *Hindenburg*'s frame.
Sin and a shame, sin and a shame,
Hindenburg burnt up to her frame.

Unlike other songs that had the hallmarks of being composed on the spot at the request of Alan Lomax, who was conducting the recording session, these lyrics seem to have been more deliberately composed. The reference to "running along a little slow" is accurate: the *Hindenburg* was twelve hours behind schedule; and being "up in the world a little too high" probably refers to the decision to save time by undertaking a riskier "flying moor," with the airship dropping its landing ropes and mooring cable from about 200 feet up, then being winched down to the mooring mast. It is important to note, however, that this line, and the repeated references to the *Hindenburg* as the "largest ship that was in this world," are an implicit critique of white hubris about technological mastery, similar to that made by Lead Belly and other Black songsters, gospel singers, and toasters in response to the foundering of the *Titanic*. Furthermore, Lead Belly's song also seems to level an implicit accusation to (and sneer at) the Nazi regime and its "master race" ideology, thus identifying the white hubris as specifically German. The line "The people in New York City, they all begin to stroll" is almost celebratory, and recalls the stanza in Lead Belly's "The Titanic," where boxer Jack Johnson mocks white people by dancing the "Eagle Rock" after hearing about the sinking of the liner.

DEATH BY FIRE: FIRES AND INDUSTRIAL DISASTERS

Paying Tribute to the Ninety-One Dead:
The 1940 Bartley, West Virginia, Mine Disaster

One of the deadliest coal mine explosions in US history took place at 2:30 p.m. on January 10, 1940, in the No. 1 Mine of the Pond Creek Pocahontas Coal Corporation, near Bartley, West Virginia. Ninety-one of the 138 miners at work were killed; the explosion was probably caused by sparks from equipment igniting gas, but a second explosion, seven hours later, made an investigation impossible. Some miners who were not killed instantly were asphyxiated while trying to reach the shaft. Thirty-seven workers on the west side of the mine, and ten at the bottom of the shaft survived. The fifty-one widows and 169 orphans left behind were the first relatives of victims of a mine disaster to be entitled to survivors' benefits paid monthly, as provided for by an amendment to the Social Security Act that had only been in force for ten days.[195]

The Bartley mine disaster generated three topical and one non-topical recordings. Two of the topical songs were recorded in Welch, West Virginia, by George Korson (1899–1967).[196] "The Bartley Explosion" (AFS 12011-A-29), recorded on May 29, 1940, was composed and sung to his own guitar accompaniment by a white miner, songwriter and guitarist Orville J. Jenks (1898–1960).[197]

> Oh, think of that awful explosion
> That happened down under the ground,
> Oh, think of the heartaches and sorrows,
> As the ninety-one miners were found.
>
> God called all his angels together,
> And marched to the pearly white gate,

To welcome the ninety-one miners
From Bartley who met such a fate.

He said, "Now come right in, strangers,
Your work down on earth is all through."
He said, "Well done, and God bless you,
Your friends are all missing you, too."

He showed them His coal mines in Heaven,
He told them that He was the boss.
"There'll be no explosions in Heaven,
Have no fear, not a life has been lost."

Called ninety-one angels together,
And says, "Go as fast as you can,
Help comfort the mothers and children,
And the wives of the ninety-one men."

Jenks's lyrics are set to the tune of Jimmie Rodgers's "Hobo's Meditation" ("Will there be any freight trains in heaven? / Any boxcars in which we might hide?"), and his singing and playing owe a clear debt to Rodgers.

On December 30, 1971, folklorist J. Roderick Moore, formerly a longtime Welch resident, collected a different song, also titled "The Bartley Explosion," from Orville J. Jenks's brother, Mack.[198]

> RODERICK MOORE: Well, do you think you might remember some more songs about the mines that you wrote?
>
> MACK JENKS: Well, now, I had one about the Bartley explosion, but I've forgot some of it. It was sung to the tune of "One Step More."[199] You've heard the old song "For It's Only One Step More?" It was sung to that. Now that happened in 1940, when Bartley Mine blowed up over on Dry Fork and killed ninety-one. I had a song on that but now I studied here for the last month trying to get that song back together because I knew you was coming, and I tried to get that song back together and I never have been able to get it back together.
>
> R.M.: Could you sing what you do have together?
>
> M.J.: Yeah.
>
> R.M.: I'd like to, you know, have some record of it at least.
>
> M.J.: Well, it was made up about the Bartley explosion.

(singing)
In the year of 1940,
On the tenth day of the year,
There was a bunch of poor coal miners
Left their loved ones, sweet and dear.

Oh a miner's life's not easy,
You can see what happened there.
They were entombed beneath the mountain
Without the slightest breath of air.

Oh, these men, these poor coal miners,
Oh, their work on earth is o'er.
They are now at rest with Jesus
Over on the other shore.

The day after he recorded Orville Jenks, George Korson collected two African American songs related to the tragedy. "Cheer the Union Travelers" is primarily a pro-union anti-scab song, but the performance that Korson recorded includes a spoken dedication to the victims of the Bartley Mine disaster.[200] "Bartley Mine Disaster" (AFS 12012-A-16) deals more directly with the tragedy, however. It was sung by the Evening Breeze (or Breezes) Sextet,[201] formed seven years earlier by members of the choir of the Loves of Zion Baptist Church, Vivian, West Virginia.

Chorus:
Hallelu-lu-lu, hallelujah, oh my Lord.
We're going to see our friends again, oh, Lord, hallelu.

Down in the mine they could not pass,
Their lives were snuffed out by fire and gas.

They looked all around, found a cap and a coat,
They looked in the cap and they found a little note.

We're not going to tell you everything that's been said,
We're just paying tribute to the ninety-one dead.

The last stanza stresses that the song is a "tribute to the ninety-one dead." Implicit in its first line, however, are anger with the mine owners' indifference to unsafe working conditions, and with the social and industrial power structures enabling that indifference. The cryptic reference to "a cap and a note" is factually based, and would have been understood by listeners at the time as a topical reference. Trapped underground and facing death, Ernest W. Hoops, 41, wrote a farewell note to his wife and five children "on paper torn from a rock dust sack, folded carefully, and placed in his hard-hat." The note read: "If we don't make it out, darling wife, please take my body down home and have Rev. Spears to preach my funeral. Ernest." Hoops was buried in Jackson, Ohio (coincidentally Orville Jenks's birthplace), where Rev. George Spears, himself one of the forty-seven miners who survived the tragedy, did indeed officiate at his funeral.[202]

Made to sound older than it is by the addition of spurious surface noise, revivalist Artie Thomas's "The Bartley Mine Disaster" is a recent original song dealing with this tragedy.[203] The lyrics report the facts accurately, including the name of the mine (Pond Creek No. 1) where the tragedy occurred and the exact numbers of those who died and survived. The song is built around the tragedies suffered by the Mullins family of Bartley: Mrs. Mullins, whose seventeen-year-old daughter, Lucille, had died in a school bus accident three months earlier, lost her husband and son in the explosion. It seems very likely that Artie Thomas drew these details from the above-referenced Dolores Riggs Davis article, published in 2011, the year that the song was uploaded to YouTube.

Given the nature of this disaster, and its social context, we might expect to find openly political songs about it, with a nonreligious perspective. This is not the case, but the songs' religious approach does not reflect a lack of social awareness. All the songs implicitly condemn the unsafe conditions that led to the miners' deaths, by making a comparison with the afterlife; Orville Jenks explicitly contrasts God's management of His coal mines ("There'll be no explosions in Heaven") with the mismanagement of terrestrial owners. The religious contextualization of the disaster neither precludes nor excludes social criticism.

Death by Fire: The 1940 Natchez Rhythm Club Fire[204]

Like the sinking of the *Titanic* in 1912 and the Mississippi River flood in 1927, the deaths of over 200 people in the 1940 Natchez Rhythm Club fire inspired a relatively substantial number of songs; but where the former disasters were sung about by African Americans and whites, songs about the Natchez Fire, occasional cover versions apart (see below), are exclusively African American. The vitality of Black oral tradition and the circulation of recordings have contributed to a regional news item's being the theme of no fewer than ten original compositions, recorded, some of them more than once, over a span of almost sixty years. The recordings cover a broad spectrum of genres, from vocal group harmony to blues and gospel, and offer commentary from both sacred and secular perspectives.

On Tuesday evening, April 23, 1940, Walter Barnes and his band were booked at the Rhythm Club on St. Catherine Street in Natchez, Mississippi. The 190-by 80-foot venue was packed with about seven hundred people, including around 100 African American high school students and three teachers on an outing from Alcorn College.[205] At about 11:15 p.m., fire broke out near the front door of the building, which could only be opened inward.[206] The building had been decorated with Spanish moss, which was probably ignited by a carelessly discarded cigarette.[207]

Walter Barnes instructed his band to continue playing, apparently in an attempt to maintain calm, but the building was already enveloped in flames. The windows had been boarded up as a precaution against gatecrashers; a few people tried to force their way out, but only a handful succeeded as dead and unconscious bodies piled up, especially near the bandstand. Fire and smoke spread very quickly, and the tragedy was complete in a few minutes, with most victims dying from asphyxia or being trampled to death. Walter Barnes, vocalist Juanita Avery, and eight members of the band died; only the drummer and bassist survived.[208]

The white-owned *Natchez Democrat* was the first paper to cover the event, the day after the fire. Most of the papers that sent special correspondents were Black-owned journals like the *Chicago Defender*, the *New York Amsterdam News*, and the *Washington Afro-American*; being weeklies, they did not publish their stories until Saturday, April 27. The *Pittsburgh Courier* published a long report on May 4.

Two conclusions emerge from contemporary journalistic coverage: the Natchez Fire overwhelmingly affected African Americans nationwide, both individually and collectively. Not surprisingly, people in and around Natchez, irrespective of race, appear to have responded sympathetically and constructively. However, although the fire was widely and sympathetically covered in the national press, it had much less resonance among whites.

Second, Black-owned newspapers covered the story with more emotion than did the *Natchez Democrat* and other white publications. Understandable though it may be, it is striking that there is no reference whatsoever to memory in the *Natchez Democrat*, whereas the reporting and commentary in the Black press makes it clear from the outset that African Americans would not forget the tragedy.

Only sixteen days later, in Chicago, the Lewis Bronzeville Five made the first two recordings about the Rhythm Club fire. They were released on Bluebird B8445 and are credited to Mabel Sanford Lewis, who was the group's manager and not a performing member.[209] "Mississippi Fire Blues" is a string band–accompanied blues sung by Royale Brent, with vocal backing from a quartet.

(Moaned verse)

It was in Natchez, Mississippi, just about a quarter to twelve (x2)
When I thought I heard my poor girl crying for help.

Then I put on my duds and I was driven close by,
When I got there, the folks was gathered around.

Her eyes was sad and her face was full of pain,
Just to think of this, I just can't keep from crying.

Then I followed the crowd to the burying ground,
And I watched the pallbearers put my sweet gal down.

Then I fell on my knees, lifted my head to God,
Said, "Oh, Lord, have mercy on this town."

That was the last time I saw my poor gal's face,
And I loved that gal; no one else can take her place.

Only the first of the six stanzas has an AAB structure. The absence of repetition thereafter, and the frequent failure to rhyme, probably reflect both improvisation and a need to fit all the verses into three minutes. After the introductory moaned verse, the song begins with a reference to the moment when tragedy struck, a feature of many African American narrative lyrics in this period. There is only one nonpersonal reference ("Oh, Lord, have mercy on this town"); otherwise, the song is a recollection of events and feelings, purportedly from the singer's perspective. It should be noted, however, that the stanza about the burying ground is widespread and traditional. The reference to being driven (rather than driving) to the scene may be an allusion to the victims of the fire being mainly from Black Natchez's moneyed class.

"Natchez Mississippi Blues" is clearly intended to be a complement and sequel, on the reverse of a thematic record.

Night time is falling, day is almost done, (ooh, yeah, yeah) (x2)
My baby left last night; she left to have some fun. (ooh, yeah, yeah)

At two o'clock in the morning by the clock on the wall (x2)
Yes, I thought I heard my poor baby call.

Ooh, the nights are long; I can't sleep at all (x2)
Since my sweet mama burned in that Rhythm Hall.

Yes, the day is breaking, sun refuse to shine (ooh, yeah, yeah) (x2)
I'm leaving Natchez, Mississippi, moving on down the line.

"Natchez Mississippi Blues" reuses a line from the first stanza of "Mississippi Fire Blues," and misstates the time of the fire, but it is more carefully and originally constructed, using exact rhymes and more vivid imagery.

The text is divided into two parts. The first comprises stanzas one and two, which respectively set the scene and describe the singer's presentiments of catastrophe. In the second half, a still-unspecified tragedy has taken place: line A of the third stanza continues to create suspense, resolved by a flashback that explains the singer's distress. Both lines of the final stanza present distinctively Black tropes. The first uses the familiar pathetic fallacy, in which the elements mirror the singer's mood, but it also references Judgment Day ("[when] the sun refuse to shine") drawing from the eighth chapter of the *Book of Revelation*,[210] an allusion reinforced by the antiphonal choral response. According to Małgorzata Ziółek-Sowińska, the "main theme of the song is that dancers were having a good time in the Rhythm Club in Natchez and death came and unfortunately they did not get saved. . . . One could assume that [death] makes [the singer] reflect on the sudden end of his earthly existence, his own mortality, and life after death."[211] This is generally true, but in my opinion the meaning of the song is hidden in the closing line, which contrasts the worldly images of migration in general, and the wandering blues singer in particular. African Americans were about half the population of Natchez in 1940. This was a time of increasing migration north and west by Southern Blacks, attracted by employment opportunities in the defense and other industries, but the singer's awareness that Natchez people would (also) wish to put physical distance between themselves and tragedy is insightful.[212]

The Bronzeville Five's songs focus on intimate first-person description of the story and on psychological reactions to it. This is the main difference between them and all subsequent recordings: the later blues songs concentrate on social responsibility and community life, while the gospel songs are pervaded with a strong sense of catharsis.

On Tuesday, June 4, 1940, six weeks after the fire and again in Chicago, two vocalists each recorded a song; the performances were coupled on Decca 7763.[213] The singer on side A, "The Natchez Fire," is Gene Gilmore, accompanied by Leonard Caston on piano and Robert Lee McCoy on harmonica:

Lord, I know, I know, how you Natchez people feel today (x2)
Some of them are thinking of the fire that took their children's life away.

Lord, it was late one Tuesday night, people had come from miles
    around (x2)
They was enjoying their lives when that Rhythm Club went down.

Lord, wasn't it sad and misery when the hearses began to roll? (x2)
It was over two hundred dead and gone, Lord, and they can't come here
    no more.

I'm gon' tell all you people to listen to what I have to say (x2)
Don't be uneasy about your children, because they all is at rest today.

Goodbye, goodbye, fare you well, goodbye (x2)
I just come to let all you people know what happened in that Natchez
    fire.

"The Natchez Fire" is a blues song alternating narrative and commentative stanzas. The words "know," "Natchez," "people," and "fire" are all present both in the first and last stanzas, and interact by contrast and association in a manner widespread in blues lyrics.[214] The repetitions may seem predictable and almost inevitable, given the theme of the song, but their collocation is original and perfectly conveys the final meaning.

"Natchez," used with "people" at the beginning of the song to address a town in mourning, is juxtaposed at the end with the "fire" that has caused the grief. The weak use of "know" ("I am aware") in stanza one contrasts with a much stronger connotation in the phrase "let all you people know" ("everyone should be aware") in the last verse. Commentative stanzas (one, four, and five) prevail over narrative ones (two and three) because the tragedy is predicated as a known fact. Rather than telling a story, the author is concerned with how the inhabitants of Natchez will react to the deaths of their loved ones ("Don't be uneasy about your children") and with the importance of spreading the news among Black people ("I just come to let all you people know"). With varying explicitness, this focus on *collective* rather than *personal* memory is shared by all later Black recordings on the Natchez Fire.

The record's reverse, "The Death of Walter Barnes," is by Baby Doo, the nickname of Natchez resident Leonard Caston (1917–1987).

Lord, I want everyone now to listen, listen to my lonesome song (x2)
Lord, I want to state what happened to poor old Walter Barnes.

Lord, it was just about midnight, just about twelve o'clock (x2)
Poor Walter played his theme song, the dance hall began to rock.

Lord, and the peoples all was dancing, enjoying their life so high (x2)
Just in a short while, the dance hall was full of fire.

The composer credit for this song is to "Caston"; despite textual and stylistic similarities with Gene Gilmore's "The Natchez Fire," the latter song is credited to "Gilmore." Caston pays homage to Walter Barnes, and Gilmore to the young victims, a contrast that is probably intentional on their and/or Decca's part. Despite taking a more narrative approach, Caston immediately draws attention to the unfortunate fate of Walter Barnes, who is thereby rightfully acclaimed as an African American hero. Interestingly, both Gilmore and Caston present the same image of the victims "enjoying their life" during the dance, although Gilmore focuses on the younger among them.

Immediately after the tragedy, and with folk reaction to it specifically in mind, African American folklorist John Wesley Work III suggested conducting fieldwork in Natchez, but failed to obtain funding.[215] Later in 1940, John A. and Ruby T. Lomax did visit the city, but recorded no songs about the fire.[216] Not until two years later, on July 23, 1942, did Alan Lomax record "The Natchez Theatre Fire Disaster" (AFS 6623-B-2) in Clarksdale, Mississippi. The singer was the blind Charles Haffer Jr.[217] The "ballet" available at the Library of Congress sheds more light on the song and its meaning.[218] Firstly, it confirms that the word "Theatre" was not meant to form part of the title. Secondly, it provides information as to which Scriptures Haffer drew inspiration from (Psalms 9:17; Job 27:8–9; Proverbs 1:24–27, and the first clause of line 28; Luke 13:1–3). Thirdly, it contains several minor variations from the recording, including spelling mistakes, slightly different choice ("full of" instead of "filled with" in stanza 1) or omission ("brethren" in the stanza after the chorus) of words, and the like. More importantly, it comprises portions of verses and the missing final stanza that Haffer did not sing to Lomax. In order to save space, they have been reproduced here in italics, exactly where and how Haffer printed them.

Spoken: The title of this song is "The Natchez Fire Disaster."

One Tuesday night in April, 'tween eleven and twelve o'clock,
A tragedy happened in Natchez, will never be forgot.
A crowd of youngsters gathered, filled with joy and glee,
When fire of a unknown origin destroyed two hundred and three.

Chorus:

It was a sad time in Natchez,
So many people died.
Dead bodies were piled up
Almost shoulder high.

The night were calm and beautiful, the skies were bright and fair,
The crowd were being jubilant, and knew not death were there.
They were eating and drinking and smoking, dancing and having a time,
And in less than a half an hour, brethren, hundreds of people were
    dying.

Chorus (x2)

The place was once a church house, used for the service of God,
Later turned into a blacksmith shop, and finally to a dancing hall.
That's where the people had gathered, so we are informed,
And were dancing to the music of the famous Walter Barnes.

Chorus

The building were crudely constructed, covered over with galvanized tin,
Twenty feet wide, two hundred feet long, with one door to enter in.
Satan had them bewildered, and lured them into his den,
And then sent a sudden destruction, which destroyed both women and
    men.

Chorus (x2)

Fire broke out in front, the people run to the rear.
Moans, groans, and screams were pitiful to hear.
The smoke had them blinded so they could not see;
Men, Women, and children cried lord have mercy on me.

They trampled on each other in an effort to break through,
But seeing they was, seeing they was destroyed, they said, "Lord, what
    shall we do?"
The orchester [sic] *continued and was playing soft and low,*
While many helpless victims lay dieing [sic] *on the floor.*

Chorus (x2)

There was a number of people there whose name were on church rolls.
But what's the hope of a hypocrite when God take away his soul?
Joined to their idols like Ephra(i)ms –estray [sic]
Sitting on the seat of the scornful, standing in the sinners(') way.

Chorus

Some was refined and cultured, I said some was refined and cultured,
   highly honored on earth,
Claimed to have been converted and had a spiritual birth.
Some teachers in the Sunday school, some singing in the choir.
Alas, like Saul, they played the fool and perished in the fire.

Chorus

After the ball was over, the news broadcast around,
Doctors, medicines, and nurses rushed there from nearby towns.
All hospitals were crowded
[That's all he can remember. The recording ends here.]
All hospitals were crowded, some were treated at home,
The exact number of injured will probably never be known.

Women obey your husbands, husbands love your wives
Together raise your families and live quite [sic] *lives*
Shun all bad company, and dives where sinners go
The fate that happened in Natchez could be mine or yours.

The "ballet" of "The Natchez Fire Disaster" constitutes an invaluable source of
information. First of all, it clarifies that the song's verse structure is made up
of two consecutive couplets.[219] Secondly, it also fills some gaps in the flow of
narration that was otherwise lacking. Finally, it significantly adds to the overall
meaning of the composition. The first unrecorded couplet introduces a subtle
reference to physical blindness caused by smoke as opposed to the revelers'
implied moral blindness. The second hints at Walter Barnes's heroic decision to
continue playing in the raging inferno. The third links the Biblical verses in Job
27:8–9 with the verse (not referenced by Haffer) in Psalms 1:1, which condemns
the hypocrisy of those who go astray. The stanza where the recording is interrupted rounds out the preceding couplet with the appalling depiction of the
extent of the disaster. The final verse sounds moralizing and even threatening
in the last line, as often occurs in sacred disaster songs.

Alan Lomax's interview and recollections, and an unpublished manuscript in the Alan Lomax Archive—which internal evidence suggests was written by Lewis W. Jones—constitute most of the available information about this prolific composer of religious songs.[220]

The following portion of the interview between Alan Lomax and Haffer illustrates the purpose of "The Natchez Theatre Fire Disaster" and similar compositions by him:

ALAN LOMAX (A.L.): Now. How many copies of this song did you sell?
CHARLES HAFFER JR. (C.H.): The Natchez song?
A.L.: Yeah. Was that a very popular one?
C.H.: Oh, popular, popular. Sold about two thousand copies. I don't have any direct record. I'm just guessing, but I sold around two thousand copies of it all right.
A.L.: After you make a song from singing around the country, do people, do you hear other people singing them then?
C.H.: Sure. Lots of people sing 'em; they buy 'em and sing 'em.
A.L.: Do they sometimes change them?
C.H.: Sometime they change it, sometime they revise it, call themselves, and sometimes they take it and reprint it, put their name on it, claimed they composed it. I come across lots of that.
A.L.: Well, what's your purpose in making a song like this Natchez Fire?
C.H.: It's a warning. The title, it's called a warning song. When we write about disasters, our object is to warn.
A.L.: To warn who?
C.H.: Warn the people, the unconverted or the careless and unconcerned Christians.
A.L.: Do you find that the ministers approve of what you do?
C.H.: Yes, sir. Yes, sir. Three-fourths and a part of the other fourth.
A.L.: Do you think it's really true that if a man dies in sin, he goes right straight to the bad place?
C.H.: Oh, well, now that, that brings a whole lot of . . . I don't know about that. I think he goes to the grave.
A.L.: You're not sure of that, 'cause that's what your song tells the people.
C.H.: That song, well, it . . . The thing in that song, that song tell the people that they were destroyed by Satan. That song don't consign 'em to no eternal torture, but it does consign that the wicked is to be destroyed.[221]

Haffer's text is a moralistic interpretation of the Rhythm Club tragedy, based on news reports read to him by his wife.[222] Most of the song's complete stanzas present a ballad-like ABCB rhyme structure, as does the refrain, which is inserted every two stanzas (except on one occasion) and sung once or twice. In the first narrative stanza, the emphasis is on memory and on the time and place where the tragedy occurred. The information provided is historically accurate, but the general perspective, and the linguistic approach, are obviously different from those in the blues songs analyzed above and below. Before comment on the meaning of the event, Haffer summarizes the facts, using a high-level lexicon ("Filled with joy and glee," "fire of a unknown origin"), in part at least probably derived from newspaper accounts.

As the song becomes homiletic, even a seemingly neutral reference to memory ("A tragedy happened in Natchez / Will never be forgot") acquires an accusatory meaning. After the estranging effect of the refrain, the stanza after the chorus seems to go on recounting the story, again using high-level language; but in fact it contains a moralistic observation, disguised as narrative ("The crowd were being jubilant" and "They were eating and drinking and smoking / Dancing and having a time"). After the second refrain (repeated twice), we are told that the dance hall had once been a church before being put to increasingly irreligious uses; this is a key observation in Haffer's text.[223] Ethical condemnation continues to be implicit in the fourth stanza, which provides a detailed description of factors in the building's construction that contributed to the death toll and then switches perspective identifying Satan as the prime mover of the tragedy.[224]

The fifth stanza is narrative, but the second line in the sixth verse conveys the people's feeling of powerlessness to deal with misfortune ("Lord, what shall we do?"). Not surprisingly, and in a very effective climax, the seventh stanza is the song's most accusatory, making the previous implicit indictment of hypocrisy explicit ("But what's the hope of a hypocrite / When God take away his soul?").

After the refrain, more evidence of hypocrisy and its consequences is provided in the eighth quatrain. The revelers' high standing, social ("Some was refined and cultured / Highly honored on earth"), spiritual ("Claimed to have been converted / And had a spiritual birth"), and religious ("Some teachers in the Sunday School / Some singing in the choir") is noted, before a Biblical allusion to 1 Samuel 26:21 ("Alas, like Saul, they played the fool") condemns them, and explains their fate. The ninth stanza reverts to narration in the aftermath of the tragedy, but the recording breaks off.

The first postwar song about the Rhythm Club fire was "The Natchez Burning" (Chess 1744), composed and performed by Howlin' Wolf (Chester Burnett, 1910–1976). Cut in Chicago on July 19, 1956, it was released three years later.[225]

> Did you ever hear about the burning that happened way down in
> Natchez, Mississippi, town? (x2)[226]

The whole building got to burning. There my baby laying on the
ground.

Shirley Joan was there.
Louisa was there.
Rosie Mae was there.
Louise was there.
Did you ever hear about the burning that happened way down in
Natchez, Mississippi, town?
I stood back, was looking, and the whole building done tumbled down.

Ooooh, oooh.
Oooh, oooh, ooooh

The meaning and purpose of this blues is again to preserve the memory of the tragedy, of those who died, and of those affected by their deaths. The *coup de théâtre* of mentioning the singer's girlfriend as one of the fatalities denotes the cataclysmic effect of personal bereavement, but it is also a spark that generates the next, closely related stanza, which has the dramatic qualities of a Greek chorus. The novel idea of commemorating some victims by name in a recitative aside is intended to suggest that Howlin' Wolf knew them personally, and implicitly makes the song's subjects the cruel fate of *all* those who died, and the suffering of their relatives. With these four fictitious names (not by chance all women, and excluding Walter Barnes), Howlin' Wolf makes it clear that grief is collective, no less than individual. In the third stanza, the slightly modified restatement of the opening lines reinforces the idea, while the rhyming line presents Howlin' Wolf himself as an epitome of all those who could only look on in petrified impotence.[227] The final moaned verse evokes people mourning the loss of their loved ones.

During 1956–57 fieldwork in Louisiana, Harry Oster recorded singer and guitarist Robert Gilmore performing "Wasn't That a Awful Day in Natchez" (Louisiana Folklore Society LFS-1). All that is known about Gilmore, from the booklet notes with the album, is his place of origin, Plaquemines Point, Louisiana, presumably the recording location.[228]

Chorus:
Wasn't that a awful day in Natchez,
Hear them sinners groan. (x2)

In the year of 1940
On April, the twenty-fourth,

Death stepped in that dance hall,
'Round that mighty host.

Chorus

Tell me that destruction was really sad,
Done used all the graves that the section had.
Messenger brought the news, looking sad,
"Dry your eyes at some other grave."

Chorus

Textually and structurally, the song, presumably Gilmore's composition, has some features in common with Charles Haffer's, especially in the unambiguous condemnation of the "sinners," but it is otherwise a different and apparently original song. In her book, Ziólek-Sowińska suggests that the

> line "hear them sinners groan" is a significant Apocalyptic theme in the song. . . . Death is personified and . . . can be perceived as one of the riders of the *Book of the Apocalypse*. . . . The message of this warning song is . . . that death may come to sinners quickly when they are not ready for the sudden arrival of the messenger of death and therefore the singer makes them think of their own mortality.[229]

On April 20, 1959, John Lee Hooker recorded his first version of "Natchez Fire [Burnin']" (Riverside LP 008) in Detroit.[230]

> Did you read about the fire, nineteen and thirty-seven?
> Did you read about the fire, nineteen hundred and thirty-seven?
> Walter Barnes and his big band, they was swinging that night.
> The building had one door. It was on the side.
> The fire broke out late that night.
> People was screaming, they couldn't get out.
> Everybody running, running to the door.
> The door got jammed, nobody got out.
> All you could hear crying, "Lord, have mercy.
> Hmm, hmm, save me, save me, save me."
> It must have been a plan, a plan from above.
> Hmm, a plan from above.
> 'Cause hoo, no, no one was saved,

Not as I know, hmm, hmm.
The band was swinging late that night, hmm,
When the fire broke out,
In Natchez, Natchez, Mississippi, hmm.
A great big barn, a great big barn,
A many lives was gone down that night.
Hmm, you'll never forget, you'll never forget,
Hmm, hmm, hmm, Natchez, Mississippi, Natchez, Mississippi,
Hmm, hmm.

As is discussed in the chapter about the Tupelo tornado, the misdating in this talking blues is probably due to Hooker confusing the two events. The reference to God as the cause of the tragedy ("It must have been a plan, a plan from above") and the final stress on memory ("you'll never forget"), aligned with most of the texts analyzed so far, are the key messages of this blues.

As with "Tupelo," Hooker recorded other versions of his Natchez Fire disaster song. "Fire at Natchez" was recorded at Culver City, Los Angeles, on March 9, 1961.[231] A different wrong year (1936) is again given in the lyrics, showing that the periodic regeneration of themes in African American popular music is not necessarily concerned with historical accuracy.

On July 28, 1963, Hooker performed a version of his composition at the Newport Folk Festival in Rhode Island, released as "The Mighty Fire" (Vee-Jay VJLP 1078).[232] Despite many textual similarities with the previous two versions and continued insistence on the wrong year, there are a few significant differences. The most obvious is his use of Howlin' Wolf's device of listing the names of victims, which gives the song a more coherent structure. For the first time (and unlike Wolf), Hooker mentions Walter Barnes among the dead. The sense of sharing in the grief of the community is still perceivable in the spoken introduction, in the use of the word "people," and in the calling of the names of the dead; but—leaving aside the majority of the Newport concert audience being white—the solidarity is weakened by the parenthetic reference to his girlfriend ("Louise was there—my girlfriend-buddy") and in the two personal recollections of the days after the event ("That Saturday morning I bought myself a paper" and "I felt so bad").

John Lee Hooker was not the only singer to conflate different disasters. On August 21, 1973, near Senatobia, Mississippi, David Evans collected "The Tupelo Fire," a field recording from George Toney, a sixty-two-year-old singer who also played guitar and drums. Evans reports that Toney "sang in a soft falsetto voice" and "was rusty on the guitar."[233] He sang only a fragment of the song comprising one stanza and a chorus:

See some old peoples coming down the street, couldn't hardly walk,
Every time you hear those people the barrelhouse was their talk.
Wasn't it sad to hear those people when they moaned?

Chorus
I declare it sure was sad
To hear those people . . .

After making a mistake, Toney interrupted his performance and told Evans
that the song was "about the fire in Tupelo many years ago. . . . It's a long record
of it."[234] The explanation went on:

> GEORGE TONEY: They had a ballroom down there, a long building, just
> about like this place out here. And they just had the night, Sunday
> night. That's all those people were doing out there, balling. And just
> one door in, and one door out. And somehow or another, it had car-
> pets and everything on the floor. It was a big thing, a big time. And
> somehow or another, a fire broke out up there by the front. And when
> the fire broke out there by the front, couldn't nobody get out. [inaudi-
> ble] They say it's over two or three hundred got burnt. And that song
> started out from Tupelo.
>
> DAVID EVANS: Did that song come out on a record, or did you hear it
> somewhere?
>
> G.T.: I just don't remember. Could be. It was some jubilee singers that
> was the ones that brought that song out. What I mean by jubilee sing-
> ers—spiritual singers. They the ones started that song.[235]

Toney obviously conflated the Tupelo and Natchez disasters and relocated the
Natchez Fire to Tupelo, but the lyrics are unrelated to any of the songs about
either disaster. The description of the Rhythm Club and of the event is accurate,
though the tragedy occurred on a Tuesday. As the ball at the Rhythm Club was
organized mainly for young people, the stanza seems to describe the reaction
of the parents and grandparents of the victims, or the older members of the
community in general, and expresses sympathy with them. The whole stanza
and refrain are somewhat reminiscent of other disaster song lyrics, especially
the "(Wasn't It Sad) When That Great Ship Went Down" cluster of songs, Leola
Manning's "The Arcade Building Moan," and the Echoes of Zion's "Atlanta's
Tragic Monday."

Howlin' Wolf's 1956 recording prompted a few covers by musicians both
white and Black. Among the latter are "The Natchez Burning," recorded on April
7, 1976, by Macon, Georgia, native Willie Wright at Sweet Home, Arkansas,[236]

Figure 2.05. Elmo Williams at the Rootsway Roots and Blues and Food Festival, Boretto, Reggio Emilia, June 26, 2010 (Luigi Monge). Luigi Monge collection

and Nappy Brown's "Natchez Burning."[237] "Natchez Fire," recorded by Elmo Williams (1933–2016) (see fig. 2.05) and Hezekiah Early (1934–) in Waterproof, Louisiana, for Fat Possum Records in 1997, is not a word-for-word cover of Howlin' Wolf's song, and is worth closer scrutiny.[238] Williams was from Natchez, which may show that the theme's relevance is decreasing to the local level, but it also confirms that African American lyrics have the power to preserve the memory of a decades-old historical event. Unlike Howlin' Wolf, who "paid his tribute to a community he cared for,"[239] Williams "sang from a local perspective, telling real tales about the real people known to him affected by the tragedy:"[240]

I play that song, "The Natchez Fire"; old fellows played it. A man from the Delta wrote it. I put my words and changed some stuff in it. And I recorded it. That's a way to educate the people about it. I changed some words. I put: "Louise was there. Big Brown was there. Big Blue was there. Willie Mae was there." Willie Mae walked up and went uptown to get some money. Her man was there, under a window; they trampled him, and he knocked out the window—a woman was saved, that's what saved her! Willie Mae was uptown when it happened; she had a juke joint on Franklin Street, just a block away. She was my aunt; that's why I put her into the lyrics. Big Blue ran a big juke joint across from the Rhythm Night Club. The other man had a club right next to the Rhythm Club, on the corner of Pine and Jefferson.[241]

It is no surprise that there are no original topical or nontopical compositions by white musicians. The few attempts to engage with Howlin' Wolf's song only confirm that the disaster is peripheral to white culture.[242]

Memory is the thread that connects most of the lyrics about the Natchez Fire. An increasing awareness of the importance of solidarity and of the healing power of time is perceptible. A strong sense of the importance of collective awareness permeates much of twentieth-century African American popular music, both sacred and secular. The way that the Rhythm Club fire resonates with issues of history, memory, and identity accounts for the resilience of the theme.

Despite an inevitable decline in awareness of the Rhythm Club tragedy with the passing of time, Howlin' Wolf's "The Natchez Burning," especially, has contributed to the creation of other topical songs. Big Jack Johnson's "Ice Storm Blues, Part One and Part Two," about the February 1994 ice storm in Clarksdale, Mississippi, is sung to Wolf's tune."[243] In February 1995, Alabama duo Little Whitt and Big Bo (respectively Jolly Wells, from Ralph, and Cleo McGee, from Emelle) recorded "The Burning" in Tuscaloosa. This downhome blues is clearly inspired by "The Natchez Burning," whose opening stanza it adopts virtually complete, adapting it to deal with the racist arson of a Natchez schoolhouse.[244]

When least expected, African American popular lyrics undergo a more or less radical change and come back to life. Such unpredictable revivals are especially meaningful when the theme is one so significant in African American history, whose musical treatment has been scarcely influenced by the majority culture.

Nobody's Fault: Unidentified and Miscellaneous Accidental Disasters

Unlike the chapter on natural disasters that only inspired a single song, this section applies chronological order based on the song's date of recording or publication in books, and takes no account of whether songs were recorded commercially or for folk song collectors. Three recordings have purposely been excluded from this study. 1) Even if it described a real shipwreck, which cannot be proved at the time of writing, Lonnie Johnson's "Life Saver Blues" (OKeh 8557), recorded in New York City on November 9, 1927, makes no mention of any fatalities. 2) As reported in the St. Louis press in 1929 and 1930, there were at least two fires involving Black people on Market Street, the location mentioned in Buck McFarland's "St. Louis Fire" (Paramount 12982), recorded in Grafton, Wisconsin, ca. March 1930, but this incident didn't cause any victims.[245] 3) Bumble Bee Slim's two takes of "Burned Down Mill" (Vocalion 02885) don't make reference to a specific mill, and variants of the phrase "the mill burned down" occur in many blues songs.[246] The lyrics don't mention any deaths or injuries, only the anonymous owner's economic loss and the unemployment of the workers.

Early African American Songs about Accidental Disasters
One of the earliest African American songs about an accidental disaster is a stevedores' chant published in 1876 by the globetrotting writer Lafcadio Hearn (1850–1904), and described by him as sung "to a slow and sweet air":

Chorus:
Shawneetown is burnin' down,
Who tole you so? (x2)

Cythie, my darlin' gal,
Who tole you so?
Cythie, my darlin' gal,
How do you know?
Chorus

How the h--l[247] d'ye 'spect me to hold her,
Way down below?
I've got no skin on either shoulder,
Who tole you so?
Chorus

De houses dey is all on fire,
Way down below.
De houses dey is all on fire,
Who tole you so?
Chorus

My old missus tole me so,
Way down below.
An' I b'lieve what ole missus says,
Way down below.
Chorus[248]

As a roustabouts' song, this may be about the explosion of the steamer *James Jackson* on September 21, 1851, as the vessel was leaving Shawneetown, Illinois.[249] Alternatively, the song may refer to Confederate guerrilla leader William Quantrill's October 17, 1862, raid on Shawneetown, Johnson County, Kansas, when thirteen buildings were burned down. However, Shawneetown, now a suburb of Kansas City, Kansas, was not on a river.[250] These lyrics, of what is possibly the earliest African American song to mention a disaster, show that Black singers were not yet comfortable with fully thematic songs, and were more inclined to present disasters in a larger context of everyday life.

There are probably fewer African American songs than white ones about sea and river disasters,[251] but some interesting and little-known compositions from the late nineteenth century display Black people's early creativity in this area. Because of their early dates and localized nature, these songs did not circulate widely, and were not recorded, but those available in printed sources are among the first known Black songs about human-caused disasters.

One of the most important sources in this respect is Mary Wheeler's *Steamboatin' Days*, which includes musical transcriptions.[252] The book's first song about a river wreck concerns the packet *John Gilbert*, which ran from Cincinnati to Florence, Alabama. On her last trip in 1888, the *John Gilbert* struck a reef, grounded in a dangerous stretch of water called "Chester Chute," and eventually broke in two because of "faulty loading of an extremely heavy cargo." Wheeler collected and transcribed "John Gilbert," describing it as "a labor song," though it may also contain some implied criticism of the clerk, captain, and mate. Its composer, Uncle Tom Wall, formerly a hand on the packet, explained that the sinking of the boat was "a warnin' frum the Lawd God."

> *Chorus*:
> John Gilbert is the boat, Di De Oh, Di De Oh,
> John Gilbert is the boat, Di De Oh,
> Runnin' in the Cincinnati trade.
>
> You see that boat a comin',
> She's comin' roun' the bend,
> An' when she gits in,
> She'll be loaded down agin.
>
> Lee P. Kahn wuz the head clerk,
> Captain Duncan wuz the Captain,
> Billy Evit wuz the head mate,
> Runnin' in the Cincinnati trade.

She hauled peanuts an' cotton,
An' she hauled so many.
When she got to Johnsonville,
Her work would just begin.

She hauled so many peanuts
Her men run frum her.
They went out in the wilderness,
An' they nevuh come back no mo'.

She hauled so many peanuts,
The rousters run frum her,
They couldn't git nobody to load her,
But the free labors.

They put her to Florence, Alabama,
Runnin' in the St. Louis trade,
An' when she got to Chester,
She broke half in two.

The second tragedy recalled in Wheeler's book is the loss of the packet *Gold Dust*, which caught fire on August 7, 1882, when her boilers exploded immediately after the boat left Hickman, Kentucky. Seventeen people were killed and forty-seven injured. Black rousters memorialized the tragedy, composing a short song that became very popular on several boats.

Ain't that a pity, oh Lawd, (x3)
Ain't that a pity 'bout the *Gold Dust* men.

Some got scalded,
Some got drownded,
Some got burnt up in the Gold Dust fire.

The burning of the *City of Bayou Sara*, a sidewheel packet owned by the St. Louis and New Orleans Anchor Line, also elicited a song. Carrying hay and other inflammable cargo, the boat burned close to shore at New Madrid, Missouri, at 11:00 p.m. on December 5, 1885. The passengers and most of the crew were saved, but roustabouts who were sleeping on one of the decks did not wake up in time and were burned to death. Surviving Black rousters composed a song about the tragedy. Tobe Royal, the white mate of the "B'y' Sara," threatened to whip any rousters who sang it, but when he was not present they ignored his order, and the song survived as a result. Its melody recalls old spirituals, such as "Swing Low, Sweet Chariot."

> Way down the rivuh, and I couldn't stay long,
> B'y' Sara burned down,
> She burned down to the water's edge,
> B'y' Sara burned down.
>
> The people begun to run an' squall,
> B'y' Sara burned down,
> When they begin to look they wuz about to fall,
> B'y' Sara burned down.
>
> Look away over yonder, what I see,
> B'y' Sara burned down,
> The captain an' the mate wuz comin' after me,
> B'y' Sara burned down.
>
> There's two bright angels by my side,
> B'y' Sara burned down,
> 'Cause I want to go to Heaven when I die,
> B'y' Sara burned down.

Like the song published by Hearn, these songs are important as the earliest-known African American disaster songs, a genre that began to flourish more strongly in the 1890s and the early twentieth century.

If You Want to Make Your Money, Work on Mr. Carrier's Line: The 1903 Carrier Line

The blues ballad "The Carrier Railroad" (AFS 6670-B-1) was collected by Alan Lomax and Lewis Jones near Sledge, Mississippi, on August 15, 1942.[253] It was sung and played on the fiddle by its composer, blind African American musician Sid Hemphill (1876 or 1878–1961)[254] with Lucius Smith on banjo, Alec (or Alex) Askew on guitar, and Will Head on bass drum. The 1907 financial panic appears to be referenced in a few stanzas, but the song is chiefly concerned with the wreck of Number Seven (nicknamed the *Seven Spot*), a train on the Sardis and Delta Railroad, a short-haul line owned by logging entrepreneur Robert Carrier, and used to haul timber from Bobo Lake (later Carrier Lake) to Sardis, in Panola County, Mississippi.

Sid Hemphill told Alan Lomax that the incident took place in 1903,[255] but 1905 or 1906, as stated by Lucius Smith, seems more likely. By ca. 1906, engineer

Dave Cowart, mentioned in the song, was working on the Lamb-Fish Lumber Company's railroad, based in Charleston, Mississippi.[256] From August 7 to 11, 1905, "about 200 men employed by the lumber firm of C. M. Carrier & Son" at Sardis struck in protest against wage cuts; this incident appears to be alluded to, in the song, where it is conflated with incidents during the 1907 panic.[257]

The train wreck certainly took place at Malone's Trestle. There were no deaths,[258] but many people were scalded by escaping steam, including a preacher, Lovey Lemons, who is referred to in the lyrics, although he is not named. Engineer Dave Cowart had often been warned by Mr. Carrier about excessive speed and told that he risked being transferred from engine No. 7 to No. 9, or dismissed. If the song is to be believed, both these things happened, but Cowart was back running his original train when the accident occurred.

> [No]body had a nickel.
> You couldn't get a dime.
> If you want to make your money, boys,
> Work on Mr. Carrier's time.
> *Refrain*
>
> Oh, my honey babe . . .
> Mr. Dave Cowart went on Mr. Carrier's engine.
> Mr. Carrier, he looked and laughed.
> "Telling you, Dave Cowart,
> Don't run my train too fast."
> *Refrain*
>
> Mr. Dave told Mr. Carrier,
> "Man, don't you know I know your rule?
> Tell you, Mr. Carrier,
> A train ain't no mule."
> *Refrain*
>
> Mr. Dave Cowart went down to Baptist.
> Mr. Carrier stood on the railroad track.
> "Send back Dave Cowart,
> Get Mr. Bailey back."
> *Refrain*
>
> Mr. Dave told Mr. Carrier,
> "Man, fire me if you will.
> Every time it come a shower of rain,

He can't run it up Johnson Hill."
Refrain

Mr. Carrier said, "Dave Cowart,
See what you has done.
You left Sardis at twelve o'clock.
Done made it back at one."
Refrain

Mr. Dave said, "Well, Mr. Carrier,
Let me have my way.
Let me run the Seven Spot,
I'll make three trips a day."
Refrain

Mr. Carrier said, "No, Dave Cowart,
Tell you in time.
Can't let you run the Seven no more."
"Well, I'll have to run the Nine."
Refrain

Everybody around Sardis said,
"Mr. Carrier, I know you got your way.
Mr. Bailey's 'most too old a man
To run your train like Dave."
Refrain

Last one Monday morning,
It come a shower of rain.
Nine come to Ballentine,
Blowing like a fast train.
Refrain

When the Nine got over to Sardis
With a large load of logs,
Mr. Carrier told the people at the plant,
"Yonder freight off the Yellow Dog."
Refrain

They said to Mr. Carrier,
"Man, ain't you 'shamed,

Looking out the window,
Don't you know your own train?"
Refrain

Mr. Carrier went to Dave Cowart,
"Dave, I done told you so.
Train cost too much,
You can't run my train no more."
Refrain

Mr. Carrier's timber mens quit too.
Thought they all was mad.
They didn't like his paydays,
'Cause he was paying 'em off in brass.
Refrain

Mr. Carrier's timber mens left,
And they thought they was going home.
Stopped down the railroad,
Farming at Malone's.
Refrain

Mr. Carrier went down to Malone's.
He didn't mean no harm.
He didn't know his timber men
Knowed how to farm.
Refrain

Hardly couldn't pay 'em no greenbacks,
Couldn't pay 'em no gold.
Couldn't pay 'em no silver,
All his banks was closed.
Refrain

Mr. Carrier's engine left Sardis then,
She left there mighty hot.
Got down to Malone's Trestle,
Where he could wreck that Seven Spot.
Refrain

Well, they telephoned to Mr. Carrier,
"Don't you think it'd be nice

[To] telephone to Sardis
And get Dr. Rice?"
Refrain

Mr. Carrier said to Dave Cowart,
"Man, ain't you 'shamed?
You done wrecked my Seven Spot.
Done scald the preacher['s] hand."
Refrain

Mr. Carrier said to the conductor—doctor,
"Think you can save his life?"
Conductor [*sic*] says, "He's a lazy man.
He won't hardly die."[259]
Refrain

He wore a mighty fine coat, boys,
Mighty fine shirt.
Rid that train every day.
He didn't never work.
Refrain

I played on Mr. Carrier's railroad,
Sardis, on Main and Beale.
I made dollars down there
[With]out working in the field.
Refrain

Buddy came down to Emma's.
Aunt Emma hollered and screamed.
"Needn't cry, Miss Emma,
Buddy got scalded by the steam."

The full refrain should be "Oh, my honey babe, why don't you come home?," but Hemphill plays the second half on the fiddle. Like Mr. Carrier, Dave Cowart, the other engineer, Pop Bailey, and Dr. Rice are white. The song was composed at the request of a Mr. Willard, a white section foreman on the line, and usually sung for white audiences. Apart from the economic incentives, Hemphill's composition may have been motivated by sympathy with the logging company's workers, many of them no doubt African American. The song implies that Mr. Carrier was insolvent, and paid his workers "in brass" (company-issued tokens in lieu of legal tender) in an effort, apparently unsuccessful, to get them back to work. Hemphill's proud boast that he can make a living as a musician, rather than having to work as a fieldhand for the white man, brings his ballad to a telling (near-)conclusion.

Like all the other ballads written by Hemphill, "The Carrier Railroad" is idiosyncratic, and unrelated to the corpus of traditional disaster songs like "Casey Jones" and those about the *Titanic*. His granddaughter, Jessie Mae Hemphill, recorded an unreleased nine-stanza version of "The Carrier Railroad" for George Mitchell in 1967, and she and her cousin Ada Mae Anderson both recorded fragments of it for David Evans, but it does not seem to have circulated beyond the Hemphill family.

The Train That Left Durham:
The 1911 Hamlet, North Carolina, Train Collision

On July 27, 1911, a special excursion train left Durham for Charlotte, North Carolina. Carrying 912 Black passengers on an outing organized by St. Joseph's African Methodist Episcopal Sunday School, it collided head-on with a freight train in Hamlet. Eight people were killed and sixty—some of whom later died—were seriously hurt.[260] This disaster prompted "The Hamlet Wreck":[261]

> See the women and children going to the train.
> Fare-you-well, my husband, if I never see you again.
> The engineer turned his head
> When he saw so many were dead.
> So many have lost their lives.
>
> *Chorus:*
> Isn't it sad, isn't it sad?
> Excursion left Durham, going to Charlotte, North Carolina,
> Isn't it sad, isn't it sad?
> So many have lost their lives.
>
> Some of us have mothers standing at the train.
> "Farewell-well-well, my daughter, I may never see you again."
> And the train began to fly,
> And some didn't come back alive.
> So many have lost their lives.
>
> The fireman said to the engineer, "We are something late;
> We don't want to meet up with the local freight."
> The local was on the line,

And they could not get there on time.
So many have lost their lives.

When the news got to Durham, some said it was a lie,
But some was in the hospital almost ready to die.
And their poor old mothers, you know,
They were running from door to door.
So many have lost their lives.

Now, colored people, I will tell you to your face,
The train that left Durham was loaded with our race,
And some did not think of dying
When they rode on down the line.
So many have lost their lives.

They put the dead in their coffins and sent them back to town,
And then they were taken to the burying ground.
You could hear the coffin sound
When they let those bodies down.
So many have lost their lives.

The song was published as a broadside by the Reformer Publishing Company, a Black-owned printing firm in Durham, with authorship credited to Franklin Williams and William Firkins, who were employees of the Liggett and Myers Tobacco Company. There seems no reason to doubt this attribution, although Frank C. Brown does so, suggesting that it "grew up in the tobacco factory, perhaps." The verse structure recalls that of "(Wasn't It Sad) When That Great Ship Went Down," but the Hamlet wreck occurred a year before the sinking, suggesting that this stanza form already existed before any song on the foundering was composed.

God's Riding through the Land:
The 1927 Pittsburgh Gas Tank Explosion

On November 14, 1927, a 1.5-million-cubic-meter gas tank exploded at the Pittsburgh, Pennsylvania, plant of the Equitable Gas Company. The blast demolished a square mile of the city. Twenty-eight people died, several hundred were injured, and thousands were left homeless.[262]

Billed on record as "The Guitar Evangelist," Reverend Edward W. Clayborn recorded "God's Riding through the Land" (Vocalion 1162) in Chicago on January 21, 1928.[263] A spoken passage ("Nineteen hundred twenty-seven, fourteenth day of November, God rode through Pittsburgh, over on the north side") gives the exact place and date of the disaster, and attributes it to divine intervention, but surprisingly does not specify its nature. A native of Alabama, Clayborn (prob. 1885–1978)[264] had moved to Pittsburgh by 1918, and lived there for the rest of his life.

A Building That Never Gives Way: A Sermon

When it comes to natural and accidental disasters, Reverend J. M. Gates is to topical sermons what Lonnie Johnson is to topical blues. On February 20, 1928, in Atlanta, Gates recorded "A Building That Never Gives Way" (Victor 21414), a sermon constructed around the spiritual "I'm Working on a Building," which discusses two different incidents: a building collapse in Atlanta, and an explosion in the Mossboro mine near Helena, Alabama.[265] The sermon provides scanty information on the two incidents, and the moral he draws is the consequence of mankind's indifference to God. The building that has collapsed and the explosion in the mine are examples of *earthly* structures, where the workers took instructions from bossmen. But Gates maintains that people should keep working on the *heavenly* building, and that God needs workers, not bossmen, to work on God's building that never gives way.

When the Arcade Building Went Down:
The 1930 Knoxville Arcade Building Fire

The fire which broke out at the Arcade Building in Knoxville, Tennessee, in the small hours of March 20, 1930, killed four people, all of them white. The first press accounts appeared the same day.[266]

Built around 1910, the Arcade Building "was a modest two-story brick building on Union between Market and Walnut" that housed several businesses, including a barbers' supply store run by Carl Melcher, a 59-year-old German immigrant who spoke little English, but had a reputation as an expert mechanic and the best razor grinder in town. More disturbingly, he was also an enthusiastic fire watcher, who would follow the sound of sirens to a blaze, even at night. At about 2:00 a.m., a loud explosion was heard and the whole block was soon on fire. The Fire Department arrived swiftly, and all the people living on the Arcade Building's second floor made it to safety, apart from Sylvester Wilkerson, a retired army recruiter, his wife, and stepson, and Carl Melcher. The latter's scorched hands and charred face—and the fact that he had taken delivery of a fifty-five-gallon drum of gasoline the day before the fire—encouraged suspicion that he had been guilty of arson. However, an autopsy established that he had died of shock (physiological, not electric), and the barrel of gasoline was found intact in the rubble. An inquiry cleared Melcher of starting the fire.

Leola Manning recorded her composition, "The Arcade Building Moan" (Vocalion 1492), two weeks after the tragedy, on April 4, 1930. It was released on June 15. The session took place at WNOX Studios in the St. James Hotel on Wall Avenue in Knoxville.[267]

> It was on one Thursday morning, March, the twentieth day.
> I think it was about two a.m., I believe I can firmly say.
> The women and their children was screaming and crying.
> Not only that, they was slowly dying.
> Oh, listen, listen how the bells did ring
> When the Arcade Building burned down.
>
> I want you to listen, listen how the bells was ringing,
> When the people fell to the ground.
> They jumped through the windows, ran down the stairways and out
>   the doors.
> They was looking for safety or they could not live no more.
> Oh, it was sad, sad, oh, how sad
> When the Arcade Building burned down.
>
> The brave heroic firemen, they could not go home to eat.
> The Salvation women with coffees and cakes kept them up on their feet.
> But the Lord saved Clyde Davis, death was so nigh,
> Carl Melcher and his wife was separated by the fire.
> Oh, listen, listen how the bells did ring
> When the Arcade Building burned down.
>
> *Spoken:* Play it. Oh, it was sad that morning. Several people lost their
>   lives when the Arcade Building burned down. What a moan in
>   Knoxville!
>
> They jumped through the windows, ran down the stairways and out
>   the door.
> They were looking for safety or they could not live no more.
> Oh, it was sad, sad, oh, how sad
> When the Arcade Building burned down.

Born in Chattanooga, Tennessee, on September 10, 1902 (Social Security Death Index) or 1903 (grave marker), Leola Ramey was the daughter of Bishop M. L. and "Mama" Ramey. She married Will Manning in 1918, but they divorced in the 1930s, and she married her guitarist on records, Eugene Ballinger. Leola Ballinger spent the rest of her life as a street evangelist, and died on February 1, 1995. Eugene Ballinger, born in 1902, had preceded her in death in 1975.

The song's accurate description—drawing on a combination of newspaper reports and personal recollections—mentions Clyde Davis, one of the eight injured survivors, and Carl Melcher, whom Manning implicitly acquits of fire-raising. Manning's compassionate vocal delivery, and her lyrics, which are narrative and only mention God in passing, contrast strongly with her motive for writing the song. Her daughter recalled Manning "telling her that she was troubled about the state of her city when she made the St. James recordings," and that she "believed God was angry with the people because so much was going on."[268] Immediately after "The Arcade Building Moan," Manning recorded "Satan is Busy in Knoxville."

Stockyard Fire Blues: The 1934 Chicago Stockyard Fire

On Saturday, May 19, 1934, a serious fire began in the Chicago Union Stock Yards & Transit Company complex ("The Yards").[269] It broke out in the cattle pens near 43rd and Morgan streets shortly after 4:00 p.m., and was probably started by a cigarette butt thrown from an automobile on the 43rd Street viaduct. The hay in the pens below ignited, and a moderate wind blew the fire northeast. It headed to the stockyards on Chicago's southwest side, skirted the Swift and Armour companies' packing plants, and spread to the huge Livestock Exchange. The Dexter Pavilion, the Stockyards Inn, the Saddle and Sirloin Club, the Department of Agriculture Building, two banks, and a radio station were destroyed, and three blocks of houses on Halstead Street were alight before three thousand firemen managed to extinguish the fire. The blaze (the worst since the 1871 Chicago Fire) occurred on a Saturday, so the death toll was low: a watchman died, three people went missing, and twenty-five were admitted to hospital. Twelve hundred people were made homeless, and there was $6 to $8 million in property damage.

"Stockyard Fire" (Bluebird BB B5812), recorded by Tampa Red (1904–1981)[270] in Chicago on October 27, 1934, makes it clear that more than five months after the disaster its economic effects were still very serious, with meat prices rising dramatically. Accompanied by Henry "45" Scott on piano, Tampa Red creates beautifully coherent lyrics, and in the final verse he even suggests a solution to the problem, although it would have needed a repeal of the law of supply and demand:[271]

> Big trouble in the meathouse and it's all about that stockyard fire (x2)
> All of the poor people kicking, because meat is going up so higher.
>
> Let me tell you, people, what that old stockyard fire will do (x2)
> It will have you eating one and it will have you skipping two.

That old stockyard fire left people in misery,
That stockyard fire left people in misery,
It's got 'em setting wondering, "Lord, what will the end be?"

Spoken: Play it, "45," play it for me.

That old stockyard fire sure did raise some sand (x2)
Lord, it's got so many people eating out of the garbage can.

Now, if the stockyard dealers could read these poor people's mind,
If the stockyard dealers could read these poor people's mind,
They would drop meat more lower and avoid worser troubling time.

The plight of Chicago's poor is the consistent focus here. The warning of "worser troubling time" if prices are not lowered is ambiguous. Is Tampa just predicting harder times for the poor, or is he hinting that they may take direct action if there is no change?

Silicosis Blues: The 1936 Hawk's Nest Tunnel Disaster

Silicosis was an occupational disease resulting from the inhalation of silica dust, which caused fibrosis of the lungs, leading to breathing difficulties that were often fatal. In the absence of protective measures, it became particularly widespread in mining and quarrying areas of the Carolinas, Virginia, West Virginia, Kentucky, Tennessee, and Alabama.

"Silicosis Is Killin' Me" (ARC 6-05-51) was recorded by Joshua White (1914–1969) in New York City on February 26, 1936, and released with a pseudonymous credit to Pinewood Tom.[272]

I says, silicosis, you made a mighty bad break on me,
Oh, silicosis, made a mighty bad break on me,
You robbed me of my youth and health, all you brought poor me was
    grief.

Now, silicosis, you a dirty robber and a thief,
Oh, silicosis, dirty robber and a thief,
You robbed me of my right to live and all you brought poor me was
    grief.

I was there digging that tunnel for six bits a day (x2)
Didn't know I was digging my own grave, silicosis eat my lungs away.

I says, mama, mama, mama, cool my fevered head,
I says, mama, mama, come and cool my fevered head,
I'm gonna meet my Jesus, God knows I'll soon be dead.

Six bits I got for digging, digging that tunnel hole (x2)
Take me away from my baby, it sure done wrecked my soul.

Now, tell all my buddies, tell all my friends you see (x2)
I'm going 'way up yonder, please don't weep for me.

At first sight, "Silicosis Is Killin' Me" does not seem to relate to a specific event, and it may be wondered whether it is a topical song. However, it was composed at the peak of a national controversy over silicosis in the wake of the Hawk's Nest Tunnel disaster at the confluence of the New and Kanawha Rivers in Fayette County, West Virginia.[273] America's worst industrial disaster—and long drawn-out, unlike most disasters—this tragedy affected 3,000 men, three-quarters of them Black migrant workers. Estimates of the death toll from silicosis between 1930 and 1935 range from 476 to 764, and the true total may have been higher. The afflicted men had been employed by the Rinehart & Dennis Company of Charlottesville, Virginia, to excavate "a three-mile hole through a sandstone mountain near the town of Gauley Bridge for the Union Carbide and Carbon Corporation" from June 1930 to 1933.[274]

The scandal broke in *New Masses*—the Marxist magazine associated with the Communist Party—and in other publications in January 1935, and reached the mainstream press in January 1936, when the House of Representatives began to conduct a hearing.[275] "Silicosis Is Killin' Me" was likely inspired generally by the press coverage, and specifically by the hearings that had begun the previous month. With its flip side "No More Ball and Chain," discussed below, ARC 6–05–51 is the first record to comment on and protest about disasters whose impact was differentiated by race and racism. White continued in this protest vein for the remainder of his career.[276]

There are, of course, songs about earlier disasters (such as the *Titanic*) with a racial component, but White's recordings introduce race as a major element, albeit not explicitly. The only two songs recorded at a session apparently arranged with them specifically in mind, they are clearly topical, even though White does not mention names and places. He probably avoided doing so because the prospect of controversy with Union Carbide might have deterred ARC from releasing the record.

There are no composer credits on the disc's labels, and no copyright registrations for either song at the Library of Congress, ASCAP, or BMI. Elijah Wald attributes "Silicosis Is Killin' Me" to the white composer and recording artist

Bob Miller,[277] whom White could easily have met in New York City's left-wing circles. If Miller composed the silicosis song, White's collaboration with him would represent an interesting and overlooked precedent, as historically and musically important as the interaction between Alan Lomax and Huddie "Lead Belly" Ledbetter.

Miller claimed to have composed thousands of songs, but he probably only copyrighted those he thought would be profitable. If he wrote or co-wrote the two Josh White songs, then he would almost certainly have copyrighted them. In the absence of definite evidence, my belief is that White composed the songs, having proposed to Miller that he record songs on these topics, and that Miller encouraged White to compose them. Miller may have been the session A&R man,[278] in which case he may well have contributed some ideas or added polish to the songs.

No More Ball and Chain: The 1936 Scottsboro, Alabama, Truck Fire
"No More Ball and Chain"[279] (see fig. 2.06) is unambiguously topical. Its subject is a tragedy that occurred in Scottsboro, Alabama, on January 31, 1936. A truck carrying Black convicts from a prison camp, eleven miles south of Scottsboro, to a rock crusher operating on Lee Highway, several miles north of the town, caught fire when a gasoline container inside the vehicle exploded.[280]

> Twenty souls done gone home to meet their God (x2)
> From that fiery van gone home to meet their God.
>
> They were trapped behind a locked door of a motor cage,
> Trapped behind a locked door, door of a motor cage,
> And they were burnt to a frazzle, Lord, while that hellfire raged.
>
> Mighty cold outside, North wind, he moaned and cried (x2)
> While inside twenty poor boys, Lord, in agony died, yes, Lord, died.
>
> No more ball and chain to carry on their weary feet,
> Hallelujah, sitting by God's mercy seat.
> I says, no more ball and chain, caused a lot of pain.
> No more ball and chain and no worries again.
> Singing hallelujah, sitting by God's mercy seat.
>
> *Repeat stanza 1*
>
> *Repeat stanza 4 with slight variations*

Figure 2.06. Pinewood Tom (Josh White)'s "No More Ball and Chain" Perfect Records ad. Cary Ginell collection; used with permission

The Scottsboro tragedy was reported in the *New York Times* and in major Black newspapers including the *Pittsburgh Courier*, the *Chicago Defender*, and the *Baltimore Afro-American*. The *Times* treated it as an accident, reporting that the explosion of one of the two gasoline cans being transported by the guards was caused by a convict, who lit a piece of paper to warm his hands.[281] On February 5, the local coroner ruled that the deaths were accidental.[282]

In contrast, the Black weeklies' coverage mixed skepticism, suspicion, and allegations. They framed the fire as a racial incident, and conflated it with the then-current, fiercely controversial case of the "Scottsboro Boys."[283] The *Courier*, dedicating a banner headline to the disaster, wrote of the white guards' "belated effort to release the men" and of a "mysterious fire" that had occurred in "the seething, bloodthirsty town . . . steeped in prejudice and infamous for its persecution of the Scottsboro boys." Ultimately, however, the paper accepted that the fire had been accidental.[284]

The most accusatory newspaper was the *Chicago Defender*, which maintained that the temperature outside had been "five below zero" instead of the more frequently reported "five above zero," and reported that a witness had stated that "the explosion was the result of a careless tossing of a cigaret [*sic*] through the steel cage of the truck by one of the white guards." The *Defender's* staff correspondent also wrote that the convicts' "cries went unheeded as the guards stood by" and that one of the guards commented that "[i]t was a pitiful sight seeing the n----rs burn up . . . , but they were bad, so they're better off in hell."[285] There was no mention of a convict's alleged carelessness having caused the fire. The *Baltimore Afro-American* did not cover the event fully, reporting instead on a prison cage similar to that in which the convicts were transported.[286]

The song is subtly accusatory, implying that the white driver and guards on the truck did not try to save the inmates. In fact, the two convicts who survived were rescued by the two guards. By February 8, the guards and a roads supervisor had been suspended by the Governor of Alabama pending an investigation for criminal negligence. By February 21, $23,200 in compensation had been paid to the dead men's families.[287]

For want of conclusive evidence as to who composed the song, the same remarks made for "Silicosis Is Killin' Me" apply. White recorded "No More Ball and Chain" again later in his career,[288] but it doesn't seem to have been a feature of his concert performances.

Somebody Died, Babe: The 1879 Asheville Junction Cave-In

In addition to several hundred Black convict laborers who died of diseases (about four hundred of pneumonia), in accidents, or killed by the guards who forced them to work at gunpoint, on March 13, 1879, twenty inmates and a warder were crushed to death in the cave-in of the Swannanoa Tunnel, the longest of six railroad tunnels that were dug and completed between 1875 and 1892 east of Asheville, North Carolina. Recorded by white local amateur singers since the 1910s, "Swannanoa Tunnel" is a popular hammer song (a work song associated with the building of railroads). It is a localized variant of the song commonly known as "This Old Hammer" or "Take This Hammer."[289] In time, as these song types originated from forced labor under cruel conditions, they became paradigmatic for oppression and resilience.

On an unspecified day in November 1939—the month before folklorist Frank C. Brown recorded Duke University employee Will "Shorty" Love's "God Moved on the Waters" for the Library of Congress in Durham, North

Carolina—Brown also collected Love's "Asheville Junction" (AFS 8792-A-1), now known to be the only African American recording commemorating the cave-in of the Swannanoa Tunnel.[290]

> Asheville Junction,
> Swannanoa Tunnel,
> All caved in, babe,
> All caved in.
>
> Last December,
> I remember.
> Wind blowed cold, babe,
> Wind blowed cold.
>
> When you hear my
> Watchdog howling,
> Somebody's 'round, babe,
> Somebody's 'round.
>
> When you hear that
> Hoot owl squawling,
> Somebody's died
> Somebody's dead.
>
> I'm going back to
> Swannanoa Tunnel,
> That's my home, babe,
> That's my home.
>
> Hammer falling
> From my shoulders,
> All day long, babe,
> All day long.

In this and the other early songs at the beginning of the miscellaneous chapter, the disaster seems to be incidental or one topic among many in the song. The songs seem to describe life and work in various environments (riverboat, convict work gang, work in the mines, levee camps, and so on) and occasionally mention disasters that occurred in these environments. It is not until "Casey Jones," "Titanic," and some early hurricane songs that Black singers/composers begin to create whole songs around a disaster.

CONCLUSION

To sum up, "one-off" African American religious and secular songs about accidental disasters seem to paint a less vivid and systematic picture than do isolated songs dealing with natural disasters. This may be due to a less pervasive perception of memory as "commemoration" and "remembrance." Some of them consider events mainly brought about by or affecting the white population, such as the Arcade Building fire, or the Pittsburgh explosion, both of which prompted the customary religious warnings. Others, such as "The Carrier Railroad" by Sid Hemphill, were written, and mostly performed, for white people. However, Hemphill did include stanzas about African Americans' precarious social and economic conditions. As with some natural disasters, most of the human-caused catastrophes memorialized in song seem to have had only local resonance. A communal rather than personal perspective prevails in Tampa Red's recording about the stockyard fire and in the song about the Hamlet train wreck.

Chapter Three

INFESTATIONS, PANDEMICS, EPIDEMICS, AND DISEASES

HE HAD HIS FAMILY THERE: THE BOLL WEEVIL INFESTATION[1]

Introduction

Between them, the sinking of the *Titanic* and the boll weevil infestation contribute the largest number of disaster songs in American folk and popular music. Unlike songs about the *Titanic*, however, those about the boll weevil lack narrative content, because of the protracted nature of the event. Most boll weevil songs draw on the same pool of stanzas, so only formal and musical typologies can be constructed, rather than textual ones. The body of songs can only be differentiated by considering the range of themes and making a tentative state-by-state subdivision. The boll weevil did most damage from the early 1900s; the lack of close overlap of the historical event with the recordings dealing with it makes it difficult to deduce how the boll weevil's chronological and geographical path across America links to the songs that describe its impact. Still, the cultural importance of such a vast and diverse corpus of songs is undeniable. The origins of some recordings, especially by musicians from Texas, Louisiana, and the Mississippi Delta, can easily be traced to verses sung by professional and amateur Southern musicians from the 1890s onward.

Historical Background

Anthonomus grandis, the parasite that became known as the boll weevil, had been present in Mexican cotton fields long before it was discovered in American cotton by laborers in Corpus Christi, Texas, in the early 1890s, and formally identified by the United States Department of Agriculture in 1894. In Texas, it appears to have lived for many years in a related plant, *Cienfuegosia drummondii*, before opportunistically spreading to commercially grown cotton.[2]

For about a decade the boll weevil remained local to southeastern Texas. Despite affecting fewer than half of the state's counties, it destroyed 19 percent of the Texan cotton crop in 1903. In the 1890s, some counties were already reporting the loss of 70 percent of their crops. When the quarter-inch-long insect began to extend its habitat north and east through the Cotton Belt, it moved at between 40 and 120 miles a year. The bug arrived in Louisiana in 1903, and by the end of 1907 it had invaded Oklahoma, Mississippi, and Arkansas. It entered the Mississippi Delta in 1909, southwestern Alabama the following year, Missouri and Kentucky in 1913, Tennessee and Georgia in 1914, South Carolina in 1917, North Carolina in 1919, and Virginia in 1922.

In Mississippi, the pest caused very large losses, above all from 1913 to 1917, and 1919 to 1923; in Alabama the most severe damage occurred in 1916–17, and again from 1919 to 1923; in Georgia the greatest destruction was exacted in 1920 to 1923, the worst year being 1921, when 45 percent of the crop was lost.

According to approximate but reliable calculations made at the end of the twentieth century, tens of billions of pounds of cotton were destroyed, with a value of nearly $1 trillion in 2000. The destructive process would begin between June and July, after the males had awakened from their diapausal (dormant) state. As soon as cotton plants started to appear, weevils were attracted to them, feeding on their terminal parts and leaves for up to seven days. After mating, female weevils sought out cotton squares (the vernacular name for the bud of the cotton plant and the three bracts enclosing it),[3] in which they laid their eggs, sealing the hole with yellow wax. Efforts to control the bug only began to have much success in the 1960s, thanks to a combination of pheromone trapping and the careful application of insecticides in the fall, to limit the number of overwintering weevils. By 2009 the weevil was eradicated except in Texas, where cross-border infection from Mexican farms poses a continuing threat.

Early Boll Weevil Songs

The boll weevil ballad originated soon after the pest started to ravage Texas. The earliest example was collected there by folklorist Gates Thomas in 1906; he had heard verses two, three, and four as early as 1897, from a group of Black singers working on his father's plantation in Winchester, Fayette County.[4]

> Have you heard the lates', the lates' all yo' own,
> It's all about them weevils gonna make yo' fa'm their home.
> Gonna make it their home, Babe, gonna make it their home.

The boll-weevil says to the sharp-shooter,[5] "Pardner, let us go,
And when we strike that cotton patch, we'll take it row by row;
For it's our home, Babe, for it's our home."

The first time I seen him he wuz settin' on a square;
Well, the next time I seen him he wuz a-crawlin' everywhere,
Just a-huntin' him a home, Babe, just a-huntin' him a home.

The boll-weevil sez to the farmer, "I ain't bothered a bit;
So when you plant that cotton, be sure you plant it thick;
For it's my home, Babe, for it's my home."

The sharp-shooter sez to the boll-weevil, "You ain't treatin' me fair;
For since I seen you last time, you've scattered everywhere.
Done found you a home, Babe, done found you a home."

The farmer sez to his ole wife, "We are in a terrible fix:
Foolin' with the weevils gonna keep us in the sticks,
Without a home, Babe, without a home."

The ole wife sez to her husban', "I done my level bes'
Workin' with them weevils, and I ain't got but one dress.
It's full of holes, Babe, it's full of holes."

The farmer sez to his ole wife, "Well, what do you think of that?
I found a little boll-weevil right in my Sunday hat;
Done found him a home, Babe, done found him a home."

The farmer said to the merchant, "It is the general talk;
The boll-weevil's et all the cotton, and left us leaves and stalk.
We've got no home, babe, we've got no home."

The merchant sez to the farmer, "What do you think of that?
Ef you ketch all them boll-weevils, make you present of a Stetson hat.
You'll have a home then, you'll have a home."

The boll-weevil sez to the sharp-shooter, "Pardner, what of that?
They say ef the farmer ketches us, gwain to give him a Stetson hat.
He'll have a time, Babe, he'll have a time."

So they took the little boll-weevil and they put him on the ice.
He sez to the farmer, "I say, but ain't this nice!
But it ain't my home, though; no, it ain't my home."

Then they took the little boll-weevil and buried him in hot sand.
He sez to the farmers, "Well, and I'll stand it like a man,
Though it ain't my home, Babe; no, it ain't my home."

The farmer said to the merchant, "I didn't make but one bale,
But befo' I'd bring that bale in, I'd fight you and go to jail;
For I've got to have a home, Babe, I've got to have a home!"

The boll-weevil sez to the farmer, "What make yo' neck so red?"[6]
"Tryin' to beat you devils; it's a wonder I ain't dead;
For you're takin' my home, Babe, just a-takin' my home!"

"Well, ef you want to kill us, I'll sho-God tell yo' how:
Just bundle up yo' cotton sack and th'ow away yo' plow;
Then hunt yo' a home, Babe, then hunt yo' a home."

Subsequent printed versions vary considerably in length and content, but most of them use the two-line rhymed stanza typical of ballads, and they almost invariably include the "looking for a home" refrain or a variant, which is the ballad's focal point. Its implicit theme is Black people's identification of themselves with the insect. Its apparent indestructibility symbolizes endurance in the face of racism and poverty, and its progress through the Cotton Belt is emblematic of hope for a better life through migration. The irony that African American migration was often enforced by the need to find work is also left implicit. Singers spread the news of the boll weevil, sometimes even before it had reached the location where they were singing, and changed the lyrics according to the pest's local impact. They painted accurate and truthful pictures of what was going on, and unconsciously served as repositories of historical memory.

W. C. Handy claimed to have heard the song as early as 1902,[7] and a few years later, John Lomax heard a blind Black man singing "Boll Weevil" in Hearne, Texas.[8] The first scholarly work on boll weevil songs was done by a member of the Lomax family. The Archive of Folk Song at the Library of Congress holds a fourteen-page typewritten article titled "Brer Boll Weevil" by B. B. Lomax (Bess Brown Lomax, John Lomax's first wife). It is annotated "Published in a Sunday issue of *New York World* about 1914, University Station, Austin, Tex.," and is almost certainly a version of the paper read by Mrs. Lomax at the inaugural meeting of the Texas Folklore Society on April 8, 1911.[9] The article paints an interesting early picture of what it calls the "Great Pest" and the songs it inspired, and prints five of the most recurrent stanzas.

Over the years, and with input from Lead Belly after 1933, John A. and Alan Lomax created a composite boll weevil song from what they regarded as the best verses and musical elements obtained from Lead Belly and others. This hodge-podge was often published in songbooks, collections, and liner notes, and became very influential on folk revivalists.[10] According to the Lomaxes, Lead Belly (born January 1888) was taught the song in the 1900s by an uncle, Terrell Ledbetter, from west Texas.[11] Whether or not Lead Belly learned it before John Lomax heard it from another source in 1905,[12] it is not easy to single out the version that best represents what he learned from tradition: Lead Belly's first recording of the song, in February 1935 (AFS 135-A), already shows traces of the Lomaxes' intervention. "The Ballit of de Boll Weevil" was included in *American Ballads and Folk Songs*, published in 1934, the year after the Lomaxes met Lead Belly. This text was "largely collected in 1909" by John Lomax; the published version specifies "words from Texas and Mississippi; tune from Texas."[13] Lead Belly's various recordings, all of them shorter than this text, are discussed in the next section.

> Oh, have you heard de lates', de lates' of the songs?
> It's about dem little Boll Weevils, dey's picked up bofe feet and gone
> A-looking for a home, jes a-looking for a home.
>
> De Boll Weevil is a little bug, f'um Mexico, dey say,
> He come to try dis Texas soil en thought he better stay,
> A-looking for a home, jes a-looking for a home.
>
> De n----r say to de Boll Weevil, "Whut makes yo' head so red?"
> "I's been wandering de whole worl' ovah till it's a wonder I ain't dead,
> A-looking for a home, jes a-looking for a home."
>
> First time I saw Mr. Boll Weevil, he wuz on de western plain;
> Next time I saw him, He wuz riding on a Memphis train,
> A-looking for a home, jes a-looking for a home.
>
> De nex' time I saw him, he was running a spinning wheel;
> De nex' time I saw him, he was riding in an automobile,
> A-looking for a home, jes a-looking for a home.
>
> De fus' time I saw de Boll Weevil he wuz setting on de square,
> De nex' time I saw de Boll Weevil he had all his family dere:
> Dey's looking for a home, jes a-looking for a home.

Then the Farmer got angry, sent him up in a balloon;
"Good-by, Mr. Farmer, I'll see you again next June,
A-looking for a home, jes a-looking for a home."

De Farmer took de Boll Weevil an' buried him in hot san';
De Boll Weevil say to the Farmer, "I'll stan' it like a man,
Fur it is my home, it is my home."

Den the Farmer took de Boll Weevil and lef' him on de ice;
Says de Boll Weevil to de Farmer, "Dis is mighty cool an' nice.
Oh, it is my home, it is my home."

Mr. Farmer took little Weevil and put him in Paris Green;[14]
"Thank you, Mr. Farmer; it's the best I ever seen.
It is my home, it's jes my home."

Den de Farmer say to de Merchant, "We's in an awful fix;
De Boll Weevil's et all de cotton up an' lef' us only sticks.
We's got no home, oh, we's got no home."

Den de Merchant say to de Farmer, "Whut do you tink o' dat?
Ef you kin kill de Boll Weevil, I'll give you a bran-new Stetson hat,
A Stetson hat, oh a Stetson hat."

Oh, de Farmer say to de Merchant, "I ain't made but only one bale,
An' befo' I bring yo' dat one, I'll fight an' go to jail,
I'll have a home, I'll have a home."

De Sharpshooter say to de Boll Weevil, "What you doing in dis square?"
An' the Boll Weevil say to de Sharpshooter, "Ise making my home in here,
Here in dis square, here in dis square."

Oh, de Boll Weevil say to de Dutchman, "Jes' poison me ef yo' dare,
An' when yo' come to make yo' crop, I'll punch out every square,
When de sun gits hot, when de sun gits hot."

De Boll Weevil say to de Farmer, "You better lemme alone,
I've et up all yo' cotton, and now I'll begin on de co'n,
I'll have a home, I'll have a home."

Boll Weevil say to de Doctor, "Better po' out all yo' pills,
When I get through wid de Farmer, he cain't pay no doctor's bills.
He'll have no home, he'll have no home."

Boll Weevil say to de Preacher, "You better close yo' ch'ch do',
When I git through wid de Farmer, he cain't pay de Preacher no mo',
Won't have no home, won't have no home."

De Merchant got half de cotton, de Boll Weevil got de rest;
Didn't leave de n----r's wife but one old cotton dress.
And it's full of holes, oh, it's full of holes.

Rubber-tired buggy, decorated hack,
Took dem Boll Weevils to de graveyard, an' ain't going bring 'em back.
Dey gone at las', oh, dey gone at las'.

Ef anybody axes you, who wuz it writ dis song,
Tell 'em 'twuz a dark-skinned n----r wid a pair o' blue duckins on,
A-looking for a home, jes a-looking for a home.

Dorothy Scarborough's *From a Southern Porch* (1919) includes an early transcription of three boll weevil verses. Ten-year-old Thomas Jefferson Randolph, probably a name assigned by Scarborough, sings three of the most common boll weevil stanzas:[15]

I found a little weevil
An' put him on de ice.
I thought dat dat would kill him,
But he said: "Oh, ain't dat nice!
Dis is my home,—Dis is my home!"

I found another little weevil
An' put him in de sand.
I thought dat dat would kill him,
But he stood it like a man,
"Dis is my home,—Dis is my home!"

De farmer said to de merchant,
"Oh, what do you think of dat?
I found a little weevil
In my new Stetson hat,—
Huntin' a home, huntin' a home!"

Scarborough included more transcriptions of the boll weevil song, mainly collected in Texas, in a 1925 collection.[16] Among them are two uncommon stanzas, present in neither Thomas's nor the Lomaxes' texts. The first, which closes the version "given by Louise Garwood, of Houston, Texas," is one of the few (possibly the only) verses that suggests a way to kill the bug without provoking his defiant reply:

> Ef you wanta kill de Boll Weevil, you betta staht in time;
> Use a little sugar an' lots o' turpentine,
> An' he'll be dead, an' he'll be dead.[17]

The second was collected by Mrs. Henry Simpson of Dallas, Texas, from workers on a plantation in the Brazos Bottom:

> "Oh, Wifie!" said Honey, "I don't know where we're at.
> If the Boll Weevil goes on like this, we'll all be busted flat.
> We'll have no home, we'll have no home."

Scarborough adds that, according to Lizzie Coleman, principal of an African American school in Greenville, Mississippi, "*The Boll Weevil* was composed by a man in Merivale." Gates Thomas and the Lomaxes knew versions of the song by ca. 1900, when the pest had not reached Mississippi; this seems to be an example of the common practice of regarding adaptation as the creation of a new song.

Also critical to understanding the evolution of the boll weevil ballad is Carl Sandburg, who included two versions in his popular and influential 1927 collection, *The American Songbag*.[18] Sandburg's decisions about which stanzas to print (he specifies that his first text comes from John A. Lomax's singing) are as significant as the fact of his publishing them.[19] It is worth noting that two verses in the "Boll Weevil Song," the first of Sandburg's texts, are not included in the 1934 Lomax collection:

> De farmer take de boll weevil, an' he put him in de fire.
> De boll weevil say to the farmer: "Here I are, here I are,
> Dis'll be my home, dis'll be my home."
>
> De cap'n say to de missus: "What d' you t'ink o' dat?
> De boll weevil done make a nes' in my bes' Sunday hat,
> Goin' to have a home, goin' to have a home."[20]

Sandburg probably appropriated the second verse from Gates Thomas's collection published the year before; the first appears, somewhat altered, in later versions of the song, demonstrating the enduring influence of *The American Songbag*.

Of "De Ballet of de Boll Weevil," Sandburg reports: "Text and tune . . . are from Texas, Oklahoma, Mississippi, and Alabama; we forego [*sic*] boll weevil blues heard in Nashville, Tennessee, and on Lang Syne Plantation at Fort Motte, South Carolina."[21] The sixth and seventh stanzas of this song (the "doctor" and "preacher" ones) are in the Lomaxes' version above, and are omitted here. The remainder are as follows:

De farmer say to de weevil: "What you doin' on de square?"
De li'l bug say to de farmer: "Got a nice big fambly dere;
Goin' to have a home, goin' to have a home."

Farmer say to de boll weevil: "You's right up on de square."
Boll weevil say to de farmer: "Mah whole fambly's there,
I have a home, I have a home."

Boll weevil say to de lightnin' bug: "Can I get up a trade wid you?
If I was a lightning bug, I'd work the whole night through,
All night long, all night long."

Don't you see dem creepers now have done me wrong?
Boll weevil got my cotton, an' de merchan' got my corn;
What shall I do? I've got de blues.

Boll weevil say to de merchan': "Bettah drink yo' col' lemonade;
W'en I get through wid you, goin' to drag you out o' dat shade,
I have a home, I have a home."

Boll weevil say to de farmer: "You can ride in dat Fohd machine.
But w'en I get through wid yo' cotton, can't buy no gasoline.
Won't have no home, won't have no home."

Boll weevil say to de farmer: "I'm sittin' here on dis gate,
W'en I get through wid de farmer, he's goin' to sell his Cadillac Eight,
I have a home, I have a home."

Boll weevil say to his wife: "Bettah stan' up on yo' feet,
Look way down in Mississippi, at de cotton we'd got to eat,
All night long, all night long."

De farmer say to de merchan': "I want some meat an' meal!"
"Get away f'm here, yo' son-of-a-gun, yo' got boll weevils in yo' fiel',
Goin' to get yo' home, goin' to get yo' home."

Boll weevil say to de farmer, "I wish you all is well!"
Farmer say to de boll weevil: "I wish you wuz in hell!
I'd have a home, I'd have a home."

Some of these stanzas would not survive, but others found favor with singers
both Black and white.

Newman Ivey White's *American Negro Folk-Songs* includes several fragments
of boll weevil songs collected in 1915–16 in Alabama.[22] Scattered among the
usual stanzas are:

I done chopped out my cotton and my new ground corn.
If you don't let me have it, down the road I'm gone.

De fus' time I saw de boll weevil, 't was in Arkansaw;
The next time I saw de boll weevil, he was arguin' wid my father-in-law.

Only the first of these two verses would enter popular tradition. In a version
of "Alabama Bound" heard in Florida and reported from Auburn, Alabama, in
1915–16, White prints two verses dealing with the boll weevil:

A farmer wants some meat and meal;
Merchant says, "Dere nothin' doin', boss,
Boll weevil's in yo' fiel'."
For I'se Alabama bound.

Boll weevil bug de farmers do despise;
Backs way down in de cotton boll,
Yo' jest can see his eyes.[23]

Howard W. Odum of the University of North Carolina sent Robert Winslow
Gordon the words of three songs titled "The Boll Weevil" on July 10, 1929. They
are held in the Gordon Manuscript Collection at the Archive of Folk Song. A
note at the foot of the last text reads: "From J. D. Arthur—Sung to the tune of
'Goo Goo Eyes,'" possibly the first popular song to use the AB + refrain form
in 1901.[24] The lyrics include the "Looking for a Home" refrain. The first song
has eight verses.

Away down in Dixie they're having an awful time,
It's all about the Boll Weevil, he seems to stand the clime.
He's got a home, he's got a home.

After an introductory stanza, it focuses on the farmer's attempts to kill the bug. Minor variations from the earlier Black compositions transcribed above are introduced in four non-consecutive common stock stanzas describing the pest's settlement "on the square" together with his whole family, his being buried in "hot sand," his being laid first in a "red-hot pan" and then "on the ice." In the fifth stanza the boll weevil is reserved the "special treatment" of being "hit with a brick," to which he replies that the farmer is liable to make him sick. The final two verses are:

The farmer says to the boll weevil, "I'll plow you under deep."
The boll weevil says to the farmer, "Right out again I'll creep.
I've got a home, I've got a home."

The farmer says to the boll weevil, "I'll burn you up with fire,"
The boll weevil says to the farmer, "You're a dog-goned liar,
I've got a home, I've got a home."

The final stanza is a variation of one of the two verses in Sandburg's "Boll Weevil Song" that he did not get from John Lomax.

Because of the scarcity of its stanzas and its failure to survive in tradition, the second text collected by Odum is worth printing in full:[25]

The boll weevil says to the farmer, "I'm your bosom friend,
I've raised the price on every bale, that's gone down to the gin.
Since I've had a home, since I've had a home."

The farmer took the boll weevil and laid him on the fence,
And says, "Every leg on you just looks like eighteen cents,
You can have a home, you can have a home."

The farmer says to the boll weevil, "Now I'll let you run,
If you will eat up the other fellow's cotton and just leave mine alone,
You can have a home, you can have a home."

The boll weevil works in the day time, when the sun is shining bright,
And all he fails to get that day, he comes back and gets at night,
He's got a home, he's got a home.

The farmer says to his children, "I'd send you off to schools,
But since the boll weevil struck this land, you'll grow up like durned
    fools,
And stay at home, and stay at home."

The boll weevil says to the farmer, "I'll learn you a little sense;
I'll learn you to raise your own food stuffs, and cut down your expense.
I've got a home, I've got a home."

The boll weevil says to the Georgians, "I'll bet you what I'll do,
I'll have you fellows on the bum in the next year or two,
You'll have no home, you'll have no home."

The boll weevil says to the lawyers, "It's me you cannot sue,
With all your legal talent against me you'll find no clue.
You've got no case, you've got no case."

Some of the six stanzas in the third song Odum sent to Gordon are closely
similar to those in versions above, but it includes:

The boll weevil says to the banker, "You don't know what a panic is,
For when I get located right, I'll paralyze your bis [business],
You'll have no home, you'll have no home."

The boll weevil says to the merchant, "You'll find when debts are due,
That I have cut them out of crop and out of credit too.
They'll have a home, they'll have a home."

Undated fragments of four Black ballads "Told to [WPA] worker by negro cook"
are in a file held by the Reference Department of the Music Division of the
Library of Congress. They were collected by Mary Agnes Davis from McLen-
nan County, Texas, probably ca. 1936.[26] The longest, titled "De Boll Weevil,"
makes use of Black dialect and consists of seven stanzas, with little text that is
not found elsewhere.

The origin of the "looking for a home" phrase (plus variants) and of other
key, uncommon, or particularly significant verses has elicited interesting discussions. Among them is the meaning of the "lightning bug" stanza first transcribed by Ethel Park Richardson and Sigmund Spaeth[27] and the concluding
claim to have composed the song, reported by the Lomaxes and Sandburg.
Most scholars posit a nineteenth-century religious source for the "looking for

a home" refrain, in either spirituals (such as "Swing Low Sweet Chariot" or "Hunting for the Lord") or camp meeting songs. Lead Belly's and other singers' repetition of the phrase in his choruses seems to support this suggestion, but this song has all the features of a secular song in the blues ballad format and the refrain seems to be original to the song.

Consideration of printed sources indicates that the song probably originated among African Americans in Texas, and may have had a single composer. If so, he or she was soon assisted by other workers, concerned about the economic, political, and social changes, notably unwilling migration, caused by the boll weevil.

BOLL WEEVIL RECORDINGS

Introduction

Analysis of the most significant boll weevil recordings requires a brief preliminary study of their stanzaic and melodic forms.

In the early stages of the song's evolution a two-line AB form, with or without a refrain, seems to have been prevalent, although it is probable that other patterns were also used. The three-line blues-ballad and blues song structures (AB + refrain or AAB) started to catch on in the early twentieth century, coexisting and developing. White singers mainly stuck to the ballad format while Black ones often used the blues form. The field holler must have played an important role in the development of the song as well. The "looking for a home" refrain may have been attached to the couplet soon after (rather than at the same time as) the first verses were conceived; if the song is of Black origin, this refrain may have been appended to an AA, AAA, or AB-structured field holler. As will be seen, the "boll weevil here, boll weevil everywhere" phrase was probably a later addition.

Discussion of melodic form inevitably starts with Gates Thomas, who wrote that "'The Boll Weevil' and 'Frankie and Albert' . . . may be sung to the same air,"[28] i.e., to the AB + refrain form. This assertion may be extended to other Black blues-ballads having eight-bar couplets, with a four-bar refrain, such as "Railroad Bill," "Delia," "Stagger Lee," and others. Peter Muir has shown that, despite some variations in melody and chord sequence, "The Ballad of the Boll Weevil" is a twelve-bar composition, belonging to a melodic family which became popular from the mid-1890s, and which is most familiar in the "Frankie" songs, inspired by an 1899 shooting in St. Louis.[29]

Pre–World War II

The first known recording, titled "Boll Weevil," was sung by a person of unknown race named "Martin," probably in Texas (or less likely, Oklahoma) between 1908 and 1910. Sadly, the recording, on cylinder 7 in John A. Lomax's list of cylinders recorded in those years and states, is unplayable.[30]

Some commercial recordings with "Boll Weevil" in their titles were released in the early 1920s, but they are instrumentals or non-topical songs. The earliest African American release was probably "Boll Weevil Blues" (Mel-O-Dee 4259), a piano roll cut by Eubie Blake in New York early in 1921 with composer credits to Cliff Hess (1894–1959).[31] Tim Brymn's Black Devil Orchestra's "The Boll Weevil Blues" (OKeh 8005), also credited to Hess, followed in May.

Also in 1921, white singers Al Bernard and Ernest Hare each recorded a version of "Boll Weevil Blues," by Postal McCurdy and Emabel Palmer; they were followed by Vernon Dalhart, who made three versions in 1924. McCurdy was from Woodruff County, Arkansas;[32] his lyric purports to be the words of a Black farmer, patronizingly presented as happy-go-lucky in prosperity and poverty alike. In November 1924, the Miami Lucky Seven recorded the song for Gennett. The boll weevil is used as to symbolize hard times and/or hard luck in the refrain, "I got the weary, I got the dreary, I got the mean boll weevil blues," but the lyrics are not otherwise relevant to this study.[33]

The first influential African American recording referencing the boll weevil is not about the cotton infestation. Gertrude "Ma" Rainey's composition, "Bo-Weavil Blues" (Paramount 12080), which she recorded in Chicago in mid-December 1923, pegs the exploration of a relationship to a topical subject, as she would again with "Titanic Man Blues" in 1925.[34] Born in Alabama in 1882, Rainey made her home in Columbus, Georgia, and was an itinerant vaudeville singer from the early 1900s. Geographically, her music cannot be described more narrowly than "Southern." However, "Bo-Weavil Blues" is important because it popularized the boll weevil as a subject for future recordings.[35]

> Hey, hey, bo weevil, don't sing them blues no more (x2)
> Bo weevil's here, bo weevil's everywhere you go.[36]
>
> I'm a lone bo weevil, been out a great long time (x2)
> I'm gon' sing these blues to ease a bo weevil's lonesome mind.
>
> I don't want no man to put no sugar in my tea (x2)
> Some of them's so evil, I'm afraid they might poison me.

I went downtown and bought me a hat,
I brought it back home, I laid it on the shelf,
Looked at my bed,
I'm getting tired sleeping by myself.

Rainey's biographer points out this song's key role in the development of boll weevil lore:

> In traditional boll weevil songs, black people identify with the little, apparently defenseless black bug who always defeats the farmer by eating his cotton crop, despite the farmer's attempts to exterminate him. Although the song carries this connotation, and although Ma Rainey apparently sang some traditional verses in live performance, the weevil here is female, a symbol of proud loneliness, apart from its mate, with no mention of the farmer or the cotton.[37]

There is more to Rainey's song than that, but it can only be considered after studying subsequent recordings.

Texas

There are surprisingly few recordings from the state where the infestation began that are related to the version collected by Gates Thomas. The explanation may lie in emigration from Texas in search of work, and musicians adapting the theme to make it relevant to the impact of the boll weevil in their new homes. Guitarist and kazooist Charlie "Dad" Nelson recorded two takes of his "Cotton Field Blues" (Paramount 12401) in Chicago, sometime between September 27 and October 2, 1926.[38] By the time he recorded, Nelson had been a northern resident for some time and was an itinerant musician based in Cleveland. When Mack McCormick interviewed his presumed nephews, Oscar "Preacher" Nelson Jr. and Newton "Horse" Nelson, however, they reported that he had been born in Milam County, Texas, in 1877.[39] Paul Oliver and McCormick state that "'Cottonfield Blues' was a version of 'Boll Weevil Ballet' and probably dated from 1906."[40] This presumably means that they considered it to be a variant of the song collected by Gates Thomas in that year.

Boll weevil, boll weevil, where did you come from? (x2)
"From Beaumont, Texas, from just over yonder farm."

Farmer said, "Boll weevil, don't you know you've done me wrong?"
Farmer said to the boll weevil, "Don't you know you've done me wrong?
Eat up all of my cotton and eat up all my corn."

Says, "I'm going to town, buy a little gasoline,"
Says, "I'm going to town to buy a little gasoline,
These the worst boll weevils, believe, that I ever seen."

An undoubtedly Texan version comes from east Texas singer-guitarist Finous "Flat Foot" Rockmore,[41] who recorded "Boll Weevil" (AFS 3988-A-2) for John and Ruby Lomax in Lufkin on October 7, 1940.[42] This eleven-stanza recording shows a clear Texan origin, sharing many verses with the version collected by Gates Thomas.

Have you heard the latest, latest of our home?
Boll weevil done eat all my cotton, he done started on my corn.
He says, "I've got me a home, boll weevil's home."

Well, the farmer taken the boll weevil, buried him down in ice,
Boll weevil says to the farmer, "I'm a-living me a happy life.
This is my home, boll weevil's home."

Then the farmer taken the boll weevil, buried him down in the sand,
Boll weevil says to the farmer, "I'm gonna stand it like a natural man.
This here's my home, boll weevil's home."

Then the farmer taken the boll weevil, he stopped him up in his flask,
Boll weevil says to the farmer, "I've found my home at last.
This is my home, boll weevil's home."

If you want to kill the boll weevil, farmer, let me tell you how:
Just throw away your cotton sacks and burn up your plow,
And you'll have a home, boll weevil's home.

Well, the farmer says to the merchant, "What do you think of that?
I found the boll weevil setting in my Stetson hat,
Making that his home, boll weevil's home."

Now the first time I seen the boll weevil, he was sitting on a square,
And the next time I seen the rascal, he done moved his family there,
Making that his home, boll weevil's home.

Well, the farmer says to his wife, "I'm in a terrible distress.
Wintertime done caught me here, and I got one old coat and vest,
And it's full of holes, it's full of holes."

Said, I heard her says to her husband, "I'm in the same distress:
Boll weevil done eat all of the cotton, left me one old cotton dress,
And it's full of holes, it's full of holes."

I ain't gonna tell you no story, I ain't gonna tell you no lie,
Farmer, you can't kill the boll weevil, ain't no need to try.
He's got him a home, boll weevil's home.

Farmer said to the merchant, "I didn't make but one bale,
And 'fore you carry my last bale to town, gonna fight you and go to jail.
And make that my home, boll weevil's home."

Rockmore's most striking stanza suggests that the only way to kill the boll
weevil is to give up cotton farming ("throw away your cotton sacks and burn
up your plow"), thereby depriving the weevil of a home. If applied, of course,
this scorched-earth policy would have the same result as the unconditional sur-
render proposed in the penultimate verse. In the last stanza, the Black farmer's
threat to fight the white merchant is also a significant, bold statement.

Oklahoma

The earliest version of the ballad by an Oklahoma-born artist is probably a
manuscript held at the Library of Congress, dated May 9, 1939. "Boll Weevil and
Farmer" is by white folksinger Woody Guthrie (1912–1967), who first recorded
"Boll Weevil Song" (AFS 3409-B-2) for the Library of Congress on March 21,
1940. Since the manuscript predates the recording, its content is given here.[43]

The boll weevil said to the farmer, "I'll swing right on your gate,
When I get through with your cotton, you'll sell that Cadillac Eight.
Gonna get your home, gonna get your home."

The farmer said to the boll weevil, "I see you're on the square."
"Yes, sir," said the boll weevil, "My whole dern family's there!
Gonna get your home, gonna get your home."

Well, the farmer said to the groceryman, "I want some meat and meal."
"Get out of here, you son of a gun, you got boll weevil in your field!
Gonna get your home, gonna get your home."

Well, the farmer said to the banker, "I'd like to cash this check."
"Get away from me, you son of a gun, you got boll weevil in your neck.
Gonna get your home, gonna get your home."

Well, the farmer said to the dry goods man, "I want to get the kids
   some shoes."
"Get away from here, you son of a gun, you got boll weevil in your
   clothes.
Gonna get your home, gonna get your home."

Well, the farmer said to the finance man, "I want to make out a note."
"Get away from here, you son of a gun, you got boll weevil in your coat.
Gonna get your home, gonna get your home."

Well, the boll weevil knocked at my front door, he said, "I've come to eat.
I'm gonna starve you plumb to death and get the shoes right off your feet.
Gonna get your home, gonna get your home."

Well, the farmer said to the President, "What am I gonna do?"
The President said, as he shook his head, "I swear I do not know.
Gonna get your home, gonna get your home."

Guthrie's version begins with traditional verses, but thereafter it reflects his left-wing politics, privileging social and economic issues at the expense of the racial dimension stressed by Black singers, who are, of course, covertly protesting the socioeconomic effects of racism. Guthrie's references to financiers' exploitation of the common people, and the political system's failure to protect them (it is not the boll weevil who is "gonna get your home" in the final stanza), are central to his refocusing of the song as an anti-establishment vehicle. The lyric was written before Guthrie moved to New York City in early 1940, and his rural Oklahoma background informs its style, and some of its content, but its political objectives transcend localism.[44]

Louisiana

The boll weevil arrived in Louisiana in 1903, around the time Lead Belly (born in Caddo Parish, on the border with Texas) learned the song from his west Texan uncle. Most of Lead Belly's boll weevil recordings, made from the mid-1930s to 1948, are slight variations of the version collected by Gates Thomas. This may reflect the influence of the Lomaxes, who introduced Lead Belly to verses they had acquired in the course of collecting. All three shared the wish to create a repertoire of "best" versions, but the motives behind the process—preservation and popularization for the Lomaxes, monetization for Lead Belly—were sometimes incompatible. One of the earliest and most representative of Lead Belly's several recordings is "Boll Weevil" (AFS 135-A), recorded in Wilton, Connecticut, in February 1935.[45]

Talk about the latest, latest of this song.
These devilish boll weevils, they's gonna rob you of a home.
They's looking for a home. (x2)

The first time I seed him, he's sitting on a square.
The next time I seed him he's spreading everywhere.
He's looking for a home. (x2)

Spoken: The farmer took the boll weevil, done everything in the world
he could to him. But every time he was gwine across the field, he could
tell his wife something.

The farmer and his old lady went out across the field.
The farmer said to his old lady: "I've found a lot of meat and meal.
And I'll have a home. (x2)
I'll have a home." (x4)

Spoken: He goes on. He done everything in the world he could to him.

The farmer taken the boll weevil, put him in the sand.
Boll weevil said to the farmer, "You's treating me like a man;
And I'll have a home." (x2)

Farmer taken the boll weevil, put him in the ice.
Boll weevil said to the farmer, "You's treating me mighty nice;
And I'll have a home." (x2)

Old man said to the old lady, "What do you think of that?"
"I got a devilish boll weevil out of my old Stetson hat;
And it's full of holes." (x6)

Old lady said to the old man, "I'm trying my level best
To keep these devilish boll weevils out of my old cotton dress;
And it's full of holes." (x2)

Farmer taken the boll weevil, set him on Paris Green
Boll weevil said to the farmer, "It's the best I ever seen;
And I'll have a home." (x2)

If anybody should ask you, who composed this song,
Tell 'em it was a dark-skinned n----r with a pair of blue duckins on,
He's looking for a home. (x6)

Figure 3.01. "Willie George King, Winnfield, Louisiana, October 15, 1940" (Ruby T. Lomax). Courtesy Prints and Photographs Division, Library of Congress, Washington, DC

There is a clear debt here to "The Ballit of de Boll Weevil," the text published by the Lomaxes in 1934 based on the version collected in 1909. As such, it seems to be a standard version, created in collaboration with the Lomaxes with a view to public performance. This can be inferred from the opening stanzas, and from the spoken explanations, which Lead Belly swiftly developed to communicate his meaning to white audiences. This hypothesis is supported by Lead Belly's subsequent recordings, which vary very little in text, melody, and stanzaic form.[46]

A notable exception is "Boll Weevil Song" (Folkways FA 242), recorded in New York on October 15, 1948.[47] It has no new verses, but before the performance Lead Belly says: "Now down—it's the same girl, what is singing this song for Alan, from Tuscaloosie, Alabama. This is the way they sing 'The Boll Weevil' down there—I 'spect she was the one singing it too." This seems certain to refer to Vera Hall, actually from Livingston, Alabama. Alan Lomax had presented Hall in concert at Columbia University, New York, on May 15, 1948, and recorded her at his apartment during her stay in the city.[48] It seems likely that Lomax introduced Lead Belly to Hall during that visit. His "Boll Weevil

Song" is melodically and structurally very similar to her song about the boll weevil discussed below. After the song, Lead Belly adds: "That's the way they sing it down in Tuscaloosie, Alabama. Sing it in a blues rhythm, you know. [. . . *Sc.* Usually] I sing it the way we would sing it down in Louisiana. But that's the way they sing in Tuscaloosie, Alabama." Lead Belly's comments make it clear that he considers the musical and structural aspects of the song, not its text, distinctively Alabamian. This is confirmed by his omission of the "boll weevil here, boll weevil everywhere" line, which—as discussed below—is a distinctive feature of Alabama singers' texts.

On October 15, 1940, John Lomax recorded an unaccompanied "Boll Weevil" (AFS 3999-B-1) in Winnfield, Louisiana, sung by Willie George Albertine King, a woman whose claim to be 101 years old is belied by her photograph (see fig. 3.01). She said that she had learned the song from a blind man in 1924 in Beaumont, Texas, "and maybe in New York."[49] There are many repeated choruses and stanzas, which are not transcribed here.

> First time I saw boll weevil, I saw him in New York,
> Next time I saw boll weevil, he was climbing up a cotton stalk.
>
> *Refrain:*
> Tell me how long the bullying boll weevil been born.
>
> A farmer went to his merchant, say, "All I want was meat and meal."
> And the merchant say to the farmer, "You got boll weevils in your field."
>
> Boll weevil said to the farmer, "You can turn me in a fold,
> But I'll be here the next following year when your doggone cotton grow."
>
> The boll weevil said to the farmer, "You don't have no right to cry,
> 'Cause when you go to your merchant, the boll weevil's in your field."
>
> And the farmer went in his house and he looked in his wife's hat,
> And the boll weevil said to the farmer, "Right here's my little one's hat."

This unusual version of the boll weevil ballad presents a new refrain in place of the "looking for a home" one, and stanzas, some of them unrhymed, that are not found anywhere else.

Arkansas[50]

In May 1939, John A. Lomax recorded two African American singers at Cummins State Farm in Gould. Irvin "Gar Mouth" Lowry (real name probably

Irwin Lowery) sang "Boll Weevil" (AFS 2672-A-2) at Camp No. 5 on May 20. Two days later, Alf "Chicken Dad" Valentine, an Arkansawyer serving time for murder, sang "Boll Weevil Song" (AFS 2673-B-2) at Camp No. 9.[51] Both songs are typical two-line field hollers without refrain, which stray from the boll weevil theme to become generic love songs. Valentine said that he learned his song "between Helena (Arkansas) and Walnut Corner."[52] Only Lowry's song is transcribed here; Valentine's includes no original verses.

> Mister farmer went to town, he asked for meal [*sic*] and meal,
> The clerk said "Go 'way, mister farmer, boll weevil's in your field."
>
> Mister farmer went back home, went walking 'cross the field,
> Says, "Look at a poor farmer haven't make a pound of seed."[53]
>
> Boll weevil taken a circle way around the moon,
> Says, "I'll be back to see you, mister farmer, the twenty-fifth of June,
> The twenty-fifth of June," says, "I'll be back to see you, mister farmer,
> the twenty-fifth of June."
>
> I was standing on the corner, my baby come riding by,
> She was drinking bottle in bond, drinking bottle in bond,
> The first thing that I done knowed, I was jailhouse bound,
> I was jailhouse bound, Lord, I was jailhouse bound and she wouldn't
> write to me.

The stanza containing the "moon/June" rhyme was a popular variant, especially among Black singers, of the one rhyming "balloon" and "June" that Lomax had collected in 1909. "Moon/June" rapidly became a cliché after "By the Light of the Silvery Moon" was a pop hit in 1909–10, and may have infiltrated the boll weevil songs as a result.

Mississippi

In view of its catastrophic effects on the state, there are surprisingly few recordings from Mississippi about the boll weevil (even including postwar revivals recorded in Chicago), especially in comparison with the considerable number of recordings from Alabama. This may be because the memory of the ravages caused by the boll weevil in Alabama was still vivid among the rural, amateur singers who contributed most of the songs on the insect, whereas the imprints for which mainly professional blues and hillbilly musicians recorded were no longer interested in a relatively outdated and demoralizing topic such as this.

The (mis)spelling of its title may have been intended to evoke Ma Rainey's hit, but Charley Patton's "Mississippi Boweavil Blues" (Paramount 12805), recorded in Richmond, Indiana, on June 14, 1929, is one of the most musically and lyrically original boll weevil songs.[54]

> There's a little boll weevil, she's moving in-a, in the [air], Lordy,
> You can plant your cotton and you won't get a half a cent, Lordy.
>
> Boll weevil, boll weevil, where's your native home, Lordy?
> "A-Louisiana and Texas is where I's bred and born, Lordy."
>
> Well, I saw the boll weevil, Lord, a-circle, Lordy, in the air, Lordy,
> And next time I seed him, Lord, he had his family there, Lordy.
>
> Boll weevil left Texas, Lord, he bid me fare-you-well, Lordy,
> *Spoken:* Where you going now?
> "I'm going down in Mississippi, gonna give Louisiana hell, Lordy."
>
> Boll weevil said [to] the farmer, "I ain't got to treat you fair, Lordy."
> *Spoken:* How is that, boy?
> "Suck all the blossom and leave you a empty square, Lordy."
> And next time I seed you, know you had your family there, Lordy.
>
> Boll weevil and his wife went set out on the hill, Lordy,
> Boll weevil told his wife, "Let's take this forty here, Lordy."
>
> Boll weevil told his wife, said, "I believe I may go north, Lordy."
> *Spoken:* Boy, I'm gon' tell all about it.
> "Let's leave a-Louisiana and go to Arkansas, Lordy."
>
> repeat stanza three
>
> repeat stanza five, slightly varied, with no speech
>
> Boll weevil, boll weevil, where's your native home, Lordy?
> "'Most anywhere they're raising cotton and corn, Lordy."
>
> Boll weevil, boll weevil, oughta treat me fair, Lordy,
> Next time I seed you, you had your family there, Lordy.

Patton's song probably resonated with farmers and sharecroppers of both races, expressing his and their urgent hope for better times elsewhere through verbs of movement, in the same way as his later flood song, "High Water Everywhere Part I." Patton's flickering yet percussive slide guitar and the omission of the "looking for a home" refrain are original treatments of and deviations from the AB ballad format.

On July 23, 1937, Lomax recorded Blind Jesse Harris of Shuqualak, Mississippi, near the border with Alabama. Harris accompanied himself on a defective piano accordion to perform one of the most idiosyncratic versions of the ballad. "Boll Weevil" (AFS 1327-B-1) features the "boll weevil here, boll weevil everywhere" phrase recurrent in several versions by Alabama musicians, and the "native home" line first recorded, but probably not originated, by Charley Patton. Harris sometimes uses the archaic AA song pattern: he begins with a repeated "I'm going away to worry you off my mind," a more pertinent line than it may seem if it encodes migration to escape white control as a farewell to a woman being abandoned.[55]

Boll weevil's here, boll weevil's everywhere (x2)

Boll weevil, boll weevil, where's your native home?
"Way down in Mississippi among the cotton and corn."

John Lomax reports that Harris taught "Boll Weevil Blues" to Vera Hall.[56] Born a slave ca. 1861, he was dead by 1939, when Lomax returned hoping to record him again.[57] Given his age and his repertoire of blues ballads and late nineteenth- and early twentieth-century popular songs, Harris might have been able, if asked, to shed some light on the origins and evolution of old songs like the boll weevil ballad, at least in Sumter County.

On August 15, 1942, Alan Lomax collected one of the catchiest Mississippian recordings in Sledge, Quitman County. Sid Hemphill sings, and his fiddle is prominent, on his band's rendition of "The Boll Weevil" (AFS 6671-A-2).[58]

I'm a-gonna sing you something, latest of my own.
Tell you 'bout the boll weevil, he's trying to take our home,
To take our home, take our home.

Well, the farmer went to the merchant, said, "Merchant, I'll tell you the fact,
I cannot kill a boll weevil, will you give me a Stetson hat?
I'll have a time."

That farmer caught the boll weevil and he rolled him in the sand
And when he's seen that morning, he's acting like a man.
He's having a time.

That farmer went back to the merchant, "Merchant, I'll tell you a cer-
  tainty fact,
That's the way to kill a boll weevil, now give me a cotton sack.
I'll have a time."

Then the farmer went to the merchant, "Merchant, I will have no more.
Ate up all my cotton, he done started on my corn.
Having a time."

That farmer said, "Now, boll weevil, you are doing it wrong
Eating all this cotton and started on this corn.
Having a time."

Then farmer went to the boll weevil, says, "Boll weevil, where in the
  world your home?"
"I stays over in Texas, won't be here very long,
Got to have a time."

That farmer went out in the field one morning, the boll weevil was fly-
  ing in the air,
Went out there the next evening, done moved his family there,
Having a time.

That farmer said, "Boll weevil, what in the world you trying to do?
I'm trying to carry six rows and my children all carrying two.
Having a time."

That farmer said, "Boll weevil, boll weevil, I thought I buried you in the
  sand."
"I'll be back next spring when you spading up your land.
Having a time."

That farmer said, "Boll weevil, how come your head's red?"
"Eating all the farmer's cotton, and he's trying to kill me dead,
But I'm having a time."

Then, the farmer went to the merchant for to get his wife a dress.
"Boll weevil's here now, farmer, and he's sure got the best,
Having a time."

And the farmer went to the merchant then for some dipping and
  chewing.
"Boll weevil's here now, farmer, ain't nothing doing.
You can't have a time."

Well, the farmer went to the merchant then, boys, for to get him a
  bucket of lard,
"Can't get nothing, farmer, the boll weevil got your job.
He having a time."

Repeat stanza 8
Repeat stanza 9

This long song is strikingly different musically from other versions, but Alan Lomax considered its text similar to an early Texan version.[59] Lomax also noted that Hemphill's ballads were played for dancers rather than listeners and were mainly adaptations rather than originals. In fact, they were more likely for listeners, as the wordy texts are obviously meant to be listened to, and all of Hemphill ballads were original except "Boll Weevil." However, the verse about carrying (being responsible for) cotton rows appears to be unique. In April 1847, *The Southern Cultivator* Vol. 5, No. 4 (Augusta, Georgia), included a letter asserting that "Three women will carry two rows, and if first rate women, four will carry three rows. A woman and a small chap will carry a row." Hemphill seems to be saying that so much of the crop has been destroyed by the boll weevil that one man can pick all the usable cotton bolls in six rows, and a child those in two.

Asked by Lomax, "When did you make that up, Sidney?" Hemphill replies, "along—a little further up than the others." On the basis of the dates of the events dealt with in "The Carrier Railroad" and his other ballads, Hemphill's version of "The Boll Weevil" may date back to around 1910. However, during the interview following the recording, one of the musicians states that the song was made in 1905 and another (not Hemphill) agrees. If true, this suggests that Hemphill heard the song from a Texan who had relocated to Mississippi before the boll weevil's arrival there. By his own account, Hemphill "heard a tip of them talking about boll weevils—I was making up songs in them times. I just went out on it." He states firmly, probably because Lomax has asked him a leading question, that he had never heard any other boll weevil song, but as Lomax noted many years later, this seems unlikely.[60]

Twenty-five years passed before another song about the insect was recorded in Mississippi. On September 1, 1967, George Mitchell recorded Joe Callicott (1899–1967) singing "Old Boll Weevil" (Revival RVS 1002 [LP]) in Nesbit.[61]

> Say, you may take boll weevil, bury him in the sand,
> You may take boll weevil, bury him in the sand,
> Says, in a few more days, help you break your land.
>
> The boll weevil wrote a letter to the farmer in the . . . ,
> A boll weevil wrote a letter to the farmer in the North,
> Says, "I'm gon' let the high waters up, and you can't get 'cross."
>
> Says, I seen boll weevil, sitting in a rocking chair,
> Ah, well I seen boll weevil, sitting in a rocking chair,
> Said, the next time I seen him, he have passed me high in the air.
>
> Figuring on the poor farmer's crop, get on another year,
> Figuring on the poor farmer's crop, gon' try to draw another year,
> Gonna let the farmer know, he got the best food here.
>
> I walked down to my merchant, get me a little meat and lard,
> I walked down to my merchant trying to get me a little meat and lard,
> Tell me, "No, no, good partner, boll weevil got you barred."
>
> I went back to my merchant trying to get a little meat and meal (x2)
> Told me, "No, no, good buddy, boll weevil's in your field."
>
> Oh, boll weevil, boll weevil, he's a peculiar man (x2)
> Says, he works in a way . . . farmer can't understand.

The last original line both plays on and contrasts with English hymnodist William Cowper's "God moves in a mysterious way / His wonders to perform," which is recurrent in gospel songs as an expression of man's submission to God's power. Callicott's secular variant expresses an ironic fatalism.

Alabama

Seven recordings about the boll weevil were made by Alabama artists up to 1943—one commercially issued on "race" records, and six collected by folklorists. More than numbers, however, it is their quality and originality that make these recordings important, together with their being among the earliest Black treatments of the subject.

There is no doubt about the Alabama provenance of "Boll Weevil" (Black Patti 8055), which harmonica wizard Burl "Jaybird" Coleman (1896–1950) recorded for a Gennett field unit in Birmingham, Alabama, on August 5, 1927.[62] The performance is built around Coleman's substitution of a harmonica riff for the refrain, and the lyrics are mainly traditional. The second stanza is similar to some of the verses collected by Newman Ivey White in Alabama, and the human characteristics attributed to the boll weevil in the third stanza—strength, manipulative ability, reasoning, and mobility—create a strikingly grotesque image, and act as a reminder of the racial encoding underlying the song. This is one of the few Alabama recordings to omit the "boll weevil here, boll weevil everywhere" cliché.

> Boll weevil, boll weevil, you think you treating me wrong,
> Eat up all of my cotton and you done started on my corn.
>
> Done stopped on my cotton, Lord, found my new-ground corn,
> "If you don't let me have it, down the road I'm gone."
>
> Boll weevil's got muscles, boll weevil's got hands,
> Sometimes they walking and a-talking just like a natural man.
>
> Boll weevil told the farmer, "Needn't plant so hard,
> I'm gonna eat your cotton, you can't plant it in your yard."
>
> Boll weevil was a thing he did not wear no clothes,
> At the end of his cotton patch, taken row by row.
>
> Boll weevil went away, Lord, and left the sand,
> "Now, I'll be back, farmer, soon as you break your land."

Charles Griffin's "Boll Weevil Rag" (AFS 238-B), which he accompanied on guitar at Kilby Prison, Montgomery, Alabama, October 28, 1934, is one of the most developed lyrics about the boll weevil.[63]

> Boll weevil's here, Lord, boll weevil's here, Lord, boll weevil's every-
>   where, Lordy Lordy,
> Boll weevil's here, boll weevil's everywhere.
> You can go to Louisiana, find boll weevil there.

Hey, he's in my cotton patch, in my cotton patch, started on my corn,
Lordy Lordy,
He's in my cotton patch, started on my corn,
He gonna keep on a-cutting, turn me out of my home.

Lordy Lordy, Lordy Lordy, Lordy Lordy, Lord,
Lordy Lordy, Lord, Lordy Lordy, Lord,
I'm getting tired of being treated like a salty dog.

Repeat stanza 1

Lord, the farmer went to the merchant, went to the merchant, cut off a
   meal and meat [*sic*],
Lordy, farmer went to the merchant, cut off a meal and meal [*sic*],
"Go away, farmer, boll weevil's in your field."

Here, weevil, looky here, weevil, where you stay last night?
Lordy, tell me, boll weevil, where'd you stay last night?
Says, "I stayed in the woods, kept your cotton in sight."

Hey, trouble, trouble, trouble, trouble, had it all my days,
Lordy, trouble, trouble, had it all my days,
Now it seems like trouble gon' carry me to my grave.

Lord, they taken boll weevil, taken boll weevil, put him in the ice and
   snow,
Lordy, taken boll weevil, put him in the ice and snow,
You can go up the country, find him everywhere you go.

I seen boll weevil, seen boll weevil, sitting on the square,
Lordy, I seen boll weevil, flying in the air,
Next time I seen boll weevil, sitting on the cotton square.

Now, biting spider, biting spider, crawling on the wall,
Lordy, biting spider crawling on the wall,
Just like a boll weevil, crazy about his alcohol.

Lord, they taken boll weevil, taken boll weevil, sent to the rising sun,
Lordy, taken boll weevil, sent to the rising sun,
Boll weevil cried out "Farmer, what have I done?"

Lord, I woke up this morning, woke up this morning, someone calling me,
Lord, I woke up this morning, someone calling me,
Now, it must be them boll weevils way down in my field.

Oh, get away from my window, away from my window, quit knocking
    on my door,
Lordy, get away from my window, quit knocking on my door,
Boll weevil's here, everywhere I go.

Repeat stanza 3

'Cause the weevil told the farmer, told the farmer, "Don't you plant no
    corn,"
Lordy, weevil told the farmer, "Don't you plant no corn,
'Cause down in your cotton patch sure gon' be my home."

Hey, tell me weevil, [recording defective]
Tell me boll weevil, where's your native home,
Over in Louisiana on my daddy's farm.

Apart from the recurrence of the "boll weevil here, boll weevil everywhere"
line, direct melodic links and textual concordances with "Bo Weavil" Jackson's
recording (analyzed later in the chapter) are apparent. Griffin uses some very
generic stanzas, not all of them related to the boll weevil, but also the "biting
spider" image that only Jackson—at least on the evidence of recordings—had
previously used in a boll weevil song.

Whether or not John A. Lomax prompted the performances, as he often did,
the stylistic diversity of the following three recordings, collected in or near the
small town of Livingston, Alabama (population between 1930 and 1940 about
1,000), attests to the vitality of the theme locally, and more generally, to the
power of oral tradition.

On July 20, 1937, and October 31, 1940, Richard Amerson (1884–1960s) (see
fig. 3.02) recorded two melodically and textually very similar versions of "Boll
Weevil" (AFS 1307-A-1 and AFS 4045-A-1).[64] Neither recording has innovative
lyrics, but Amerson's second version has an interesting opening stanza:

Farmer killed the weevil, he buried him in the sand,
Said, "If I don't kill the weevil, he'll kill the farming man."

Boll weevil played sick, Lord, he goes in the sand,
"I'm gonna watch them farmers heaping up they's land."

Figure 3.02. *"Richard Amerson and John A. Lomax Sr. at the home of Mrs. Ruby Pickens Tartt, Livingston, Alabama, October 27, 1940" (Ruby T. Lomax).* Courtesy Prints and Photographs Division, Library of Congress, Washington, DC

Farmer went to the merchant, "Give me flours and lard,"
Said, "Get off of my counter here, boll weevil got you barred."

He went back to the merchant, "Uh, gimme meal and meat,"
Said, "Get out here, n----r, boll weevil's in your field."

He says, "I'm going to the city, I'm going to buy me some lard,
I believe I'll grease my gatepost, boll weevil's in my yard."[65]

Boll weevil, boll weevil, you gonna let me live,
Done ate all of my cotton, now you in my crib.

This is one of the few recorded versions where the farmer kills the boll weevil, claiming self-defense as a (not unreasonable) justification.

On July 23, 1937, Lomax collected a version from Vera Hall (ca. 1901–1964), who would record two more in 1940 and 1959.[66] The October 31, 1940, rendition, "Boll Weevil Blues" (AFS 4049-B-3), transcribed here, is her best and most representative, and is melodically similar to Jaybird Coleman's recording:

First time I seen the boll weevil, he's sitting on the square.
Next time I seen him, he had his family there.

Boll weevil here, boll weevil everywhere,
They done ate up all the cotton and corn, all but the new-ground
    square.

Well, the farmer asked the merchant for some meat and meal,
Tain't nothing doing, old man, boll weevil's in your field.

Hey, hey, boll weevil, where is your native home?
"Way down in the bottom, among the cotton and corn."

Tennessee

The only prewar song from Tennessee is "Boll Weevil" (OKeh 45346), recorded by white singers W. A. Lindsey and Alvin Conder in Memphis on February 24, 1928.[67] The song is a six-stanza medley of traditional verses which seem mainly to be drawn from Sandburg, including the uncommon "Sunday hat" phrase.

Georgia

The boll weevil arrived in Georgia in late 1914, and its impact on the state generated some powerful responses. The first recording, "Boll Weevil Blues" (Columbia 15016-D), was made in New York on March 7, 1924, by white fiddler Gid Tanner (prob. 1885–1960).[68]

The farmer said to the boll weevil, "You's right up on the square."
Boll weevil said to the farmer, "My whole family's there.
I have a home, I have a home."

You get out your barrel of poison, scatter it upon the row,
Boll weevil said to the farmer, "You scatter your poison, though
I have a home, I have a home."

Gonna eat you up to my cotton stalks, gonna cover the grubs all up,
Boll weevil said to the farmer, "I'll doodle myself right up,
I have a home, I have a home."

Boll weevil said to the lightning bug, "Can I get up a trade with you?
If I was a lightning bug, I'd work the whole night through,
All night long, all night long."

If you don't seem to see them critters now have done me wrong
Boll weevil's got my cotton and the merchant's got my corn,
What shall I do? I've got the blues.

Boll weevil said to the merchant, "Better drink your cold lemonade.
When I get through with you, gwine drag you out of the shade.
I have a home, I have a home."

Boll weevil said to the farmer, "You'll fly [*sic*] a Ford machine.
When I get through with the farmers, can't buy no gasoline."
"What shall I do? Boll weevil blues."

Boll weevil said to the doctor, "You gotta pull out all of them pills,
When I get through with the farmer, can't pay no doctor bills,
I have a home, I have a home."

Boll weevil said to the preacher, "You better close up your tent show.
When I get through with the farmer, can't pay the preacher no more.
I have a home, I have a home."

Boll weevil said to the farmer, "I set you on the gate.
When I get through with the farmer, he'll sell the Cadillac Eight
To have a home, I have a home."

Boll weevil said to his wife, "You got to stand up on your feet,
Look-a-way down here in Georgy, it's the cotton we've got to eat,
All night long, all day too."

The farmer said to the boll weevil, "I wish you was well."
The farmer said to the boll weevil, "I wish you all—hah!
I have a home, I have a home."

The laugh in the penultimate line makes "in hell" perfectly clear by pretending to censor it. Stanzas about the boll weevil advanced as rapidly as the bug itself; the "lightning bug" and "preacher" stanzas would have traveled orally from Texas to Georgia well before Tanner's recording session.

Fiddlin' John Carson's "Dixie Boll Weevil" (OKeh 40095, recorded in Atlanta, late March or early April 1924)[69] is not particularly original, but its last verse is a more pointed version of the "hell" joke:

The boll weevil said to the farmer, "I certainly wish you well,"
The farmer said to the boll weevil, "I wish you was in Griffin, Georgia."
"Yes and you were deep in hell."

Usually, when this couplet occurs, "hell" is either defiantly sung, or omitted for the listener to supply. The joke was probably common in performance, but seldom collected: an example occurs in a boll weevil song collected in 1940, where the dig is at Hope Dale, North Carolina.[70]

African American songs from Georgia about the boll weevil came late to recording. A 1929 sermon by Reverend J. M. Milton described the economic consequences of the infestation in some detail in order to compare the insect to the "wickedness of the world and the sins of man. . . . Like the boll weevil eat up the cotton boll, so sin eats up the life of a good man or a good woman."[71] It was not until 1935, however, that James "Kokomo" Arnold recorded "Bo Weavil Blues" (Decca 7191) in Chicago on April 18.[72] Born in Lovejoy, near Jonesboro, Georgia, in 1896, Arnold had left home in 1919, and led a wandering life before settling in Chicago in 1929; nevertheless, he specifies that his song is about the effect on his native state, and locates himself, as protagonist, there for its duration:

> Boll weevil, come out of my flour barrel. (x2)
> Said, that boll weevil's here, mama, boll weevil's everywhere.
>
> Says, I went to my captain and I asked him for a peck of meal. (x2)
> He said, "Leave here, Kokomo, you got boll weevils in your field."
>
> Now, Mister Weevil, how come your bill's so long? (x2)
> You done eat up all my cotton, started on my youngest corn.
>
> Says, the merchant told the doctor, "Don't sell no more C. C. pills (x2)
> 'Cause the boll weevils down here in Georgy done stopped these cot-
>   ton mills."
>
> Now, Mister Boll Weevil, if you can talk, why don't you tell? (x2)
> Say you got poor Kokomo down here in Georgy catching a lot of hell.

In the last verse, Arnold seems to ask the boll weevil to admit his guilt for the trouble people (of whom he offers himself as an example) are in. The preceding stanza makes a scatological joke: the doctor is advised to stop selling compound cathartic (C.C.) pills, marketed as a remedy for constipation. Either people are so scared by hard times that they have the opposite problem, or they are so poor that they can't afford to buy much food, and are unlikely to suffer from intestinal blockage.

On November 5, 1940, in an Atlanta hotel room, John A. and Ruby T. Lomax recorded twelve-string guitarist Blind Willie McTell (1903–1959) performing "Boll Weevil" (AFS 4070-A-1) for the Library of Congress. McTell was then partway through a commercial recording career that had begun in 1927.[73]

> Boll weevil, boll weevil, where you get your great long bill?
> "I got it from Texas, I got it from the western hills." (x2)
>
> Boll weevil, he told the farmer, says, "Don't you buy no more pills.
> Ain't gonna make enough money to pay your drugstore bill.
> You ain't going to make enough money to even pay your drugstore bill."
>
> Boll weevil, he told the farmer, "Don't you plow no more.
> Ain't gonna make enough flour in your back door.
> You ain't gonna make enough flour to even put in your back door."
>
> Boll weevil, he told the farmer, "Don't buy no Ford machine.
> You ain't going to make enough money to even buy gasoline." (x2)
>
> Boll weevil said to the farmer, "Don't buy no more pills.[74]
> Ain't going to make enough money to even buy your meal.
> Won't make enough money to even buy your meal."
>
> So now, boll weevil, boll weevil, where you say you get your great long
>   bill?
> "I got it from Texas, out in the western hills.
> Way out in the Panhandle,[75] out in the western hills."

A subsidiary part of John A. Lomax's recording activities was the documenting of boll weevil songs; one episode of his ten-part 1941 radio series, *The Ballad Hunter*, was entirely devoted to them.[76] McTell was one informant who consented to sing a boll weevil song, but he depicts an "extraordinarily aggressive," almost impudent insect, and "[s]ince this recording followed immediately upon Lomax's request for 'complaining songs,' it may have been McTell's subtle way of complying without giving the impression of having hard personal feelings."[77]

McTell's song is structurally innovative, converting the ballad (or blues ballad) into a blues by removing the refrain altogether, but employing an unusual ABB form instead of the more common AAB. Textually it is not very innovative, although the inaccurate references to north and west Texas are unique.

The most eloquent Georgian song about the black bug is "Boll Weevil" (AFS 5154-A-1 and AFS 5162-B-1) by guitarist and harmonica player Buster "Buz" Ezell (unknown–prob. late 1950s). It was recorded twice during the period March 6–9, 1941, by John Wesley Work III, during the Fort Valley Music Festival at historically Black Fort Valley State College, near Macon, Georgia.[78] Stanzas repeated at the end of the performance are omitted from this transcription of the more original and better preserved second version:

> Well, the first time I saw boll weevil, he was setting on a cotton square,
> Next time I saw Mister Weevil, he had his whole family there.
> What you reckon he said? "'Bout to kill me dead!"

> He said to all doctors, "Might as well throw away your pills,
> For when I get through with this country, the farmers can't pay their
>   bills:
> They won't have no homes, they won't have no homes."

> "Well, I'm going back to Texas, where I was bred and born,
> Mama, I'm going to leave Georgia, but Georgia ain't none of my home,
> I'm on my way, I'm on my way."

> Boll weevil said to the farmer, "Farmer, I wish you well,"
> Farmer said to the weevil, "Yes, but I wish you dead [in hell],
> Got to leave my home on account of you."

> Well, the weevil says to the farmer, "Why, I'm your bosom friend,
> Ever since I been in this country, cotton brought you thirty-five cents:
> You ought to praise my name, you ought to praise my name."

> Boll weevil says to the farmer, "You must do just as you please.
> But if you don't raise no cotton, I'll eat up all of your peas:
> You'll have to sell your corn for to pay your debts."

> Weevil says to the farmer, "You might think I'm telling a tale,
> But when you come to find out, you'll be arrested and put in jail:
> You can't pay your fine, you can't pay your fine."

> Boll weevil said to high sheriff one day, a-riding in his automobile,
> He said, "When I get through with this cotton field, I'm gonna puncture
> every one of your wheels;
> You're left to ride on the rims, you're left to ride on [the rims]."

Well, the weevil said to the judge, "You can do just as you please,
But when I get through with this country, you'll be crawling on your
   knees,
You're going to be in rags, you're going to be in [rags]."

Ezell's first two stanzas are traditional, but they are followed by a series of highly
original verses. The third expresses wishful thinking by Georgia farmers, putting words into the boll weevil's mouth about leaving Georgia and returning
to Texas. Ezell's verse about thirty-five-cent cotton is unusual in stressing that
income, not crop yield, is what matters to farmers.[79] The boll weevil's concluding
taunts against white authority, in the shape of the high sheriff and the judge,
are striking reminders of African American self-identification with the bug.
Ezell's earlier recording of the song, which has technical faults, includes some
different stanzas, including one where the weevil mockingly tells the farmer
not to lose his mind, because if his "cotton don't take the rust . . . it makes it
better for us."[80]

North Carolina

The birthplace of singer-guitarist James "Bo Weavil" Jackson, who made the
first commercial blues recording about the boll weevil, is not known, but it is
unlikely to be Alabama or Mississippi. Indeed, a fact-based study offers evidence that Jackson came from North Carolina and provides tentative dates of
birth and death (1897–1932).[81] Jackson's "Devil and My Brown Blues" (Vocalion
unissued) is included in this chapter also because talent scout Harry Charles,
who in fact was from Birmingham, Alabama, discovered him while Charles
was operating in North Carolina. "Devil and My Brown Blues" was recorded
in New York on September 30, 1926, at Jackson's second and last session. It
was scheduled for issue on Vocalion 1055, which would have been credited,
like Jackson's other Vocalion recordings, to Sam Butler.[82] Vocalion 1055 was
cancelled, but fortunately a test has survived.[83]

No gypsy woman, no gypsy woman can't fry no meat for me, Lordy
   mama,
No gypsy woman can't fry no meat for me,
I ain't scared, I'm skittish, she might pizen me.

'Cause I woke up this morning, woke up this morning, heard some-
   body calling me, Lordy mama,
Woke up this morning, heard somebody calling me,
Must have been a weevil, thing they call stingaree.

A boll weevil's here, a boll weevil's there, he can bum a ride 'rywhere,
  people tell me that,
Boll weevil's here, boll weevil's everywhere,
I got me a dream last night, it was all in your flour barrel.

The farmer went to the merchant, says, "I want meat and meal," Lordy
  mama,
Farmer went to the merchant, says, "I wants meat and meal,"
The merchant screamed, "Oh, no, the boll weevil's in your field."

Biting spider, biting spider, crawling on the wall, mm-mm,
Biting spider, now, crawling on the wall,
Grinds it natural, but he's crazy about his alcohol.

I heard a mighty rumbling down under the ground, Lordy mama,
Mighty rumbling deep down under the ground,
The boll weevil and the devil was tickling with somebody's brown.

Said he was low and squatty, said he was cut for speed, Lordy mama,
Low and squatty, said he was cut for speed,
Says, he has everything that a poor boll weevil need.

Now boll weevil, now boll weevil, sitting down on the square,
The first time I seed Mister Boll Weevil, sitting down on the square,
Next time I seed him, mama, he had his whole family there.

The weevil told that farmer, "Buy no Ford machine," Lordy mama,
He told the farmer not to buy no Ford machine,
'Cause he's gonna fix it so he can't buy no gasoline.

The singer seems to identify closely with the insect in what was probably his "signature" song. It is a medley of verses from different sources, most of them traditional, but it includes one stanza, and shares the melody, of "Stingaree Blues (A Down Home Blues)," composed by Clinton A. Kemp and recorded ca. November 5, 1921, by vaudeville singer Esther Bigeou.[84] The "boll weevil here, boll weevil everywhere" catchphrase is borrowed from Ma Rainey's hit. Jackson/Butler's fear that a gypsy woman may poison him also echoes a line in Rainey's recording.[85]

Though born in North Carolina, Hugh "Black Bottom" McPhail (1892 or 1894–1961) was long gone by the time he made records. McPhail was living in Ohio by 1917, and later moved to Detroit. However, the singer of "Boll Weavil"

(Vocalion unissued), recorded in Chicago on May 26, 1938,[86] is aware of the insect's impact on the rural South. Vocalion seem to have decided that its blend of traditional and original lines in a twelve-bar blues format was unlikely to sell.

> I went to my merchant; I asked him for some meat and meal,
> Lord, I went to my merchant; I asked him for some meat and meal,
> And he said, "Go away from me, farmer, you've got boll weevils in your
>   field."

> Boll weevil, boll weevil, you know you didn't treat me right. (x2)
> You ate my cotton in the daytime and you ate my corn at night.

> There ain't but the one thing will turn a boll weevil down. (x2)
> That's a sweet potato; it grows way down in the ground.

> Boll weevil told the farmer, "You can ride round in your Ford
>   machine (x2)
> But when I get through with your cotton, you can't buy gasoline."

> Boll weevil took a circle, went all the way 'round the moon (x2)
> And he told all the farmers, "Now, I won't be back till June."

The "sweet potato" stanza is not found in any other boll weevil song. McPhail's other stanzas, or variants of them, are widespread. This is an early appearance of the "moon/June" rhyme found later in field recordings, but it seems likely to have been in circulation well before McPhail's recording session.[87]

Virginia

The boll weevil reached Virginia in late 1922, but the state was not seriously affected until 1929–30.[88] The only issued prewar recording from the state is "Boll Weevil Been Here" (AFS 727-B-1), sung by Willie Williams at the State Penitentiary, Richmond, Virginia, on May 30, 1936.[89]

> Boll weevil's been here, done bored his hole and gone. (x2)
> You can tell by that boll weevil won't be here long.

> *Repeat stanza 1*

> If I could sing like a sea lark in the air,
> I would be like boll weevil, fly from town to town.

Boll weevil here, boll weevil everywhere (x2)
Looked in my meal barrel and boll weevil, he was there.

Boll weevil flew up, he sent a circle 'round the moon (x2)
Said, "Goodbye, farmers, I'll see you another year."

This splendid and relatively original bluesy holler alternates two rhymed traditional stanzas with unrhymed ones. The image of the "sea lark" is unusual, and this is the first recording that refers to "a circle around the moon."

Post–World War II

The boll weevil continued to be a popular theme after World War II, and the ballad spread from folk (blues and old-time music) traditions, entering popular music and becoming well-known outside the USA. Urbanization, commercialization, and cultural diffusion, the latter accelerated particularly by the worldwide spread of rock 'n' roll, meant that the theme lost some of its original folkloric features as it reached an audience very distant from its social, racial, economic, and geographical origins. It is obviously fruitless to look for regionally distinctive features in boll weevil songs adapted by composers, and performed by musicians, who were products of mass society.

The continuing appeal of songs about the boll weevil was fostered by Lead Belly, until his death in 1949, by the white country singer Tex Ritter, and by African American crossover artists Fats Domino and Brook Benton. These artists' recordings, together with some prewar ones, influenced most other postwar versions.

Tex Ritter (1905–1974) was a friend of John A. Lomax, and unsurprisingly, his 1945 hit, "Boll Weevil" (Capitol 40084),[90] uses the text that Lomax collected. Sung in a stereotypical version of Black speech,[91] it features no significant textual innovation and no particular concern for the effect of the infestation on farmers. However, its success made record companies aware of the theme's sales potential. The next decade was a period of transition. Recordings of traditional boll weevil songs, such as those by Lead Belly, Brother John Sellers and Josh White, appeared in parallel with attempts to modernize the theme in order to market it to younger listeners, both Black and white, and particularly to urban teenagers, eager for a music that they could perceive as simultaneously more deep-rooted and more subversive than mass-market easy listening.

"Boll Weevil" (Parkway 104, January 1950) by "Baby Face" Leroy Foster (1923–1958) is the earliest example of the ballad's transformation in Chicago.[92] Backed by two electric guitars, Little Walter's amplified harmonica, and Foster's drumming, the song is reduced to three stanzas, at least partly so that Little

Walter can display his skills. Only a reference to wearing blue duckins in the sign-off verse hints at a rural origin,[93] but the "if anybody asks you" conclusion and the revival of Ma Rainey's opening stanza both link the performance to older sources.

"Boll Weevil" (Vanguard VRS-8005) by Brother John Sellers (1924–1999), recorded in New York on January 22, 1954,[94] derives either from one of the Lomaxes' books or a Lead Belly recording. The LP on which it appears was aimed at the white audience for jazz and "folk blues." Josh White also stuck to the Lead Belly model when he recorded "Boll Weevil" (ABC Paramount LP 124) in New York on April 18, 1956.[95] White's version was recorded as a tribute to Lead Belly, and it adds little either lyrically or musically to his versions.

"Bo Weevil" (Imperial 5375) was composed by Antoine "Fats" Domino (1928–2017) and Dave Bartholomew.[96] Recorded by Domino in New Orleans on October 15, 1955, it was the first post–World War II African American recording related to the boll weevil to be widely heard. It is particularly significant because it eliminates both historical context and racial subtext.

> On Saturday night where I was born down on the farm,
> Guitars plinking and we started drinking till the break of dawn.
> About twelve o'clock everything gets hot; up steps old Jones,
> We started clapping and he started singing this sweet little country song.
>
> Boll weevil, boll weevil, where've you been all day?
> Your mama's been looking,
> Had to stop cooking
> Since you went away.
> Boll weevil, boll weevil, why did you go and stay?
> You'll get a licking[97]
> Sure as I'm sitting
> On this bale of hay.

This "sweet little country song" depicts a lighthearted, racially neutral Arcadia in which the historical boll weevil is irrelevant. Instead of devastating the cotton industry and serving as a stand-in for African Americans "looking for a home," the boll weevil supplies a nickname for a child who has run away from home. This seems unlikely to have been an intentional contrast, in a song designed to appeal to the majority-white pop music market.

Boll weevil songs recorded by Dr. Harry Oster between March 1959 and March 1961, during fieldwork mainly carried out at the Louisiana State Penitentiary, Angola, attest to the simultaneous existence of tradition and innovation. These songs, recorded at a prison where cotton was and is grown, combine awareness of the theme's factual meanings and metaphorical implications with some changes of perspective.[98]

Among them is the four-stanza "Boll Weevil Blues" (Tradition LP 2066), by Memphis-born Robert "Guitar" Welch (1889–1966), recorded on March 21, 1959.[99] Building on the "boll weevil here, boll weevil everywhere" line, it recombines traditional images to contrast the insect's freedom of movement with Welch's inability to travel "down the road" or prevent his woman's unfaithfulness.

Structurally and textually much more original, the "Boll Weevil Blues" that Oster collected from Monroe, Louisiana, native Otis Webster (1919–1992) on November 12, 1960, is a sharecropper's lament.[100]

> I met the boll weevil out in the field,
> He asked me for a natural meal,
> He looked at my cotton, he looked at my bloom;
> He made me a home but he didn't skip soon.
>
> *Chorus 1*
> Well, the boll weevil coming,
> Yon the boll weevil coming,
> Yes, the boll weevil coming,
> Him and his family too.
>
> Well, the boll weevil told me I didn't have to pull my cotton,
> He had a way of picking, didn't have no nothing,
> He walked in the square, he hid his head,
> He said, "The cotton, man, am 'most dead.
>
> *Chorus 2*
> I ain't gonna poison,
> Ain't no need of you to poison (x2)
> Because it won't do me no good."
>
> Well, the boll weevil he's smart as a bee,
> He know how to eat, but he never get me,
> He look at his family, begin to laugh,
> He said, "A foolish man trying to poison my [ass]."
>
> *Chorus 3*
> You know the boll weevil blues,
> I got the boll weevil blues (x2)
> Picking my cotton and . . .

Spoken:

Yes, I went out there, you know, with my poison gun, I shot at the boll
weevil, and that scoundrel got up and run. He said, "You's a fool [to]
think you gonna give me something to eat, I don't eat a thing, I just
punch in your squares."

Chorus 4

Because I'm on there,
I'm on there,
Well, it's on there,
He's a-punching at all of my squares.

Well, I went up my bossman's for settlement,
He said, "You didn't have nothing, the boll weevil's got your rent."
I looked at the bossman, begin to laugh,
He say, "Son, you better leave town, [or] make you some cotton fast."

I looked at my bossman, looked so funny,
He say, "You got goobers, you got no money."
I looked at the bossman one more time,
He say, "You gotta make another crop and do your time."

Chorus 5

Now the boll weevil blues,
I got the boll weevil blues (x2)
I can't do no time.

Well, the boll weevil got his hat and shoes,
He say, "I'm so glad I done moved off you."
I cleared 'nother crop, beginned a third or half,
He said, "I got every dog' thing he had."

Chorus 6

I got the boll weevil blues, (x3)
You can't do no [time].

Webster's guitar accompanies Angola inmate Roosevelt Charles (1917–1983)
on "The Boll Weevil and the Bale Weevil" (Vanguard VRS 9136), which Oster
recorded on November 19, 1960. An original blues, partly spoken, partly sung,
and deeply rooted in the soil of the Cotton Belt, it is another, much more
explicit complaint about the power relations involved in sharecropping.[101]

SPOKEN: Man, let me tell you about farming. There's too many "its" in farming. You got to break it up. You got to harrow it off. Then you got to build it up. Then you go and get this cotton seed and you plant them in the ground. It got to come up. Then you's got to raise it. You got to chop your cotton. Then along come the boll weevil. He gonna knock your square. Then come the bale weevil. He gonna take the bale. You hear that old bale weevil hollering to that boll weevil:

SUNG: "Woh, Mister Boll Weevil, please don't take it off of me."

SPOKEN: Then you hear the farmer crying,

SUNG: "Yeah, Mister Bale Weevil, please don't knock me in the head with the pea."[102]

SPOKEN: Then here come the poor farmer coming up to settle. Here the Bossman with his pencil: "You raised so many bales of cotton this year, but you still owe me a little bit. Try to raise a little more next year." Then you hear that poor farmer holler:

SUNG: "Woh, Mister Bale Weevil, I done broke up your land, I done planted your cotton seed, I done raised your cotton, I done poisoned the bolls, killed the boll . . . Bale weevil, now here you come taking it all from me."

SPOKEN: Woh! Too many "its" in raising that cotton. I ain't shucking, man. Look a-here. I want to tell you, Christmas time, hear the old Bossman hollering:

"Well, come up here John. I'm gonna let you have a few dollars for Christmas. Buy your old lady a gingham dress and the kid a pair of overalls."

Then that old farmer say,

SUNG: "Woh, Bossman, please what you gonna do about me?"

SPOKEN: He say, "Well, I got an old suit at the house I'm gonna give you. Say, the rats done cut a hole in the rear end and I had it patched." Hear that old farmer holler,

SUNG: "Woh, Bossman, that ain't, ain't no way to treat me."

Charles's word play, linking the boll weevil and the "bale weevil" (the planta-tion owner) as a pair of pests, reaches an aggressive climax when he sings that he "killed the bale weevil." Apart from being an indication of his confidence in Oster, this is an instance of the increasingly explicit antipathy to the white boss class found in some African American boll weevil songs in the 1950s, and more so in the 1960s. This willingness to speak out about the injustices of sharecropping may be a side effect of the civil rights movement.

Singer-guitarist Robert Pete Williams (1914–1980), paroled from Angola in 1958 thanks to Oster's efforts, recorded an unissued "Boll Weevil Blues" in

Denham Springs, Louisiana, on March 8, 1961. It describes the effects of the boll weevil on both the cotton crop and the psychological state of the sharecropper. Is the poisonous Paris Green in verse two intended to kill the boll weevil or the farmer?[103]

> Oh, hard as me an' my baby work, boll weevil is eatin' up all my cotton
>   an' corn. (x2)
> Well, I done did all in the world I can, baby, an' the boll weevil won't
> leave me 'lone.
>
> Woh, I'm goin' downtown, see can I find me some Paris Green,
> Woh, I goin' downtown, see can I find me some Paris Green,
> Woh, some people tell me, Paris Green make away with the boll weevil
>   blues.
>
> Oh, I'm tire' of workin' so hard, boll weevil won't leave me 'lone,
> Woh, oh baby, boll weevil won't leave me 'lone,
> Woh, if the boll weevil keeps botherin' me, God knows gonna leave this
>   town.
>
> Woh, oh, I'm leavin' soon, darlin' you done better make up your min' an'
>   go too,
> Woh, I'm leavin' soon, woman, you done better make up in your min'
>   an' go too,
> Boll weevil's so bad, darlin', they won't leave us alone.
>
> Well, the boll weevil done worried me so much, they forgin [sic] to give
>   me the blues,
> Woh, the boll weevil done worried me so much, darlin', they forgin to
>   give me the blues.[104]

The last boll weevil song Oster collected in the field was "Insect Blues" (Bluesville LP 1063). Mississippi-born Smoky Babe (Robert Brown, 1927– poss. May 1973) accompanied himself on guitar at Scotlandsville, Louisiana, on March 27, 1961.[105]

> Boll weevil knocked down all my cotton, woh peoples, I didn't even
>   make no corn,
> Boll weevil knocked down all my cotton, peoples, I just didn't make no
>   corn,
> Lord, I say my little family and my wife just could not get along.

I said the worms cut my greens, we had all insects that year,
I said the worms cut down my greens, we had all trouble that year,
Well, I say me and my wife and family, you know we's all here.

Well, we got to do better, we got to do better, peoples, I know,
We gotta do better, we gotta do things better, peoples, I know,
Well, I don't want my wife and family going on drifting from door to door.

Well, I say now that's all right, things be better, Lord, after a while,
I say it's all right, people, things be better after a while,
Say, my wife she in good health, but I got one little poor afflicted child.

I didn't raise no cotton, I didn't raise no corn,
I didn't raise no cotton, I did not raise no corn,
It must have been one of them old bad crop years, 'cause the boll wee-
   vils they come along.

You know I'm talking about work now, woh people, that sure is hard,
I'm talking about work now, people, you know now it sure is hard,
I'm trying to raise my little family, woh man, something got me barred.

This original lyric moves adroitly between the personal and the communal, focusing on the boll weevil's effect on the musician's family and the wider economy and offering glimpses of cautious optimism, injured pride, and striving for amelioration. The concluding complaint that "something got me barred" from prosperity alludes to more than the boll weevil.

Texas songster Mance Lipscomb's "Ballad of the Boll Weevil" (Reprise R 2012), recorded in Houston on July 8, 1961, centers on the usual, sometimes fanciful countermeasures—ice, sand, poison—adopted by farmers.[106]

First saw old boll weevil, he was in the air,
Next time I saw that boll weevil, he was sitting on a cotton square.
He found him a home, had to have a home.

Farmer said to the boll weevil, "What you doing on my farm?"
Boll weevil said to the farmer, "I ain't gon' do you much harm,
I'm a-looking for a home, I'm got to have a home."

Farmers all got together, said, "Let's poison our crop,
We don't stop that boll weevil, he'll eat up everything we got.
He's looking for a home, done found him a home."

And they decided to take him, stick him in some ice,
Stayed in the ice twenty-four hours, come out looking very nice.
He had him a home, had a cool home.

Then they decided to catch him, stick him in the sand,
Stayed there thirty long hours, he stood it like a natural man,
He had a home, he had a hot home.

Farmers all decided, wondering what to do,
"You done ate up all of our cotton crop, going in the corn patch, too,
Done found a home, done found a home."

Now the boll weevil said to the farmer, "I'm your bosom friend.
I caused you to get four cents on every bale of cotton that you takes to
    the gin.
I got a home, I done found me a home."

The invincible bug adds insult to injury by claiming that the shortage he has caused enables farmers to make an additional, derisory four cents on each cotton bale. (Compare Buster Ezell's "Ever since I been in this country, cotton brought you thirty-five cents.")

Piedmont songster Pink Anderson's "Boweevil" (Bluesville LP 1071), recorded in Spartanburg, South Carolina, on August 14, 1961, is noteworthy for its first stanza, which is very similar to the second stanza of "Bo Weavil" Jackson's "Devil and My Brown Blues." This strongly suggests that Esther Bigeou's vaudeville blues recording "Stingaree Blues (A Down Home Blues)" was their common source.[107]

Woke up this morning, woke up this morning, heard somebody calling
    me,
Woke up this morning, heard somebody calling me,
It must've been the mama weevil, that they call the stingaree.

In the wake of Tex Ritter's hit, there were a number of recordings of boll weevil songs. Both the recording by white country music duo Homer and Jethro for King in the late 1940s and early 1950s, and Eddie Cochran's rockabilly version on Liberty (1959) are clearly indebted to Ritter; so too, though less closely, is Burl Ives on Decca in 1956. The Weavers' 1957 recording on Vanguard owes more—not least in the line "Well, the boll weevil ate all the cotton, banker stole the rest"—to Woody Guthrie. As well as musicians' own preferences, these versions reflect the wish of the record industry to cater to different sectors of the growing mass market for music. The recordings were not textually innovative, and (the Weavers excepted) they seem oblivious to boll weevil songs' historical and cultural meanings.

The record industry's attempts to monetize the boll weevil paid off with the worldwide success of "The Boll Weevil Song" (Mercury 71820), by North Carolina–born Black balladeer Brook Benton (1931–1988), who recorded his first version in New York in 1961. Despite its title, the rendition, which reached No. 2 on the *Billboard* Hot 100 chart, is not sung but recited, except in the "looking for a home" hook. This reflects a slight contemporary vogue for such treatments.[108] The lyrics of the LP version (Mercury SR 61640), given here, differ very little from the 45 r.p.m. version:[109]

> Let me tell you a story about the boll weevil, that some of you may not know,
> But the boll weevil is an insect, and he's found mostly where cotton grows.
> Now where they come from nobody really knows,
> But this is the way the story goes.
>
> The farmer said to the boll weevil,
> "I'll see you on the square."
> Boll weevil said to the farmer,
> Said, "Yep, my whole darn family's here.
> We got to have a home, got to have a home."
>
> The farmer said to the boll weevil,
> Said, "Why'd you pick my farm?"
> The weevil just laughed at the farmer
> And said, "We ain't gonna do you much harm,
> We're looking for a home."
>
> And the boll weevil spotted a lightning bug,
> He said, "Hey, I'd like to make a trade with you.
> But you see, if I was a lightning bug,
> I'd search the whole night through.
> Searching for a home, I'd have me plenty of homes."
>
> And the boll weevil called the farmer
> And said, "You better sell your old machines
> 'Cause when I'm through with your cotton
> You can't even buy gasoline.
> I'm 'on' take me a home, gotta have a home."

> And the boll weevil said to the farmer,
> Said, "Farmer, I'd like to wish you well."
> Farmer said to the boll weevil,
> "Yeah, I wish that you [was] in [hell]
> Looking for a home, looking for a home.
> Ah, you'll have a home, alright, you'll have a home.
> Real hot home, ah, have a home."

Despite his use of traditional lyrics, Benton's knowing, detached delivery follows the racially and historically decontextualized trail blazed by Fats Domino. The use of style to negate history by Benton (and arranger Clyde Otis, responsible for the presence of strings and a wordless female chorus) parallels Eddie Cochran's approach. As Andrew Scheiber has noted, the boll weevil ballad's vernacular sources become indistinct: the pest loses its heroic status and is frozen as the harmless museum piece that the farmers who "put him on the ice" wanted. The bug's "longevity and cultural visibility" are enhanced at the expense of the meanings imputed to him by folk values, and "Charley Patton and Eddie Cochran's boll weevils are distant cousins in the same way as are Br'er Rabbit and Bugs Bunny."[110] This is as much—perhaps even more—true of Brook Benton's boll weevil and Charley Patton's. Anyone aware only of Benton's performance would never suspect that in the South at this time, some African Americans were creating more racially confrontational treatments of the boll weevil.

A plethora of covers and of not very significant boll weevil recordings followed, by both African American and white singers.[111] An interesting exception to the run-of-the-mill majority is "D.D.T. and the Boll Weevil" (Southern Sound SS 104) by Lyn Earlington with Sherman Conrad and His Bourbon Street Seven, recorded in 1961. Despite the name assigned to the band, the session was probably held in Philadelphia, where Southern Sound was based. Composer credits are to Earlington and Lawrence. This answer song to Brook Benton's recording elaborates on some traditional phrases, and on the usual cut-and-thrust between the farmer and the boll weevil, but this time the farmer wins the battle, triumphantly telling the insect that it is eating the D.D.T. that he has sown along with the cotton. (D.D.T. had initially been very effective, but despite Earlington's lyrics, the weevils had developed resistance to it by the mid-1950s.)

> Now I'm gonna tell you a little secret that Brook Benton don't seem to
>   know.
> It's about that hungry boll weevil and the things he can't do no more.
> Now D.D.T. is an insect spray, and it's mostly used around the farm.

D.D.T. means "Drop Dead Twice," the boll weevils won't hang around
    the barn.
They'll leave you alone, take the family back home.

The boll weevil says to the farmer, says, "Farmer, I think I'll split the scene.
I done heard about that magic stuff you got that's wiping all these cot-
    ton fields clean.
I'll leave you alone, yeah, take my family back home."

The farmer told the boll weevil, "I'm gonna buy back all my machines,
'Cause when I drop this load on you, I'm gonna start making gasoline.
I'll be a happy man. Yeah, don't you understand?"

The boll weevil said to the farmer, "I guess I'm reaping what I sowed."
Farmer said to the boll weevil, "No, you eating up what I sowed."
The boll weevil saw that same old lightning bug sitting up high in a tree.
Lightning bug said, "Hey, boll weevil, you still gonna make that trade
    with me?"

The boll weevil says to the farmer, said now, "He sure don't wish me well,
'Cause I sure would look mighty crazy trying to hide in your field with
    a spotlight on my tail.
I'll leave you alone, yes, take my family back home.
I'm in misery, and you've got D.D.T.
I'm in misery; you've got D.D.T."

    Also of interest is "Boll Weevil" collected by David Evans from Mississippi
guitarist Babe Stovall (1907–1974) in Franklinton, Louisiana, on January 26,
1966.[112]

First heard tell of boll weevil twenty-third of June,
Looked over in my cotton field, he was sitting in a cotton bloom,
He had a home in the cotton bloom.

Went to the merchant, asked him "What do you think of that?
I found a boll weevil in my Sunday hat,
He had a home in the cotton bloom."

Went to the merchant, asked him for a meat and a meal,
"You go home, old n----r, the boll weevil's in your field,
You go home and let me alone."

> Went down to the briar patch, heard a great racket,
> Nothing but a bullfrog pulling off his jacket.

Stovall draws on various folk sources and includes lines that had been printed by Gates Thomas and Sandburg. He supplies a new refrain and adds an unrelated closing stanza, seemingly from a children's song or minstrelsy. This conclusion reminds us, however, that Stovall's melody is very similar to that of "The Hop Joint," a member of the "Frankie" family of tunes to which many boll weevil songs belong. The verbal persistence of the theme is paralleled by this musical persistence.[113] As "Frankie" referred to events that occurred in 1900 and the tune was probably composed soon thereafter, the origin of the "Boll Weevil" tune may date back to the early 1900s.

Conclusions

Drawing conclusions from this survey of printed and recorded songs, and suggesting new perspectives, is made difficult by the obscurity of the ballad's origins, and by the sheer quantity and variety of songs. It may be fruitful to begin with a reconsideration of earlier analyses.

Discussing animal and human tricksters, Black folk heroes, and bad men, cultural historian Lawrence W. Levine states that "[t]ales were perpetuated because they were entertaining and brought relief from tedious and difficult tasks. But they lived also because they were bearers of tradition and group memory."[114] As with other disasters discussed in this book, memory is the common thread underlying the development of the boll weevil theme. Levine adds:

> [Black storytellers] made no special effort to keep the old tales alive. Those that continued to reflect their interests, needs and aesthetic sensibilities survived. Those that did not had to give way or undergo alteration, often beyond recognition. . . . Animal and human trickster tales continued to exist. . . . They endured, but they underwent continuous change reflective of the changes taking place in Afro-American consciousness.[115]

An obvious difference between African American and white boll weevil songs is that African American singers identify more closely with the bug.[116] This is sometimes embodied in nicknames, either because the singer was celebrated for a particular song about the boll weevil (e.g. James "Bo Weavil" Jackson) or because physical features, and perhaps sexual innuendo, suggested a link (for example, Boll Weevil Bill).[117]

From the 1940s onward, politically oriented white composers and performers focused on the socioeconomic consequences of the boll weevil, often linking them to the alleged failings of capitalism. Less politically engaged white artists detached the weevil from its historic context, as did the African Americans Fats Domino and Brook Benton, aiming for crossover success. Other Black musicians, although racially conscious to different degrees, usually made the racial subtext obvious.

Scholars have usually discussed Black people's identification with the boll weevil in terms of covert behavior and hidden protest, and seldom with reference to overt behavior and uncoded language. An example of the latter can be found in the closing "who composed this song" stanza. By the time John Lomax collected it, this verse was already used to denote that Black farmers and sharecroppers, of whom the singer is representative, are actually, and not at all metaphorically, "a-looking for a home."

In early Texas songs, the insect is a slick trickster, like the animal heroes of African American folk tales. However, "[a]s the ballad moves eastward from Texas, the boll weevil tends to be transformed from a trickster who outwits the farmer into a verbally and physically abusive 'badman'" who becomes more and more defiant and outrageous.[118] There has been little scholarly interrogation of the implications of the bug's status as either a trickster like Brer Rabbit or Shine or an anthropomorphized badman like Stagger Lee or Railroad Bill. Broadly speaking, the trickster image may be older and go back to African tradition (animal tricksters) and the slavery era. The badman image becomes more prominent in the post-Reconstruction era (1890s and later), and eventually becomes more common than the trickster. The development of boll weevil songs over the twentieth century reflects this partial shift from trickster to badman, the former's image never going away entirely. Also, over time in the early decades of the twentieth century the boll weevil's depredations became more widespread, eventually affecting most of the South's cotton crop, thus making the insect seem more powerful and fearsome (and therefore a "badman"). This may explain why versions of boll weevil songs from the eastern states in the 1920s and later generally reflect more of a badman image.

Black identification with the weevil, as an outlet for frustration and powerlessness, and a projection of hope, has also been accepted rather than explored. However, the development of the boll weevil theme, as evidenced in African American recordings, suggests that the interaction of tradition and innovation has transformed the way it has been treated in time. Fats Domino's "Bo Weevil," recorded in October 1955, was the first African American song to blend elements of folklore with modern themes appealing to the new generation. It is significant and not coincidental that 1955 functions both as the cutoff point for the analysis of disaster songs in this book as well as for the most reasonable partition date between "folk" and "popular" compositions and recordings on the boll weevil infestation. By 1955 only a few Black singers had adopted a definite critical position against racial prejudice and injustice in their song lyrics. From the mid-1950s the thematic treatment of the boll weevil theme became even lighter and started to fall into oblivion. The main factor in the decline of boll weevil songs after 1955 is the shift in the center of gravity of Black culture (and the population itself) from rural to urban, and from the South to the North or West Coast.

The boll weevil infestation was a long-drawn-out disruption to the economy of the rural American South, which initially generated cultural responses in the areas directly affected. As members of mass urban society became aware of those cultural responses, they adapted and assimilated them, experiencing the meanings of the boll weevil vicariously. It has been argued that an early sign of this metamorphosis is Ma Rainey's depiction of the boll weevil as a "sexual persona": "Rainey's 'Bo-weavil Blues'... shows the almost complete assimilation of the beetle to a new language, one that has almost no explicit reference to agriculture or a specific historical memory."[119] The boll weevil's economic—and consequently cultural—impact on the cotton industry and its milieu continued for many years after Rainey's 1923 recording, and the synthesis of cultural trends is often a lengthy process. The unexpectedly high number of boll weevil songs recorded after World War II shows that the pest's effects continued to resonate in folk culture, but the popularity of Fats Domino's, Brook Benton's, and Tex Ritter's recordings reflects changes in American society at large. In this instance, tradition and innovation—constant, often antagonistic presences in any culture—both worked slowly to "erod[e] the animal trickster's central importance in Black lore,"[120] and to shape new modes of artistic expression within the culture.

In recent years, the boll weevil's main cultural function has been to offer a sense of validation through appropriation for white artists, especially blues-rock revivalists like the North Mississippi Allstars and the White Stripes.[121] For them,

> the weevil functions as a generic signifier of roots, a citation that helps the performer position himself or herself as a link in an ongoing tradition. The weevil of song has thus passed from the realm of memory into the kingdom of style, where its communicative possibilities have become all the more fungible—assuring that despite whatever success might greet the eradication campaigns against the actual insect, the weevil of song will be with us for a long time to come.[122]

Though that prediction might prove right, especially as regards Black cover songs taking the boll weevil as an example of resilience against the still-frequent acts of racial discrimination and physical violence toward African Americans, conditions are not ideal for a return to the historical import and folk values inherent in boll weevil songs. By folk values, I mean the whole of social and moral principles characterizing a group of individuals and informing their sense of belonging to a community or race. The impact of historical facts within a group varies dramatically in time and modes and contributes to shape the way such a group expresses ideas and its approach to life. Black people's diminished interest in the cultural and historical significance of the black insect since the mid-fifties is the logical consequence of the passing of time and of the ongoing change in American and African American popular culture, which make the revival of boll weevil songs highly unlikely. Despite their overall decreasing number, sudden catastrophic events such as natural disasters seem to be a more flexible and suitable topic to inspire the composition of original songs.

Gospel singer Mahalia Jackson provides an example of reaction to the boll weevil. Jackson saw the boll weevil as a blessing in disguise, undermining the sharecropping system, and a

> curse . . . on that part of the South where the white people robbed the colored people for the cotton. . . . They were a proud and selfish people, those plantation owners, and I believe . . . that God finally sent the boll weevil to jumble [*sic*, perhaps for "humble"] them. . . . Thanks to the boll weevil, a lot of those thieving plantation people died out, too.[123]

Jackson is cynical about human motives, but practical and realistic about the need to survive adversity. Her view on how to respond to the hardships imposed continuously by racism and intermittently by natural disaster, with the former often reinforcing the effects of the latter, is historically accurate and the result of an uncompromising clear mind.

JESUS IS COMING SOON: PANDEMICS AND EPIDEMICS

Jesus Is Coming Soon:
The 1918–20 Influenza Pandemic and the 1929 Influenza Epidemic

"The Great Influenza," which ravaged the whole world from early 1918 to late 1920, was the most widespread and deadly tragedy in history.[124] The death toll is uncertain, but recent research suggests it may be between 50 and 100 million people, or 3 to 6 percent of the world's population.[125] The pandemic was (and sometimes still is) mistakenly called "the Spanish Flu" because at the time of its outbreak during World War I, neutral Spain did not have political or military reasons to censor news of the disease. This created a false impression that Spain had been especially hard hit.

Recent research by the Centers for Disease Control has established that the influenza was caused by a virus with genes of avian origin, which mutated to become infectious to both humans and swine.[126] It is still uncertain where the disease broke out,[127] but it was first observed in Haskell County, Kansas, in January 1918 by local physician Loring Miner, who reported it in the US *Public Health Service*'s weekly journal Public Health Reports.[128] The disease spread to the country's second-largest military training camp, Camp Funston, part of the base at Fort Riley, Kansas, where several thousand soldiers were being trained before being deployed, mainly to the European theater of war.

Relatively unaggressive at this stage, the influenza caused pneumonia in 237 men, about 20 percent of those at Camp Funston, of whom only thirty-eight died.[129] However, the virus then mutated, becoming virulently dangerous to humans. In the second and third waves, which started in August and December 1918, an epidemic overran the continental United States and most of Europe, then developed into a pandemic that killed some thirty-five million people in Asia (twenty million in the Indian subcontinent alone), around two million in Europe, and several million in Africa and Oceania.[130] In the United States, 28 percent of the population of about 105 million were infected, and 675,000 died.[131]

Most deaths occurred during the second wave, mainly in October and November 1918. One of the peculiarities of the "Great Influenza" was its high incidence and mortality rate in young adults, usually least affected by milder forms of the disease. This was partly because young people's stronger immune systems reacted to the virus by overproducing antibodies, leading to a massive inflammatory reaction (a cytokine storm), and partly because malnutrition, overcrowding, and poor hygiene favored the development of severe bacterial pneumonia in patients already stricken with influenza.[132]

The first known song is the text of "That Influenza Train," reprinted by Newman Ivey White ten years after the pandemic began.[133] His source was a borrowed copy of *The Golden Trumpet Jubilee Hymns*, an undated thirty-two-page pamphlet containing twenty-eight songs. Compiled by Rev. W. M. Jones of Richmond, Virginia, it sold for twenty-five cents, and was being used by a small Black congregation in Durham, North Carolina.

> One day while sitting in my home
> I felt very bad,
> My head began to ache me,
> I didn't know what I had.
>
> *Chorus*
> That influenza, that Influenza
> Come to lay your body down,
> That Influenza.[134]

The first thing the influenza done,
In the North, I am told
It went in almost every home
And left somebody cold.

It came rumbling down the line,
The people were amazed,
They had the doctor come at once,
But still they filled their graves.

It moved like a cyclone,
Without fear or dread,
It ran across some doctor's den
And left their bodies dead.

The Board of Health met one day,
The churches all were closed,
The saints of God wandering about
Had to praise God out of doors.

This sent forth doctors all around,
They didn't know what to do.
A message came from across the sea
And said it was the flu.

This terrible disease must come from God
For the Doctors couldn't say.
Remember in just two month's [sic] time
Ten thousand filled their graves.

It took away your appetite,
It made you feel so mean,
Just in three or seven days,
It left you very lean.

Some time I think it beat the war
But didn't last as long.
In a short time all over the land,
Millions were going home.

Some boys were overseas,
Returning home you know,

But those who left on the influenza train
Have never come back any more.

The last two stanzas confirm that this text is about the 1918 influenza epidemic. At the end of September 1918,

> 3,108 troops boarded a train leaving [Camp Grant, Illinois] for Camp Hancock outside Augusta, Georgia. . . . The men leaving Grant on that train were jammed into the cars with little room to move about. . . . When the train arrived, over seven hundred men . . . were taken directly to the base hospital, quickly followed by hundreds more; in total, two thousand of the 3,108 troops would be hospitalized with influenza. After 143 deaths among them the statistics merged into those of other troops from Camp Hancock . . . and became impossible to track. But it is likely that the death toll approached, and possibly exceeded, 10 percent of all the troops on the train.[135]

The song's composer may have heard about this incident (see the discussion below of "Influenza Epidemic in Baton Rouge"), but if so, it seems to have inspired a metaphor ("It came rumbling down the line") rather than a specific reference. The "influenza train" on which some soldiers metaphorically left Europe for the afterlife is implicitly contrasted with the ships that carried surviving veterans home to the U.S. An intertextual relationship to songs and sermons that refer to "death's black train," "the little black train," and so on seems clear.

The first recording about the epidemic was "Jesus Is Coming Soon" (Columbia 14391-D), cut in Dallas, Texas, on December 5, 1928. Blind Willie Johnson accompanies himself on guitar, and his partner, Willie B. Richardson (later Harris), sings on the choruses.[136] This is one of Johnson's most compelling and interesting songs, and its originality suggests that Johnson composed it.

Chorus (after each stanza)
Well, we done told you, God's done warned you, Jesus coming soon.
We done told you, God's done warned you, Jesus coming soon.

In the year of 19 and 18, God sent a mighty disease.
It killed many a thousand on land and on the seas.

Great disease was a-mighty, and the people was sick everywhere.
It was an epidemic, and it floated through the air.

The doctors, they got troubled, and they didn't know what to do.
They gathered themselves together, and called it the Spanish influ.

Soldiers died on the battlefields, died in the camps too.
Well, the Captain says, "Lieutenant, ah, we don't know what to do."[137]
Well, God is warning the nations, He's warning them every way,
To turn away from the evil and seek the Lord and pray.

Well, the note was sended to the people, "You'd better close your public
   schools,
To prevent this epidemic, better close the churches too."

Read the Book of Zachariah, Bible plainly says
That the people in cities died 'count of their wicked ways.

The song's central focus is the imminent Second Coming of Christ, and the need to earn salvation by repentance. The influenza, regarded as one of the "pestilences" referred to in Matthew 24:7–8, is a sign of Christ's coming. Johnson's mention of the disease is intended to support his eschatological argument, but the length and detail of his account are unusual. The references to its outbreak in the army, and to the closure of public schools and churches, are factually accurate. In the last stanza the reference is probably to Zechariah 14:2: "For I will gather all nations against Jerusalem to battle; and the city shall be taken, and the houses rifled, and the women ravished; and half of the city shall go forth into captivity, and the residue of the people shall not be cut off from the city." It has correctly been observed that "Zacharias . . . preached about the ultimate end of the world and the divine retribution. . . . The *Book of Zachariah* belongs to the Apocalyptic literature as it contains series of mysterious visions on the end of time."[138]

On his unaccompanied "Influenza Epidemic in Baton Rouge" (AFS 98-A-1), the obscure Sugar Smith[139] employs a highly rhythmic, semi-sung style that predates rap music by some forty years. It was collected by the Lomaxes for the Library of Congress in the Louisiana capital on December 7, 1934.

Chorus:
[Now] It was a sad time: Your heart was aching and your mind was
   engaged, now.
It was a sad time when that 'fluenza was in a rage.

Oh, well, oh well.
Flagged them at Port Allen, Baton Rouge the same,
Looking for dead bodies on every train.
You was at the depot when the coffin came.
Your general brought my son and some other man.

I didn't feel satisfied by being at the place,
But "Open the coffin, let me look in his face."
The message brought the news, spoken right sad,
"Lower the coffin, gonna bury right away."

Chorus

Oh, well, oh well.
You're reading in your mind, it's a natural fact.
That influenza take you 'bout your neck and your back.
Look over your mind, see ain't that true?
The only ones could walk, it was one or two.
A-walking very faithful 'cause it was fair,
They advertised God sont[140] a disease in the air.

Chorus

Repeat stanza 2

Chorus

Oh, well, oh well.
The doctors heard of it, they wanted to know.
They never have heard of such a sickness before.
The colonels got uneasy, they spoke and replied,
"We'll cut out all gatherings in a great big crowd."
And then that influenza begin to search,
We have nowhere to go, we've closed every church.
The doctors worked but got beyond a comprehension,
Didn't call that sickness but that influenza.

Chorus

Oh, well, oh, well.
You may wanna know where that flu first broke out:
Camp Grant, Illinois, it first broke out.
The boys went to camp out on a [re]doubt,
They made it in their mind for to build a dead house.
You oughta been there to see what a shame.
They put some in a dead house and some on a train.
The peoples was crying because trouble's in they home.

Told them, "Don't be rejoicing 'cause the flu is not gone."
I read the Holy Bible, saying: "Mmm, what it say?"
Says, "My God come riding in another way."

Chorus

Despite its late recording date, the reference to Camp Grant, Illinois, confirms
that this song is about the 1918–20 epidemic. It did not begin there, as the singer
asserts, but he is clearly aware of the outbreak of influenza among soldiers on a
train from Camp Grant to Fort Hancock, described above in connection with
"That Influenza Train." Camp Grant may have held additional significance for
Smith, and other African Americans, because on November 13, 1918,

> The Army Nurses Corps accepted 18 Black nurses on an "experimen-
> tal" basis following the influenza epidemic. The Army sent half of them
> to Camp Grant, Illinois, and the other half to Camp Sherman, Ohio.
> Although their living quarters were segregated, they were assigned to
> duties in an integrated hospital. Because of the postwar reduction in
> force, the Army released all 18 women in August 1919.[141]

On September 30, 1929, Elder Tarleton Roberts, assisted by Sisters Bessie
Johnson, Melinda Taylor, and Sally Sumler (the Memphis Sanctified Singers),
recorded an unissued sermon with singing, "Death Went Creeping through
the Air," for Victor in Memphis. The sung component of this recording seems
certain to have been a lyric published in an undated Church of God in Christ
paperback songster, where it is attributed to Elder Tarleton Roberts.

The text in the songster, titled "It Was God's Mighty Hand," and subtitled
"The Influenza Epidemic, in tune of 'O It Bows Down My Heart, and the Tear
Drops Will Start,'" is as follows:[142]

Nineteen hundred and twenty-nine,
Men and women sure were dying,
Of that stuff which doctors call the "Flu"
People died everywhere,
Death went creeping through the air,
For the groans of the sick sure were sad.[143]

Chorus:
It was God's mighty hand,
He is judging this old land,

North and South, East and West can be seen,
Yes He killed rich and poor,
And He's going to kill more,
If you don't turn away from your shame.

It was Memphis, Tennessee,
Doctors said it soon would be,
A few days influenza we'll control,
But God showed them He's head
So He sent the doctors to bed
And the nurses broke down with the same.

Influenza is a disease,
Makes you weak in your knees,
Carries a fever everybody sure does dread,
Puts a pain in every bone,
A few days you are gone,
To a place in the ground called the grave.

It is clear that the songster text was the source for "Memphis Flu" (OKeh 8857), recorded at the Edwards Hotel, Jackson, Mississippi, on December 16, 1930. "Elder Curry and Congregation," credited on the record label, were—as well as the voices of the congregation—Church of God in Christ (COGIC) preacher Elder David R. Curry Sr. (1884–1972) (guitar and vocal), Jo Ann Williams (lead vocal), and Elder Charles Beck (piano).[144] The melody of "Memphis Flu" derives from Robert Carridine's 1890s composition "On a Hill Lone and Gray." The only significant variation from Roberts's text in Curry's version is his substitution of the generic "Over land, over sea" for "It was Memphis, Tennessee."

There were six influenza epidemics in the United States in the 1920s, all much less severe than the Great Influenza, but the outbreak between November 25, 1928, and February 16, 1929, which peaked on January 9, 1929, caused many deaths:

[A]bout 50,000 influenza-pneumonia deaths occurred in the United States during the epidemic of the winter of 1928–1929. The case incidence of influenza and grippe in the 1928–1929 epidemic . . . seemed to be more than half of that of 1918–1919. The percentage of cases complicated by pneumonia and the case fatality, however, were much less in the recent epidemic, being in 1928–1929 somewhere between one-fourth and one-half of the corresponding figures for 1918–1919.[145]

The epidemic was on the wane in Memphis by January 1929, even as it peaked elsewhere,[146] but it seems certain that Elder Roberts's lyric was inspired by the winter 1928–29 epidemic. Elder Curry perhaps generalized the location to "over land, over sea" hoping that the recording would have wider appeal; if so, it's surprising that OKeh issued it as "Memphis Flu." Nevertheless, it is clear that this song is about recent events, and not, as some blues and gospel researchers have suggested,[147] a misdated account of the 1918–20 pandemic as it affected Memphis.

Two later recordings of the song both seem likely to derive ultimately from the COGIC songster; their words align very closely with it, and both refer to "Memphis, Tennessee," as the location of the outbreak. Ace Johnson's guitar-accompanied "Influenza" (AFS 3552-B-3) also refers to 1929 as the year of the outbreak. Recorded for the Library of Congress at Clemens State Farm, Brazoria, Texas, on April 16, 1939,[148] Johnson's version was learned "off a holiness boy in Amarillo."[149]

Arkansas-born pianist Essie Jenkins's 1962 recording "Influenza Blues" (Arhoolie LP 1018)[150] was reissued as "The 1919 Influenza Blues" because she mentions that year, rather than "nineteen hundred and twenty-nine." Jenkins probably learned the song from the COGIC songbook and changed the date for reasons of her own. Unusually, she refers to "the groans of the rich" rather than "of the sick."

In "God Don't Never Change" (Columbia 14490-D), recorded in New Orleans on December 10, 1929, Blind Willie Johnson could be referring to either influenza outbreak when he sings:

> God in the time of sickness,
> God in the doctor too,
> In the time of the influenza, He truly was a God to you.[151]

However, Johnson's phrasing ("the time of the influenza") characterizes the event as a portentous one, and he is probably alluding to the 1918 pandemic, which would have been more widely known to his listeners.

Frances Wallace's earlier "Too Late Too Late Blues (The Flu Blues)," with composer credits to "[Charles 'Cow Cow'] Davenport," has not hitherto been seen as topical, or associated with the 1928–29 epidemic. Recorded in Chicago on April 24, 1929, it was released on Brunswick 7076 on May 11.[152] This is undoubtedly another song generated by the 1928–29 influenza outbreak. The lyrics are closely modeled on Victoria Spivey's "T-B Blues" (OKeh 8494), recorded in St. Louis on April 27, 1927. Wallace's derivative and nonspecific text suggests that its inspiration was opportunistic rather than personal. In her song, the place name is changed from Denver to Colorado. The state's capital was closely associated with treatment for tuberculosis, for which its mountain air was thought to be therapeutic, but had no such link with influenza.

Four main conclusions can be drawn from the study of blues and gospel songs dealing with the deadliest global disaster ever, and with the later outbreak of 1928–29:

1) As Barry observes, "despite ... occasional harshness, the 1918 influenza pandemic did not in general demonstrate a pattern of race or class antagonism. ... The disease was too universal, too obviously not tied to race or class."[153]

2) The scarcity of African American songs on the pandemic, compared to other song clusters dealing with large-scale disasters (like the 1927 Mississippi River flood), is partly explained by the death rate among African Americans being lower than that for whites, a reversal of the usual pattern in American epidemics.[154]

3) Gospel songs about pandemics and epidemics prevail over blues songs because gospel singers are more inclined to draw moral and theological conclusions from such events.

4) Songbooks and other printed material were important sources for singers, both recorded (commercially or otherwise) and unrecorded.

Jake Leg Blues: The 1930 Jamaica Ginger Paralysis

The outbreak of polyneuritis, often called Jamaica ginger paralysis, which began in late February 1930 and was first reported in the press on March 7,[155] caused serious, usually at best only partially reversible physical damage, and no fatalities, but its widespread impact meant that it was fairly extensively sung about by African American and hillbilly singers. Dr. John P. Morgan has studied the disease in both its medical and musical contexts, and this chapter is indebted to his research.[156]

The epidemic was caused by the adulteration of a batch of the patent medicine Jamaica ginger, nicknamed "jake," with tri-ortho-cresyl phosphate (TOCP). Marketed under numerous brand names, jake's high alcohol content and low cost (thirty-five cents for a two-ounce bottle), had long made it a popular alternative to legal alcohol. Prohibition only encouraged its consumption, and an unintended consequence of making alcoholic drink illegal was that there was no government oversight of its safety. TOCP attacked the cells of the spinal cord, causing a lesion that weakened the muscles, especially near the arm and leg joints. This caused shooting pains and affected the steps of sufferers, causing "a distinctive gait necessitated by a foot drop, in which the forward leg is lifted high to allow the foot to clear the ground,"[157] which became known as "the jake walk," "the jake leg," and "the limber leg."

Reliable statistical data are not available, but high-end estimates suggest that about 50,000 Americans were affected. The disease was first reported in the Midwest, with Oklahoma, Missouri, Indiana, southern Ohio, southeastern Kansas, and Kentucky most affected.[158] It then spread to Arkansas, Texas, Tennessee, Mississippi, Louisiana, and Georgia, followed by southern California and New York state. Large cities such as St. Louis, Kansas City, and Los Angeles counted victims by the hundreds, but above all Cincinnati was severely struck; its General Hospital was filled to capacity, with more than 1,000 confirmed cases. Smaller towns and villages were not spared: around 1,000 Mississippians developed the disease, along with six hundred of Johnson City, Tennessee's 25,000 people.

The association of the paralysis with Jamaica ginger was established by Federal pharmacologist Dr. Maurice Smith in March 1930, but it was only on May 24 that Drs. Smith and Elvove discovered that TOCP was the trigger.[159] By July new cases had largely stopped in the Midwest and southern states, but there was no cure for those already afflicted. Several people were involved in the wholesale and retail distribution of the deadly concoction, but the main culprits were Harry Gross and his brother-in-law Max Reisman, owners of the Hub Products Corporation, 65 Fulton Street, Boston, where the poisonous batch of jake had been prepared. In April 1931, Gross and Reisman pleaded guilty to charges against them, and were given two-year suspended sentences, on condition that that they help the authorities trace the "New York bootleggers" who they claimed were the source of the product. A year later, having failed to do so—unsurprisingly, since he himself was the source—Gross was sent to prison by Judge James A. Lowell, who declined to review Reisman's case, and whose lenient sentencing attracted severe criticism.[160]

The first recording prompted by the paralysis was "Jake Liquor Blues" (Paramount 12941), made circa April 1930 in Grafton, Wisconsin, by Jackson, Mississippi, guitarist Ishman Bracey (1899–1970).[161] The song was mistitled by Paramount, who misheard the first line.

> Jake legger, jake legger, what in the world you trying to do? (x2)
>   Everybody in this city messed up on account of jake and you.
>
>   I drink so much jake, it's settled all in my knee,
>   I drink so much jake until it's settled all in my knee,
>   I reached for my loving, my baby turned her back to me.
>
>   That's the doggonest disease, ever heard since I been born. (x2)
>   You're numb in the front of your body; you can't carry this loving on.

> Aunt Jane, she come a-running, telling everybody in the
>   neighborhood,
> Aunt Jane, she come running and screaming, telling everybody in
>   the neighborhood,
> "That man of mine got the limber trouble, and his loving can't do
>   me any good."
>
> The doctor told me to tell you something, for your own craving
>   knowledge's sake[162] (x2)
> If you don't quit drinking that poison jake you're drinking, it's
>   gonna leave you with the limber leg.

In the first stanza, the singer blames the illness on bootleggers (here specifically called "jake leggers"), before concentrating on a symptom that contemporary standards excluded from the mass media: sexual impotence. As Morgan notes in his various articles, modern research has found evidence that erectile dysfunction was a frequent result of TOCP poisoning: African American blues musicians were the only people to make explicit public reference to it. As will be seen below, some white musicians did make veiled allusions to impotence.

During the same sessions ca. April 1930, Bracey's associate Tommy Johnson (1896–1956) recorded "Alcohol and Jake Blues" (Paramount 12950), which includes spoken comments, possibly by Bracey. Johnson died at age sixty of a massive heart attack, although his alcoholism was undoubtedly a major contributing cause. Johnson's song draws some lyrical and musical elements from his "Canned Heat Blues" (Victor V38535), a song about another cheap substitute for liquor, which he had recorded in 1928.[163] "Knock-ahol," which Johnson clearly sings, appears to be "a portmanteau word made by combining elements of 'knock out' and 'alcohol,' and signifying 'a drink that has a powerful effect.'"[164]

> Knock-ahol, knock-ahol, crying sure Lord's killing me.
> *Spoken:* Is that so, boy?
> Knock-ahol, mama, sure, Lord's killing me.
> *Spoken:* You oughta let it alone, then.
> Knock-ahol don't kill me, Lord, I'll never die.
>
> I woke up, early this morning, crying knock-ahol 'round my bed.
> *Spoken:* What happened then?
> Woke up this morning, knock-ahol was 'round my bed.
> Says, I'm gon' get drunk, I'm gonna have to speak my sober mind.

Mmmmmm, mmmm [*Spoken:* Oh, moan it a long time.] Mmmmmm,
Mmmmmm, I ain't gon' be here long.
Spoken: Moan it a long time, boy.
Says, I'm leaving town, mama, I'm going to wear you off my mind.

I drink so much of jake till it done give me the limber leg.
Spoken: Now that sure mess you up.
Drinking so much of jake till it done give me the limber leg.
Spoken: Sure mess you up, boy. That's all it is to that.
If I don't quit drinking, Lord, it's sure gon' kill me dead.
Spoken: You ain't no lying man.

Ehhhh ehhhh, ehhh.
Ehhhh [*Spoken:* You ain't got to (moan)], sure gonna kill me dead,
And if it don't kill me, Lord, it's sure gonna put me down.
Spoken: You ain't got to put 'em on me 'cause you've got 'em.

I woke up, Lord, this morning, crying knock-ahol on my mind,
Woke up this morning, knock-ahol was on my mind,
I've got them knock-ahol blues, and I can't rest easy here.

Bracey said of Johnson's alcoholism:

> Drinking was his weakness. That's what killed him. Tommy would drink
> anything that he could get to. When he was out of whisky, he would
> drink anything. That's the reason he put out those Canned Heat Blues. He
> drank canned heat, shoe polish, alcorub, till they put this business in it.
> He'd drink anything, denature, beer, wine, whisky, anything he'd get to.[165]

"Alcohol and Jake Blues," which was Johnson's last recording, is a haunting song,
harsher than "Canned Heat Blues," and a nightmarish yet realistic picture of a
man going to pieces physically and psychologically. Johnson did not actually
suffer from jake leg, and against the odds he lived to the age of sixty, dying in
1956. Bracey did not contract the ailment either; a preacher from 1951, he seems
always to have been less of a hellraiser than Johnson.

The Ray Brothers' instrumental "Jake Leg Wobble" (Victor V-40291) recorded
in Memphis on May 28, 1930, was the first white response to the outbreak. On
June 5, in the same town, the Allen Brothers (vocalist and banjoist Austin,
1901–1959; guitarist and kazooist Lee, 1906–1981) cut Austin's composition
"Jake Walk Blues" (Victor V-40303), which allegedly sold over 20,000 copies.[166]

"Iron socks" appears in contemporary advertising, meaning "socks that can be ironed," but here it is a joking term for leg braces.

> I can't eat, I can't talk,
> Been drinking mean jake, Lord, now I can't walk.
> Ain't got nothing now to lose
> 'Cause I'm a jake walking papa with the jake walk blues.
>
> "Listen here, papa, can't you see,
> You can't drink jake and get along with me.
> You're a jake walking papa with the jake walk blues,
> I'm a red-hot mama that you can't afford to lose."
>
> "Listen here, daddy, while I tell you once more,
> If you're gonna drink jake, don't you knock at my door."
> Listen here, mama, have to call your hand,
> I'm a jake walking papa from a jake walk land.
>
> I'm not good looking and I'm not lowdown,
> I'm a jake walking papa just hanging around.
> Now I've made this song and it may not rhyme
> But I'm a jake walking papa just having a good time.
>
> My daddy was a gambler and a drunkard too,
> If he was living today, he'd have the jake walk too.
> When I die, you can have my hand,
> Gonna take a bottle of jake to the Promised Land.
>
> *Spoken:* Now, I'm feeling kind of drunk, brother,
> Be wearing jake socks after a while.
> You know they call them iron socks,
> You know, I bet you don't know one from the other, brother.
> Which is the other?

In 1975, forty-five years later, the lyrics of this song were quoted to Dr. John P. Morgan by two victims of jake leg in Johnson City, Tennessee. Morgan writes that the words "are not sympathetic and express the view that for a tough-drinking, tough-living man, the Jake Walk was inevitable."[167] It should be added that the second and third stanzas, which quote a "red-hot mama" rejecting a jake walker, refer obliquely to impotence. The following year Morgan interviewed

Lee Allen, who recalled seeing several jake leggers in and near Chattanooga and elsewhere in eastern Tennessee.[168]

On June 6, 1930, white Mississippians William T. Narmour (fiddler, 1889–1961) and Shell W. Smith (guitarist, 1895–1968) recorded the instrumentals "Jake Leg Rag" (OKeh 45469) and "Limber Neck Blues" (OKeh 45548) in San Antonio, Texas. Four days later, and in the same temporary recording studio, the popular African American group the Mississippi Sheiks, who on this occasion were Walter Vinson (guitar) and the Chatmon brothers, Armenter (aka Bo Carter, vocal, 1893 or 1894–1964), Lonnie (violin, 1888–by 1951), and Sam (vocal and guitar, 1900–1983), responded to the epidemic with "Jake Leg Blues" (OKeh 8939):[169]

> You thought the lively man would die,
> When you made the country dry.
> When you made it so that he could not get
> Not another drop of rye.
> But I know that you will feel bad
> When you see what he have had.
> When you see him coming with a lot of talk,
> If you listen I will tell you, folks.
>
> *Chorus:*
> Oh well, it's here he come, I mean to tell you, here he come,
> He's got those jake limber leg blues.
> Here he come, I mean to tell you, here he come,
> He's got those jake limber leg blues.
>
> When you see him coming, I am going to tell you,
> If you sell him jake, you better give him a crutch too.
> Oh, well, it's here he come, I mean to tell you, here he come,
> He's got those jake limber leg blues.
>
> *Spoken:* Oh, step on it.
>
> *Chorus*
> He could be named Charlie and he could be named Ned.
> But if he drinks this jake, it will give him the limber leg.
>
> *Chorus*

The tone of the piece is blithe and satirical. The first stanza is critical of Prohibition laws, and the "you" addressed are Prohibitionists ("dries") and white legislators, who are blamed for the jake leg outbreak, seen as an indirect consequence of legal alcohol being unavailable, and therefore unregulated for purity.

Jimmie Rodgers (1897–1933), then the biggest name in country music, inspired many disciples, among them Virginian blue yodeler Byrd Moore (as Bert Moss).[170] His "Jake Leg Blues" (Superior 2559) was recorded in Richmond, Indiana, on September 27, 1930:

> Listen to my story, listen to my song (x2)
> Tell you about the old jake liquor, tell me if I'm right or wrong.
>
> He wrecked this great nation, put the widows, orphans on the
>   street (x2)
> No home to go, nothing for 'em to eat.
>
> Don't see why he could be so cruel to wreck so many homes (x2)
> Leave widows and orphans out in the cold wide world to roam.
>
> I saw two little chilluns come to me and said (x2)
> "Mother has gone to heaven, Father is sick in bed."
>
> Did not stop to study, eager with his old jake plan (x2)
> All he wanted was money, did not care for man.
>
> I see some in hospitals, some all on the street (x2)
> I meet them on crutches asking for something to eat.
>
> "I'll always be a cripple," young man cried and said (x2)
> "I shall be a burden on my people, I would rather be dead."

Unlike the popular Allen Brothers' song, this recording "is the only jake performance that expresses sorrow so clearly and contains little of the whimsy and cynicism of other songs."[171]

In November 1930 Pope, Mississippi, hillbilly musician Bernard (Slim) Smith (1899–1991) was in New York City. On November 11, he recorded "Jake Itus Blues" for ARC, and ca. November 19, he cut "Jakeitus Blues" for Gennett. These are presumably versions of the same song, which almost certainly dealt with the paralytic illness, but neither was released.[172] More successful was the superb "Got the Jake Leg Too" (Victor V-23508), sung to the tune of "Frankie and Johnny" by the white Ray Brothers (fiddler Will E. and singer and guitarist S. Vardaman Ray), originally from Chester in Choctaw County, but living in Winona, Mississippi. The song may have been intended as a follow-up to their earlier instrumental, "Jake Walk Wobble." The record label credits S. V. Ray as composer, but in fact the lyrics were by Clayton Riley, a songwriter living in Winona:[173]

> I went to bed last night, feeling mighty fine,
> Two o'clock this morning, the jake leg went down my spine,
> I had the jake leg too, I had the jake leg too.
>
> I woke up this morning, I couldn't get out of my bed,
> This stuff they call jake leg had me nearly dead,
> It was the jake leg too, it was the jake leg too.
>
> Looks like old Aunt Dinah been in a hive of bees,
> This stuff they call jake leg has gone down in her knees,
> She got the jake leg too, she got the jake leg too.
>
> A preacher drinked some ginger, he said he did it for flu,
> That was his excuse for having the Jake Leg too,
> He got the jake leg too, he got the jake leg too.
>
> Talk about your liquor, talk about your booze,
> This stuff they call jake leg has gone down in my shoes,
> I got the jake leg too, I got the jake leg too.
>
> Boys, Jamaica ginger sure will do its part,
> Boys, Jamaica ginger will kill your honest heart,
> I got the jake leg too, I got the jake leg too.
>
> Now you've heard my story, but I haven't told half,
> This on your tomb will be your epitaph:
> I had the jake leg too, had the jake leg too.
>
> My song has grown monotonous but one more thing I'd say,
> For all you jake leggers I will always pray,
> I had the jake leg too, I had the jake leg too.

The text pokes fun at respectable people exposed as drinkers by the jake leg, but it is also sympathetic to sufferers, possibly because Lester Ray, a younger brother, suffered from the disease, although he ultimately made a complete recovery.

As Dave and Howard, white country musicians David McCarn (vocal and harmonica) and Howard Long (vocal and kazoo) recorded "Bay Rum Blues" (Victor 23566) in Charlotte, North Carolina, on May 19, 1931. The song refers to people who are afraid of "ginger," presumably because of jake leg, and drink "bay rum" (a brand of hair tonic) instead.[174] These songs make incidental references; "Jake Leg Blues" (Vocalion 1676), recorded in Chicago on October 21, 1931, by the African American wife and husband Mississippi Sarah and Daddy Stovepipe (Sarah and Johnny Watson) probably dealt more fully with the disease, but no copy of the record has been found.

It was eighteen months before the next recording about jake leg, which suggests that the affliction had become an accepted, if regrettable, fact of life rather than a topical crisis. On April 5, 1933, country music singer and guitarist Asa Martin (1900–1979) recorded "Jake Walk Papa" (Champion S-16627) for the Starr Piano Company in Richmond, Indiana. The song is closely based on the Allen Brothers' "Jake Walk Blues," but Martin's fifth and sixth stanzas are interesting:[175]

> I'm leaving you, mama, so fare you well,
> I'll have my jake in spite of you know,[176]
> I'm going now, mama, but you will see,
> You'll never get another loving papa like me.
>
> "Come back, daddy, I'll tell you true:
> Your loving mama can't live without you.
> You can drink your jake, have your way,
> Do anything, daddy, but don't go away."

Martin's jake leg victim is clearly not one of those affected by impotence, but its existence in others is implicit in his celebration of his own escape. Morgan notes, "Martin told me that there were many victims of the jake leg near his home in Winchester, Kentucky, when he was a young man and, in fact, like the Allen Brothers, he made a jake song because of the publicity and clear evidence of the disease in his own community."[177]

Next, and last, an African American produced an excellent musical response. From Crystal Springs, Mississippi, Willie "Poor Boy" Lofton (possibly 1897–1960s) recorded "Jake Leg Blues" (Decca 7076) in Chicago on August 24, 1934.[178]

> I say, jake leg, jake leg, jake leg, jake leg, tell me what in the world you gonna do,
> I say, jake leg, jake leg, jake leg, tell me what in the world you gonna do,

I say he done drunk so much jake, oh, Lord, till it done give him the
  limber leg.
Spoken: Yeah.

I say, I know the jake leg, oh, Lord, just as far as I can hear the poor boy
  walk,
Hmmmmmm, hmmmmmm.

I say, the people drink their jake on the roadside, oh, Lord; they even
  throw the bottle away (x2)
But the jake left 'em with a present, oh, Lord, that keep 'em company
  every day.

Hmmmmm, mama, mama, mama, mama, mama, Lord, children keep
  on crying,
Wonder what in the world poor daddy gonna do,
I say, he done drunk so much jake, oh, Lord, till it done give him the
  limber leg.

Mama, mama, mama, mama cried out and say, oh, Lord, there's nothing
  in the world poor daddy can do,
'Cause he done drink so much jake, oh, Lord, till he's got the limber leg
  too.

Lofton's song is inspired by his friend Tommy Johnson's jake leg recording, and
includes his line about the limber leg (here meaning impotence, as "nothing in
the world poor daddy can do" makes clear); but it is notable for being entirely
about the troubles of others, not the singer himself, and for its empathy with
victims and their families. Particularly arresting is Lofton's account of people
casually swigging jake and throwing the empty bottle away, only for brief pleasure to result in permanent affliction. The line about hearing "the poor boy
walk" refers to the distinctive flapping sound of the toe and heel striking the
ground with each step.

There are several song titles in the Copyright Office that may have dealt
with the event, but were not issued on records.[179] "Jake-i-tis Blues" (May 2, 1930,
E pub. 18435), may be the Slim Smith song; with words by Joe M. Reynolds and
J. C. Gilliland, and arrangement and music by Gilliland, it was registered in
Corinth, Mississippi. "Jakey Blues" (August 25, 1930, E pub. 17614), with words
and melody by James Rooney and copyright held by Frank Harding, was registered in New York. The unpublished "Jake Leg Blues" (November 1, 1930, E unp.
31004) has Julius Dewitt Henley as composer and copyright holder. The song
was registered in Afton, Texas. The words and music of "Jakefoot" (November

3, 1930, E unp. 30050) were written and registered by H. R. Kent and D. N. Duncan in Ponca City, Oklahoma.

As the jake leg epidemic faded from memory, "jake" in postwar blues became a general term for "alcoholic drink" or "illegal liquor," as it had been before the outbreak. On August 14, 1960, Black Ace (1905 or 1907–1972, real name "Babe" Kyro "Lemon" Turner) recorded "Beer Drinkin' Woman" (Arhoolie LP 1017) in Fort Worth, Texas;[180] in the first stanza he refers to his "jake drinking woman."

It is immediately obvious from the foregoing discussion that no gospel songs were recorded. The theme fits with stereotypes of the "blues life" and blues topics, but this finding is still unexpected. Drinking was considered a sin by many Christians, and a disaster thought to result from sinful behavior often prompted a reproachful gospel song. Religious singers may have been reluctant to express condemnation because the victims were often relatives, friends, or neighbors and were therefore perceived as individuals, rather than an anonymous mass. The blues format was certainly more suitable than narrative ballads for describing a once-and-for-all event that had permanent consequences (especially, perhaps, when one of them was impotence), and this probably explains why white recordings are very bluesy, in both content and form.

It continues to be essential to dispel doubts and correct false views, and to consider how attitudes to the disease are differentiated by race. With regard to the former, it is important to note that there was a higher incidence of jake leg among African Americans than was believed in the 1930s. At that time, scientists at the University of Oklahoma and the University of Cincinnati suggested that the Black community was almost immune to the illness. These findings have been challenged by later research; not least among the reasons for the undercounting of Black sufferers in contemporary statistical surveys is that many of them were not admitted to hospital.[181] It is additional counterevidence that African Americans made half the recordings about the paralysis, including the first two.[182]

As for the artists' responses to the outbreak, Black musicians make no bones about impotence being a result of the illness, and do not feel entitled to pass moral or ethical judgment on people's conduct. Willie Lofton's wholly sympathetic view of sufferers is especially striking; so too is Bo Carter's slightly veiled reproach to white lawmakers. With the exception of the Allen Brothers, white singers are more reticent about the sexual aspects of the illness, although the topic is by no means absent from their songs. Their responses to the epidemic are varied and assertive: there is pity for the victims, and gleeful exposure of hypocrisy, but most usual is defiant determination to continue drinking and having fun. This is a stance that blues, and bluesy images, are well-suited to expressing, and a further reason for the use of the form by white singers.

Figure 3.03. Echo(e)s of Zion's "Atlanta's Tragic Monday" first pressing (David Evans). David Evans collection, Courtesy David Evans

Atlanta's Tragic Monday: The 1951 Poisoned Moonshine Incident

More than twenty years after the jake leg epidemic, another tragedy caused by the adulteration of illegal alcohol occurred, mainly in Atlanta, Georgia.[183] Late on Sunday, October 21, 1951, the first victims of poisoned moonshine whiskey were admitted to the Grady Negro Clinic and other hospitals in the city.[184] Several hundred people, including a ten-year-old boy, were afflicted by a concoction that caused blindness, staggering, panting, frothing at the mouth, and convulsive writhing. Forty people died, thirty-six of them Black, a number went totally blind, and dozens suffered partial loss of vision.

The 120-gallon batch of moonshine was a blend of well water, corn whiskey, peach flavoring, and the poisonous ingredient, methyl alcohol, also called wood alcohol. It was prepared at a deserted farmhouse near Duluth,[185] about twenty miles northeast of Atlanta in Gwinnett County, and distributed by two white moonshiners. John R. "Fat" Hardy, a forty-four-year-old, 360-pound ex-convict with a long record of liquor violations, was charged with murder. Roger Smallwood, twenty-four, was indicted for manslaughter, as were two African Americans: L. O. Riggins, a wholesale bootlegger, and Richard "Snooks" Weems, Riggins's delivery man, who had assisted with the preparation of the deadly mixture. After Hardy's trial, in which the other three men testified, a grand jury indicted them for murder.[186]

Atlanta Police Lieutenant L. T. Bullard said that the mixture had mainly been sold in the Black area of the city known as Peoplestown by twelve dealers (ten

Black and two white), who were all arraigned on manslaughter charges, as was druggist C. B. Wheeler, who had sold Hardy the wood alcohol. Alcohol sales were legal in Atlanta, but there was no liquor store within a mile of either Peoplestown or Summerhill, the other Black district affected by the tragedy. Drinkers living there found it cheaper and more convenient to buy moonshine locally.[187]

Hardy and Smallwood were indicted because of the testimony of white farmer Luke Franklin Turner, who saw them mix and decant the whiskey. This took place in Turner's barn; he was paid $10 for its use or, in another account, for storing the whiskey before its transportation to Atlanta.[188] The state called for a death sentence on Hardy, but he was sentenced to life imprisonment, following a jury recommendation of mercy.[189]

Two topical songs were recorded about the event, both by Atlanta musicians, and both on the local Gerald label, owned by Joe Galkin. Gospel group the Echoes of Zion cut "Atlanta's Tragic Monday" (Gerald 103) in late 1951 or (more likely) early 1952 (see fig. 3.03).[190]

> *Chorus*:
> Wasn't it sad? (So sad one Monday morning),
> Oh, wasn't it sad? (So sad one Monday morning),
> Wasn't it sad? (So sad one Monday morning),
> The people was dying from drinking moonshine.
>
> Oh, it was down in Gwinnett County,
> During revival time;
> Men should have been praying:
> They were making bad moonshine.
>
> *Chorus*
>
> They mixed this deadly poison,
> Forgetting the bloodstained banner.
> They sped the dangerous highway
> Bringing death and sorrow to Atlanta.
>
> *Chorus*
>
> Grady Hospital sent out a call
> For doctors one and all.
> Kin folks standing around,[191]
> Lord, no remedy could be found.

Chorus

Now, let me tell you, friends,
Just what to do.
You'd better drink pure water
I know it's good to do.

Chorus

Oh, you'd better drink that water
[That] flows from Emmanuel's veins,
Yes, where those sinners,
Lord, can lose their stains.

Chorus

Oh, on that awful morning
I heard a mother cry
"Lord, God Almighty
I b'lieve my child will die."

Chorus (x2)[192]

The first half of the song relates factual information about the event, whereas
the second adopts the moralizing approach typical of most gospel songs about
disasters. The first half only hints at condemnation of the guilty parties, which
is not surprising, given the risk of a racist backlash against the group, the record
company, or Black Atlantans in general. However, the repeated use of the word
"they" conveys an implicit racial angle: as already noticed, "they" often serves as
a coded reference to white people in both secular and sacred African American
lyrics, when actions against African Americans, individually or collectively, are
being criticized.[193]

African American press coverage took note of racial issues relevant to the
tragedy. The *Pittsburgh Courier* noted that "A white man and a white woman
were dead and several whites were sick from the 'stuff,' giving impetus to the
speedy action of police, who ordinarily only snipe at Atlanta's bootleg racket."[194]

Atlanta's Black-owned *Daily World*, reliant on advertising by white-owned
businesses, dared not accuse whites of crime until they had been arrested and
charged. Accordingly, editor William Gordon, aware that the police had not
charged "Fat" Hardy, gave the story to his friend Ralph McGill, the white editor
of the *Constitution*, before publishing it himself. Gordon also sent a delivery

truck to broadcast warnings about the moonshine[195]—perhaps the one that "kept the 'Bad, Bad Whiskey' tune playing constantly while an announcer issued periodic warnings."[196]

The second half of the song uses the tragedy as an opportunity to reproach moonshine drinkers more directly, and to suggest an alternative path in life. This directness is possible because it is African Americans, as both the main sufferers from the poisoning and the likely purchasers of the record, who are taken to task.

Unsurprisingly, the song's language draws on religious sources, and does so in a very detailed and specific way. "The bloodstained banner," forgotten by the men who made and transported the moonshine, appears in the African American gospel song "We Are Soldiers in the Army." The reference to the "water [that] flows from Emmanuel's veins" is adapted from William Cowper's 1772 hymn "Praise for the Fountain Opened," usually known as "There Is a Fountain Filled with Blood," which uses the crucified Christ's wounds as signifiers of atonement:

> There is a fountain filled with blood drawn from Emmanuel's veins;
> And sinners plunged beneath that flood lose all their guilty stains.

This hymn is often sung in Black churches, and its opening verse is incorporated into other gospel songs.

The distinctiveness of the song lies in its contrast between indictment and sympathy, sin and redemption. Its spiritual blend is appropriate and well balanced, unlike the blended spirits that caused the tragedy.

The second recording was "Fat Hardy's Boogie" (Gerald 104) by Roy Mays and His Orchestra with vocals by Tommy Brown (1931–2016).[197] Credited to Smith-Brown-Barnet,[198] this song was presumably recorded early in 1952. It is a rhythm and blues piece in the same spirit as "Good Rockin' Tonight," a 1947 hit for both Roy Brown and Wynonie Harris. The reference to "Fat" Hardy's death-dealing product sits oddly within the song's exuberant tone, but gallows humor was doubtless one response to the disaster.

> *Chorus (with slight variations after each stanza):*
> Don't want no Fat Hardy's toddy at the party [No!]
> Can't have no Fat Hardy's toddy at the party [No!]
> Want no Fat Hardy's toddy, can't have that Fat Hardy's toddy.
> Don't want no Fat Hardy's toddy at the party.
>
> Well, Caldonia was there, a brand-new wig
> Deacon Jones came down to cut a little jig

Fannie Brown was there to cut a little rug
Grandma even brought her jug
On down, down to the Hole in the Wall

Well, Minnie got loaded, wobbled on the floor
Mitzi got high and tore down the door
'Bout the break of day the juice gave out
Above all the noise I heard 'em shout:

Well, the joint got hot as day was breaking,
Feet was shuffling, the house was shaking.
Above all the noise I heard 'em cry
"There's no one at the party to die."

The phrase "Fat Hardy's toddy" was almost certainly current in Atlanta soon after the poisoning, and before the song was written in (at the latest) February 1952. Tommy Brown maintained that the death toll was "about 139 people," and elsewhere that it was "138 or 139 people."[199] It seems that he was adding one hundred, for dramatic effect, to a total widely announced at the time. His claim, in the same sources, that "Fat" Hardy tried to sue him over the song appears equally unlikely; either that, or Hardy was extremely optimistic. Brown also said that he himself had never touched alcohol, but claimed that a relative of his ran a club where many people drank the poisoned moonshine and died as a result.[200]

MY HEALTH IS FAILING ME: MISCELLANEOUS EPIDEMICS AND DISEASES[201]

A chapter in Paul Oliver's *Blues Fell This Morning* was the first general study of blues and contagious diseases.[202] The present study considers blues and country singers' responses to specific diseases, and looks at the relevant songs in more detail than Oliver did, but it makes no claim to be exhaustive. The impact of these diseases on society was widespread, but often recurrent and long-term, unlike the 1918–20 influenza pandemic, for example. The diseases also differ from one-off incidents like the 1930 Jamaica ginger paralysis and the 1951 Atlanta moonshine poisonings. Accordingly, the discussion that follows is thematic rather than chronological.[203]

Meningitis Blues

Outbreaks of meningitis (inflammation of the meninges, the membranes enclosing the brain and spinal cord) were common in America before the development of antibiotics, and Memphis was severely hit in the first half of 1930. In the whole of 1929, only thirty-eight cases, twenty-five of them people from east Arkansas, had been treated in Memphis, but by April 22, 1930, there had been eighty-six deaths among 175 stricken people.[204] Only at the end of May, when the epidemic was almost over, was a topical blues recorded.

Memphis Minnie made the first recording of her composition, "Meningitis Blues" (Victor 23421), on May 26, 1930, as a guest vocalist with the Memphis Jug Band.[205] With her then-husband, Kansas Joe McCoy, on second guitar, Minnie also re-recorded the song (in two takes) for Vocalion in Chicago, on June 5, 1930. It was probably the record company who punningly titled it "Memphis Minnie-Jitis Blues" on Vocalion 1588.[206]

> Mmm, the meningitis killing me (x2)
> I'm bending, I'm bending, baby, my head is nearly down to my knee.
>
> I come in home one Saturday night, pulled off my clothes and I lied down (x2)
> And next morning just about day, the meningitis began to creep around.
>
> My head and neck was paining me, seemed like my back was breaking too (x2)
> Lord, I had such a misery that morning, I didn't know what in the world to do.
>
> My companion take me to the doctor, "Doctor, please tell me my wife's complaint,"
> My companion taken me to the doctor, "Doctor, please tell me my wife's complaint,"
> The doctor looked down on me, shook his head, said, "I wouldn't mind telling you, son, but I can't."
>
> "You take her 'round to the city hospital, just as quick, quick as you possible can,
> Take her 'round to the city hospital, just as quick, quick as you possible can,
> Because the condition she's in now, you never will get her back home 'live again."

> He run me 'round to the city hospital, the clock was striking ten,
> Drove me 'round to the city hospital, the clock was striking ten,
> I said to my companion, "Say, I won't see your smiling face again."

Apart from minor differences, Minnie's version with the Memphis Jug Band omits the penultimate verse above and includes an additional stanza:

> Then the nurses all began to stand around me, the doctors had done
>   give me out (x2)
> Every time I would have a potion, I would have a foaming at the mouth.

Memphis Minnie's realism and intensity, her accurate description of the symptoms, and bluesman Brewer Phillips's account below of what Memphis Minnie apparently told him suggest that she contracted and recovered from meningitis. In an interview, Phillips said:

> At the time, she had the meningitis . . . she was at John Gaston Hospital (In Memphis) and she had meningitis and yellow fever. The doctors give up on her. There wasn't no cure for her. And [her husband] went and got her a quart of corn whiskey and that saved her. The yellow fever and the meningitis, she made it, she stayed in the hospital, on charity, and you know how it was in the South. And she got treatment sometime. And she made the *Meningitis Blues* in the hospital. She recorded it in the hospital. And during that time, when she went into a coma, they pushed her away, back in the back room to die, and covered her up with a sheet. And the next morning that whiskey had sweated that fever out. The sheet was yellow and everything. And she survived. That whiskey cured her. How many times she told me.[207]

Phillips's account probably has some grounding in what Memphis Minnie told him, but it is inconsistent ("The doctors give up on her . . . And she got treatment sometime"), and some of its assertions ("She recorded it in the hospital") seem intended to impress his interviewer. Though there was a devastating yellow fever outbreak in Memphis in 1879 and 1880, the "yellow fever" he refers to is surely jaundice, which is a symptom of meningitis in infants but rarely in adults. It remains an open question whether Memphis Minnie developed meningitis or some other feverish illness, or was simply motivated to write her song by the recent outbreak.[208] Whatever the reason, "Memphis Minnie-Jitis Blues" stands out on its own for its originality and psychological impact on the African American population of the time, as it was the only recording to bring "an obscure disorder into public light" and its lyrics "created a drama around a prevalent early-twentieth-century malady, a disorder that affected African Americans in the Mid-South disproportionately." As a result, when Memphis Minnie performed the song or Black people listened to her recording, "it was at once an expression of the new economy and an index of the rising visibility of regional culture and health."[209]

On December 11, 1933, St. Louis–based Frank Pluitt recorded "Meningitis Blues" (Victor 23428), with Roosevelt Sykes (as Willie Kelly) on piano.[210] No copy of the record has been found, but Pluitt was probably inspired by the summer and autumn outbreak of encephalitis in St. Louis and St. Louis County, with 1,097 cases resulting in 221 deaths. The disease was transmitted by mosquitoes, which had bred vigorously in an unusually hot, dry summer. Now named after the city where it was first identified, St. Louis encephalitis is widespread, though not common, from Canada to South America. Encephalitis is an inflammation of the brain, rather than the meninges, but it has similar symptoms, and it seems likely that the general public sometimes conflated it with the more familiar disease.[211]

Pneumonia Blues

The incidence of pneumonia as a cause of death among African Americans was relatively high in the first three decades of the twentieth century; at 257 and 197 per 100,000 in 1910 and 1920 respectively, it was the second most frequent cause of death after tuberculosis. Migration to industrial towns, both northern and southern—where living conditions were often unhealthy, and overcrowding facilitated the spread of disease—was certainly a contributory factor, but by 1930 the pneumonia mortality rate among Blacks was down to 138 per 100,000. It fell again to 92 per 100,000 in 1940, and in those years was respectively the fourth and fifth most common cause of death.[212]

His death certificate gives the cause of Blind Lemon Jefferson's death, on December 19, 1929, as "probably chronic myocarditis." He was found dead in the street, on the second day of a two-day blizzard which had deposited nearly fifteen inches of snow on Chicago.[213] Three months earlier, on September 24, Jefferson had recorded "Pneumonia Blues" (Paramount 12880) in Richmond, Indiana.[214] It is a myth—which Jefferson seems to have believed—that exposure to cold or wet weather can lead to pneumonia,[215] and the song may not even be autobiographical, but his imminent death during a snowstorm gives it an unintended premonitory quality.

> Aching all over, believe I've got the pneumonia this time,
> I'm aching all over, believe I got the pneumonia this time,
> And it's all on account of that lowdown gal of mine.

Sneaking 'round the corners, running up alleys too,
I say, I'm sneaking 'round corners and running up alleys too,
Watching my woman, trying to see what she gon' do.

Stood out in the streets, one cold, dark, stormy night,
I stood out in the streets, one dark and stormy night,
Trying to see if my good gal gon' make it home all right.

I believe she's found something, good partner, it's made her fall,
She must did found something, and I believe it made her fall,
I've stood out in the cold all night, and she didn't come home at all.

And it's BVDs[216] in the winter, prowling 'round in the rain,
Wearing BVDs in the winter, prowling 'round in the rain,
Running down my baby give me this pneumony pain.

Now when I die, bury me in a Stetson hat,
I say, when I die, bury me in a Stetson hat,
Tell my good gal I'm gone, but I'm still a-standing pat.

The song was credited to "Jefferson-LaMoore," the latter a pseudonym for Aletha Dickerson (1902–1994), pioneering producer J. Mayo Williams's secretary and Paramount's unofficial race recording director.[217] In typical blues mode, the song is an indictment of his woman for causing Jefferson's pneumonia, rather than a description of the disease.

The disease was still the leading infectious cause of death in America when Big Bill Broonzy recorded "Pneumonia Blues (I Keep on Aching)" (ARC 6-07-57) in Chicago on April 22, 1936:[218]

I'm feeling sick and bad, my head is hurting too,
Go get the doctor, so he can tell me just what to do
Because I keep on aching, yes, I ache both night and day.
Yeah, doctor, doctor, please drive this old pneumonia away.

I have got the pneumonia, I've got it in both my sides,
My friends treat me so bad till I just can't keep from crying.
Poor me, I keep aching, yes, I ache both night and day.
Yeah, doctor, doctor, please drive this old pneumonia away.

I have used Vicks bags, I done used everything my friends said.
Now I believe I'll take a hot toddy and go to bed

Because I keep on aching, yes, I ache both night and day.
Yeah, doctor, doctor, please drive this old pneumonia away.

My friends told my wife they had did all they could.
They said, "Put him in a hospital before he ruins the neighborhood."
I keep on aching, yes, I ache both night and day.
Yeah, doctor, doctor, please drive this old pneumonia away.

The doctor said my fever was a hundred and three.
The nurse said, "Put him in a private room, that's where he ought to be
Because he keeps on aching." Yes, I aches both night and day.
Yeah, doctor, doctor, please drive this old pneumonia away.

The original lyrics to this song[219] describe symptoms, folk remedies ("hot toddy," "Vicks bags"), and the isolation arising from other people's fear of catching the disease. There may be an autobiographical element to Broonzy's song, but in the 1930s pneumonia was a public health issue. Antipneumococcal serotherapy had been developed in the late 1920s, but the process was complex, expensive, and hospital-dependent. Public health advocates who wanted to make the serum cheaper and more easily administered set out to create awareness of pneumonia as a public health issue. Dr. Thomas Parran, appointed surgeon general by President Roosevelt in April 1936, was a leading advocate of pneumonia control through federal funding of state programs; Broonzy's song predates Parran's expansion of such funding, but when "Pneumonia Blues (I Keep on Aching)" was recorded there was heightened public awareness of the disease. When easily administered sulfonamides replaced serotherapy from 1939 onwards, pneumonia control programs ceased to be relevant.[220]

"Dust Pneumonia Blues" (Victor 26623), recorded in New York City on May 3, 1940, by folk singer Woody Guthrie (1912–1967), deals with a different kind of pneumonia, and despite his sometimes humorous first-person presentation, Guthrie's perspective is more politically and community-oriented.[221]

I got that dust pneumony, pneumony in my lung. (x2)
And I'm a-gonna sing this dust pneumony song.

I went to the doctor, and the doctor, said, "My son (x2)
You got that dust pneumony and you ain't got long, not long."

Now there ought to be some yodeling in this song;
Yeah, there ought to be some yodeling in this song;
But I can't yodel for the rattling in my lung.

My good gal sings the dust pneumony blues. (x2)
She loves me 'cause she's got the dust pneumony, too.

If it wasn't for chopping, my hoe would turn to rust. (x2)
I can't find a woman in this black old Texas dust.

Down in Oklahoma, the wind blows mighty strong. (x2)
If you want to get a mama, just sing a California song.

Down in Texas, my gal fainted in the rain. (x2)
I threwed a bucket of dirt in her face just to bring her back again.

"Dust Pneumonia Blues" is part of Guthrie's "Dust Bowl Ballads" song cycle, inspired by the natural and man-made disaster that hit the American prairies, and their inhabitants, in the latter half of the 1930s. Dust pneumonia was a fibrosis of the lungs, caused by the inhalation of dust particles. It mainly affected the young and elderly; accurate mortality rates are not available, but hundreds and possibly thousands of people died.[222]

The song's blues structure is probably derived from Jimmie Rodgers, whose trademark blue yodel is wryly referenced in the third stanza. Guthrie juxtaposes sober description of the illness with cynical, estranging humor, but there is a political undercurrent: the stanza about chopping with an underemployed (rusty) hoe carries a sexual double meaning, but it also suggests that the dust storm's economic hardship disrupts relationships. The contrast between dust-ridden Oklahoma and California alludes to the westward migration that many people hoped would offer escape from the dust storms and the hard times they brought.

It is difficult to draw conclusions from such a small corpus of songs, and Woody Guthrie's politically conscious songwriting may not be typical of white responses; but it appears that African American blues singers favored a more personal and individualistic approach to pneumonia, whether or not they were drawing on their own experiences.

Poliomyelitis

Outbreaks of poliomyelitis, also known as polio or infantile paralysis, were recurrent in the twentieth century, mainly in the summer months, until Jonas Salk developed a vaccine in the mid-1950s. Blues singer Brownie McGhee was infected as a child. President from 1932 to his death, Franklin Roosevelt (1882–1945), contracted polio in the early 1920s. Roosevelt was careful not to be seen in a wheelchair, but his disability was well known, and lyricist McKinley

Kantor didn't need to mention him by name in his, and composer Harry Rosenthal's, sentimental pop eulogy, "The Man Who Couldn't Walk Around." African American artist Josh White, whose repertoire extended beyond blues, and who was a friend of Eleanor Roosevelt's, premiered the song at her request in 1947, and recorded three versions, the first of them (Apollo 157) on June 12 that year.[223]

Polio is otherwise not a subject dealt with by blues singers, but there is probably an indirect connection to King Perry's double entendre "Vaccinate Me Baby" (RPM 381), which was recorded in Los Angeles in 1953. At that time, there was considerable public interest in Salk's attempts to create a vaccine for the disease, which was then in the testing stage.[224]

Syphilis and Gonorrhea

Syphilis and gonorrhea were not perceived as different diseases until the mid-nineteenth century; they ran rampant until the second half of the twentieth century. Venereal diseases are transmitted through sexual contact with an infected person or congenitally, by infection of the birth canal. In the late 1920s, the rate of syphilitic infection was eight times higher among Black people than among whites, because of bad living conditions, poor health education, and differential access to health care.[225] In 1930 and 1940, syphilis was only the eighth leading cause of death among nonwhites, but between 1919 and 1936 the number of reported cases of syphilis in all races "rose steadily from 113.2 per 100,000 population in 1919 to 212.6 cases per 100,000 population in 1936."[226] In part the figures reflect more widespread notification of cases to public health agencies, but "in 1934 syphilis was blamed for causing about 17,700 deaths. Also, there were an estimated 7,000,000 persons with syphilis, meaning that about one of every ten adults would have the disease during his or her life. About 500,000 new cases were entering treatment annually."[227] A 1944 report on "Physical Examinations of Selective Service Registrants During Wartime" said that "50.2 registrants per 1,000 examined were found to have syphilis; the rate for white registrants being 20.8 and for Negroes 214.7." Comparable rates for gonorrhea were 2.3 and 28.7 per 1,000. As late as 1941, 15 percent of any form of blindness in the United States was due to syphilis, either congenitally or sexually transmitted.[228] This accounts, in part, for the high number of sightless African Americans who gravitated to music as a livelihood.[229]

Walter Davis drew inspiration from this tragic state of affairs to create the lighthearted, suggestive "Think You Need a Shot" (Bluebird B6498), recorded in Chicago on April 3, 1936.[230]

> You've got bad blood, mama, and I believe you need a shot,
> You've got bad blood, babe, I believe you need a shot,
> Now, turn over here, mama, let me see what else you got.

I doctors on women, I don't fool around with men. (x2)
All right, take it easy here, mama, whilst I stick my needle in.

Lord, your ways is so loving, and your skin is nice and soft,
Lord, your ways is loving, and your skin is nice and soft,
Lord, if you keep on grunting, mama, you gon' make me break my
    needle off.

Lord, my needle is in you, baby, and you seem to feel all right (x2)
And when your medicine go to coming down, I want you to hug me
    tight.

Here your medicine come now, baby, put your leg upside the wall,
Say, your medicine come now, mama, put your foot upside the wall,
I don't want to waste none of it, mama, I want you to have it all.

It's obvious what kind of "injection" and "medicine" Davis intends to adminis-
ter. Although to outsiders there would have seemed to be no direct reference
to venereal disease, "bad blood" was then a very common name for syphilis
among Black Americans. (It is now also used to refer to AIDS.) "Unlike whites,
few blacks associated syphilis and gonorrhea with immorality or any loss of
social standing (though they did recognize VD as a health problem). Most
simply concluded that they had 'bad blood,' which they felt was as treatable as
bad teeth."[231] Davis's "shot" refers to weekly injection of salvarsan for as long as
seventy weeks, which was then the treatment for syphilis. Salvarsan, the "magic
bullet" developed by Paul Ehrlich in Germany, and on the market by 1910, was
a compound of arsenic. Not without its own dangers, it was still much safer
and more effective than previous treatments, which had involved poisonous
compounds of mercury.[232]

"Think You Need a Shot" has been thought to be the only blues song related
at length, albeit allusively, to syphilis; but there were two earlier recordings
that are relevant. Bo Carter (real name Armenter Chatmon) may have been
infected with syphilis, of which lower back pain is a common symptom.[233] His
"Backache Blues" (OKeh 8906, June 4, 1931),[234] whose melody derives from
Victoria Spivey's "T-B Blues," seems to relate to the disease. Carter regards his
backache as the symptom of a serious illness ("I'm 'fraid I am too late"), which
leads women to avoid him:

I got the backache so bad, I can't even pull off my shoes. (x2)
I'm just laying 'round here, with those backache blues.

When I was on my feet, I couldn't walk down the street,
For all these pigmeats, just jiving at me,
But mmm, now, this backache's killing me,
I'm on my way to the doctor's, I'm 'fraid I am too late.

This backache ain't bad, but your girl will treat you so low down—lord,
  lord!
This backache ain't bad, but your girl will treat you so low down,
They will all stay 'ways from you, on the other side of town.

Lord, lord!

Mmm now, my kidneys hurting me. (x2)
I'm on my way to the doctor's, I'm 'fraid I am too late.

When I was in my prime, I could love two-three girls, any old time,
Now I'm sick and down, can't get around,
Lord, lord, this backache's killing me,
I'm on my way to the doctor, I'm 'fraid I am too late.

The second song's relevance has only been recognized recently, because its title was changed to disguise the content. In New York on March 14, 1935, Alabaman singer-pianist Walter Roland (1900 or 1902–1972) recorded "O. B. D. Blues" (ARC 5-11-66), on which he sings neither "O" nor "B." In light of his actual lyrics, it seems likely that ARC changed the title to disguise the song's content:[235]

Boys, I can't get nobody, lord, that will care for me. (x2)
Says, you know I can't see why they's scared of that old VD.

It was so dark last night, lord, I could not hardly see,
It was so dark last night, people, I could not hardly see,
But you know, I could hear people a-whispering, lord, about that old VD.

So woman, you leaving, I reckon I have to let you be,
Hey, you leaving, I guess I have to let you be,
Because you done got tired, lord, of this here old VD.

The next woman I get, I'm gon' get her from Tennessee. (x2)
Then I won't have to worry 'bout this here old VD.

Boys, I'm leaving, I'm gon' catch that old Santy Fe. (x2)
Says I'm going down in Florida, where they uses that old VD.

The song's lyrics may depict a man who is either suffering from or thought to have venereal disease. Whatever the reason, he is behaving unethically toward his "next woman" from distant Tennessee. If he is suffering from venereal disease, he has no qualms about not telling her that he has VD and may infect her; if he thinks he suffers from venereal disease, his behavior is unprincipled because she will be unaware that he is gossiped about and shunned as a result. The final stanza presents a puzzle (leaving aside the fact that the Santa Fe railroad went nowhere near Florida, and is only there to supply a rhyme). The likely meaning of "uses that old VD" is that people in Florida are used to it, in other words, that they don't regard VD as a cause for scandal and an excuse for gossip.

Attitudes to venereal disease were changing when Roland composed this song. From being seen as a problem of (im)morality, it was coming to be regarded—not yet universally, as ARC's title change demonstrates—as an issue of public health. In November 1934, New York State health commissioner Dr. Thomas Parran was barred from the air by CBS because he proposed to use the words "syphilis" and "gonorrhea" in a radio talk. The publicity that followed probably did more to raise public awareness, and encourage frank speaking, than the broadcast would have, and when Parran became surgeon general of the United States in April 1936, he campaigned energetically for VD to be regarded as an illness like any other, and greatly increased funding for its control. (Parran's appointment, announced in late January, possibly may have prompted Walter Davis to write the song he recorded on April 3. It is unlikely that there is a direct link between the censored broadcast and Walter Roland's composition, but both are symptomatic of changes in public attitudes.)[236]

Discovered in 1928, penicillin was first used to treat gonorrhea and syphilis by the US armed forces during World War II; it reduced the treatment time dramatically and was highly effective.[237] The 1944 Public Health Service Act paved the way for the drug being made generally available in peacetime. In 1948 a public health campaign began, urging people to get checked and treated for venereal disease; sponsored by the United States Public Health Service, it was overseen by media historian Erik Barnouw, formerly a radio producer but by 1948 supervisor of the Communications Materials Center at Columbia University.

An important part of the initiative was the V.D. Radio Project, a series of twenty-two programs, some of them "ballad dramas or 'hillbilly operas,'"[238] sung and narrated by famous musicians, and including interviews with medical experts.[239]

Columbia University Education Discs also released a 78 r.p.m. record (catalog number VD 602) aimed at spreading the word through jukeboxes and disk jockeys. One side is "I've Got Good News" by the Dixie-Aires (see fig. 3.04). Released in 1949, it was recorded in New York, probably in the same year, with

Figure 3.04. The Dixie-Aires' "I've Got Good News" (Luigi Monge). Luigi Monge collection

words and music credited to Alan Lomax, who wrote and narrated a number of scripts for the radio series. He probably only composed the verses about syphilis and grafted them onto a traditional biblical story-song or possibly an original song by one member of the Dixie-Aires.[240]

> (*Lead*) People! I've got good news
> (*Chorus*) Well, I've got good news (well), the good news, good news
>   this morning
> I've got good news (well), good news, trouble don't last always.
>
> (*Lead*) Well, when Jesus walked in Jerusalem streets
> (*Chorus*) Passing through the land
> (*Lead*) His face was sad, his voice was sweet
> (*Chorus*) Passing through the land
> (*Lead*) The sick folk[s] knew that the Healer had come
> (*Chorus*) Passing through the land
> (*Lead*) They cried "Hosanna" to Jehovah's son
> (*Chorus*) Passing through the land
>
> (*Chorus*) Well, I've got the good news (well), the good news, good news
>   this morning
> I've got good news (well), good news, trouble don't last always.

(*Lead*) Well, a poor man rotted with a bad disease
(*Chorus*) Trouble don't last always
(*Lead*) Cried, "Lord, Lord, help me please"
(*Chorus*) Trouble don't last always
(*Lead*) Well, he fell right down in Jesus' path
(*Chorus*) Trouble don't last always
(*Lead*) And the twelve disciples all drew back
(*Chorus*) Trouble don't last always
(*Lead*) But Jesus, the Healer, he wasn't afraid
(*Chorus*) Trouble don't last always
(*Lead*) Laid His hands on the man, and the sores fell away
(*Chorus*) Trouble don't last always

(*Chorus*) Yes, there is good news moving through the land, through the
    land
There is good news moving through the land, through the land
Well, science is marching on, and the people growing strong
There is good news moving through the land, through the land.

(*Lead*) Yes, the news is flashing the world around
(*Chorus*) Science is marching on
(*Lead*) A cure for syphilis has been found
(*Chorus*) Science is marching on
(*Lead*) It will cure your bloodstream in a matter of days
(*Chorus*) Science is marching on
(*Lead*) If you don't have the money, you don't have to pay
(*Chorus*) Science is marching on

(*Chorus*) Yes, there is good news moving through the land, through the
    land
There is good news moving through the land, through the land
Well, you've heard those doctors' words, that syphilis can be cured
There is good news moving through the land, through the land.

(*Lead*) Well, now stop right still and listen to me
(*Chorus*) Science is marching on
(*Lead*) Syphilis is a hypocrite's disease
(*Chorus*) Science is marching on
(*Lead*) Hide[s] in your blood and it won't show
(*Chorus*) Science is marching on
(*Lead*) Then strike you down before you know

(*Chorus*) Science is marching on
(*Lead*) But a doctor's test will surely tell
(*Chorus*) Science is marching on
(*Lead*) If you're sick or if you're well
(*Chorus*) Science is marching on
(*Lead*) So don't be afraid, don't be ashamed
(*Chorus*) Science is marching on
(*Lead*) Just take your blood test in the Healer's name
(*Chorus*) Science is marching on

(*Chorus*) Yes, I've got good news (well), the good news, good news this
    morning
I've got good news (well), good news, trouble don't last always.

The reverse is "That Ignorant, Ignorant Cowboy." A pop-country ballad written by Barnouw and sung by urban folk singer Tom Glazer, it tells the story of a cowboy who does not realize he has contracted syphilis from a woman.[241] Each side is obviously aimed at a different racial market. The Dixie-Aires' song is positive and optimistic, while Glazer's is at best tragicomic, with its good news ("Only a doctor can cure syphilis") confined to one line, and easily missed. It's clear that Lomax was a much more experienced songwriter than Barnouw, and better able to focus on getting the message across.

In October 1949, Washington, DC, vocal group the Cap-Tans recorded "Put It Down," written by Bette Bullock Murphy. Allied A-12326, a transcription disc for radio play, was produced by the DC Health Department. The compiler of the sixteen-CD box set in which it has been issued rightly observes that "The anti-VD recording is a remarkable reflection of the social and medical reality of life in the black side of segregated Washington at the end of the 1940s."[242]

Tuberculosis

Tuberculosis (TB), also called "the white death," was widespread in the United States in the twentieth century. It was also known as consumption because of the weight loss it causes, and was often referred to thus by blues singers.[243] Pulmonary tuberculosis, the commonest form of the disease, affects the lungs, and is easily transmitted by coughing, sneezing, spitting, or simply in conversation.[244]

In the 1920s, the death rate from consumption in Harlem "was two and a half to three times higher than in the rest of the city."[245] In 1930s Harlem, the mortality rate from the disease was four times higher than in New York City as a whole. The single block bounded by Lenox Avenue, Seventh Avenue, and

142nd and 143rd Streets was known as "the lung block" because its death rate from TB was twice that of white Manhattan.[246]

Despite the efforts of various agencies, the African American death rate from tuberculosis became much higher than that among whites. "The TB death rate among whites in both the North and South declined from 1920 to 1933, [while] the rate among blacks in the North actually climbed upward from 1923 to 1926 and again between 1929 and 1930."[247] This increase is attributable to migration from the South and the precarious living conditions in the North. In the early thirties, the incidence of tuberculosis among African Americans was especially high in the South: "During the Depression years about one-fourth of TB deaths in the United States occurred among blacks. In the South, black mortality from TB, where they composed about 26 percent of the population, amounted to 53 percent of the total TB deaths in this region."[248] Campaigns encouraging people to present themselves for treatment, like the one begun in Detroit in 1936, had positive results, with many African Americans responding,[249] but the disease continued to be a threat; outbreaks swept through Oak Cliff, a Black district of Dallas, in the 1940s.[250]

Songs about Tuberculosis by African American Singers
In the blues, tuberculosis is indelibly associated with Victoria Spivey (1906–1976) and her best-selling "T-B Blues" (OKeh 8494), recorded in St. Louis on April 27, 1927.[251]

> Too late, too late, too late, too late, too late,
> It's too late, too late, too late, too late, too late,
> Well, I'm on my way to Denver,[252] and, mama, mustn't not [sic] hesitate.
>
> TB's all right to have if your friends didn't treat you so lowdown (x2)
> Don't you ask 'em for no favors, they even stop coming around.
>
> Mmmmm, TB's killing me. (x2)
> I'm like a prisoner, always wishing he's free.
>
> When I was up on my feet, I could not walk down the street
> For the mens looking at me from my head to my feet.
> But, oh now, the TB's killing me.
> I want my body buried in the deep blue sea.
>
> Mmmmm, mmmmmmmmm,
> Got the tuberculosis, the consumption's killing me.

Inspired by memories of the death of a childhood playmate, Spivey composed the song in Moberly, Missouri, where she was a staff songwriter for the St. Louis Music Company.[253] In 1960 she explained the context in which she wrote it:

> I'll never know what made me make that record. 'Cause my mother heard it and when she heard it she dialed Tommy Rockwell who at that time was handlin' me and ask if I was sick, if I had the T.B. And then I got afraid I *might* catch the T.B. and every time I hear it I'd shake. I don't know why I said it. But at that time I had been lookin' at people who had the T.B. in part of the country and at that time, if you had the T.B. nobody would have no part with you; they would put you away in hospital and you was just doomed then, you gonna die. So I figgered it was a nice thing to write about.[254]

Spivey's song, and its striking imagery, resonated with the reality of its listeners' lives, and it inspired many covers and adaptations. Its success prompted a sequel, "Dirty T.B. Blues" (Victor V38570), recorded in New York City on October 1, 1929.[255]

> Here I lay a-crying,
> Something is on my mind,
> It's midnight, wonder where the nurse can be?
>
> I feel down, not a friend in this town, I'm blue and all alone.
> Sisters are gone, brothers are too, no one to call my own.
>
> I can't keep from crying, left alone while I am dying.
> Yes, it may look crazy for me to plead on my knee.
> But it's a lot of difference between tough breaks and TB, oh, Lord.[256]
>
> Yes, he railroaded me to the sanitarium.
> It's too late, too late, mother, I done finished my run.
> This is the way all good women are done, when they got the dirty TB.
>
> Yes, I run around for months and months
> From gin mill to gin mill to honky-tonk.
> Now it's too late, just look what I've done done.
> Now I've got the dirty TB.
>
> Mmmmm, ah-ah-ah-ah-ah.
> Oh, Lord, mmmmm, ah-ah, ah-ah.

Spivey's sequel focuses on isolation, the result of rejection by friends, family, a sexual partner who has "railroaded" (coerced) her into a sanatorium, and even a nurse who is neglecting her patient. The song's protagonist blames her predicament on leading a fast life, and the adjective in "dirty TB" may imply a comparison with the social shunning ("This is the way that all good women are done") that could result from VD.

Bessie Tucker (1906 or 1907–1933) recorded a moving and very spare "T.B. Moan" (Victor 23392) in her hometown Dallas, Texas, on October 21, 1929.[257]

> You've got your pistol, a-ha, you've got it drawed on me (x2)
> I'm a real sick woman, sick as I can be.
>
> I may get better, aha, but I can't get well (x2)
> I've got the tuberculosis, and I can't get well.
>
> Tell me, rider, ah-hah, what makes you so mean? (x2)
> I asked you for water, you gave me gasoline.

The song portrays a woman trapped in a violent and loveless relationship (the latter aspect alluded to by the "water/gasoline" trope), who must also cope with suffering from TB. The triple repetition of "I can't get well" leaves the listener in no doubt of her situation, but Tucker's forthright delivery defies mistreatment, invalidism, and impending death.

When Georgia blues guitarist Eugene "Buddy" Moss (1912 or 1913–1984) recorded "T.B.'s Killing Me" (Banner 32736) in New York City on January 18, 1933, he was about twenty years old.[258]

> I went to the doctor, up the street.
> I sat right down and he looked at me.
> He said, "I hate to tell you, but you come to see,
> You ain't got nothing but them old TBs."
> And now, mmm, TBs is killing me.
> I used to have friends but none of them that I can see.
>
> Now, mmmm, mmmm.
> Mmm, TBs is killing me,
> And it won't be long 'fore [in] some lonely graveyard I'll be.
>
> I had a good girl and a happy home,
> But since TB got me, she's left me all alone.
> Said, now, mmm, TBs is killing me,
> And it won't be long before [in] some lonely graveyard I'll be.

Now, boys, these days and I'm just hanging on,
And it won't be long before I'll be gone.
Saying now, mmm, TBs is killing me,
And it won't be long before [in] some graveyard I will be.

Moss takes the repeated "T.B. is killing me" from Spivey. More generally, he is indebted to her for his images of abandonment by friends and a lover, but his lyrics are original, particularly when he introduces dialogue between doctor and patient.

Birmingham, Alabama, guitarist Sonny Scott's "Coal Mountain Blues" (Vocalion 25012), recorded in New York City on July 18, 1933, tells the story of an unemployed man who is refused employment in a coal mine because he has tuberculosis.[259] Coal Mountain, in St. Clair County, is thirty miles northeast of Birmingham. Scott leaves us wondering whether the purpose of his subsequent journey to the coast is to find work as a longshoreman, to take a break from his troubles ("seashore town," rather than "seaport town" is perhaps a clue), or because he has already decided to kill himself.

Spoken: Ah, play it just like I feel it.

Well, I went on Coal Mountain, saw the men pulling coals from the
    mine,
Lord, I went on Coal Mountain, saw the men pulling coals from the
    mine,
I saw the men wearing their mine lamps where all the lights did shine.

Lord, I went to the mine foreman, told him, "I need a job mighty bad."
    (x2)
But he said, "You have to go to the doctor, and boy, you sure won't pass."

Lord, I left that mining section, went to the seashore town (x2)
I believe I'm got the TB, I'm gonna jump overboard and drown.

Spoken: "Oh, shucks, what is this, you reckon?" "I can't tell what it's all
    about."

Lord(y), I've seen a seagull flying, baby, over my watery grave (x2)
And it seemed to say that you going away to stay.

Victoria Spivey's second sequel, and her last prewar song about consumption, is "T.B.'s Got Me" (Decca 7222), recorded in Chicago on July 7, 1936.[260]

Here I lay a-crying,
Something is on my mind,
It's midnight, I wonder where the nurse can be.

T.B.'s got me, all my friends done throwed me down,
T.B.'s got me, and all my friends done throwed me down,
But they treated me so nice when I was up able to run around.

Ooh, my poor lungs are hurting me so,
Mmmmm, my poor lungs are hurting me so,
I don't get no peace or comfort no matter where I go.

Lord, my good man don't want me no more,
Mmm, my good man don't want me no more,
Well, I wish I was dead, and in the land I'm doomed to go.

The repetition of imagery and ideas, and the platitude "My poor lungs are hurting me so," make this an uninspired attempt to milk the success of her previous songs about TB.

On June 29, 1939, in New York City, Kentucky-born guitarist Bill Gaither (1910–1970) recorded "Too Late Too Late" (Decca 7637) under the moniker Leroy's Buddy.[261]

Too late, too late, the doctor can't do no good (x2)
I've got the TBs, I've got to leave my neighborhood.

TB will slowly, slowly carry you down (x2)
And even your best friends won't even come around.

When I was upon my feet, I could not walk down the street
For the women looking at me from my head to my feet.
But oh, now, this TB is killing me,
My body pains all the way down, I'm in so much misery.

When my girl looked at me, stood in my door,
And told me to my face she didn't want me no more,
Oh, oh, I can't be here long.
I got the tuberculosis and my lungs are almost gone.

The stylistic inspiration of Gaither's idol, Leroy Carr, and the influence of Victoria Spivey's hit are both evident in these lyrics, which have the usual focus on ostracism.

On January 23, 1941, singer and pianist Champion Jack Dupree (1910–1992) recorded "Bad Health Blues" (OKeh 06197), the less known, but textually more imaginative and touching, of his two original compositions about tuberculosis.[262] As the liner notes to one reissue observe, "'Bad Health'... proves that you can sing about TB without plagiarizing Victoria Spivey's famous number."[263] Exceptionally, the song is not about the singer's own disease but about his woman's. He vows to stay with her to the end; only after death, "out in the T.B. cemetery," will she undergo the isolation regretted in many blues songs about the disease.

> My woman's in bad health, so do the doctors say (x2)
> And it look like to me T.B.'s gonna kill her dead.
>
> My woman's got the T.B., T.B. is all in her bones,
> My woman's got the T.B., eeeh, T.B. is all in her bones,
> I know I'm gon' miss you, baby, when you're dead and gone.
>
> The people all talking, say you ain't nothing but skin and bone,
> The people all talking, eeeh, say you ain't nothing but skin and bone,
> But I'm gonna be with you, woman, until you're dead and gone.
>
> I wish I would have listened to what my mother say (x2)
> I wouldn't have been worried and down, walking around this way.
>
> When my baby dead and gone, I'm gon' lay her out in a blood-red dress,
> When my baby is dead and gone, I'm gonna lay her out in a blood-red
>   dress,
> I'm gonna lay her out in the T.B. cemetery, different from the rest.

Dupree's fourth stanza about not taking his mother's advice is generic or, more likely, it may have been composed in the woman's words, with the typical shift of persona from the singer to someone else, in this case the sick lover. In the last stanza, the realistic evocation of a bereaved lover preparing to lay out his woman's body for burial is striking. The "blood-red dress," whose color invokes a main symptom of TB, makes for a richly symbolic conclusion.

Probably in April 1948, African American pianist and vocalist Nellie Lutcher (1912–2007) recorded "Chest X-Ray Song" (Capitol 154-3) in Los Angeles. The recording, which appears on both sides of the disc, was a similar public health initiative to the Dixie-Aires' song about syphilis; in this case, the aim was to encourage people to be X-rayed for tuberculosis. James C. Petrillo, president of the American Federation of Musicians, granted an exemption from the ban on recording which he had imposed from January 1, 1948. With words by Charles Alldredge, assistant to Secretary of the Interior Julius A. Krug, set to the tune of Lutcher's hit "Hurry on Down to My House," the custom-pressed record was sponsored by the District Health Department, the United States Health Service and the National Tuberculosis Association of New York. Lutcher premiered the song in the Loews Theater projection booth at the National Press Building in early May 1948.[264]

> *Spoken:* X-ray, X-ray, X-ray time,
> X-ray, X-ray. I've had mine.

> *Sung:* I'm ready now and raring to go
> Little old X-ray told me so
> Just took a minute, click, click, click,
> For the picture to show I wasn't sick.

> Thought I wasn't but I wanted to know
> Honey baby, I am raring to go.
> Yes, I'm ready now and raring to go
> 'Cause the little old X-ray told me so.

> *Scat*

> Old T.B. can't get me down,
> Stopped at the X-ray on the way to town.
> Took my picture, fast as they could,
> Showed just what I thought it would.

> I am healthy, and I'm fine,
> I know 'cause I went through the X-ray line.
> I'm ready now, and raring to go,
> The little old X-ray told me so.

> *Scat*

> Honey, soon as you awaken
> Go and get your picture taken

Tell the man to let you know
Just what the little pictures show.

Costs you nothing, no, not a dime
To make you happy in your mind.
So run down, honey, quick, quick, quick,
And let that X-ray click, click, click.

X-ray, X-ray time, X-ray, X-ray, I've had mine.
Honey, hurry, hurry on down,
Get your place in the X-ray line.

Seventeen years after his "Bad Health Blues," Champion Jack Dupree recorded "T.B. Blues" (Atlantic LP 8019) in New York City on February 4, 1958.[265]

Well, I got the TBs and the TB is all in my bones, all in my bones,
Yes, I got the TBs, TB is all in my bones,
Well, the doctor told me that I ain't gon' be here long.

Well, the TBs is all right to have, but your friends treat you so lowdown, so lowdown,
Yes, the TB is all right to have, your friends treat you so lowdown, so lowdown,
Yeah, don't ask 'em for no favor, they will even stop coming round, stop coming round.

Well, I sent for the doctor, see what the doctor could do for me,
Yes, I sent for the doctor, see what he could do for me, do for me,
He say, "I'm sorry, I'm sorry." Lord, have mercy on me. Oh, yeah!

Well, I know you're gon' miss me, baby, when I'm dead and gone, when I'm dead and gone,
Yes, you're gonna miss me, baby, baby, when I'm dead and gone,
Well, you see, I've got the TBs, now I'm dead and gone.

There is little new in these lyrics, apart from the assertion to his girlfriend that "you're gonna miss me when I'm dead and gone." Even this is a blues commonplace, however.

Robert "Guitar" Welch's "T.B. Blues" is an interesting conflation of original and traditional verses; unissued, it was collected by Harry Oster in the State Penitentiary at Angola, Louisiana, on February 27, 1959.[266]

Woh, baby, T.B.'s killin' me,
Lord, baby, T.B.'s killin' me,
Bad luck in my family, Lord, you done all fell on me.

When I was on my feet, I could not walk down the street
For the women lookin' at me, I'm crying, hey baby, that T.B. killin' me,
Doctor say, "Baby is dyin' by degree.'"

You know it's a mean mistreater that doin' me thisdaway,
It's a mean mistreater, Lord, that been doin' me thisdaway,
That's all right, baby, I'm gonna see you some old day.

I went an' asked the doctor, "Save her if you can,"
Yeah, asked the doctor, "Please save her if you can,"
Give her anything, baby, any drugstore would buy."

They took my baby, down to the buryin' groun',
Taken my baby, down to the buryin' groun',
I love you, baby, Lord, an' I just can't keep from cryin'.

Graveyard ain't nothin', Lord, but great long lonesome place,
You can lay flat on your back, little woman, an' let the sun shine in your
    face.

Just a good girl gone, ain't that a cryin' shame (x2)
Just a good girl gone, oh baby, way down in Shady Lane.

The two Spivey-inspired opening stanzas convey the bluesman's despair for his own disease, but from the last line of the second verse Welch's subject becomes his woman, dying of tuberculosis. The opening stanzas are followed by two partly traditional verses, and the last three deal with the recurrent blues topic of a lover's death and burial. The penultimate one is a variant of the concluding verse in Jimmie Rodgers's "T.B. Blues," although it may not come from Rodgers's recording; variants are widespread, and it was first collected from an African American informant by Newman Ivey White in 1918.[267] The reference to "Shady Lane," a common term for the location of a graveyard, probably derives from Leroy Carr's "Shady Lane Blues" (Vocalion 02762, February 21, 1934).

In July 1964, folklorist Bruce Jackson recorded "T.B. Bees" (Elektra LP EKL 296), a toast by Ramsey Prison Farm, Texas, inmate Louis "Bacon & Porkchop" Houston.[268]

Boy, the T.B. bees has been my complaint.
It seem to get well, it seems a narrow chance.
I got a hacking cough, sometimes spits up blood.
I wanta say goodbye to the ones I love.
I sweats at night and have a high, high fever,
Boy, and I got a very, very poorly appetite.
I got a hacking cough, sometimes spits up blood.
That ain't nothing but a letter from death.
I got a pain in my side and I got a pain in my chest,
You know that ain't nothing but a letter from death.
Out o' all the rules you got to obey,
And that is, some kind a pain got to carry you away.
But as I got to go and you gonna stay,
Won't you give me one of those old Chesterfields
To help me on my way?
You can't turn down a pal!

At the end of the toast, the listener is caught off-guard by the abrupt, firing-squad humor of Houston's request for a "free world" cigarette, which clashes with the downbeat and realistic description of his symptoms.

Songs about Tuberculosis by White Singers

The most influential recording about tuberculosis by a white singer was the blue yodel "T.B. Blues" (Victor 23535), composed by Jimmie Rodgers and Raymond E. Hall (1903–1983), an Oklahoma drifter, and later a prisoner, whom Rodgers had met on his travels, and who wrote a number of lyrics for him.[269] Rodgers cut two takes in San Antonio, Texas, on January 31, 1931.

My good gal's trying to make a fool out of me,
Lord, my gal's trying to make a fool out of me,
Trying to make me believe I ain't got that old T.B.
I've got the T.B. blues.

When it rained down sorrow, it rained all over me (x2)
'Cause my body rattles like a train on that old S.P.
I've got the T.B. blues.

I've got that old T.B., I can't eat a bite,
Got that old T.B., I can't eat a bite,
Got me worried so, I can't even sleep at night.
I've got the T.B. blues.

I've been fighting like a lion, looks like I'm going to lose,
I'm fighting like a lion, looks like I'm going to lose,
'Cause ain't nobody ever whipped the T.B. blues.
I've got the T.B. blues.

Gee, but the graveyard is a lonesome place,
Lord, that old graveyard is a lonesome place,
They put you on your back, throw that mud down in your face.
I've got the T.B. blues.

Rodgers made no secret of the tuberculosis from which he died in New York, two years after recording this song. Early in 1929, he asked the imprisoned Ray Hall for "your version of 'T.B. Blues,'" and as Hall remembered, "Jimmie changed words here and there and some of the phrases." From the opening rejection of well-intentioned optimism to the finality of death and burial, the resulting lyric focuses tightly and unflinchingly on the disease, its symptoms, and what it portends.[270] Rodgers's song was as admired and influential among white country singers as Spivey's was among Black artists. It also inspired bluesman Robert Johnson, as reported by his stepsister: "I learned to sing along with those Jimmie Rodgers records. I couldn't yodel, but I'd sort of hum it. Brother Robert could really yodel. He identified with Jimmie Rodgers through the 'TB Blues'—we had two older half-siblings die of TB in Memphis around the time Jimmie Rodgers passed from it."[271]

Without Hall's collaboration, Rodgers also wrote a heroically defiant sequel, "Whippin' That Old T.B." (Victor 23751), and recorded two takes in Camden, New Jersey, on August 11, 1932.[272]

Listen all you rounders, you ought to be like me,
Don't worry about consumption, even if they call it T.B.

T.B., T.B., some say tonic is fine,
You take all your medicine you want, I'll take good liquor for mine.

Oh, the hospital and the doctors done everything they could, (*Spoken:* Lord, Lord)
Happiness and the sunshine, Lord, it's done me all the good.

Don't let that old T.B. ever get you down, (*Spoken:* Don't let it get you down)
First they want your insurance, then they want to plant you in the ground.

(*Spoken:* Play it boy, play that thing)

Just say in your mind your troubles you forgot, (*Spoken:* Get 'em, boy)
Because good old contentment, Lord, it's gonna help you a lot.

Ain't no use to worry, no use to lay down and die,
'Cause nine times out of ten ain't nobody will cry.

From a "come-all-ye" opening typical of ballads, the song soon shifts into blues territory, and defiance of the disease and its dangers is expressed through a skillful stylistic device: Rodgers alternates typical blues language in the first lines of stanzas 2, 3, 4, and 6 with witty and unusual second lines. The text is characterized by biting sarcasm about the ineffectiveness of doctors and medicines (stanzas 2 and 3), the avarice of relatives and friends, and their indifference to the sick protagonist's fate (stanzas 4 and 6).

Ernest Tubb (1914–1984), who began his career as an emulator of Jimmie Rodgers, wrote a reversal of the Rodgers song, "The T B Is Whipping Me" (Bluebird B-7000), recorded in San Antonio, Texas, on March 2, 1937.[273]

You all heard the story of whipping that old TB,
Heard Jimmie singing "Whipping that old TB,"
Well, I'm here to tell you, the TB is whipping me. (*Spoken:* Tell 'em
    about it, son)

Once I had a mama, thought the world of me,
Lord, I once had a mama that thought the world of me,
But her love vanished when I took this old TB. (*Spoken:* Some love, gal!)

I went to see the doctor and he thumped upon my back,
Went to see the doctor and he thumped upon my back,
He says, "Boy, you're traveling on a one-way track." (*Spoken:* Tell me the
    truth, doctor)

I went on down the street, found a fortune-telling man,
I strolled on down the street, found a fortune-telling man,
I says, "Boy, I know my past, tell me my future if you can." (*Spoken:* Tell
    it to me, brother)

My lungs are rattling, and you ought to hear this cough of mine,
Lord, my lungs are rattling, and you ought to hear this cough of mine,
Oh, the doggone bug must be working overtime.

Listen here, pretty mama, I know I can't last long,
Lord, I know, good mama, that I can't last long,
You're gonna be sorry after I am gone. (*Spoken:* You're gonna miss me,
    honey)

Tubb's immediate reference to Rodgers's earlier song both acknowledges and
exploits his inspirer's popularity and influence. Like Rodgers, Tubb juxtaposes
A lines containing negative tropes commonly found in blues in general, and
blues about TB in particular, with original imagery in the B lines. Working
in the same blue yodel genre, Tubb masterfully substitutes irony for sarcasm,
and forgiveness for defiance, but like Rodgers he relies on a refined use of
understatement in a song that is both an ingenious answer to the original and
a respectful tribute to its performer.

The elusive duo Julian Johnson and Leon Hyatt recorded an original "TB
Killed My Daddy" (Bluebird B-7510), in Charlotte, North Carolina, on January
27, 1938.[274]

I had a loving father, just as kind as he could be,
Till one dark old evening he taken that old T.B.

They took him to the T.B. camp, they laid him on a bed,
It wasn't very long, folks, till dear old daddy was dead.

He had four little children, a loving wife so true,
And all that worried him was what they were going to do.

He called me to his bedside, "Hey, son, be good and true,
For when your dear old dad's gone, they're all depending on you."

He says, "I hate to leave them, but I have run my race,
So time is come for you, son, to take your daddy's place."

I held him to my bosom, said, "Dad, don't leave me now,"
He smiled and said, "My boy, just live to meet me up there."

He turned to ring the bell, he raised his aching head,
But when the bell quit ringing, my dear old daddy was dead.

I know I'll meet my father up in Heaven some sweet day,
If I just live the life he lived, I know I'm going that way.

I know he's up in Heaven, I know that, don't you see?
He's gone to the place, good people, where they don't have that old T.B.

This son's recollection of a father dying of tuberculosis is part of the extensive corpus of hillbilly sorrow songs about deathbed farewells to children, parents, or relatives. Despite its pathetic and gloomy topic, the song is pleasant listening, thanks to the sprightly mandolin played by one of the musicians, and because its lyrics are well-sequenced and neither contrived nor schmaltzy.

Two preliminary observations can be made after analyzing this batch of hillbilly songs about tuberculosis: 1) They are mainly covers of, or answers to, Jimmie Rodgers's "T.B. Blues" and "Whippin' That Old T.B." 2) All but one are blues songs that employ typical blues irony.

CONCLUSION

In *The Blues Come to Texas*, Paul Oliver maintains that diseases like cancer, heart disease, arthritis, diabetes,[275] anemia, and asthma, though common among Blacks, are overlooked in blues songs, unlike tuberculosis, pneumonia, and blindness. Oliver hypothesizes that the latter diseases feature in blues because they are more likely to affect younger people.[276] Heart disease was the leading cause of death among nonwhites in the 1930s and 1940s,[277] but it can be a disease of sudden onset, whereas tuberculosis is a chronic illness (like the seldom sung-about, but widespread, syphilis), and blindness is a largely irreversible condition. The high incidence and the physical, economic, social, and psychological impacts of tuberculosis (and to a lesser extent pneumonia) on African Americans seem to account for the greater number of songs.

Victoria Spivey's signature phrase, "T.B. is killing me," and her obsessive repetition of "too late" to denote the insidious course of the illness, evidently struck a chord with musicians and record buyers. Isolation from friends and relatives, confinement, and displacement are the common concerns in Black songs on tuberculosis.

Even though many songs dealing with tuberculosis are covers or variants, depending on the race of the singer, of the hits by Victoria Spivey and Jimmie Rodgers, the disease elicited enough recordings to enable a comparison of responses by Black and white musicians. The greater number of African American recordings on tuberculosis, rather than other diseases, suggests a higher degree of preoccupation with this illness, probably as a result of its higher incidence in Black communities. White people were of course victims of all the diseases discussed here and elsewhere, although almost always in lower percentages than Black people. Interestingly, the Black and white repertoires don't seem to have influenced one another textually, but most white songs are in the blues form.

If cover versions are included, TB seems to have inspired an equivalent number of songs among white and Black singers, but on the whole the latter seem to have adopted a more original approach. Of all the Black and white songs about TB, Champion Jack Dupree's "Bad Health Blues" is a notable exception to the tropes of describing one's own disease and being neglected by friends and lovers. He is also the only singer who expresses the intention of staying with a life partner to the end.

Jimmie Rodgers's songs about the reality of suffering from TB, and its foreseen outcome, show his indomitable character in life and his uncompromising attitude toward death. Songs about pneumonia, though few in number, seem to suggest a confluence between songs about disease of viral origin and about job-related illnesses caused by fibrosis—the silicosis of the Hawk's Nest Tunnel and Dust Bowl pneumonia. The influenza outbreaks of 1918–20 and 1928–29 were more frequently dealt with by gospel singers. The latter outbreak prompted a single, derivative blues recording. The Dixie-Aires' gospel song on syphilis was a disc recorded for promotional purposes. Gospel singers' rare treatment of other illnesses makes a comparison of secular and sacred attitudes impossible.

A general problem in discussing songs about venereal disease is that they were not much recorded, because of the prevailing reluctance to speak openly about sexually transmitted diseases, and because the record companies would not issue anything that was not more or less disguised. With the exception of Tom Glazer's musical public health advisory "That Ignorant, Ignorant Cowboy," there seem to be no recordings by white singers about VD, perhaps because (as with impotence resulting from jake leg) they and their audiences were more prudish than African American blues singers and their listeners. It may be that there was a correlation between white people's racist and puritanical attitudes and the reinforcement of racism by puritanical views about sex. It may also be indicative that there appear to be no songs stigmatizing either African Americans or European immigrants as transmitters of the TB from which both groups suffered disproportionately. Record companies, sharing the majority view of African Americans as hypersexual and promiscuous, saw them as a market for blues on sexual topics. The companies' indifference to Black sexuality, except in terms of sales potential, also accounts for the fact that a few recordings by African Americans that mention VD, usually by implication rather than openly, were issued.[278]

Chapter Four

AFRICAN AMERICAN
DISASTER SONGS AND
MEMORY

Tragedies that have occurred over centuries of American and African American history, and especially the disasters that have been investigated in this book, have contributed to the shaping and development of "black culture and black consciousness" and "Afro-American folk thought."[1] Likewise, the different functions of memory, such as remembrance, retention, and commemoration, have all contributed to the molding of collective African American understanding of the past. This process has taken place even though the inherent transience of disaster songs rarely enables them to become sufficiently popular and long-lived. Only by retaining a more universal scope might they enter tradition.[2]

When least expected, African American blues and gospel lyrics are reborn like the phoenix from the ashes of memory. The concept of memory in its different meanings is the common thread running through the tragic events recounted by African American singers in the seventy-six years covered in this study. Memory pervades Black disaster songs regardless of the singer's mode of expression, moral purpose (if any), and viewpoint. As well as observing that these songs exorcised both contingent and existential problems by reporting on events, it is necessary to understand why and how Black singers have contributed to the development of a collective culture of disaster.[3]

It is also crucial to say at the outset that the general concept of memory, which may be deemed an obvious component when discussing songs that describe historical events, acquires a broader meaning in a book that consists of individual studies of the many disasters that took place in the period treated. As a result, there are exceptions to almost any generalization made in this concluding chapter. Quoting Sterling Brown, who wrote that "[t]here are so many blues that any preconception might be proved about Negro life, as well as its opposite,"[4] Michael Taft has correctly argued that "[a]ny conclusions about the meaning of the blues, based on a thematic analysis of this song form is [*sic*] difficult" and that "[v]irtually every aspect of black life was grist for the singer's mill."[5]

Brown went on to say that "the Blues [a]s documents about humanity . . . are invaluable," that "[i]t is a popular misconception that the Blues are merely songs that ease a woman's longing for her rambling man . . . ," and that "the Blues furnish examples of other concerns. . . . Blues will be found ranging from flood songs to graphic descriptions of pneumonia."[6] There is no all-encompassing critical method for finding meaning in African American popular music, and quantitative analysis without the support of a qualitative (thematic) analysis, based on accurate transcriptions, restricts the scope of possible interpretations.

There is no dichotomy between blues performers describing their own lives and the collective life of their community. The same is true of memory in relation to disaster songs. Whenever blues and gospel singers recall a tragic event from their own viewpoint, they also, more or less consciously, do so on their community's behalf, turning personal memory into collective memory. The most glaring example in African American disasters is the Rhythm Club fire in Natchez, where the sites "are not closed containers of memory, but . . . spaces where everyday human activity relevant to a community imbues the land with emotions" and where "[p]laces are not simple geographical spaces, but complex constructions where individual memories encounter a broader collective remembrance."[7] Hence, the "blues enable the esthetic expression of collective memory through intensely personal accounts," and "Blues songs are vessels of history where individual presences are possible."[8]

In 1932 a chaplain preaching at a commemoration of the twentieth anniversary of the sinking of the *Titanic* remarked: "The world has a short memory even for the things which thrill and shock it most deeply, and it is well for us to stop and stand and look and remember."[9] Finding ways not to forget is especially important in partly oral cultures. Telling stories in speech and song has been an important way for African Americans to achieve this since slavery times. One need not be a historian to be a representative of one's community. Those blues and gospel singers who have been keen observers of the life around them have become their communities' spokespeople.

It has been maintained that "[h]istorians have much to learn from [common people's] reminiscences not merely because they are so often accurate but also because they are so often legendary; because they blend and interweave myth with fact. The folk are not historians; they are simultaneously the products and creators of a culture, and that culture includes a collective memory."[10]

As shown in the study of the Tupelo disaster, some commercially recorded original compositions may be traced back to earlier sources and, in turn, late recordings may play a key role in bringing long-forgotten disasters back to the fore. In sacred music, the melodies of older songs, and songbooks and

miscellaneous printed material, were the most common earlier sources, especially in the Church of God in Christ. For example, the melody in the chorus
of "Wasn't That a Mighty Storm" can be found in later field recordings about
the *Titanic*, and in much later recordings such as "Gilliam's Storm," where new
lyrics were fitted to the melody, to create a song describing a different disaster. The same is true of the melodic and/or lyric similarities between Elders
McIntorsh and Edwards's "The 1927 Flood" and Lulu Morris's "The Tupelo
Disaster"; Marie Knight's "The Florida Storm" and Henry Green's "Storm Thru
Mississippi"; and Blind Willie Johnson's "God Moves on the Water" and James
Brown Jr.'s "Hurricane."

Consideration of oral history becomes a way of testing the validity of the
assumptions above.[11] Michael Frisch has stated that "memory . . . moves to
center stage as the object, not merely the method of oral history."[12] The blues
and gospel singers' lyrics examined in this book often contain factual mistakes
or are altogether fabricated but, as British author Christian O'Connell points
out, paraphrasing oral history scholar Alessandro Portelli, "with memory as
(unofficial) object, whether the oral account is based on historical fact or is
mere fiction becomes irrelevant. It is what the informants choose to tell and
what they believe that becomes history."[13] To quote Portelli himself about the
conciseness of oral-based popular cultures:

> The poetics of subtraction in popular cultures based on orality derives
> from the fact that they live only if they manage to compress all their
> knowledge within the limited space of memory. . . . Insofar as memory
> and the voice are the only cultural tools available, oral cultures draw life
> from performance. . . . The way oral culture works consists in not let-
> ting the word fall: in memory, with the aim of assuring the continuity of
> culture; in the performance, with the aim of assuring the continuity and
> length of communication. Therefore, the bluesman is at the center of
> what we might call a systolic and diastolic process: memory compresses,
> and performance expands.[14]

The contiguity of the past with the present, and their continuity in collective
memory,[15] are not the exclusive properties of learned people or of particular
cultures.[16] It has been said, with reference to singers in the Hebrides:

> Those who confuse literacy with culture can scarcely credit the reten-
> tiveness of oral tradition. . . . As one or another old man or old woman
> dies it is as if a library were lost. Wherever songs and stories have been
> preserved not in books but in living minds, continuity of participa-
> tion in the whole past of a culture has been preserved. [T]here is little

distinction between personal and ancestral memories: memory merges into history and history into the "time immemorial" of legend. Through the songs a whole past is experienced as contemporaneous and insepa- rable from the sense of personal identity.[17]

This idea can be applied to blues and gospel performers, recorded or otherwise. When a blues singer dies, a "library" of memories is similarly lost forever; but in a world where oral culture and mass media interact, a link to the past can be created by recordings, interviews, and so on. There may be a clash between past and present, as one flows into the other, and a split between memory and history. As for the latter contrast, it has been argued that "[m]emory is blind to all but the group it binds . . . , that there are as many memories as there are groups, that memory is by nature multiple and yet specific; collective, plural, and yet individual. History, on the other hand, belongs to everyone and to no one, whence its claim to universal authority."[18]

In order to draw conclusions, a theoretical overview of the concept of memory needs to be completed and enhanced by a practical discussion of the findings from the previous chapters. Even a cursory study of disaster songs recounting tragic events in the United States after the mid-1950s shows that the death toll of any specific natural and accidental disaster is lower than for those that occurred in the period analyzed in this book, with the exception of Hurricane Katrina in 2005. This aligns with Ted Steinberg's contention that natural disasters caused more casualties in the period 1880–1930, after which they began proportionally to damage more property and kill fewer people.[19] However, my research is limited to analyzing Black disaster songs (and a few white songs dealing with the same events); since disasters which were either not sung about or memorialized by white singers only are not discussed, it lacks comprehensive data about all types of disasters, both before and after 1930.

It has been observed that "when it comes to confronting the troubles of life with resiliency and flexibility, . . . the comic is the stratagem supreme. [O]ne redefines blunders and disappointments as opportunities to grow. Laughing at one's predicaments, one is better able to confront them, to evaluate them, and to cope with them."[20] Despite the tragic nature of the subject, what blues (and even gospel) lyrics about disasters sometimes spark, alongside memories, is a counterblast of irony, sarcasm, and humor. At first, this notion ("laughing to keep from crying") may not look like an original addition to blues and gospel criticism, but one of the aims of this book is to show, through lyric analysis rather than a priori assumptions or statistics, that Black people have coped with disasters in diverse and sometimes conflicting ways. "To joke and tell tall tales about the event,"[21] and to sing about it are among the methods that African American people (not just singers) adopt to exorcise hardship.

However, that is not a sufficient explanation. Undoubtedly, "the need for black solidarity in the face of events had symbolic parallels with their growing frustrations with the social conditions of the time,"[22] but in my view that solidarity was the product of a sense of belonging, of the urgent need to feel part of a community struggling for freedom, but not yet possessing the necessary unity of purpose. African American disaster songs before the mid-1950s contain only few and isolated premonitory hints of the struggle for human and civil rights.[23] The most notable examples are the overtly racial themes in some *Titanic* songs and toasts. In songs about the boll weevil infestation, a subtext of resistance to white oppression is present, but does not gain momentum. Lonnie Johnson's "Broken Levee Blues" is one of the harshest and most overt indictments of white racism in disaster songs, but it is an exception in both blues generally and Johnson's large repertoire. Most criticism of white people in Black disaster song lyrics was cryptic and isolated.

The only two "white-only" disaster themes to gain major appeal in Black tradition have a Black character who escapes. In "Casey Jones," composed probably ca. 1901 at the nadir of Jim Crow, he is a minor character, the fireman who is "ordered" to jump by the heroic white engineer. This implies that the "white folks" were good and noble to the Black man in the song at a time when in fact many whites were openly racist toward Black people. In African American versions of the song, Casey is given "Black" characteristics and is converted from a typically white "tragic" hero to a typically Black "trickster/badman" hero. By 1912 and the years that followed, when *Titanic* songs were popular, the Black man jumps of his own free will and good sense and magical powers ("traveling coon"), or escapes by being Jim-Crowed (Jack Johnson). Nineteen twelve is the year when the blues emerged as a recognized new song form, and that in turn was recognition of a new Black racial consciousness, of which the real Jack Johnson became a symbol. In later toasts (ca. 1940 and later) inspired by this theme, the Black hero takes on the nickname or actual name "Shine" (the only name we know him by) and openly insults the white captain and passengers as he swims away. These developments mirror the rise of Black protest, political awareness, and militancy. Other "white-only" disasters (the Arcade Building Fire, the *Hindenburg* disaster) don't feature any Black characters in the songs, and perhaps failed to gain wider popularity for that reason.

An analysis of lyrics about disasters leads to the conclusion that African Americans who composed songs about catastrophic events were mainly reactive and unsystematic, yet also deeply original. Neither secular nor (more surprisingly) sacred Black artists show a stereotypical and codified approach to writing disaster songs. Nor are their songs always easy to categorize as strictly secular or sacred.

As to the significance of African American disaster songs in history, one may agree with Angela Davis when she maintains that

> Bessie Smith's and Sippie Wallace's contributions, together with many other songs about the catastrophic effects of the floods in the lives of black people, preserve a tragic moment in the history of African Americans. They also preserve and reflect a cultural consciousness that was capable of transforming such tragedies into catalytic events, rather than consigning them to historical memory as merely private misfortunes. If not for the blues, many individual tragedies affecting black working-class communities might never have been recast as social, collective adversities. Such a course would have significantly diminished black people's ability to constitute themselves as a community in struggle.

However, the italicized portion of Davis's continuation is too all-inclusive and does not fully reflect Black people's multifaceted approach to disaster songs: "Songs like 'Backwater [sic] Blues' are much more than the folk history to which they are often relegated. Transforming individual emotions into collective responses to adversity, they transcend the particular circumstances that inspired them *and become metaphors about oppression*" [my italics].[24]

There is no doubt that African Americans' disaster songs were a sign of developing cultural consciousness, and that the shaping of a more coherent and determined community struggling for economic and social independence was already taking place in the 1920s when Bessie Smith and Sippie Wallace recorded their flood blues. Likewise, Davis asserts that "[w]e would encounter many more blues with themes of critical social commentary if the artists had been allowed to record all the material they included in their live repertoire,"[25] although it is obviously impossible to analyze such an absence systematically.

My analysis indicates, rather, that while some Black disaster songs are or "become metaphors about oppression," most do not. It is unconvincing to argue that this ongoing process had reached maturity by the mid-1950s, and that by then the "individual emotions" (personal memories) that had turned into "collective responses to adversity" (through collective memory) were *inevitably* generating conscious and shared metaphors of oppression. This suggestion is only occasionally corroborated by the analysis of disaster song lyrics. In songs like Barbecue Bob's lighthearted and ironic "Mississippi Heavy Water Blues," a response to the 1927 Mississippi River flood (possibly the natural disaster that elicited the most explicit reactions to racial oppression), there emerge only a few hints, either direct or indirect, of this topic.

Conversely, in two books that cover part of the same historical period as this one, Guido van Rijn's analysis of songs dealing with US presidents and social, political, and economic issues shows a gradual change in blues and gospel musicians' attitudes toward politics. In the 1950s, partly as a result of the Korean War, there are many more recordings about politics than there are about disasters. In his book about lyrics dealing with the presidency of Franklin D. Roosevelt (1933–1945), van Rijn concludes: "Blues songs were not political in an organizational sense. They contain little expression of conventional political ideology or advocacy of programs and solutions. The songs do, however, deal with the effects of events, policies and personalities on the singer's life and physical needs."[26]

This attitude to politics in songs during the Roosevelt era is similar to that found in disasters during the whole period I have examined. However, when considering blues and gospel songs about Presidents Truman (1945–53) and Eisenhower (1953–61), van Rijn points out that more artists seem to become more aware of broader issues: "In contrast to the Roosevelt era . . . , [o]ne particularly noticeable innovation is the growth of interest in the political process itself."[27] Possibly because of different attitudes toward politics and tragic events, this change of attitude occurs only sporadically in Black disaster songs. Not surprisingly, Black people's need to struggle for and sing about their rights, and in the end for and about their very existence, was more urgent than the need to write and record songs about occasional and unpredictable natural and accidental disasters. Nowadays, we are more aware of the social and political implications inherent in writing and recording a disaster song, especially when dealing with a natural disaster that may also be the result of human mistakes. In the period covered by this book, however, African Americans mainly responded individually, rather than communally, to catastrophic events.

Statistical analysis shows that the commercial recording of disaster songs coincided with the 1927 Mississippi River flood. Still-remembered events like the sinking of the *Titanic* and the Casey Jones train wreck had been popular earlier, but the high number of boll weevil songs before the 1940s is mainly due to field collectors' requests for them. The much lower number of blues and gospel field recordings from 1945 to 1960 does not confute this trend, and the scarcity of disaster songs then and later is further evidence of Black singers' decreasing interest in writing, and record companies' decreasing interest in recording, disaster songs.

What initially seemed to be a minor and peripheral topic has turned out to be an important piece of the huge and variegated mosaic of African American popular music. Disasters were often covered in the Black press and other media, making African Americans aware of the details of tragedies. This enabled the generation of poignant, cryptic, or consolatory comments, according to the type of catastrophe and the people who had been affected by it. In most, but not all cases, secular and sacred artists took different approaches to the events they were singing about. Blues musicians were mainly concerned with how the tragedy affected African Americans, especially when dealing with tragedies that hit their own towns and communities, as in Tampa Red's "Stockyard Fire" or the broadside about the Hamlet, North Carolina, train wreck. This is especially so when racial issues are involved or implied, as with the 1940 Natchez Rhythm Club fire and the 1936 Scottsboro truck fire. This may explain why a global disaster without racially specific aspects, like the 1918 influenza pandemic, did not kindle African American people's imagination as much as other tragic events.

Another common theme in African American (and occasionally white, including the sinking of the *Titanic*) disaster songs is that of solidarity with poor people. This seems to be overt or suggested in some secular recordings about tragedies as diverse as floods, fires, and the 1930 dry spell. Different degrees of sympathy for poor Black people are present in a few songs about floods (such as Bessie Smith's "Back-Water Blues," Blind Lemon Jefferson's "Rising High Water Blues," and both of Charley Patton's songs titled "High Water Everywhere"), in Son House's two-part "Dry Spell Blues," and in some songs about the 1940 Natchez Fire. The most explicit and thematically central support for poor people is expressed in Tampa Red's "Stockyard Fire."

As noted in connection with the 1893 Sea Islands Hurricane, which had hit many years before and largely been forgotten, amateur Black singers were more likely than professionals to sing about relatively minor, local, and lesser-known disasters. Obscure field recordings such as Hagar Brown's "Ballad of the '93 Storm," Lavinia Simmons's "Twenty-seventh of August, 1893," and Sister Crockett's "Flood in Omaha" confirm that it was mainly nonprofessional singers, and particularly religious women, indifferent to singing as an economic activity, who sang about disasters that had affected their community and race or that were part of their family's artistic heritage, like Osceola Mays's "Gilliam's Storm."

Only the *Titanic*, Casey Jones, and boll weevil disasters had much recorded commercial life long after the event, and occurred in many recorded variants. Significantly, the topics were also popular with whites and yielded commercial hits. The long-drawn-out nature of the boll weevil infestation undoubtedly kept songs about it alive. Howlin' Wolf's "The Natchez Burning," John Lee Hooker's "Tupelo Blues," and Bessie Smith's "Back-Water Blues" were commercially motivated compositions (which is not to deny their composers' empathy and engagement), not variants of folk songs.

Few artists in the early years of "race" recording deal with the racial aspects of disasters, either openly or covertly, Lonnie Johnson in "Broken Levee Blues" and Josh White in "Silicosis Is Killin' Me" and "No More Ball and Chain" being exceptions. Fear of retaliation, obstruction by record companies, or both are likely to have been factors in the infrequency of such recordings, although ARC coupled Josh White's songs on a two-sided "protest record."

The 1927 Mississippi River flood was a matter of national concern, and the explicit indictment in Johnson's recording probably did not go unnoticed among Black people, although it could not have been a catalyst for change at the time. However, while Black singers usually did not openly express anger about racial disparities in the effects of disasters like the 1927 Mississippi River flood, blues singers' responses can nevertheless illuminate—usually in an encoded manner—contemporary African American frustrations and concerns. The blues can do this more easily than gospel music, whose parlance is inherently more restricted and less suited to (or concerned with) commentary on the specific and the here-and-now.

Despite their highly racialized impacts, some mainly local tragedies, like the Scottsboro truck fire and the Hawk's Nest Tunnel disaster, were largely overlooked by singers and scholars alike. It is evidence of this neglect that this book is the first study to connect some songs with a racial theme or subtext to the underlying historical events.

African American treatments of exclusively white tragedies with a world-wide impact, like the sinking of the *Titanic* and the wreck of the *Hindenburg*, vary from vindictive to ironically derisive. Black singers considered disasters that mainly afflicted and disturbed white people from a perspective that had little to do with commemoration or remembrance; rather they were seen as reminders, religious or secular warnings.

Black gospel singers and preachers perceived disasters mainly as acts of God, warnings to sinners to repent and prepare for the Second Coming. As Alan Lomax notes, apropos the Tupelo disaster,

> [B]allad making is not just rhyming the news; it fixes an important event in the memory of the people and shapes it to conform to their moral dilemmas and emotional needs. "The wicked shall be destroyed," these black poets shout, and the people, listening, are comforted; God will avenge their wrongs.[28]

The term "wicked" recurs in many of the religious songs analyzed in this book, among them Lavinia Simmons's "Twenty-seventh of August, 1893," Elders McIntorsh and Edwards's "The 1927 Flood," Blind Willie Johnson's "Jesus Is Coming Soon," Sister Crockett's "Flood in Omaha," Lulu Morris's "Tupelo Destruction," Reverend A. C. W. Shelton's "Wasn't It a Storming Time?" and Osceola Mays's "Gilliam's Storm."

A specific example of the difference in approach is found when blues singer Lonnie Johnson and poet Sterling Brown both seem to regard the 1927 St. Louis twister as separate from God, and simply a disastrous event, whereas for Rev. J. M. Gates the twister is God, using the cyclone to manifest His anger. This is a fundamental difference between secular and sacred interpretations, even when the secular material borrows religious language and includes appeals to God.

Despite her reliance on poor sources to transcribe some of the lyrics and her limited choice of disaster songs analyzed, Małgorzata Ziólek-Sowińska has brilliantly shown that there is considerable religious content in blues songs and has also highlighted apocalyptic imagery in both blues and spiritual/gospel music. Also, she has rightly observed that "the power of the language of the Apocalypse" in blues and gospel disaster songs shows "the presence of eschatological thinking in the consciousness of black Americans" and that "natural calamities . . . in blues lyrics are frequently depicted as the forerunners of the approaching end of time," which in some songs may also be read as the end "of a certain period of time or the passing of an age, or a way of life on the earth now."[29] However, when quoting Levine to demonstrate that he "makes a distinction between the religious view of the end of time and the end of 'a time' that is worldly in the sense of the here and now,"[30] Ziólek-Sowińska does not seem to appreciate the difference that Levine clearly delineates between the old spirituals and the newer gospel songs about disasters. Levine writes:

> The disaster songs resembled the traditional religious mentality in finding patterns of meaning in worldly events and in depicting an active deity involved in the lives of human beings. But while the spirituals had easily and naturally assumed the existence of God in every aspect of Man's life, the newer songs seemed more strident, perhaps less secure, in their need to prove God's being in the tragedies which everywhere beset humanity. They appeared to be less certain of the presence of the kind of community of belief into which the spirituals had fit. Unlike the spirituals the disaster songs no longer freely negotiated between time dimensions. The omnipotence and omnipresence of God were usually documented . . . through the events of one's lifetime. The liberating amalgam of time and space was missing; the focus was insistently, rigidly, upon the present generation.[31]

Catastrophic events do not only "demonstrate despair and hopelessness of people who experience them."[32] In the course of my study, the analysis of a more comprehensive corpus of disaster songs has also revealed that mixed interpretations of disaster do emerge in African American lyrics from time to time, especially among blues musicians: an example is Sippie Wallace's "The Flood Blues," where sacred and secular answers to the distress caused by the flood are juxtaposed in the last stanza. In this respect, Son House stands out as one of the most original blues lyricists in his unusual, and perhaps unique, capacity as a conflicted bluesman with a past as a preacher rather than vice versa, which sets him apart from the many blues singers who later converted. This originality is evident in the topical lyrics he produced throughout his career, most notably "Dry Spell Blues," and is the result of a high level of linguistic competence, derived from a successful conflation of an intellectual yet unconventional reading of the Bible with attentiveness to Black colloquial speech.

Hillbilly singers dealing with a disaster that had hit both the white and Black communities adopt a ballad-like descriptive or narrative approach, which occasionally becomes fatalistic or moralizing. Most of their songs argue that one never knows when death and disaster will strike; that we cannot understand "God's mysterious ways"; and that the only way to deal with them is to get right with, and be ready for, God. Black and white singers alike see disasters as unpredictable and unaccountable, but also as timely warnings to repent. However, there is a distinction between white singers' view that God displays His power by striking blameless victims at random, and Black singers' attitude, that God specifically vents His anger on sinners. White singers also sometimes stress the need to "rebuild," to restore the status quo (as in "Pop" Stoneman's "The Story of the Mighty Mississippi" or Elton Britt's "1936 Tornado"), whereas Black singers are more apt to see an opportunity for a new beginning (as in Memphis Minnie and Kansas Joe's "When the Levee Breaks," Bessie Smith's "Homeless Blues," Charley Patton's "High Water Everywhere Part I," Mattie Delaney's "Tallahatchie River Blues," Casey Bill Weldon's "Flood Water Blues No.2," or Big Bill Broonzy's "Terrible Flood Blues").

Unlike African American blues singers, white singers rarely project themselves into the song as witnesses to or participants in the disaster. In "The Terrible Mississippi Flood," Arthur Fields (Abe Finkelstein) may be including himself by implication among "the grieving survivors" in the last two lines; but if so, this is an exception. It is perhaps supporting evidence that there is no mention of religious solace in the song; Fields, like Bob Miller, was Jewish and a citybilly without the fundamentalist Christian upbringing of most Southern hillbilly singers. In Willie Phelps and the Virginia Rounders' "Terrible Tupelo Storm," memory uncharacteristically mirrors a pessimistic (or perhaps realistic) outlook on life, with the storm perceived as an indelibly tragic event that will haunt the survivor forever. This never occurs in Black songs about natural disasters, where memory reflects a mostly positive attitude toward life.

The moralistic, fatalistic, sentimental, or practical (rebuilding) responses of southern white singers to natural disasters are paralleled by their avoidance of pointed or accusatory comments about delicate topics like sex, impotence, and venereal disease. They also avoid discussion of civil and criminal liability in disasters like the jake leg poisoning. (The Atlanta moonshine poisoning, caused by white criminals but afflicting Black consumers, significantly elicited no white songs.) Conversely, in their treatment of the Jamaica ginger paralysis

African American singers acknowledge sexual impotence without sermonizing. However, Black gospel singers dealing with the Atlanta moonshine poisoning self-censor (toward outsiders) by using the coded "they" to refer to the white bootleggers, while at the same time openly accusing their own community of containing drunkards and sinners.

Black and white songs about diseases appear to have the most similar approaches to their subject, although more analysis of white lyrics is needed to substantiate this. African Americans singing about diseases feel abandoned to their fate, and are understandably preoccupied with their own predicaments. Memory is accorded little importance, and there is almost no expression of grief or sympathy with the sick, even when the spread of disease is aggravated by public health issues like poor hygiene. This is in marked contrast to songs about epidemics caused by white criminality, like the jake leg paralysis and the Atlanta poisonings.

It is not clear why there are no gospel songs about jake leg. It is unusual in this respect, a distinction it shares (among disasters that were sung about) with the 1937 Ohio and Mississippi River floods. All we can say is that it can be impossible to determine why some tragedies are sung about and others are not. It is important, however, to note the Bartley Mine disaster, where Black singers seem to have felt obliged to imply, rather than express, social criticism in their commemoration of the victims.

Most contemporary white musicians ignored tragedies whose geneses and outcomes were rooted in race, like the Scottsboro truck fire and the Hawk's Nest tunnel disaster; sympathetic "cover" recordings made many years after the event (as with the Natchez Rhythm Club fire), and the writing by revivalists of new songs about old events, are aspects of a separate phenomenon. The likelihood is that musicians contemporary with such events did not know, or if they did know, did not care about what had happened. They, or more likely their recording companies, did not want to have to deal with possible racial controversies.

Most of the tragedies that were sung about by both white and Black musicians were natural disasters, and these events are the most fruitful for drawing comparisons between both Black and white songs and sacred and secular ones. Unsurprisingly, the 1927 Mississippi River flood was the commonest topic among Black singers because of its devastating and widespread effects on the African American community, and the concurrent boom in the production and sale of race records. However, later natural disasters, some less serious, some less sung about, like the floods of 1929, 1930, 1936, and 1937 and the 1930 dry spell, have been important to understanding Black musicians' and Black people's diverse ways of facing tragic events.

There are few "cover" recordings of Black songs made by white They occur almost exclusively with the Natchez fire and the 1930 dry spell. The comparatively high number of covers in these cases, all by folk revival singers and singer-songwriters of the 1960s and later, is probably due to admiration for Howlin' Wolf and Son House, rather than a perceived need to commemorate the tragic events themselves.

On the other hand, disasters, whether natural, accidental, or infestations, continue to resonate among African American songwriters, and original songs have been written long after the events, often by songwriters with little or no geographical or ancestral connection to the disaster. Examples include songs inspired by the 1927 Mississippi River flood (such as Eric Bibb's 2008 "Flood Water"), the 1912 sinking of the *Titanic* (Cousin Joe's 1985 "What a Tragedy" and Fruteland Jackson's 1999 "Titanic Blues"), the 1940 Natchez Rhythm Club fire (Big Jack Johnson's two-part "Ice Storm Blues" from 1994 and Little Whitt and Big Bo's 1995 "The Burning"), and even the boll weevil (Lyn Earlington's 1961 "D.D.T. and the Boll Weevil"). These later compositions often eschew narrative and description in favor of a political, racial, or ideological slant.

Black victims and rescuers in disaster song are seldom depicted as heroes, and when they are, the reports are not ostentatious. This may be seen in the matter-of-fact reporting of the heroic behavior of Walter Barnes and his band members in the Natchez fire disaster, and of the achievements of John Little (the "Crenshaw Life Saver") in the 1935 Coldwater River flood. The fictional Shine's unrealistic and boastful deeds attached to the *Titanic* disaster descend from different, earlier tropes in African and African American folklore.

It has been argued, with reference to railroad disaster songs, that "[t]he big takers of human life have not been immortalized in song, as if strength of numbers conferred silent anonymity to the victims" and that "the human capacity for empathy seems to decrease as the number of deaths increases."[33] Numerous white ballads about train wrecks were composed and recorded, but only a few entered tradition. In contrast, there are few Black songs about railway accidents, regardless of how many people died. Sid Hemphill's "The Carrier Railroad (Line)" was only sung locally by members of the Hemphill family to a predominantly white audience, and the 1911 Hamlet train wreck apparently generated only a single broadside. The exception is "Casey Jones," whose origins are complex and somewhat controversial. One reason for the rarity of African American songs about train wrecks is that there were few Black engineers (although there were more firemen, one of whom was involved in the wreck of Jones's Cannonball Express); but it is probably also relevant that in general, Black singers preferred to portray themselves, realistically or otherwise, as participants in an event, rather than drawing a moral conclusion from it. The Hamlet wreck song is exceptional in being a response to a large number of deaths: Casey Jones's is the only death in the other two songs, both of which display humorous elements.

Considering the catastrophic consequences of the boll weevil, the infrequency of prewar African American commercial recordings about it is striking; the many noncommercial recordings and collected texts demonstrate that there was—not surprisingly—considerable interest and concern among African Americans. By 1923 the boll weevil had become an established and expected problem in the Southern cotton economy, rather than a newly unsettling scourge. The reason for the dearth of commercial recordings may be that when the boll weevil was a new phenomenon, the systematic recording of rural Southern singers had not yet begun. When it did begin, in the mid-1920s, the boll weevil theme was probably deemed old-fashioned by musicians and recording companies alike. Until the postwar pop recordings, which are uprooted from race and history, the boll weevil became largely a topic for amateur singers, of interest to two highly contrasted audiences: the singers' neighbors and folklorists, whether local, like Ruby Pickens Tartt, or visiting, like John Lomax.

It was the remarkable sales of Bessie Smith's "Back-Water Blues" in 1927 that led producers to ask singers and preachers—sometimes urgently—for topical compositions and sermons. Before that year, stage and record producers probably asked Black vaudeville and cabaret singers for upbeat approaches, and discouraged gloomy topics. Before Smith's smash hit, events like the 1925 Tri-State Tornado, and other natural and accidental disasters, called forth only scattered and sometimes belated songs, mainly preserved as field recordings.

Some disaster songs by Black composers, though printed in broadsheets, went unrecorded, or were recorded only after the success of "Back-Water Blues." About one hundred African American disaster songs are unissued or untraced. The earliest recordings are not disaster songs proper, and only use disasters metaphorically. The first disaster songs recorded before "Back-Water Blues" are field recordings for the Archive of Folk Song. The first African American original and commercial disaster songs, recorded in 1926 by Virginia Liston, Charlie "Dad" Nelson, and "Bo Weavil" Jackson, were not topical: they dealt with the sinking of the *Titanic*, fourteen years earlier, or with the infestation of the boll weevil. Both subjects were probably deemed old-fashioned by prospective buyers of "race records," and therefore by the record companies. Accordingly, Paul Oliver's surprise at the neglect of the 1913 Brazos River flood, the 1915 Colorado River flood, and a series of tornadoes that devastated Texas in 1921 is unjustified, because his list of natural disaster songs only includes recordings made after "Back-Water Blues." The list's brevity is therefore not an indicator of disaster songs' rarity, whether in Texas or elsewhere.[34]

Disaster songs account for a relatively low (albeit not negligible) percentage of African American blues and gospel recordings. The effects of the Depression and the New Deal on the market for race records are clearly noticeable in the number and period of disaster songs recorded. After "Back-Water Blues," more than sixty disaster songs were recorded in just two and a half years between February 17, 1927, and the Wall Street crash. (Bessie Tucker's "T.B. Moan," cut on October 21, 1929, has the distinction of being the last disaster song recorded before "Black Thursday," three days later.) More than 40 percent of these recordings deal with the 1927 Mississippi River flood. In all, the Tallahatchie River flood, the jake leg paralysis, the dry spell, and outbreaks of meningitis and influenza prompted fourteen recordings by African Americans in 1930 alone. In parallel with the general decrease in recording activity, only three new African American disaster songs, two of them unissued or untraced, were cut in 1931, and just one in 1932, before the pace began to pick up in 1933. Numerous disaster songs were recorded by folksong researchers from 1933 to 1942, and again later, especially in the late 1950s and early 1960s. There were several commercial recordings about two major floods (the 1936 Pennsylvania flood and the 1937 Ohio and Mississippi River flood), the 1936 tornado in Tupelo, and the 1940 Natchez fire, but sixty-seven (55 percent) of the 122 disaster songs recorded between 1933 and 1942 are field recordings.

Fewer field recordings were made between 1943 and 1955, and the new, independent record companies apparently did not solicit disaster songs, which became something of a rarity on commercial releases. More than 40 percent of all the Black disaster songs analyzed in this book, including unissued items, were recorded between 1956 and 2020, but this is a potentially misleading figure: most of them are covers of prewar songs, or new songs revisiting past calamities. Before Hurricane Katrina in 2005, original disaster songs are scarce in that time period, as a combined result of there being fewer such events to write about and decreasing interest from the public and record companies. The need to move on from the horrors of World War II, and African Americans' increasing focus on civil rights and other social and political issues, probably contributed to this trend.

Of the 181 disaster songs transcribed in this book, 155 (85.6 percent) were performed by African American and twenty-six (14.4 percent) by white musicians. One hundred and twenty-two Black songs and two toasts (80 percent) are secular; twenty-nine Black songs and two sermons (20 percent) are sacred. The 1927 Mississippi River flood, the boll weevil, and miscellaneous diseases account for over 30 percent of the secular disaster songs analyzed in the book.

The twenty-six white songs transcribed were all performed by men. One hundred and twenty-two African American recordings (8.7 percent) were sung by men and thirty-three (21.3 percent) by women. Six of the women's songs were recorded by the Library of Congress. The high proportion of songs by women, whether vaudevillians, "down-home" blues singers, gospel singers, or nonprofessionals, is striking. In comparison, only 8 and 5 percent, respectively, of the socially and politically oriented songs in Guido van Rijn's two books, which cover US presidencies from 1933 to 1960, are by women.[35] The much higher percentage of women's disaster songs is probably not due to a gender-specific preoccupation. The relevant factors seem to be Bessie Smith's commercially successful recording of "Back-Water Blues"; the fact that (mostly natural) disasters affected, or at least dealt with, personal and sexual relationships (such as Luella Miller's "Tornado Groan" and "Muddy Stream Blues," Mattie Delaney's "Tallahatchie River Blues," Bessie Jackson's "Mean Twister," Bessie Tucker's "T.B. Moan," and the clusters of songs using disasters as an image); and the focus of female Christian singers on the social and teleological implications of natural disasters (Marie Knight's "Florida Storm" and Katie Bell Nubin's "Miami Storm"; Lily Mae Atkinson's "God Rode on a Mighty Storm" and Viola Jenkins's "West Palm Beach Storm"; Lulu Morris's "Tupelo Destruction" and Osceola Mays's "Gilliam's Storm").

Despite the extensive recording and high sales of sermons, especially from the mid-1920s to the early 1940s, only five about disasters were issued, three by Rev. J. M. Gates, one by Moses Mason, and one by Rev. Sutton Griggs.[36] As many as sixteen commercial 78 r.p.m. records (one of them unissued) were "concept discs," with both sides devoted to either a single disaster or two unrelated ones. With the exception of the Dixie-Aires/Tom Glazer public health advisory disc on syphilis, these releases were all attempts to cash in on public interest and sympathy.[37]

The 1927 Mississippi River flood appears to be the only tragedy to have inspired a number of original blues songs that might be regarded as proportionate to the seriousness of the event. The numerous recordings about the boll weevil derive from a few stock verses, and songs about the *Titanic* are more diversified, reflecting contrasting approaches (whether white/Black or sacred/secular) to that disaster. The jake leg epidemic and the 1929 Elba, Alabama, flood produced a balanced ratio of Black and white recordings, consistent with the similar Black and white death tolls in these disasters. In the end, however, it is not the number of recordings resulting from each disaster that is impressive and telling, but their cumulative effect.

This is perhaps less true for African American songs about accidental disasters, which are less homogeneous than those dealing with natural disasters. This is partly because of the specificity of each accidental disaster; but apart from that, these recordings are not as deeply imbued as songs on natural disasters with the concept of memory (meaning "commemoration" and "remembrance"), because they frequently reported events that affected white people, like the Arcade Building fire or the Casey Jones saga, or were written and played for white people, like Sid Hemphill's "The Carrier Railroad (Line)." Even the

1918–20 influenza pandemic, one of the deadliest global disasters ever, did not inspire many songs and

> has survived in memory more than in any literature. Nearly all those who were adults during the pandemic have died now. Now the memory lives in the minds of those who only heard stories, who heard how their mother lost her father, how an uncle became an orphan, or heard an aunt say, "It was the only time I ever saw my father cry." Memory dies with people.[38]

African American popular culture and music are diverse and complex, irrespective of the theme, historical period, or cultural aspects manifested. Historically relevant yet ephemeral, disaster songs—be they secular, religious, circumstantial, or impressionistic—are a crucial body of evidence in support of this assertion. It is fruitless to look for a single interpretation, and I resist a single conclusion in favor of detecting four tendencies common to blues and gospel disaster songs.[39]

1) The disasters covered in this book reveal what blues and gospel musicians regarded as important, but events that did not attract the attention of Black performers are also pertinent to this study because they tell us what the singers, and the communities to and for whom they spoke, regarded as irrelevant or peripheral to their lives and worldviews.

2) There are more songs—and they are, in general, more original—about natural disasters than about diseases and accidental disasters. Despite this, songs about accidental disasters have endured more strongly, because the random and unpredictable nature of the events they recount is more shocking. *Titanic* songs are still occasionally composed and recorded, but new songs—as distinct from covers of recordings made at the time—about disasters like the 1927 Mississippi River flood or the 1936 Tupelo tornado, devastating though they were, have been few and far between.

3) Only Howlin' Wolf's "The Natchez Burning" seems to have acted both as a preserver of memory of the original event and a catalyst for the creation of original compositions about both the Natchez fire and other, later disasters. This sets it apart from songs like "Back-Water Blues," "God Moves on the Water," and the Casey Jones and boll weevil sagas, which generated a number of cover versions that display only minor verbal and music changes.

4) Record companies encouraged the creation of topical disaster songs with a view to monetizing them; folklorists encouraged the singing of such songs in order to document them; but what motivated most African American

musicians who made and performed disaster songs was the importance of urging their listeners not to forget. Their recourse to the unifying power of memory signified a growing and increasingly mature awareness of the nature of the society within which they, and their listeners, were struggling to establish personal and collective meaning and dignity.

Ralph Ellison is entrusted with the final comment, which summarizes why it is important to study cultural responses to disaster:

Perhaps if we learn more of what has happened and *why* it happened, we'll learn more of who we really are. And perhaps if we learn more about our unwritten history, we won't be so vulnerable to the capriciousness of events as we are today. And in the process of becoming more aware of ourselves, we will recognize that one of the functions of our vernacular culture is that of preparing for the emergence of the unexpected, whether it takes the form of the disastrous or the marvelous.[40]

NOTES

INTRODUCTION

1. Among such invaluable sources are: R. M. W. Dixon, John Godrich, and Howard Rye, *Blues and Gospel Records 1890–1943*, 4th ed. (New York: Oxford University Press, 1997); Tony Russell, *Country Music Records. A Discography, 1921–1942* (New York: Oxford University Press, 2004); Tony Russell, *Country Music Originals: The Legends and the Lost* (New York: Oxford University Press, 2007); Guthrie T. Meade, with Dick Spottswood and Douglas S. Meade, *Country Music Sources: A Biblio-Discography of Commercially Recorded Traditional Music* (Chapel Hill: Southern Folklife Collection, The University of North Carolina at Chapel Hill Libraries in association with the John Edwards Memorial Forum, 2002); Les Fancourt and Bob McGrath, *The Blues Discography 1943–1970*, 3rd ed. (West Vancouver, Canada: Eyeball Productions, 2019); Edward Komara, ed., *Encyclopedia of the Blues*, Volumes 1 and 2 (New York: Routledge, 2006); W. K. McNeil, ed., *Encyclopedia of American Gospel Music* (New York: Routledge, 2005); Robert Ford and Bob McGrath, *The Blues Discography 1971–2000* (West Vancouver, BC, Canada: Eyeball Productions, 2011); Cedric J. Hayes and Robert Laughton, *The Gospel Discography 1943–2000*, 2 vols., 3rd ed. (West Vancouver, BC, Canada: Eyeball Productions, 2014); Robert Ford, *A Blues Bibliography*, 2nd ed. (New York: Routledge, 2007); Robert Ford, *A Blues Bibliography: Update to the Second Edition* (New York: Routledge, 2020); Tony Russell and Chris Smith, with Neil Slaven, Ricky Russell and Joe Faulkner, *The Penguin Guide to Blues Recordings* (London: Penguin Books, 2006); Bob Eagle and Eric S. LeBlanc, *Blues: A Regional Experience* (Santa Barbara, CA: Praeger, 2013); Sheldon Harris, *Blues Who's Who: A Biographical Dictionary of Blues Singers*, 6th ed. (New York: Da Capo, 1991); Craig Martin Gibbs, *Field Recordings of Black Singers and Musicians: An Annotated Discography of Artists from West Africa, the Caribbean and the Eastern and Southern United States, 1901–1943* (Jefferson, NC: McFarland, 2018); Howard Rye, and Chris Smith, draft revision of Robert M. W. Dixon, John Godrich, and Howard Rye, *Blues and Gospel Records 1890–1943*, 4th ed. (Oxford: Clarendon Press, 1997), for fifth edition to be published as *Blues and Gospel Recordings 1890–1943*, consulted with permission, forthcoming.

2. For books, articles, or book excerpts dealing with various disaster songs in addition to those referenced in chapters on specific disasters, see Chris Strachwitz and Peter Welding, eds., *The American Folk Music Occasional* (New York: Oak, 1970), 53–57; Henry "Hank" Sapoznik, "The Daily Record," introduction to *People Take Warning! Murder Ballads and Disaster Songs, 1913–1938*, Tompkins Square 1875 (3CD), 2007; Jacques Demêtre and Jean-Paul Levet, "Katrina Blues: Ou un Siècle de Catastrophes Naturelles dans le Blues," *Soul Bag* 181 (December 2005): 10–15; Christoph Wagner, "Doom and Gloom: In the Shadow of the Apocalypse," liner notes

to *Doom and Gloom: Early Songs of Angst and Disaster (1927–1945)*, Trikont US-0364, 2007; Paul Oliver, "High Water Everywhere," in *Broadcasting the Blues: Black Blues in the Segregation Era* (New York and London: Routledge, 2006), 113–16; Luciano Federighi, *Blues on My Mind* (Palermo, Italy: L'Epos, 2001), 141–47, Małgorzata Ziółek-Sowińska, *Images of the Apocalypse in African American Blues and Spirituals* (Frankfurt am Main, Germany: Peter Lang, 2017), esp. chapters 2 and 3.

3. Luigi Monge, "Topical Blues: Disasters," in *Encyclopedia of the Blues* vol. 2 (K–Z), ed. Edward Komara (New York: Routledge, 2006), 995–1002. In the present book the term "topical" has been used only when the song was actually composed immediately after the tragic event.

4. See Guido van Rijn, *The Carter, Reagan, Bush Sr., Clinton, Bush Jr. and Obama Blues: African-American Blues and Gospel Songs, 1976–2012* (Overveen, The Netherlands: Agram Blues Books, 2012), 215–25, 260.

5. David Evans, unpublished interview with Rev. Ruben Lacy, Ridgecrest, CA, February 26, 1966. Email message to author, August 3, 2018.

6. For scholarly literature adopting multidisciplinary approaches, see J. M. Albala-Bertrand, *The Political Economy of Large Natural Disasters with Special Reference to Developing Countries* (Oxford, UK: Clarendon Press, 1993); E. L. Quarantelli, ed., *What Is a Disaster? A Dozen Perspectives on the Question* (London: Routledge, 1998); Ted Steinberg, *Acts of God: The Unnatural History of Natural Disaster in America*, 2nd ed. (New York: Oxford University Press, 2006); Roger Del Moral and Lawrence R. Walker, *Environmental Disasters, Natural Recovery and Human Responses* (New York: Cambridge University Press, 2007); Christine A. Klein and Sandra B. Zellmer, *Mississippi River Tragedies: A Century of Unnatural Disaster* (New York and London: New York University Press, 2014); Richard M. Mizelle Jr., *Backwater Blues: The Mississippi Flood of 1927 in the African American Imagination* (Minneapolis and London: University of Minnesota Press, 2014); Susan Scott Parrish, *The Flood Year 1927* (Princeton, NJ, and Oxford, UK: Princeton University Press, 2017).

7. Referring to the Middle Ages, Jussi Hanska, *Strategies of Sanity and Survival: Religious Responses to Natural Disasters in the Middle Ages* (Helsinki, Finland: Studia Fennica, 2002), 27, stated the more generally valid idea that "[C]atastrophe sermons are an extremely important group of sources. . . . They allow us to know the message communicated by the Church to the faithful in times of crisis. They reflect the doctrine as it was taught to the people, not in the overtly sophisticated form of university theology."

8. Among such recordings are: Buddy Boy Hawkins's "Jailhouse Fire Blues" (Paramount 12489), recorded in Chicago ca. April 1927, which deals with a fire in a jailhouse where the singer's woman is locked up, and could be an attempt to deceive the jailer to get his woman out of jail, available on William Harris and Buddy Boy Hawkins, *Complete Recorded Works in Chronological Order (1927–1929)*, Document Records DOCD-5035, 1991; Dobby Bragg (Roosevelt Sykes)'s "Fire Detective Blues" (Paramount 12827), recorded in Richmond, Indiana, on September 7, 1929, and available on his *Complete Recorded Works in Chronological Order—Volume 1 (1929–1930)*, Document Records DOCD-5116, 1992, which is an account of the burning of Sykes's house; Big Joe Williams's "Brother James" (Bluebird B7022), recorded at the Leland Hotel, Aurora, Illinois, on May 5, 1937, and available on his *Complete Recorded Works in Chronological Order—Volume 1 (1935–1941)*, Blues Document BDCD-6003, 1991, which deals with a friend's death in a car wreck; Sleepy John Estes's "Fire Department Blues (Martha Hardin)" (Decca 7571), recorded in New York City on April 22, 1938, and available on his *Complete Recorded Works 1929–1941*

in Chronological Order—Volume 2 (1937–41), Document Records DOCD-5016, 1990, which is an account of a disastrous fire that destroyed a woman friend's house; and Memphis Minnie's "Call the Fire Wagon" (Vocalion 04858), recorded in Chicago on February 6, 1939, and available on Memphis Minnie, *Complete Recorded Works 1935–1941 in Chronological Order—Volume 4 (1938–39)*, Blues Document BDCD-6011, 1991, which describes the consequences of a house fire, perhaps inspired by a fire that destroyed her sister Ethel's house in the mid-1920s.

9. David Evans, "Bessie Smith's 'Back-Water Blues': The Story Behind the Song," *Popular Music* 26, no. 1 (2007): 106.

10. The reason for analyzing some songs by white singers is that advanced in Tony Russell, *Blacks, Whites and Blues* (London: Studio Vista, 1970), 10, reprinted in Paul Oliver, Tony Russell, Robert M. W. Dixon, John Godrich, and Howard Rye, *Yonder Come the Blues: The Evolution of a Genre*, 2nd ed. (Cambridge: Cambridge University Press, 2001), 148: "[T]he only way to understand fully the various folk musics of America is to see them as units in a whole; as traditions with . . . a certain degree of independence, but possessing an overall unity."

11. Lowell Juilliard Carr, "Disaster and the Sequence-Pattern Concept of Social Change," *American Journal of Sociology* 38 (1932): 209, quoted in Susan Scott Parrish, *The Flood Year 1927*, 5, 298, 361. See also Steinberg, *Acts of God*, 69.

CHAPTER ONE: NATURAL DISASTERS

1. William and Fran Marscher, *The Great Sea Island Storm of 1893* (Macon, GA: Mercer University Press, 2004), vii. For another book-length study of the Sea Islands hurricane see Rachel C. Mather, *The Storm Swept Coast of South Carolina* (Woonsocket, RI: Charles E. Cook, 1894). See also Lawrence S. Rowland and Stephen R. Wise, "The Great Sea Island Hurricane of 1893 and Its Aftermath," in *Bridging the Sea Islands' Past and Present, 1893–2006: The History of Beaufort County, South Carolina, Volume 3* (Columbia: University of South Carolina Press, 2015), 1–18.

2. See the Historical Marker Database at https://www.historicalmarkerproject.com/markers/HM5JY_the-great-sea-island-storm_St-Helena-Island-SC.html.

3. Kincaid Mills, Genevieve C. Peterkin, and Aaron McCullough, eds., *Coming Through: Voices of a South Carolina Gullah Community from WPA Oral Histories Collected by Genevieve W. Chandler* (Columbia: University of South Carolina Press, 2008), 13–36.

4. Mills, Peterkin, and McCullough, *Coming Through*, 125–97.

5. Mills, Peterkin, and McCullough, *Coming Through*, 320–25.

6. A footnote explains that Chandler was unaware that the song variously known as "The Storm of '93" or "The Ballad of the '93 Storm" was about the August, rather than the October disaster: "A spiritual Genevieve Chandler believed to have been written about the Flagg storm. More likely, it originated in Beaufort, South Carolina, where far more people were killed by an earlier hurricane." Mills, Peterkin, and McCullough, *Coming Through*, 325. Very similar lyrics are also transcribed in Genevieve C. Peterkin in conversation with William P. Baldwin, *Heaven Is a Beautiful Place: A Memoir of the South Carolina Coast* (Columbia: University of South Carolina Press, 2000), 207.

7. See "Chlotilde Martin, 1895–1991" at https://bdcbcl.wordpress.com/2008/11/10/chlotilde-martin-1895-1991-3859k4scvdgpj-34/

8. Lawrence W. Levine, *Black Culture and Black Consciousness: Afro-American Folk Thought from Slavery to Freedom* (Oxford: Oxford University Press, 1977), 172–73.

9. Rivers Lawton Varn (1898–1981) was white.

10. William and Fran Marscher, *The Great Sea Island Storm of 1893*, 121–23.

11. "The Florida Hurricane—September 18, 1926: Official Report of the Relief Activities," American National Red Cross, Washington, DC, n.d.

12. See Steinberg, *Acts of God*, 51–59.

13. See Jack Palmer, *Vernon Dalhart: First Star of Country Music* (Denver: Mainspring Press, 2005), 174.

14. Russell, *Country Music Records*, 261.

15. This song is reissued on various artists, *People Take Warning! Murder Ballads and Disaster Songs, 1913–1938*, Tompkins Square TSQ 1875 (3CD), 2007.

16. "God's Wrath in the St. Louis Cyclone" (OKeh 8515), recorded by Rev. J. M. Gates in Atlanta, Georgia, on October 6, 1927, and reissued on *Complete Recorded Works in Chronological Order—Volume 5 (1927)*, Document Records DOCD-5449, 1996. In the sermon, Gates says that God "rode through Miami, Florida, in a storm."

17. The song is available at https://www.loc.gov/item/flwpa000365/, but is not included in Dixon, Godrich, and Rye, *Blues and Gospel Records 1890–1943*.

18. Alton C. Morris, *Folksongs of Florida* (Gainesville: University of Florida Press, 1950), 103. Morris states that the song "recounts the events of the Miami hurricane of 1928," but he is probably mistaken, because the song specifically mentions Miami and not those parts of Florida that were hit in 1928, at the time of the two Lake Okeechobee hurricanes and floods (see "Their Eyes Were Watching God: The 1928 Florida Hurricanes and Floods" in this chapter). Brown was enumerated (as Tom James Brown) in the 1940 census; his mother, and his paternal grandfather, were born in Georgia, which seems to support his account of learning the song in Dawson, Georgia.

19. Morris, *Folksongs of Florida*, 103.

20. *Orlando Sentinel* (Orlando, Florida), September 25, 1926, 1.

21. *Miami News* (Miami, Florida), "Miami Negroes Brand Charges of Race Riot," October 6, 1926, 2. Thanks to Chris Smith for sending these articles.

22. "Florida Storm" is available on Marie Knight, *Hallelujah What a Song! 1946–1951* (Gospel Friend PN-1500, 2002), as "The Florida Storm." She is accompanied by the Sammy Price Trio (Price, piano; Billy Taylor, bass; Herbert Cowens, drums). The CD booklet credits Knight as composer.

23. Knight was born in Attapulgus, Georgia, on June 1, 1920, and died in New York City on August 30, 2009. From the age of five she was an active member of the Old Tabernacle Church of God in Christ in Newark, New Jersey.

24. See "There Is a God Somewhere: The 1936 Tupelo, Mississippi, and Gainesville, Georgia, Tornadoes" later in the book. The chorus and stanza 3 of Reverend Charles Haffer's undated typescript "A Judgment Song," which is available at the Library of Congress at www.loc.gov/resource/afc2004004.ms090438/?sp=27&r=-0.417,0.839,1.492,0.734,0, are also very similar.

25. The same tune and similar lyrics referring to Miami were also used by gospel singer Flora Molton in "Path by the Sea," a song recorded live for Radio France in 1987 and available on Flora Molton, *Gospel Songs*, Ocora C 583053, 2014.

26. Katie Bell Nubin, *Soul, Soul Searching*, Verve MGV 3004, n.d. Reissued on Sister Rosetta Tharpe, *Complete Vol. 7 (1960–1961)*, Frémeaux FA 1307 (3CD), 2012.

27. See "Miami's new dry dock, results of hurricane, Sept. 18, 1926" at http://www.loc.gov/pictures/item/2007660796/.

28. This song was originally released on Marie Knight, *Today*, Blue Labor BL-106, 1976, and was reissued on a CD bearing the same title (The Blues Alliance TBA-13006, 1996).

29. Judge Jackson, *The Colored Sacred Harp* (Ozark: published by the author, 1934), 87–89.

30. Joe Dan Boyd, *Judge Jackson and the Colored Sacred Harp* (Montgomery: Alabama Folklife Association, 2002), 26–27. Originally used to teach musically illiterate singers, the shape-note singing method started to be used in New England in the eighteenth and nineteenth centuries and spread to the South and West, especially in churches located in rural areas. The system, also "known as 'fasola' because of its use of vocal syllables to represent the different scale notes," is called "shape note" because "the vocal parts were notated using different shapes for the various scale tones." In the beginning, the vocal parts "were often limited to a five-note (pentatonic) scale (four scale notes and the octave)," but by the early nineteenth century, the "common Western scale of eight notes (seven notes and the octave) was also translated into the shape-note tradition." See Richard Carlin, "Shape-Note Singing," in *Encyclopedia of American Gospel Music*, ed. W. K. McNeil, 336–37.

31. Boyd, *Judge Jackson and the Colored Sacred Harp*, 40–41.

32. Both recordings are available on *The Colored Sacred Harp and the African American Shape-Note Tradition* (Alabama Traditions 109, 2003), the CD accompanying Boyd's book.

33. The recording is available on *Drop On Down in Florida: Recent Field Recordings of Afro-American Traditional Music*, Florida Folklife LP 102–3, 1981, reissued as *Drop On Down in Florida* on Dust-to-Digital DTD-24, 2012.

34. "Florida Storm" is included on Wiregrass Sacred Harp Singers, *The Colored Sacred Harp*, New World Records 80433-2, recorded April 17–18, 1993, at Union Grove Baptist Church, Ozark, Alabama.

35. This chapter is a revised and abridged version of my earlier study "Their Eyes Were Watching God: African-American Topical Songs on the 1928 Florida Hurricanes and Floods," *Popular Music* 26, no. 1 (2007): 129–40, which includes titles of newspaper articles and complete transcriptions and analyses of all the lyrics discussed here.

36. See "Palm Beach Dark, Swept by Hurricane; 2 Ships in Distress," *New York Times*, August 8, 1928, 1; "Gale Quit Florida; New Storm Arises: Centre of State Flooded," *New York Times*, August 10, 1928, 1; "Floods and Hazard to Gale in Florida: Lake Okeechobee Overflow Menaces Wide Area—Aid Cut Off from Towns," *New York Times*, August 14, 1928, 1.

37. For a discography of "The Porto Rico Storm" by white singers, see Guthrie T. Meade, with Dick Spottswood and Douglas S. Meade, *Country Music Sources*, 85, and Russell, *Country Music Records*, 765. For its composer Carson Robison and his technique for writing "event" songs in a formulaic way, see Hugh Leamy, "Now come all you good people," in *A History and Encyclopedia of Country, Western, and Gospel Music*, rev. 2nd ed., ed. Linnell Gentry (Nashville: Clairmont, 1969), 6–13.

38. "Florida Makes Ready," *New York Times*, September 15, 1928, 2; "Hundreds Hurt, 33 Killed in Florida Storm, 100-Mile Swath Wrecked, Palm Beach Hard Hit," *New York Times*, September 18, 1928, 1; "Flood Menace in Florida: 24 Drown in Okeechobee," *New York Times*, September 18, 1928, 1; "200 to 400 Killed in Florida Hurricane," *New York Times*, September 19, 1928, 1; "Florida

Dead, 200; Loss in Millions: Sixty-Eight Dead at Okeechobee," *New York Times*, September 19, 1928, 14; "Florida Dead Put at 400, with 23,000 in Distress," *New York Times*, September 20, 1928, 1; "350 Dead in Okeechobee Area," *New York Times*, September 20, 1928, 12; "Florida Deaths Mounting, Now 800, Many Are Missing," *New York Times*, September 21, 1928, 1, 22; "$5,000,000 Sought for Storm Relief; Florida Dead 1,000," *New York Times*, September 22, 1928, 1; "Threat of Disease Grows in Florida: Put Dead at 1,385 and 2,500" and "544 Bodies Recovered: National Guard Officer Puts Dead at 1,500 in Lake Area," *New York Times*, September 22, 1928, 10; "Waters Rise Again in Okeechobee Area; Florida Aid Pressed," *New York Times*, September 23, 1928, 1, 24; "Florida Storm Dead Now Placed at 1,836," *New York Times*, October 29, 1928, 18.

39. Lawrence E. Will, *Okeechobee Hurricane and the Hoover Dike* (St. Petersburg, FL: Great Outdoors Publishing Company, 1961), reprinted Belle Glade, FL: Glades Historical Society, 1990. See also Eliot Kleinberg, *Black Cloud: The Great Florida Hurricane of 1928* (Cocoa, FL: Florida Historical Society Press, 2016), originally published in New York: Carroll & Graf, 2003, and Robert Mikle, *Killer 'Cane: The Deadly Hurricane of 1928* (Lanham, MD: Taylor Trade Publishing, 2006), originally published by Cooper Square Press, 2002.

40. Ruby Gowdy's recording is available on various artists, *Female Blues Singers—Vol. 6: E/F/G (1922–1928)*, Document Records DOCD-5510, 1996. The original 78 r.p.m. was also issued on Champion 15613 and Conqueror 7265, the former credited to Ruby Gowdy, the latter to the pseudonym Martha Bradford. The composer credit is to "Burke," probably Harry Burke, a pseudonym for J. C. Johnson, the composer of Bessie Smith's "Me and My Gin" (Columbia 14384-D), recorded one month before Gowdy's song.

41. Researcher Bob Eagle found many matches for Gowdy in census returns, but the only definitely African American Ruby Gowdy, aged 22, single, occupation "Laborer, Farm," was enumerated on April 3, 1930, at which time she was a prisoner at City Prison, Female Department, Militia district 1,347, Enumeration District 38, De Kalb County, Georgia. She was born in Virginia around 1907 and her parents had been born there, too. Chris Smith points out that a Ruby Gowdy married Johnny Youngblood in New York City (where "Florida Flood Blues" was recorded), on September 10, 1928, but there is no information about the couple's race.

42. "Negro Spiritual Song Grows out of Flood," *Atlanta Constitution*, October 25, 1928, 24. See also Kleinberg, *Black Cloud*, 298–99, where it is said that a similar song was "found in the files of the American Red Cross" . . . and "was first performed three days before" it was printed in a *Palm Beach Post* story published on October 24, 1928.

43. This stanza is drawn from William Cowper's eighteenth-century hymn "Light Shining out of Darkness."

44. Viola Jenkins may be the "maid, private family" living in Gainesville in 1940, aged 43. She, her husband Eddie and their children had moved from Waterstown in Columbia County, Florida, sometime after 1935, and were still in Gainesville in 1953. US Federal Census, 1930 and 1940; Gainesville city directory, 1953. Alternatively, she is the ten-year-old student enumerated in the July 7, 1900, US census, born in January 1890 to single mother Lula Jenkins from Georgia, and living in Gainesville, Alachua County, Florida.

45. A. C. Morris, *Folksongs of Florida*, 101–2. Another reference to Viola Jenkins's "West Palm Beach Storm" is included in G. Malcolm Laws Jr., *Native American Balladry: A Descriptive Study and a Bibliographical Syllabus* (Philadelphia: American Folklore Society, 1964), 272.

46. Zora Neale Hurston, *Their Eyes Were Watching God* (Philadelphia: J.B. Lippincott, 1937); reprint: New York: Harper & Row, 1990.

47. For a chapter on Zora Neale Hurston and the 1928 Okeechobee Hurricane, see Kleinberg, *Black Cloud*, 245–51. Historian Richard M. Mizelle Jr. states in *Backwater Blues*, 61, that Hurston was living at the Everglades Cypress Lumber Company near Loughman, Florida, at the time of the disaster, but this is confuted by Kleinberg, 205.

48. A tornado is said to be "significant" when it has at least an F2 parameter.

49. Accounts of the event can be found in Montrose W. Hayes, "The St. Louis Tornado of September 29, 1927," *Monthly Weather Review* 55, no. 9 (September 1927): 405–7. See also "St. Louis, MO Tornado Destruction, Sep 1927" at http://www.gendisasters.com/missouri/11251/st-louis-mo-tornado-destruction-sep-1927.

50. Born in Mississippi but a resident of St. Louis, bluesman Henry Townsend recounts this disaster in his autobiography *A Blues Life: Henry Townsend as Told to Bill Greensmith* (Urbana and Chicago: University of Illinois Press, 1999), 23–24. Townsend did not compose a song about it, however.

51. Recorded on October 3, 1927, in New York City and reissued on Lonnie Johnson, *Complete Recorded Works 1925–1932 in Chronological Order—Volume 3*, Document Records DOCD-5065, 1991. In October or November 1927 (Guido van Rijn, email to author, March 19, 2015), Elzadie Robinson covered Lonnie Johnson's song on Paramount 12573. It is available on Elzadie Robinson, *Complete Recorded Works in Chronological Order—Volume 1 (1926–1928)*, Document Records DOCD-5248, 1994. Born in Logansport, Louisiana, in 1897, Robinson was a resident of Chicago in 1926–1929, when she recorded for Paramount. Textually, there are only minor differences between the two recordings. The persistence of this disaster as a topic for African American blues singers is attested by "St. Louis Cyclone" (Swingmaster 2106), brother-and-sister guitar duo George and Ethel McCoy's version of Lonnie Johnson's song. With George on vocals, it was recorded in East St. Louis, Illinois, on August 14 or 15, 1981, almost fifty-four years after the catastrophe.

52. Paul Oliver, *Conversation with the Blues* (Cambridge: Cambridge University Press, 1997), 121, originally published by Cassell, 1965. See also Dean Alger, *The Original Guitar Hero and the Power of Music. The Legendary Lonnie Johnson: Music and Civil Rights* (Denton: University of North Texas Press, 2014), 114–15, which fails to mention Mary Johnson's role in inspiring the song, reported in Oliver.

53. For apocalyptic imagery in Lonnie Johnson's song and Elzadie Robinson's cover, see Małgorzata Ziółek-Sowińska, *Images of the Apocalypse in African American Blues and Spirituals*, 60–61, 63–64.

54. For Rev. J. M. Gates see Gayle Dean Wardlow, "Dead Cat on the Line," *Blues & Rhythm* 197 (March 2005): 10–11. See also Dr. Guido van Rijn, "Praying for the Pastor: The Life of Rev. J. M. Gates," *Living Blues* 152 (July-August 2000): 48–51.

55. Recorded on October 6, 1927, in Atlanta, Georgia, and reissued on Rev. J. M. Gates, *Complete Recorded Works in Chronological Order—Volume 5 (1927)*, Document Records DOCD-5449, 1996. For a partial transcription and short comment on this recording see Paul Oliver, *Songsters and Saints: Vocal Traditions on Race Records* (Cambridge: Cambridge University Press, 1984), 162.

56. Chris Smith, liner notes to Rev. J. M. Gates, *Complete Recorded Works in Chronological Order—Volume 5 (1927)*.

57. On October 8, 1931, Sam Collins recorded "Atlanta Fire" (ARC unissued), which is possibly the only African American song dealing with this event.

58. Townsend, *A Blues Life*, 35–36, where the description of Miller as possibly "slightly older than me" (Townsend was born in 1909) conflicts with the date of birth given here, which is reported in Bob Eagle and Eric LeBlanc, *Blues: A Regional Experience*, 522.

59. See Helge Thygesen and Russell Shor, *Vocalion 1000 and Brunswick 7000 Race Series* (Overveen, The Netherlands: Agram Blues Books, 2014), 47. Thanks to Guido van Rijn for the information that the October recording was also issued.

60. Reissued on Luella Miller, *Complete Recorded Works in Chronological Order (1926–1928)*, Document Records DOCD-5183, 1993.

61. This work is included in *The Collected Poems of Sterling A. Brown*, ed. Michael S. Harper (New York: Harper & Row, 1980), 68–69.

62. See Clarence Major, ed., *Juba to Jive: A Dictionary of African-American Slang* (New York: Penguin Books, 1994), 327.

63. Thomas P. Grazulis, *Significant Tornadoes 1680–1991, A Chronology and Analysis of Events* (St. Johnsbury, VT: The Tornado Project of Environmental Films, 1993), quoted in Martis D. Ramage Jr., *Tupelo, Mississippi, Tornado of 1936* (Tupelo: Northeast Mississippi Historical and Genealogical Society, 1997), 42.

64. Ramage, *Tupelo, Mississippi, Tornado of 1936*, i–ii.

65. E. J. Mays, comp., "Mississippi's Tornado Disaster," in Ramage, *Tupelo, Mississippi, Tornado of 1936*, 69.

66. This song has been reissued on various artists, *Two Decades of Country Music*, Bronco Buster CD 9043, 1998.

67. This song has been reissued on Elton Britt, *Early Recordings 1933–1937*, B.A.C.M. CD D 109, 2005.

68. Little information is available on this singer. The most likely match is Lula Morris, aged 48, born in Mississippi, no occupation, listed in the April 2, 1930, US Census, enumeration district 27, Belzoni City, Humphreys County, Mississippi. She married at 15 for the first time. Her father was born in Alabama, and her mother in Mississippi. Thanks to Bob Eagle for providing census information.

69. "Seabird" is a dialect pronunciation of Seeburg, a brand of jukebox.

70. Alan Lomax, *The Land Where the Blues Began* (New York: Pantheon Books, 1993), 35–36.

71. No mention of a mass hanging like the one described by Johnson is reported in any of the following studies: Adam Gussow, *Seems Like Murder Here: Southern Violence and the Blues Tradition* (Chicago and London: University of Chicago Press, 2002); Manfred Berg, *Popular Justice: A History of Lynching in America* (Lanham, MD: Rowman and Littlefield, 2015, originally published in 2011); Amy Louise Wood, *Lynching and Spectacle: Witnessing Racial Violence in America 1890–1940* (Chapel Hill: University of North Carolina Press, 2009); and Julius Eric Thompson, *Lynchings in Mississippi: A History 1865–1965* (Jefferson, NC: McFarland, 2007).

72. See Chris Herrington, "Beginning of the End: Expatriate Memphians Bob Frank and John Murry Come Together Half a Country Away," *Memphis Magazine*, October 2007, http://www.memphismagazine.com/October-2007/Beginning-of-the-End. Although coverage of contemporary newspapers is not comprehensive, a search at www.newspapers.com reveals no reports of a lynching at Tupelo in 1926.

73. For biographical information on Haffer, see Lomax, *The Land Where the Blues Began*, 48–58.

74. Lomax, *The Land Where the Blues Began*, 52.

75. See "Image 9, Alan Lomax Collection, Manuscripts, Mississippi, Tennessee, and Arkansas, 1941-1942: 'The Tupelo Disaster'" at https://www.loc.gov/resource/afc2004004.ms090438 /?st=gallery.

76. As reported in John W. Work, Lewis Wade Jones, and Samuel C. Adams Jr., *Lost Delta Found: Rediscovering the Fisk University–Library of Congress Coahoma County Study, 1941–1942,* eds. Robert Gordon and Bruce Nemerov (Nashville: Vanderbilt University Press, 2005), 117, John Work noted that "His wife reads books, magazines and newspapers to him daily."

77. Ramage, *Tupelo, Mississippi, Tornado of 1936,* 47, 55.

78. Ramage, *Tupelo, Mississippi, Tornado of 1936,* 8.

79. Bluesman Robert Lockwood said that he and Sonny Boy II were on their way to Tupelo in 1936 and got there the day after the tornado struck. See Larry Hoffman, "Robert Lockwood, Jr.," *Living Blues* 121 (June 1995): 17; reprint: Jas Obrecht, ed., *Rollin' and Tumblin': The Postwar Blues Guitarists* (San Francisco: Miller Freeman, 2000), 168. This might explain why Sonny Boy reputedly sang about the tornado.

80. Marc W. Ryan, *Trumpet Records: Diamonds on Farish Street* (Jackson: University Press of Mississippi, 2004), 25.

81. Researcher Bob Eagle reports that "a Brother Henry Green (gospel songwriter) was based at Route 1, Box 113, Georgetown, South Carolina, in 1966." Email to the author, February 26, 2004.

82. "Storm Thru Mississippi" is available on the compilation *1950s Gospel Classics (1950–1958),* Document Records DOCD-5464, 1996. Its correct recording date reported in Robert Pruter, Robert Campbell, and Armin Büttner, "The Chance Label," *Blues & Rhythm* 200 (June 2005): 12–13, 21, proves that this song does not deal with the 1952 Mississippi storm, as reported in Timothy Dodge, *The School of Arizona Dranes: Gospel Music Pioneer* (Lanham, MD: Lexington Books, 2013), 134. More information about Henry Green and his song is provided in the April 14, 2019, update by the same authors at http://campber.people.clemson.edu/chance.html, which also includes the following link https://www.youtube.com/watch?v=NSNcUKgk6Zg, where in a 2014 post Green is reported as being nearly 100 years old and "residing with his wife in the suburbs of Illinois."

83. "Tupelo, Miss., Wrecked," *New York Times,* April 6, 1936, 4.

84. This inaccuracy is reported in Mizelle, *Backwater Blues,* 11.

85. Charles Shaar Murray, *Boogie Man: The Adventures of John Lee Hooker in the American Twentieth Century* (New York: St. Martin's Press, 2000), 214.

86. John M. Barry, *Rising Tide* (New York: Simon & Schuster, 1997), 170–71.

87. Luigi Monge, "Death by Fire: African-American Popular Music on the Natchez Rhythm Club Fire," in *Nobody Knows Where the Blues Come From: Lyrics and History,* ed. Robert Springer (Jackson: University Press of Mississippi, 2005), 95–96. See also Luigi Monge, "Topical Blues: Disasters," in *Encyclopedia of the Blues,* vol. 2 (K–Z), ed. Edward Komara, 997.

88. Reissued on *The Country Blues of John Lee Hooker,* Original Blues Classics OBCCD-542, n.d.

89. On August 26, 1966, in Franklinton, Louisiana, David Evans and Marina Bokelman recorded bluesman L. V. Conerly, whose "High Water" (Flyright 512) mentions Tupelo in a flood context and is obviously based on Hooker's faulty understanding.

90. Reissued on Albert King, Steve Cropper, Pop Staples, *Jammed Together,* Stax SCD-8544-2, 1990.

91. This song was reissued on John Lee Hooker, *The Cream*, Fuel 2000 Records 302 061 139 2, 2001.

92. See "Gainesville, GA Tornado, Apr 1936," at https://www.gendisasters.com/georgia/6630/gainesville-ga-tornado-apr-1936, and "The 1936 Gainesville Tornado: Disaster and Recovery" at http://dlg.galileo.usg.edu/tornado.

93. See Bruce Nemerov, "I'm a Holy Ghost Preacher!," *Blues & Rhythm* 141 (August 1999): 4–6. In a January 11, 2011, email, Nemerov, whom I thank for his kind help, confirmed that no "ballet" of the song has been found and that due to her failing health, Sister Terrell could only remember the two lines quoted above.

94. The best-sounding reissue of Bessie Smith's "Back-Water Blues" is on Bessie Smith, *The Complete Recordings—Volume 5*, Frog Records DGF44, 2003.

95. For a biography of Bessie Smith, see Chris Albertson, *Bessie*, rev. 2nd ed. (New Haven, CT, and London: Yale University Press, 2003).

96. *Webster's Third New International Dictionary of the English Language* (Springfield: Merriam-Webster, 1993), 160.

97. Evidence of the widespread assumption that Smith's song was about the 1927 flood is found in Leadbelly's "Backwater Blues" (Playboy PB 119), recorded at the University of Texas at Austin on June 15, 1949, and reissued on *Leadbelly 'Live': Complete Recorded Works in Chronological Order (1947 and 1949)*, Document Records DOCD-5676, 2004. Big Bill Broonzy also ascribed this song to the Mississippi River flood of 1927. See also Jerry Ricks's account of how Brownie McGhee used to introduce his version of "Backwater Blues" in Philip R. Ratcliffe, *Mississippi John Hurt: His Life, His Times, His Blues* (Jackson: University Press of Mississippi, 2011), 156.

98. David Evans, "Bessie Smith's 'Back-Water Blues': The Story Behind the Song," 97–116. Although Richard M. Mizelle Jr. was aware that Smith's song was recorded before the Mississippi levees broke, there is no mention of Nashville or the Cumberland River flood in his *Backwater Blues*, 30–31. For a discussion of the analysis of "Back-Water Blues" in Susan Scott Parrish, "Bessie's Eclogue," in *The Flood Year 1927*, 125–46, see this book's chapter on the 1927 Mississippi River flood.

99. For the Bible's central status in African American life, culture, and rhetoric see Allen Dwight Callahan, *The Talking Book: African Americans and the Bible* (New Haven, CT, and London: Yale University Press, 2008).

100. See, for example, "1,000 Made Homeless by Nashville Flood," *New York Times*, December 26, 1926, 23.

101. Angela Y. Davis, *Blues Legacies and Black Feminism: Gertrude "Ma" Rainey, Bessie Smith, and Billie Holiday* (New York: Vintage Books, 1998), 108. See also Ziólek-Sowińska, *Images of the Apocalypse in African American Blues and Spirituals*, 58.

102. "Unite for Rescue Work after Flood," *Chicago Defender*, January 15, 1927, 2, also published with the title "Two Races Aid Flood Victims," *Pittsburgh Courier*, January 15, 1927, 3. Quoted in Evans, "Bessie Smith's 'Back-Water Blues': The Story Behind the Song," 113.

103. See Lonnie Johnson's "Back Water Blues" (OKeh 8466), recorded in St. Louis on May 3, 1927, and reissued on *Complete Recorded Works 1925–1932 in Chronological Order—Volume 2 (1926–1927)*, Document Records DOCD-5064, 1991; Viola McCoy's "Back Water Blues" (Cameo 1189), recorded in New York City ca. mid-June 1927, and reissued on Viola McCoy, *Complete Recorded Works in Chronological Order—Volume 3 (1926–1929)*, Document Records DOCD-5418, 1995; and Kitty Waters's "Back Water Blues" (Pathé Actuelle 7531), recorded in New York City ca.

June 1927, and reissued on various artists, *Female Blues Singers Vol. 14 (1923–1932)*, Document Records DOCD-5518, 1996.

104. Around forty-five versions are known to have been recorded before 1970, including one titled "Backwater Blues" (AFS 3021-A-2), collected by Herbert Halpert from Will C. Thomas in Iuka, Mississippi, on May 17, 1939, on the same day that he recorded a song about the Tupelo tornado. Thomas claimed that he had never heard the song on record, and that it was about a flood in Arkansas seven or eight years earlier. He was perhaps associating it with the 1929 overflowing of Big Lake in Arkansas. Also unissued is the cover version of Bessie Smith's recording titled "When It Rains Five Days (Backwater Blues)," collected by John A. Lomax from Christine Shannon (misidentified as Christine Cannon in Library of Congress filing) in the Camp for Women at the State Penitentiary, Parchman, Mississippi, on April 13, 1936. Several other versions were recorded, among others, by Lead Belly, Josh White, and Big Bill Broonzy.

105. Evans, "Bessie Smith's 'Back-Water Blues': The Story Behind the Song," 99.

106. This recording has been reissued on the 10-CD set Uncle Dave Macon, *Keep My Skillet Good and Greasy*, Bear Family 15978 JM, 2004, and on the 4-CD set *Uncle Dave Macon Vol. 2: Classic Cuts 1924–1938*, JSP 7769B, 2006.

107. For a biography of Uncle Dave Macon, see Michael D. Doubler, *Dixie Dewdrop: The Uncle Dave Macon Story* (Urbana: University of Illinois Press, 2018). For a biography of Sam McGee, see Russell, *Country Music Originals*, 31–32.

108. See Barry Lee Pearson, "Appalachian Blues," and Cecelia Conway, "Black Banjo Songsters in Appalachia," *Black Music Research Journal* 23, no. 1/2 (spring/fall 2003): 40 and 161, respectively.

109. Three more hillbilly songs titled "Back Water Blues" were composed in the following years. The first was recorded by Byrd Moore in Richmond, Indiana, on October 30, 1928, and released on Gennett 6686. Again in Richmond, the Three Tobacco Tags recorded their version of "Back Water Blues" for the Champion label (16674) on August 9, 1932. I haven't been able to listen to this recording. Dewey and Gassie Bassett recorded another "Back Water Blues" (Bluebird B-8682) on September 28, 1938, in Rock Hill, South Carolina, but it is not about a flood.

110. For book-length studies of this disaster, see Pete Daniel, *Deep'n As It Come: The 1927 Mississippi River Flood* (Fayetteville: University of Arkansas Press, 1996); John M. Barry, *Rising Tide: The Great Mississippi Flood of 1927 and How It Changed America* (New York: Simon and Schuster, 1997); Patrick O'Daniel, *When the Levee Breaks: Memphis and the Mississippi Valley Flood of 1927* (Charleston: History Press, 2013); Mizelle, *Backwater Blues*; and Parrish, *The Flood Year 1927*. See also Steven J. Morrison, "Downhome Tragedy: The Blues and the Mississippi Flood of 1927," *Southern Folklore* 51 (1994): 265–84; R. A. Lawson, *Jim Crow's Counterculture: The Blues and Black Southerners 1890–1945* (Baton Rouge: Louisiana University Press, 2010), 135–43; Patrick O'Daniel, *Memphis and the Superflood of 1937: High Water Blues* (Charleston: History Press, 2010), 21–31; Christine A. Klein and Sandra B. Zellmer, *Mississippi River Tragedies: A Century of Unnatural Disaster* (New York and London: New York University Press, 2014), 67–78; and Philip Horne, "Flood Songs, Dylan, and the Mississippi Blues," *Raritan: A Quarterly Review* 33, no. 2 (2014), https://raritanquarterly.rutgers.edu/issue-index/author-index/horne-philip.

111. Old footage showing the seriousness of the disaster can be seen in the television film *Warming by the Devil's Fire*, directed by Charles Burnett, 2003.

112. See Barry, *Rising Tide*, 200–201. For a summary of other abuses against blacks and relevant references, see David Evans, "High Water Everywhere: Blues and Gospel Commentary

on the 1927 Mississippi River Flood," in *Nobody Knows Where the Blues Come From: Lyrics and History*, ed. Robert Springer, 7–9, 68–69.

113. Evans, "High Water Everywhere," 3–75. Among the African American songs not mentioned in this study and outside the blues and gospel traditions is Paul Robeson's "High Water" (His Master's Voice B3663, recorded on September 11, 1930), a McHardy and Brennan composition that had appeal to a wide spectrum of the public, both black and white, and that was undoubtedly inspired by the 1927 Mississippi River flood.

114. Reprinted in Richard L. Riley, comp., *Early Blues*, vol. 2 (Roseville, CA: PianoMania, 1996), 79–81.

115. See the June 6, 1900, US census of the City of St. Louis, Missouri, and the January 14–15, 1920, April 14, 1930, and April 4, 1940, US censuses of Augusta, Woodruff County, Arkansas.

116. "300 Marooned by Flood at Peach Orchard Bluff with Scanty Provisions," *Commercial Appeal* (Memphis), April 19, 1927, 10.

117. Eight days later Johnson recorded "Back Water Blues," a cover of Bessie Smith's earlier recording about a different flood. Both Johnson songs are available on *Complete Recorded Works 1925–1932 in Chronological Order—Vol. 2 (1929–1930)*, Document Records DOCD-5064, 1991.

118. This is Dalhart's first version recorded on April 27 (Victor 20611). An almost identical and currently more easily accessible version was recorded on August 3 (Edison 52088) and reissued on Vernon Dalhart, *Puttin' on the Style*, Document Records DOCD-1105, 2007. An unreleased "Mississippi Flood" was recorded by Lawrence Woods for Gennett on July 7, 1932. It is not known whether this is a version of the Robison/Dalhart song, nor even whether it refers to the flood of 1927. See Meade, Spottswood, and Meade, *Country Music Sources*, 86–87, and Russell, *Country Music Records*, 973.

119. Robison is considered to be white, but there may have been some doubt about it in the 1920s. He often associated with black musical figures and was billed as "the white boy with the colored fingers." For a discography of Dalhart's versions see Russell, *Country Music Records*, 268–69, 271.

120. Jefferson's "Rising High Water Blues," on which, unusually, he does not play guitar, is on his *Complete Recorded Works in Chronological Order—Volume 2 (1927)*, Document Records DOCD-5018, 1990. The late April 1927 recording date is given in Guido van Rijn and Alex van der Tuuk, *New York Recording Laboratories Rodeheaver, Marsh and 2000 Series* (Overveen, The Netherlands: Agram Blues Books, 2013), 76–77. Writer Paul Oliver considered this song Jefferson's first "truly sequential blues with a clear story line." See Alan Govenar and Kip Lornell, comps., *The Blues Come to Texas: Paul Oliver and Mack McCormick's Unfinished Book* (College Station, TX: A&M University Press, 2019), 302, 362.

121. See Luigi Monge, "The Language of Blind Lemon Jefferson: The Covert Theme of Blindness," *Black Music Research Journal* 20, no. 1 (spring 2000): 35–81. See also Luigi Monge and David Evans, "New Songs of Blind Lemon Jefferson," *Journal of Texas Music History* 3, no. 2 (fall 2003): 8–28.

122. The song is credited to "Martin." For biographical information on Bessie Mae Smith, see Alex van der Tuuk, *The New Paramount Book of Blues* (Overveen, The Netherlands: Agram Blues Books, 2017), 287–92; and Bob Eagle, "Roosevelt Sykes Aliases and Associates," *Frog Blues and Jazz Annual* 5, ed. Paul Swinton (2017): 169.

123. "High Water Blues" was reissued on St. Louis Bessie and Alice Moore, *Complete Recorded Works in Chronological Order—Volume 1 (1927–1929)*, Document Records DOCD-5290, 1994.

124. This song is available on Sippie Wallace, *Complete Recorded Works in Chronological Order—Volume 2 (1925–1945)*, Document Records DOCD-5400, 1995.

125. In Richard M. Mizelle Jr.'s book referenced above, Wallace is oddly defined as "one of the more commercially successful *Texas R&B singers of the 1920s*" (emphasis added) and two of her lines are inaccurately transcribed as "They sent out a law" instead of "They sent out alarms" and "do you hear this plea?" instead of "doing as it please" (48).

126. Their lyrics are printed alongside some African American songs on the 1927 Mississippi River flood in "The Words," in Strachwitz and Welding, *The American Folk Music Occasional*, 53–57. The transcription of "The Terrible Mississippi Flood" contains small but significant errors in its last line, which have been corrected here.

127. See Russell, *Country Music Records*, 337–38. To my knowledge, this song has not been reissued on CD. It can be heard at https://archive.org/details/78_the-terrible-mississippi -flood_arthur-fields-ryder_gbia0011462a.

128. Stoneman's "The Story of the Mighty Mississippi" is available on *People Take Warning! Murder Ballads and Disaster Songs, 1913–1938*, Tompkins Square 1875 (3CD), 2007. For a brief biography of these musicians, see Russell, *Country Music Originals*, 9–11 and 21–23 respectively.

129. Barry reports that an "estimated 330,000 people were rescued from rooftops." See Barry, *Rising Tide*, 285.

130. Ivan M. Tribe, *The Stonemans: An Appalachian Family and the Music That Shaped Their Lives* (Urbana: University of Illinois Press, 1993), 56.

131. The liner notes to *People Take Warning!*, 27, state that Stoneman's source was a black performer "waiting in the recording studio," but only the Million Dollar Pier Orchestra, a white dance band, also recorded that day.

132. See Bruce Bastin with Kip Lornell, *The Melody Man: Joe Davis and the New York Music Scene* (Jackson: University Press of Mississippi, 2012), 78, 82; and Russell, *Country Music Records*, 148. The Bonnie and Clyde song is at https://www.youtube.com/watch?v=IMLPe8KmuBo. "Joe Hoover" as lyricist is at https://adp.library.ucsb.edu/index.php/talent/detail/50210/Hoover_Joe_ lyricist. "Young Man You'd Better Take Care," the fourth "Joe Hoover" composition recorded by Dwight Butcher, is registered with ASCAP as a J. Russel Robinson copyright; see https://www. ascap.com/ace/#ace/writer/14371710/HOOVER%20JOE.

133. The songs are available on Edna Hicks, Hazel Meyers, and Laura Smith, *Complete Recorded Works in Chronological Order—Vol. 2 (1923–1927)*, Document Records DOCD-5431, 1996. Their lyrics are transcribed in Evans, "High Water Everywhere," 36–38. For more information on Laura Smith, see Laurie Wright, "Pieces of the Jigsaw," in *Storyville 1996/7*, ed. Laurie Wright (Chigwell, UK: L. Wright, 1997), 227–29.

134. Barry, *Rising Tide*, 324–27.

135. The song is available on Barbecue Bob, *Complete Recorded Works in Chronological Order—Vol. 1 (1927–1928)*, Document Records DOCD-5046, 1991.

136. Pete Lowry, "Some Cold Rainy Day," *Blues Unlimited* 103 (August-September 1973): 15.

137. Bruce Bastin, *Red River Blues: The Blues Tradition in the Southeast* (Urbana: University of Illinois Press, 1986), 108.

138. Both songs were reissued on various artists, *Barrelhouse Women—Vol. 2 (1924–1928)*, Document Records DOCD-5497, 1996. For the correct recording date, see van Rijn and van der Tuuk, *New York Recording Laboratories Rodeheaver, Marsh and 2000 Series*, 85, 87.

139. Oliver, *Conversation with the Blues*, 68.

140. Pearson's name does not show up in Greenville in the 1920 or 1930 census or the 1927 and 1929 city directories. Bob Eagle and David Evans, personal communications, August 6, 2018. However, "there are one or more Alice Pearsons listed in Memphis in the 1920 and 1930 US Census and in city directories of the time." David Evans, Ed Payne, Richard Linster, T. DeWayne Moore, and Bob Eagle, "Lightning Struck Him: Walter Rhodes, The Delta Crowing Rooster," *Frog Blues and Jazz Annual* 6, forthcoming.

141. Evans, "High Water Everywhere," 45.

142. Paul Oliver, *Bessie Smith* (New York: A. S. Barnes, 1961); originally published by Cassell, 1959, 47.

143. Reissued on Bessie Smith, *The Complete Recordings—Volume 6*, Frog Records DGF45, 2003.

144. "Steeple" is probably a Southern pronunciation of the word "staple," meaning a nail. For the transcription of both "potholes" and "steeple," see Chris Smith, "Homeless Blues (Bessie Smith)," in column "Words Words Words," *Blues & Rhythm* 339 (May 2019): 24.

145. For an interesting discussion of this song see Mizelle, *Backwater Blues*, 49–50.

146. For Rev. Mason's date of birth and death see Gene Tomko, *Encyclopedia of Louisiana Musicians* (Baton Rouge: Louisiana State University Press, 2020), 277, 297: "Born possibly Aug. 11, 1871, Chicot County, Arkansas (Louisiana Death Certificate 20–7933); died possibly July 14, 1934, Lake Providence, E. Carroll Parish." Evans, "High Water Everywhere," 48, reports a different date of birth (June 1, 1878) from the 1930 US Census and World War I civilian draft card; van der Tuuk, *The New Paramount Book of Blues*, 218, reports a different date of birth (1872), but the same date of death as Tomko.

147. This sermon is available on various artists, *Alabama: Black Secular and Religious Music: Complete Recorded Works in Chronological Order (1927–1934)*, Document Records DOCD-5165, 1993.

148. *Chicago Defender*, March 17, 1928, pt. 1, 11.

149. See van der Tuuk, *The New Paramount Book of Blues*, 218–20.

150. J. Winston Harrington, "Deny Food to Flood Sufferers," *Chicago Defender*, June 4, 1927, 1, 2; Ida B. Wells-Barnett, "Flood Report Found Untrue to Conditions," *Chicago Defender*, July 9, 1927, 1, 4.

151. Reissued on Luella Miller, *Complete Recorded Works in Chronological Order (1926–1928)*, Document Records DOCD-5183, 1993.

152. Reissued on Lonnie Johnson, *Complete Recorded Works 1925–1932 in Chronological Order—Volume 4 (1928–1929)*, Document Records DOCD-5066, 1991.

153. See Mizelle, *Backwater Blues*, 37.

154. Reissued on Barbecue Bob, *Complete Recorded Works in Chronological Order—Volume 2 (1928–1929)*, Document Records DOCD-5047, 1991.

155. Crawford's song was recorded in New York City ca. July 11, 1928, and reissued on various artists, *Male Blues of the Twenties: Complete Recorded Works in Chronological Order—Volume 1 (1922–1930)*, Document Records DOCD-5482, 1996. Dixon's song was recorded in New York City

on August 24, 1929, and reissued on various artists, *Blue Girls: Complete Recorded Works—Volume 2 (1925-1930)*, Document Records DOCD-5504, 1996.

156. Reissued on *People Take Warning! Murder Ballads and Disaster Songs, 1913-1938*, Tompkins Square 1875 (3CD), 2007. In the transcription, the words in square brackets are sung only in the repeated stanzas, whereas the words in round brackets are sung by the congregation.

157. Reissued on *People Take Warning! Murder Ballads and Disaster Songs, 1913-1938*, Tompkins Square 1875 (3CD), 2007.

158. Ethel Douglas, quoted in Paul and Beth Garon, *Woman with Guitar: Memphis Minnie's Blues* (San Francisco: City Lights Books, 2014), 49; originally published by Da Capo Press, 1992.

159. Garon and Garon, *Woman with Guitar*, 50.

160. The ca. October 1929 date reported in *Blues and Gospel Records 1890-1943*, 708, has been questioned. For the correct recording date see Guido van Rijn and Alex van der Tuuk, *New York Recording Laboratories Matrix Series Volume One: The L Matrix Series (1929-1932)*, rev. 2nd ed. (Overveen, The Netherlands: Agram Blues Books, 2015), 7. This recording is available on the box set *Screamin' and Hollerin' the Blues: The Worlds of Charley Patton* (Disc 2), Revenant Album No. 212 (7CD), 2001. For Patton's date of birth see van der Tuuk, *The New Paramount Book of Blues*, 246-49, and David Evans, "Charley Patton: The Conscience of the Delta," in *Charley Patton: Voice of the Mississippi Delta*, rev. ed., ed. Robert Sacré (Jackson: University Press of Mississippi, 2018), 32. For further comments on the flood see Evans, "Charley Patton: The Conscience of the Delta," 33, 105-9. "High Water Everywhere Part II," which has mistakenly been thought to be an account of the 1927 Mississippi River flood, in fact describes a later flood. The two recordings are discussed as one song in Julia Simon, *Time in the Blues* (New York: Oxford University Press, 2017), 142-45.

161. Evans, "High Water Everywhere," 62.

162. See Robert Springer, ed., "Text, Context and Subtext in the Blues," in *The Lyrics in African American Popular Music* (Bern, Switzerland: Peter Lang, 2001), 12-16.

163. Susan Scott Parrish, "Bessie's Eclogue," in *The Flood Year 1927*, 125-46.

164. Among the most touching recollections from bluesmen is David "Honeyboy" Edwards's "The Water Overflowed Her Heart," in his autobiography *The World Don't Owe Me Nothing: The Life and Times of Delta Bluesman Honeyboy Edwards* (Chicago: Chicago Review Press, 1997), 15-17. Museum features on the disaster can be found at the B.B. King Museum and Delta Interpretive Center in Indianola, Mississippi, at the Delta Cultural Center in Helena, Arkansas, and at the 1927 Flood Museum, Greenville, Mississippi. A historical trail marker was placed in Scott, Mississippi, on April 21, 2009.

165. Among them are two versions of Barbecue Bob's "Mississippi Heavy Water Blues," the first recorded by Robert Pete Williams and Robert "Guitar" Welch (Folklyric LP 111) in Angola, Louisiana, on March 21, 1959, and reissued on various artists, *Country Negro Jam Session*, Arhoolie CD 372, 1993; the second by Josh Thomas (Blue Ridge Institute BRI 008) in Hollins (Roanoke County), Virginia, in spring 1970, and reissued on various artists, *Virginia Traditions: Southwest Virginia Blues*, Global Village Music CD 1008, 1990. A two-part guitar-accompanied Cajun-French narration of the disaster, "Durante l'Eau Haute de '27" ("During Flood Waters of 1927"), was recorded by Marion Marcotte and released on Jin 45-129 in 1960. It was reissued on *The Cajun French Humor of Marion Marcotte*, Swallow Records SW 6004, 1996. David "Honeyboy" Edwards recorded a version of Charley Patton's "High Water Everywhere" in Salina, Kansas, on February 20 or 21, 1999, issued on APO DVD 2010D, 2000.

166. See Guido van Rijn's booklet notes to Big Bill Broonzy, *Amsterdam Live Concerts 1953*, Munich Records MRCD 275 (2CD), 2006, 28; and Bob Riesman, *I Feel So Good: The Life and Times of Big Bill Broonzy* (Chicago and London: University of Chicago Press, 2011), 194–95.

167. Eric Bibb, "Flood Water," in *Booker's Guitar*, Telarc Blues TEL-31756-02, 2010. See also Peter Daniels, *The Legend of Booker's Guitar* (self-published, 2014), 151–52.

168. See Kelly Kazek, "A Look at Alabama's Deadliest Floods," https://www.al.com/living/index.ssf/2015/12/a_look_at_alabamas_deadliest_f.html.

169. See "Elba, Alabama Flood—March 1929," at http://www.gendisasters.com/alabama/8282/elba-al-flood-mar-1929.

170. See the National Weather Service website https://www.weather.gov/safety/flood-states-al.

171. See George A. Lott, "The Great-Volume Rainstorm at Elba, Alabama," *Monthly Weather Review* 82, no. 6 (June 1954): 153, http://citeseerx.ist.psu.edu/viewdoc/download?doi=10.1.1.39 4.6294&rep=rep1&type=pdf.

172. George Carter's four recordings are available on various artists, *Georgia Blues and Gospel (1927–1931)*, Document Records DOCD-5160, 1993. It has been suggested that George Carter is a pseudonym for Georgia bluesman and Columbia recording artist Charlie Hicks, aka Charlie Lincoln (1900–1963). See Evans, "High Water Everywhere," 20. This song is inexplicably included in Mizelle's study of the 1927 Mississippi River flood *Backwater Blues*, 41, where George Carter is said, also inexplicably, to be a pseudonym for blues and gospel pianist and composer Thomas A. "Georgia Tom" Dorsey.

173. Reissued on Rev. J. M. Gates, *Complete Recorded Works in Chronological Order—Vol. 7 (1927–1929)*, Document Records DOCD-5469, 1996.

174. See "4 Horses Used to Land Turtle of 1350 Pounds," *Brownsville Herald* (Brownsville, Texas), March 17, 1929, 41; and "4 Horses Required to Pull Big Turtle Out of the Gulf," *Atlanta Constitution*, March 19, 1929, 13. See also Chris Smith, "The Flood of Alabama," in column "Words Words Words," *Blues & Rhythm* 344 (November 2019): 28–29.

175. See Russell, *Country Music Records*, 455, and Meade, Spottswood, and Meade, *Country Music Sources*, 88. "The Alabama Flood" has been reissued on *People Take Warning! Murder Ballads and Disaster Songs, 1913–1938*, Tompkins Square TSQ 1875 (3CD), 2007. I have not been able to listen to "The Fate of Elba, Alabama." For some biographical information on Jenkins, see Archie Green, *Only A Miner: Studies in Recorded Coal-Mining Songs* (Urbana and Chicago: University of Illinois Press, 1972), 123–25.

176. Mary Lee Spain sings "town," the correct rhyme word; Andrew Jenkins sings "street."

177. Lonnie Johnson, *Complete Recorded Works 1925–1932 in Chronological Order—Vol. 5 (1929–1930)*, Document Records DOCD-5067, 1991.

178. Evans, "High Water Everywhere," 56–57. Johnson's original "Falling Rain Blues" was not about a flood.

179. See Commonwealth of Kentucky, Department of Health, Bureau of Vital Statistics, Certificate of Death, issued in the name of Iva B. Devenport [*sic*], born in Logan County, Kentucky, on November 23, 1892, and deceased in Drakesboro, Muhlenburg County, Kentucky, on April 14, 1937.

180. Reissued on Ivy Smith and Cow Cow Davenport, *1927–1930*, Blues Document BDCD-6039, 1993.

181. Walter Roland, *Complete Recorded Works in Chronological Order—Vol. 1 (1933)*, Document Records DOCD-5144, 1993. For biographical information on Sonny Scott, see *Chasin' That*

Devil Music: Searching for the Blues, ed. Gayle Dean Wardlow (San Francisco: Miller Freeman Books, 1998), 71.

182. For a discography of songs on the Alabama flood, see Russell, *Country Music Records*, 406, 455, 772; and Meade, Spottswood, and Meade, *Country Music Sources*, 87–88. The latter source gives the date of the flood as March 15.

183. Reissued on Vernon Dalhart, *Puttin' on the Style*, Document Records DOCD-1105, 2007. Dalhart's first recording dealing with this disaster was "The Alabama Flood," recorded in New York City exactly one week after the catastrophe, on Thursday, March 21, and released on Harmony 879-H under the pseudonym Mack Allen. Five days later, Dalhart recorded two takes of "Alabama Flood Song" (composed by Jack Waite) and one of "Flood Song" (composed by Andrew Jenkins), but only the latter was released, on Victor V-40075. Composed by Andrew Jenkins, it has not been heard, but it is probably a version of the song Jenkins had recorded five days earlier. On March 28, the day after three more versions were rejected or not issued by Edison, Dalhart recorded Waite's "The Alabama Flood," released on Columbia 15386-D. See Russell, *Country Music Records*, 286; and Palmer, *Vernon Dalhart*, 298, 311, 357. Less than two weeks elapsed before Frank Luther (Francis Luther Crow, 1899–1980) also recorded "The Alabama Flood" (Banner 6369), on April 9 in New York City. It is a version of the song recorded by Dalhart and credited to Jack Waite. See Meade, Spottswood, and Meade, *Country Music Sources*, 87. For more information on Frank Luther, see Russell, *Country Music Originals*, 150–52. Despite its title, hillbilly yodeler Happy Bud Harrison's two-part "Levee Breaking Blues" (Vocalion 5332), recorded in Chicago on May 29, 1929, and released in September, is merely a bucolic depiction of a hypothetical disaster rather than the narrative account of a disaster song dealing with the 1927 Mississippi River flood or the 1929 Alabama flood. The 78 r.p.m. was advertised in the *Chicago Defender* on August 3, 1929, pt. 1, 6. For a partial transcription and discussion, see Tony Russell, *Rural Rhythm: The Story of Old-Time Country Music in 78 Records* (New York: Oxford University Press, 2021), 141–43.

184. The impact of this disaster on the black community is attested by Ma Rainey's midnight ramble benefit, held at the Nashville Bijou Theater in April 1929, with proceeds going to the flood victims. See Sandra R. Lieb, *Mother of the Blues: A Study of Ma Rainey* (Amherst: University of Massachusetts Press, 1981), 43, drawing information from the *Chicago Defender*.

185. Around 2,500 people lived in Elba City and 4,000 in the precinct at the time of the 1930 US Census. See https://www2.census.gov/library/publications/decennial/1940/population -volume-1/33973538v1ch03.pdf, 73.

186. "Tallahatchie River Blues" was reissued on various artists, *Mississippi Blues—Vol. 1 (1928–1937)*, Document Records DOCD-5157, 1993. For its release date of May 1, see Thygesen and Shor, *Vocalion 1000 and Brunswick 7000 Race Series*, 119.

187. Evans, "High Water Everywhere," 20. See also "Flood Menace Shifts to Mississippi Area: Swollen Tallahatchie Forces 400 Families Out: Ice Thwarts Rescuers," *Commercial Appeal* (Memphis), January 23, 1930, 1, 3.

188. In Mizelle's *Backwater Blues*, 47–48, Delaney is incorrectly described as a "Classic blues singer" and her recording mistakenly associated with the 1927 Mississippi River flood. Another account of Mattie Delaney, which is rejected here, is in Stephen Calt and Gayle Wardlow, *King of the Delta Blues: The Life and Music of Charlie Patton* (Newton: Rock Chapel Press, 1988), 197–98.

189. Patton's recording is available on the box set *Screamin' and Hollerin' the Blues: The Worlds of Charley Patton* (Disc 2), Revenant Album No. 212 (7CD), 2001.

190. van Rijn and van der Tuuk, *New York Recording Laboratories Matrix Series Volume One: The L Matrix Series (1929–1932)*, rev. 2nd ed., 7. Evans in "High Water Everywhere," 63–64, and Calt and Wardlow in *King of the Delta Blues*, 199, had earlier doubted that "High Water Everywhere Part II" was about the 1927 flood. See also Evans, "Charley Patton: The Conscience of the Delta," 136–39; Evans, *Charley Patton: Voice of the Mississippi Delta*, 109–12.

191. See "Snow Turns to Ice, Slows City Traffic: Threat of Another Storm Passes, but Temperature Drop Is Due Today: South Colder Than Arctic," *New York Times*, January 23, 1930, 25; "Flood Menace Shifts to Mississippi Area: Swollen Tallahatchie Forces 400 Families Out: Ice Thwarts Rescuers," *Commercial Appeal* (Memphis), January 23, 1930, 1, 3; "Ice Blocking Rescue of Flood Sufferers: Mississippi County Situation at Acute Stage: Plane Drops Supplies," *Commercial Appeal*, January 24, 1930, 1, 3; "Workers Rescue 150 from Big Lake Area: Boats Crash Through Melting Ice; Waters Receding: Plan Refugee Camps: National Guard Offers Facilities at Blytheville—300 More Persons May Be Marooned—Rising Temperatures Bring Relief," *Commercial Appeal*, January 25, 1930, 1, 3.

192. "Flood Refugees Suffer in Cold," *Greenwood Commonwealth*, January 22, 1930, 1.

193. Evans, "High Water Everywhere," 64.

194. See "Making History: The Heinz History Center Blog" at https://www.heinzhistorycenter .org/blog/western-pennsylvania-history/st-patricks-day-flood-1936.

195. Sixty-nine deaths and 500 injured people including the area surrounding Pittsburgh are reported at https://en.wikipedia.org/wiki/Johnstown_flood_of_1936.

196. See "Pittsburgh, PA Flood, Mar 1936," http://www.gendisasters.com/pennsylvania/2806/ johnstown%2C-pa-flood%2C-mar-1936.

197. See "Attractions: Johnstown Flood Museum" at https://www.jaha.org/attractions/ johnstown-flood-museum/flood-history/1936-1977-floods/.

198. Weldon also recorded an alternate take of "Flood Water Blues No. 2," unissued at the time. It differs little from the recording issued on 78 r.p.m. All three recordings are available on Casey Bill Weldon, *Complete Recorded Works 1935–1938 in Chronological Order—Volume 1*, Document Records DOCD-5217, 1993. Composer credits on both sides of the Conqueror issue (8658) are to Willie Weldon (and the pseudonymous artist credit is a flood-related Levee Joe). For biographical information on this long-elusive musician, see Jim O'Neal, "Unraveling Casey Bill: The Hawaiian Guitar Wizard," *Living Blues* 228 (December 2013): 72–77.

199. David Evans, *Big Road Blues: Tradition and Creativity in the Folk Blues* (New York: Da Capo Press, 1987), 58; originally published by University of California Press, 1982.

200. Reissued on Carl Martin and Willie "61" Blackwell, *Complete Recordings in Chronological Order (1936–1941)*, Document Records DOCD-5229, 1994.

201. See Chris Courtney, "Central China Flood, 1931" at http://www.disasterhistory.org/ central-china-flood-1931.

202. For accounts of this flood, see Rick Bell, *The Great Flood of 1937: Rising Waters— Soaring Spirits* (Louisville, KY: Butler Books, 2007); David Welky, *The Thousand-Year Flood: The Ohio-Mississippi Disaster of 1937* (Chicago and London: University of Chicago Press, 2011); O'Daniel, *Memphis and the Superflood of 1937: High Water Blues*; Klein and Zellmer, *Mississippi River Tragedies: A Century of Unnatural Disaster*, 83–89; "Hell and High Water," *Time* 29, no. 5, February 1, 1937; and American Red Cross, *The Ohio-Mississippi Valley Flood Disaster of 1937: Report of Relief Operations of the American Red Cross* (Washington, DC: American Red Cross, 1938), which reported that 137 people died directly as a result of the flood, but stated that the

exact number was impossible to determine because of the difficulty to ascertain whether deaths were attributable to the flood or other reasons.

203. See "300,000 Acres Under Water in West State; Tenants Leave Homes," *Jackson Sun* (Tennessee), January 21, 1937, 1; "Number of Refugees Growing by the Hour," *Jackson Sun*, January 25, 1937, 10; "Refugees Receive Typhoid Inoculation," *Jackson Sun*, January 26, 1937, 2.

204. O'Daniel, *Memphis and the Superflood of 1937*, 69.

205. Benjamin Albert Botkin, *A Treasury of Mississippi River Folklore: Stories, Ballads, Traditions, and Folkways of the Mid-American River Country* (New York: Bonanza, 1978), 557; originally published by Crown, 1955. Botkin gives no source for the quoted lyric fragment, which was perhaps influenced by the Delmore Brothers' hit "Brown's Ferry Blues" (Bluebird B-5403), recorded in Chicago, on December 6, 1933, reissued on *Brown's Ferry Blues*, County CCS-CD-116, 1995.

206. See "Image 28, Alan Lomax Collection, Manuscripts, Mississippi, Tennessee, and Arkansas, 1941-1942: 'The 1937 Flood'" at https://www.loc.gov/resource/afc2004004.ms090438/?sp=28.

207. Bumble Bee Slim recorded two takes of "Rising River Blues," only one of which was released, on Vocalion the following June. Differences are minor, and only the first, issued take is transcribed here. The two versions are available on Bumble Bee Slim (Amos Easton), *Complete Recorded Works in Chronological Order—Volume 7 (1936-1937)*, Document DOCD-5267, 1994; and *Complete Recorded Works in Chronological Order—Volume 8 (1937-1951)*, Document DOCD-5268, 1994.

208. For his biography, see Riesman, *I Feel So Good*.

209. The "dime-store labels" were Banner, Oriole, Perfect, Romeo, and Melotone. "Terrible Flood Blues" was issued on Melotone and Perfect with the same catalog number, and on Conqueror 8776. The two recordings are available on Big Bill Broonzy, *Complete Recorded Works in Chronological Order—Volume 5 (1936-1937)*, Document Records DOCD-5127, 1992.

210. See Russell, *Country Music Records*, 309, and Meade, with Spottswood and Meade, *Country Music Sources*, 88. I have not been able to hear this song, which features a vocal duet accompanied by mandolin and guitar. The other side of Bluebird B6852 is credited to Roscoe and Samuel Dellinger, who are presumably two of the musicians who comprised the Dellinger Family. Roscoe Conklin Dellinger (1891–1952) and Samuel Garland Dellinger (1917–1989) were brothers, born in Gaston County, North Carolina, but living in Charlotte in the mid-1930s.

211. Kokomo Arnold, *Complete Recorded Works in Chronological Order—Volume 3 (1936-1937)*, Document Records DOCD-5039, 1991.

212. Sleepy John Estes, *Complete Recorded Works in Chronological Order—Volume 2 (1937-1941)*, Document Records DOCD-5016, 1990.

213. I have eventually opted for transcription as "crop," which sounds clearer to me in Estes's version on Testament, but as suggested by Chris Smith, the slang term "crumb" meaning "a few dollars," "a little amount of money," makes sense and is a perfect rhyme. For the meaning of "crumb" see Harold Wentworth and Stuart Berg Flexner, comps., *The Pocket Dictionary of American Slang* (New York: Pocket Books, 1967), 85.

214. In Kip Lornell, "Living Blues Interview: Hammie Nixon and Sleepy John Estes," *Living Blues* 19 (January-February 1975): 16, Estes refers to getting "a ride out of Hickory (in fact, Hickman), Kentucky," a small settlement eighteen miles south of Paducah right on the Ohio River. In 1972, Charlie Pickett, formerly a musical associate of Estes and Nixon, told Bob Eagle that the accident happened in Paducah (see Eagle and LeBlanc, *Blues: A Regional Experience,*

240, 461). The Lornell interview is reprinted in *The Voice of the Blues: Classic Interviews from "Living Blues" Magazine*, eds. Jim O'Neal and Amy Van Singel (New York and London: Routledge, 2002), 43–67. Max Haymes, *Railroadin' Some: Railroads in the Early Blues* (York, UK: Music Mentor Books, 2006), 104–8, notes that in American English the term "car" refers to a train carriage, and argues that Estes's frightening experience was the consequence of a train, rather than an automobile, accident. This is refuted by Estes's own account in Lornell's interview. For an analysis of the song's formulas, see Michael Taft, *The Blues Lyric Formula* (New York: Routledge, 2006), 282.

215. Les Fancourt and Bob McGrath, *The Blues Discography 1943–1970*, 3rd ed. (West Vancouver, BC, Canada: Eyeball Productions, 2019), 185.

216. This song was issued for the first time on Sleepy John Estes, *Goin' to Brownsville*, Testament Records TCD 6008, 1998.

217. Reissued on Lonnie Johnson, *Complete Recorded Works 1937 to June 1947 in Chronological Order—Volume 1 (1937–1940)*, Blues Document BDCD-6024, 1992.

218. Chris Smith, booklet notes to Lonnie Johnson, Blues Document BDCD-6024.

219. Evans, "High Water Everywhere," 22.

220. Annye C. Anderson, with Preston Lauterbach, *Brother Robert: Growing Up with Robert Johnson* (New York: Hachette, 2020), 79.

221. Reissued on Walter Davis, *Complete Recorded Works 1933–1952 in Chronological Order—Volume 2 (1935–1937)*, Document DCOD-5282, 1994. For a biography of Walter Davis, see Guido van Rijn, *The St. Louis Blues of Walter Davis* (Overveen, The Netherlands: Agram Blues Books, 2022).

222. Reissued on Carl Martin and Willie "61" Blackwell, *Complete Recorded Works in Chronological Order*, Document DCOD-5229, 1994.

223. Harry Oster, *Living Country Blues* (New York: Minerva Press, 1975), 283–84.

224. This hemistich is the same as Walter Davis's "West Coast Blues."

225. See Nan Elizabeth Woodruff, *As Rare as Rain: Federal Relief in the Great Southern Drought of 1930–31* (Urbana and Chicago: University of Illinois Press, 1985), esp. ix–38. The inexorable and merciless progress of the 1930 Dry Spell is evident in Table 1 of Woodruff's chapter 1, which compares rainfall in the drought-affected states during June, July, and August 1930 with the same months in previous years.

226. For more literature on the drought, see Robert Cowley, "The Drought and the Dole," *American Heritage* 23, no. 2 (February 1972) 16–19, 92–99; anon., "The Great Drought of 1930," *Literary Digest*, August 16, 1930, 5–6; anon., "Good and Evil Effects of the Drought," *Literary Digest*, August 23, 1930, 5–6; A. L. Schafer, "When Hunger Followed Drought," *The Survey* LXV, no. 11, March 1, 1931, 581–83, 627–28; and headlines in the *Clarksdale Daily Register* listed in Table 6.2 in Monge, "Preachin' the Blues," 235. I am indebted to David Evans for his meticulous research in the *Clarksdale Daily Register* and the *Memphis Press-Scimitar*.

227. See John C. Hoyt, "Droughts of 1930–34," United States Department of the Interior, United States Government Printing Office, Washington DC, 1936, 41–45, accessible at https://pubs.usgs.gov/wsp/0680/report.pdf.

228. The drought is mentioned in stanza 5 of Reverend Charles Haffer's undated typescript "The Depression," which is available at the Library of Congress at https://www.loc.gov/resource/afc2004004.ms090438/?st=gallery.

229. Son House's statements on the date of the session are found in Samuel Charters, *The Blues Makers*, Part I (New York: Da Capo, 1991), 188; Bob Hall and Richard Noblett, "A Handful

of Keys: Louise Johnson Again!," *Blues Unlimited* 115 (September-October 1975): 21–22; Alex van der Tuuk, "Son House: How Paramount's Elusive Artist Evolved into a Blues Icon," *Frog Blues and Jazz Annual* 4 (2015): 127–28; and in an interview conducted by David Evans, Alan Wilson, and Taj Mahal in Cambridge, Massachusetts, in November 1964, published in David Evans, "An Early Interview with Son House—Part One," "An Early Interview with Son House—Part Two," *Frog Blues and Jazz Annual* 5 (2017): 29–44, 176–94, esp. 181. See also van Rijn and van der Tuuk, *New York Recording Laboratories Matrix Series Volume One: The L Matrix Series (1929–1932)*, rev. 2nd ed., 29–31. For an overview of the entire 1930 session see Edward Komara, "Blues in the Round," *Black Music Research Journal* 17, no. 1 (spring 1997): 3–36.

230. This two-part blues is available on the box set *Screamin' and Hollerin' the Blues: The Worlds of Charley Patton* (Disc 4), Revenant Album No. 212 (7CD), 2001.

231. The word "quirl" is a dialect form of both "coil" and "curl." For the latter, see Frederic G. Cassidy, ed., *Dictionary of American Regional English*, vol. I (Cambridge: Belknap Press of Harvard University, 1985).

232. The last line of Son House's "Dry Spell Blues Part II" has caused much controversy. I am therefore grateful to the many researchers who have contributed ideas and shared informed opinions.

233. This sermon is transcribed in Work, Jones, and Adams, *Lost Delta Found*, 68. It is worth pointing out that Reverend Savage was from Coahoma County, where Son House was born and raised. House's final line conveys a feeling of hope that befits my interpretation of the song as a positive and optimistic blues sermon/prayer addressed to God and, quoting Chris Smith's words in a Yahoo prewar blues list post (July 17, 2008), it is consistent with the "prophet's function in the Old Testament . . . to 'tell it like it is,' not necessarily to foretell the future."

234. For Son House's alcoholism, see Daniel Beaumont, *Preachin' the Blues: The Life and Times of Son House* (Oxford: Oxford University Press, 2011), esp. 144–45, 147–50, 161–63, 169–70.

235. This blues is available on *Screamin' and Hollerin' the Blues: The Worlds of Charley Patton* (Disc 5), Revenant Album No. 212 (7CD), 2001.

236. Patton was born into a devout family. His father was a deacon, and he received a strict religious education, which is mirrored in the sacred recordings he made for Paramount and Vocalion. Unlike Son House, Patton preached during the same period when he sang blues, whereas House's allegiance went back and forth between the sacred and the secular. For a discussion of Patton's religious upbringing and recordings, see David Evans, "Charley Patton: The Conscience of the Delta," in *The Voice of the Delta*, ed. Robert Sacré (Liège, Belgium: Presses Universitaires de Liège, 1987), 136–39; Evans, *Charley Patton: Voice of the Mississippi Delta*, 48–52.

237. For further comments on, and textual and/or musical transcriptions of, Charlie Patton's "Dry Well Blues" see Evans, "Charley Patton: The Conscience of the Delta," 136–39; see also the following, in the Revenant boxed set *Screamin' and Hollerin' the Blues*: Evans, "Charlie Patton: The Conscience of the Delta," 30; Dick Spottswood, "Song Notes and Transcriptions," 77; Edward Komara, "Thematic Catalogue of the Recorded Music of Charley Patton," 108.

238. See Evans, "Charley Patton: The Conscience of the Delta," 197–98; rev. ed.: *Charley Patton: Voice of the Mississippi Delta*, 116–17; "Bond Issue for Improvement, Repair and Extension of the Water Works System of the Town of Lula, Coahoma County, Mississippi," *Clarksdale Daily Register*, July 15, 1930, 7; "Lula Booms," *Clarksdale Daily Register*, July 20, 1930, 7; "When the Well Goes Dry," *Clarksdale Daily Register*, August 10, 1930, 4.

239. "Spider" Carter's "Dry Spell Blues" is included in various artists, *St. Louis 1927–1933*, Document Records DOCD-5181, 1993.

240. See Russell, *Country Music Records*, 620. The song is credited to Bob Ferguson and His Scalawaggers, one of Miller's pseudonyms.

241. Among others, John Mooney, Rory Block (both disciples and admirers of House), and Colin Linden have recorded versions. John Mooney, *Gone to Hell*, Blind Pig Records BPCD 5063, 2000; Rory Block, *From the Dust*, Telarc 83614, 2005; Colin Linden, *Easin' Back to Tennessee*, CrossCut 11091, 2006.

242. Two sermon and spoken-word recordings are not considered here. "Telling Story of the Big Storm" (AFS 5088-A) was collected by Robert Sonkin from "Uncle" Lee Pettway Sr., at a meeting at Rev. Richard Gregg's house in the Lebanon Community of Gee's Bend, Alabama, on July 21, 1941. It is a spoken account of the "Dixie Tornado Outbreak" of April 23–26, 1908, which affected Louisiana, Mississippi, Alabama, Georgia, and other states. Reverend Sutton E. Griggs (1872–1933) recorded the sermon "Saving the Day" (Victor V38516) on September 18, 1928, in Memphis. The sermon is about the 1912 floods in the Mississippi Valley region. It is available on various artists, *Black Vocal Groups Volume 5 (1923–1941)*, Document Records DOCD-5553, 1997. For an analysis of this sermon see Evans, "High Water Everywhere," 19.

243. See, among many sources, Herbert Molley Mason Jr., *Death from the Sea: The Galveston Hurricane of 1900* (New York: Dial Press, 1972); Stephen J. Spignesi, "The Galveston Hurricane," in *Catastrophe! The 100 Greatest Disasters of All Time* (New York: Citadel Press, 2002), 118–20; "1900 Galveston Hurricane," Wikipedia, https://en.wikipedia.org/wiki/1900_Galveston_hurricane; "How the Galveston Hurricane of 1900 Became the Deadliest U.S. Natural Disaster," History.com, https://www.history.com/news/how-the-galveston-hurricane-of-1900-became-the-deadliest-u-s-natural-disaster.

244. The song is available on various artists, *Field Recordings—Vol. 5: Louisiana, Texas, Bahamas*, Document Records DOCD-5579, 1997. The following discussion of the recording date is adapted, with permission, from Sin-Killer Griffin's entry in the draft fifth edition of *Blues and Gospel Records 1890–1943*:

> In the Library of Congress *Check-List*, discs 185 to 187 are collectively entered as *Church Service, Easter*, sung and spoken by Sin-Killer Griffin and Congregation. Bands 185-A-2 and 185-B-1 are listed in the *Check-List* as by Members of Congregation at Palm Sunday Service; other bands are listed as by Sin-Killer Griffin. File cards give May as the month of recording for disc 187, which seems almost certain to be incorrect, and April for discs 185 and 186, which may be incorrect. In 1934 Palm Sunday was on 25 March, and Easter Day was on 1 April. In *Adventures of a Ballad Hunter* (New York: Macmillan, 1947 and reprint, Austin, TX: University of Texas Press, 2017), Sin-Killer Griffin is quoted as saying, "Today is my Easter service," but Griffin's chaplaincy was presumably peripatetic, and his statement may be theological rather than chronological. Notwithstanding the titles assigned to disc 187 (*Easter Day Service*), it does not establish that the service was held on Easter Day.

245. Lomax, *Adventures of a Ballad Hunter*, 191–98. See also John A. Lomax and Alan Lomax, *Our Singing Country: Folk Songs and Ballads* (1941; Mineola: Dover Publications, 2000), 9–13; Lynn Abbott and Doug Seroff, *Out of Sight: The Rise of African American Popular Music*

1889–1895 (Jackson: University Press of Mississippi, 2002), 339–40; "Griffin, J. L.," Handbook of Texas Online, http://www.tshaonline.org/handbook/online/articles/fgr61, published by the Texas State Historical Association, uploaded on June 15, 2010, and accessed on July 7, 2015. "Sin-Killer" Griffin's real name was John L. Griffin. His death certificate, traced by Chris Smith, shows that he was born on November 3, 1871, and died in Harris County, Texas, on November 29, 1958.

246. Lomax, *Adventures of a Ballad Hunter*, 221–23; reprint ed., 191–93.

247. See "Wasn't That a Mighty Storm" in Steve Sullivan, *Encyclopedia of Great Popular Song Recordings, vol. 2* (Lanham, MD: Scarecrow Press, 2013), 452; for Sheffer as composer of coon songs, see "Annotated Index of Commercial Spirituals, 1870-1887 (R-Z)" at https://sites.google.com/site/grahamsandraj/home/commercial-spirituals/r-z, citing Sheffer and Blakely's *"New Coon Done Gone" Songster* (New York: Popular Publishing, n.d.); for the Olympia Quartette, see Sandra Jean Graham, *Spirituals and the Birth of a Black Entertainment Industry* (Urbana and Chicago: University of Illinois Press, 2018), 234. Sullivan's assertion that the Texas prison recording's refrain "derives from" Sheffer's composition seems highly questionable.

248. Sullivan, *Encyclopedia of Great Popular Song Recordings, vol. 2*, 452.

249. For a similar stanza in relation to the *Titanic* disaster, see Bruce Jackson, "The *Titanic* Toast," in "Veins of Humor," ed. Harry Levin, *Harvard English Studies 3* (Cambridge, MA: Harvard University Press, 1972), 223; and Washington ("Lightnin'")'s "God Moves on the Water," transcribed and analyzed elsewhere in this book.

250. The line "Their prophets gived them warning" seems to be accusatory, but if so, it is an unjust accusation. There was little or no warning of the hurricane. See Neil L. Frank, "The Great Galveston Hurricane of 1900" at https://research.fit.edu/media/site-specific/researchfitedu/coast-climate-adaptation-library/united-states/gulf-coast/texas/Frank.-2003.-Galveston-1900-Hurricane.pdf. Therefore, it is more likely that "prophets" means "prognosticators."

251. Chris Smith, "Seawall Special (Lela Bolden)," in column "Words Words Words," *Blues & Rhythm* 301 (August 2015): 26–27.

252. See, among others, "Gilliam Wrecked: Tornado Sweeps Across Upper Portion of Louisiana," *Austin American-Statesman*, May 14, 1908; "50 Killed! Clean Path Is Made by the Storm," *Buffalo Enquirer*, May 14, 1908; and Grazulis, *Significant Tornadoes 1680–1991, a Chronology and Analysis of Events.*

253. Originally issued in 1988, the recording is available on Osceola Mays, *Spirituals and Poems*, Documentary Arts CD 1006, 2005.

254. She probably said "army" to mean "armor."

255. Alan Govenar and Shane W. Evans, *Osceola: Memories of a Sharecropper's Daughter* (New York: Hyperion, 2000), 41.

256. See "Trinity River (Texas)," Wikipedia, https://en.wikipedia.org/wiki/Trinity_River_(Texas).

257. This recording is available on various artists, *Texas Blues 1927–1935*, Document Records DOCD-5161, 1993. For a biography of Walker, see Helen Oakley Dance, *Stormy Monday: The T-Bone Walker Story* (New York: Da Capo, 1990), originally published by Louisiana State University Press, 1987.

258. See "Army Corps of Engineers Flood History," II, 40, which lists both disasters. I am grateful to Dallas city archivist John Slate and Alan Govenar for sending this document. The East Fork Trinity River rises near McKinney, a few miles north of Dallas, and flows through Lavon Lake and Lake Ray Hubbard before joining the Trinity River just southeast of Dallas.

259. Walker is obviously borrowing the final stanza from Blind Lemon Jefferson's "Rising High Water Blues," but he did not clearly hear "prayer in my heart," and tries to create something having the same meaning while retaining a similar sound to Lemon's word "prayer."

260. Helen and Stanley Dance, "Electrifying Texas Blues: Aaron 'T-Bone' Walker," in *Bluesland: Portraits of Twelve Major American Blues Masters*, eds. Pete Welding and Toby Byron (New York: Dutton, 1991), 104.

261. See "Trinity River (Texas)," Wikipedia.

262. See Lyle Saxon, Edward Dreyer, and Robert Tallant, *Gumbo Ya-Ya* (New York: Bonanza Books, 1945), 476–77. Originally published by Houghton Mifflin, Boston, 1945; reprint: Gretna Louisiana, Pelican Press, 1987; sixth ed., 2012. The song text is reprinted in Harold Courlander, *Negro Folk Music U.S.A.* (New York: Columbia University Press, 1963), 75–76.

263. See "1909 Grand Isle hurricane," Wikipedia, https://en.wikipedia.org/wiki/1909" _Grand_Isle_hurricane.

264. The chorus can also be found in gospel singer Jessie Mae Hill's "God Rode in the Windstorm" (OKeh 8490), recorded in Chicago on May 5, 1927, and reissued on various artists, *Gospel Classics 1927–1931*, Document Records DOCD-5190, 1993. This song is not about the 1909 Grand Isle Hurricane and its melody is different. On October 10, 1960, in Chicago, Pete Welding recorded Teddy "Blind" Darby performing the unissued "God Rode in the Wind."

265. David Evans, unpublished interview with Rev. Ruben Lacy, Ridgecrest, California, February 26, 1966. Email to the author, August 3, 2018.

266. "250 Dead in Tornado-Swept States; Omaha Chief Victim of Storm's Fury," *New York Times*, March 25, 1913, 1.

267. See "Omaha Loss, $3,000,000," *New York Times*, April 6, 1913, viii, 12.2; "Omaha Identifies 112 Bodies," *New York Times*, March 28, 1913, 5; "March 1913 Tornado Outbreak Sequence," Wikipedia, https://en.wikipedia.org/wiki/March_1913_tornado_outbreak_sequence; Adam Fletcher Sasse, "A History of North Omaha, Part 2," https://northomahahistory.com/ 2015/02/13/a-history-of-north-omaha-part-2/.

268. Lomax, *Adventures of a Ballad Hunter*, 232–36; reprint: Austin: University of Texas Press, 202–6; for her husband as co-pastor, see 1920 US census.

269. I am grateful to Rob Ford and Chris Smith for sharing census records and other material, and for their thoughts about Sister Crockett. In 1907 the Crocketts were in Los Angeles, where their son Lemuel Wyatt Crockett was born, according to his World War II draft card.

270. "Flood in Omaha Fair Sample of Negroes' Religious Songs," *Dallas Morning News*, May 3, 1936, II, Section Three. The twenty-seven discs containing seventy items recorded in January 1936 and listed in The American Folklife Center, Texas Collections in the Archive of Folk Culture at https://www.loc.gov/folklife/guides/Texas.html may include some of Sister Crockett's songs.

271. In the introduction to his novel *Walking on Borrowed Land*, writer William A. Owens states that he repeatedly recorded Sister Crockett in San Antonio between 1937 and 1941. William A. Owens, *Walking on Borrowed Land* (Fort Worth: Texas Christian University Press, 1954), xv–xvi. No song titles are provided, but one of the songs that Sister Crockett sang to Lomax is titled "I'm Walking on Borrowed Land." See also Dixon, Godrich, and Rye, *Blues and Gospel Records 1890–1943*, 188; "Flood in Omaha Fair Sample of Negroes' Religious Songs," *Dallas Morning News*, May 3, 1936, II, Section Three.

272. The subheading to the article "Omaha Counts 200 Lives Lost," *New York Times*, March 26, 1913, 3, reads "Snow Adds to Destitution."

273. Henry Shaw's two versions of "God's A-Getting Worried with Your Wicked Ways" (AFS 330 and 331), recorded in Oakhill, Georgia, ca. April 10, 1926, and "God Is Worried with Your Wicked Ways" (AFS 3010-B-1), an unaccompanied song recorded by an unidentified group of older men and women at St. Austin's Church in Cockrum, Mississippi, on May 14, 1939, must be versions of singer and composer Madkin Blind Butler's sacred song, and are not about any disaster, as probably is not the still untraced "God Is Worried at Your Wicked Ways" (Decca 7113), recorded by Blind Gussie Nesbitt in New York City on September 9, 1935.

274. "250 Dead in Tornado-Swept States: Died in Mother's Arms," *New York Times*, March 25, 1913, 2.

275. Based on search of newspapers.com, https://www.newspapers.com, on October 27, 2018. The name is given as "Dillard" in other sources. See Adam Fletcher Sasse, *North Omaha History, vol. 2* (Olympia, WA: CommonAction Publishing, 2016), 483; and "Early Omaha. Gateway to the West: Tornado of March 23, 1913," www.omahapubliclibrary.org/earlyomaha/tornadoes/1913_tornado_6.html.

276. *Coffeyville Daily Journal*, March 25, 1913, 1.

277. On March 24, 1913, an article in the *Evening Gazette* of Cedar Rapids, Iowa, posted by Stu Beitler at http://www.gendisasters.com/nebraska/13509/omaha-ne-disastrous-tornado-mar-1913?page=0,0, reported that "[a]bout 40 negroes [died] in the burned ruins of the Idlewild Hall."

278. "Omaha Counts 200 Lives Lost," *New York Times*, March 26, 1913, 3, refers to the removal of sixteen bodies from the movie house; other reports retrievable at https://www.newspapers.com, searched on October 27, 2018, speak of "at least thirty" or fifty deaths. For the former death toll, see "Many Killed in Moving Picture Theater and Poolroom," *Brooklyn Daily Eagle*, March 24, 1913, 1; for the latter number of casualties, see "Many Dead in Theater," *Evening Times-Republican* (Marshalltown, Iowa), March 24, 1913, 1; and "Ruins of Diamond Theater after Omaha Tornado; Fifty People Are Killed While Witnessing the Show," *Star-Gazette* (Elmira, NY), March 28, 1913, 1. The reports of fifty deaths seem to have been exaggerated. According to Adam Fletcher Sasse, "everyone [in the Diamond Theatre] escaped before the building was demolished." See https://northomahahistory.com/2016/06/01/a-history-of-the-1913-easter-sunday-tornado-in-north-omaha-nebraska/.

279. See Richard M. Breaux, "The New Negro Renaissance in Omaha and Lincoln, 1910–1940," in *The Harlem Renaissance in the American West: The New Negro's Western Experience*, eds. Bruce A. Glasrud and Cary D. Wintz (New York and London: Routledge, 2011), 123.

280. "1915 New Orleans hurricane," Wikipedia, https://en.wikipedia.org/wiki/1915_New_Orleans_hurricane.

281. I could trace no information on Shelton, but he may be the Reverend Isaiah Shelton who recorded two sides for Victor on March 8, 1927, in New Orleans. "Isaiah" could have been misunderstood as "A.C." See Dixon, Godrich, and Rye, *Blues and Gospel Records 1890–1943*, 791.

282. Saxon, Dreyer, and Tallant, *Gumbo Ya-Ya*, 476–77. Like Louis Armstrong, Rev. Shelton was addicted to the initial capitalization of words he deemed important; their presence in the text as printed in *Gumbo Ya-Ya* is evidence of its origins in a ballet. I have regularized the orthography for the benefit of readers.

283. See Geoff Partlow, *America's Deadliest Twister: The Tri-State Tornado of 1925* (Carbondale: Southern Illinois University, 2014); Peter S. Felknor, *The Tri-State Tornado: The Story of America's Greatest Tornado Disaster* (Lincoln, NE: iUniverse, 2004); Wallace Akin, *The Forgotten Storm: The Great Tri-State Tornado of 1925* (Lanham, MD: Rowman & Littlefield, 2015); Stephen J.

Spignesi, "The Tristate Tornadoes," in *Catastrophe! The 100 Greatest Disasters of All Time* (New York: Citadel Press, 2002), 184–86; and "The Great Tri-State Tornado" at http://www.gendisasters .com/illinois/5997/various-towns-il-horrible-tornado-damage-mar-1925.

284. The singers may have been Clarence Banks, lead, Bob Bentley, tenor, Harold Vosburg, baritone, and Charlie Blake, bass, who sang two songs recorded on side A of disc 264. See Dixon, Godrich, and Rye, *Blues and Gospel Records 1890–1943*, 958, 38.

285. "New Madrid Fault Caused Earthquake: Shocks Here Early Yesterday Felt Over 250-Mile Radius: Memphis' 37th Quake: Shifting of Rocks Cause Temblors That Shook Houses, Caused Chimneys to Topple—No Connection Between Flood and Quake," *Commercial Appeal* (Memphis), May 8, 1927, 1–2; Evans, "High Water Everywhere," 42.

286. Reissued on various artists, *Barrelhouse Women—Vol. 2 (1924–1928)*, Document Records DOCD-5497, 1996. The song was also issued on Broadway 5017 as by Martha Barr.

287. This stanza is similar in melody, structure, and delivery to the first stanza of Bessie Smith's "Back-Water Blues," a song Pearson was clearly familiar with. The apocalyptic references to signs of the end of time are discussed in Ziólek-Sowińska, *Images of the Apocalypse in African American Blues and Spirituals*, 59–60.

288. Reissued on Texas Alexander, *Complete Recorded Works in Chronological Order—Volume 3 (1930–1950)*, Matchbox Records, MBCD 2003, 1994.

289. See "Various Towns, TX Tornados Cause Death and Damage, May 1930," transcribed from the Texas *Amarillo Grove*, May 7, 1930, and available at http://www.gendisasters.com/ texas/5535/various-towns-tx-tornados-cause-death-damage-may-1930. See also Govenar and Lornell, *The Blues Come to Texas*, 302.

290. See "1932 Deep South tornado outbreak," Wikipedia, http://en.m.wikipedia.org/ wiki/1932_Deep_South_tornado_outbreak; and "Tornado Dead 362; Relief Centralized," *New York Times*, March 26, 1932, 15.

291. See "95 Dead in 4 States Hit by Tornado," *New York Times*, March 22, 1932, 8.

292. Reissued on Lucille Bogan (Bessie Jackson), *Complete Recorded Works in Chronological Order—Volume 2 (1930–1933)*, Blues Document BDCD-6037, 1993.

293. The last stanza presents close textual similarities with Bessie Smith's prototypical "Back-Water Blues."

294. "95 Dead in 4 States Hit by Tornadoes; Towns Lie in Ruins," *New York Times*, March 22, 1932, 1, 8.

295. "Heroism of Negro Saves 100 in Flood," *New York Times*, January 27, 1935, 24; "On the Coldwater," *Time* 25, no. 5, February 4, 1935.

296. "Heroism of Negro Saves 100 in Flood," *New York Times*, January 27, 1935, 24.

297. "Half Frozen Boatman Saves Scores in Mississippi Flood," *Baltimore Afro-American*, February 2, 1935, 6.

298. "Mississippian Hailed as Hero for Saving 100 Lives," *Chicago Defender*, February 2, 1935, 1. In the article the sentence "The refugees—white and black alike, old and young, rich and poor—are being taken to such safe posts as are available" reminds one of the Lulu Morris chorus in the "Tupelo Destruction" gospel song that recounts the tornado of 1936 but is certainly older in sacred lyric tradition.

299. Reissued on Joe Pullum, *Complete Recorded Works in Chronological Order—Volume 1 (1934–1935)*, Document Records DOCD-5393, 1995.

300. Evans, "High Water Everywhere," 21.

301. I am greatly indebted to William Lee Ellis for his painstaking research in the following newspapers, from which all details of this catastrophe are drawn: "Tornadoes Sweep 6 States; 115 Dead, Hundreds Injured: 66 Killed, 500 Hurt in Storm in Mississippi—Illinois, Indiana, Kentucky, Tennessee and Missouri Also Wracked by Winds," *New York Times*, March 17, 1942, 1, 14; "100 Killed, 650 Injured as Storms Sweep 5 States in South, Midwest: Mississippi Hardest Hit by Twisters as 69 Are Said Dead," *Atlanta Constitution*, March 17, 1942, 1; James H. Purdy Jr., "100 Dead, 1,000 Injured as Tornado Strikes Seven Southern States," *Washington Afro American*, March 21, 1942, 1, 7; "55 Known Dead and More Reported Missing; Hundreds Are Injured and Left Homeless As Tornadoes Strike Mississippi, Tennessee," *Commercial Appeal*, March 17, 1942, 1, 2, 10; "155 Known Storm Dead," *Memphis Press-Scimitar*, March 17, 1942, 1, 6, 7. The *Chicago Defender* made no mention of the tornadoes in its March 21, 1942, edition.

302. See "March 1942 tornado outbreak," Wikipedia, https://en.wikipedia.org/wiki/March_1942_tornado_outbreak.

303. Purdy, "100 Dead, 1,000 Injured as Tornado Strikes Seven Southern States," 7.

304. See Work, Jones, and Adams, *Lost Delta Found*, 218.

305. Lomax, *The Land Where the Blues Began*, 52.

306. Work, Jones, and Adams, *Lost Delta Found*, 95.

307. After the second chorus, Reverend Haffer sings: "On a Monday evening in March between four and five o'clock / There's . . .," and then interrupts himself before starting the correct stanza.

308. See "Their Eyes Were Watching God" elsewhere in this book for discussion.

309. "Death and Destruction Left in Wake of Tornadic Winds," *Commercial Appeal*, March 17, 1942, 10.

310. "Ball of Fire Seen as Tornado Destroys Cabin, Hits Compress," *Commercial Appeal*, March 17, 1942, 10; and "Balls of Fire as Big as Wagon Wheels," *Memphis Press-Scimitar*, March 17, 1942, 6.

311. "Courageous Townfolk Treat Storm Victims by Lamplight," *Commercial Appeal*, March 17, 1942, 1.

312. See "Images 5 and 29, Alan Lomax Collection, Manuscripts, Mississippi, Tennessee, and Arkansas, 1941-1942: 'A Song of the Great Disaster'" at https://www.loc.gov/resource/afc2004004.ms090438/?st=gallery.

313. Though unaware of the differences between Haffer's recording and Lomax's transcription as well as of the existence of Haffer's broadside of the song at the Library of Congress, Małgorzata Ziółek-Sowińska's *Images of the Apocalypse in African American Blues and Spirituals*, 51–52, contains interesting insights into Haffer's text as "a perfect example of an Apocalyptic song."

314. "Courageous Townfolk Treat Storm Victims by Lamplight," *Commercial Appeal*, March 17, 1942, 1.

315. See "March 1952 Southern United States tornado outbreak," Wikipedia, https://en.wikipedia.org/wiki/March_1952_Southern_United_States_tornado_outbreak. See also Grazulis, *Significant Tornadoes 1680–1991: A Chronology and Analysis of Events*; and J. A. Carr, "A Preliminary Report on the Tornadoes of March 21–22, 1952," *Monthly Weather Review* 80, no. 3 (March 1952): 50. Coverage by the *New York Times* is included in "Judsonia Tornado of 1952; The Worst Tornado in Arkansas History," in William Ewing Orr, *That's Judsonia: An Informal History of a Small Town in Arkansas* (Judsonia, AR: White County Print Company, 1957).

316. See Cedric J. Hayes and Robert Laughton, *The Gospel Discography 1943–2000*, vol. 1, 3rd ed. (West Vancouver, BC, Canada: Eyeball Productions, 2014), 428. "God's Chariot" is available

on *Get Right with God: Hot Gospel*, Heritage HTCD 01, 1988, and *Texas Gospel Volume 1: Come on Over Here*, Acrobat ACMCD 4209, 2005.

317. For more information on this recording, see George A. Moonoogian and Roger Meeden, "Duke Records—the Early Years: An Interview with David J. Mattis," *Whiskey, Women, and . . .* 14 (June 1984): 18–20; and Dodge, *The School of Arizona Dranes. Gospel Music Pioneer*, 134.

318. David Evans, unpublished interview with Rev. Ruben Lacy, Ridgecrest, CA, February 26, 1966. Email to the author, August 3, 2018.

319. See Cedric J. Hayes and Robert Laughton, *The Gospel Discography 1943–2000*, vol. 1, 3rd ed., 428. "Praying Time" is available on various artists, *Powerhouse Gospel on Independent Labels 1946–59*, JSP Records 77135 (4CD), 2010.

320. See the *Dixon Evening Telegraph* (Dixon, Illinois), February 2, 1955, submitted by Stu Beitler and retrieved at http://www.gendisasters.com/illinois/6041/commerce-olive-branch -ms-tornado-damages-small-towns-feb-1955; "Official Death Toll of Tornado Now Set At 22," *Clarion-Ledger* (Jackson, Mississippi), February 2, 1955; and "Start Helping Tornado Victims," *Greenwood Commonwealth* (Mississippi), February 3, 1955. The article "29 Killed as Tornadoes Rip Through Dixie Areas" in the *Philadelphia Inquirer* of February 2, 1955, 1, reported that a "teacher and at least three pupils" were killed at Commerce Landing.

321. See "29 Killed as Tornadoes Rip Through Dixie Areas: Big Log Saves School Children," *Philadelphia Inquirer*, February 2, 1955, 1–2.

322. The song is available on Kokomo Arnold, *Complete Recorded Works in Chronological Order—Volume 4 (1937–1938)*, Document Records DOCD-5040, 1991.

323. These quotations are taken from Ziólek-Sowińska, *Images of the Apocalypse in African American Blues and Spirituals*, 67–68.

324. Paul Oliver, *Broadcasting the Blues: Black Blues in the Segregation Era* (New York and London: Routledge, 2006), 70.

325. Oliver, *Broadcasting the Blues*, 70.

326. The song is available on various artists, *I Can Eagle Rock: Jook Joint Blues from Alabama and Louisiana*, Travelin' Man TM CD 09, 1996.

327. See "Various Towns, AK, LA, TX, OK, AL Tornadoes, Apr. 1939," http://www.gendisasters .com/alabama/11241/various-towns-ar-la-tx-ok-al-tornadoes-apr-1939.

328. Reissued on *The Chronological Lightnin' Hopkins 1946–1948*, Classics Records 5014, 2002. On April 6, 1964, in Philadelphia, Hopkins recorded live another version of this song titled "The Twister," which is available on *The Swarthmore Concert*, Original Blues Classics OBCCD-563, 1993.

329. John Lee Hooker's "Twister Blues" (Savoy SJL-2255), recorded in Detroit ca. November 1948, and reissued on *Detroit 1948–1949*, Savoy/Atlantic 92910, 2000, is a pastiche of these songs.

330. The question of which tornado is involved is left unresolved in Alan Govenar, *Lightnin' Hopkins: His Life and Blues* (Chicago: Chicago Review Press, 2010), 80–81; Timothy J. O'Brien and David Ensminger, *Mojo Hand: The Life and Music of Lightnin' Hopkins* (Austin: University of Texas Press, 2013), 46, 81, 251; and Govenar and Lornell, *The Blues Come to Texas*, 303. See also Ray Templeton, "'Bad Luck and Trouble.' Lightnin' Hopkins," *Blues & Rhythm* 280 (June 2013) 4–5. For details of the St. Augustine tornado, see https://www.gendisasters.com/texas/7492/ san-augustine-tx-tornado-mar-1943.

331. Mack McCormick, "Sam 'Lightnin'' Hopkins—A Description," *Jazz Monthly* 5, no. 8 (October 1959): 4–6, reprinted in *Sing Out!* 10, no. 3 (October/November 1960): 4–8.

332. Mack McCormick, "A Conversation with Lightnin' Hopkins, Part 2," *Jazz Journal* 14, no. 1 (January 1961): 18, also quoted in Govenar and Lornell, *The Blues Come to Texas*, 303. For the audience's reaction to this song, see Mack McCormick, liner notes to Lightnin' Hopkins, *The Rooster Crowed in England*, 77 LA 12–1 (LP), 1959, quoted in Govenar, *Lightnin' Hopkins: His Life and Blues*, 80.

333. Reissued on St. Louis Jimmy Oden, *Complete Recorded Works 1932–1955 in Chronological Order—Volume 2 (1944–1955)*, Document Records DOCD-5235, 1994.

334. Guy Davis, *You Don't Know My Mind*, Red House Records RHR 113, 1998.

335. Guy Davis, *Teller of Tales: The Guitar Artistry of Guy Davis*, Vestapol DVD 13124, 2011.

336. For further information on Boone, see Ann Sears, "John William 'Blind' Boone, Pianist-Composer: 'Merit, Not Sympathy Wins,'" *Black Music Research Journal* 9, no. 2 (fall 1989): 225–47.

337. See John Davis, *Marshfield Tornado: John Davis Plays Blind Boone*, Newport Classic NPD85678, 2008.

338. See Sears, "John William 'Blind' Boone, Pianist-Composer: 'Merit, Not Sympathy Wins,'" 235.

339. Bob Eagle, post to the Yahoo prewar blues list, March 16, 2005; and Eagle and LeBlanc, *Blues: A Regional Experience*, 192.

340. See respectively "Tornadoes Ravage South; 26 Killed and 150 Injured," *New York Times*, April 8, 1935, submitted by Greg Eichelberger, and retrievable at http://www.gendisasters.com/mississip pi/20529/louisiana-mississippi-tornadoes-apr-1935; and "Storms Kill 16, Injure 100 in South," *New York Times*, May 4, 1935, submitted by Greg Eichelberger, and retrievable at http://www.gendisasters .com/kentucky/20536/kentucky-arkansas-texas-mississippi-amp-tennessee-storms-may-1935.

CHAPTER TWO: ACCIDENTAL DISASTERS

1. Major studies and transcriptions of the "Casey Jones" ballad include Norm Cohen, "Casey Jones," in *Long Steel Rail: The Railroad in American Folksong* (Urbana and Chicago: University of Illinois Press, 2000), xxvi–xxvii, 132–57, originally published in 1981; John A. Lomax and Alan Lomax, *American Ballads and Folk Songs* (New York: Dover Publications, 1994), 34–36, originally published by Macmillan, 1934; John A. and Alan Lomax, *Folk Song U.S.A.* (New York: Signet Books, 1966), originally published by Duell, Sloan & Pearce in 1947, 315–19, 336–37; G. Malcolm Laws Jr., *Native American Balladry*, 90, 212–13; Carl Sandburg, *The American Songbag* (San Diego, New York, and London: Harcourt Brace, 1990), 366–68, originally published in 1927; E. C. Perrow, "Songs and Rhymes from the South," *Journal of American Folklore* 26 (April-June 1913): 165–67; B. A. Botkin, *A Treasury of American Folklore*, 241–45; Sterling Sherwin and Harry McClintock, *Railroad Songs of Yesterday* (New York: Shapiro, Bernstein, 1943), 4, 14; John Garst, "Casey Jones," in *Encyclopedia of the Blues*, vol. 1 (A–J), ed. Edward Komara, 187; Richard Polenberg, "Casey Jones (1900)," in *Hear My Sad Story: The True Tales That Inspired "Stagolee," "John Henry," and Other Traditional American Folk Songs* (Ithaca, NY, and London: Cornell University Press, 2015), 163–70, 274–75; John Garst, "Casey Jones," retrievable at www .bubbaguitar.com/articles/caseyjones.html.

2. Polenberg, "Casey Jones (1900)," 166.

3. Sim T. Webb recorded two 78 r.p.m. discs titled "The Story of Casey Jones' Last Trip" (Davidson Clay Co., Memphis, 1952). His account, which appears to be read from a script,

presumably prepared from interviews with him, can be heard in part at https://www.youtube
.com/watch?v=7OMx2zlmYFo.

4. Lomax and Lomax, *American Ballads and Folk Songs*, 34, reports that in 1910 O. L. Miller, mayor of Canton, Mississippi, wrote to John A. Lomax that "Wallis Sanders [*sic*] is the composer of the popular song 'Casey Jones.'"

5. The best summary of this controversy is in Cohen, *Long Steel Rail*, 137–48. See also "Casey Jones" at http://fresnostate.edu/folklore/ballads/LG01.html.

6. *Railroad Man's Magazine* 5 (March 1908): 384.

7. A similar stanza is found in a lyric transcription of "Casey Jones" dated November 1939 and filed in the Fletcher Collins Jr. Collection, Archive of Folk Culture, American Folklife Center, Library of Congress. Many thanks to Judith Gray for sending me a copy of this document.

8. Odum's text is reprinted in Dorothy Scarborough, *On the Trail of Negro Folk-Songs* (Cambridge: Harvard University Press, 1925), 249–50, where it is reported that writer Irvin Cobb told her that "*Casey Jones* was written by a Negro in Memphis, Tennessee, to recount the gallant death of 'Cayce' Jones, an engineer who came from Cayce, Tennessee. He was called that in order to distinguish him from others of his name and calling, there being three engineers named Jones, one called 'Dyersburg,' one 'Memphis,' and one 'Cayce,' after the towns they hailed from." Scarborough also wrote that "[T]he music for *Casey Jones* was given me by Early Busby," a baritone singer and trombonist from Texas who probably gave her the tune of the popular Newton-Seibert song. Scarborough's information about Memphis is questionable; there is a Cayce in Kentucky and also in Mississippi, but not in Tennessee. Thanks to Chris Smith for doing research on Albert Early Busby.

9. Howard W. Odum, "Folk-Song and Folk-Poetry as Found in the Secular Songs of the Southern Negroes," *Journal of American Folk-Lore* 24 (October-December 1911): 352; reprinted with minor variations in Howard W. Odum and Guy B. Johnson, *The Negro and His Songs* (Hatboro, VT: Folklore Associates, 1964), 207–8; originally published in 1925 by University of North Carolina Press. See also Howard W. Odum and Guy B. Johnson, *Negro Workaday Songs* (Chapel Hill: University of North Carolina Press, 1926), 126.

10. Advertisement in the *Los Angeles Times*, April 4, 1909, 44.

11. In 1928, Laycook Music and Printing Co. of Jackson, Tennessee, printed music and lyrics of "My Husband Casey Jones," composed by "Mrs. Casey Jones in collaboration with Lysle Tomerlin." The song's lyrics were also printed on March 11, 1928, in J. W. West's "Casey Jones Lives in Railroaders' Hearts," *The Tennessean* (Nashville), where it is reported that the song had been copyrighted the week before. In the article, Mrs. Jones claimed that another black worker, Ike Wentworth, helped Wallace Saunders put together "snatches of 'made-up' songs about railroad men that [Saunders] knew." Similarly to the Seibert-Newton's sheet music, the printed lyrics of "My Husband Casey Jones" refer to "Reno Hill," and the last verse reprises the line "Go to bed, children, and hush your crying," but rhymes it with "Cause your papa's now driving on the Heavenly line." The stanza about Mrs. Jones's infidelity is obviously not included, and the hit version's last verse is rebutted by the phrase "the heartache of children and of wife." I am grateful to Chris Smith for providing scans of the music sheet and newspaper article.

12. Reported in Cohen, *Long Steel Rail*, 139.

13. See Odum and Johnson, *The Negro and His Songs*, 248–49.

14. See Cohen, *Long Steel Rail*, 386–89.

15. Lomax and Lomax, *American Ballads and Folk Songs*, 36–39.

16. This stanza does not correspond to the one transcribed by the Lomaxes in *American Ballads and Folk Songs*, but it is thought to belong to Cornelius Steen's "Casey Jones" because the record jacket contains notes by Alan Lomax that it was collected there in that month and year, and forms part of the original version of the ballad sung by a friend of Saunders.

17. Cornelius Steen, "Casey Jones" (AFS 1866-A and 1866-B), recorded in Canton, Mississippi, ca. August 5–7, 1933. Printed in Cohen, *Long Steel Rail*, 143.

18. Cohen, *Long Steel Rail*, 146.

19. "Eagle eye" and "tallow pot" are respectively railroad slang for an engineer and a fireman, according to "Kelley the Rake."

20. See Cohen, *Long Steel Rail*, 139–40. For another disaster song reprising stanzas from both "Casey Jones" and "Joseph Mica," see Newman Ivey White, "Engineer Rigg," in *American Negro Folk-Songs* (Hatboro, VT: Folklore Associates, 1965), 220–21; originally published by Harvard University Press in 1928.

21. See Cohen, "Ben Dewberry's Final Run," in *Long Steel Rail*, 158–62.

22. See Cohen, "Ben Dewberry's Final Run," in *American Folk Songs: A Regional Encyclopedia*, vol. 1 (Westport, CT: Greenwood Press, 2008), 312–13; and "The Recent Wreck at Buford," *Keowee Courier* (Pickens, South Carolina), September 23, 1908, 3.

23. Among them are "Sloppy" [Waymon] Henry's "Hobo Blues" (OKeh 8683), recorded in Atlanta, Georgia, on March 12, 1929, and available on various artists, *Male Blues of the Twenties*, Document Records DOCD-5482, 1996; and Ed Cobb's noncommercial recording, "Casey Jones" (AFS 1330-B-1), recorded in Livingston, Alabama, on July 23, 1937. See Cohen, "J. C. Holmes Blues," in *Long Steel Rail*, 163–65.

24. Smith's recording is available on *The Complete Recordings—Volume 4*, Frog Records DGF43, 2002.

25. "N., C. & St. L. Mileage," *News-Democrat* (Paducah, Kentucky), June 20, 1903, 8. The abbreviation stands for "Nashville, Chattanooga & St. Louis [Railroad]."

26. In fact, the N., C. & St. L. only operated a line between Bruceton, Tennessee, and Paducah from 1896; see https://www.american-rails.com/nashville-chattanooga-and-st-louis-railway .html.

27. Cohen, *Long Steel Rail*, 145.

28. David Evans, email to the author, January 5, 2019.

29. Henry Rhodes, "Casey Jones: 'A Heavy Right-Wheeler of a Mighty Fame,'" *New York Sunday News*, November 27, 1927, 4.

30. See, for instance, a squib in the *Tennessean*, June 7, 1911, 6: "A New York man died with heart disease accelerated by the piano-pounding of a 10-year-old girl who lived in a neighboring flat. Here's dollars to doughnuts she played 'Casey Jones.'"

31. D. K. Wilgus and Lynwood Montell defined a blues ballad as "a highly variable, subjective, lyrical, yet dramatic narrative which celebrates and comments on an event rather than presenting a straightforward, circumstantial account." See Wilgus and Montell, "Clure and Joe Williams: Legend and Blues Ballad," *Journal of American Folk-Lore* 81 (1968): 296. See also D. K. Wilgus, "A Type Index of Anglo-American Traditional Narrative Songs," *Journal of the Folklore Institute* 7 (August-December 1970): 161–76.

32. E. C. Perrow, "Songs and Rhymes from the South," *Journal of American Folklore* 26 (April–June 1913): 165–67.

33. The following text is transcribed in Cohen, *Long Steel Rail*, 143–44, from Harry K. McClintock, *Haywire Mac*, Folkways FD 5272, 1972, available at http://www.folkways.si.edu/ harry-haywire-mac-mcclintock/american-folk-struggle-protest/music/album/smithsonian.

34. Cohen, *Long Steel Rail*, 145–46.

35. Early white popular versions of "Casey Jones" were recorded by Billy Murray and the American Quartette (Victor 16483) in 1909 (released in 1910), Arthur Collins and Byron Harlan (Indestructible Record 3163) in 1910, and Gene Greene (Pathé Actuelle) in 1913. For white hillbilly recordings of "Casey Jones," see Meade, with Spottswood and Meade, *Country Music Sources*, 44–45.

36. Reported in "Temple Theater, New Orleans," *Indianapolis Freeman*, November 12, 1910, and quoted in Lynn Abbott and Doug Seroff, *The Original Blues: The Emergence of the Blues in African American Vaudeville* (Jackson: University Press of Mississippi, 2017), 71, 326.

37. Abbott and Seroff, *The Original Blues*, 76, 181, 183–85, 327, 351, 352.

38. Reissued on Fiddlin' John Carson, *Complete Recorded Works in Chronological Order— Volume 1 (1923-1924)*, Document Records DOCD-8014, 1997.

39. Riley Puckett (Columbia 113-D), recorded in New York on March 7, 1924; Paul Stone Wright (Special unnumbered), recorded ca. September 1924; George Reneau (Vocalion 14813), recorded in New York City in April 1924; the prolific Vernon Dalhart (Banner 1580, Victor 20502, Plaza unissued, Edison 51611), recorded in New York City in June and July 1925; and Al Bernard (Brunswick 178), recorded in New York City in June and September 1927. For a complete discography see Russell, *Country Music Records*, 1029, and Cohen, *Long Steel Rail*, 151–57. Frank Hutchison's "Hell Bound Train" (OKeh 45452), recorded in New York City on September 10, 1928, is loosely related to "Casey Jones."

40. Gid Tanner and His Skillet-Lickers (Columbia 15237-D), reissued on various artists, *People Take Warning! Murder Ballads and Disaster Songs, 1913–1938*, Tompkins Square TSQ 1875 (3CD), 2007.

41. Furry Lewis's "Casey Jones" for Vocalion was recorded in Chicago on October 9, 1927; Mississippi John Hurt's "Casey Jones" for OKeh was recorded in Memphis on February 14, 1928.

42. Reissued on various artists, *People Take Warning! Murder Ballads and Disaster Songs, 1913–1938*, Tompkins Square TSQ 1875 (3CD), 2007. The apparent spelling error "Kassie Jones" is probably deliberate, so that A&R man Ralph Peer's publishing company could benefit; the composer credit on disc is to "F. Lewis." Updated biographical information on Lewis is in Eagle and LeBlanc, *Blues: A Regional Experience*, 187, 447; and J. Tyler Fritts, "Furry Lewis: An Ethnomusicological Study of a Memphis Musician" (PhD diss., University of Memphis, August 2016), 25–82.

43. A reference to Stavin' Chain, whose sexual heroics are celebrated in several obscene blues and folk songs.

44. An eastman is a man who lives off women, not necessarily as a pimp. A similar meaning is reported in Lomax and Lomax, *American Ballads and Folk Songs*, 34.

45. Bluesman Thomas Shaw's father is known to have sung a similar verse as early as 1915 or 1916. See Guido van Rijn, "Thomas Shaw Interview," *Blues & Rhythm* 193 (October 2004): 5.

46. For Lewis's later versions, see Fancourt and McGrath, *The Blues Discography 1943–1970*, 381–83; and Ford and McGrath, *The Blues Discography 1971–2000*, 276.

47. J. Tyler Fritts, "Lyric Formulas as Traditional Compositional Processes in the Folk Blues: A Case Study of Furry Lewis," *Ethnomusicology* 64, no. 1 (winter 2020): 160–61, 164–65.

48. Cohen, *Long Steel Rail*, 149–50.

49. De Ford Bailey's "Casey Jones" was recorded for Victor in Nashville, Tennessee, on October 2, 1928; Cow Cow Davenport's "Casey Jones Blues" was recorded for Gennett in Richmond, Indiana, on June 7, 1930. Pianist Little Brother Montgomery (1906–1985) recorded an unissued "Casey Jones" for Francis Wilford-Smith at Trumpets Farm, Herstmonceux, Sussex, England, on August 26, 1960. See Fancourt and McGrath, *The Blues Discography 1943–1970*, 480; and Caroline Beecroft and Howard Rye, *Blues for Francis: The Life and Work of Francis Wilford-Smith* (York, UK: Music Mentor Books, 2015), 41, 61.

50. Hart and Ogle, "Casey Jones" (Broadway 8303), recorded in Grafton, Wisconsin, ca. August 1931; Carson Robison's medleys "A Hill Billy Mixture Part 1" (Regal English MR 645) and "Hill Billy Songs Medley Part 1" (Columbia British DX 365), both recorded in London, England, on June 24, 1932; Francis H. Abbott, "Casey Jones" (AFS L-68), recorded in Charlottesville, Virginia, on March 24, 1932.

51. African American versions include Rochelle French and Gabriel Brown, "Casey Jones" (AFS 356-A), recorded by Alan Lomax, Zora Neale Hurston, and Elizabeth Barnicle in Eatonville, Florida, in June 1935. Available on various artists, *Field Recordings—Vol. 7: Florida*, Document Records DOCD-5587, 1997 (originally issued on Flyright/Matchbox LP 257, 1975), it is mainly a guitar display piece. Ed Cobb, "Casey Jones" (AFS 1330-B-1), recorded in Livingston, Alabama, on July 23, 1937, is a conflation of stanzas from "J. C. Holmes" and the unrelated "Hobo Blues." John Floyd, "Casey Jones" (AFS 3076-B-2), recorded at the colored YMCA in Vicksburg, Mississippi, on May 30, 1939, is unaccompanied (no further information is available). Arthur "Brother-in-Law" Armstrong accompanies himself on guitar on "Casey Jones" (AFS 3987-B-4), recorded in Jasper, Texas, on October 4, 1940, but again there is no further information. Asa Ware, "Casey Jones" (AFS 6631-A-6), recorded in Clarksdale, Mississippi, on July 25, 1942, is a fragment. For a complete list of recordings, both black and white, see Cohen, *Long Steel Rail*, 156.

52. Lomax and Lomax, *American Ballads and Folk Songs*, 34–36. For the relationship between John A. Lomax and Truvillion, see Patrick B. Mullen, "The Racial Relationship of John Lomax and Henry Truvillion," in *The Man Who Adores the Negro: Race and American Folklore* (Urbana and Chicago: University of Illinois Press, 2008), 63–78.

53. This song is available on various artists, *Piano Blues Vol. 1 (1927–1936)*, Document Records DOCD-5192, 1993.

54. According to the Oxford English Dictionary, this rarely used verb means "to go out." Stephen Calt, *Barrelhouse Words: A Blues Dialect Dictionary* (Urbana and Chicago: University of Illinois Press, 2009), 176.

55. A Mother Hubbard is "a loose-fitting, long-sleeved, and nearly floor-length type of dress regarded as an emblem of feminine modesty and worn primarily by rural females. Introduced around 1884, they remained popular through the early years of the 20th century, and are still worn by members of the Amish sect." Stephen Calt, *Barrelhouse Words*, 165.

56. Lomax and Lomax, *Folk Song U.S.A.*, 336–37. In an interview with Son House in his 1942 field notes, Lomax refers to Jesse James's "Lonesome Day Blues," the flip side of "Southern Casey Jones." Clearly, the Jesse James recording was the source of the stanzas (described as "sometimes sung by barrelhouse blue-blowers") in *Folk Song U.S.A.* David Evans, email to the author, August 28, 2017.

57. Another version deriving from the Seibert and Newton song, and conforming to the music fashions of the period, was recorded by vocal group the Jubalaires in 1947 or 1948.

Unissued then, it is available on various artists, *Rumba Doowop 1933–1954*, Rhythm and Blues Records, RANDB015, 2011; and on the Jubalaires, *Singing Waiters: 1947–1948*, Heritage HT CD 48, 2004. The Golden Gate Quartet also recorded an a cappella version of "Casey Jones," in Paris, France, on April 29, 1960. It is available on the Golden Gate Quartet, *Spirituals to Swing 1955–1969*, EMI France 791569-2, 1988.

58. The exact recording date is not known. The Cook LP where it was included was released in 1954, and reissued with additional tracks as *Mercury Blues*, Oldie Blues OL 2812, 1980. See Fancourt and McGrath, *The Blues Discography 1943–1970*, 169.

59. Lipscomb's song was reissued on *Trouble in Mind*, Rhino Handmade RHM2 7829, 2002. In Govenar and Lornell, *The Blues Come to Texas*, 282, it is reported that the Texas songster learned "Casey Jones" as early as 1902, when he was only seven.

60. The song was reissued on Mississippi John Hurt, *Avalon Blues 1963*, Rounder Records CD 1081, 1991. A very similar version was recorded for the Library of Congress in Washington, DC, on July 15, 1963, and is available on Mississippi John Hurt, *D.C. Blues: The Library of Congress Recordings Vol. 2*, Fuel 2000 302 061 495 2 (2CD), 2005.

61. Ratcliffe, *Mississippi John Hurt*, 38.

62. Cohen, *Long Steel Rail*, 54.

63. Cohen, *Long Steel Rail*, 148, 156. "Casey Jones-The Union Scab," a parody containing no references to the accident, was written by Industrial Workers of the World activist Joe Hill as early as 1911.

64. John Garst, "Casey Jones," 6–7, www.bubbaguitar.com/articles/caseyjones.html.

65. Samuel C. Adams Jr., "Changing Negro Life in the Delta" (MA thesis, June 1947), quoted in Work, Jones, and Adams, *Lost Delta Found*, 289–90.

66. It must also be remembered that there were very few obscene folksongs collected in the U.S. in the nineteenth and early twentieth centuries, and that if folklorists encountered them, they were considered unfit for print.

67. Bruce Jackson, *Get Your Ass in the Water and Swim Like Me: African American Narrative Poetry from Oral Tradition* (New York and London: Routledge, 2004), 36, originally published by Harvard University Press, 1974.

68. See Bruce Jackson, *Get Your Ass in the Water and Swim Like Me*, 153. The second section of the toast derives from the British ballad "The Farmer's Curst Wife" (Child 278) and is sometimes found in songs about Stackolee. For an account of "Slim Wilson," see Jackson, 9–12.

69. Levine, *Black Culture and Black Consciousness*, 427.

70. The various blues ballads about "Betty and Dupree" should be noted, although they are not about a disaster. Like Casey Jones, Frank Dupree was white, although Brownie McGhee was not the only blues singer to believe otherwise. African Americans were sympathetic to Dupree, hanged for murder in Atlanta in 1922, because he was young, and perceived as a fellow victim of the Southern legal system. Other white protagonists of ballads sung by blacks include President William McKinley and the various people in Sid Hemphill's ballads.

71. This chapter draws on my earlier publication "Topical Blues: Disasters: The Sinking of the Titanic (1912)," in *Encyclopedia of the Blues*, vol. 2 (K–Z), ed. Edward Komara, 997–98.

72. The most important publications are: Sandburg, *The American Songbag*, 254–56; Oliver, *Songsters and Saints: Vocal Traditions on Race Records*, 222–26; Jackson, *Get Your Ass in the Water and Swim Like Me*, 35–38, 180–96; Levine, *Black Culture and Black Consciousness*, 258, 427–29; Chris Smith, "The Titanic: A Case Study of Religious and Secular Attitudes in African

American Song," in *Saints and Sinners: Religion, Blues and (D)evil in African-American Music and Literature*, ed. Robert Sacré (Liège, Belgium: Société Liégeoise de Musicologie, 1996), 213–27; Laws, *Native American Balladry*, 172–73, 264, 276; Courlander, *Negro Folk Music U.S.A.*, 75–78; Richard D. Barnet, Bruce Nemerov, and Mayo Taylor, "The Band Played 'Nearer My God to Thee' As the Ship Went Down," in *The Story Behind the Song: 150 Songs That Chronicle the 20th Century* (Westport, CT, and London: Greenwood Press, 2004), 31–32; Newman Ivey White, *American Negro Folk-Songs*, 347–48, 412; Norm Cohen, "The Sinking of the *Titanic* and the Floundering of American Folksong Scholarship," *Southern Folklore* 56, no. 1 (1999): 3–26; Solomon Goodman's handwritten list, *Titanic Disaster Music: A Listing by Copyright Registration Number, and Showing Names of Authors, Composers, Copyright Proprietors and Publishers, and Dates of Copyright Registration*, copy no. 13, August 1985, American Folklife Center, Library of Congress, and the collection of sheet music at the Library of Congress; Newman I. White, gen. ed., *The Frank C. Brown Collection of North Carolina Folklore* (Durham, NC: Duke University Press, 1952–61): *Folk Ballads from North Carolina*, vol. 2, eds. Henry M. Belden and Arthur Palmer Hudson, 1952, 662–68, esp. 667–68, and *The Music of the Ballads*, vol. 4, ed. Jan Philip Schinham, 1957, 314–18, esp. 317–18; Meade, with Spottswood and Meade, *Country Music Sources*, 70; D. K. Wilgus, "Tentative Type List of *Titanic* Ballads," unpublished typewritten document, courtesy of David Evans. See also D. K. Wilgus Papers #20003, Southern Folklife Collection, Wilson Library, University of North Carolina at Chapel Hill at http://www2.lib.unc.edu/mss/inv/w/Wilgus,D.K.html. Wilgus and others grouped several recordings from Ireland, Haiti, Newfoundland, and elsewhere into song types.

73. For this study I have drawn on: Walter Lord, *A Night to Remember* (New York: St. Martin's Griffin, 2005), originally published by Holt, Rinehart & Winston in 1955; Steven Biel, *Down with the Old Canoe: A Cultural History of the* Titanic *Disaster* (New York and London: W. W. Norton, 1997); Steven Biel, ed., *Titanica: The Disaster of the Century in Poetry, Song, and Prose* (New York and London: W. W. Norton, 1998); Greg Ward, *The Rough Guide to the Titanic* (London: Rough Guides, 2012); Nic Compton, *Titanic on Trial: The Night the Titanic Sank* (London: Bloomsbury, 2012); Paul Heyer, *Titanic Century: Media, Myth, and the Making of a Cultural Icon* (Santa Barbara, CA: Praeger, 2012); Richard Polenberg, "The *Titanic* (1912)," in *Hear My Sad Story*, 223–32, 280. See also Erwin Bosman, https://www.nodepression.com/blues-and-black-folk-music-shine-on-the-american-titanic/, published May 10, 2012.

74. Gareth Russell, *The Darksome Bounds of a Failing World: The Sinking of the* Titanic *and the End of the Edwardian Era* (London: William Collins, 2019), 177–78.

75. Polenberg, "The *Titanic* (1912)," 223.

76. For early comments on the possible presence of black people on board the *Titanic*, see the following newspaper articles quoted in Biel, *Titanica*, 156–59: "Editorial," *St. Paul Appeal*, April 20, 1912; "Editorial," *Pittsburgh Courier*, April 27, 1912; "Editorial Notes," *New York Age*, April 25, 1912. See also Logan Marshall, *Sinking of the Titanic and Great Sea Disasters* (Ann Arbor, MI: University Microfilms, 1980 [1912]), 55–56.

77. Marshall, *Sinking of the Titanic and Great Sea Disasters*, 55–56.

78. Mike Herbold, message to Encyclopedia Titanica, https://www.encyclopedia-titanica .org/community/threads/black-crew-members.18827/, accessed March 10, 2019.

79. Ward, *The Rough Guide to the Titanic*, 194–95.

80. The most comprehensive compilation of recordings about the disaster is *Titanic Songs*, TSCD 22798, n.d. [1998]. This CD includes all songs discussed here for which other reissues

are not cited, but *Titanic Songs* is hard to find, and more easily accessible reissues are cited when available. *Titanic Songs* and the Japanese CD *Titanic Requiem* (P-Vine PVCP-8745) were both issued in 1998, the year after the release of the eponymous James Cameron film. Two African American sacred recordings about the sinking of the *Titanic* were never released: Rev. Edward W. Clayborn (The Guitar Evangelist)'s "Sinking of the Titanic" (Vocalion, New York City, June 17, 1927), and the Jubilee Gospel Team's two-part "Sinking of the Titanic" (Perfect, New York City, March 19, 1930). Another black recording dealing with this disaster is J. B. Smith's unaccompanied "Titanic" (unissued), recorded at the Ramsey Prison Farm, Texas, on August 23, 1965 (see Fancourt and McGrath, *The Blues Discography 1943–1970*, 534). Among white field recordings are: "Sinking of the Titanic" (3174-B-3), by Ruby Hughes, collected by Sidney Robertson Cowell in Crossville, Tennessee, on November 23, 1936; "The Titanic" (3189-A-2), by Louisiana native Gilbert Fike, collected by Sidney Robertson Cowell in Little Rock, Arkansas, on November 26, 1936; and "The Sinking of the Titanic" (2877-A-2), by Mrs. A. J. Huff, collected by Herbert Halpert in Gatlinburg, Tennessee, on April 21, 1939.

81. Joseph C. Hickerson as quoted in Green, *Only a Miner*, 411.

82. For a discography of white country songs on the sinking of the *Titanic*, see Meade, with Spottswood, and Meade, *Country Music Sources*, 70.

83. White, *American Negro Folk-Songs*, 347–48.

84. White, *American Negro Folk-Songs*, 347–48. A similar chorus, reported by J. A. Logan of Clinton, Mississippi, from the singing of an old black man, is printed in Newbell Niles Puckett, *Folk Beliefs of the Southern Negro* (Chapel Hill: University of North Carolina Press, 1926), 64–65. A partial transcription is also printed in Howard W. Odum, *Wings on My Feet: Black Ulysses at the Wars* (Indianapolis: Bobbs-Merrill, 1929), 27–28.

85. The text of the ballad in White, *The Frank C. Brown Collection of North Carolina Folklore*, 663, has a headnote including the words "Note by Dr. Brown: 'Made by W.O. Smith and Irma Smith (da.).'"

86. Stoneman's "The Titanic" is available on various artists, *People Take Warning! Murder Ballads and Disaster Songs, 1913–1938*, Tompkins Square TSQ 1875 (3CD), 2007, which wrongly assigns the date of his earlier unissued version, ca. September 4, 1924. Stoneman recorded another version, titled "Sinking of the Titanic" (Edison 51823) in New York City on June 22, 1926. It was issued as by Ernest V. Stoneman the Blue Ridge Mountaineer. Among other white versions based on this song model are: Arlie Baker, "The Titanic" (AFS 1411-B-1), collected by Alan and Elizabeth Lomax in Pine Mountain, Kentucky, on September 23, 1937, available at https://www.huffingtonpost.com/stephen-d-winick/titanic-100-anniversary_b_1424430.html; W. E. Claunch, accompanied by his own fiddle and Mrs. Christeen (Christine) Haygood (guitar), "The Great Titanic" (AFS 2972-B-4, 2973-A-1), collected by Herbert Halpert near Guntown, Mississippi, in 1939, and available on various artists, *Mississippi Fiddle Tunes and Songs from the 1930s*, Document Records DOCD-8071 (3CD), 2015; and Walter Caldwell with James Williams (guitar), "Titanic" (AFS 1023-A-1), collected by John Avery Lomax in Ashland, Kentucky, on June 28, 1937. This recording, which includes the less common verse about St. Paul's shipwreck, is available among the Library of Congress's Kentucky Alan Lomax Recordings 1937–1942 collection at https://archive.org/details/lomaxky.

87. Among them are: "The Sinking of the Titanic" (Columbia 15032-D, June 4, 1925); "The Great Titanic" (Gennett 3311, ca. May 14–17, 1926); "The Wreck of the Titanic" (Grey Gull 4131, issued as by Jeff Calhoun, ca. May 1927); "Sinking of the Titanic" (Champion 15121, ca. May 23,

1928). George Reneau recorded a similar version, titled "Sinking of the Titanic" (Vocalion 15148) in New York City on October 14, 1925.

88. These recordings are held in the Robert Winslow Gordon Cylinder Collection at the Library of Congress, Washington, DC. Gordon asked singers to announce their names, the location, and date after their performances. The information here has been supplied by Chris Smith after listening to the recordings.

89. This song is available on various artists, *People Take Warning! Murder Ballads and Disaster Songs, 1913–1938*, Tompkins Square TSQ 1875 (3CD), 2007. For the correct recording date, see van Rijn and van der Tuuk, *New York Recording Laboratories Rodeheaver, Marsh and 2000 Series*, 89–91.

90. Chris Smith, "William & Versey Smith, and William & Irma Smith: Not Husbands and Their Wives," *Names & Numbers* 89 (April 2019): 11–12.

91. My thanks to Chris Smith for enabling me to hear this song. The original recording is held in the Laura Boulton Archive at the Center for Ethnomusicology, Columbia University, New York City.

92. These songs are held in the Herbert Halpert Southern States Collection at the Library of Congress, Washington, DC.

93. The first recording is available on a CD shared with Reverend Gary Davis, *Gospel, Blues and Street Songs*, Original Blues Classics OBCCD-524, 1987; the second is on *The Blues of Pink Anderson: Ballad and Folksinger, Vol. 3*, Original Blues Classics OBCCD-577, 1995. On August 26, 1960, pianist Little Brother Montgomery recorded an unissued "It Was Sad When That Great Ship Went Down" at Trumpets Farm, Herstmonceux, Sussex, England. See Fancourt and McGrath, *The Blues Discography 1943–1970*, 480, and Pamela Wilford-Smith, "Memories of the Sixties," in Beecroft and Rye, *Blues for Francis: The Life and Work of Francis Wilford-Smith*, 58, 61.

94. This stanza was used by Ernest Stoneman the Blue Ridge Mountaineer in "Sinking of the Titanic" (Edison 51823), recorded on June 22, 1926.

95. Reissued on the Dixieaires, *My Trouble Is Hard*, Heritage LP HT 319.

96. The song is available on Bill Jackson, *Long Steel Rail*, Testament TCD 5014, 1994.

97. Ward, *The Rough Guide to the Titanic*, 197.

98. Reissued on various artists, *The Introduction to Living Country Blues*, Bellaphon CDLR 711921 (2CD), 2008.

99. Norman Darwen, "Rejected No More: Flora Molton Interview," *Blues & Rhythm* 245 (Christmas 2009): 12–14, esp. 14. In another interview, she remembered singing "'Was Sad When That Great Ship Went Down,' like my daddy used to play." See Eleanor Ellis, "'From a Little Girl I've Been Singing, Singing Singing,'" *Living Blues* 86 (May/June 1989): 22–28, esp. 24.

100. These lyrics are as published in the booklet *Songs Sung by R. D. Burnett—The Blind Man—Monticello, Kentucky*, reprinted in *Old Time Music* 10 (autumn 1973): 10. For a biography of Burnett, see Russell, *Country Music Originals*, 92–94.

101. This song is available on various artists, *Doom and Gloom: Early Songs of Angst and Disaster (1927–1945)*, Trikont US-0364, 2007. For a biography of the duo see Russell, *Country Music Originals*, 57–58.

102. Available on CD 1, *Pigtown Fling*, included in James P. Leary, *Folksongs of Another America: Field Recordings from the Upper Mid-West, 1937–1946* (Madison: University of Wisconsin Press, and Atlanta, GA: Dust-to-Digital, 2015, in collaboration with the American Folklife Center at the Library of Congress and the Association for Cultural Equity/Alan Lomax Archive). The

song text is on 39–40, and the recording is also available at http://www.huffingtonpost.com/stephen-d-winick/titanic-100-anniversary_b_1424430.html.

103. This song has been reissued on *People Take Warning! Murder Ballads and Disaster Songs, 1913–1938*, Tompkins Square TSQ 1875 (3CD), 2007. For a biography of the duo, see Russell, *Country Music Originals*, 189–90.

104. Because of time limitations, the Dixon Brothers omitted the song's final stanza, published in the May 24, 1938, *Rockingham Post-Dispatch*. It reads: "Now, dear sinners, hear my plea / You may wreck out on life's sea / In a slanting dive you may go down out there / So why don't you heed the call / Jesus sends out to you all / So you can smile and face that chilly air?" See Patrick Huber, "Notes on the Songs," in *The Dixon Brothers: A Blessing to People* (Hambergen, Germany, 2012, with CD box set of the same name, Bear Family BCD 16817 DK, 2012). The notes also quote Dorsey Dixon on his motives for writing the song.

105. In 1908, near College Station, Texas, in the Brazos bottoms, John A. Lomax recorded a variant of the Queen/Wilson song by an African American woman called "Dink" with the refrain "Fare-you-well, O honey, fare-you-well." See Lomax, *Adventures of a Ballad Hunter*, 238–41.

106. Peter Muir, *Long Lost Blues: Popular Blues in America, 1850–1920* (Urbana and Chicago: University of Illinois Press, 2010), 49, 187. See also Peter Muir, "Before 'Crazy Blues': Commercial Blues in America, 1850–1920" (PhD diss., City University of New York, 2004), 220, and Abbott and Seroff, *The Original Blues*, 182–83, 351–52.

107. Both takes of "Titanic Man Blues" are available on Ma Rainey, *Complete Recorded Works in Chronological Order—Vol. 3 (1925–1926)*, Document Records DOCD-5583, 1997. For critical essays on her life and music see Lieb, *Mother of the Blues*, and Davis, *Blues Legacies and Black Feminism*.

108. Ma Rainey is known to have sung "her own composed song, 'Titanic'" (presumably "Titanic Man Blues"), in Pensacola, Florida, as early as 1914, but the most popular version was the one Virginia Liston introduced in Chicago in May 1913. "Moses Graham, better known as Two-Story Mose," was singing "Titanic, Fare Thee Well" in Charlotte, North Carolina, two months before Virginia Liston's first documented performance of it. Ida Cox performed her own version in Georgia in 1915. See Abbott and Seroff, *The Original Blues*, 173, 181–84, 199, 348, 351, 352, 355.

109. Abbott and Seroff, *The Original Blues*, 43, 178–80.

110. Available on *Virginia Liston Volume 2 (1924–1926) and Lavinia Turner (1921–1922)*, Document Records DOCD-5447, 1996; the notes include some biographical information by Steve Tracy.

111. Ward, *The Rough Guide to the Titanic*, 120; Encyclopedia Titanica, https://www.en cyclopedia-titanica.org/articles/wormstedt.pdf; "How Many Ships besides the Titanic Broke in Half while Sinking?" at https://www.quora.com/How-many-ships-besides-the-Titanic -broke-in-half-while-sinking.

112. Available on the second CD of the box set *Lead Belly's Last Sessions*, Smithsonian Folkways SF 40068–71 (4CD), 1994.

113. This song was reissued on Leadbelly, *The Titanic*, Rounder Records CD 1097, 1994. For a biography of Lead Belly see Charles Wolfe and Kip Lornell, *The Life and Legend of Leadbelly* (New York: HarperCollins, 1994). A cover of Lead Belly's song titled "Titanic" is available on Eric Bibb and JJ Milteau, *Lead Belly's Gold*, Dixiefrog DFGCD 8780, 2015.

114. The year after the Library of Congress recording, the first music and lyric transcriptions of this song were printed in John A. Lomax and Alan Lomax, *Negro Folk Songs as Sung by Lead Belly* (New York: Macmillan, 1936), 181–83.

115. For Lead Belly's belief that Jack Johnson was refused passage, see Wolfe and Lornell, *The Life and Legend of Leadbelly*, 247, and Lead Belly's introduction to his 1948 recording of the song.

116. For a discussion of the dichotomy "Absence vs. Presence" as related to the *Titanic* topic, see Biel, *Down with the Old Canoe*, 114–15.

117. For general information about this song and its origin, and for biographical information on Blind Butler and his relationship with Blind Willie Johnson, see Govenar and Lornell, *The Blues Come to Texas*, 285, 313–19.

118. See Dorothy Scarborough, *From A Southern Porch* (New York and London: G. P. Putnam's Sons, 1919), 305–7.

119. Abbott and Seroff, *The Original Blues*, 116.

120. Newman I. White, gen. ed., *The Frank C. Brown Collection of North Carolina Folklore* (Durham, NC: Duke University Press, 1952–1961): vol. 2, *Folk Ballads from North Carolina*, eds. Henry M. Belden and Arthur Palmer Hudson, 1952, 667–68, and vol. 4, *The Music of the Ballads*, ed. Jan Philip Schinham, 1957, 314–18, esp. 317–18.

121. For more on encoded protest in blues lyrics, see Springer, "Text, Context and Subtext in the Blues," 1–16.

122. This song is held in the Frank C. Brown Collection of North Carolina Songs at the Library of Congress in Washington, DC.

123. This song is available on *The Complete Blind Willie Johnson*, Sony/Columbia Legacy C2K 52835 (2CD), 1993. For the most reliable biographical information on Johnson, see Michael Corcoran, "On the Trail of Blind Willie Johnson," *Blues & Rhythm* 188 (April 2004): 4–5.

124. The similarity of this chorus to James Brown Jr.'s "Hurricane" (AFS 3898 A) has been noted earlier.

125. This refers to Titan, misunderstood as a "God in a tin" (that is, he understands the second syllable of Titan as "tin"). This and the previous stanza suggest that Johnson learned from a previous source (possibly Butler's ballet), probably written and read to him by someone.

126. See Govenar and Lornell, *The Blues Come to Texas*, 316. For the argument that Johnson and Butler were more closely associated and traveled together, see Michael Corcoran, "Blind Willie Johnson: Revelations in the Dark," on-line at https://www.mtzionmemorialfund.org/2018/09/blind-willie-johnson-revelations-in-dark.html.

127. This field recording is held in the John A. Lomax Southern States Collection at the Library of Congress in Washington, DC, and can be heard at https://www.loc.gov/item/ihas.200197230/. I am grateful to Chris Smith for helping me with the transcription.

128. This stanza is based on Matthew 28:1–7; Mark 16:1–8; Luke 24:1–10; and John 20:1–9.

129. For partial transcriptions of this song, see John A. Lomax and Alan Lomax, *Our Singing Country: Folk Songs and Ballads* (Mineola, NY: Dover Publications, 2000), 26–27; originally published by Macmillan, 1941. See also Courlander, *Negro Folk Music U.S.A.*, 76–77. For a version of the *Titanic* including a stanza related to the Galveston flood, see Bruce Jackson, "The *Titanic* Toast," in Harry Levin, ed., "Veins of Humor," *Harvard English Studies 3* (Cambridge, MA: Harvard University Press, 1972), 223. This version was collected in Huntsville, Texas, on March 17, 1966, from a man in his seventies who claimed to have learned it in Texas in 1918.

130. This recording is held in the John A. Lomax Southern States Collection at the Library of Congress in Washington, DC.

131. Reissued on various artists, *Southern Journey Volume 8: Velvet Voices—Eastern Shores Choirs, Quartets, and Colonial Era Music*, Rounder CD 1708, 1997. Jones recorded the song again on St. Simons Island, Georgia, on July 30 or 31, 1973. The later version has the same stanzas in a different sequence, and with minor changes. It was released on *So Glad I'm Here*, Rounder LP 2015, 1975, and reissued on Bessie Jones, *Put Your Hand on Your Hip and Let Your Backbone Slip*, Rounder CD 1166-1587-2, 2001. For information about Jones, see Bessie Jones and Bess Lomax Hawes, *Step It Down* (New York: Harper & Row, 1972; reprint: Athens: University of Georgia Press, 1987); and Bessie Jones and John Stewart, eds., *For the Ancestors: Autobiographical Memories* (Urbana: University of Illinois Press, 1983; reprint: Athens: University of Georgia Press, 1989). Ruthie Foster recorded an a cappella version of Jones's *Titanic* song in New Orleans, with support from the Blind Boys of Alabama. It is available on Ruthie Foster, *Let It Burn*, Blue Corn Music BCM 1281, 2011.

132. For Lipscomb's versions, see Fancourt and McGrath, *The Blues Discography 1943–1970*, 392–95; for a performance filmed at the University of Washington, Seattle, in 1968, see *Texas Blues Guitar*, Vestapol DVD 13041, 2003.

133. "God Moves on the Water (The Titanic)," recorded in Berkeley, California, on May 2, 1964, and reissued as "The Titanic" on Mance Lipscomb, *You Got to Reap What You Sow: Texas Songster Volume 2*, Arhoolie CD 398, 1993.

134. Govenar and Lornell, *The Blues Come to Texas*, 285 and note.

135. See Glen Alyn, *I Say Me for a Parable: The Oral Autobiography of Mance Lipscomb, Texas Bluesman* (New York: Da Capo Press, 1994), 219–21, 223. In his book Alyn makes use of dialect spelling to represent Lipscomb's voice. In Jim Kelton, "From Mance, with Love," *Blues Revue* 69 (July-August 2001): 16, Lipscomb is reported to have "learned 'The Titanic' by hearing Blind Boy Fuller play it in Houston . . . the same year the great ship went down." This cannot have been the well-known North Carolina artist, born in 1904. Even though Lipscomb never met Blind Butler, it seems likely that Kelton misunderstood a reference to him, perhaps understanding "Boy Fuller" instead of "Butler." See also Bruce Cook, *Listen to the Blues* (New York: Da Capo Press, 1995; originally published by C. Scribner's Sons, 1973), 111.

136. Alyn, *I Say Me for a Parable*, 220–21.

137. Transcription and quotation from Sandburg, *The American Songbag*, 254–56. The song's refrain is also in Howard W. Odum's novel, *Wings on My Feet: Black Ulysses at the Wars*, 28–29.

138. See "Jones, Bessie Zaban" at https://www.thebreman.org/Research/Cuba-Family-Archives/Oral-Histories/ID/870/Jones-Bessie-Zaban.

139. For textual correspondences, including two references to "forty eight pumps," see the *Titanic* toasts in Jackson, *Get Your Ass in the Water and Swim Like Me*, 180–96.

140. This recording (song GA-329 on cylinder A-552) is held in the Robert Winslow Gordon Cylinder Collection at the Library of Congress in Washington, DC. Song GA-330 on the same cylinder was sung by S. Scarlett, a female singer, in Brunswick, Georgia, on May 21, 1926.

141. The song is held in the John A. Lomax and Alton Morris Florida Collection at the Library of Congress in Washington, D.C.

142. See Eagle and LeBlanc, *Blues: A Regional Experience*, 88, 246.

143. Another Bahamian song, held at the Library of Congress, is "Titanic Sinking" (AFS 431-A), sung by Patrick Williams and a group of Andros Island men and collected by Alan Lomax

and Mary Elizabeth Barnicle at Sponge Docks, Nassau, Bahamas, in July 1935. See *Check-List of Recorded Songs in the English Language in the Archive of American Folk-Song to July, 1940* (Washington, DC: Library of Congress Music Division, 1942), 403. The song is available at http://www.huffingtonpost.com/stephen-d-winick/titanic-100-anniversary_b_1424430.html, but it has no narrative content about the disaster other than the phrase "Titanic sinking."

144. See "The Gullah/Geechee Connection," at https://gullahgeecheeconnection.wordpress.com/bahamas-folklore-gullahgeechee-connection/; and John Holm, "On the Relationship of Gullah and Bahamian," *American Speech* 58, no. 4 (1983): 303–18.

145. White, *American Negro Folk-Songs*, 347, 412.

146. White, *American Negro Folk-Songs*, 348–49.

147. It is worth noting that "Alabama Bound" was published in 1909. For songs employing lyrics such as "Where were you when the rolling mill burned/went down?" see, for example, Charley Patton's "Moon Going Down" (Paramount 13014).

148. See White, *American Negro Folk-Songs*, 345–46, citing E. C. Perrow, *Journal of American Folklore*, 1909. The issue is at https://archive.org/details/journalofamefolk28ameruoft/page/188, where the stanza is on 189, and said to be from "MS. of Dr. Herrington, 1909." The citation, based on White's bibliography, is E. C. Perrow, "Songs and Rhymes from the South," *Journal of American Folklore* XXVII (1915): 129–90.

149. William Jackson and Charles E. Wright, "The End of the Titanic in the Sea" (Medina, NY: Krompart Publishing, 1912), held at the American Folklife Center, Library of Congress, Washington DC.

150. See Adam Tabelski, "The End of the Titanic in the Sea," *Medina Bugle: A Publication of the Medina Historical Society* (September 2012), https://historicmedina.org/wp-content/uploads/2016/01/2012-09-medina-bugle.pdf, accessed January 16, 2016.

151. Lomax, *The Land Where the Blues Began*, 52–53. Haffer's *Titanic* song is cursorily mentioned in "The Natchez Theater Fire Disaster" (Library of Congress 6623-B-2), recorded in Clarksdale, Mississippi, on July 23, 1942.

152. Lomax, *The Land Where the Blues Began*, 54.

153. A. E. Perkins, "Negro Spirituals from the Far South," *Journal of American Folklore* 35 (1922): 223. See also Newman I. White, gen. ed., *The Frank C. Brown Collection of North Carolina Folklore* (Durham, NC: Duke University Press, 1952–1961): eds., Henry M. Belden and Arthur Palmer Hudson, *Folk Ballads from North Carolina*, vol. 2 (1952), 662; and Oliver, *Songsters and Saints*, 226.

154. Abbott and Seroff, *The Original Blues*, 81, 85, 116, 329, 334, 335, which includes descriptions of May's performance. See also Seroff and Abbott, "The Life and Death of Pioneer Bluesman Butler 'String Beans' May: 'Been Here, Made His Quick Duck, and Got Away,'" *Tributaries: Journal of the Alabama Folklife Association* 5 (2002): 20–21, 24–25.

155. Reported by Abbe Niles in "Ballads, Songs and Snatches," *The Bookman* 67, no. 3 (May 1928): 290–91, from W. C. Handy's recollections of May's singing at the Monogram Theater in Chicago. See also Abbott and Seroff, *The Original Blues*, 116, which also quotes the variant collected by Dorothy Scarborough and published in her book *From a Southern Porch* (1919).

156. Lynn Abbott, email to the author, February 18, 2014.

157. The Elgin National Watch Company engraved "Guaranteed to wear 20 years" on the cases of its pocket watches. This guarantee of the case was widely taken, as was perhaps intended, to

refer to the watch's mechanism (its movement). The sexual pun on hip movements emerged from this.

158. Brown's available recordings are on various artists, *The Great Songsters (1927–1929)*, Document Records DOCD-5003, 1990. For biographical information on Brown, see Kevin Fontenot, "Times Ain't Like They Used to Be: Rabbit Brown, New Orleans Songster," *Jazz Archivist* XIII (1998–1999): 1–6.

159. It was reissued on *People Take Warning! Murder Ballads and Disaster Songs, 1913–1938*, Tompkins Square TSQ 1875 (3CD), 2007. For a biography of Hutchison, see Russell, *Country Music Originals*, 60–62.

160. Available on Darby and Tarlton, *Complete Recordings*, Bear Family BCD 15764 (3CD), 1995. Biographical notes on him are in Russell, *Country Music Originals*, 63–64.

161. See W. K. McNeil, ed., *Southern Folk Ballads*, vol. II (Little Rock, AR: August House, 1988), 105–7. According to McNeil, a version of Seth Newton Mize's song was collected and transcribed by George W. Boswell from the singing of Mrs. James K. Nash in Hickman County, Tennessee, on June 21, 1951. She probably learned it from her mother Ollie Palestine Smith Stevens, who was born in 1873. See also Charles K. Wolfe, ed., *Folk Songs of Middle Tennessee: The George Boswell Collection* (Knoxville: University of Tennessee Press, 1997), 62–64.

162. Ed Kahn, liner notes to Darby and Tarlton, *Complete Recordings*, Bear Family BCD 15764 (3CD), 1995, 37.

163. White, *American Negro Folk-Songs*, 349.

164. Reissued on Charley Jordan, *Complete Recorded Works in Chronological Order—Volume 2 (1931–1934)*, Document Records DOCD-5098, 1992. The interpretation here is a revised version of my "Ocean Blues: A Textual Linguistic Analysis of 'Hi' Henry Brown's 'Titanic Blues,'" in *Ocean of Sounds*, ed. Pierangelo Castagneto (Turin, Italy: Otto Editore, 2007), 31–40, which offers a more racially oriented interpretation.

165. See Don Kent, liner notes to various artists, *St. Louis Town 1929–1933*, Yazoo Records L-1003, n.d. [ca. 1968]; and Eagle and LeBlanc, *Blues: A Regional Experience*, 186. Henry Townsend thought that Brown was Charley Jordan. See Townsend, *A Blues Life*, 70.

166. Chris Smith, booklet notes to *Charley Jordan: Complete Recorded Works in Chronological Order—Volume 2*.

167. Card playing before and after the collision with the iceberg, and until shortly before the sinking, is reported in most accounts of the disaster. The White Star Line normally allowed no card playing on Sundays, but an exception was made on this occasion. See Lord, *A Night to Remember*, 6, 9; Ward, *The Rough Guide to the Titanic*, 53, 108; Compton, *Titanic on Trial*, 38. Not surprisingly, it is reported that prayers were offered as the ship sank. See Lord, *A Night to Remember*, 57; Ward, *The Rough Guide to the Titanic*, 110.

168. This recording is held (shelf number 17814-A-1) at the Archives of Traditional Music, Indiana University, Bloomington, Indiana. I am grateful to Chris Smith for pointing it out. For a similar white recording, see Pete Seeger's "Deep Blue Sea" (Folkways FA 2452), available on Pete Seeger, *American Favorite Ballads, vol. 3*, Smithsonian Folkways SFW 40152, 2004. A music and lyric transcription of this song can be found in Ethel Raim, Irwin Silber, and Pete Seeger, *American Favorite Ballads. Tunes and Songs as Sung by Pete Seeger* (New York: Oak Publications, 1961), 76.

169. Saxon, Dreyer, and Tallant, *Gumbo Ya-Ya*, 373–74; Langston Hughes and Arna Bontemps, eds., *The Book of Negro Folklore* (New York: Dodd, Mead, 1958), 366–67; Langston Hughes,

Book of Negro Humor (New York: Dodd, Mead, 1966), 91–92; Roger D. Abrahams, *Deep Down in the Jungle: Negro Narrative Folklore from the Streets of Philadelphia* (Hatboro, VT: Folklore Associates, 1964), 116–23; Roger D. Abrahams, *Positively Black* (Englewood Cliffs, NJ: Prentice Hall, 1970), 44–45; Jackson, "The *Titanic* Toast," 205–23; William Labov, Paul Cohen, Clarence Robins, and John Lewis, "Toasts," in *Mother Wit from the Laughing Barrel: Readings in the Interpretation of Afro-American Folklore*, ed. Alan Dundes (Englewood Cliffs, NJ: Prentice Hall, 1973), 329–47; Neil A. Eddington, "Genital Superiority in Oakland Negro Folklore: A Theme," in *Mother Wit from the Laughing Barrel*, 646–48; Jackson, *Get Your Ass in the Water and Swim Like Me*, 180–96; Levine, *Black Culture and Black Consciousness*, 427–29; Lomax, *The Land Where the Blues Began*, 52–54; Steven Biel, *Down with the Old Canoe*, 107–8, 115–17. Issued recordings include "Shine and the Titanic," collected by Mack McCormick in 1959 and available on *Unexpurgated Folk Songs of Men* (un-numbered LP, 1960, reissued as Raglan Records R51); "Tom," "Titanic," recorded by Bruce Jackson at Ellis Unit, Texas Department of Corrections, March 24, 1966, issued on *Get Your Ass in the Water and Swim Like Me!*, Rounder LP 2014 (1976), CD 2014 (1998); "Slim," "Titanic," recorded by Bruce Jackson at Missouri Penitentiary, Jefferson City, June 24, 1964, issued on *Get Your Ass in the Water and Swim Like Me* CD with revised edition of the eponymous book (New York: Routledge, 2004); Rudy Ray Moore's variously titled versions of the toast with music, including, among others, "The Great Titanic," issued on *The Rudy Ray Moore Album: Eat Out More Often*, Kent Records KST001, 1970, reissued on CD by Traffic Entertainment Group, 2005, and "The Big Ship Wreck," issued on *The Third Rudy Ray Moore Album: The Cockpit*, Kent Records KST006, 1971; George Clinton, "Get Yo Ass in the Water and Swim Like Me," CD single, Douglas Music ADC 16, 1997. The last item is a recitation of the toast with musical accompaniment and a vocal chorus, probably issued to cash in on the release of the James Cameron film.

170. Hughes and Bontemps, *The Book of Negro Folklore*, 366–67.

171. Jay Gould's daughter appears in some versions of "Casey Jones," and has probably migrated from one of them to this toast.

172. Probably *sic* for "AT & T," the American Telephone and Telegraph Company, which at that time had a monopoly on American telephone services.

173. An exclusive establishment in Harlem (variously described as a bar, restaurant, and nightclub) owned by the boxer Sugar Ray Robinson.

174. See, among others, Abrahams, *Deep Down in the Jungle*, 112–16; Levine, *Black Culture and Black Consciousness*, 427–29; Smith, "The Titanic: A Case Study of Religious and Secular Attitudes in African American Song," 222–24.

175. White, *American Negro Folk-Songs*, 349–50. See also Oliver, *Songsters & Saints*, 93–96. Percy F. Dilling was white; born in January 1903, he was a teenager when he reported the song in 1919. He sang it for White at Trinity College, Durham, on December 5 of that year; see Newman Ivey White, ed., *The Frank C. Brown Collection of North Carolina Folklore, vol. V: The Music of the Folk Songs* (Durham, NC: Duke University Press, 1962), 286.

176. Newman Ivey White, "Racial Traits in the Negro Song," *Sewanee Review* 28, no. 3 (July 1920): 396–404.

177. A racist term, originally for a black man exhibiting stereotyped behavior, particularly in so-called "coon songs," but "coon" (an abbreviation of "raccoon") became applied to black people in general. See John Minton and David Evans, *"The Coon in the Box": A Global Folktale in African-American Tradition* (Helsinki, Finland: Academia Scientiarum Fennica, 2001).

178. Odum and Johnson, *Negro Workaday Songs*, 59–61. Odum and Johnson collected two more versions of "Travelin' Man," from a quartet in Dayton, Tennessee, and a North Carolina black youth. For another early variant see Odum, *Wings on My Feet*, 286.

179. Jackson, "The *Titanic* Toast," 211.

180. Abrahams, *Deep Down in the Jungle*, 114.

181. See Saxon, Dreyer, and Tallant, *Gumbo Ya-Ya*, 373–74; and Abrahams, *Deep Down in the Jungle*, 112–13.

182. The second recorded version is available at https://www.loc.gov/item/ihas.200197233/. For more on this version, as remembered and transcribed by Alan Lomax, see *The Land Where the Blues Began*, 53–54.

183. One was issued in 2015 on a 45 r.p.m. single (Soulful Torino Records STR012), and can be heard at https://www.youtube.com/watch?v=J_n6nFU7woc. This transcription is of take 5, first issued on various artists, *Titanic and 23 Other Unsinkable Sax Blasters*, Westside Records CD 539, 1998. Dave Penny's liner notes include biographical information on Williams.

184. The *Queen Mary* was a 1940s–1950s passenger ship. From 1938 to 1952 (partly thanks to World War II, which interrupted passenger crossings), she held the Blue Riband for the fastest westbound Atlantic crossing by a passenger liner.

185. Reissued on Johnny Otis Show/Snatch and the Poontangs, *Snatch and the Poontangs*, Ace Records CDCHD855, 2002.

186. Cousin Joe, *Relaxin' in New Orleans*, Great Southern Records 11011, 1985, reissued on Cousin Joe, *I Never Harmed an Onion: Rare and Unreleased Recordings from Great Southern Records 1985*, Night Train International NTI CD 7159, 2008. For his biography, see Pleasant "Cousin Joe" Joseph and Harriet Ottenheimer, *Cousin Joe: Blues from New Orleans* (Chicago and London: University of Chicago Press, 1987; reprint: Gretna: Pelican Publishing, 2012). The month in which "What a Tragedy" was recorded is uncertain: July 1/2 is reported on the cover of the original LP, and October 1/2 is reported in Joseph and Ottenheimer. Cousin Joe appears to have recorded two sessions for Great Southern Records. Bob Ballard located the wreck on September 1, and the October date seems more likely. I am grateful to Harriet Ottenheimer and Chris Smith for discussion of this puzzle.

187. Smith, "The Titanic: A Case Study of Religious and Secular Attitudes in African American Song," 226.

188. Ford and McGrath, *The Blues Discography 1971–2000*, 72. Scanty biographical information on Buford is available in the liner notes to various artists, *Virginia Traditions: Southwest Virginia Blues*, Blue Ridge Institute BRI 008, reissued on Global Village Music CD 1008, 1990.

189. See "Bobby Buford, The Titanic at Home in Pulaski" at https://www.youtube.com/watch?v=TDojkmEf-Yk.

190. Available on Fruteland Jackson, *I Claim Nothing but the Blues*, Electro-Fi 3364, 2000.

191. Three white singers recorded songs in the immediate aftermath of this catastrophe: Bob Miller cut "Crash of the Akron" (Columbia 15782-D) in New York City on April 5, 1933 (the day after the disaster); Frank Luther's "The Akron Disaster" (Banner 32748) was recorded in New York City on April 10, 1933; and Frank Welling made "The Ill Fated Akron" (Champion 16588) in Richmond, Indiana, on April 13, 1933. Miller's recording is reissued on *People Take Warning! Murder Ballads and Disaster Songs, 1913–1938*, Tompkins Square TSQ 1875 (3CD), 2007.

192. For a thorough account of the disaster, including the well-known film footage, see https://en.wikipedia.org/wiki/Hindenburg_disaster, where Herbert Morrison's famous WLS radio broadcast is also available.

193. The song is available on Wilf Carter, *Cowboy Songs*, Bear Family BCD 15939 BCD (8CD and book), 1997. For biographical information on Carter, see Russell, *Country Music Originals*, 175–76.

194. First released on Elektra and Document LPs, these recordings are available on Leadbelly, *Nobody Knows the Trouble I've Seen*, Rounder Records CD 1098, 1994, and Leadbelly, *The Smithsonian Folkways Collection*, Smithsonian Folkways SFW CD 40201, 2015. For another discussion of the song that regards it as a more considered composition, see Wolfe and Lornell, *The Life and Legend of Leadbelly*, 208.

195. For further information on this disaster, see http://www.gendisasters.com/west-virginia /5379/bartley-wv-coal-mine-gas-explosion-disaster-jan-1940. For the amendment that brought monthly payment of survivors' benefits forward from January 1, 1942, to January 1, 1940, see "Senate Report No. 734, Social Security Act Amendments of 1939," https://www.finance.senate .gov/imo/media/doc/SRpt76-734.pdf.

196. For George Korson's work as a folklorist, see Green, *Only A Miner*, and Chris Smith, "Cheer the Union Travelers: The Field Recordings of George Korson," *Blues & Rhythm* 176 (February 2003): 10–11.

197. Jenks's song is transcribed in George Korson, *Coal Dust on the Fiddle: Songs and Stories of the Bituminous Industry* (Philadelphia: University of Pennsylvania Press, 1943; reprint: Hatboro, VT: Folklore Associates, 1965), 274–75, and is held at the American Folklife Center, Library of Congress. My thanks to Judith Gray of the American Folklife Center for its accession number. Biographical information on Jenks may be found in Korson, *Coal Dust on the Fiddle*, 447–48.

198. J. Roderick Moore, "Mack Jenks, Union Bard," in *Goldenseal* 3, no. 2 (April-June 1977): 25–34, reprinted in Ken Sullivan, ed., *The Goldenseal Book of the West Virginia Mine Wars* (Missoula, MT: Pictorial Histories Publishing, 1991), and available at http://www.wvgenweb .org/wvcoal/mack7.html, 7.

199. Jenks probably derived the tune from "Only One Step More" by the Blue Sky Boys (Bluebird B8552, Montgomery Ward M8670, February 5, 1940).

200. These songs are available on various artists, *Coal Digging Blues: Songs of West Virginia Miners*, West Virginia University Press Sound Archive, WVUPRESS-SA 8, 2006. Their transcriptions are in Korson, *Coal Dust on the Fiddle*, 274 and 308–9. "Cheer the Union Travelers" (AFS 12011-A-10) was sung by the Rising Star Quartet, formed by coal miners who were also members of the Royal Baptist Church in Caples, West Virginia. Its lyrics adapt the popular gospel song "Let Us Cheer the Weary Traveler." Song leader B. H. Jenkins's monologue about the Bartley mine disaster is probably the part Korson refers to as "made . . . the night before the recording."

201. All LP and CD issues of this group credit the Evening Breezes Sextet, as does Korson, 138. Korson, 274, credits this song to the Evening Breeze Sextet.

202. Dolores Riggs Davis, "A Time to Weep—Bartley 1940," posted to the *Logan, WV History and Nostalgia* website on March 27, 2011. See https://www.oocities.org/heartland/Ridge/4478/ weep.htm, accessed June 8, 2020.

203. The song and its lyric transcription were uploaded at https://www.youtube.com/ watch?v=mihrEQwDOgU.

204. This is a revised and abridged version of my essay of the same title in *Nobody Knows Where the Blues Come From: Lyrics and History*, 76–107. The following appeared just before or after that book's publication: Work, Jones, and Adams, *Lost Delta Found*, especially 1–2, 9, 10, 14, 291–93; Jim O'Neal, "The Natchez Burning: Mississippi Blues Trail Marker," http://www .msbluestrail.org, 2008, and http://www.stackhouse-bluesoterica.blogspot.com; Vincent Joos,

"Natchez Fire," *ABS Magazine* 25 (February 2010, originally published in 2009): 10–21 (in French); Vincent Joos, "A Profile of African American Remembrance in a Small Mississippi Town" (thesis, Master of Arts in the Folklore Program, University of North Carolina at Chapel Hill, 2011), available at https://core.ac.uk/download/pdf/210600118.pdf; Luigi Monge, "The Natchez Burnin'," in *Howlin' Wolf. I'm the Wolf. Testi Commentati* (Rome, Italy: Arcana, 2010), 322–30 (in Italian); Scott Barretta, "The Natchez Blues," *Living Blues* 210 (December 2010): 13–14; Russell Shor, "Walter Barnes and the Natchez Fire," *Frog Blues and Jazz Annual* 2, ed. Paul Swinton (2011): 32–36; Preston Lauterbach, *The Chitlin' Circuit and the Road to Rock 'n' Roll* (New York: Norton, 2011), 66–72; Luigi Monge, "Natchez Rhythm Club Fire," in *The Mississippi Encyclopedia*, eds. Ted Ownby and Charles Reagan Wilson, associate eds. Ann J. Abadie, Odie Lindsey, and James G. Thomas, Jr. (Jackson: University Press of Mississippi, 2017), 913. The DVD *The Rhythm Club Fire*, a 30-minute documentary directed by Bryan Burch, is available at http://rhythmclubfire.com.

205. John R. Williams, "Natchez Quivers in Stunned Grief as Dead Are Buried," *Pittsburgh Courier*, May 4, 1940, 1–2.

206. David Kellum, "Identity of Scores of Victims Still Lacking," *Chicago Defender*, April 27, 1940, 1.

207. According to a wire story reporting the words of elevator operator Ernest Wright, the cigarette was discarded intentionally. The arsonist was one girl who was heard telling a friend: "Now you did it. You set the place on fire." United Press wire story, *Nashville Banner* (April 24, 1940), 1, as reported in Work, Jones, and Adams, *Lost Delta Found*, "Appendix 1: A Spark in Natchez," 291–93, 328.

208. Dwight "Gatemouth" Moore, one of the band's vocalists, said that he survived because he was on the band bus, talking to a girl between sets. See Johnny Otis, "The Otis Tapes 4: Dwight 'Gatemouth' Moore," *Blues Unlimited* 109 (August-September 1974): 13; and Dave Penny and Tony Burke, "Stand Up and Shout the Blues: Dwight 'Gatemouth' Moore," *Blues & Rhythm* 15 (December 1985): 4. Rev. Moore confirmed this to me in an April 18, 2002, interview at the Comfort Inn, Yazoo City, Mississippi, published as "La Lunga Fede Musicale: Intervista al Reverendo Arnold Dwight 'Gatemouth' Moore" (Unshakeable Faith in Music: Interview with Reverend Arnold Dwight "Gatemouth" Moore), *World Music Magazine* 69 (November-December 2004): 34–35. Former Memphis Jug Band members Willie Shade and Charlie Burse said that the Rhythm Club had booked them as members of a novelty band. They escaped death because they were delayed by a flat tire. Willie Borum claimed to have been with Shade's group, but he cannot be relied on; his description of the building is inaccurate, and he named Charley Patton (d. 1934) as among the musicians who were playing. See Samuel Charters, *The Country Blues* (New York: Da Capo, 1975), 126–27, originally published by Rinehart, 1959; and Bengt Olsson, *Memphis Blues and Jug Bands* (London: Studio Vista, 1970), 70.

209. The songs were reissued on various artists, *Black Secular Vocal Groups—Volume 3 (1923–1940)*, Document Records DOCD-5604, 1998.

210. Ziólek-Sowińska, *Images of the Apocalypse in African American Blues and Spirituals*, 83.

211. Ziólek-Sowińska, *Images of the Apocalypse in African American Blues and Spirituals*, 83.

212. In October 1940, John and Ruby T. Lomax were doing fieldwork in Natchez. Mrs. Lomax wrote to her family that "any songs besides spirituals are hard to get here; for that terrible dance hall fire of several months ago has sent the Negro population to the mourners' bench."

213. The two sides were reissued on various artists, *Chicago Blues—Volume 2 (1939-1944)*, Document Records DOCD-5444, 1996.

214. For an explanation of the contrastive/associative structural principle in blues lyrics, see Evans, *Big Road Blues*, 58, 146, 219, 318.

215. See Work, Jones, and Adams, *Lost Delta Found*, especially 1–2, 5–6, 13, 319; and Bruce Nemerov, "John Wesley Work III: Field Recordings of Southern Black Folk Music, 1935–1942," *Tennessee Folklore Society Bulletin* LIII, no. 3 (fall 1987): 82–103, especially 89 and 91. See also Robert Gordon, *Can't Be Satisfied: The Life and Times of Muddy Waters* (Boston: Little, Brown, 2002), 35–36.

216. See endnote 212 above.

217. Despite the presence of "Theatre" (spelling *sic*) on the Library of Congress file card, when Haffer announces the title of the song, he does not use the word. At the Library of Congress, I am indebted to Judith A. Gray, Reference Specialist at the American Folklife Center, and Christel Schmidt, Public Services Assistant in the Motion Picture, Broadcast and Recorded Sound Division, for their invaluable help and patience.

218. "Image 3, Alan Lomax Collection, Manuscripts, Mississippi, Tennessee, and Arkansas, 1941-1942: 'The Natchez Fire Dissaster'" [*sic*] at https://www.loc.gov/resource/afc2004004 .ms090438/?st=gallery.

219. My previous lyric transcription used a different verse structure. See Monge, "Death by Fire," 86–88.

220. See Work, Jones, and Adams, *Lost Delta Found*, 113–17; Lomax, *The Land Where the Blues Began*, 48–58, 495–96; and prob. Lewis W. Jones, typescript report of Coahoma County Project (Nashville: Fisk University, ca. 1943; courtesy of Alan Lomax Archive). For additional biographical information on Haffer, see Monge, "Death by Fire," 89.

221. Charles Haffer Jr. interviewed by Alan Lomax, Clarksdale, July 23, 1942, AFS 6623-B-2.

222. Compare "Dance Hall Fire Trap Was Once a Church," *Chicago Defender*, May 4, 1940, 1; and "This Mother Keeps Her Daughters Home at Night," *Chicago Defender*, May 4, 1940, 8.

223. The belief that the dance hall had been a church was widespread and reported in various sources such as "Dance Hall Fire Trap Was Once a Church," *Chicago Defender*, May 4, 1940, 8; O. C. W. Taylor, "Disaster Suspects Released," *Pittsburgh Courier*, May 4, 1940, 2; and "240 at Dance Die in Fire," *Washington Afro-American*, April 27, 1940, 1. Rev. Utah Smith also held this belief, and on the Sunday after the fire, he was criticized by the congregation at a church he was visiting. See Thelma Watson, "Natchez Catastrophe Blamed on Dancing, Saints Criticize," *Plaindealer* (Kansas City, KS), May 3, 1940. Unprompted, Ethel Lee Porter and Frank R. Robinson, two survivors of the fire, both denied that the Rhythm Club had been a church when I interviewed them in Natchez, respectively on April 20, 2002, at the NAPAC (Natchez Association for the Preservation of Afro-American Culture) and April 21, 2002, at the Copiah-Lincoln Community College.

224. For a thorough discussion of dancing and dance halls as the "devil's lair" according to Christian evangelists, see Adam Gussow, "Devil Dance Blues," in *Beyond the Crossroads: The Devil and the Blues Tradition* (Chapel Hill: University of North Carolina Press, 2017), 97–106.

225. Howlin' Wolf's song was reissued on *The Real Folk Blues/More Real Folk Blues*, MCA Records 088112 820, 2002. For his biography, see James Segrest and Mark Hoffman, *Moanin' at Midnight: The Life and Times of Howlin' Wolf* (New York: Thunder Mouth's Press, 2005). For an analysis of his lyrics, see Monge, *Howlin' Wolf. I'm the Wolf. Testi Commentati*. In November

1968 in Chicago, Howlin' Wolf recorded an unissued "Natchez Is Burning," presumably a cover of his earlier version, for Chess Records' subsidiary Cadet. It had been intended for inclusion in the "psychedelic" ("dogshit," in Wolf's estimation) LP *The Howlin' Wolf Album* (Cadet Concept LPS-319).

226. This line may have been inspired by the opening stanza of John Lee "Sonny Boy" Williamson's "Bad Luck Blues" (Bluebird B8265, July 21, 1939), the account of the killing of a cousin of Sonny Boy's: "People, did you hear about the bad luck, the bad luck that happened just about six months ago."

227. During one of Howlin' Wolf's tours in the South, he asked guitarist Hubert Sumlin to drive him to the site of the disaster, and they "stared at the remains of the Rhythm Club." See Segrest and Hoffman, *Moanin' at Midnight*, 277.

228. I am very grateful to Chris Smith for alerting me to, and providing a copy of, this rare field recording collected by Dr. Harry Oster.

229. Ziółek-Sowińska, *Images of the Apocalypse in African American Blues and Spirituals*, 77.

230. Reissued on *Burning Hell*, Original Blues Classics OBCCD-555, 1992.

231. This version was released on Galaxy LP (8)201 and has been reissued on John Lee Hooker, *The Galaxy Album*, Soul Jam Records 600876, 2016.

232. Reissued (as "The Great Fire of Natchez") on John Lee Hooker, *Live at Newport*, Vanguard Records VCD 79703-2, 2002.

233. David Evans, email to the author, August 19, 2020.

234. The word "record" does not only mean "phonograph record" but is a common expression for a song.

235. David Evans, email to the author, August 19, 2020.

236. Issued on the compilation *Keep It to Yourself: Arkansas Blues, Volume 1: Solo Performances*, Rooster Blues Records R7605, 1983, which was reissued with the same title on Stackhouse Records SRC-1910, 2006. Jim O'Neal, in "The Natchez Burning: Mississippi Blues Trail Marker," writes that the song "was recorded by Louis Guida in 1976 as part of a Bicentennial field recording project, and the title on the original tape was 'Madison, Mississippi,' because that's what Wright is singing, rather than 'Natchez, Mississippi.' (Or it could just as well have been 'Mattson, Mississippi.') I changed it on the album to 'The Natchez Burning' because that's what the song was."

237. Recorded live, date and place unknown, and issued on the King Bees, *Carolina Bound*, Original High John Records, no #, 2011.

238. Issued on Elmo Williams and Hezekiah Early, *Takes One to Know One*, Fat Possum Records 0313-2, 1997.

239. Joos, "A Profile of African American Remembrance in a Small Mississippi Town," 26.

240. Frank Kossen, "Obituaries: Elmo Williams," *Living Blues* 245 (October 2016): 74. See also Scott Barretta, "Elmore Williams: All I've Had All My Life Nearabouts Is Blues," *Living Blues* 210 (December 2010): 16.

241. Joos, "A Profile of African American Remembrance in a Small Mississippi Town," 26–27.

242. Among white covers are the Groundhogs, "Natchez Burning," London, June 1969, Liberty 83253, reissued on *Blues Obituary*, BGO BGOCD6, 1997; and Captain Beefheart, "Natchez Burning," Boston, 1972, a forty-four-second fragment, apparently from a radio interview, first issued on *Captain Beefheart and His Magic Band: Grow Fins—Rarities (1965–1982)*, Revenant 210, 1999.

243. Issued on Rooster Blues Records R-60-C (audiocassette), 1994. Big Jack Johnson confirmed to the author that he was singing about real events and people, and that he drew

inspiration from Howlin' Wolf's song: "Ice was everywhere. It broke down posts. I thought it was something to write about and that's what I did. . . . I just wanted my voice to sound like [Howlin' Wolf's]. . . . I wanted to go as deep as he did. It's a great song." See Marino Grandi and Luigi Monge, "The Oil Man Si Racconta," *Il Blues* 103 (June 2008): 13. I am indebted to Edward Komara for providing information on this song and a transcription of its lyrics.

244. Little Whitt and Big Bo, *Moody Swamp Blues*, Vent Records VR 30009, 1995. For the definition of "downhome blues" as a better alternative to "country blues," see Jeff Todd Titon, *Early Downhome Blues: A Musical and Cultural Analysis*, 2nd ed. (Chapel Hill and London: University of North Carolina Press, 1994), xv–xviii.

245. "Four Negro Families Rescued from Burning Dwelling," *St. Louis Post-Dispatch*, May 25, 1929, 3; and "Negroes Flee from Fire," *St. Louis Post-Dispatch*, January 3, 1930, 15.

246. The first occurrence is in "Railroad Blues" by Floyd Canada, collected by Walter Prescott Webb in Beeville, Texas, and printed in *Journal of American Folk-Lore* 28 (1915): 293.

247. Censored in the original.

248. Lafcadio Hearn, "Levee Life," in *Children of the Levee*, ed. O. W. Frost (Lexington: University of Kentucky Press, 1957), 66–67. Originally published as "Levee Life/Haunts and Pastimes of the Roustabouts/Their Original Songs and Peculiar Dances," *Cincinnati Commercial*, March 17, 1876, 2:1–4.

249. See "Shawneetown, IL Steamer James Jackson Explodes Sep 1851," researched and transcribed by Stu Beitler, at http://www.gendisasters.com/illinois/5852/shawneetown-il -steamer-james-jackson-explodes-sep-1851.

250. See Michael E. Banasik, ed., *Cavaliers of the Brush: Quantrill and His Men* (Iowa City: Press of the Camp Pope Bookshop, 2003), 66.

251. For white songs on sea disasters, see Meade, Spottswood, and Meade, *Country Music Sources*, 70–72; and Laws, *Native American Balladry*, 161–74, 263–65.

252. Mary Wheeler, *Steamboatin' Days: Folksongs of the River Packet Era* (Freeport, NY: Books for Libraries Press, 1969), 40–41, 41–43, 43–46. Originally published by Louisiana State University Press in 1944.

253. Available (as "The Carrier Line") on the CD various artists, *Afro-American Folk Music from Tate and Panola Counties, Mississippi*, Rounder Records 1515–2, 2000. For historical background to the song, see James W. Silver, "Paul Bunyan Comes to Mississippi," *Journal of Mississippi History* XIX, no. 2 (April 1957): 93–119.

254. For information on Sid Hemphill, see George Mitchell, *Blow My Blues Away* (Baton Rouge: Louisiana State University Press, 1971), 88–90; Lomax, *The Land Where the Blues Began*, 314–26, 333–34; Jessie Mae Hemphill, "Ain't Got Tears to Cry With," *Living Blues* 100 (November/ December 1991): 16–21; Evans, liner notes to *Afro-American Folk Music from Tate and Panola Counties, Mississippi*, 34–39; Jared Snyder, "Hemphill, Sid" and "Fife and Drums," in *Encyclopedia of the Blues*, vol. 1, ed. Edward Komara, 419 and 323 respectively; and Jim O'Neal, "Sid Hemphill: Hill Country Patriarch," *Living Blues* 253 (February 2018): 38–41.

255. See "Interview" (AFS 6670-A-2) on various artists, *Rock Me, Shake Me: Field Recordings Vol. 15, Mississippi 1941–1942*, Document Records DOCD-5672, 2002.

256. Mary Evelyn Starr, comment, posted April 26, 2013, on [Nathan Salsburg,] "Sid Hemphill and Mr. Carrier's Line," at https://roothogordie.wordpress.com/2009/11/26/sid-hemphill-and -mr-carriers-line/.

257. "Lumber Men Strike" and "Strike Settled," *Jackson Daily News*, August 7, 1905, 4, and August 11, 1905, 4, respectively.

258. Though the disaster it describes caused no fatalities, the inclusion of this song is justified by the fact it is the only disaster song composed at the specific request of white people and deals with the African Americans' tense relationship with white people in a period of economic depression and social unrest.

259. Hemphill makes a mistake in the first line of this stanza, and corrects it, but repeats the mistake in the third line.

260. See "Eight Negro Excursionists Killed in a Head-on Collision at Hamlet," *Charlotte Daily Observer*, July 28, 1911, transcribed at http://www.gendisasters.com/north-carolina/6996/hamlet-nc-train-wreck-jul-1911.

261. See Newman Ivey White, gen. ed., *The Frank C. Brown Collection of North Carolina Folklore* (Durham: Duke University Press, 1952–1961): vol. II: *Folk Ballads from North Carolina*, eds. Henry M. Belden and Arthur Palmer Hudson, 1952, 674–76; vol. IV: *The Music of the Ballads*, ed. Jan Philip Schinhan, 1957, 318–19. See also Levine, *Black Culture and Black Consciousness*, 258; and Cohen, *Long Steel Rail*, 274.

262. See "Pittsburgh, PA Disastrous Gas Explosion, Nov 1927" at http://www.gendisasters.com/pennsylvania/5164/pittsburgh%2C-pa-disastrous-gas-explosion%2C-nov-1927. For newspaper coverage, see "21 Killed in Gas Tank Explosion at Pittsburgh; 600 Hurt, 13 Missing; Ruins Dynamited in Hunt for Bodies," *New York Times*, November 15, 1927, 1:8, 2; "Pittsburgh Dead 26; Many Still Missing," *New York Times*, November 16, 1927, 27:3; "Suffering in Wake of Blast," *Pittsburgh Courier*, November 19, 1927, 1, 8; "28th Blast Victim Dies in Pittsburgh," *New York Times*, November 25, 1927, 14:4.

263. Reissued on Rev. Edward W. Clayborn (The Guitar Evangelist), *Complete Recorded Works 1926–1928 in Chronological Order*, Document Records DOCD-5155, 1993. For its release date, see Thygesen and Shor, *Vocalion 1000 and Brunswick 7000 Race Series*, 51.

264. On his 1918 draft card, Clayborn gave his birth year as 1880 and his race as "Indian" (Bob Eagle, post to the prewar blues list, February 16, 2007). On his World War II "old men's draft" card, he gives an 1888 birthdate. The Social Security Death Index shows 1885.

265. Reissued on Rev. J. M. Gates, *Complete Recorded Works in Chronological Order—Vol. 6 (1928–1929)*, Document Records DOCD-5457, 1996. See also "Two Workers Lose Lives and Third Is Badly Hurt When Buried Under Slide," *Atlanta Constitution*, February 2, 1928. This article is reproduced in Chris Smith, "A Bank That Never Fails (Rev. J.M. Gates)," in column "Words Words Words," *Blues & Rhythm* 254 (November 2010): 24.

266. The most thorough account of the event, and of the woman who wrote and recorded the only song about it, is Jack Neely, "The Moan: A Forgotten Fire, Remembered in a Song," in *Knoxville: This Obscure Prismatic City* (Charleston, SC: History Press, 2009), 63–76. See also R. R. Macleod, *Document Blues-5* (Edinburgh, UK: PAT, 1998), 46–48.

267. Reissued on various artists, *Rare Country Blues—Volume 1 (1928–1937)*, Document Records DOCD-5170, 1993. Leola Manning was accompanied by her future husband, Eugene Ballinger, on guitar, and pianist Gace Haynes. See Ted Olson and Tony Russell, *The Knoxville Sessions 1929–1930*, 46, 89–90, in CD boxed set Bear Family BCD16097, 2016.

268. Neely, "The Moan: A Forgotten Fire, Remembered in a Song," 11.

269. See Jeff Stern, "Chicago, 1934: The Union Stock Yards Fire," *Firehouse Magazine*, September 1, 2009; and "Catastrophe: Chicago Fire," *Time*, May 28, 1934, quoted in full by Chris Smith in "Stockyard Fire," in column "Words Words Words," *Blues & Rhythm* 201 (August 2005): 21.

270. Tampa Red's real name was Hudson Woodbridge; he was also known as Hudson Whittaker, which was the name of his mother's family.

271. Reissued on Tampa Red, *Complete Recorded Works 1926–1928 in Chronological Order—Volume 6 (1934–1935)*, Document Records DOCD-5206, 1993.

272. Available on Josh White, *Complete Recorded Works 1929 to March 1940 in Chronological Order—Volume 3 (1935–1940)*, Document Records DOCD-5196, 1993. White recorded two more versions of the song, both titled "Silicosis Blues." The first, on American Folklife Center disc 6094-A, was made at a December 20, 1940 concert commemorating the 75th anniversary of the Thirteenth Amendment, in the Coolidge Auditorium of the Library of Congress, Washington, DC. It is available on the Golden Gate Quartet and Josh White, *Freedom*, Bridge CD 9114, 2002. The second commercial version (Elektra EKL 193) was recorded in 1960 in Chicago, and was reissued on Josh White, *Elektra Years*, Rhino Handmade RHM2 7879 (2CD), 2004. It appears that White considered the topic to be of continuing relevance to the labor movement.

273. Among the several 1930s articles on silicosis, see "NJ Begins Study of Disease," *New York Times Index*, October 24, 1933, 23:5; "Dr. F.G. Banting Invents Device to Free Mine Air of Particles Causing Disease," *New York Times Index*, November 2, 1933, 22:1; "B.F. Tillison Urges Use of X-Ray to Combat Disease," *New York Times Index*, February 20, 1934, 11:3; "Bill Offered to Bring Disease under Terms of New York State Workmen's Compensation Insurance Law," *New York Times Index*, March, 30, 1934, 7:3; "Gov. Lehman Vetoes Bill Bringing Silicosis under Workmen's Compensation Insurance," *New York Times Index*, May 16, 1935, 8:4; "L.H. Pink Announces Temporary Workmen's Compensation Insurance," *New York Times Index*, August 17, 1935, 24:6.

274. For an account of the tragedy, see Catherine Venable Moore, "The Book of the Dead: In Fayette County, West Virginia, Expanding the Document of Disaster," *Oxford American* 94 (fall 2016), available at https://www.oxfordamerican.org/magazine/item/1049-the-book-of-the-dead; Martin Cherniack, *The Hawk's Nest Incident: America's Worst Industrial Disaster* (New Haven, CT: Yale University Press, 1986); West Virginia Department of Arts, Culture, and History, http://www.wvculture.org/history/notewv/hawksnest.html, which includes a list of books and articles on the disaster; and "The Hawk's Nest Tunnel Tragedy: The Forgotten Victims of America's Worst Industrial Disaster" at https://ehstoday.com/industrial-hygiene/hawk-s-nest-tunnel-tragedy-forgotten-victims-america-s-worst-industrial-disaster, which states that "[S]ome 5,000 men worked on the project from March 1930 to December 1931, earning 25 cents an hour and working 60 hours a week." Josh White's "six bits a day" (75 cents) is an exaggeration of the low pay offered, which is not to suggest that the $2.50 a day—assuming a six-day working week—actually paid was adequate. For the death toll, I have relied on Moore, "The Book of the Dead," and on the Hawk's Nest Tunnel Disaster marker, viewable online at https://en.wikipedia.org/wiki/Hawks_Nest_Tunnel_disaster#/media/File:Hawks_Nest_Tunnel_Disaster.jpg. The Hawk's Nest Tunnel was first linked to the Josh White song by Archie Green in his liner notes to various artists, *Hard Times*, Rounder Records LP 4007, 1975.

275. Articles published before Josh White's recording include: Albert Maltz, "Man on the Road," *New Masses*, January 8, 1935; Bernard (a.k.a. Philippa) Allen, "Two Thousand Dying on A Job," *New Masses*, January 22, 1935; "Tunneling through an Atmosphere of Deadly Dust," *Newsweek*, January 25, 1936, 33; "Village of the Living Dead," *Literary Digest*, January 25, 1936, 6. See also US Congress, Subcommittee of the Committee on Labor, *An Investigation Related to Health Conditions of Workers Employed in the Construction and Maintenance of Public Utilities,*

74th Congress, 2nd session, January 1936, reprinted in Jim Comstock, ed., *West Virginia Heritage*, vol. 7 (Richwood: West Virginia Heritage Foundation, 1972), 1–3.

276. Elijah Wald, *Josh White: Society Blues* (Amherst: University of Massachusetts Press, 2000).

277. Wald, *Josh White*, 45. See also Elijah Wald, "Josh White and the Protest Blues," *Living Blues* 158 (July–August 2001): 36–42, esp. 38, also available at https://www.elijahwald.com/joshprotest.html; and Ronald D. Cohen and Dave Samuelson, liner notes to various artists, *Songs for Political Action: Folk Music, Topical Songs and the American Left: 1926–1953*, Bear Family Records BCD 15720 JL (10CD), 1996, 56, 59, where Miller is thought to have drawn inspiration for the mining-themed song after supervising Aunt Molly Jackson's 1931 Columbia 15000-D recording session. I am grateful to Joel Collin Roberts for exchanging information and opinions about the song's credits.

278. Miller had worked as an A&R man for Columbia and OKeh, and may have continued in this role at ARC after Grigsby-Grunow, which owned Columbia and OKeh, went into liquidation in 1934.

279. Available on Josh White, *Complete Recorded Works 1929 to March 1940 in Chronological Order—Volume 3 (1935–1940)*, Document Records DOCD-5196, 1993.

280. "20 Negro Convicts Killed, 2 Burned in Locked Cage on Transport Truck, Scottsboro (Alabama); Gov. Graves Orders Investigation," *New York Times Index*, February 1, 1936. I am greatly indebted to David Evans for alerting me to this information, and for sending newspaper articles covering the event.

281. "Truck Blaze Kills 20 Negro Convicts; Prisoners Being Transported in a Locked Vehicle Are Trapped Near Scottsboro. Gasoline Can Exploded. Only Two Victims, Both Badly Burned, Were Rescued by White Guards," *New York Times*, February 1, 1936, 3.

282. *Dadeville Record*, February 6, 1936, 8.

283. The "Scottsboro Boys" were nine young African American hobos, groundlessly charged in 1931 with raping two white women who were hoboing on the same freight train. They were held at Scottsboro, Alabama. Despite clear evidence of their innocence, eight of them were initially sentenced to death (a thirteen-year-old boy was acquitted). The American left fought for their release in further trials, but they collectively spent over one hundred years in confinement. The last of the "Scottsboro Boys" was not freed until May 1950. For a thorough treatment of this *cause célèbre* and its topical songs, see Guido van Rijn, "The Scottsboro Boys," in *Roosevelt's Blues: African-American Blues and Gospel Songs on FDR* (Jackson: University Press of Mississippi, 1997), 131–38.

284. "Ala. Convicts Burned Alive in Wheeled Cage; Plan Probe; Neglect Charge Made in Burning," *Pittsburgh Courier*, February 8, 1936, 1, 4.

285. J. W. Harrington, "See Plot in Burning at Scottsboro; Prison Head Fixes Blame for 22 Deaths in Flames," *Chicago Defender*, February 8, 1936, 1:1, 4:6.

286. "Dixie Prison Cages Cold These Days," *Baltimore Afro-American*, February 8, 1936, 1.

287. "Suspends 3 in 20 Negro Deaths," *New York Times*, February 8, 1936, 18; "Damages Awarded for Negro Deaths," *Selma Times-Journal*, February 21, 1936, 1, 3.

288. White recorded another version of "No More Ball and Chain" as "Ball and Chain Blues" (Elektra EKL 114) in New York on December 20–21, 1956. It is available on Jesse Fuller and Josh White, *Four Classic Albums*, Avid Entertainment EMSC 1344 (2CD), 2019, where the song is credited as "arr. White."

289. Meade, with Spottswood and Meade, *Country Music Sources*, 507–8.

290. The song is held in the Frank C. Brown Collection of North Carolina Songs at the Library of Congress in Washington, DC, and, unlike some of Love's other songs, is only cursorily mentioned by the editors in Brown's anthology. For coverage of the historical event, availability of the recording, and biographical information on Will Love, see Kevin Kehrberg and Jeffrey A. Keith, "Somebody Died, Babe: A Musical Cover-Up of Racism, Violence, and Greed," *The Bitter Southerner* (August 4, 2020), at https://bittersoutherner.com/2020/somebody-died-babe-a-musical-coverup-of-racism-violence-and-greed.

CHAPTER THREE: INFESTATIONS, PANDEMICS, EPIDEMICS AND DISEASES

1. Selected literature on the boll weevil includes: Arthur Palmer Hudson, "Mister Boll Weevil," in *Folksongs of Mississippi and Their Background* (Chapel Hill: University of North Carolina Press, 1936), 199–200; Frank Luther, *Americans and Their Songs* (New York: Harper and Brothers, 1942), 257ff.; Alton Chester Morris, *Folksongs of Florida* (Gainesville: University of Florida Press, 1950), 188–90; Paul Oliver, "Sources of American Folk Song (3): Boll Weevil Blues," *Music Mirror* 1, July 1954, 35–37; Oliver, *Songsters and Saints*, 250–51, 254, 269; Levine, *Black Culture and Black Consciousness*, 240–41; Portia Naomi Crawford, "A Study of Negro Folk Songs from Greensboro, North Carolina and Surrounding Towns," *North Carolina Folklore* XVI (1968): 82–83; Chris Plail, "The New Boll-Weavil Song" and "The Passing of a Folk-hero," *Shindig: The BBC Folk Club Magazine* (October 1967): 12–13; Joe Dan Boyd, "Ballad of the Black Sharecropper," *Farm Journal* (January 1969): 39; Joe Dan Boyd, "'Boll Weevil': The Ballad That Followed a Bug!," sixty-five-page unpublished typed manuscript; Govenar and Lornell, *The Blues Come to Texas*, 289–90, 408.

2. For the boll weevil infestation itself, I have relied on James C. Giesen, *Boll Weevil Blues: Cotton, Myth, and Power in the American South* (Chicago and London: University of Chicago Press, 2011). This account accurately and exhaustively outlines the historical impact of the pest, but deals inadequately with songs about it, on 37–42, 95–97, and 165–68. See also Richard Polenberg, "The Boll Weevil (1920s)," in *Hear My Sad Story*, 233–39, 280–81.

3. Joan Houston Hall, ed., *Dictionary of American Regional English*, vol. 5, Sl–Z (Cambridge, MA: Belknap Press of Harvard University Press, 2012), 223.

4. Gates Thomas, "South Texas Negro Work-Songs: Collected and Uncollected," *Publications of the Texas Folklore Society*, vol. V (1926); reprint: J. Frank Dobie, ed., *Rainbow in the Morning* (Hatboro, VT: Folklore Associates, 1965), 173–75.

5. In Gates Thomas's article, a "sharp-shooter" is defined as "a small insect like a midge, contemporary with the boll weevil and once thought as harmful."

6. Controversies have arisen over the way most singers sang this line (see Sid Hemphill's "The Boll Weevil") where it is the farmer who says that the boll weevil's neck is red. As originally transcribed by Gates Thomas, it makes more sense that the line began "Boll weevil says to the farmer." It is likely that the two characters in this line were later reversed because of the risks involved in singing it to white listeners. In John A. Lomax and Alan Lomax, "De Ballit of de Boll Weevil," in *American Ballads and Folk Songs*, 113, it is a black man who asks the question to the boll weevil ("De n----r say to de Boll Weevil / "What makes yo' head so red?"). The Lomaxes wrote in a footnote that "[t]he Negro must have his rhyme. He is thinking of the red-headed peckerwood." In fact, besides its literal meaning, the latter term also connotes "a very poor

white Anglo-Saxon Protestant," and was used by Black speakers as a derogatory term for a white person. See Major, *Juba to Jive*, 342–43. For a summary of the controversy, see Boyd, "'Boll Weevil': The Ballad That Followed a Bug!," 29.

7. W. C. Handy and Arna Bontemps, *Father of the Blues: An Autobiography* (New York: Macmillan, 1941), 75.

8. Lomax and Lomax, *Folk Song U.S.A.*, 287.

9. Kenneth L. Untiedt, "The Family Nature of the Texas Folklore Society," in *Celebrating 100 Years of the Texas Folklore Society*, ed., Kenneth L. Untiedt (Denton: University of North Texas Press, 2009), 73; "To Hold First Formal Meeting," *Austin American-Statesman*, February 14, 1911, 3. John Lomax wrongly estimated the date of the *New York World* publication as "probably 1910" in *Folk Song U.S.A.*, 287. In August 1909, Mississippian author Harris Dickson (1868–1946) published "Br'er Boll Weevil," "an article which tells of the damage done cotton and credit by a mere bug," in *Success* (Arthur E. Weld, "August Magazines Are Fine," *Waterloo [Iowa] Reporter*, July 24, 1909, 65). Its relationship, if any, to Bess Lomax's paper is undetermined.

10. The most important collections, articles, and liner notes published by the Lomaxes and including boll weevil songs are: John A. Lomax, "Some Types of American Folk-Song," *Journal of American Folk-Lore* XXVIII, no. CVII (January-March 1915): 1–17, esp. 15; Lomax and Lomax, "De Ballit of de Boll Weevil," in *American Ballads and Folk Songs*, 112–17, originally published by Macmillan in 1934; John A. Lomax and Alan Lomax, "De Ballit of de Boll Weevil," in *Negro Folk Songs as Sung by Lead Belly* (New York: Macmillan, 1936), 184–87; Alan Lomax, "The Boll Weevil Holler," in *The Folk Songs of North America* (New York: Dolphin Books, 1975); originally published by Doubleday, 1960, 519, 535–36; Lomax and Lomax, *Folk Song U.S.A.*, 285–87, 300–301; John A. Lomax and Alan Lomax, eds., "De Ballit of de Boll Weevil," liner notes to *Leadbelly: A Collection of World-Famous Songs by Huddie Ledbetter* (New York: Folkways Music Publishers, 1959), 12; Alan Lomax, "The Ballad of the Boll Weevil," in *The Penguin Book of American Folk Songs* (Baltimore: Penguin Books, 1964), 86. See also "Ballad Hunter. Pt. 6. Boll Weevil: Songs about the little bug that challenged King Cotton" at https://www.wnyc.org/series/ballad-hunter.

11. Lomax and Lomax, *Negro Folk Songs as Sung by Lead Belly*, 184.

12. Alan Lomax wrote (see "The Boll Weevil Holler," *The Folk Songs of North America*, 519) that his father said that he first became aware of a song about the boll weevil in a telephone call from an African American who sang a version of the ballad that he claimed to have composed.

13. Lomax and Lomax, "De Ballit of de Boll Weevil," in *American Ballads and Folk Songs*, 112–17.

14. A copper arsenate–based insecticide used to kill the boll weevil.

15. Scarborough, *From a Southern Porch*, 55–56.

16. Scarborough, "The Boll Weevil," in *On the Trail of Negro Folk-Songs*, 76–79.

17. This is a folk remedy for various illnesses, including venereal disease.

18. "Boll Weevil Song" and "De Ballet of de Boll Weevil," in Sandburg, *The American Songbag*, 8–10, 252–53. Five of Sandburg's stanzas had been published in Bessie J. Zaban, "'Ballad of the Boll Weevil' Will Live, Says Carl Sandburg" (*Atlanta Journal*, August 29, 1922, 12). Sandburg recorded a version of "The Boll Weevil," which is available on various artists, *Songs for Political Action: Folk Music, Topical Songs and the American Left: 1926–1953*, Bear Family Records BCD 15720 JL (10CD), 1996.

19. It is likely that Lead Belly had access to the Sandburg book either through the Lomaxes or in Texas after his release from prison.

20. If one compares this stanza with Lead Belly's version of "The Midnight Special," one may in fact conclude that he probably had access to Sandburg's collection in the 1920s.

21. Sandburg, *The American Songbag*, 252.

22. Newman Ivey White, *American Negro Folk-Songs* (Harvard University Press, 1928), 351–53.

23. White, *American Negro Folk-Songs*, 353–54.

24. Text obtained by David Evans in 1969 from Mrs. Rae Korson, then head of the Archive of Folk Song at the Library of Congress, Washington, DC.

25. All three of Odum's texts read like the productions of someone with literary pretensions, especially the order inversion of "right out again I'll creep" in the first text.

26. For Davis's employment as a WPA worker with the Federal Writers' Project in 1936, see Alan Brown, *Southern Ghost Stories* (Jackson: University Press of Mississippi, 2000), 179; and "Ruby Hammock, Brandon, Texas" at https://www.loc.gov/resource/wpalh3.33060106/?sp=1.

27. Ethel Park Richardson and Sigmund Spaeth, *American Mountain Songs* (New York: Greenberg Publisher, 1927), 91. See also Henry M. Belden and Arthur Palmer Hudson, eds., "Folk Songs from North Carolina," in *The Frank C. Brown Collection of North Carolina Folklore* vol. 3 (Durham, NC: Duke University Press, 1952), 245–47.

28. Thomas, "South Texas Negro Work-Songs: Collected and Uncollected," 173.

29. Muir, *Long Lost Blues*, 192–95, 199.

30. Information supplied by Howard Rye and Chris Smith, from the draft revision of *Blues and Gospel Records, 1890–1943*.

31. Reissued on Eubie Blake, *Memories of You*, Biograph BCD 112, 1990. On February 5, 1921, *Music Trade Indicator* reported that "a special shipment is being rushed." Mike Montgomery, "Eubie Blake Piano Rollography (Revised)," *Record Research* 159/60 (December 1978): 4–5.

32. See "Fakes Chapel" at http://www.wendtroot.com/wright/d0005/d0005notes/Fakes Chapel.htm.

33. One of Dalhart's versions can be heard at http://www.loc.gov/jukebox/recordings/detail /id/10023.

34. Another recording that uses the boll weevil as an image for one party in a relationship (and also for that party's penis) is Lee Brown's "Let Me Be Your Bo Weavil" (Decca 7790, New York, March 24, 1939), available on *Complete Recorded Works 1937 to January 1940 in Chronological Order*, Document Records DOCD-5344, 1995.

35. Rainey recorded two takes of the song, both available on Ma Rainey, *Complete Recorded Works in Chronological Order—Volume 1 (1923–1924)*, Document Records 5581, 1997. For the recording date see Guido van Rijn and Alex van der Tuuk, *New York Recording Laboratories 1100–1199 Matrix Series* (Overveen, The Netherlands: Agram Blues Books, 2014), xix, 165. Bessie Smith recorded a cover version, "Bo-Weavil Blues" (Columbia 14018-D, New York, April 7, 1924), reissued on *The Complete Recordings Volume 2*, Frog Records DFG 41, 2001. Rainey herself recorded a sequel, "New Boweavil Blues" (Paramount 12603, Chicago, early January 1928), which is reissued on *Complete Recorded Works in Chronological Order—Volume 4 (1926–1927)*, Document Records 5584, 1997. For this song's exact recording date, see Guido van Rijn and Alex van der Tuuk, *New York Recording Laboratories 20000 and Gennett Matrix Series* (Overveen, The Netherlands: Agram Blues Books, 2012), xv, 19. John A. and Ruby T. Lomax collected a "Boll Weevil Blues" (AFS 3989-A-1) from Louisiana-born Oscar "Buddy" Woods (ca. 1903–1955) in Shreveport, Louisiana, on October 8, 1940. It contains few textual variations from Rainey's original, but nevertheless seems to be almost an "answer" song from a male

perspective. It is available on various artists, *I Can Eagle Rock: Jook Joint Blues from Alabama and Louisiana*, Travelin' Man TM CD 09, 1996. Accompanied by Louisiana Red and Carey Bell, Valerie Wellington recorded "Bo-Weavil Blues" (L+R LP 42.061) in Chicago on April 1, 1983.

36. This opening stanza was well-known to postwar Chicago blues musicians (see the recordings by "Baby Face" Leroy Foster, Johnny Shines, and Big Mojo Elem mentioned later). It is cited by John W. Work III as a "typical blues verse" in his *American Negro Songs and Spirituals* (New York: Bonanza Books, 1940), 29–30.

37. Lieb, *Mother of the Blues: A Study of Ma Rainey*, 87–88. The quotation is followed by an analysis of the song. Its impact on blues singers is evident from a stanza in Memphis Minnie's "Ma Rainey" (OKeh 05811, Chicago, June 27, 1940): "When she made 'Bo-Weavil Blues,' I was living way down the line / Every time I hear that record, I just couldn't keep from crying." This tribute to Rainey, who died on December 22, 1939, is available on Memphis Minnie, *Complete Recorded Works 1935–1941 in Chronological Order—Volume 5 (1940–1941)*, Blues Documents BDCD-6012, 1991.

38. The first take is available on various artists, *Rare Paramount Blues (1926–1929)*, Document Records DOCD-5277, 1994; the second on various artists, *Too Late Too Late Volume 12 (1917–1948)*, Document Records DOCD-5659, 1999. For the recording date, see van Rijn and van der Tuuk, *New York Recording Laboratories Rodeheaver, Marsh and 2000 Series*, 44–45.

39. McCormick's interview is available in Govenar and Lornell, *The Blues Come to Texas*, 69–70, 394. It is uncertain whether this Texas Charles Nelson is the same man who recorded for Paramount. See David Evans, Ed Payne, Richard Linster, T. DeWayne Moore, and Bob Eagle, "Lightning Struck Him: Walter Rhodes, The Delta's Crowing Rooster," *Frog Blues and Jazz Annual* 6, forthcoming.

40. Govenar and Lornell, *The Blues Come to Texas*, 70. This is unlikely, as Nelson's song is in the AAB blues form, which was not attested until a few years later.

41. This song is issued on Rounder (see note 42) as by Phineas Rockmore, but the artist signed his name "Finous" on his World War I and World War II draft cards, on which he gave his occupations respectively as "laborer, ice plant" and "play a string band about over the city" [*sic*].

42. Issued on various artists, *Deep River of Song. Black Texicans: Balladeers and Songsters of the Texas Frontier*, Rounder CD 1821, 1999.

43. Reissued on Woody Guthrie, *Library of Congress Recordings*, Rounder Records CD 1041–43, 1988.

44. As a further example of delocalization for political purposes, on April 2, 1940, Alan Lomax sang "Boll Weevil" with the vocal accompaniment of the Golden Gate Quartet in "Poor Farmer Songs," program 22 of the CBS American School of the Air's *Folk Music of America* series. Lomax played guitar, and Woody Guthrie harmonica. This performance is held by the Library of Congress as band 4507-A-4 (also indexed as 4508-A-5). The Golden Gate Quartet also sang on Lead Belly's version of the song in "Program Finale," the twenty-fifth and last in the series, on April 23, 1940. This version is on Library of Congress disc 13499-A. It has not been possible to listen to these performances, but the script of "Poor Farmer Songs" has Alan Lomax saying that "this is the way my father heard it down in the Brazos bottoms of Texas around 1907," and the song text in the script contains no significant new material. The script is accessible at https://www.loc.gov/collections/alan-lomax-manuscripts/?q=folk+music+of+ame rica. In these broadcasts, Lomax was aiming to raise awareness of American folk music among schoolchildren and their teachers, and to use it to transcend racial and regional boundaries. He

was also aiming to create a national identity based on solidarity, common purpose, and unity in diversity during the Depression—in practice, that is, to support the New Deal. This endnote draws on research by Chris Smith for the revision of "Blues and Gospel Records 1890–1943," and on Todd Harvey, "Alan Lomax Radio-Related Materials, 1939–1969: A Guide" (American Folklife Center, Library of Congress, 2016, accessible at https://www.loc.gov/collections/alan -lomax-manuscripts/articles-and-essays/guides-to-lomax-family-collections/?loclr=blogflt). The latter source states that program 21, "Outlaw Songs," broadcast on March 19, 1940, included a "Boll Weevil" sung by Alan Lomax, but the script, accessible at https://www.loc.gov/collections/ alan-lomax-manuscripts/?q=folk+music+of+america does not support this.

45. Available on Leadbelly, *The Titanic*, Rounder Records CD 1097, 1994.

46. For further boll weevil recordings by Lead Belly, see *Blues and Gospel Records 1890–1943*, 518, 522, 524, 525, 527, 530, 532; and Fancourt and McGrath, *The Blues Discography 1943–1970*, 373, 375.

47. Available on *Leadbelly's Last Sessions*, Smithsonian Folkways SF CD 40068–71 (4CD), 1994.

48. Livingston is sixty miles southwest of Tuscaloosa, which may have been the departure point for Hall's train journey to New York.

49. Reissued on various artists, *Boll Weevil Here, Boll Weevil Everywhere: Field Recordings Volume 16 (1934–1940)*, Document Records DOCD-5675, 2004. See Lomax, *Adventures of a Ballad Hunter*, 252–53; and Tremain F. Robinson, "Southern Folksongs Recorded for Library," *Shreveport Times*, June 8, 1941, 8. Thanks to Chris Smith for alerting me to the latter publication. See also Bob Groom's notes to the CD reissue and John A. Lomax's interview following the recording.

50. All known postwar songs from Arkansas are field recordings by white performers, which are peripheral to a study of African American songs. Among them are: "Boll Weevil Song" (10811-A-3), collected by Merlin Mitchell from Pete Martin at Evansville, Arkansas, in 1950, available at http://digitalcollections.uark.edu/cdm/ref/collection/OzarkFolkSong/id/544; "Boll Weevil" (AFS 12050-B-28), collected by Mary C. Parler from Bob Parker and George Bulloch at Fayetteville, Arkansas, in 1958; "Boll Weevil Song" (AFS 12039-B-5), collected by Mary C. Parler from Mrs. Mamie Pridemore at Lincoln, Arkansas, in 1959, see https://maxhunter.missouristate. edu/songinformation.aspx?ID=400; "Boll Weevil Blues" (AFS 13131-A-5), collected by Mary C. Parler from Charles Mayo at Benton, Arkansas, in 1960. In 1958, at Wild Cherry, Arkansas, Parler also collected "Boll Weevil" (AFS 12050-A-5) from Al Bittick of Winkelman, Arizona.

51. Both songs are available on various artists, *Boll Weevil Here, Boll Weevil Everywhere: Field Recordings Volume 16 (1934–1940)*, Document Records DOCD-5675, 2004.

52. Walnut Corner is eleven miles west of Helena, in Phillips County.

53. The word "seed" may be meant literally or may imply "seed (cotton)," which is cotton that has been picked but not ginned (processed to separate the fibers from seeds and other waste). For the latter meaning, see http://agropedia.iitk.ac.in/content/glossary-useful-terms-related-cotton.

54. Reissued on the box set *Screamin' and Hollerin' the Blues: The Worlds of Charley Patton* (Disc 1), Revenant Album No. 212 (7CD), 2001. Paramount credited the first pressing to "The Masked Marvel," and ran a competition in September and October 1929, in which contestants were invited to identify the performer. See also Robert K. D. Peterson, "Charley Patton and His Mississippi Boweavil Blues," *American Entomologist* (Fall 2007): 142–44, available at www .montana.edu/historybug/documents/Peterson_2007.pdf.

55. Available on various artists, *Field Recordings—Volume 4: Mississippi and Alabama (1934–1942)*, Document Records DOCD-5578, 1997.

56. Lomax, *Adventures of a Ballad Hunter*, 174.

57. US census, June 1880; Jerrilyn McGregory, booklet notes to *Deep River of Song: Alabama. From Lullabies to Blues*, Rounder Records 1829-2, 2001.

58. Reissued on various artists, *Rock Me, Shake Me: Field Recordings—Volume 15: Mississippi (1941–1942)*, Document Records DOCD-5672, 2002. The same CD also includes a spoken account of the infestation, also titled "The Boll Weevil" (AFS 6734-A-1), recorded by Asa Ware for Lewis Jones in Coahoma County, ca. September-October 1941.

59. For the comparison, see Lomax, *The Land Where the Blues Began*, 321–23, 490–92.

60. Lomax, *The Land Where the Blues Began*, 321–23.

61. Reissued (as "Old Bo Weevil") on various artists, *Mississippi Delta Blues Volume 2: Blow My Blues Away*, Arhoolie CD 402, 1993. Callicott had recorded an unissued "Mississippi Boll Weevil Blues" for Brunswick in Memphis, ca. September 25, 1929. A copy of the lead sheet, which State Street Music Publishing filed for copyright registration on July 3, 1930, is in my possession. It is titled "Mississippi Bool Weavel Blues" [*sic*], and miscredits "Albert Akers" (itself probably an error for "Garfield Akers") as the composer. James Alston transcribed the song and notated it for piano, presumably from a test pressing. The words and music are similar to Callicott's 1967 version, but the text is shorter, as is normal for lead sheets, which contained only enough information to identify the composition in the event of a dispute. Babe Stovall grew up and learned music in Mississippi and recorded a boll weevil song the year before Callicott, but in Louisiana.

62. Reissued on various artists, *The Stuff That Dreams Are Made Of*, Yazoo Records 2202 (2CD), 2006. For biographical information on Coleman, see James Patrick Cather, "Tracking Down a Legend: The 'Jaybird' Coleman Story," *Tributaries: Journal of the Alabama Folklife Association* 5 (2002): 62–68.

63. Available on various artists, *Boll Weevil Here, Boll Weevil Everywhere: Field Recordings Volume 16 (1934–1940)*, Document Records DOCD-5675, 2004.

64. In the Lomax interview preceding the second version, Amerson claims to have "located" (probably meaning "made up") the song himself. Both songs are available on various artists, *Boll Weevil Here, Boll Weevil Everywhere: Field Recordings Volume 16 (1934–1940)*, Document Records DOCD-5675, 2004.

65. This may be some hoodoo practice, or it may allude to the proverb that "the squeaky hinge gets the grease," meaning problems that are complained about receive attention. If so, the implication is that it's a waste of time to complain about the boll weevil.

66. Hall's 1937 "Boll Weevil" (AFS 1323-A-1) is available on various artists, *Boll Weevil Here, Boll Weevil Everywhere: Field Recordings Volume 16 (1934–1940)*, Document Records DOCD-5675, 2004; her 1940 recording, "Boll Weevil Blues," is on various artists, *Field Recordings—Volume 4: Mississippi and Alabama (1934–1942)*, Document Records DOCD-5578, 1997; "Boll Weevil Holler" (Atlantic LP 1346) was recorded in Livingston on October 10, 1959, and appears on various artists, *Sounds of the South*, Atlantic 7 82496-2 (4CD), 1993. See also Alan Lomax's biography of Hall (disguised as "Nora"), in *The Rainbow Sign: A Southern Documentary* (New York: Duell, Sloan & Pearce, 1959); Jerrilyn McGregory, "Livingston, Alabama Blues: The Significance of Vera Ward Hall," and Steve Grauberger and Kevin Nutt, comps., "A Vera Hall Discography," both in *Tributaries: Journal of the Alabama Folklife Association* 5 (2002): 72–81, 82–91.

67. Reissued on various artists, *Hard Times Come Again No More Vol. 2*, Yazoo CD 2037, 1998.

68. At the time of writing, this song was available only on https://www.youtube.com/watch?v=3VoDXqGaj4l. For biographical information on Tanner, see Russell, *Country Music Originals*, 32–36.

69. Reissued on various artists, *People Take Warning!* Tompkins Square TSQ 1875 (3CD), 2007.

70. See Henry M. Belden and Arthur Palmer Hudson, eds., "Folk Songs from North Carolina," in *The Frank C. Brown Collection of North Carolina Folklore*, vol. 3, 247. Another verse including the word "hell" and the music transcription of "The Boll Weevil" as sung by white singer Mr. Burch Blaylock in Ridgeville, North Carolina, on November 10, 1936, is filed in the Fletcher Collins Jr. Collection, Archive of Folk Culture, American Folklife Center, Library of Congress. I am grateful to Mrs. Judith Gray for sending me a copy of this document.

71. Rev. J. M. Milton, "Silk Worms and Boll Weevils" (Columbia 14562-D), recorded in Atlanta on November 5, 1929, and reissued on various artists, *Preachers and Congregations—Volume 5 (1926–1931)*, Document Records DOCD-5559, 1997.

72. Reissued on Kokomo Arnold, *The Complete Recorded Works in Chronological Order—Volume 2*, Document Records DOCD-5038, 1991. For biographical information on Arnold, see Keith Briggs, liner notes to the four Document Records CDs.

73. Reissued on Blind Willie McTell, *Complete Library of Congress Recordings 1940*, Document Records BDCD-6001, 1990. For biographical data on McTell, see Michael Gray, *Hand Me My Travelin' Shoes: In Search of Blind Willie McTell* (London: Bloomsbury, 2007), and David Evans, booklet notes to *Atlanta Blues 1933*, John Edwards Memorial Foundation JEMF-106, 1979.

74. McTell probably meant "pills" even if the word comes out sounding like "chills" or shills."

75. The Panhandle contains the twenty-six northernmost counties in Texas, an area virtually untouched by the boll weevil.

76. The complete program can be heard at https://www.wnyc.org/story/pt-6-boll-weevil-songs-about-the-little-bug-that-challenged-king-cotton/. It was issued on LP as one side of AAFS L51, *The Ballad Hunter Parts V and VI*.

77. David Evans, liner notes to various artists, *Deep River of Song: Georgia. I'm Gonna Make You Happy*, Rounder CD 1828, 2001.

78. Both songs are available from "'Now What a Time': Blues, Gospel, and the Fort Valley Music Festivals," American Folklife Center, Library of Congress, https://www.loc.gov/collections/blues-gospel-and-the-fort-valley-music-festivals/ or on the CDs various artists, *African American Music Festivals 1938–1943: Folk Songs* and *African American Music Festivals 1938–1943: Blues Songs* (2CD), A2ZCDS.com. The second version, transcribed here, is more readily accessible on various artists, *Field Recordings Vol. 2: North and South Carolina, Georgia, Tennessee, Arkansas (1926–1943)*, Document Records DOCD-5576, 1997. Ezell sang the song again as "Boll Weevil the Farmers' Trouble" at the 1951 festival. See Bruce Bastin, "Fort Valley Blues—Part 2," *Blues Unlimited* 112 (March-April 1975): 15. For Ezell, see Tony Russell, liner notes to various artists, *Fort Valley Blues: 1941–43 Field Recordings from Georgia*, Flyright-Matchbox SDM 250, 1974; and van Rijn, *Roosevelt's Blues: African-American Blues and Gospel Songs on FDR*, 161–62, 234–35. For the Fort Valley State College Festivals, see Bastin, *Red River Blues*, 72–86, and "Truckin' My Blues Away: East Coast Piedmont Styles," in *Nothing but the Blues*, ed. Lawrence Cohn (New York: Abbeville Press, 1993), 204 (where Ezell is pictured), 223–24.

79. See Robert Higgs, "The Boll Weevil, the Cotton Economy, and Black Migration 1910–1930," *Agricultural History* 50, no. 2 (1976): 335–50.

80. Cotton rust is a fungal disease; see https://en.wikipedia.org/wiki/Puccinia_schedonnardii.

81. van der Tuuk, *The New Paramount Book of Blues*, 196–97.

82. The "Sam Butler" pseudonym was probably intended to conceal Harry Charles's double-dealing from Paramount.

83. Available on various artists, *Backwoods Blues (1926–1935)*, Document Records DOCD-5036, 1991.

84. Bigeou's recording (originally on OKeh 8025) appears on *The Complete Recorded Works of Esther Bigeou, Lillyn Brown, Alberta Brown and the Remaining Titles of Ada Brown in Chronological Order (1921–1928)*, Document Records DOCD-5489, 1996. For biographical information on Kemp (who appears on the record label as "Kempf"), see Chris Smith, "Stingaree," in column "Words Words Words," *Blues & Rhythm* 306 (January 2016): 24.

85. Both Rainey and Jackson are probably concerned about control by hoodoo (folk magic), rather than attempted murder.

86. Issued on Jack Newman, James Hall, Frankie Jones, Black Bottom McPhail, *Complete Recorded Works in Chronological Order (1938)*, Document Records DOCD-5351, 1995.

87. North Carolina singer, banjo and fiddle player Thomas Jefferson Jarrell (1901–1985) learned "Boll Weevil" from a black woman singing at a traveling tent show. See Cecelia Conway, "Jarrell, Thomas Jefferson," in *Dictionary of North Carolina Biography*, vol. 3, ed. Williams Powell (Chapel Hill: University of North Carolina Press, 1988), available at https://www.ncpedia.org/biography/jarrell-thomas-jefferson.

88. "Cotton Boll Weevil in Two Virginia Counties," *Times Dispatch* (Richmond, Virginia), November 19, 1922, 21; "Says Boll Weevil Seriously Infests State Cotton Fields," *News Leader* (Staunton, Virginia), July 21, 1930, 3.

89. Available on various artists, *Deep River of Song: Virginia and the Piedmont: Minstrelsy, Work Songs, and Blues*, Rounder CD 1827, 2000. Information on Williams can be found in John A. Lomax and Alan Lomax, comps., *Our Singing Country: Folk Songs and Ballads* (Mineola, NY: Dover Publications, 2000), xxv; originally published by Macmillan, xiii. See also Bastin, *Red River Blues*, 62–63. In 1947, MacEdward Leach and Horace P. Beck collected "Boll Weevil" (AFS 9072-A-1) from William Sloan in Washington (commonly referred to as Little Washington), Rappahanock County, Virginia.

90. Reissued on Tex Ritter, *Blood on the Saddle*, Bear Family BCD 16260 (4CD), 1999.

91. The concluding "sign-off" stanza identifies the song's composer as "a dark-complected feller with a pair of blue duckins on."

92. Available on various artists, *The Blues World of Little Walter*, Delmark DD-648, 1993. For biographical information on Foster, see Mike Rowe, *Chicago Blues: The City and the Music* (New York: Da Capo Press, 1981), 74–76; originally published as *Chicago Breakdown* (London: Eddison Press, 1973).

93. It seems possible, however, that Tex Ritter's recording inspired the reference to blue duckins.

94. Reissued as Brother John Sellers, *Sings Blues and Folk Songs*, Vanguard VMD 8005, 2006. Folk singer Pete Seeger recorded a cover version for Folkways in 1970.

95. Reissued on *The Josh White Stories Volume 1 and 2*, Jasmine Records CD 3148, 2020. For his biography, see Wald, *Josh White: Society Blues*. There is an anecdote about a BBC radio performance of "Boll Weevil" by White on 219–20.

96. Reissued on Fats Domino, *Out of New Orleans*, Bear Family Records BCD 15541 (8CD), 1993, with a slightly different additional stanza recorded on the same day. The song reached

number 35 in the pop charts, and was covered by the Dixie Belles on *(Down on) Papa Joe's,* Sound Stage 7 5000, 1963. Washboard Doc, Lucky and Flash recorded a jug band version, "Bollweevil" (L+R LP 42.010), in New York on February 5, 1980. Lynn August's "Bo Weevil" (Maison de Soul MdS 1036) is a 1989 zydeco version.

97. A licking is a beating; in the third repetition of the stanza, Domino sings "Mama going to whip you." The stanza was probably omitted from the original release because the line is at odds with the mood of the song.

98. Oster recorded his own, guitar-accompanied version of "The Boll Weevil," released in 1959 on various artists, *Louisiana Folksong Jambalaya,* Louisiana Folklore Society LFS A-2.

99. Reissued on various artists, *20 to Life: Prison Blues Songs from Angola State Penitentiary,* Fuel 2000 302 061 161, 2001.

100. Issued on various artists, *Country Negro Jam Session,* Arhoolie CD 372, 1993. See also "Meet Me in the Bottom," recorded by Webster the same day, in Harry Oster, *Living Country Blues,* 124–25. Webster recorded another, unissued, "Boll Weevil Blues" two weeks later.

101. Available on Roosevelt Charles, *Mean Trouble Blues,* Vanguard Records VRS 9136, 1964. Oster had recorded Charles performing an unissued version in April 1959.

102. The balance weight of a steelyard, here being used to weigh cotton bales. See Joan Houston Hall, ed., *Dictionary of American Regional English,* vol. IV, P-Sk (Cambridge, MA: Belknap Press of Harvard University Press, 2002); and Chris Smith, "The Pea (Roosevelt Charles)," in column "Words Words Words," *Blues & Rhythm* 359 (May 2021): 27.

103. Transcribed in Oster, *Living Country Blues,* 127. For information on Williams, see Luigi Monge, "Williams, Robert Pete," in *Encyclopedia of the Blues,* vol. 2: K–Z, 1084–85.

104. "Forgin" is either a garbling of "begin" by Williams, or—perhaps more likely with this *sui generis* songmaker—an idiolect with the same meaning.

105. Reissued on *The Blues of Smoky Babe,* Original Blues Classics OBCCD-595, 2001.

106. Reissued on *Trouble in Mind,* Rhino RHM2 7829, 2002. In Govenar and Lornell, *The Blues Come to Texas,* 289, 408, Lipscomb is reported to have learned the song in 1902, at the age of seven.

107. Available on *The Blues of Pink Anderson: Ballad and Folksinger, Vol. 3,* Original Blues Classics OBCCD-577, 1995.

108. Compare Wink Martindale, "Deck of Cards" (1959; there had been 1948 hit versions by T. Texas Tyler and Tex Ritter), and Jimmy Dean, "Big Bad John" (1961).

109. Originally issued on Brook Benton, *The Boll Weevil Song and 11 Other Great Hits,* Mercury Records SR 60641, 1961; reissued on *Let Me Sing and I'm Happy,* Jasmine Records CD 744, 2013. Composer credits on the 45 r.p.m. single are to Benton and arranger Clyde Otis. For Benton's biography, see Herwig Gradischnig and Hans Maitner, *Brook Benton: There Goes That Song Again* (York, UK: Music Mentor Books, 2015). Tennessee-born blues singer John Henry Barbee sang a textually very similar "Boll Weavil" (Storyville SLP 4074) in concert in Copenhagen, Denmark, on October 8, 1964. It is available on John Henry Barbee and Sleepy John Estes, *Blues Live!,* Storyville STCD 8051, 2000.

110. Andrew Scheiber, "From Cotton Boll to Rock 'n' Roll," *Arkansas Review* 40, no. 2 (August 2009): 112.

111. Recordings by African Americans include "Boll-weevil" (Stax LP 702), recorded by Gus Cannon in Memphis, ca. March 23, 1963, reissued on *Walk Right In,* Stax SCD-8603-2, 1999. In summer 1962, Cannon had recorded the song as "Boll Weevil Blues," issued on *Tennessee*

Legends, Southland SLP 14, reissued as various artists, *The George Mitchell Collection—Tennessee Recordings (1962–1963),* Fat Possum FP 1092, 2006. "Bo Weevil" (Vanguard VSD 2153), recorded by Odetta in December 1963, is reissued on *One Grain of Sand,* Vanguard VMD 2153, 2006. A later Odetta version titled "Alabama Bound/Boll Weevil" was recorded in New York City on December 21, 2000, and issued on *Lookin for a Home,* M.C. Records 0044, 2001. Cannon's songs are from the folk tradition documented by the Lomaxes and epitomized by Lead Belly, although it is most unlikely that Cannon was aware of the folklorists or Lead Belly. Odetta's are probably drawn directly from one or more of Lead Belly's recordings. "Mr. Boweevil" (Vanguard Records VSD-79218), recorded by Johnny Shines in Chicago in December 1965, and reissued on various artists, *Chicago—The Blues Today—Volume 3,* Vanguard Records VMD 79218, 1989, begins with Ma Rainey's opening verse, like Leroy Foster's song; but from the third stanza onward it includes relatively original lyrics, developing a possibly racial theme of self-defense from the wickedness of the boll weevil. Hayes McMullan's "Bo Weevil Blues" (Light in the Attic LITA 152), recorded in Jackson, Mississippi, in 1968, is a fragmentary hodgepodge of traditional verses. Despite the singer's lifelong residence in the Delta and his association with Charley Patton, it is unrelated to the latter's recording. Alabama-born Johnie Lewis recorded an unissued "Boll Weevil" for Arhoolie in Chicago on August 13, 1970. Guitarist Percy Lassiter's "Boll Weevil" (Crossroads C-101 LP), recorded in his native Rich Square, Northampton County, North Carolina, in 1977 or 1978, is a partly sung, partly spoken performance, including the "boll weevil here, boll weevil everywhere" refrain. "Boll Weevil" by Robert "Big Mojo" Elem, recorded in Chicago in 1994, and first issued that year on Big Mojo Elem Chicago Blues Band, *Mojo Boogie!,* St. George Records STG 7703, is a cover of Leroy Foster's recording. "The Boll Weevil," recorded by Jimmy Lee Robinson in Salina, Kansas, on February 14, 1998, and issued on Jimmy Lee Robinson, *Remember Me,* Analogue Productions Originals 2006, n.d., is an idiosyncratic, partly spoken version of the Lead Belly/Lomax song. Predictably, Little Pink Anderson's "Bo Weavil" (unknown location and date; issued on Little Pink Anderson, *Carolina Bluesman,* Music Maker Recordings MMCD 24, 2001) is a version of his father's recording. "Boll Weevil," recorded by Eric Bibb on September 13–17, 2011, and issued on *Deeper in the Well,* Dixiefrog DFGCD 8720, 2012, derives from old-time banjo player Tommy Jarrell's version, available on Tommy Jarrell, Fred Cockerham, and Oscar Jenkins, *Down to the Cider Mill,* County Records 2734, 2005. The song is related to the Lead Belly version, but it also includes one of the stanzas found in "Bo Weavil" Jackson's song.

112. Various artists, *South Mississippi Blues,* Rounder LP 2009, 1971.

113. Compare Mississippi John Hurt's "Frankie and Albert," which has the same melody as Stovall's "Boll Weevil," and his "The Hop Joint."

114. Levine, *Black Culture and Black Consciousness,* 369. The chapters "'Some Go Up and Some Go Down': The Animal Trickster," 102–21, and "A Pantheon of Heroes," 367–440, are particularly relevant to this study. See also Abrahams, *Deep Down in the Jungle,* 65–86; and Ayana Smith, "Blues, Criticism, and the Signifying Trickster," *Popular Music* 24 (2005): 179–91.

115. Levine, *Black Culture and Black Consciousness,* 374.

116. For a generic study of this subject, not mentioning the boll weevil, see Bill R. Hampton, "On Identification and Negro Tricksters," *Southern Folklore Quarterly* 31, no. 1 (March 1967): 55–65.

117. For a study of nicknames in blues music, see David Evans, "From Bumble Bee Slim to Black Boy Shine: Nicknames of Blues Singers," in *Ramblin' on My Mind: New Perspectives on the*

Blues, 179–221. This study suggests that the nickname "Boll Weevil Bill" alludes to the blackness of both insect and singer. It is not clear whether this nickname disguises Willie Moore (as A&R man Art Satherly's files indicate) or Julius "Juke" Davis, a member of Mitchell's Christian Singers. The latter identification came from Lewis Herring, another member of the group. See Bastin, *Red River Blues*, 218.

118. David Evans, liner notes to various artists, *Deep River of Song: Georgia: I'm Gonna Make You Happy*, Rounder CD 1828, 2001.

119. Scheiber, "From Cotton Boll to Rock 'n' Roll," 110.

120. Levine, *Black Culture and Black Consciousness*, 376.

121. North Mississippi Allstars, "Mississippi Bollweevil," *Electric Blue Watermelon*, ATO Records 0026, 2005, is a version of Charley Patton's song. The White Stripes, "Boll Weevil," *Live in Mississippi*, Third Man Records TMR-100, 2007, derives from Lead Belly.

122. Scheiber, "From Cotton Boll to Rock 'n' Roll," 112.

123. Mahalia Jackson with Evan McLeod Wylie, *Movin' on Up* (New York: Hawthorn Books, 1966), 13–14.

124. The best account is John M. Barry, *The Great Influenza: The Story of the Deadliest Pandemic in History* (London: Penguin Books, 2005).

125. See Niall Johnson and Jürgen Müller, "Updating the Accounts: Global Mortality of the 1918–1920 'Spanish' Influenza Pandemic," *Bulletin of the History of Medicine* 76, no. 1 (2002): 105–15; and S. Knobler, A. Mack, A. Mahmoud, and S. Lemon, eds., "The Story of Influenza." *The Threat of Pandemic Influenza: Are We Ready? Workshop Summary*. Washington, DC: National Academies Press, 2005. http://books.nap.edu/openbook.php?record_id=11150&page=57.

126. See "History of 1918 Flu Pandemic" at https://www.cdc.gov/flu/pandemic-resources/1918 -commemoration/1918-pandemic-history.htm; and "The Deadliest Flu: The Complete Story of the Discovery and Reconstruction of the 1918 Pandemic Virus" at https://www.cdc.gov/flu/ pandemic-resources/reconstruction-1918-virus.html.

127. "History of 1918 Flu Pandemic" at https://www.cdc.gov/flu/pandemic-resources/1918 -commemoration/1918-pandemic-history.htm; and "The Deadliest Flu: The Complete Story of the Discovery and Reconstruction of the 1918 Pandemic Virus" at https://www.cdc.gov/flu/ pandemic-resources/reconstruction-1918-virus.html.

128. Alfred W. Crosby, *America's Forgotten Pandemic: The Influenza of 1918*, 2nd ed. (Cambridge and New York: Cambridge University Press, 2003); and Barry, *The Great Influenza*, 92–97.

129. Barry, *The Great Influenza*, 96.

130. See "Spanish Flu" at https://en.wikipedia.org/wiki/Spanish_flu; Barry, *The Great Influenza*, 396–97; and Stephen J. Spignesi, "The Great Influenza Epidemic," in *Catastrophe! The 100 Greatest Disasters of All Time*, 6–9, esp. 8.

131. See *The Great Pandemic: The United States in 1918–1919*, US Department of Health and Human Services; and Barry, *The Great Influenza*, 396–97.

132. See "Spanish Flu" at https://en.wikipedia.org/wiki/Spanish_flu.

133. Newman Ivey White, *American Negro Folk-Songs* (Hatboro, VT: Folklore Associates, 1965; originally published Cambridge, MA: Harvard University Press, 1928), 424–25.

134. This chorus appears in Howard W. Odum's novel *Wings on My Feet: Black Ulysses at the Wars*, in a passage about the outbreak of influenza on the Western Front (Bloomington: Indiana University Press, 2007; reprint of Indianapolis: Bobbs-Merrill, 1929), 149–51. On page 286, Odum's protagonist, Leftwing Gordon, brags about his survival: "Influenza train a-runnin', I never had

no ticket." Odum and Newman Ivey White were both academics on North Carolina campuses, respectively at University of North Carolina, Chapel Hill, and Duke University, Durham.

135. Barry, *The Great Influenza*, 216–17.

136. Available on *The Complete Blind Willie Johnson*, Sony/Columbia Legacy C2K 52835, 1993.

137. This stanza was possibly influenced by "The Influenza Train."

138. Ziólek-Sowińska, *Images of the Apocalypse in African American Blues and Spirituals*, 73.

139. The file card for this song gives the singer's name as Sidney Smith, but he is announced as Sugar Smith (probably a nickname) after the performance.

140. Past tense and past participle of the verb "send," especially frequent among black speakers in the South and South Midland, also spelled "sahnt" and "saunt."

141. *United States Armed Forces Celebrating 60 Years of Integration 1948–2008* (Patrick Air Force Base, FL: Defense Equal Opportunity Management Institute, Research Directorate, 2008), 18. Online at https://apps.dtic.mil/dtic/tr/fulltext/u2/a489099.pdf, accessed January 15, 2020.

142. See Lynn Abbott, *I Got Two Wings: Incidents and Anecdotes of the Two-Winged Preacher and Electric Guitar Evangelist Elder Utah Smith* (Brooklyn: CaseQuarter, 2008), 18–20, 115. I am grateful to Lynn Abbott for supplying a copy of the COGIC songster.

143. Church of God in Christ's minister Ballinger's "God Rode in a Windstorm" (Peacock 119), reissued on Ballinger featuring Willie Dixon, *The King's Highway*, Bear Family Salvation Series BCD17575 (2CD), 2021, mentions doctors and the flu in 1929 in a chorus similar to this one and the one in "God, He Rolled in the Wind and the Storm" (AFS 264-B-1), the only African American song dealing with the 1925 Great Tri-State Tornado. Strangely enough, he used a different disaster to reference the flu. His recording titled "He Rode" (Peacock 110, recorded ca 1963 in Chicago) is a version of this song but it doesn't mention the 1929 flu. He also recorded two unreleased Chess titles in Chicago: "In Miami, Florida" (ca. June 1955) and "Influenza" (ca. August 1961), which are likely to be covers of disaster songs.

144. Available on Elder Curry and Elder Beck, *Complete Recorded Works in Chronological Order (1930–1939)*, Document Records BDCD-6035, 1993.

145. Selwyn D. Collins, "The Influenza Epidemic of 1928–1929 with Comparative Data for 1918–1919," *American Journal of Public Health* XX, no. 2 (February 1930): 129.

146. "Shelby Schools to Open Monday: Memphis Influenza Epidemic Is Waning," *Leaf-Chronicle*, Clarksville, TN, January 9, 1929, 2.

147. See Ken Romanowski, liner notes to Elder Curry and Elder Beck, *Complete Recorded Works in Chronological Order (1930–1939)*, Document Records BDCD-6035, 1993; and Beecroft and Rye, *Blues for Francis: The Life and Work of Francis Wilford-Smith*, 174.

148. Available on the Library of Congress website at https://www.loc.gov/item/lomax bib000548/. Howard Rye and Chris Smith, quoted from the draft revision of *Blues and Gospel Records, 1890–1943*: "John Lomax announces the recording date as 15 April 1936 after band 3552-B-3, but 16 April, given in Ruby T. Lomax's field notes for all these recordings, is thought to be correct."

149. See John Cowley, quoting Ruby T. Lomax's field notes, in liner notes to various artists, *Two White Horses Standin' in Line*, Flyright-Matchbox SDM 264, 1976, 5.

150. "Influenza Blues" was recorded in Berkeley, California, on March 17, 1962. First issued on various artists, *Bad Luck N' Trouble*, Arhoolie LP 1018, 1965, it was reissued as "The 1919 Influenza Blues" on Arhoolie CD 510, 2005.

151. Reissued on *The Complete Blind Willie Johnson*, Sony/Columbia Legacy C2K 52835, 1993.

152. Available on various artists, *Barrelhouse Women—Volume 1 (1925–1930)*, Document Records DOCD-5378, 1995. For biographical information on Wallace (probably born Frances B. M. Wilson in 1899), see Eagle and LeBlanc, *Blues: A Regional Experience*, 149, 440.

153. Barry, *The Great Influenza*, 395.

154. David McBride, *From TB to AIDS: Epidemics among Urban Blacks since 1900* (Albany: State University of New York Press, 1991), 38.

155. "Poison Liquor Feared Cause of Odd Illness," *Daily Oklahoman*, March 7, 1930, 15. This story does not mention Jamaica ginger, but the following day the *Cushing [OK] Daily Citizen* reported it as the cause ("Hundreds Are Paralyzed as Result Drink," [sic] March 8, 1930, 1–2). A federal ban on the shipment of Jamaica ginger to Oklahoma City had already been put in place. At this stage, adulteration of the product was not suspected.

156. John P. Morgan and Thomas C. Tulloss, "The Jake Walk Blues," *Old Time Music* 28 (spring 1978): 17–24; John P. Morgan and Thomas C. Tulloss, "The Jake Walk Blues: A Toxicologic Tragedy Mirrored in American Popular Music," *Annals of Internal Medicine* 85, no. 6 (December 1976): 804–8; John P. Morgan, "Jake-leg: Mystery Disease of the 1930s," *Kaleidoscope* I, no. 1 (winter 1983–84): 4–7, 14; John P. Morgan, "Cincinnati's Jake Walk Blues," *Cincinnati Horizons* (February 1978): 6–8; John P. Morgan, "The Jamaica Ginger Paralysis," *Journal of the American Medical Association* 248, no. 15 (October 15, 1982): 1864–67; John P. Morgan and Patricia Penovich, "Jamaica Ginger Paralysis: Forty-seven Year Follow-up," *Archives of Neurology* 35 (August 1978): 530–32. For a sociological study of alcoholism and the blues, see Jon D. Cruz, "Booze and Blues: Alcohol and Black Popular Music, 1920–1930," *Contemporary Drug Problems* 15, no. 2 (summer 1988): 149–86.

157. Leon Gussow, "The Jake Walk and Limber Trouble: A Toxicology Epidemic," *Emergency Medicine News* 26, no. 10 (October 2004): 48.

158. For the development of the epidemic in Oklahoma, see David T. Bowden, L. A. Turley, and H. A. Shoemaker, "The Incidence of 'Jake' Paralysis in Oklahoma," *American Journal of Public Health* XX, no. 11 (November 1930): 1179–86, available at https://ajph.aphapublications.org/doi/pdf/10.2105/AJPH.20.11.1179, accessed February 22, 2020; and L. A. Turley, H. A. Shoemaker, and D. T. Bowden, *Jake Paralysis* (Norman: University of Oklahoma Press, 1931).

159. John P. Morgan and Thomas C. Tulloss, "The Jake Walk Blues," *Annals of Internal Medicine* 85, no. 6: 804–5; John P. Morgan, "Cincinnati's Jake Walk Blues," *Cincinnati Horizons*, 8.

160. "Guilty Plea Entered in Jamaica Ginger Case by Defendant in Boston," *Cincinnati Enquirer*, April 11, 1931, 10; "'Jake' Manufacturer Sentenced to Jail," *Rutland [VT] Daily Herald*, April 2, 1932, 1; "Judge Lowell Inquiry Starts," *Boston Globe*, September 26, 1933, 1; John Parascandola, "The Jamaica Ginger Paralysis Episode of the 1930s," *Pharmacy in History* 36, no. 3 (1994): 123–43.

161. This and all the issued songs analyzed in this chapter were reissued on *Jake Leg Blues*, Jass J-CD-642, 1994 (originally *Jake Walk Blues*, Stash LP ST-110, 1977, with two fewer titles). For the date of Bracey's recording, see van Rijn and van der Tuuk, *New York Recording Laboratories Matrix Series Volume One: The L Matrix Series (1929–1932)*, xix–xx, 17. Hillbilly guitarist Lemuel Turner recorded "Jake Bottle Blues" (Victor VI-V-40052) in Memphis on February 9, 1928, but this is an instrumental recorded well before the epidemic and the title almost certainly refers to his use of a jake bottle as a slide, although it seems to make a sly allusion to drinking the contents as well. Other references to "jake," "jake head," and its variants in pre- and postwar blues recordings are discussed in Chris Smith, "Jig Head / Jickhead / Jake Head," in column

"Words Words Words," *Blues & Rhythm* 253 (October 2010): 25, and "Jickhead," in column "Words Words Words," *Blues & Rhythm* 257 (March 2011): 24.

162. I would like to thank members of the Yahoo prewar blues group (now closed down) for their opinions on the transcription of this line.

163. "Alcohol and Jake Blues" and "Canned Heat Blues" are available on Tommy Johnson, *Complete Recorded Works in Chronological Order (1928–1929)*, Document Records DOCD-5001, 1990 (reissued in 2008 as *Victor and Paramount Recordings 1928–1929 in Chronological Order*). For a biography of Johnson, see David Evans, *Tommy Johnson* (London: Studio Vista, 1971).

164. Chris Smith, email to the author, April 21, 2013. Compare "Nok-Em-All Blues" (Victor 23324) by Eddie and Oscar (Ed Schaffer and Oscar Woods), recorded in Dallas on February 8, 1932, and reissued on various artists, *Too Late Too Late Volume 4 (c. 1892–1937)*, Document Records DOCD-5321, 1995. For a transcription, see Macleod, *Document Blues-9*, 76.

165. Quoted in Evans, *Tommy Johnson*, 57.

166. For biographical information on the Allen Brothers, see Russell, *Country Music Originals*, 72–74; and D. L. Nelson, "The Allen Brothers," *John Edwards Memorial Foundation Quarterly* 7, no. 24 (winter 1971): 147–50. "Jake Walk Blues" (Library of Congress AAFS 1522 A-2), by white Kentucky musician and jake leg sufferer Maynard Britton, was collected on October 15, 1937, by Alan and Elizabeth Lomax at Big Creek, near Winchester, Kentucky, where white recording artist Asa Martin also lived. It is a cover of the Allen Brothers' song.

167. John P. Morgan, liner notes to *Jake Walk Blues*, Stash ST-110, 1977.

168. John P. Morgan and Thomas C. Tulloss, "The Jake Walk Blues," *Old Time Music* 28 (spring 1978): 20.

169. Issued as by Mississippi Sheiks with Bo Carter. Reissued on *Complete Recorded Works in Chronological Order—Volume 1 (1930)*, Document Records DOCD-5083, 1991.

170. For more biographical information on Byrd Moore, see Morgan and Tulloss, "The Jake Walk Blues," *Old Time Music*, 21, and C. H. Green Jr., "Fiddling Clarence Green: Mountain Musician," *John Edwards Memorial Foundation Quarterly* 7, no. 24 (winter 1971): 163–67.

171. Morgan and Tulloss, "The Jake Walk Blues," *Old Time Music*, 22. "Jake Leg Blues" (Library of Congress AAFS 1524 A-1) is another field recording from Maynard Britton collected by Alan and Elizabeth Lomax for the Library of Congress at Big Creek, near Winchester, Kentucky, on October 15, 1937. It is a cover of the Byrd Moore recording.

172. See Russell, *Country Music Records*, 842; and Morgan and Tulloss, "The Jake Walk Blues," *Old Time Music*, 22. For a biography of Smith, see Russell, *Country Music Originals*, 143–45.

173. John P. Morgan, liner notes to *Jake Walk Blues*, Stash ST-110, 1977. For a discussion of the song, see Russell, *Rural Rhythm: The Story of Old-Time Country Music in 78 Records*, 199–204.

174. "Bay Rum Blues" was not reissued on the Stash LP; it is on the Jass CD *Jake Leg Blues*, and is also available on *Cotton Mill Songs and Hillbilly Blues: Piedmont Textile Workers on Record, Gaston County, North Carolina 1927–1931*, Old Hat Records CD 1007, 2009.

175. For a short biography of Asa Martin, see Russell, *Country Music Originals*, 90–92.

176. In this line, "you know" is a substitution for "all hell."

177. Morgan and Tulloss, "The Jake Walk Blues," *Old Time Music*, 22.

178. The scant and conflicting biographical information available on Lofton is in Evans, *Big Road Blues*, 289; Eagle and LeBlanc, *Blues: A Regional Experience*, 215, 454; and John H. Vanco, liner notes to various artists, *Mississippi Blues—Vol. 2 (1926–1935)*, Document Records DOCD-5158, 1993.

179. See Morgan and Tulloss, "The Jake Walk Blues," *Old Time Music*, 22, 24. Its 1920 copyright date means that "Jakey Ginger Blues" (words by Paul A. Smith, music by Len Murphy) is not related to the "jake leg" poisoning. It is reprinted in Riley, *Early Blues*, vol. 2, 26–27.

180. Reissued on Black Ace, *I Am the Boss Card in Your Hand*, Arhoolie CD 374, 1992. See also Eagle and LeBlanc, *Blues: A Regional Experience*, 311–12.

181. For this topic, and a general discussion of the disease, see Dan Baum, "Jake Leg: How the Blues Diagnosed a Medical Mystery," *New Yorker*, September 15, 2003, 50–57.

182. Morgan and Tulloss, "The Jake Walk Blues: A Toxicologic Tragedy Mirrored in American Popular Music," 805; Dan Baum, "Jake Leg: How the Blues Diagnosed a Medical Mystery," 53. In Howard W. Blakeslee, "'Jake Leg' May Be Color Ill: Scientists Believe Pigment in Skin May Combine with Poison," *Miami [OK] Daily News-Record*, September 12, 1930, 6, despite the apparent meaning of the headline, the color and pigment referred to were those of white people (and white chickens!).

183. Two people were reported to have died in nearby dry counties, and a white truck driver from Atlanta, who took some moonshine on the road with him, died in Nashville, Tennessee. See William A. Fowlkes Jr., "Poison Whiskey Kills 35," *Pittsburgh Courier*, November 3, 1951, 1, 4; "38th Victim Claimed by Death Mix," *Atlanta Constitution*, November 2, 1951, 12.

184. I am very grateful to Daniel Fleck for scans of the following newspaper articles: Keeler McCartney, "13 Die Here in Liquor Poisonings," *Atlanta Constitution*, October 23, 1951, 1, 8; Keeler McCartney, "12 Suspects Held As Poison Liquor Claims 27th Life," *Atlanta Constitution*, October 24, 1951, 1, 5; Keeler McCartney, "Ex-Convict Sought in Poison Cases," *Atlanta Constitution*, October 25, 1951, 1, 8; Keeler McCartney, "Webb Finds Source of Fatal Drink," *Atlanta Constitution*, October 26, 1951, 1, 7; "Ugly from Every Viewpoint" (editorial), *Atlanta Constitution*, October 26, 1951, 4; Keeler McCartney, "Man Sought in Liquor Poison Case," *Atlanta Constitution*, October 27, 1951, 2; "Last Poison Liquor Cache Is Believed Seized Here," *Atlanta Constitution*, October 29, 1951, 3; Keeler McCartney, "Police Find Second Car, More Booze," *Atlanta Constitution*, October 31, 1951, 2; "Bootlegging Revealed As State's Worst Evil" (editorial), 4; "Grady Clinic Strained As Ailing Victims Crowd In," *Atlanta Daily World*, October 23, 1951, 1; Marion E. Jackson, "Liquor Death Toll Soars to 24: Grady Clinic Facilities Taxed by Liquor Poisoning Victims," *Atlanta Daily World*, October 24, 1951, 1, 6; George Coleman, "25 Gallons of Deadly Fluid Rounded up Here," *Atlanta Daily World*, October 23, 1951, 1, 6; Marion E. Jackson, "Trace Poison Liquor to White Bootlegger; To Charge Murder: Crime Spokesman Deplores Mass Deaths, Asks Citizens to Act," *Atlanta Daily World*, October 25, 1951, 1, 6; "Death Toll Set at 32; Many Reported Blind," *Atlanta Daily World*, October 25, 1951, 1, 6; "Bootleg Liquor Must Go!" (editorial), *Atlanta Daily World*, October 25, 1951, 1, 6; Marion E. Jackson, "Police Will Probe Bootleg War: Peoplestown Soul Laid Bare by Shocking Liquor Tragedy," *Atlanta Daily World*, October 26, 1951, 1, 4; "John R. Hardy, White Being Held in Poison Liquor Case," *Atlanta Daily World*, October 26, 1951, 1, 4; "Record and Discription [sic] of J. R. Hardy," *Atlanta Daily World*, October 26, 1951, 1, 4; George Coleman, "Poison Liquor Picture Same People Still Drinking 'Stuff,'" *Atlanta Daily World*, October 26, 1951, 1, 4; "Two More Deaths Reported Results of Poison Moonshine," *Atlanta Daily World*, October 26, 1951; "The Post-Mortem" (letter to editor), *Atlanta Daily World*, October 26, 1951, 4; "Enforcement the Answer" (letter to editor), *Atlanta Daily World*, October 26, 1951, 4; "All-Out Fight Pledged Until Every Source of Bootleg Booze Dries Up," *Atlanta Daily World*, October 27, 1951, 1; "Stop Being a Sucker" (editorial), *Atlanta Daily World*, October 27, 1951; "Smallwood Admits Taking 'White Lightning' to Farm," *Atlanta Daily World*, October 28, 1951, 1; "Mother, 2

Daughters Lose Lives from Moonshine," *Atlanta Daily World*, October 28, 1951; George A. Sewell, "Dots and Dashes" (editorial), *Atlanta Daily World*, October 28, 1951; "10 Negroes, 3 Whites Held on Manslaughter; One Held for Murder," *Atlanta Daily World*, October 30, 1951, 1; "Poison Deaths Near the 40 Mark; 2 More Dead," *Atlanta Daily World*, October 30, 1951, 1, 6; "A Horrible Price to Pay" (editorial), *Atlanta Daily World*, October 30, 1951, 6; "Police Uncover Another 140 Gallons of Whiskey," *Atlanta Daily World*, October 31, 1951; "27 Are Dead in Atlanta from Poisonous Liquor," *New York Times*, October 24, 1951, 23; "Second Bootlegger Hunted; 34 Now Dead," *New York Times*, October 27, 1951, 6; "Gives Up in Liquor Deaths: Alleged Seller of Whisky That Killed 35 in Atlanta," *New York Times*, October 28, 1951, 51; "Liquor Deaths Bring Indictment," *New York Times*, November 3, 1951, 32; "Guilty in Whisky Deaths: Bootlegger Gets Life Term for Selling Mixture Fatal to 38," *New York Times*, December 14, 1951, 23. Other articles cited were located by Chris Smith.

185. "38th Victim Claimed by Death Mix," *Atlanta Constitution*, November 2, 1951, 12.

186. "3 Alleged Hardy Accomplices Indicted on Murder Charges," *Atlanta Constitution*, January 19, 1952, 3; "Three to Stand Trial In 'Poison Liquor' Deaths," *Alabama Tribune*, March 21, 1952, 1. No reports of the outcome of the trial have been traced.

187. William A. Fowlkes Jr., "Poison Whiskey Kills 35," *Pittsburgh Courier*, November 3, 1951, 1, 4; "Poison Drink Areas Without Liquor Store," *Atlanta Constitution*, November 22, 1951, 22.

188. Fowlkes, "Poison Whiskey Kills 35"; "Hardy Rented Barn, Used Broomstick to Mix Poison Brew, Witnesses Say," *Atlanta Constitution*, December 12, 1951, 1, 12.

189. Hardy made a brief escape from prison in 1953; he was paroled in 1967. Keeler McCartney, "'Fat' Hardy's Escape Dries Up Moonshine," *Atlanta Constitution*, October 3, 1953, 1; "Poison Moonshine Peddler Captured," *Pittsburgh Courier*, October 24, 1953, 4; "Didn't Kill Anybody Says Fat: Bitter Bootlegger Leaves Reidsville," *Atlanta Constitution*, April 28, 1967, 3.

190. "Atlanta's Tragic Monday" is available on various artists, *Get Right with God: Hot Gospel*, Heritage HTCD 01, 1988, and at http://www.youtube.com/watch?v=_k1Tw3MoFI4. Hayes and Laughton, *The Gospel Discography 1943–2000*, vol. 1, 262, gives an incorrect recording date of ca. 1949/1950. The group's singers, accompanied by an unidentified guitarist, were Walter Andrews (lead), Alfred Ingram (second lead), Richard Frazier, Benjamin Moore, Azell Mitchell, and George Kennedy. On the first pressing of the record, the group's name is spelled "Echos" rather than "Echoes" (see label scan). On later pressings the song is credited to the group's manager, Harrison Smith, and Barnett. Simon Barnett's full name appears in "Tunes Written on Whiskey Deaths," *Pittsburgh Courier*, March 1, 1952, 21, although there "Atlanta's Tragic Monday" is said to be by an anonymous writer (see note 198). Barnett was a salesman for the Atlanta-based Southland Record Distributing Company ("Obituaries," *Atlanta Constitution*, February 6, 1976, 1-D), who probably received composer credits in return for promoting Gerald product.

191. A photograph accompanying Fowlkes, "Poison Whiskey Kills 35," is captioned "Atlanta police prevent crowds of curious from crossing the street to Grady Hospital's clinic where victims of poison liquor were being transported, some of them never to return alive. The crowd remained, continuously changing and filling up, for three days after news of the tragedy spread."

192. The Southern Bell Singers' "The Tragedy of Kennedy" (Vee Jay 934), recorded in December 1963, is an adaptation of this song to the assassination of President Kennedy. See Guido van Rijn, *Kennedy's Blues: African-American Blues and Gospel Songs on JFK* (Jackson: University Press of Mississippi, 2007), 127–28.

193. See Springer, "Text, Context and Subtext in the Blues," 12–16.

194. Fowlkes, "Poison Whiskey Kills 35," 1, 4.

195. Rachel Buchanan O'Hare, "A Life to Treasure," *Atlanta Constitution*, June 13, 1999, F5.

196. Fowlkes, "Poison Whiskey Kills 35," 1, 4. Amos Milburn's "Bad Bad Whiskey" (Aladdin 3068), recorded on September 21, 1950, and released in November, had recently been a major hit. See "The Bad, Bad Whisky: Lethal Atlanta Bootleg Kills 35," *Life*, November 5, 1951, 42.

197. The song was reissued with the title "Fat Hardy's Tardy" (an error for "Toddy") on *Classic Tommy Brown*, Chitlin Circuit Productions Inc., 2002.

198. The full names of the credited writers were Thomas [i.e. Tommy] Brown, Harrison Smith (manager of the Echoes of Zion), and Simon Barnett (see note 190), here misspelled "Barnet." "Tunes Written on Whiskey Deaths," *Pittsburgh Courier*, March 1, 1952, 21.

199. See respectively Brian Baumgartner, "Tommy Brown: Laughing at the Blues," *Juke Blues* 50, 2002, 17; and Steve Cushing, *Blues Before Sunrise: The Radio Interviews* (Urbana: University of Illinois Press, 2010), 161–62.

200. David Evans, unpublished interview with Tommy Brown, Helsinki, Finland, April 4, 2013.

201. The title of this chapter comes from a line in St. Louis Jimmy Oden's "Going Down Slow" (Bluebird BB B8889), recorded in Chicago on November 11, 1941.

202. "Going Down Slow," in Paul Oliver, *Blues Fell This Morning: Meaning in the Blues*, 243–50.

203. For African Americans and epidemics, see McBride, *From TB to AIDS: Epidemics among Urban Blacks since 1900*.

204. See Chris Smith, "Meningitis Blues (Memphis Minnie)," in column "Words Words Words," *Blues & Rhythm* 322 (September 2017): 27.

205. Reissued on Memphis Jug Band, *Complete Recorded Works 1927–1930 in Chronological Order—Volume 3 (1930)*, Document Records DOCD-5023, 1991. Memphis Minnie was breaking her contract with Vocalion by recording for Victor, and she is not named on the label of the Memphis Jug Band version.

206. Reissued on Memphis Minnie and Kansas Joe, *Complete Recorded Works 1929–1934 in Chronological Order—Volume 2 (1930–31)*, Document Records DOCD-5029, 1991. The second take (Vocalion unissued) is available on various artists, *Too Late, Too Late Blues Volume 1*, Document Records DOCD-5150, 1993. Siblings George and Ethel McCoy recorded a cover of Memphis Minnie's song in East St. Louis, Illinois, on September 9 or 12, 1969, issued on *Early in the Morning* (Adelphi AD 1004, 1970). A second Ethel McCoy version, recorded on September 28, 1975, was issued on various artists, *Songs of Death and Tragedy*, Library of Congress Volume 9, LBC 9, 1978. The McCoys claimed that Joe McCoy and Memphis Minnie were their uncle and aunt, but this was opportunistic: born in Booneville, Mississippi, they were both living in East St. Louis by 1930. See Bob Eagle, "Directory of African-Appalachian Musicians," *Black Music Research Journal* 24, no. 1 (Spring 2004): 32.

207. Steve Cushing, interview with Brewer Phillips, Chicago, July 8 and 9, 1989. For this quotation, and further discussion, see Garon and Garon, *Woman with Guitar*, 196–98.

208. Paul and Beth Garon leave the question unresolved in *Woman with Guitar*, 198.

209. Keith Wailoo, *Dying in the City of the Blues: Sickle Cell Anemia and the Politics of Race and Health* (Chapel Hill: University of North Carolina Press, 2001), 1–3, 54, 55.

210. For biographical information on Pluitt, see Bob Eagle, "Roosevelt Sykes Aliases and Associates," *Frog Blues and Jazz Annual* 5 (2017): 172.

211. See Chris Smith, "Meningitis Blues (Frank Pluitt)," in column "Words, Words, Words," *Blues & Rhythm* 351 (August 2020): 26. See also "St. Louis Encephalitis Virus" at https://www

.sciencedirect.com/topics/immunology-and-microbiology/st-louis-encephalitis-virus; and David P. Barr, "The Encephalitis Epidemic in St. Louis," *Annals of Internal Medicine, Vol. 8, 1934–35*, 37–45, online at http://citeseerx.ist.psu.edu/viewdoc/download?doi=10.1.1.851.847& rep=rep1&type=pdf.

212. McBride, *From TB to AIDS*, 46–47.

213. "Christmas Day White, Weather Man Predicts," *Belvedere [IL] Daily Republican*, December 20, 1929, 6.

214. Available on Blind Lemon Jefferson, *Complete Recorded Works in Chronological Order—Volume 4 (1929)*, Document Records DOCD-5020, 1990. Sam "Lightnin'" Hopkins recorded three variants of Jefferson's song, all titled "Pneumonia Blues." The first of them (Bluesville BVLP 1061) was recorded in Houston, Texas, on February 20, 1962, and reissued on *How Many More Years I Got*, Ace Records CDCH 409, 1989. The second was recorded in Houston, Texas, in 1969, and reissued on *Fishing Clothes: The Jewel Recordings, 1965–1969*, Westside WESD 228, 2001. The third was recorded in Berkeley, California, on May 20, 1969, and reissued on *In the Key of Lightnin'*, Tomato CD 2098, 2002.

215. Rates are in fact highest in tropical countries, owing in part to indoor pollution from cooking fuels; see *World Health Statistics 2011*, 14, 103 (World Health Organization, https://www .who.int/whosis/whostat/EN_WHS2011_Full.pdf). The spread of winter pneumonia is probably fostered by people being together indoors to escape the cold.

216. BVDs are underwear manufactured by, and named after, Bradley, Voorhees, and Day. In blues, the expression usually alludes to a union suit, a one-piece long underwear garment for men.

217. van der Tuuk, *The New Paramount Book of Blues*, 87–94.

218. Reissued on Big Bill Broonzy, *Complete Recorded Works in Chronological Order—Volume 4 (1935–1936)*, Document Records DOCD-5126, 1992.

219. It appears to be a reconfiguration of Bumble Bee Slim's two-part "I Keep on Drinking (To Drive My Blues Away)" (Vocalion 03037, July 11, 1935).

220. Scott H. Podolsky, "The Changing Fate of Pneumonia as a Public Health Concern in 20th-Century America and Beyond," *American Journal of Public Health*, 95, no. 12 (December 2005), https://www.ncbi.nlm.nih.gov/pmc/articles/PMC1449499/.

221. Reissued on Woody Guthrie, *Dust Bowl Ballads*, Rounder Records CD 1040, 1988.

222. For the history of the Dust Bowl, see Timothy Egan, *The Worst Hard Time: The Untold Story of Those Who Survived the Great American Dust Bowl* (New York: Houghton Mifflin, 2006); and Donald Worster, *Dust Bowl: The Southern Plains in the 1930s* (New York: Oxford University Press, 1979).

223. This New York recording is available on Josh White, *The Remaining Titles (1941–1947)*, Document Records DOCD-1013, 1999. It is transcribed and discussed in Guido van Rijn, *The Truman and Eisenhower Blues: African-American Blues and Gospel Songs, 1945–1960* (London: Continuum, 2004), 3–4, 155. See also Wald, *Josh White: Society Blues*, 150. White recorded the song twice more. A version made in Chicago in 1960 was released on the LP *The House I Live In* (Elektra EKL 203) and reissued on various artists, *The Truman and Eisenhower Blues: African-American Blues and Gospel Songs, 1945–1960*, Agram Blues ABCD 2018, 2004. An April 1, 1961, concert performance at the Royal Festival Hall, London, England, appeared on *Live* (ABC Paramount LP 407), and is available at https://www.youtube.com/watch?v=9FsRpua54Sk.

224. See Chris Smith, "Vaccinate Me, Baby (King Perry)," in column "Words, Words, Words," *Blues & Rhythm* 30 (October 2015): 24.

225. Oliver, *Blues Fell This Morning: Meaning in the Blues*, 249–50.

226. Louis I. Dublin and J. Lotka, *Twenty-Five Years of Health Progress* (New York: Metropolitan Life Insurance Company, 1937), 371; and William J. Brown et al., *Syphilis and Other Venereal Diseases* (Cambridge, MA: Harvard University Press, 1970), 61–65, as reported in McBride, *From TB to AIDS*, 47, 77.

227. McBride, *From TB to AIDS*, 91.

228. See Gabriel Farrell, *The Story of Blindness* (Cambridge, MA: Harvard University Press, 1956), 231. Further selected general literature on blindness includes Frances Koestler, *The Unseen Minority: A Social History of Blindness in the United States* (New York: David McKay Company, 1976); and John H. Dobree and Eric Boulter, eds., *Blindness and Visual Handicap: The Facts* (Oxford: Oxford University Press, 1982). About syphilis, see James H. Jones, *Bad Blood: The Tuskegee Syphilis Experiment* (New York: Free Press, 1993), expanded ed.; originally published in 1981.

229. Discussions of blind musicians can be found in Luigi Monge, "Blindness Blues: Visual References in the Lyrics of Blind Pre-War Blues and Gospel Musicians," in Springer, *The Lyrics in African American Popular Music*, 91–119; Joseph Witek, "Blindness as a Rhetorical Trope in Blues Discourse," *Black Music Research Journal* 8, no. 2 (1988): 177–93; Christopher John Farley, "Visionary Blindness: Blind Lemon Jefferson and Other Vision-Impaired Bluesmen," in Peter Guralnick, Robert Santelli, Holly George-Warren, and Christopher John Farley, eds., *Martin Scorsese Presents the Blues: A Musical Journey* (New York: Amistad, 2003), 165–70; and Terry Rowden, *The Songs of Blind Folk: African American Musicians and the Cultures of Blindness* (Ann Arbor: University of Michigan Press, 2009). The latter study notes (131) that "[t]he disproportionate rates of blindness among blacks was [*sic*] . . . exacerbated by the fact that diseases like tuberculosis, which afflicted blacks in greater numbers than whites, and sickle-cell anemia, which in the United States is an almost exclusively black disease, can also cause blindness."

230. Available on Walter Davis, *Complete Recorded Works 1933–1952 in Chronological Order—Volume 2 (1935–1937)*, Document Records DOCD-5282, 1994. Jimmie Gordon's recording (Decca 7268) of the same title, available on Jimmie Gordon, *Complete Recorded Works in Chronological Order—Volume 2 (1936–1938)*, Document Records DOCD-5649, 1999, is a cover of Davis's song. Unreleased recordings by Barrel House Annie (probably a pseudonym for Mary Mack) (ARC unissued, Chicago, March 3, 1937) and James Wright (Library of Congress AFS 6776-B-2, Central Farm No. 1, Sugarland, Texas, July 1942) are probably also covers. Postwar covers or variants of Davis's song on record include Jack Dupree Trio, "I Think You Need a Shot" (Continental 6064), recorded in New York City in 1945, reissued on Champion Jack Dupree, *1945–1953*, Krazy Kat CD 08, 1992; Brownie McGhee, "Bad Blood" (Alert 406), recorded in New York City in 1946, reissued on Brownie McGhee, *New York Blues 1946–1948*, EPM 159692, 2000; Brownie McGhee, "New Bad Blood" (Jax 322), recorded in New York City in 1952, reissued on Brownie McGhee and Sonny Terry, *Whoopin' the Blues*, Blue Label SPV 49402, 2007; Champion Jack Dupree, "Bad Blood" (Atlantic LP 8019), recorded in New York City on February 4, 1958, reissued on *Blues from the Gutter*, Atlantic CD 82434, 1992; Johnnie Young, "Bad Blood" (Testament T2203), recorded in Chicago on November 17, 1963, reissued on various artists, *Modern Chicago Blues*, Testament TCD 5008, 1994; and James Crutchfield, "I Believe You Need a Shot" (Swingmaster LP 2109), recorded in Groningen, The Netherlands, on October 28, 1983, reissued on *St. Louis Blues Piano*, Swingmaster CD 2205, 2001. On January 23, 1940, Stetson Kennedy and Robert Cook recorded "I Got A Gal, She Mean Me No Good (I

Got Those Syphilis Blues)" (AFS 3393-A), self-accompanied on piano by Bahamian Theodore Rolle in Key West, Florida, on January 23, 1940; but despite its subtitle, the song, available at https://www.floridamemory.com/discover/audio/, doesn't deal with syphilis. Thanks to Chris Smith and John Cowley for their assistance with locating this song. Circa September-October 1941, Charlie Watkins, from Shell Ridge, in Sunflower County, Mississippi, recited a "Poem on Syhyliss" [sic] for the Fisk University–Library of Congress research project. AFS-6738-B-2 is filed as by Charlie Palms, but the artist introduces himself by name on the first of his three recordings. Reissued on Walter Davis, *Complete Recorded Works 1933–1952 in Chronological Order—Volume 3 (1937–1938)*, Document Records DOCD-5283, 1994, is also his "Good Gal" (Bluebird B6996), recorded at the Leland Hotel, Aurora, Illinois, on May 5, 1937, which seems to be another song related to venereal disease and addressed to a prostitute. The reference to Hot Springs, Arkansas, is relevant because Hot Springs was a center for the treatment of syphilis. See "Hot Spring waters and the treatment of venereal diseases: The U.S. Public Health Service Clinic and Camp Garraday," https://pubmed.ncbi.nlm.nih.gov/7868479/, and van Rijn, *The St. Louis Blues of Walter Davis*, 130–31, 141–42.

231. Edward H. Beardsley, *A History of Neglect: Health Care for Blacks and Mill Workers in the Twentieth-Century South* (Knoxville: University of Tennessee Press, 1987), 117; quoted in Rowden, *The Songs of Blind Folk*, 49. In the context of this sentence, "as treatable as bad teeth" means "easily treatable."

232. See "Salvarsan" in *Chemical and Engineering News* 83, no. 25 (June 2005), https://pubsapp.acs.org/cen/coverstory/83/8325/8325salvarsan.html. The new drug did away with the grim joke, "A night with Venus, a lifetime with mercury."

233. See T. DeWayne Moore, "Bo Carter: Genius of the Country Blues," *Blues & Rhythm* 330 (June 2018): 16, 21, 24.

234. Available on Bo Carter, *Complete Recorded Works in Chronological Order—Volume 1 (1928—4 June 1931)*, Document Records DOCD-5078, 1991. Less than three years later, Carter recorded a similar version (Bluebird B5825, March 26, 1934), reissued on various artists, *Too Late Too Late Volume 2 (1897–1935)*, Document Records DOCD-5216, 1993.

235. The song is available on Walter Roland, *Complete Recorded Works in Chronological Order—Volume 2 (1934–1935)*, Document Records DOCD-5145, 1993. The reverse of the record was "S. O. L. Blues," recorded four days later. "S. O. L." stands for "shit out of luck," and it appears that ARC conceived the release as a two-sided "initials" issue.

236. See Chris Smith, "O. B. D. Blues (Walter Roland)," in column "Words, Words, Words," *Blues & Rhythm* 351 (August 2020): 26–27.

237. See Maj. Mark S. Rasnake, USAF MC, et al., "History of U.S. Military Contributions to the Study of Sexually Transmitted Diseases," in *Military Medicine* 170, no. 4 (April 2005): 61–65.

238. Erik Barnouw, *Media Marathon* (Durham, NC: Duke University Press, 1996), cited in Alan J. Sofalvi, "The Venereal Disease (VD) Radio Project" (see next note).

239. The best account of the V.D. Radio Project is Alan J. Sofalvi, "The Venereal Disease [VD] Radio Project: A Look at a 20th-Century Initiative on Sexually Transmitted Infection [STI] Prevention," *Health Educator* 49, no. 2 (fall 2017): 28–34, available at https://files.eric.ed.gov/fulltext/EJ1196133.pdf, accessed March 16, 2020. It includes an overview of the VD Radio Project and a synopsis of the radio programs, but the 78 r.p.m. record is not mentioned. A less scholarly (and sometimes facetious) entry point, which however includes valuable links to recordings, is Ben Houtman, "The Story Behind the V.D. Radio Project," published by NYPR Archives and

Preservation on February 17, 2019 (available at https://www.wnyc.org/story/story-behind-vd
-radio-project/, accessed March 15, 2020). The programs featured major country stars like Roy
Acuff, Hank Williams, Eddy Arnold, and others; folk singer Woody Guthrie; the Hall Johnson
Choir, in "Born on Friday"; the Dixie-Aires, in the musical segments of "The Prodigal Son," a
modern-day version of the well-known biblical story; and Sister Rosetta Tharpe, alternating
traditional gospel songs with the story of a woman who loses three children to congenital
syphilis. Courtesy of the David J. Sensor CDC Museum and Columbia University, the latter
program can be heard at https://www.wnyc.org/story/vd-on-the-radio/. Tharpe's contribution
to the campaign is discussed in Gayle F. Wald, *Shout, Sister, Shout! The Untold Story of Rock-
and-Roll Trailblazer Sister Rosetta Tharpe* (Boston: Beacon Press, 2007), 65–66. The program's
title is uncertain: it is called "Rosetta Tharpe Sings a Cautionary Tale" at the website referenced,
and "I Shall Be a Witness" by the Recorded Sound Division, Library of Congress, whose digital
sound cassette, RGB 3024, is credited to Rosetta Tharpe and the Heavenly Queens Choir (see
Wald, *Shout, Sister, Shout!*, 234).

240. I was made aware of this recording by Ray Templeton, "Ain't That Good News: Crossing
Over. Mixing Sacred and Secular, with the Dixieaires and More," *Blues and Rhythm* 33 (June
2018): 6-7. See also "To Ask Ops' Aid in Fighting VD," *Billboard*, August 13, 1949, 99–100. The
article is datelined August 6, and its content suggests that the disk had been recently recorded.

241. For the history of Tom Glazer's song and its text, see Barnouw, *Media Marathon: A
Twentieth-Century Memoir*, 105–9. The song can be heard at https://www.wnyc.org/story/
ignorant-cowboy/. For biographical information on Glazer, see https://en.wikipedia.org/wiki/
Tom_Glazer.

242. Jay Bruder, notes to various artists, *R&B in D.C.*, Bear Family Records BCD 17052
(16CD), 2021.

243. Cf. Robert Johnson, "Preachin' Blues" (Vocalion 04360, San Antonio, November 27, 1936);
and Sleepy John Estes, "Milk Cow Blues" (Victor V38614, Memphis, May 13, 1930).

244. For literature on tuberculosis, see Thomas Dormandy, *The White Death: A History of
Tuberculosis* (New York: New York University Press, 2000).

245. Garon and Garon, *Woman with Guitar*, 196.

246. Federal Writers' Project, *New York City Guide* (New York: Random House, 1939), 258.
There was another "lung block" between Cherry, Catherine, Monroe, and Market Streets on
the Lower East Side, where many immigrants from Europe lived. See Max Page, *The Creative
Destruction of Manhattan, 1900–1940* (Chicago and London: University of Chicago Press,
1999), 100–101.

247. C. St. C. Guild, "A Five-Year Study of Tuberculosis Among Negroes," *Journal of Negro
Education* 6, no. 3 (July 1937): 548, referenced in McBride, *From TB to AIDS*, 37.

248. McBride, *From TB to AIDS*, 86.

249. Oliver, *Blues Fell This Morning*, 246–47.

250. Bill Minutaglio, *In Search of the Blues: A Journey to the Soul of Black Texas* (Austin:
University of Texas Press, 2010), 116.

251. Reissued on Victoria Spivey, *Complete Recorded Works in Chronological Order—Volume
1 (1926–1927)*, Document Records DOCD-5316, 1995. Apart from the follow-up songs discussed
here, Spivey rerecorded her initial hit several times, all versions being titled "T.B. Blues." The first
remake, recorded in New York City on June 3, 1963, remains unissued; live recordings were made
at Kossuth Hall, New York City, on August 31, 1963, and in Bremen, Germany, on October 13,

1963, during the American Folk Blues Festival. They were issued respectively on *Victoria Spivey and Her Blues*, Spivey Records LP 1030, 1980s, and various artists, *American Folk Blues Festival '62 to '65*, Evidence Records ECD 26100, 1995. Spivey made two studio versions in Chicago on March 26, 1964; one of them appears on various artists, *Encore! for the Chicago Blues*, Spivey LP 1009, 1968. Lawrence Gellert recorded an unidentified man singing an unaccompanied "Too Late Too Late Too Late Too Late" (7–2141-B) in the Carolinas or Georgia. The recording, held at Indiana University Archives of Traditional Music, is inaudible, but it is likely to be a version of Spivey's song. If so, it was probably recorded in 1928 or 1929; it appears on one of the aluminum discs that Gellert used during his early expeditions. (Information from Chris Smith.) Among the first issued versions of the many covers or textually similar renditions of Spivey's song are Willie Jackson, "T.B. Blues" (Columbia 14284-D), recorded in New York City on January 21, 1928, reissued on various artists, *Male Blues of the Twenties—Volume 2 (1923–1928)*, Document Records DOCD-5532, 1997; George Noble, "T.B. Blues" (Vocalion 02954), recorded in Chicago on March 20, 1935, reissued on various artists, *Chicago Piano (1929–1936)*, Document Records DOCD-5191, 1993; Sonny Boy Williamson (John Lee Williamson), "T.B. Blues" (Bluebird B8333), recorded in Chicago on July 21, 1939, reissued on Sonny Boy Williamson, *Complete Recorded Works in Chronological Order—Volume 3 (1939–1941)*, Document Records DOCD-5057, 1991, which uses Spivey's tune, and her "When I was on my feet" trope, but mentions tuberculosis only in the refrain; Lead Belly, "T.B. Woman Blues," recorded in New York City on March 25, 1935 (ARC, first issued on Leadbelly, *King of the Twelve-String Guitar*, Columbia/Legacy CD CK 46776, 1991); Josh White, "T.B. Blues" (Asch 550–1), recorded in New York City, ca. April 1944, reissued on Josh White, *Free and Equal Blues*, Smithsonian Folkways SF CD 40081, 1998; Big Joe Williams, "T.B. Blues" (Folkways FS 3820), recorded in Chicago on July 13–20, 1961, reissued on *Big Joe Williams and His Nine-String Guitar*, Smithsonian Folkways SF CD 40052, 1995; Memphis Slim, "T.B. Blues" (Spivey Records LP 1006, 1966), recorded in New York City, ca. June 1965. On March 18, 1935, in New York City, Josh White recorded a song titled "Homeless and Hungry" (Perfect 0328), which includes a stanza dealing with tuberculosis. After World War II, White and Lead Belly recorded further covers of the Spivey song. Bo Carter's brother Sam Chatmon made two versions of the tuberculosis song. The first was recorded in Hollandale, Mississippi, in 1978 by Alan Lomax, Worth Long, and John Bishop during the shooting of the film *The Land Where the Blues Began*, which was released on the eponymous DVD in collaboration with www.culturalequity.org. The song is also available at https://www.youtube.com/watch?v=6ifJEr-pUQ, and is a mixture of Bo Carter's and Victoria Spivey's lyrics. Chatmon's second version, "T.B.'s Killing Me (T.B. Blues)," was recorded by Gianni Marcucci in Hollandale, Mississippi, in June 1982, and is currently unissued.

252. Denver, Colorado, known as "the mile-high city," functions here as a metonym for the treatment of TB; its mountain air was thought to be therapeutic, and many sanatoriums were located there.

253. Daphne Duval Harrison, *Black Pearls: Blues Queens of the 1920s* (New Brunswick: Rutgers University Press, 2000 [1988]), 153–54; see also Victoria Spivey, "Blues Are My Business," *Record Research* 53 (July 1963): 12; and anon., "Victoria Spivey Cleffed 'T.B. Blues,' Not Leadbelly, Tune Detectives Discover," *Variety* 242, April 13, 1966, 55.

254. Victoria Spivey, "I Commence to Whippin'," in Oliver, *Conversation with the Blues*, 118.

255. Reissued on Victoria Spivey, *Complete Recorded Works in Chronological Order—Volume 3*, Document Records DOCD-5318, 1995.

256. For the transcription of this difficult line, I am indebted to Jim Dixon and Mick Pearce, in a discussion of Spivey's TB songs at https://mudcat.org/thread.cfm?threadid=60385.

257. Reissued on Bessie Tucker, *Complete Recorded Works in Chronological Order*, Document Records DOCD-5070, 1991.

258. Reissued on Buddy Moss, *Complete Recorded Works in Chronological Order—Volume 1 (1933)*, Document Records DOCD-5123, 1992. Vocalion 1735 was issued pseudonymously, as by Jim Miller.

259. Reissued on various artists, *Alabama and the East Coast (1933–1937)*, Document Records DOCD-5450, 1996.

260. Reissued on Victoria Spivey, *Complete Recorded Works in Chronological Order—Volume 3*, Document Records DOCD-5318, 1995.

261. Reissued on Bill Gaither (Leroy's Buddy), *Complete Recorded Works in Chronological Order—Volume 3 (1938–1939)*, Document Records DOCD-5253, 1994.

262. Reissued on Champion Jack Dupree, *Early Cuts from a Singer Pianist and Songwriter Who Took the Blues to the World*, JSP Records JSPCD 77120 (4CD), 2009.

263. Alan Balfour, liner notes to Champion Jack Dupree, *Junker Blues 1940–1941*, Travelin' Man TM 807, 1985.

264. "Chest X-Ray Song" is available in streaming at http://drdemento.com/online.html?c=e20&s=s. A label scan can be seen at https://www.audioasylum.com/messages/vinyl/811183/quot-get-out-those-old-records-quot-photos-part-2-3. See also Al Sweeney, "Lutcher-Style to Spark T.B. Exams," *The Afro-American*, May 15, 1948; Arthur Edson, "'Chest X-Ray Song' Latest TB Singing Commercial," *Abilene (Texas) Reporter* (News), May 6, 1948, 35, which is the same article as "Singing Blurb, on Rising Note, Plugs for TB Chest X-Rays," *Pittsburgh Berkshire Evening Eagle*, May 7, 1948, 10, available at https://newspaperarchive.com/pittsfield-berkshire-evening-eagle-may-07-1948-p-10/; "Nellie Lutcher Helps X-Ray Program," *Indianapolis Recorder*, August 19, 1950, 13. For biographical information on Nellie Lutcher, see Steve Propes, "Obituaries: Nellie Lutcher," *Blues & Rhythm* 221 (August 2007): 12. Lutcher's brother Joe also got into public health issues, reportedly recording a song titled "Answer to Cancer" in support of a cancer fund drive. The song's copyright registration is dated May 19, 1948, but no record seems to have been issued. See *Indianapolis Recorder*, February 4, 1950, 7. I am grateful to Chris Smith for alerting me to the Lutcher song and providing further relevant information.

265. The original LP is reissued on Champion Jack Dupree, *Blues from the Gutter*, Atlantic CD 82434, 1992.

266. Transcribed and discussed in Oster, *Living Country Blues*, 71, 181.

267. White, *American Negro Folk-Songs*, 391.

268. This toast has been reissued on vinyl as *Negro Folklore from Texas State Prisons*, Moochin' About moochin22LP, 2020.

269. Both takes of "T.B. Blues" are in Jimmie Rodgers, *The Singing Brakeman, 1927–33*, Bear Family Records BCD 15540 (6CD), 1992. Thanks to David Evans and Chris Smith for general assistance with this discussion, and especially for information about Hall. See also Nolan Porterfield, *Jimmie Rodgers: The Life and Times of America's Blue Yodeler* (Jackson: University Press of Mississippi, 2007; originally University of Illinois Press, 1979), 252–53, and Barry Mazor, *Meeting Jimmie Rodgers, How America's Original Roots Music Hero Changed the Pop Sounds of a Century* (New York: Oxford University Press, 2012 [2009]), 117, 119, 192. Among numerous versions of "T.B. Blues" covering or inspired by Rodgers's song are those by his admirer, and

initially imitator, Gene Autry (1907–1998). Autry's second cover version, recorded in New York City on April 14, 1931, was released on Banner 32244. It is available on Gene Autry, *Blues Singer 1929–1931*, Columbia/Legacy CK 64987, 1996. Other interesting prewar versions of Rodgers's song are Frankie Marvin, "T.B. Blues" (Crown 3204), recorded in New York City, ca. August 1931, available on www.youtube.com, and the Callahan Brothers, "T.B. Blues No. 2" (Banner 33414), recorded in New York City on August 16, 1934, credited to Homer Callahan on the mp3 compilation *1940's Country Volume 3*, also available on www.youtube.com.

270. The last stanza is very similar to a widespread traditional blues formula, transcribed as part of "The Cholly Blues" in Lomax and Lomax, *American Ballads and Folk Songs*, 201–3. Rodgers had previously used it in "Blue Yodel No. 9" (Victor 23580, July 12, 1930). On the writing of "T.B. Blues," see Porterfield, *Jimmie Rodgers*, 278–80.

271. Anderson, with Lauterbach, *Brother Robert: Growing Up with Robert Johnson*, 54–55.

272. Also available in the Bear Family Records box set and on www.youtube.com.

273. Reissued, with annotation by Mack McCormick, on various artists, *Songs of Death and Tragedy*, Library of Congress Volume 9, LBC 9, 1978, and available on www.youtube.com. For biographical information on Tubb, see Russell, *Country Music Originals*, 238–40.

274. Available on various artists, *Classic Field Recordings* (4CD), JSP 77131, 2010, and on www.youtube.com.

275. Blues singers who suffered, and in some cases died, from diabetes include B.B. King, Bo Diddley, Peg Leg Howell, Ida May Mack, Willie Trice, Big Joe Duskin, Willie Dixon, Louis Myers, and Luther "Guitar Junior" Johnson. Only Big Joe Williams seems to have sung about his condition, in "Sugar Diabetes," recorded in Crawford, Mississippi, in May 1971, and issued on Big Joe Williams and Friends, *Going Back to Crawford* (Arhoolie CD 9015). In "She's a Sweet One" (USA 742, May 28, 1963), Junior Wells uses the disease as a humorous metaphor. Coughing throughout the song mentioning tonsillitis, Bumble Bee Slim recorded "I Done Caught My Death of Cold" (Vocalion 03767, February 6, 1936), an individual response to a personal tragedy.

276. Govenar and Lornell, *The Blues Come to Texas*, 304.

277. See text and Table 2.1, "Leading Causes of Death among Nonwhites: Rate per 100,000 in Successive Decades, 1910–1940," in McBride, *From TB to AIDS*, 46–47.

278. Similar social approaches to the topic are discussed in Allan M. Brandt, *No Magic Bullet: A Social History of Venereal Disease in the United States Since 1880* (New York: Oxford University Press, 1987).

CHAPTER FOUR: AFRICAN AMERICAN DISASTER SONGS AND MEMORY

1. Levine, *Black Culture and Black Consciousness*.

2. Bruce Jackson, in the magazine *Listen*, quoted by Pete Welding in the sleeve notes to various artists, *Can't Keep from Crying: Topical Blues on the Death of President Kennedy*, Bounty LP 6035, 1967. See also Cohen, *Long Steel Rail*, 21.

3. Benjamin Filene, *Romancing the Folk: Public Memory and American Roots Music* (Chapel Hill: University of North Carolina Press, 2000), 5, 8, defines public memory as "the vague and often conflicting assumptions about the past that Americans carry with them and draw on, usually unconsciously in their daily actions and reactions . . . formed by a recursive process [which] involves revisiting and revaluating the culture of the past in light of the present."

4. Sterling A. Brown, "The Blues as Folk Poetry" (1930), reprinted in Robert G. O'Meally, ed., *The Jazz Cadence of American Culture* (New York: Columbia University Press, 1998), 541.

5. Taft, *The Blues Lyric Formula*, 192.

6. Brown, "The Blues as Folk Poetry," 541.

7. Joos, "A Profile of African American Remembrance in a Small Mississippi Town," 18.

8. Joos, "A Profile of African American Remembrance in a Small Mississippi Town," 27.

9. "Memorial Service at Titanic Tower," *New York Times*, April 16, 1932, 33; quoted in Biel, *Down with the Old Canoe*, 144.

10. Levine, *Black Culture and Black Consciousness*, 389.

11. One of the most comprehensive publications on oral history is Robert Perks and Alistair Thomson, eds., *The Oral History Reader*, 3rd ed. (London: Routledge, 2015 [1998]).

12. Michael Frisch, "Oral History and Hard Times: A Review Essay," 19–37, in Perks and Thomson, eds., *The Oral History Reader*. Literature on the concept of memory includes Filene, *Romancing the Folk*; George Lipsitz, *Time Passages: Collective Memory and American Popular Culture* (Minneapolis: University of Minnesota Press, 1990); David Thelen, ed., *Memory and American History* (Bloomington: University of Indiana Press, 1990); and Geneviève Fabre and Robert O'Meally, eds., *History and Memory in African-American Culture* (New York and Oxford: Oxford University Press, 1994).

13. See Christian O'Connell, *Blues, How Do You Do? Paul Oliver and the Transatlantic Story of the Blues* (Ann Arbor: University of Michigan Press, 2015), 109–10; and Alessandro Portelli, "What Makes Oral History Different," in Perks and Thomson, *The Oral History Reader*, 63–74.

14. Alessandro Portelli, "Robert Johnson: La Sua Voce Parla per Noi" ("Robert Johnson: His Voice Speaks for Us"), foreword to Luigi Monge, *Robert Johnson: I Got the Blues. Testi Commentati* (Rome, Italy: Arcana, 2008), 15–27, quotation on 16–17. Adapted and reprinted in Alessandro Portelli, "Robert Johnson: I Suoni del Silenzio" ("Robert Johnson: The Sounds of Silence"), in *Note Americane: Musica e Culture negli Stati Uniti* ("American Notes: Music and Cultures in the United States") (Milano and Rimini, Italy: ShaKe Edizioni, 2011), 63–71, quotation on 64. The translation is mine.

15. Gayle Wald, "Past Is Present," *Oxford American: Vision of the Blues: Southern Music Issue* 28 (winter 2016): 26.

16. African American writer Toni Morrison explained in 1988 that the main motivation for her to write her Nobel Prize–winning novel *Beloved* had been American people's forgetting of the days of slavery. Among other things, her works aim to bridge the gap between the past and the present, and to consider the past as flowing into the present.

17. Kathleen Reine, "The Ways of the Isles," *Times Literary Supplement*, December 20, 1977, 1520, quoted in Bessie Jones, *Put Your Hand on Your Hip and Let Your Backbone Slip*, Rounder CD 1166–1587–2, 2001, originally published in the liner notes to Bessie Jones, *Step It Down*, Rounder Records LP 8004, 1979.

18. Pierre Nora, "Between Memory and History: Les Lieux de Mémoire," in Fabre and O'Meally, *History and Memory in African-American Culture*, 286, 289–90.

19. Steinberg, *Acts of God*, 69, 71, 81. According to another study, the average annual death toll from tornadoes in the United States in the first half of the twentieth century was two hundred people. John Brooks, "A Reporter at Large: Five-ten on a Sticky June Day," *New Yorker*, May 28, 1955, 39–75; quoted in Martha Wolfenstein, *Disaster: A Psychological Essay* (London and New York: Routledge, 2013), 203, originally published in 1957.

20. Robert G. O'Meally, "On Burke and the Vernacular: Ralph Ellison's Boomerang of History," in Fabre and O'Meally, *History and Memory in African-American Culture*, 252.

21. Oliver, *Broadcasting the Blues*, 113.

22. Oliver, *Broadcasting the Blues*, 116.

23. A contrary view is advanced in Alger, *The Original Guitar Hero and the Power of Music: The Legendary Lonnie Johnson: Music and Civil Rights*. Similarly, Kevin D. Greene, *The Invention and Reinvention of Big Bill Broonzy* (Chapel Hill: University of North Carolina Press, 2018), seems to position Broonzy as a precursor of the civil rights movement. These interpretations are unconvincing, and not valid as far as disaster songs are concerned.

24. Both quotations are from Davis, *Blues Legacies and Black Feminism*, 111.

25. Davis, *Blues Legacies and Black Feminism*, 111.

26. van Rijn, *Roosevelt's Blues*, 205. See also Evans, *Big Road Blues*, 29–30.

27. van Rijn, *The Truman and Eisenhower Blues*, 150.

28. Lomax, *The Land Where the Blues Began*, 52. Sister Cally Fancy's "Everybody Get Your Business Right" (Brunswick 7110), a warning song alluding to a series of recent natural disasters, was recorded in Chicago on August 15, 1929. It is available on various artists, *Gospel Classics—Volume 2 (1927–1935)*, Document Records DOCD-5313, 1994. Lomax's statement applies equally to many white compositions, especially to Carson Robison's and Andy Jenkins's disaster songs.

29. Ziólek-Sowińska, *Images of the Apocalypse in African American Blues and Spirituals*, 12, 54, 68.

30. Ziólek-Sowińska, *Images of the Apocalypse in African American Blues and Spirituals*, 56.

31. Levine, *Black Culture and Black Consciousness*, 174.

32. Ziólek-Sowińska, *Images of the Apocalypse in African American Blues and Spirituals*, 12.

33. Cohen, *Long Steel Rail*, 169, 170. See also Laws, *Native American Balladry*, 24, where the author states that "the ballad with a single victim or hero has a much better chance of popularity than one in which many are killed. Mass tragedies can be looked upon with some detachment, but the death of an individual whose character has been delineated is far more moving and meaningful."

34. Govenar and Lornell, *The Blues Come to Texas*, 303–4.

35. van Rijn, *Roosevelt's Blues*, 207–8, and *The Truman and Eisenhower Blues*, 153.

36. For a non-topical sermon, see Rev. J. M. Milton's "Silk Worms and Boll Weevils" in the relevant chapter.

37. The Baby Doo and Gene Gilmore release on the Natchez Fire is an example of a coupling on the same disaster, while Josh White's songs on the Hawk's Nest Tunnel and Scottsboro disasters are examples of a coupling on different disasters.

38. Barry, *The Great Influenza*, 393. Lonnie Johnson lost several family members to the influenza pandemic, but never recorded a song about it.

39. See also Luigi Monge. "Topical Blues: Disasters," in Komara, *Encyclopedia of the Blues*, vol. 2, 1001–2.

40. Ralph Ellison, *Going to the Territory* (New York: Vintage International, 1995), 144. Originally published by Random House in 1986.

BIBLIOGRAPHY

BOOKS

Abbott, Lynn. *I Got Two Wings: Incidents and Anecdotes of the Two-Winged Preacher and Electric Guitar Evangelist Elder Utah Smith*. Brooklyn: CaseQuarter, 2008.

Abbott, Lynn, and Doug Seroff. *Out of Sight: The Rise of African American Popular Music 1889–1895*. Jackson: University Press of Mississippi, 2002.

Abbott, Lynn, and Doug Seroff. *The Original Blues: The Emergence of the Blues in African American Vaudeville*. Jackson: University Press of Mississippi, 2017.

Abrahams, Roger D. *Deep Down in the Jungle: Negro Narrative Folklore from the Streets of Philadelphia*. Hatboro, PA: Folklore Associates, 1964.

Abrahams, Roger D. *Positively Black*. Englewood Cliffs, NJ: Prentice Hall, 1970.

Akin, Wallace. *The Forgotten Storm: The Great Tri-State Tornado of 1925*. Lanham, MD: Rowman & Littlefield, 2015.

Albala-Bertrand, J. M. *The Political Economy of Large Natural Disasters with Special Reference to Developing Countries*. Oxford, UK: Clarendon Press, 1993.

Albertson, Chris. *Bessie*, 2nd ed. New Haven, CT, and London: Yale University Press, 2003.

Alger, Dean. *The Original Guitar Hero and the Power of Music: The Legendary Lonnie Johnson, Music, and Civil Rights*. Denton: University of North Texas Press, 2014.

Alyn, Glen. *I Say Me for a Parable: The Oral Autobiography of Mance Lipscomb, Texas Bluesman*. New York: Da Capo Press, 1994.

Anderson, Annye C., with Preston Lauterbach. *Brother Robert: Growing Up with Robert Johnson*. New York: Hachette, 2020.

Banasik, Michael E., ed. *Cavaliers of the Brush: Quantrill and His Men*. Iowa City: Press of the Camp Pope Bookshop, 2003.

Barnet, Richard D., Bruce Nemerov, and Mayo Taylor. "The Band Played 'Nearer My God to Thee' As the Ship Went Down." In *The Story Behind the Song: 150 Songs That Chronicle the 20th Century*, 31–32. Westport, CT, and London: Greenwood Press, 2004.

Barnouw, Erik. *Media Marathon*. Durham, NC: Duke University Press, 1996.

Barry, John M. *Rising Tide: The Great Mississippi Flood of 1927 and How It Changed America*. New York: Simon & Schuster, 1997.

Barry, John M. *The Great Influenza: The Story of the Deadliest Pandemic in History*. London: Penguin, 2005.

Bastin, Bruce. *Red River Blues: The Blues Tradition in the Southeast*. Urbana: University of Illinois Press, 1986.

Bastin, Bruce. "Truckin' My Blues Away: East Coast Piedmont Styles." In *Nothing but the Blues*, edited by Lawrence Cohn, 204, 223–24. New York: Abbeville Press, 1993.

Bastin, Bruce, with Kip Lornell. *The Melody Man: Joe Davis and the New York Music Scene*. Jackson: University Press of Mississippi, 2012.

Beaumont, Daniel. *Preachin' the Blues: The Life and Times of Son House*. Oxford: Oxford University Press, 2011.

Beecroft, Caroline, and Howard Rye. *Blues for Francis: The Life and Work of Francis Wilford-Smith*. York, UK: Music Mentor Books, 2015.

Bell, Rick. *The Great Flood of 1937: Rising Waters, Soaring Spirits*. Louisville, KY: Butler Books, 2007.

Berg, Manfred. *Popular Justice: A History of Lynching in America*. Lanham, MD: Rowman & Littlefield, 2015.

Biel, Steven. *Down with the Old Canoe: A Cultural History of the "Titanic" Disaster*. New York and London: W. W. Norton, 1997.

Biel, Steven, ed. *Titanica: The Disaster of the Century in Poetry, Song, and Prose*. New York and London: W. W. Norton, 1998.

Bodnar, John. *Remaking American Public Memory: Commemoration and Patriotism in the Twentieth Century*. Princeton, NJ: Princeton University Press, 1992.

Botkin, Benjamin Albert. *A Treasury of Mississippi River Folklore: Stories, Ballads, Traditions, and Folkways of the Mid-American River Country*. New York: Bonanza, 1978.

Boyd, Joe Dan. *Judge Jackson and the Colored Sacred Harp*. Montgomery: Alabama Folklife Association, 2002.

Brandt, Allan M. *No Magic Bullet: A Social History of Venereal Disease in the United States since 1880*. New York: Oxford University Press, 1987.

Breaux, Richard M. "The New Negro Renaissance in Omaha and Lincoln, 1910–1940." In *The Harlem Renaissance in the American West: The New Negro's Western Experience*, edited by Bruce A. Glasrud and Cary D. Wintz, 121–39. New York and London: Routledge, 2011.

Brown, Alan. *Southern Ghost Stories*. Jackson: University Press of Mississippi, 2000.

Callahan, Allen Dwight. *The Talking Book: African Americans and the Bible*. New Haven, CT, and London: Yale University Press, 2008.

Calt, Stephen. *Barrelhouse Words: A Blues Dialect Dictionary*. Urbana and Chicago: University of Illinois Press, 2009.

Calt, Stephen, and Gayle Wardlow. *King of the Delta Blues: The Life and Music of Charlie Patton*. Newton, NJ: Rock Chapel Press, 1988.

Carlin, Richard. "Shape-Note Singing." In *Encyclopedia of American Gospel Music*, edited by W. K. McNeil, 336–37. New York: Routledge, 2005.

Cassidy, Frederic G., ed. *Dictionary of American Regional English*, vol. I. Cambridge, MA: Belknap Press of Harvard University, 1985.

Charters, Samuel. *The Country Blues*. New York: Da Capo, 1975.

Charters, Samuel. *The Blues Makers*. New York: Da Capo, 1991.

Check-List of Recorded Songs in the English Language in the Archive of American Folk-Song to July, 1940. Washington, DC: Library of Congress Music Division, 1942.

Cherniack, Martin. *The Hawk's Nest Incident: America's Worst Industrial Disaster*. New Haven, CT: Yale University Press, 1986.

Cohen, Norm. *Long Steel Rail: The Railroad in American Folksong*. Urbana and Chicago: University of Illinois Press, 2000.

Cohen, Norm. *American Folk Songs: A Regional Encyclopedia*, vol. 1. Westport, CT: Greenwood Press, 2008.

Cohn, Lawrence. *Nothing but the Blues*. New York: Abbeville Press, 1993.

Compton, Nic. *Titanic on Trial: The Night the Titanic Sank*. London: Bloomsbury, 2012.

Comstock, Jim, ed. *West Virginia Heritage*, vol. 7. Richwood: West Virginia Heritage Foundation, 1972.

Cook, Bruce. *Listen to the Blues*. New York: Da Capo Press, 1995.

Courlander, Harold. *Negro Folk Music U.S.A.* New York: Columbia University Press, 1963.

Crosby, Alfred W. *America's Forgotten Pandemic: The Influenza of 1918*, 2nd ed. Cambridge and New York: Cambridge University Press, 2003.

Cushing, Steve. *Blues Before Sunrise: The Radio Interviews*. Urbana: University of Illinois Press, 2010.

Dance, Helen Oakley. *Stormy Monday: The T-Bone Walker Story*. New York: Da Capo, 1990.

Dance, Helen, and Stanley Dance. "Electrifying Texas Blues: Aaron 'T-Bone' Walker." In *Bluesland: Portraits of Twelve Major American Blues Masters*, edited by Pete Welding and Toby Byron, 98–113. New York: Dutton, 1991.

Daniel, Pete. *Deep'n As It Come: The 1927 Mississippi River Flood*. Fayetteville: University of Arkansas Press, 1996.

Daniels, Peter. *The Legend of Booker's Guitar*. Self-published, 2014.

Davis, Angela Y. *Blues Legacies and Black Feminism: Gertrude "Ma" Rainey, Bessie Smith, and Billie Holiday*. New York: Vintage Books, 1998.

Del Moral, Roger, and Lawrence R. Walker. *Environmental Disasters, Natural Recovery, and Human Responses*. New York: Cambridge University Press, 2007.

Dixon, Robert M. W., John Godrich, and Howard Rye. *Blues and Gospel Records 1890–1943*, 4th ed. New York: Oxford University Press, 1997.

Dobree, John H., and Eric Boulter. *Blindness and Visual Handicap: The Facts*. Oxford: Oxford University Press, 1982.

Dodge, Timothy. *The School of Arizona Dranes: Gospel Music Pioneer*. Lanham, MD: Lexington Books, 2013.

Dormandy, Thomas. *The White Death: A History of Tuberculosis*. New York: New York University Press, 2000.

Doubler, Michael D. *Dixie Dewdrop: The Uncle Dave Macon Story*. Urbana: University of Illinois Press, 2018.

Dublin, Louis I., and Alfred J. Lotka. *Twenty-Five Years of Health Progress*. New York: Metropolitan Life Insurance Company, 1937.

Eagle, Bob, and Eric S. LeBlanc. *Blues: A Regional Experience*. Santa Barbara, CA: Praeger, 2013.

Eddington, Neil A. "Genital Superiority in Oakland Negro Folklore: A Theme." In *Mother Wit from the Laughing Barrel: Readings in the Interpretation of Afro-American Folklore*, edited by Alan Dundes, 642–48. Englewood Cliffs, NJ: Prentice Hall, 1973.

Edwards, David Honeyboy. *The World Don't Owe Me Nothing: The Life and Times of Delta Bluesman Honeyboy Edwards*. Chicago: Chicago Review Press, 1997.

Egan, Timothy. *The Worst Hard Time: The Untold Story of Those Who Survived the Great American Dust Bowl*. New York: Houghton Mifflin, 2006.

Ellison, Ralph. *Going to the Territory*. New York: Vintage International, 1995.

Evans, David. *Tommy Johnson*. London: Studio Vista, 1971.

Evans, David. *Big Road Blues: Tradition and Creativity in the Folk Blues*. New York: Da Capo Press, 1987.

Evans, David. "High Water Everywhere: Blues and Gospel Commentary on the 1927 Mississippi River Flood." In *Nobody Knows Where the Blues Come From: Lyrics and History*, edited by Robert Springer, 3–75. Jackson: University Press of Mississippi, 2006.

Evans, David, ed. "From Bumble Bee Slim to Black Boy Shine: Nicknames of Blues Singers." In *Ramblin' on My Mind: New Perspectives on the Blues*, 179–221. Urbana and Chicago: University of Illinois Press, 2008.

Evans, David. "Charley Patton: The Conscience of the Delta." In *Charley Patton: Voice of the Mississippi Delta*, edited by Robert Sacré, 23–137. Jackson: University Press of Mississippi, 2018.

Fabre, Geneviève, and Robert O'Meally, eds. *History and Memory in African-American Culture*. New York and Oxford: Oxford University Press, 1994.

Fancourt, Les, and Bob McGrath. *The Blues Discography 1943–1970*, 3rd ed. West Vancouver, BC, Canada: Eyeball Productions, 2019.

Farley, Christopher John. "Visionary Blindness: Blind Lemon Jefferson and Other Vision-Impaired Bluesmen." In *Martin Scorsese Presents the Blues: A Musical Journey*, edited by Peter Guralnick, Robert Santelli, Holly George-Warren, and Christopher John Farley. New York: Amistad, 2003.

Farrell, Gabriel. *The Story of Blindness*. Cambridge, MA: Harvard University Press, 1956.

Federal Writers' Project. *New York City Guide*. New York: Random House, 1939.

Federighi, Luciano. *Blues on My Mind*. Palermo, Italy: L'Epos, 2001.

Felknor, Peter S. *The Tri-State Tornado: The Story of America's Greatest Tornado Disaster*. Lincoln: iUniverse, 2004.

Filene, Benjamin. *Romancing the Folk: Public Memory and American Roots Music*. Chapel Hill: University of North Carolina Press, 2000.

"Florida Hurricane (The)—September 18, 1926: Official Report of the Relief Activities." American National Red Cross, Washington, DC, n.d.: 3–45.

Ford, Robert. *A Blues Bibliography*, 2nd ed. New York: Routledge, 2007.

Ford, Robert. *A Blues Bibliography: Update to the Second Edition*. New York: Routledge, 2020.

Ford, Robert, and Bob McGrath. *The Blues Discography 1971–2000*. West Vancouver, BC, Canada: Eyeball Productions, 2011.

Frisch, Michael. "Oral History and Hard Times: A Review Essay." In *The Oral History Reader*, edited by Robert Perks and Alistair Thomson, 3rd ed., 19–37. London: Routledge, 2015.

Garon, Paul, and Beth Garon. *Woman with Guitar: Memphis Minnie's Blues*. San Francisco: City Lights Books, 2014.

Garst, John. "Casey Jones." In *Encyclopedia of the Blues*, vol. 1 (A-J), edited by Edward Komara, 187. New York: Routledge, 2006.

Gibbs, Craig Martin. *Field Recordings of Black Singers and Musicians: An Annotated Discography of Artists from West Africa, the Caribbean and the Eastern and Southern United States, 1901–1943*. Jefferson: McFarland & Company, 2018.

Giesen, James C. *Boll Weevil Blues: Cotton, Myth, and Power in the American South*. Chicago and London: University of Chicago Press, 2011.

Goodman, Solomon. *Titanic Disaster Music: A Listing by Copyright Registration Number, and Showing Names of Authors, Composers, Copyright Proprietors and Publishers, and Dates of Copyright Registration*, copy no. 13, August 1985. American Folklife Center, Library of Congress.

Gordon, Robert. *Can't Be Satisfied: The Life and Times of Muddy Waters*. Boston: Little, Brown, 2002.

Govenar, Alan. *Lightnin' Hopkins: His Life and Blues*. Chicago: Chicago Review Press, 2010.

Govenar, Alan, and Shane W. Evans. *Osceola: Memories of a Sharecropper's Daughter*. New York: Hyperion, 2000.

Govenar, Alan, and Kip Lornell, comps. *The Blues Come to Texas: Paul Oliver and Mack McCormick's Unfinished Book*. College Station, TX: A&M University Press, 2019.

Gradischnig, Herwig, and Hans Maitner. *Brook Benton: There Goes That Song Again*. York, UK: Music Mentor Books, 2015.

Graham, Sandra Jean. *Spirituals and the Birth of a Black Entertainment Industry*. Urbana and Chicago: University of Illinois Press, 2018.

Gray, Michael. *Hand Me My Travelin' Shoes: In Search of Blind Willie McTell*. London: Bloomsbury, 2007.

Grazulis, Thomas P. *Significant Tornadoes 1680–1991: A Chronology and Analysis of Events*. St. Johnsbury, VT: Tornado Project of Environmental Films, 1993.

Green, Archie. *Only a Miner: Studies in Recorded Coal-Mining Songs*. Urbana and Chicago: University of Illinois Press, 1972.

Greene, Kevin D. *The Invention and Reinvention of Big Bill Broonzy*. Chapel Hill: University of North Carolina Press, 2018.

Gussow, Adam. *Seems Like Murder Here: Southern Violence and the Blues Tradition*. Chicago and London: University of Chicago Press, 2002.

Gussow, Adam. *Beyond the Crossroads: The Devil and the Blues Tradition*. Chapel Hill: University of North Carolina Press, 2017.

Hall, Joan Houston, ed. *Dictionary of American Regional English*, vol. 5, Sl–Z. Cambridge, MA: Belknap Press of Harvard University Press, 2012.

Handy, William Christopher, and Arna Bontemps. *Father of the Blues: An Autobiography*. New York: Macmillan, 1941.

Hanska, Jussi. *Strategies of Sanity and Survival: Religious Responses to Natural Disasters in the Middle Ages*. Helsinki, Finland: Studia Fennica, 2002.

Harper, Michael S., ed. *The Collected Poems of Sterling A. Brown*. New York: Harper & Row, 1980.

Harris, Sheldon. *Blues Who's Who: A Biographical Dictionary of Blues Singers*, 6th ed. New York: Da Capo, 1991.

Harrison, Daphne Duval. *Black Pearls: Blues Queens of the 1920s*. New Brunswick, NJ: Rutgers University Press, 2000.

Hayes, Cedric J., and Robert Laughton. *The Gospel Discography 1943–2000*, 2 vols., 3rd ed. West Vancouver, BC, Canada: Eyeball Productions, 2014.

Haymes, Max. *Railroadin' Some: Railroads in the Early Blues*. York, UK: Music Mentor Books, 2006.

Hearn, Lafcadio. "Levee Life." In *Children of the Levee*, edited by O. W. Frost, 66–67. Lexington: University of Kentucky Press, 1957.

Heyer, Paul. *Titanic Century: Media, Myth, and the Making of a Cultural Icon*. Santa Barbara, CA: Praeger, 2012.

Hudson, Arthur Palmer. "Mister Boll Weevil." In *Folksongs of Mississippi and Their Background*, 199–200. Chapel Hill: University of North Carolina Press, 1936.

Hughes, Langston. *Book of Negro Humor*. New York: Dodd, Mead, 1966.

Hughes, Langston, and Arna Bontemps, eds. *The Book of Negro Folklore*. New York: Dodd, Mead, 1958.

Hurston, Zora Neale. *Their Eyes Were Watching God*. Philadelphia: J. B. Lippincott, 1937.

Jackson, Bruce. "The *Titanic* Toast." In "Veins of Humor," edited by Harry Levin, *Harvard English Studies 3*, 205–23. Cambridge, MA: Harvard University Press, 1972.

Jackson, Bruce. *Get Your Ass in the Water and Swim Like Me: African American Narrative Poetry from Oral Tradition*. New York and London: Routledge, 2004.

Jackson, Judge. *The Colored Sacred Harp*. Ozark: published by the author, 1934.

Jackson, Mahalia, with Evan McLeod Wylie. *Movin' on Up*. New York: Hawthorn Books, 1966.

Jones, Bessie, and Bess Lomax Hawes. *Step It Down*. Athens: University of Georgia Press, 1987.

Jones, Bessie, and John Stewart, eds. *For the Ancestors: Autobiographical Memories*. Athens: University of Georgia Press, 1989.

Jones, James H. *Bad Blood: The Tuskegee Syphilis Experiment*, expanded ed. New York: Free Press, 1993.

Joseph, Pleasant "Cousin Joe," and Harriet Ottenheimer. *Cousin Joe: Blues from New Orleans*. Chicago and London: University of Chicago Press, 1987.

Klein, Christine A., and Sandra B. Zellmer. *Mississippi River Tragedies: A Century of Unnatural Disaster*. New York and London: New York University Press, 2014.

Kleinberg, Eliot. *Black Cloud: The Great Florida Hurricane of 1928*. Cocoa, FL: Florida Historical Society Press, 2016.

Koestler, Frances. *The Unseen Minority: A Social History of Blindness in the United States*. New York: David McKay Company, 1976.

Komara, Edward, ed. *Encyclopedia of the Blues*, 2 vols. New York: Routledge, 2006.

Korson, George. *Coal Dust on the Fiddle: Songs and Stories of the Bituminous Industry*. Hatboro, VT: Folklore Associates, 1965.

Labov, William, Paul Cohen, Clarence Robins, and John Lewis. "Toasts." In *Mother Wit from the Laughing Barrel: Readings in the Interpretation of Afro-American Folklore*, edited by Alan Dundes, 329–47. Englewood Cliffs, NJ: Prentice Hall, 1973.

Lauterbach, Preston. *The Chitlin' Circuit and the Road to Rock 'n' Roll*. New York: Norton, 2011.

Laws, G. Malcolm, Jr. *Native American Balladry: A Descriptive Study and a Bibliographical Syllabus*. Philadelphia: American Folklore Society, 1964.

Lawson, R. A. *Jim Crow's Counterculture: The Blues and Black Southerners 1890–1945*. Baton Rouge: Louisiana University Press, 2010.

Leamy, Hugh. "Now Come All You Good People." In *A History and Encyclopedia of Country, Western, and Gospel Music*, edited by Linnell Gentry, rev. 2nd ed., 6–13. Nashville: Clairmont, 1969.

Levine, Lawrence W. *Black Culture and Black Consciousness: Afro-American Folk Thought from Slavery to Freedom*. Oxford: Oxford University Press, 1977.

Lieb, Sandra R. *Mother of the Blues: A Study of Ma Rainey*. Amherst: University of Massachusetts Press, 1981.

Lipsitz, George. *Time Passages: Collective Memory and American Popular Culture*. Minneapolis: University of Minnesota Press, 1990.

Lomax, Alan. *The Rainbow Sign: A Southern Documentary*. New York: Duell, Sloan & Pearce, 1959.

Lomax, Alan. "The Ballad of the Boll Weevil." In *The Penguin Book of American Folk Songs*, 86. Baltimore: Penguin Books, 1964.

Lomax, Alan. "The Boll Weevil Holler." In *The Folk Songs of North America*, 519, 535–36. New York: Dolphin Books, 1975.

Lomax, Alan. *The Land Where the Blues Began*. New York: Pantheon Books, 1993.

Lomax, John A. *Adventures of a Ballad Hunter*. Austin: University of Texas Press, 2017.

Lomax, John A., and Alan Lomax. *Negro Folk Songs as Sung by Lead Belly*. New York: Macmillan, 1936.

Lomax, John A., and Alan Lomax, eds. "De Ballit of de Boll Weevil." In *Leadbelly: A Collection of World-Famous Songs by Huddie Ledbetter*. Folkways Music Publishers, 1959.

Lomax, John A., and Alan Lomax. *Folk Song U.S.A.* New York: Signet, 1966.

Lomax, John A., and Alan Lomax. *American Ballads and Folk Songs*. New York: Dover Publications, 1994.

Lomax, John A., and Alan Lomax, comps. *Our Singing Country: Folk Songs and Ballads*. Mineola, NY: Dover Publications, 2000.

Lord, Walter. *A Night to Remember*. New York: St. Martin's Griffin, 2005.

Luther, Frank. *Americans and Their Songs*. New York: Harper and Brothers, 1942.

Macleod, R. R. *Document Blues-5*. Edinburgh, UK: PAT, 1998.

Macleod, R. R. *Document Blues-9*. Edinburgh, UK: PAT, 2002.

Major, Clarence, ed. *Juba to Jive: A Dictionary of African-American Slang*. New York: Penguin Books, 1994.

Marscher, William, and Fran Marscher. *The Great Sea Island Storm of 1893*. Macon, GA: Mercer University Press, 2004.

Marshall, Logan. *Sinking of the Titanic and Great Sea Disasters*. Ann Arbor, MI: University Microfilms, 1980.

Mason, Herbert Molley, Jr. *Death from the Sea: The Galveston Hurricane of 1900*. New York: Dial Press, 1972.

Mather, Rachel C. *The Storm Swept Coast of South Carolina*. Woonsocket, RI: Charles E. Cook, 1894.

Mays, E. J., comp. "Mississippi's Tornado Disaster." In Martis D. Ramage Jr., *Tupelo, Mississippi, Tornado of 1936*, 69. Tupelo: Northeast Mississippi Historical and Genealogical Society, 1997.

Mazor, Barry. *Meeting Jimmie Rodgers: How America's Original Roots Music Hero Changed the Pop Sounds of a Century*. New York: Oxford University Press, 2012.

McBride, David. *From TB to AIDS: Epidemics among Urban Blacks since 1900*. Albany: State University of New York Press, 1991.

McNeil, W. K., ed. *Southern Folk Ballads*, vol. II. Little Rock: August House, 1988.

McNeil, W. K., ed. *Encyclopedia of American Gospel Music*. New York: Routledge, 2005.

Meade, Guthrie T., with Dick Spottswood and Douglas S. Meade. *Country Music Sources: A Biblio-Discography of Commercially Recorded Traditional Music*. Chapel Hill: Southern Folklife Collection, University of North Carolina at Chapel Hill Libraries in association with the John Edwards Memorial Forum, 2002.

Mikle, Robert. *Killer 'Cane: The Deadly Hurricane of 1928*. Lanham, MD: Taylor Trade Publishing, 2006.

Mills, Kincaid, Genevieve C. Peterkin, and Aaron McCullough, eds. *Coming Through: Voices of a South Carolina Gullah Community from WPA Oral Histories Collected by Genevieve W. Chandler*. Columbia: University of South Carolina Press, 2008.

Minton, John, and David Evans. *"The Coon in the Box": A Global Folktale in African-American Tradition*. Helsinki, Finland: Academia Scientiarum Fennica, 2001.

Minutaglio, Bill. *In Search of the Blues: A Journey to the Soul of Black Texas*. Austin: University of Texas Press, 2010.

Mitchell, George. *Blow My Blues Away*. Baton Rouge: Louisiana State University Press, 1971.

Mizelle, Richard M., Jr. *Backwater Blues: The Mississippi Flood of 1927 in the African American Imagination*. Minneapolis and London: University of Minnesota Press, 2014.

Monge, Luigi. "Blindness Blues: Visual References in the Lyrics of Blind Pre-War Blues and Gospel Musicians." In *The Lyrics in African American Popular Music*, edited by Robert Springer, 91–119. Bern, Switzerland: Peter Lang, 2001.

Monge, Luigi. "Topical Blues: Disasters." In *Encyclopedia of the Blues*, vol. 2 (K–Z), edited by Edward Komara, 995–1002. New York: Routledge, 2006.

Monge, Luigi. "Williams, Robert Pete." In *Encyclopedia of the Blues*, vol. 2 (K–Z), edited by Edward Komara, 1084–85. New York: Routledge, 2006.

Monge, Luigi. "Death by Fire: African-American Popular Music on the Natchez Rhythm Club Fire." In *Nobody Knows Where the Blues Come From: Lyrics and History*, edited by Robert Springer, 76–107. Jackson: University Press of Mississippi, 2006.

Monge, Luigi. "Ocean Blues: A Textual Linguistic Analysis of 'Hi' Henry Brown's 'Titanic Blues.'" In *Ocean of Sounds*, edited by Pierangelo Castagneto, 31–40. Turin, Italy: Otto Editore, 2007.

Monge, Luigi. "Preachin' the Blues: A Textual Linguistic Analysis of Son House's 'Dry Spell Blues.'" In *Ramblin' on My Mind: New Perspectives on the Blues*, edited by David Evans, 222–57. Urbana and Chicago: University of Illinois Press, 2008.

Monge, Luigi. *Howlin' Wolf. I'm the Wolf. Testi Commentati*. Rome, Italy: Arcana, 2010.

Monge, Luigi. "Natchez Rhythm Club Fire." In *The Mississippi Encyclopedia*, edited by Ted Ownby and Charles Reagan Wilson, 913. Jackson: University Press of Mississippi, 2017.

Morris, Alton C. *Folksongs of Florida*. Gainesville: University of Florida Press, 1950.

Muir, Peter. *Long Lost Blues: Popular Blues in America, 1850–1920*. Urbana and Chicago: University of Illinois Press, 2010.

Mullen, Patrick B. "The Racial Relationship of John Lomax and Henry Truvillion." In *The Man Who Adores the Negro: Race and American Folklore*, 63–78. Urbana and Chicago: University of Illinois Press, 2008.

Murray, Charles Shaar. *Boogie Man: The Adventures of John Lee Hooker in the American Twentieth Century*. New York: St. Martin's Press, 2000.

Neely, Jack. "The Moan: A Forgotten Fire, Remembered in a Song." In *Knoxville: This Obscure Prismatic City*, 63–76. Charleston, SC: History Press, 2009.

Nora, Pierre. "Between Memory and History: Les Lieux de Mémoire." In *History and Memory in African-American Culture*, edited by Geneviève Fabre and Robert O'Meally, 284–300. New York and Oxford: Oxford University Press, 1994.

Obrecht, Jas. *Rollin' and Tumblin': The Postwar Blues Guitarists*. San Francisco: Miller Freeman Books, 2000.

O'Brien, Timothy J., and David Ensminger. *Mojo Hand: The Life and Music of Lightnin' Hopkins.* Austin: University of Texas Press, 2013.

O'Connell, Christian. *Blues, How Do You Do? Paul Oliver and the Transatlantic Story of the Blues.* Ann Arbor: University of Michigan Press, 2015.

O'Daniel, Patrick. *Memphis and the Superflood of 1937: High Water Blues.* Charleston, SC: History Press, 2010.

O'Daniel, Patrick. *When the Levee Breaks: Memphis and the Mississippi Valley Flood of 1927.* Charleston, SC: History Press, 2013.

Odum, Howard W. *Wings on My Feet: Black Ulysses at the Wars.* Indianapolis: Bobbs-Merrill, 1929.

Odum, Howard W., and Guy B. Johnson. *Negro Workaday Songs.* Chapel Hill: University of North Carolina Press, 1926.

Odum, Howard W., and Guy B. Johnson. *The Negro and His Songs.* Hatboro, VT: Folklore Associates, 1964.

Ohio-Mississippi Valley Flood Disaster of 1937 (The): Report of Relief Operations of the American Red Cross. Washington, DC: American Red Cross, 1938.

Oliver, Paul. *Bessie Smith.* New York: A. S. Barnes, 1961.

Oliver, Paul. *Songsters and Saints: Vocal Traditions on Race Records.* Cambridge: Cambridge University Press, 1984.

Oliver, Paul. *Blues Fell This Morning: Meaning in the Blues.* Cambridge: Cambridge University Press, 1990.

Oliver, Paul. *Conversation with the Blues.* Cambridge: Cambridge University Press, 1997.

Oliver, Paul. *Broadcasting the Blues: Black Blues in the Segregation Era.* New York and London: Routledge, 2006.

Olsson, Bengt. *Memphis Blues and Jug Bands.* London: Studio Vista, 1970.

O'Meally, Robert G. *The Jazz Cadence of American Culture.* New York: Columbia University Press, 1998.

O'Meally, Robert G. "On Burke and the Vernacular: Ralph Ellison's Boomerang of History." In *History and Memory in African-American Culture*, edited by Geneviève Fabre and Robert O'Meally, 244–60. New York and Oxford: Oxford University Press, 1994.

O'Neal, Jim, and Amy Van Singel, eds. *The Voice of the Blues: Classic Interviews from Living Blues Magazine.* New York and London: Routledge, 2002.

Orr, William Ewing. "Judsonia Tornado of 1952; The Worst Tornado in Arkansas History." In *That's Judsonia: An Informal History of a Small Town in Arkansas.* Judsonia, AR: White County Print Company, 1957.

Oster, Harry. *Living Country Blues.* New York: Minerva Press, 1975.

Owens, William A. *Walking on Borrowed Land.* Fort Worth: Texas Christian University Press, 1954.

Page, Max. *The Creative Destruction of Manhattan, 1900–1940.* Chicago and London: University of Chicago Press, 1999.

Palmer, Jack. *Vernon Dalhart: First Star of Country Music.* Denver: Mainspring Press, 2005.

Parrish, Susan Scott. *The Flood Year 1927.* Princeton, NJ, and Oxford, UK: Princeton University Press, 2017.

Partlow, Geoff. *America's Deadliest Twister: The Tri-State Tornado of 1925.* Carbondale: Southern Illinois University, 2014.

Perks, Robert, and Alistair Thomson, eds. *The Oral History Reader*, 3rd ed. London: Routledge, 2015.

Peterkin, Genevieve C., in conversation with William P. Baldwin. *Heaven Is a Beautiful Place: A Memoir of the South Carolina Coast*. Columbia: University of South Carolina Press, 2000.

Polenberg, Richard. "Casey Jones (1900)." In *Hear My Sad Story: The True Tales That Inspired "Stagolee," "John Henry," and Other Traditional American Folk Songs*, 163–70, 274–75. Ithaca, NY, and London: Cornell University Press, 2015.

Polenberg, Richard. "The *Titanic* (1912)." In *Hear My Sad Story: The True Tales That Inspired "Stagolee," "John Henry," and Other Traditional American Folk Songs*, 223–32, 280. Ithaca, NY, and London: Cornell University Press, 2015.

Portelli, Alessandro. "Robert Johnson: La Sua Voce Parla per Noi." Foreword to Luigi Monge. *Robert Johnson: I Got the Blues. Testi Commentati*, 15–27. Rome, Italy: Arcana, 2008.

Portelli, Alessandro. "What Makes Oral History Different." In *The Oral History Reader*, 3rd ed., edited by Robert Perks and Alistair Thomson, 63–74. London: Routledge, 2015.

Porterfield, Nolan. *Jimmie Rodgers: The Life and Times of America's Blue Yodeler*. Jackson: University Press of Mississippi, 2007.

Puckett, Newbell Niles. *Folk Beliefs of the Southern Negro*. Chapel Hill: University of North Carolina Press, 1926.

Quarantelli, E. L., ed. *What Is a Disaster? A Dozen Perspectives on the Question*. London: Routledge, 1998.

Raim, Ethel, Irwin Silber, and Pete Seeger. *American Favorite Ballads: Tunes and Songs as Sung by Pete Seeger*. New York: Oak Publications, 1961.

Ramage, Martis D., Jr. *Tupelo, Mississippi, Tornado of 1936*. Tupelo: Northeast Mississippi Historical and Genealogical Society, 1997.

Ratcliffe, Philip R. *Mississippi John Hurt: His Life, His Times, His Blues*. Jackson: University Press of Mississippi, 2011.

Richardson, Ethel Park, and Sigmund Spaeth. *American Mountain Songs*. New York: Greenberg, 1927.

Riesman, Bob. *I Feel So Good: The Life and Times of Big Bill Broonzy*. Chicago and London: University of Chicago Press, 2011.

Rijn, Guido van. *Roosevelt's Blues: African-American Blues and Gospel Songs on FDR*. Jackson: University Press of Mississippi, 1997.

Rijn, Guido van. *The Truman and Eisenhower Blues: African-American Blues and Gospel Songs, 1945–1960*. London: Continuum, 2004.

Rijn, Guido van. *Kennedy's Blues: African-American Blues and Gospel Songs on JFK*. Jackson: University Press of Mississippi, 2007.

Rijn, Guido van. *The Carter, Reagan, Bush Sr., Clinton, Bush Jr. and Obama Blues: African-American Blues and Gospel Songs, 1976–2012*. Overveen, The Netherlands: Agram Blues Books, 2012.

Rijn, Guido van. *The St. Louis Blues of Walter Davis*. Overveen, The Netherlands: Agram Blues Books, 2022.

Rijn, Guido van, and Alex van der Tuuk. *New York Recording Laboratories 20000 and Gennett Matrix Series*. Overveen, The Netherlands: Agram Blues Books, 2012.

Rijn, Guido van, and Alex van der Tuuk. *New York Recording Laboratories Rodeheaver, Marsh and 2000 Series*. Overveen, The Netherlands: Agram Blues Books, 2013.

Rijn, Guido van, and Alex van der Tuuk. *New York Recording Laboratories 1100–1999 Matrix Series*. Overveen, The Netherlands: Agram Blues Books, 2014.

Rijn, Guido van, and Alex van der Tuuk. *New York Recording Laboratories Matrix Series Volume One: The L Matrix Series (1929–1932)*, rev. 2nd ed. Overveen, The Netherlands: Agram Blues Books, 2015.

Riley, Richard L., comp. *Early Blues*, vol. 2. Roseville, CA: PianoMania, 1996.

Rowden, Terry. *The Songs of Blind Folk: African American Musicians and the Cultures of Blindness*. Ann Arbor: University of Michigan Press, 2009.

Rowe, Mike. *Chicago Blues: The City and the Music*. New York: Da Capo Press, 1981.

Rowland, Lawrence S., and Stephen R. Wise. "The Great Sea Island Hurricane of 1893 and Its Aftermath." In *Bridging the Sea Islands' Past and Present, 1893–2006: The History of Beaufort County, South Carolina*, vol. 3, 1–18. Columbia: University of South Carolina Press, 2015.

Russell, Gareth. *The Darksome Bounds of a Failing World: The Sinking of the "Titanic" and the End of the Edwardian Era*. London: William Collins, 2019.

Russell, Tony. *Blacks, Whites and Blues*. London: Studio Vista, 1970.

Russell, Tony. *Country Music Records. A Discography, 1921–1942*. New York: Oxford University Press, 2004.

Russell, Tony. *Country Music Originals: The Legends and the Lost*. New York: Oxford University Press, 2007.

Russell, Tony. *Rural Rhythm: The Story of Old-Time Country Music in 78 Records*. New York: Oxford University Press, 2021.

Russell, Tony, and Chris Smith, with Neil Slaven, Ricky Russell and Joe Faulkner. *The Penguin Guide to Blues Recordings*. London: Penguin Books, 2006.

Ryan, Marc W. *Trumpet Records: Diamonds on Farish Street*. Jackson: University Press of Mississippi, 2004.

Rye, Howard, and Chris Smith. Draft revision of Robert M. W. Dixon, John Godrich, and Howard Rye, *Blues and Gospel Records 1890–1943*, 4th ed. (Oxford: Clarendon Press, 1997), for 5th ed. to be published as *Blues and Gospel Recordings 1890–1943*, forthcoming.

Sandburg, Carl. *The American Songbag*. San Diego, New York, and London: Harcourt Brace, 1990.

Sasse, Adam Fletcher. *North Omaha History*, vol. 2. Olympia, WA: CommonAction Publishing, 2016.

Saxon, Lyle, Edward Dreyer, and Robert Tallant. *Gumbo Ya-Ya*. New York: Bonanza Books, 1945.

Scarborough, Dorothy. *From A Southern Porch*. New York, London: G. P. Putnam's Sons, 1919.

Scarborough, Dorothy. *On the Trail of Negro Folk-Songs*. Cambridge, MA: Harvard University Press, 1925.

Segrest, James, and Mark Hoffman. *Moanin' at Midnight: The Life and Times of Howlin' Wolf*. New York: Thunder Mouth's Press, 2005.

Sherwin, Sterling, and Harry McClintock. *Railroad Songs of Yesterday*. New York: Shapiro, Bernstein, 1943.

Simon, Julia. *Time in the Blues*. New York: Oxford University Press, 2017.

Smith, Chris. "The Titanic: A Case Study of Religious and Secular Attitudes in African American Song." In *Saints and Sinners: Religion, Blues and (D)evil in African-American Music and Literature*, edited by Robert Sacré, 213–27. Liège, Belgium: Société Liégeoise de Musicologie, 1996.

Snyder, Jared. "Hemphill, Sid" and "Fife and Drums." In *Encyclopedia of the Blues*, vol. 1, edited by Edward Komara, 419 and 322–24. New York: Routledge, 2006.

Spignesi, Stephen J. *Catastrophe! The 100 Greatest Disasters of All Time*. New York: Citadel Press, 2002.

Spivey, Victoria. "I Commence to Whippin'." In Paul Oliver, *Conversation with the Blues*, 118. Cambridge: Cambridge University Press, 1997.

Springer, Robert, ed. "Text, Context and Subtext in the Blues." In *The Lyrics in African American Popular Music*, 1–16. Bern, Switzerland: Peter Lang, 2001.

Steinberg, Ted. *Acts of God: The Unnatural History of Natural Disaster in America*. New York: Oxford University Press, 2000.

Strachwitz, Chris, and Peter Welding, eds. *The American Folk Music Occasional*. New York: Oak, 1970.

Sullivan, Steve. *Encyclopedia of Great Popular Song Recordings*, vol. 2. Lanham, MD: Scarecrow Press, 2013.

Taft, Michael. *The Blues Lyric Formula*. New York: Routledge, 2006.

Thelen, David, ed. *Memory and American History*. Bloomington: University of Indiana Press, 1990.

Thomas, Gates. "South Texas Negro Work-Songs: Collected and Uncollected." *Publications of the Texas Folklore Society*, vol. V (1926). In *Rainbow in the Morning*, edited by J. Frank Dobie, 154–80. Hatboro, VT: Folklore Associates, 1965.

Thompson, Julius Eric. *Lynchings in Mississippi: A History 1865–1965*. Jefferson: McFarland, 2007.

Thygesen, Helge, and Russell Shor. *Vocalion 1000 and Brunswick 7000 Race Series*. Overveen, The Netherlands: Agram Blues Books, 2014.

Titon, Jeff Todd. *Early Downhome Blues: A Musical and Cultural Analysis*, 2nd ed. Chapel Hill and London: University of North Carolina Press, 1994.

Tomko, Gene. *Encyclopedia of Louisiana Musicians*. Baton Rouge: Louisiana State University Press, 2020.

Townsend, Henry. *A Blues Life: Henry Townsend as Told to Bill Greensmith*. Urbana and Chicago: University of Illinois Press, 1999.

Tribe, Ivan M. *The Stonemans: An Appalachian Family and the Music That Shaped Their Lives*. Urbana: University of Illinois Press, 1993.

Turley, L. A., H. A. Shoemaker, D. T. Bowden. *Jake Paralysis*. Norman: University of Oklahoma Press, 1931.

Tuuk, Alex van der. *The New Paramount Book of Blues*. Overveen, The Netherlands: Agram Blues Books, 2017.

Untiedt, Kenneth L., ed. "The Family Nature of the Texas Folklore Society." In *Celebrating 100 Years of the Texas Folklore Society*, 73–83. Denton: University of North Texas Press, 2009.

Wailoo, Keith. *Dying in the City of the Blues: Sickle Cell Anemia and the Politics of Race and Health*. Chapel Hill: University of North Carolina Press, 2001.

Wald, Elijah. *Josh White: Society Blues*. Amherst: University of Massachusetts Press, 2000.

Wald, Gayle F. *Shout, Sister, Shout! The Untold Story of Rock-and-Roll Trailblazer Sister Rosetta Tharpe*. Boston: Beacon Press, 2007.

Ward, Greg. *The Rough Guide to the Titanic*. London: Rough Guides, 2012.

Wardlow, Gayle Dean. *Chasin' That Devil Music: Searching for the Blues*, edited and with an introduction by Edward Komara. San Francisco: Miller Freeman Books, 1998.

Webster's Third New International Dictionary of the English Language. Springfield, MA: Merriam-Webster, 1993.

Welky, David. *The Thousand-Year Flood: The Ohio-Mississippi Disaster of 1937*. Chicago and London: University of Chicago Press, 2011.

Wentworth, Harold, and Stuart Berg Flexner, comps. *The Pocket Dictionary of American Slang*. New York: Pocket Books, 1967.

Wheeler, Mary. *Steamboatin' Days: Folksongs of the River Packet Era*. Freeport, NY: Books for Libraries Press, 1969.

White, Newman Ivey. *American Negro Folk-Songs*. Cambridge, MA: Harvard University Press, 1928.

White, Newman Ivey, gen. ed. *The Frank C. Brown Collection of North Carolina Folklore*. Durham, NC: Duke University Press, 1952–1961.

White, Newman Ivey. "Engineer Rigg." In *American Negro Folk-Songs*, 220–21. Hatboro, VT: Folklore Associates, 1965.

Will, Lawrence E. *Okeechobee Hurricane and the Hoover Dike*. St. Petersburg, FL: Great Outdoors Publishing Company, 1961.

Wolfe, Charles K. *Folk Songs of Middle Tennessee: The George Boswell Collection*. Knoxville: University of Tennessee Press, 1997.

Wolfe, Charles, and Kip Lornell. *The Life and Legend of Leadbelly*. New York: HarperCollins, 1994.

Wolfenstein, Martha. *Disaster: A Psychological Essay*. London and New York: Routledge, 2013.

Wood, Amy Louise. *Lynching and Spectacle: Witnessing Racial Violence in America 1890–1940*. Chapel Hill: University of North Carolina Press, 2009.

Woodruff, Nan Elizabeth. *As Rare as Rain: Federal Relief in the Great Southern Drought of 1930–31*. Urbana and Chicago: University of Illinois Press, 1985.

Work, John W., III. *American Negro Songs and Spirituals*. New York: Bonanza Books, 1940.

Work, John W., Lewis Wade Jones, and Samuel C. Adams Jr. *Lost Delta Found: Rediscovering the Fisk University–Library of Congress Coahoma County Study, 1941–1942*, edited by Robert Gordon and Bruce Nemerov. Nashville: Vanderbilt University Press, 2005.

Worster, Donald. *Dust Bowl: The Southern Plains in the 1930s*. New York: Oxford University Press, 1979.

Wright, Laurie, ed. "Pieces of the Jigsaw." In *Storyville 1996/7*. Chigwell, UK: L. Wright, 1997.

Ziółek-Sowińska, Małgorzata. *Images of the Apocalypse in African American Blues and Spirituals: "Destruction in This Land."* Frankfurt am Main, Germany: Peter Lang, 2017.

ARTICLES IN PERIODICALS

Allen, Bernard (a.k.a. Philippa). "Two Thousand Dying on a Job." *New Masses*, January 22, 1935.

Anon. "The Great Drought of 1930." *Literary Digest*, August 16, 1930.

Anon. "Good and Evil Effects of the Drought." *Literary Digest*, August 23, 1930.

Anon. "Casey Jones." *Railroad Man's Magazine* 5 (May 1908).

Anon. "Victoria Spivey Cleffed 'T.B. Blues,' Not Leadbelly, Tune Detectives Discover." *Variety* 242, April 13, 1966.

Barretta, Scott. "The Natchez Blues." *Living Blues* 210 (December 2010).

Barretta, Scott. "Elmore Williams: All I've Had All My Life Nearabouts Is Blues." *Living Blues* 210 (December 2010).

Bastin, Bruce. "Fort Valley Blues—Part 2." *Blues Unlimited* 112 (March-April 1975).

Baum, Dan. "Jake Leg: How the Blues Diagnosed a Medical Mystery." *New Yorker*, September 15, 2003.

Baumgartner, Brian. "Tommy Brown: Laughing at the Blues." *Juke Blues* 50 (2002).

Bowden, David T., L. A. Turley, and H. A. Shoemaker. "The Incidence of 'Jake' Paralysis in Oklahoma." *American Journal of Public Health* XX, no. 11 (November 1930): 1179–86.

Boyd, Joe Dan. "Ballad of the Black Sharecropper." *Farm Journal* (January 1969).

Brooks, John. "A Reporter at Large: Five-ten on a Sticky June Day." *New Yorker*, May 28, 1955.

Carr, J. A. "A Preliminary Report on the Tornadoes of March 21–22, 1952." *Monthly Weather Review* 80, no. 3 (March 1952): 50–58.

Carr, Lowell Juilliard. "Disaster and the Sequence-Pattern Concept of Social Change." *American Journal of Sociology* 38 (1932): 207–18.

Cather, James Patrick. "Tracking Down a Legend: The 'Jaybird' Coleman Story." *Tributaries: Journal of the Alabama Folklife Association* 5 (2002): 62–68.

Cohen, Norm. "'Casey Jones': At the Crossroads of Two Ballad Traditions." *Western Folklore* 32, no. 2 (April 1973): 77–103.

Cohen, Norm. "The Sinking of the *Titanic* and the Floundering of American Folksong Scholarship." *Southern Folklore* 56, no. 1 (1999): 3–26.

Collins, Selwyn D. "The Influenza Epidemic of 1928–1929 with Comparative Data for 1918–1919." *American Journal of Public Health* XX, no. 2 (February 1930): 119–29.

Conway, Cecelia. "Black Banjo Songsters in Appalachia." *Black Music Research Journal* 23, no. 1/2 (spring/fall 2003): 149–66.

Corcoran, Michael. "On the Trail of Blind Willie Johnson." *Blues & Rhythm* 188 (April 2004).

Cowley, Robert. "The Drought and the Dole." *American Heritage* 23, no. 2 (February 1972).

Crawford, Portia Naomi. "A Study of Negro Folk Songs from Greensboro, North Carolina and Surrounding Towns." *North Carolina Folklore* XVI (1968): 82–83.

Cruz, Jon D. "Booze and Blues: Alcohol and Black Popular Music, 1920–1930." *Contemporary Drug Problems* 15, no. 2 (summer 1988): 149–86.

Darwen, Norman. "Rejected No More: Flora Molton Interview." *Blues & Rhythm* 245 (Christmas 2009).

Demêtre, Jacques, and Jean-Paul Levet. "Katrina Blues: Ou un Siècle de Catastrophes Naturelles dans le Blues." *Soul Bag* 181 (December 2005).

Eagle, Bob. "Directory of African-Appalachian Musicians." *Black Music Research Journal* 24, no. 1 (spring 2004): 7–72.

Eagle, Bob. "Roosevelt Sykes Aliases and Associates." *Frog Blues and Jazz Annual* 5 (2017): 165–75.

Ellis, Eleanor. "'From a Little Girl I've Been Singing, Singing Singing.'" *Living Blues* 86 (May-June 1989).

Evans, David. "Bessie Smith's 'Back-Water Blues': The Story Behind the Song." *Popular Music* 26, no. 1 (2007): 97–116.

Evans, David. "An Early Interview with Son House—Part One" and "An Early Interview with Son House—Part Two." *Frog Blues and Jazz Annual* 5 (2017): 29–44, 176–94.

Evans, David, Ed Payne, Richard Linster, T. DeWayne Moore, and Bob Eagle. "Lightning Struck Him: Walter Rhodes, the Delta Crowing Rooster." *Frog Blues and Jazz Annual* 6, forthcoming.

Fontenot, Kevin. "Times Ain't Like They Used to Be: Rabbit Brown, New Orleans Songster." *Jazz Archivist* XIII (1998–99).

Fritts, J. Tyler. "Lyric Formulas as Traditional Compositional Processes in the Folk Blues: A Case Study of Furry Lewis." *Ethnomusicology* 64, no. 1 (winter 2020): 141–66.

Grandi, Marino, and Luigi Monge. "The Oil Man Si Racconta." *Il Blues* 103 (June 2008) (in Italian).

Grauberger, Steve, and Kevin Nutt. "A Vera Hall Discography." *Tributaries: Journal of the Alabama Folklife Association* 5 (2002): 82–91.

Green, C. H., Jr. "Fiddling Clarence Green: Mountain Musician." *John Edwards Memorial Foundation Quarterly* 7, no. 24 (winter 1971): 163–67.

Gussow, Leon. "The Jake Walk and Limber Trouble: A Toxicology Epidemic." *Emergency Medicine News* 26, no. 10 (October 2004): 48.

Hall, Bob, and Richard Noblett. "A Handful of Keys: Louise Johnson Again!" *Blues Unlimited* 115 (September-October 1975).

Hampton, Bill R. "On Identification and Negro Tricksters." *Southern Folklore Quarterly* 31, no. 1 (March 1967): 55–65.

Hayes, Montrose W. "The St. Louis Tornado of September 29, 1927." *Monthly Weather Review* 55, no. 9 (September 1927): 405–7.

"Hell and High Water." *Time* 29, no. 5, February 1, 1937.

Hemphill, Jessie Mae. "Ain't Got Tears to Cry With." *Living Blues* 100 (November-December 1991).

Herrington, Chris. "Beginning of the End: Expatriate Memphians Bob Frank and John Murry Come Together Half a Country Away." *Memphis Magazine* (October 2007). www.memphis magazine.com/October-2007/Beginning-of-the-End.

Higgs, Robert. "The Boll Weevil, the Cotton Economy, and Black Migration 1910–1930." *Agricultural History* 50, no. 2 (1976): 335–50.

Hoffman, Larry. "Robert Lockwood, Jr." *Living Blues* 121 (June 1995).

Holm, John. "On the Relationship of Gullah and Bahamian." *American Speech* 58, no. 4 (1983): 303–18.

Horne, Philip. "Flood Songs, Dylan, and the Mississippi Blues." *Raritan: A Quarterly Review* 33, no. 2 (2014). https://raritanquarterly.rutgers.edu/issue-index/author-index/horne-philip.

Johnson, Niall, and Jürgen Müller. "Updating the Accounts: Global Mortality of the 1918–1920 'Spanish' Influenza Pandemic." *Bulletin of the History of Medicine* 76, no. 1 (2002): 105–15.

Joos, Vincent. "Natchez Fire." *ABS Magazine* 25 (February 2010) (in French).

Kehrberg, Kevin, and Jeffrey A. Keith. "Somebody Died, Babe: A Musical Cover-Up of Racism, Violence, and Greed." *Bitter Southerner* (August 4, 2020). https://bittersoutherner.com/2020/somebody-died-babe-a-musical-coverup-of-racism-violence-and-greed.

Kelton, Jim. "From Mance, with Love." *Blues Revue* 69 (July-August 2001).

Komara, Edward. "Blues in the Round." *Black Music Research Journal* 17, no. 1 (spring 1997): 3–36.

Kossen, Frank. "Obituaries: Elmo Williams." *Living Blues* 245 (October 2016).

Lomax, John A. "Some Types of American Folk-Song." *Journal of American Folk-Lore* XXVIII, no. CVII (January-March 1915): 1–17.

Lornell, Kip. "Living Blues Interview: Hammie Nixon and Sleepy John Estes." *Living Blues* 19 (January-February 1975).

Lott, George A. "The Great-Volume Rainstorm at Elba, Alabama." *Monthly Weather Review* 82, no. 6 (June 1954): 153–59.

Lowry, Pete. "Some Cold Rainy Day." *Blues Unlimited* 103 (August-September 1973).

Maltz, Albert. "Man on the Road." *New Masses*, January 8, 1935.

McCormick, Mack. "Sam 'Lightnin" Hopkins—A Description." *Jazz Monthly* 5, no. 8 (October 1959).

McCormick, Mack. "A Conversation with Lightnin' Hopkins, Part 2." *Jazz Journal* 14, no. 1 (January 1961).

McGregory, Jerrylin. "Livingston, Alabama Blues: The Significance of Vera Ward Hall." *Tributaries: Journal of the Alabama Folklife Association* 5 (2002): 72–81.

Monge, Luigi. "The Language of Blind Lemon Jefferson: The Covert Theme of Blindness." *Black Music Research Journal* 20, no. 1 (spring 2000): 35–81.

Monge, Luigi. "La Lunga Fede Musicale: Intervista al Reverendo Arnold Dwight 'Gatemouth' Moore." *World Music Magazine* 69 (November-December 2004) (in Italian).

Monge, Luigi. "Their Eyes Were Watching God: African-American Topical Songs on the 1928 Florida Hurricanes and Floods." *Popular Music* 26, no. 1 (2007): 129–40.

Monge, Luigi, and David Evans. "New Songs of Blind Lemon Jefferson." *Journal of Texas Music History* 3, no. 2 (fall 2003): 8–28.

Montgomery, Mike. "Eubie Blake Piano Rollography (Revised)." *Record Research* 159/160 (December 1978).

Moonoogian, George A., and Roger Meeden. "Duke Records—the Early Years: An Interview with David J. Mattis." *Whiskey, Women, and . . .* 14 (June 1984).

Moore, Catherine Venable. "The Book of the Dead: In Fayette County, West Virginia, Expanding the Document of Disaster." *Oxford American* 94 (fall 2016). www.oxfordamerican.org/magazine/item/1049-the-book-of-the-dead.

Moore, J. Roderick. "Mack Jenks, Union Bard." *Goldenseal* 3, no. 2 (April–June 1977).

Moore, T. DeWayne. "Bo Carter: Genius of the Country Blues." *Blues & Rhythm* 330 (June 2018).

Morgan, John P. "Cincinnati's Jake Walk Blues." *Cincinnati Horizons* (February 1978).

Morgan, John P. "The Jamaica Ginger Paralysis." *Journal of the American Medical Association* 248, no. 15 (October 15, 1982): 1864–67.

Morgan, John P. "Jake-leg: Mystery Disease of the 1930s." *Kaleidoscope* I, no. 1 (winter 1983–84).

Morgan, John P., and Patricia Penovich. "Jamaica Ginger Paralysis: Forty-seven Year Follow-up." *Archives of Neurology* 35 (August 1978): 530–32.

Morgan, John P., and Thomas C. Tulloss. "The Jake Walk Blues: A Toxicologic Tragedy Mirrored in American Popular Music." *Annals of Internal Medicine* 85, no. 6 (December 1976): 804–8.

Morgan, John P., and Thomas C. Tulloss. "The Jake Walk Blues." *Old Time Music* 28 (spring 1978).

Morrison, Steven J. "Downhome Tragedy: The Blues and the Mississippi Flood of 1927." *Southern Folklore* 51 (1994): 265–84.

Nelson, D. L. "The Allen Brothers." *John Edwards Memorial Foundation Quarterly* 7, no. 24 (winter 1971): 147–50.

Nemerov, Bruce. "John Wesley Work III: Field Recordings of Southern Black Folk Music, 1935–1942." *Tennessee Folklore Society Bulletin*, LIII, no. 3 (fall 1987): 82–103.

Nemerov, Bruce. "I'm a Holy Ghost Preacher!" *Blues & Rhythm* 141 (August 1999).

Niles, Abbe. "Ballads, Songs and Snatches." *The Bookman* 67, no. 3 (May 1928).

Oliver, Paul. "Sources of American Folk Song (3): Boll Weevil Blues." *Music Mirror* 1 (July 1954).

O'Neal, Jim. "Unraveling Casey Bill: The Hawaiian Guitar Wizard." *Living Blues* 228 (December 2013).

O'Neal, Jim. "Sid Hemphill: Hill Country Patriarch." *Living Blues* 253 (February 2018).

Otis, Johnny. "The Otis Tapes 4: Dwight 'Gatemouth' Moore." *Blues Unlimited* 109 (August-September 1974).

Parascandola, John. "The Jamaica Ginger Paralysis Episode of the 1930s." *Pharmacy in History* 36, no. 3 (1994): 123–43.

Pearson, Barry Lee. "Appalachian Blues." *Black Music Research Journal* 23, no. 1/2 (spring/fall 2003): 23–51.

Penny, Dave, and Tony Burke. "Stand Up and Shout the Blues: Dwight 'Gatemouth' Moore." *Blues & Rhythm* 15 (December 1985).

Perkins, A. E. "Negro Spirituals from the Far South." *Journal of American Folklore* 35 (1922): 223–49.

Perrow, E. C. "Songs and Rhymes from the South." *Journal of American Folklore* 26 (April-June 1913): 165–67.

Perrow, E. C. "Songs and Rhymes from the South." *Journal of American Folklore* 27 (1915): 129–90.

Plail, Chris. "The New Boll-Weavil Song" and "The Passing of a Folk-hero." *Shindig: The BBC Folk Club Magazine* (October 1967).

Propes, Steve. "Obituaries: Nellie Lutcher." *Blues & Rhythm* 221 (August 2007).

Pruter, Robert, Robert Campbell, and Armin Büttner. "The Chance Label." *Blues & Rhythm* 200 (June 2005).

Rasnake, Maj. Mark S., et al. "History of U.S. Military Contributions to the Study of Sexually Transmitted Diseases." *Military Medicine* 170, no. 4 (April 2005): 61–65.

Reine, Kathleen. "The Ways of the Isles." *Times Literary Supplement*, December 20, 1977.

Rijn, Guido van. "Praying for the Pastor: The Life of Rev. J. M. Gates." *Living Blues* 152 (July-August 2000).

Rijn, Guido van. "Thomas Shaw Interview." *Blues & Rhythm* 193 (October 2004).

Schafer, A. L. "When Hunger Followed Drought." *The Survey* LXV, no. 11, March 1, 1931.

Scheiber, Andrew. "From Cotton Boll to Rock 'n' Roll." *Arkansas Review* 40, no. 2 (August 2009).

Sears, Ann. "John William 'Blind' Boone, Pianist-Composer: 'Merit, Not Sympathy Wins.'" *Black Music Research Journal* 9, no. 2 (fall 1989): 225–47.

Seroff, Doug, and Lynn Abbott. "The Life and Death of Pioneer Bluesman Butler 'String Beans' May: 'Been Here, Made His Quick Duck, and Got Away.'" *Tributaries: Journal of the Alabama Folklife Association* 5 (2002): 20–21, 24–25.

Shor, Russell. "Walter Barnes and the Natchez Fire." *Frog Blues and Jazz Annual* 2 (2011): 32–36.

Silver, James W. "Paul Bunyan Comes to Mississippi." *Journal of Mississippi History* XIX, no. 2 (April 1957): 93–119.

Smith, Ayana. "Blues, Criticism, and the Signifying Trickster." *Popular Music* 24 (2005): 179–91.

Smith, Chris. "Cheer the Union Travelers: The Field Recordings of George Korson." *Blues & Rhythm* 176 (February 2003).

Smith, Chris. "Stockyard Fire," in column "Words Words Words." *Blues & Rhythm* 201 (August 2005).

Smith, Chris. "Jig Head / Jickhead / Jake Head," in column "Words Words Words." *Blues & Rhythm* 253 (October 2010).

Smith, Chris. "A Bank That Never Fails (Rev. J. M. Gates)," in column "Words Words Words." *Blues & Rhythm* 254 (November 2010).

Smith, Chris. "Jickhead," in column "Words Words Words." *Blues & Rhythm* 257 (March 2011).

Smith, Chris. "Seawall Special (Lela Bolden)," in column "Words Words Words." *Blues & Rhythm* 301 (August 2015).

Smith, Chris. "Vaccinate Me, Baby (King Perry)," in column "Words Words Words." *Blues & Rhythm* 303 (October 2015).

Smith, Chris. "Stingaree," in column "Words Words Words." *Blues & Rhythm* 306 (January 2016).

Smith, Chris. "Meningitis Blues (Memphis Minnie)," in column "Words Words Words." *Blues & Rhythm* 322 (September 2017).

Smith, Chris. "William and Versey Smith, and William and Irma Smith: Not Husbands and Their Wives." *Names & Numbers* 89 (April 2019).

Smith, Chris. "Homeless Blues (Bessie Smith)," in column "Words Words Words." *Blues & Rhythm* 339 (May 2019).

Smith, Chris. "The Flood of Alabama," in column "Words Words Words." *Blues & Rhythm* 344 (November 2019).

Smith, Chris. "Meningitis Blues (Frank Pluitt)," in column "Words Words Words." *Blues & Rhythm* 351 (August 2020).

Smith, Chris. "O. B. D. Blues (Walter Roland)," in column "Words Words Words." *Blues & Rhythm* 351 (August 2020).

Smith, Chris. "The Pea (Roosevelt Charles)," in column "Words Words Words." *Blues & Rhythm* 359 (May 2021).

Sofalvi, Alan J. "The Venereal Disease [VD] Radio Project: A Look at a 20th-Century Initiative on Sexually Transmitted Infection [STI] Prevention." *Health Educator* 49, no. 2 (fall 2017): 28–34.

Spivey, Victoria. "Blues Are My Business." *Record Research* 53 (July 1963).

Stern, Jeff. "Chicago, 1934: The Union Stock Yards Fire." *Firehouse Magazine*, September 1, 2009.

Templeton, Ray. "'Bad Luck and Trouble.' Lightnin' Hopkins." *Blues & Rhythm* 280 (June 2013).

Templeton, Ray. "Ain't That Good News: Crossing Over. Mixing Sacred and Secular, with the Dixieaires and More." *Blues and Rhythm* 330 (June 2018).

"To Ask Ops' Aid in Fighting VD." *Billboard*, August 13, 1949.

"Tunneling through an Atmosphere of Deadly Dust." *Newsweek*, January 25, 1936.

Tuuk, Alex van der. "Son House: How Paramount's Elusive Artist Evolved into a Blues Icon." *Frog Blues and Jazz Annual* 4 (2015): 125–34.

"Village of the Living Dead." *Literary Digest* 121, January 25, 1936.

Wald, Elijah. "Josh White and the Protest Blues." *Living Blues* 158 (July-August 2001).

Wald, Gayle. "Past Is Present." *Oxford American: Vision of the Blues. Southern Music Issue* 28 (winter 2016). www.oxfordamerican.org/magazine/item/1102-past-is-present.

Wardlow, Gayle Dean. "Dead Cat on the Line." *Blues & Rhythm* 197 (March 2005).

Webb, Walter Prescott. "Notes on the Folk-Lore of Texas." *Journal of American Folk-Lore* 28 (1915): 290–99.

White, Newman Ivey. "Racial Traits in the Negro Song." *Sewanee Review* 28, no. 3 (July 1920).

Wilgus, D. K. "A Type Index of Anglo-American Traditional Narrative Songs." *Journal of the Folklore Institute* 7 (August-December 1970): 161–76.

Wilgus, D. K., and Lynwood Montell. "Clure and Joe Williams: Legend and Blues Ballad." *Journal of American Folk-Lore* 81 (1968): 295–315.

Witek, Joseph. "Blindness as a Rhetorical Trope in Blues Discourse." *Black Music Research Journal* 8, no. 2 (1988): 177–93.

DISSERTATIONS

Fritts, J. Tyler. "Furry Lewis: An Ethnomusicological Study of a Memphis Musician." PhD diss., University of Memphis, 2016.

Joos, Vincent. "A Profile of African American Remembrance in a Small Mississippi Town."
    Degree thesis, University of North Carolina at Chapel Hill, 2011.
Muir, Peter. "Before 'Crazy Blues': Commercial Blues in America, 1850–1920." PhD diss., City
    University of New York, 2004.

NEWSPAPERS

Abilene (TX) Reporter (1948)
Afro-American (The) (Washington, DC) (1948)
Alabama Tribune (Montgomery, AL) (1952)
Atlanta Constitution (1928, 1929, 1942, 1951, 1952, 1953, 1967, 1976, 1999)
Atlanta Daily World (1951)
Atlanta Journal (1922)
Austin American-Statesman (1908, 1911)
Baltimore Afro-American (1935, 1936)
Belvedere (IL) Daily Republican (1929)
Boston Globe (1933)
Brooklyn Daily Eagle (1913)
Brownsville (TX) Herald (1929)
Buffalo (NY) Enquirer (1908)
Chicago Defender (1927, 1928, 1929, 1935, 1936, 1940, 1942)
Cincinnati Commercial (1876)
Cincinnati Enquirer (1931)
Clarion-Ledger (Jackson, MS) (1955)
Clarksdale Daily Register (1930)
Coffeyville (KS) Daily Journal (1913)
Commercial Appeal (Memphis) (1927, 1930, 1942)
Cushing (OK) Daily Citizen (1930)
Dadeville (AL) Record (1936)
Dallas Morning News (1936)
Daily Oklahoman (Oklahoma City) (1930)
Evening Times-Republican (Marshalltown, IA) (1913)
Greenwood Commonwealth (1930, 1955)
Indianapolis Recorder (1950)
Jackson (MS) Daily News (1905)
Jackson (TN) Sun (1937)
Keowee Courier (Pickens, SC) (1908)
Leaf-Chronicle (Clarksville, TN) (1929)
Los Angeles Times (1909)
Memphis Press-Scimitar (1930, 1942)
Miami (OK) Daily News-Record (1930)
Miami News (1926)
Nashville Banner (1940)
Natchez Democrat (1940)
New York Age (1912)

New York Amsterdam News (1940)

New York Sunday News (1927)

New York Times (1913, 1926, 1927, 1928, 1930, 1932, 1935, 1936, 1942, 1951)

New York Times Index (1933, 1934, 1935, 1936)

News-Democrat (Paducah, KY) (1903)

News Leader (Staunton, VA) (1930)

Orlando Sentinel (1926)

Palm Beach Post (1928)

Philadelphia Inquirer (1955)

Pittsburgh Courier (1912, 1927, 1936, 1940, 1951, 1952, 1958)

Plaindealer (Kansas City, KS) (1940)

Rockingham Post-Dispatch (1938)

Rutland (VT) Daily Herald (1932)

Selma Times-Journal (1936)

Shreveport Times (1941)

St. Louis Post-Dispatch (1929, 1930)

St. Paul Appeal (1912)

Star-Gazette (Elmira, NY) (1913)

Tennessean (The) (Nashville) (1911, 1928)

Times Dispatch (Richmond, VA) (1922)

Washington Afro American (1940, 1942)

Waterloo (IA) Reporter (1909)

LINER NOTES

Balfour, Alan. Liner notes to Champion Jack Dupree, *Junker Blues 1940–1941*. Travelin' Man TM 807, 1985.

Bruder, Jay. Notes to various artists, *R&B in D.C.* Bear Family Records BCD 17052 (16CD), 2021.

Cohen, Ronald D., and Dave Samuelson. Notes to various artists, *Songs for Political Action: Folk Music, Topical Songs and the American Left: 1926–1953*. Bear Family Records BCD 15720 JL (10CD), 1996.

Cowley, John. Liner notes to various artists, *Two White Horses Standin' in Line*. Flyright-Matchbox SDM 264, 1976.

Evans, David. Booklet notes to various artists, *Atlanta Blues 1933*. John Edwards Memorial Foundation JEMF-106, 1979.

Evans, David. Booklet notes to various artists, *Afro-American Folk Music from Tate and Panola Counties, Mississippi*. Rounder Records 1515-2, 2000.

Evans, David. Booklet notes to various artists, *Deep River of Song: Georgia. I'm Gonna Make You Happy*. Rounder CD 1828, 2001.

Green, Archie. Liner notes to various artists, *Hard Times*. Rounder Records LP 4007, 1975.

Huber, Patrick. "Notes on the Songs." In *The Dixon Brothers: A Blessing to People*. Bear Family BCD 16817 DK, 2012.

Kahn, Ed. Notes to Darby & Tarlton, *Complete Recordings*. Bear Family BCD 15764 (3CD), 1995.

Kent, Don. Liner notes to various artists, *St. Louis Town 1929–1933*. Yazoo Records L-1003, n.d.

Komara, Edward. "Thematic Catalogue of the Recorded Music of Charley Patton." In *Charley Patton, Screamin' and Hollerin' the Blues: The Worlds of Charley Patton*. Revenant Album No. 212 (7CD), 2001.

Morgan, John P. Liner notes to various artists, *Jake Walk Blues*. Stash ST-110, 1977.

Olson, Ted, and Tony Russell. Notes to various artists, *The Knoxville Sessions 1929–1930*. Bear Family BCD16097 (4CD), 2016.

Rijn, Guido van. Booklet notes to Big Bill Broonzy, *Amsterdam Live Concerts 1953*. Munich Records MRCD 275 (2CD), 2006.

Russell, Tony. Liner notes to various artists, *Fort Valley Blues: 1941–43 Field Recordings from Georgia*. Flyright-Matchbox SDM 250, 1974.

Sapoznik, Henry "Hank." Introduction to "The Daily Record." In *People Take Warning! Murder Ballads and Disaster Songs, 1913–1938*. Tompkins Square 1875 (3CD), 2007.

Smith, Chris. Booklet notes to Lonnie Johnson, *Complete Recorded Works 1937 to June 1947 in Chronological Order—Volume 1 (1937–1940)*. Blues Document BDCD-6024, 1992.

Smith, Chris. Booklet notes to Charley Jordan, *Complete Recorded Works in Chronological Order, Volume 2 (1931–1934)*. Document Records DOCD-5098, 1992.

Smith, Chris. Booklet notes to Rev. J. M. Gates, *Complete Recorded Works in Chronological Order Volume 5 (1927)*. Document Records DOCD-5449, 1996.

Spottswood, Dick. "Song Notes and Transcriptions." In Charley Patton, *Screamin' and Hollerin' the Blues: The Worlds of Charley Patton*. Revenant Album No. 212 (7CD), 2001.

Vanco, John H. Booklet notes to various artists, *Mississippi Blues—Vol. 2 (1926–1935)*. Document Records DOCD-5158, 1993.

Wagner, Christoph. "Doom & Gloom: In the Shadow of the Apocalypse." Booklet notes to various artists, *Doom & Gloom: Early Songs of Angst and Disaster (1927–1945)*. Trikont US-0364, 2007.

UNPUBLISHED MATERIAL

Boyd, Joe Dan. "'Boll Weevil': The Ballad That Followed a Bug!" Sixty-five-page unpublished typed manuscript.

Jones, Lewis W. (prob.). Typescript report of Coahoma County Project. Nashville: Fisk University, ca. 1943.

Wilgus, D. K. "Tentative Type List of *Titanic* Ballads." Unpublished typewritten document.

INTERVIEWS

Johnson, Big Jack. Interview by Marino Grandi and Luigi Monge. Rovigo, Italy, June 29, 2003.

Lacy, Rev. Ruben. Unpublished interview by David Evans. Ridgecrest, California, February 26, 1966.

Moore, Arnold Dwight "Gatemouth." Interview by Luigi Monge. Yazoo City, Mississippi, April 18, 2002.

Porter, Ethel Lee. Interview by Luigi Monge. Natchez, Mississippi, April 20, 2002.

Robinson, Frank R. Interview by Luigi Monge. Natchez, Mississippi, April 21, 2002.

GENERAL INDEX

Page numbers for figures are in **bold**.

ARTIST INDEX

TRANSCRIBED SONG INDEX

ABOUT THE AUTHOR

Luigi Monge is a freelance teacher and translator in Genoa, Italy. In 1985 he graduated in Modern Foreign Languages with the dissertation "Black English and the Blues." A blues and gospel lecturer in Italian and English, in his native language he has written the books *Robert Johnson. I Got the Blues. Testi Commentati* and *Howlin' Wolf. I'm the Wolf. Testi Commentati* as well as more than 150 articles for various magazines and periodicals. In English, he has published articles for *Black Music Research Journal*, *Journal of Texas Music History*, *Popular Music*, and in miscellaneous books for University Press of Mississippi and University of Illinois Press. He has contributed entries to *The Encyclopedia of the Blues* and the *Encyclopedia of American Gospel Music*, both published by Routledge. This is his first book in English.